THE Durability FACTOR

A chair in walnut and hickory
by George Nakashima
of Bucks County, Pennsylvania.

"A better economy, to my way of thinking, would be one that would place its emphasis not upon the quantity of notions and luxuries but upon the quality of necessities. Such an economy would, for example, produce an automobile that would last at least as long, and be at least as easy to maintain, as a horse. It would encourage workmanship to be as durable as its materials; thus a piece of furniture would have the durability not of glue but of wood."

WENDELL BERRY, *A Continuous Harmony*
(Harcourt Brace Jovanovich, 1972)

THE Durability FACTOR

A guide to finding long-lasting cars, housing, clothing, appliances, tools, and toys

Edited by Roger B. Yepsen, Jr.

Bill Keisling, assistant editor

Terry Kneeland, editorial assistant

Rodale Press, Emmaus, Pennsylvania

The streamlined GG-1 electric locomotive, designed in the late 1930s by Raymond Loewy. Now in their forties, these engines are still capable of pulling trains at 100 miles per hour.

Book design: Merole Berger
Copy editor: Jan Barckley
Project photographer: Christie C. Tito

Printed in the United States of America.

Library of Congress Cataloging in Publication Data
Main entry under title:

The Durability factor.

Includes index.
1. Consumer education. 2. Durable goods, Consumer.
I. Yepsen, Roger B.
TX335.D87 640.73 82-3870
ISBN 0-87857-400-X hardcover AACR2
ISBN 0-87857-403-4 paperback

Lowest figure indicates number of this printing:

2 4 6 8 10 9 7 5 3 1 hardcover
2 4 6 8 10 9 7 5 3 1 paperback

Disclaimer

The Durability Factor is based upon opinions. The editors have solicited the opinions of not only repair people, designers, and engineers, but also others who have no credentials, save that they lived with a product for a time. In reporting the praise or criticism of these people, the editors do not presume to pass judgment on the quality of a product, or to recommend or condemn a product. Rodale Press has not conducted its own tests to evaluate products, and has relied exclusively on the opinions of others. The phone surveys and interviews performed by Rodale are not guaranteed to be statistically accurate, but the editors report these opinions in the hope that they will be of value and inspiration to the reader. When our reportage doesn't enable you to choose a product with confidence, please turn to the data-rich tests conducted by consumer and special-interest magazines for specific information.

Cover acknowledgments

Design by Merole Berger
Photo by Carl Doney
Styling by J. C. Vera

The models were Bonnie Kline, Craig Neal, and David Hartenstine.

Jøtul 602C woodstove, Scandia Stoves of Pennsylvania, Inc., Kutztown, Pennsylvania
Le Creuset saucepan. La Belle Cuisine–Fine Cookware, Allentown, Pennsylvania
Waring 7011 bar blender, A-1 Restaurant Supply Co., Whitehall, Pennsylvania
Bosch electronic jigsaw, model 1578, Robert Bosch Power Tool Corp., New Bern, North Carolina
1957 Gravely Model L tractor, Lauchnor's Gravely Tractor Agency, Allentown, Pennsylvania
Maytag automatic washer, model A510, Kleckner and Sons, Emmaus, Pennsylvania
Schwinn Varsity bicycle, George's Schwinn Cyclery, Emmaus, Pennsylvania
Eureka upright vacuum cleaner, model 4040B, Dave's Vacuum Cleaner Service, Allentown, Pennsylvania
Harris tweed jacket and gray flannel trousers, Anderson Little Co., Inc., Lehigh Valley Mall, Whitehall, Pennsylvania
Bulova 17-Jewel Caravelle watch, Richards Jewelers, Emmaus, Pennsylvania
Izod Lacoste shirt and Levi's jeans, The Lodge at Harvard Square, Lehigh Valley Mall, Whitehall, Pennsylvania
Child's Saucony running shoes, A & H Sporting Goods, Emmaus, Pennsylvania
Bonnie Kline's hairstyling by Barry H., New York City

Thanks to those who loaned their durable possessions:
Christie C. Vera, Dick Boak, Kerry Pechter, Craig Neal, J. C. Vera, Ann Snyder, Joe Carter, and Bill Hylton.

CONTENTS

Volkswagen of America

The 1948 Volkswagen Beetle.

THE DURABILITY FACTOR

1

A trustworthy 100,000-mile car, a comfortably broken-in shirt, a hand-me-down toaster that does its job each breakfast.

Everyone knows the satisfaction of owning such products, manufactured with care and maintained considerately to an old age. Life is enhanced by these special possessions. They are nice to have around; we feel at home with them. And, as the years pass, it's a pleasure to recall a purchase price that seems tiny in retrospect.

A curious issue

Durability is a curious issue for a book, because no one really takes issue with it. How can you build an argument for shoddiness and not sound depraved?

A Pennsylvania television station once broadcast an editorial that took a fervent stand against birth defects, then invited rebuttals from dissenting viewers. Hardly provocative, and so it seems to be with the issue of durability. Writers of ad copy like the word because it has a gritty, no-nonsense sound that balances such glitter as "luxurious loose-cushion look," "electronic-digital LED readout," and the perennial "new and improved." Everybody, consumer and manufacturer alike, agrees that ageless products are great.

If durability has no opponents, then why is it in such short supply? All is not well in the marketplace. In dozens of polls, we Americans grumble that things don't last as long as they used to. Our basements, yard sales, and dumps are gorged with radios, refrigerators, cars that died young and still shine as if new. Each carcass is flawed in some way, gone rotten at the core; each tells the story of a frustrated, perhaps angry, owner who had to go out and buy a replacement at an inflation-boosted price.

Every torn seam and rusted fender whispers of a dark side to this issue of durability. The villains, it should be clear, are not metals or woods or plastics, but people—we who design and manufacture short-lived things, we who can't find the time (or the screwdriver) to maintain them to a proper old age.

What's our problem? Perhaps we're giddy. Fueled by cheap energy and lured by technology's promise, we speed toward ever-higher standards of living. The sheer quantity of goods, of marvels and gimmickry, has been exhilarating, but quality hasn't gotten a boost. Who's responsible? Consumers blame business, and business blames consumers.

Durability is not an unqualified blessing for producers. They know there is an optimum level of durability from the standpoint of profit. Building a long-life product can be bad business, says Edward H. Chamberlin in *Towards a More General*

Theory of Value. A producer tends to determine that level of durability which will maximize his profit. If the product lasts too long, repeat demand will suffer; if the product wears out too quickly, reputation will suffer. A manufacturer must therefore travel a thin line in planning product life.

You would expect the temptation to downgrade durability to be especially strong in a fully mature market, one that is all but saturated. For example, one obvious way for the auto industry to sell more cars is to nudge up the annual scrappage rate a percent or two. It's not hard to see why, in Detroit, the term "planned obsolescence" is as welcome as water in a witches' coven.

Gillette offers a case in point. Known as the company that introduced the throwaway blade in 1903, Gillette also brought out the first long-life stainless-steel blade in 1930. But this innovation was taken off the market and remained out of sight for more than three decades. Gillette explained its action by claiming that the company was unsure of quality control, but a more likely explanation is that a blade offering 16 shaves would bring in lower profits than the old 4-shave standard blade.

NASA

Skylab 4, the space station that was to plummet to earth as several tons of flaming junk. In 1981, NASA successfully brought the spaceship Columbia back to earth, making this the first recyclable space craft.

In 1962, a British firm, Wilkinson, finally brought the stainless-steel blade to America, and Gillette was forced to follow suit. "When other people come in, we have to join," Gillette's chief executive commented. "But we wouldn't have chosen this route." Indeed. Before the stainless revolution swept the United States, the company sold about 90 percent of all disposable blades.

Is it possible to turn out only well-crafted, long-lived products and stay in business? Yes, and the stories of such companies are heartwarming. Pendleton, a family-owned clothier dating back to the later 1800s, was able to weather the flood of synthetic clothing in the 1960s and now enjoys the revived popularity of wool as a commonsense fabric. Other companies have dropped a line that evidently had more built-in durability than people would pay for; a few have folded because of their reluctance to titillate the public with new styling and gadgetry.

So here is the manufacturers' rebuttal, and they have the last word: if people demanded no-nonsense products and would back up their words with dollars, then companies surely would produce them.

The free-market two-step

Perhaps we shop unwisely because advertising robs us of our common sense. Ads rarely seek to instruct, after all, and appeal instead to our crasser desires. Until our recent economic troubles, product life was a rare theme in ads. Maytag had its lonely service person, Zippo had its unconditional guarantee, and the VW Beetle dressed itself as a comical antihero.

Today, many companies are bragging about durability, real or imagined, but the pitch has changed only because the public's mood has changed. The producer is following the consumer's lead in what looks not so much like a battle as a dance. From time to time, government threatens to step in with regulations, but both partners see these as costing jobs and profits.

Corporations give us what we want—whether or not it's good for us, true, and sometimes wants are seeded in our minds by sophisticated ads. Big business is amoral, neither working harder to serve you better, as they would have it, nor out to screw you to the wall, as consumer advocates would have it. No, a corporation is an amoral organism whose prime responsibility is to perpetuate itself. The engineers behind the shoddy stuff are blameless too, says Samuel Florman in *The Existential Pleasures of Engineering* (St. Martin's Press, 1976): "Something other than engineering failure is at issue here. The engineering profession is not on trial. It is our democracy that is on trial. . . . If engineers had been asked to look into the problem of overall protection of our resources, they would have been happy to do so. . . . Considering that society did not provide such support and showed practically no interest in preserving the environment, the role of the engineer during the precrisis years was not one to be ashamed of."

Caveat emptor. You might take a lesson from the wary consumers of other nations. With fewer funds and fewer ads, they aren't so impulsive in the marketplace. Europeans, for example, generally aren't as attracted by bargain prices and generally relate a higher price with durability. For them, trusted specialty stores are still an important part of life; shoppers take confidence from knowing the merchant. Americans, on the other hand, place their faith in large-scale advertising and favor big-name brands from national companies. Regional companies collapse not only because of the economics of scale, but because of our aversion to buying local.

European nations lead the United States in initiating enlightened consumer legislation and ad regulations. Norway and Sweden tend to lead the way, followed by Germany and the United Kingdom and, a few years behind, the United States. The Swedes apparently are more advanced in their thinking about product life, in particular. At a United Nations seminar on alternative patterns of development and life-styles, a Swedish paper suggested that products be made more durable and that they be shared through joint ownership; the resulting savings "should, unlike most of the technology emerging today, benefit the majority of mankind who do not belong to the world's upper classes." Ironically, some durable products, such as wool clothing, BMWs and Volvos, and well-built housing, can be afforded only by those who least need their long life spans. So it is that the bargain outlets peddle trendy junk, the opiate of today's masses.

Europeanization and Japanization

If Americans have a reputation for being wasteful, we didn't get this way because we're lazy. Laziness isn't a profound explanation for anybody's behavior. Rather, we just can't find the time to care for all our things.

Americans have more things than anyone else, and we are the first society to prove out the prediction of economist Staffan B. Linder: as we struggle to use more and more possessions, we will spend less time on such activities as dining and lovemaking. Skilled crafts will be abandoned in favor of activities that take no preparation, such as electronic games, television, spectator sports. Meanwhile, the recreational hardware piles up in closets and garages.

As the pace of life quickens, durability *must* lose out. Even labor-saving devices steal our time. They may spare precious minutes once successfully installed and humming nicely. But add up the time spent earning the purchase price, then shopping, transporting, repairing, storing, and ultimately holding a yard sale and, lo, the little gadget has eaten up a good part of our life.

Our things go unwashed, unlubricated, unadjusted. Manufacturers respond with no-wash surfaces, permanently lubricated bearings, and computer brains. Such advances are greeted with skepticism by many. These are the people who feel frustrated by labels that scold, "DO NOT OPEN—No owner-serviceable parts," who don't share manufacturers' optimism about new "extended-service intervals," who like products with screws and nuts and bolts rather than hermetically sealed plastic cases. These are the people who take the time to wash, lubricate, and adjust, who have learned the satisfaction of tending products that respond to care.

A person may become such a durability bug out of bald economic necessity, or for the satisfaction of living right, or both. In a phenomenon that has been called the Europeanization of America, consumers on the west shore of the North Atlantic now show an increasing concern for quality over quantity, both of food and of manufactured products. At the same time, American business managers and professors are traveling to Japan to learn if quality control is indeed more than a function of national disposition, if it can be fostered in the factories at home.

The free-market two-step, diagrammed

Producer: That's a fine-looking quiche you've got there. Spinach?

Consumer: This is no quiche. You're looking at the toaster-oven I bought from you six months ago. From the first day, it refused to release my English muffins, and this morning it proceeded to burn the muffins and fry itself. You sure don't make them like you used to.

Producer: Come on now, you're wallowing in nostalgia. Today's appliances utilize the latest space-age technology. We craft them of miraculous alloys and polycarbonates your parents never dreamed of, much less your grandparents.

Consumer: But my muffins—

Producer: Well, you can bet we'd build them to last if anybody'd buy them. This country still has a few shreds of free enterprise, you know.

Consumer: But I'd pay more for a durable toaster-oven. After six months of muffins, the dog wouldn't look at—

Producer: You *say* you'd buy one, but when we brought out our stainless steel, five-year-warranty model, where were you? It was built like a truck, but it died on the shelves. You wouldn't peel off another two lousy bucks for twice the product life.

Consumer: Well, why does it have to be all or nothing? Why can't you just bring out a durable line for people who'd invest in a better product?

Producer: Hey, this is an industry, not some backyard workshop. We can't make custom models. It's not cost-effective. You want to pay $5,000 for a toaster-oven?

Consumer: I guess not.

Producer: You guess not.

A sentimental junkyard

Almost every home has one—a resting place for things that we don't want in sight and yet can't live without. Rare is the person who doesn't have at least a closet, a drawer full of debris, precious and irreducible but caught forever in a horrible limbo. Here are unfinished craft projects, unrefinished antiques, superfluous tools, and appliances and toys that need nothing but a spring or a handle or a wire to be good as new.

This fish-eye view lays bare one family's sentimental junkyard. Below, the ashamed list tells the shabbier side of the durability issue: while we love things enough to drown ourselves in them, enough to work 40 hours a week to afford still more of them, we don't love them quite enough to care for them and see them through to a proper old age.

The family will go unnamed. Their outbuilding once was a stable for two horses. Today, the junk makes passage through the little building difficult, if not hazardous. There has been brave talk of a yard sale, but the trouble is this—the junk now has so much mass and complexity that it seems to have acquired a soul.

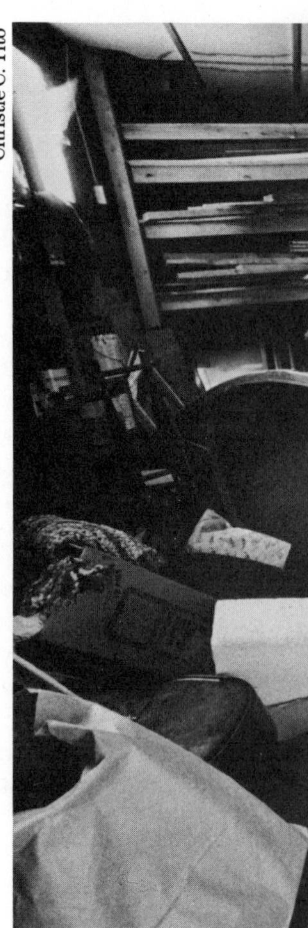
Christie C. Tito

Duck (circa 1895) was purchased during a bout of antique wooden boat fever. Upon close inspection, the hull proved to be stuffed with much cotton wool, held in place with roofing tar. The launching of *Duck* has been postponed indefinitely.

Columns from a lugubrious old mantel piece, rescued from a Victorian house. They don't suit the owners' bright little bungalow, and so bide their time here.

A handsome old soda machine dispenses the traditional seven-ounce Coke bottles. The relic was installed here with the intention of using the outbuilding as a party room.

A carpet too new to give away and too ugly to unroll.

A 220-volt commercial-grade Stanley router, bought at a public sale and stilled by a bad attack of rust.

Pieces of an oak bed, a woodworking project halted for want of a router.

Sassafras lumber, sawed from a downed tree and now quietly splitting and warping away. The wood was intended for night tables to complement the oak bed.

A railroad lantern, intended to become a lamp base.

An oats box, intended for conversion to a coffee table.

Five years' worth of empty wine bottles, hoarded with the expectation that by now they'd be filled with homemade vintages.

A Fender bass guitar amp, purchased at the wane of rock's golden age and stored here until the inevitable resurrection of 1960s pop.

Idle tools, some shiny and unused and others antiques of brass and rosewood. In this household, few chores or hobbies go undone for want of a tool. The missing component is time.

An axe. Among the simplest of tools, the axe has but two parts. Both of them are amiss here—a dull blade and a cracked handle. The owners have not fixed it out of the conviction that in this age of no-sharpen, disposable razors and scalpels, a disposable axe will soon be on the market.

An oak porch swing, picked up at a yard sale and stored here for want of a porch.

Two lawn chairs, banished to this sunless place because when in their proper spot—on the lawn—they seemed to reproach the owners for not slowing down and enjoying life. Here, securely stashed beneath old tires, the chairs can't make trouble.

A bicycle, idled partly because of a flat tire but mostly because of its owner's discovery that jogging is less time-intensive than pedaling.

A caned rocking chair, done in because of its inexplicable attractiveness to heavy house guests. Recaning it is a low-priority weekend project.

The current sobriety of American consumers may be just a lull between binges. It's too soon to tell. Just like hemlines and hair length, the demand for durability seems to follow cycles. Still, the public mood has changed for the time being.

Today, most Americans seem to realize their spendthrift days are over. Some gird themselves for what they expect to be a humbling, perhaps painful, change to leaner times. We face no less than a new era of pioneering. Nevertheless, many people will come through this transitional period quite cheerfully—millions of us, according to a Stanford Research Institute study, which estimates that 25 million Americans soon will choose a simpler, less cluttered life based on durable, reparable possessions. Their numbers are expected to grow to some 60 million by the end of the century.

Already, consumers are investing in goods with long-term value, ranging from antiques and gold watches to cars with high resale value, home insulation, and classic-styled clothing.

Shopping with an investor's eye and a conservationist's heart

Invest in products that last and the advantages are threefold: you stand to save money in repairs and replacement cost; you avoid the frustration that comes free of charge with every shoddy appliance and oafish car; and you are conserving resources and energy in a very real way, because a product that lasts longer is getting more mileage, in effect, out of the energy and materials that went into it.

Here is the pitch of the book before you. Both your financial health and the globe's health are intertwined. They meet in the store when you buy a product with its share of embodied materials, energy, and time.

The last paragraph of E. F. Schumacher's *Small Is Beautiful* asks and then answers the question, "What can I actually do?... We can, each of us, work to put our own house in order." These pages suggest one way to do just that, by consuming responsibly.

You'll note straight off that this book is not an L. L. Bean-y catalog of solid, woolly things to buy. If it were, a reader might come away with the mistaken impression that durability is something you can buy lots of. For anyone other than a lumberjack, one pair of deathless, heavy-duty malone cloth pants will serve as well as ten. And you don't even need to order *one* of each: if your terrain is no fiercer than a sidewalk, then you should resist the impulse to trade up to a pair of seven-pound Vibram-soled hiking boots. Here are five strategies to consider when sleuthing things built to last.

- The first and simplest was expressed by the presainthood Francis of Assisi in the Zefferelli movie *Brother Sun, Sister Moon*, when he said that if you have no possessions there'll be "no rust, no moth, no thief to steal." Modify this tack a bit and you have the Yankee proverb, "Use it up, wear it out, make it do, do without." You don't have to be a monastic saint or a flinty New Englander to appreciate that the simplest approach to the marketplace is to approach it not at all.
- Your second option will also keep you out of the malls: fix it up. Renew, rebuild, refinish, refurbish, rewire, reblock, reupholster, rebore, resole. Here is a skilled form of recycling. You'll pick up skills as you go, or you can take an evening course at the local vo-tech school. Tools are necessary. George Putz, coeditor of *The Mariner's Catalog*, calls a good tool kit a boat's "gland full of antibodies."
- Your third option demands more skill and time than the first and second. Make it yourself, and you can specify superior materials and will be assured of the

product's integrity. You can custom-design something to suit you, and because you built it, you'll know better than anybody else how to fix it. Not many people resort to building their own cars, but ever-greater numbers are taking on home construction, sewing, and cabinetry.

- There's still one option short of buying a new thing, and that's buying a used one, or "previously owned" if the thing happens to be an old Cadillac. This option involves pitfalls, as told by the old saw, "Buy used and you buy somebody else's problems." It's true that troubles may hide beneath a new coat of paint. Also, the marketing channels for buying and selling used things are often inconvenient, even downright risky. Best known is the used-car lot, with its string of bare light bulbs and torn pennants across the front and an unheated shack for signing papers in the back. (Perhaps the unkindest cut leveled at Richard Nixon during his 1960 presidential campaign was an ad featuring his five-o'clock-shadow face and the caption, "Would you buy a used car from this man?") The cars on the lot are caught in that awkward age between almost presentable and lovably camp. That is to say, they're grotesque—bulbous, faded, tatty, smelling of weary metal and spent liquids. Still, the secondhand buyer has the advantage of shopping with 20–20 hindsight. Given some distance from the cycles of fashion, it is possible to identify those items that have aged gracefully. Anyone can spot a classic, once it's been so certified.

- Buy new. Here is the option of last resort, from this book's point of view, but we all do it, so there's no need to wallow in guilt. The trouble here is that, despite warranties and odometer readings of one digit, the showroom is an ideal setting for a seduction—yours. It's harder to remain rational and skeptical in an air-conditioned, tastefully beige showroom than at a flea market or in the breakfast nook reading the morning's classifieds. Further, and at the risk of being a killjoy, this book would suggest to you that it is not enough to buy tastefully and with discretion. You're still playing the old tacky consumer game if durable things are purchased not out of need but to make a personal statement, or to kill time, or to resell in ten years at a killing, or to dodge a tax.

RY

Living simply and liking it

Investing care and money in but a few long-lasting products—here is a tactic that not only makes sense financially but also happens to be a first step in fashioning a contemplative or spiritual life.

Excess material baggage impedes this pursuit. A person has only so much time and energy to devote each day, and these precious commodities are siphoned off by tools, amenities, and toys.

The term "voluntary simplicity" has been applied to the intent of people who consciously limit their baggage in favor of a richer inner and interpersonal experience. As described by Richard Gregg, a student of Gandhi, voluntary simplicity "means singleness of purpose, sincerity and honesty within, as well as avoidance of exterior clutter, of many possessions irrelevant to the chief purpose of life."

It's not hard to see how a concern for the durability of one's possessions would fit into such a life.

One trip is too few

The one-trip throwaway tends to be a rather sophisticated, self-satisfied item.

Although of fleeting purpose, the plastic throwaway remains unbiodegradably cheerful as it bides its long life in roadside weeds, upon the shore, or blowing about a landfill. Unlike the reusable partners with which they are pictured, the one-trippers defy reuse, repair, and recycling. The consumer is absolved of such responsibilities, in exchange for an extra couple of pennies.

All photos, Christie C. Tito

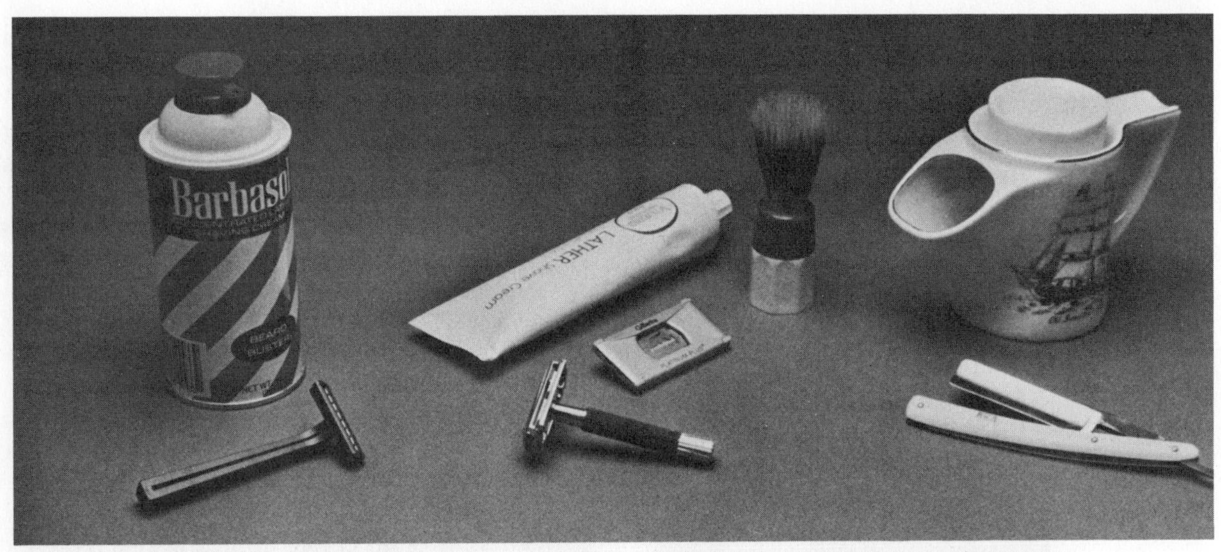
Barbasol
LATHER Shave Cream

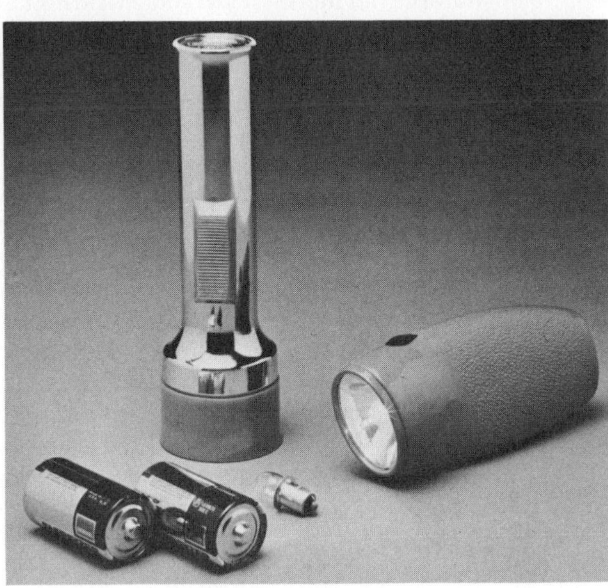

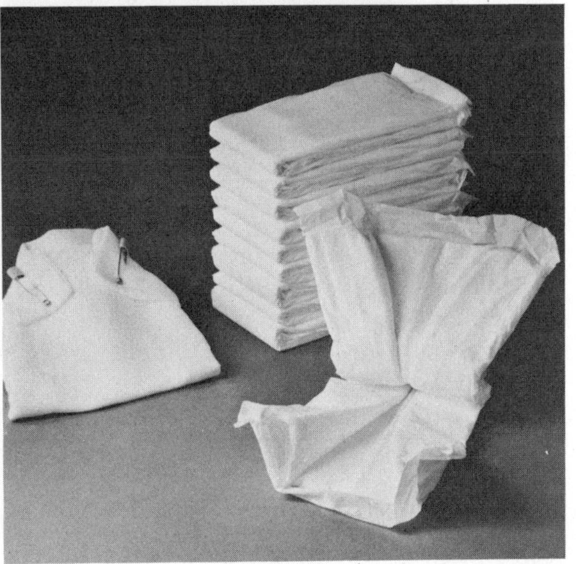

THE FASHION OF DURABILITY

Through most of history, durability has meant poverty. Only a handful of wealthy people could indulge in goods designed for delicacy or elegance rather than for indestructibility; everyone else owned just a few useful items constructed from the cheapest, most plentiful materials, in the simplest and sturdiest way. For example, in Europe of the Middle Ages, an ordinary peasant or laborer might have a bench, chest, and bedstead built from thick oak planks, crudely jointed and held together by nailed iron bands; some coarse bedding; work clothes of rugged fabrics like wool or linen; one more ornate feast-day outfit; several heavy iron pots and pans; and a few tools.

These possessions were handed down from generation to generation. Productivity was far too low to permit early replacement. As a result, styles in clothing and furnishings hardly changed over time. In some parts of the world, the basic garment of the common man went unchanged for centuries—the poncho in Peru, the dhoti in India, the long shirt in China, the kimono in Japan. The immobility of fashion among the poor was an outward sign of their social immobility; the durability of their possessions expressed the stultifying monotony and lack of opportunity in their lives. This was the durability of necessity.

Terms

Reliability is inversely proportional to the incidence of repair, while *durability* is a measure of potential useful life. An increase in reliability does not necessarily mean an increase in durability, and vice versa.

The few rich, on the other hand, celebrated their distinction from the masses by indulging in ornate, fragile goods such as glass vases, mirrors, furniture inlaid with precious woods, elaborate ruffs, and silk-embroidered robes. Louis XIV's Versailles was luxurious not only for the silver furniture and chandeliers, the gilt, the marble statues, the handmade carpets, but also for the rate of replacement. Because the rich enjoyed items not intended to last for generations, they also enjoyed changing styles of fashion. Upholstery and curtains were altered according to fashion and according to season (red and green velvet in winter, silks of all colors and brocades trimmed with gold and silver in the summer). The building itself was always being remodeled. One disgruntled courtier complained, "There isn't a part of Versailles which hasn't been modified at least ten times, and often not for the better." Louis XIV built Versailles in the first place rather than renovate the palace of the Louvre in Paris, as his ministers had advised. This was the conspicuous consumption of the nondurable.

But the reign of Louis XIV also marks the era when, for the first time in history, many people were liberated from the durability of necessity. Eighteenth-century Europe saw a growing market for less-durable but more-stylish goods: the middle classes bought domestic furnishings like mirrors and wallpaper, and colorful textiles made by country weavers in rural Europe and the bright calicoes made by handloom weavers in India.

The European craft guilds went to court to put a halt to these infringements on their legal monopoly of trade. One favorite argument of the guildsmen was that the illegal goods were inferior to those produced by guild members, who adhered to strict quality standards (for example, rules about so many threads per inch). But in the competition between quality controls and free trade, between a limited market of high quality and a broadly based market of lesser quality, the victory of the latter was inexorable. The guilds disappeared, victims, in part, of a vast movement of economic democratization—the demand of ordinary people to taste the pleasures of novelty, to be liberated from the tyranny of durability.

This movement was greatly accelerated by the Industrial Revolution, with the introduction of machines like the spinning jenny and the power loom. The power looms of the north of England drove the Indian hand-weavers out of business: in parts of the Indian countryside, the jungle literally grew back over the handlooms. The spinning jenny permitted at first a 3-fold, and soon a 10- or even 20-fold increase in output of yarn per worker, but there was no loss of quality, because the machine simply duplicated the worker's motions. (Modern yarn-making machines are a thousand times more productive than eighteenth-century spinning wheels and produce a far superior yarn.) The Industrial Revolution made it possible to produce long-lasting fabrics far more efficiently and far more cheaply than ever before. But these new fabrics were not long lasting, for reasons not technological but human. Finally liberated from the durability of necessity, people sought the delicacy, fashion, and elegance that for so long had been princely prerogatives. Thin, bright cottons, sleazy silks, and clumsy brocades satisfied their need. Machinery also cranked out flimsy wallpapers, thin carpets, pressed-tin knickknacks, ornate and easily chipped porcelains, and plated jewelry. In the words of the late-nineteenth-century French historian Georges d'Avenel, industrialization brought "the democratization of luxury," and with it an inherent decrease of durability.

Who are you?

> *"The socially conscious consumer is a pre-middle age adult of relatively high occupational attainment and socioeconomic status. He is typically more cosmopolitan, but less dogmatic, less conservative, less status conscious, less alienated, and less personally competent than his less socially conscious counterpart."*
>
> W. THOMAS ANDERSON, JR. and WILLIAM H. CUNNINGHAM, "The Socially Conscious Consumer," *Journal of Marketing*

A wallpaper manufacturer interviewed by d'Avenel confided that the dyes of his loveliest papers faded quickly, and lamented the passing of the cruder but inalterable dyes of earlier products. A silk dyer expressed similar regrets: the tints of his silks were gorgeous but ephemeral, he sighed, for durability had been sacrificed to quantity and charm. d'Avenel wondered if the sacrifice was really so terrible:

> I do not plead here the case of the "shoddy"; it does not need a lawyer, and if it needed a poet the dyers could say [and here d'Avenel quotes a well-known line from the French poet de Musset], "Who cares what's in the flask as long as it gets you drunk?" Who does care, if a new attraction is offered, if a present satisfaction is possessed by those . . . for whom it procures a quarter hour or even a minute of pleasure, if the delicious colors of this satin ribbon, of this taffeta blouse, or of this velour bow are destined to a premature disappearance? Are they made for eternity?

Because d'Avenel had made detailed historical studies of consumption patterns in France from 1200 to 1800, he viewed the democratized luxury of his own day against a backdrop of those long centuries when the luxuries of novelty and transience had been forbidden to the masses. He felt it was entirely understandable why shopgirls preferred shoddy, mass-produced silks to sturdy, handsome cottons. "The democratization of the silk dress, that ancient symbol of opulence," had helped topple the "brutal barrier" of appearance between rich and poor, and had allowed at least "an illusion of similarity." To those who would protest that such emphasis on appearances is banal, d'Avenel responded, "Before there was nothing banal but misery."

The shoddy swindle

What d'Avenel failed to point out is the degree to which a capitalist market economy encourages such "banal" desires for stylish novelty. Profits are to be made primarily by producing new goods, not by repairing old ones, and by selling the new ones in large numbers, meaning at the lowest possible unit price. Mechanization could cut costs, but other methods have been tried, including child and female labor, labor regimentation, adulteration of goods, and substitutions in materials and techniques. Reliability and durability have suffered: through the nineteenth century there was a swelling chorus of complaints about "cheap and nasty" and "shoddy" merchandise. The word "shoddy" originally described a cloth made from yarn obtained by shredding discarded woolen rags (an early example of recycling); this yarn was woven with new wool yarn into a tough fabric. During the American Civil War, a number of industrialists made fortunes by supplying army clothing made of shoddy rather than wool as promised. The "shoddy swindle" of these get-rich-quick businessmen, and not the inherent quality of the cloth, caused the word to become a derogatory term for pretentious, deceptive junk (such as d'Avenel meant when he protested, "I do not plead here the case of the 'shoddy' "). Consumers blamed producers for shoddiness, and producers turned around and blamed consumers for bad taste and bargain hunting. Both sides had their point, for it is the conjunction of consumer demand for democratized luxury and of market organization promoting it that has discouraged the manufacture of durable goods in the industrial age.

The social result has not been to produce an outward similarity between rich and poor. Luxury has changed in appearance—ironically toward durability. As the masses revel in silk dresses and wallpapers, the rich take refuge in so-called classics: timeless fashions, antique furniture, gold, aged wines, old books, venerable art works, heavy silver, musical instruments, well-worn Oriental rugs, and almost anything else old and handmade rather than new and machine-made. The rich invest in such items not so much because they will last a long time but because they are scarce, made from costly materials, and represent expensive labor. Here is a startling reversal of values: handcrafted durability becomes something sought by the rich, while ordinary folk have to be content with fashion, novelty, change.

Clearly this new elitist durability served to maintain a "brutal barrier" of appearances between the rich and the common herd in a rapidly changing world. But the upper class embraced conspicuous durability for more laudable motives, including the need to maintain lovely and useful things (although too often underpaid servants did the upkeep). Such things have been termed (in the words of one late-nineteenth-century economist) "the capital of enjoyment." Pianos, dinnerware, books, if built to last and maintained, can provide pleasure through periods of change and uncertainty. Here is the soul of durability. In a commercial age proclaiming the standard of profitability, the notion of durability recalls a higher, humanistic standard: that of civilization.

This higher standard applies to more than personal possessions. In even faster cycles, whole environments are tossed up and then traded in. The effects have been most noticeable in the cities. During the nineteenth century, major cities of the West commenced a process of perpetual urban renewal. The prototypical case is Paris. In the mid-1800s, Paris was still a semimedieval confusion of dark, dank houses and narrow, twisted, rutted alleys. By 1870, the city had 85 miles of wide, paved, well-drained, tree-lined streets. Acres of old houses had been torn down and new apartments erected. During the last three decades of the century, electrical street lighting was installed, the Metro was built, the boulevards were extended, the sewer and water systems were further modernized, and countless new apartment and commercial buildings were erected and old ones were equipped with elevators and electricity—all of this

before the major adjustments required by the advent of the automobile. Georges d'Avenel remarked in 1897 that the childhood memories of middle-aged Parisians like himself were linked to hammering and scaffolding, for in their lifetimes they had seen their city crumble and rise again: half the houses in Paris were under 25 years old, so most Parisians of that time were older than their homes. d'Avenel wondered if the stability of the physical environment might not promote human instability. Parisians had gained material comforts but had lost spiritual solace:

> Walls have not only ears but also a mouth . . . They speak and evoke certain memories with a precision which had no equal . . . Here, along these new byways, under these fresh moldings, the individual . . . ceases to hang his existence . . . onto the material things that surround him. Mobile pile of human dust, the masses squat before hearths which have no history, which are indifferent to their joys or sorrows, and they form no attachment to them.

This is a radical alteration in the relationship between man and the material world he creates.

Traditionally, a person was born into a stable physical environment—tools, furnishings, buildings—constructed and used by past generations and destined for future ones. Industrialization completely changed not only the appearance of the material world, but also its duration—not only space, but also time. The poet Charles Baudelaire, writing during the height of Paris's reconstruction, sighed,

> The old Paris is no more (the form of
> a city
> Changes faster, alas! than the heart of
> a mortal).

Under such conditions, how could an individual feel himself part of a lasting human community? How could a person retain a commitment to an ideal of civilization when its concrete form was perpetually being destroyed? Such questions have been especially troubling in the United States. While the European countryside remained comparatively stable, in the United States city and country alike have been caught up in a process of continual renewal. Americans build for mobility rather than durability. This tendency was disturbing to Thomas Jefferson, who may have rejected Old World governments but continued to admire the Old World ideal of civilization. In his *Notes on the State of Virginia* (1785), Jefferson criticized

fellow Virginians for building most of their houses from thin boards plastered with lime: "It is impossible to devise things more ugly, uncomfortable, and happily more perishable." Jefferson argued that stone and brick dwellings were equally healthy, often cheaper, and "infinitely more durable," adding,

> This latter consideration renders it of great importance to eradicate this prejudice [against stone and brick] from the minds of our countrymen. A country whose buildings are of wood, can never increase in its improvements to any considerable degree. Their duration is highly estimated at fifty years. Every half century then our country becomes a *tabula rasa*, whereon we have to set out anew, as in the first moment of seating it.

Most Americans considered civilization not as an inheritance of the past but as a dream of the future. In 1840, a Massachusetts farmer expressed the prevailing view when he explained why stone houses were inappropriate for dynamic American conditions:

> Our roads are always changing their direction, and after a man has built at great cost a stone house, a new road is opened, and he finds himself a mile or two from the highway. Then our people are not stationary, like those of old countries, but always alert to better themselves, and will remove from town as a new market opens or a better farm is to be had, and do not wish to spend too much on their buildings.

The dilemma of durability in modern life, then, and especially in American life, is how to escape the dead weight of the past without also throwing off its guidance and gifts and comfort; how to be mobile without being rootless; how to maintain civilization without maintaining unfair privilege; how to enjoy the pleasures of novelty and style without giving up stability, order, and repose. The issue of durability obviously involves physical resources, but to discuss it is to cross over into matters social, moral, and ultimately spiritual. For whatever complicated reasons, the rise of industrialization coincides with the decline of religious conviction. As the physical environment becomes more transient, people question their faith in the endurance of the soul.

The Arts and Crafts revolt

Beginning in the late nineteenth century, designers of buildings and furnishings undertook the task of redefining the significance of durability for our time.

William Morris, a British poet, designer, and revolutionary socialist, refused to

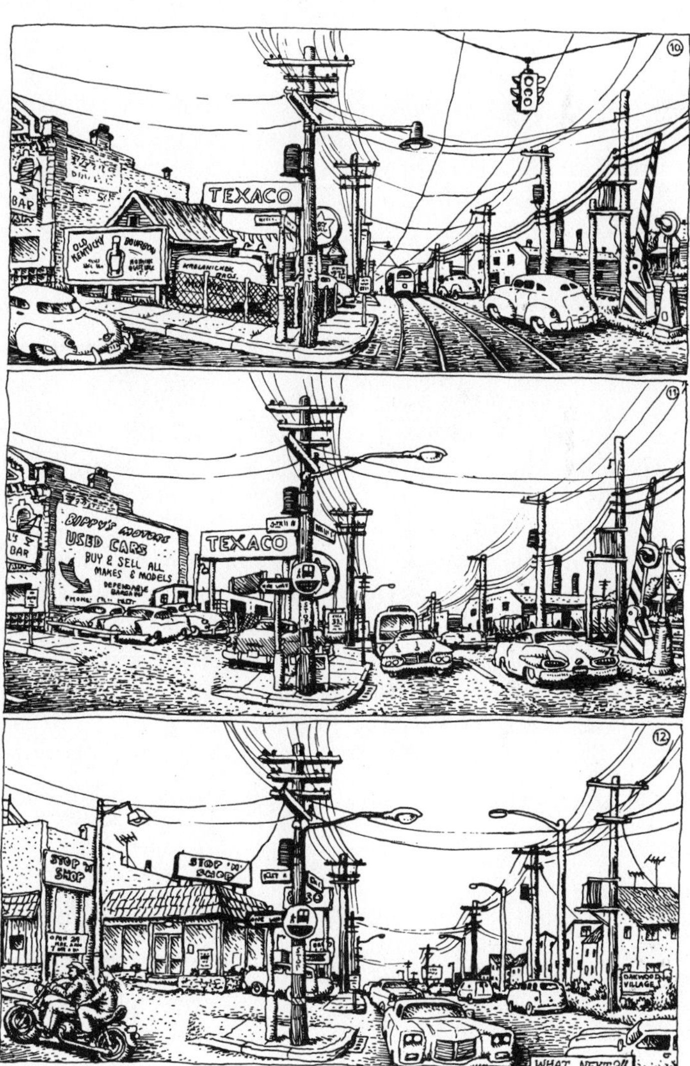

dissociate his concern for art from his concern for social justice. For Morris, the lack of durability in industrial civilization was both a social and an artistic outrage: social because "shoddiness" was the inevitable result of an inhuman economic system that had profit as its only aim; and artistic because of the pervasive ugliness of the "jerry-built," another term from the mid-1800s. Morris's response was not so much to redefine durability as to restore it, by returning to the techniques and designs of the Middle Ages. His reaction was entirely understandable in the context of the Victorian age, when ideals of the Middle Ages were held up to the grim, grimy reality of industrial England. Morris's preference for manual rather than mechanical techniques was based not only on his conviction that machine-made goods were inferior in quality and beauty—a prejudice he shared with the guildsmen of the eighteenth century—but even more on his conviction that only hand methods allowed the variety and creativity that differentiated a human from a robot.

Morris's firm produced sturdy Gothic or neo-peasant handmade furniture, carpets, wallpapers, fabrics, and the like; the Kelmscott Press, which he established toward the end of his life, turned out elaborate, hand-printed books. Morris took extraordinary measures to ensure that these goods would have the durability as well as the appearance of preindustrial models. Most of Morris's furniture was massively solid. He experimented tirelessly to find bright and long-lasting natural dyes. His carpets were so tightly woven that they were virtually indestructible. Kelmscott books were made from rag paper and ink made precisely to his specifications.

Morris revived preindustrial durability—but after the Industrial Revolution, handmade durability could no longer be afforded by the poor. The labor and materials that went into Morris's goods were far too costly for any but wealthy buyers. Morris believed this contradiction between his commercial market and his socialist politics could be resolved only by the revolutionary overthrow of capitalism. Morris's disciples in the English Arts and Crafts Movement, however, tended to adopt his aesthetics but not his politics. For them the contradiction was more troubling. One disciple, Eric Ashbee, confided to his unpublished memoirs, "We have made a great social movement, a narrow and tiresome little aristocracy working with great skill for the very rich."

This self-criticism was mild compared to the denunciations hurled at Morris, his compatriot John Ruskin, and the Arts and Crafts designers by younger Italian artists. Filippo Marinetti, spokesman of the Italian Futurists, shocked a London audience in 1912 when he pleaded,

---

"The high cost of energy has made consumers much more aware of operating costs. They'll do some calculations to estimate how much a particular appliance will cost to own. But consumers are still pretty naive about life-cycle costing. The problem for the consumer is that he's not sophisticated enough to understand discounted cash flow. Or present value. Yet that's what you need to know to get a life-cycle cost that is useful. In other words, you might as well buy durable goods because to hold money as money means you're going to have rapidly declining value on your hands, thanks to inflation."

ROBERT LUND,
Massachusetts Institute of Technology

Renewal

"I've forgotten how many miles of porches the old Grand Union Hotel had, with hundreds of rockers along them. First thing in the morning the people would walk across the road to Congress Springs to drink of the waters. Presidents and nobles stayed there—President Van Buren, Jerome Napoleon, Mark Twain, James Fenimore Cooper, Washington Irving. Victor Herbert was in the gardens when he overheard a conversation in the moonlight, and that was the stimulus for writing 'Kiss Me Again.'

The Grand Union Hotel in Saratoga Springs, New York.

"Some would feign illness as an excuse to spend the social season at the spas. One man used to come down to the Hotel bar and try to get people to invest money in building a bridge across the Atlantic Ocean so that they could make Saratoga Springs the capitol of the world. His name was Lord Wilson. I don't know if he really was of noble extraction or not, but he wore old-time clothes, with a top hat, and britches instead of pants.

"It was demolished in the 1950s. All of us who cared about the old days feel terrible. And of all things, to have a Grand Union parking lot right where it was."

An interview with VIOLET DUNN,
Saratoga County (New York) historian

The hotel in 1900.

Sleepy sidewalks in 1952, not long before the hotel's razing.

All photos, collection of George S. Bolster

The Grand Union supermarket, 1981.

> When will you disencumber yourselves of the lymphatic ideology of your deplorable Ruskin, whom I intend to make utterly ridiculous in your eyes?... this maniac for antique simplicity resembles a man who in full maturity wants to sleep in his cot again and drink at the breasts of a nurse who has now grown old, in order to regain the carefree state of infancy.

Englishmen like Ruskin and Morris, who saw at first hand the filth and misery of modern industry, yearned for simpler, lovelier, more humanly satisfying times. Italians like Marinetti, who came from a poor and unindustrialized country, could not comprehend a rejection of the benefits of modern technology. They had seen the past at first hand, as it were, having been raised among the ruins of past glories and the bitter fruits of ancient poverty. They substituted a cult of the future for the cult of the past, and glorified speed, transience, change. The great cities of the world should be leveled and destroyed. Even the Louvre should be burned, along with anything else intended as a monument to past achievements. In the hard-edged universe of the future, only machinery would be worshipped. Life would take on not only the look of the machine but also its rhythms of constant cycling, ceaseless movement, and dynamic restlessness. Durability was a maniacal concept of "antique simplicity" which itself had to be scrapped as hopelessly obsolete. "Each generation its own house" was one Futurist slogan.

Despite the hysterical aura around the Futurist vision, it encouraged a generation of architects and designers to experiment with structures intended to be movable, inflatable, or disposable, rather than conforming to traditional architectural ideals of solidity and stability. Designers of the German-based Bauhaus School were committed to the "Factory Aesthetic," the unabashed use of industrial forms and materials irrespective of traditional aesthetic furnishings. Bauhaus designers like Walter Gropius also rejected the domestic ideal in housing, the ideal of a private home passed down from generation to generation. Gropius preferred "Workers' Housing," which would tend to free people from ties to the past and to family. The French architect Le Corbusier, at one time associated with the Bauhaus, proclaimed that a house should be nothing but a "machine for living," a "House-Tool":

> The house has always been the indispensable and first tool that man has forged for himself, and tools are the result of successive improvement; . . . We throw the out-of-date tool on the scrap-heap . . . but men live in old houses still and they have not yet thought of building houses adapted to themselves . . . they have established the cult of the home.

The Arts-and-Crafts notion that human beings need to be in touch with familiar and lasting objects was derided by Le Corbusier and others as the class-bound, self-serving ravings of privileged cliques. Neither side convinced the other, and the bitterness of the argument obscured the fact that it was based on false assumptions—the assumptions that durability is necessarily associated with expensive hand work, and that machinery necessarily promotes disposability.

Friendly technology

The insight that durability can be united with modern technology came from neither England nor Italy in the Old World, but from the New World. Frank Lloyd Wright, son of a Wisconsin farm family, sounded the note of reconciliation in a 1901 speech titled "The Art and Craft of the Machine." "All artists love and honor William Morris," Wright declared. "That he miscalculated the machine does not matter." Morris's mistake lay in confusing the ugliness due to the misuse of the machine with mechanization itself. The task of the modern artist and architect, Wright asserted, is to use the machine creatively rather than in reproducing old forms.

Sometimes in his ardor for modern technology, Wright sounded like the Futurists ("My God is machinery"), but he did not agree with the Futurists' social values. He considered their "ideal cities" to be more like "graveyards of individuality." Wright's houses were not intended to emulate machinery but to express their own integrity as human dwellings, structures that belong to the owner and to the land from which they rise. In the late teens, in response to Futurist propaganda, Wright published numerous essays defending the Gothic spirit in architecture.

The American reconciliation of durability and machinery went beyond Wright in the development of interchangeable parts (especially for making guns, locks, farming machinery, sewing machines, and watches). An item could then be maintained by replacing one part instead of making the entire object over again—an important consideration in a society where labor was scarce. So, although American opportunism tended to encourage a disregard of durability, the country also encouraged durability with tools that were reliable and easily maintained by the owner. The "American vernacular" is the term used by cultural historian John Kouwenhoven to describe the functional "machines, buildings, and other objects for use in the routine of daily life," which, in his opinion, comprise a genuine, homegrown American art form.

Another characteristic of the American vernacular has been continual experimentation with light, easily worked materials, many of which have proved to be exceptionally durable as well. The classic example is the use of slender 2 × 4s and small nails to construct "balloon-frame" houses, so called because the structure seems improbably fragile compared to dwellings framed by time-consuming traditional methods of cutting, fitting, and pegging together stout timbers over a foot square. Despite the contemptuous name, balloon frames proved to be strong, and they required far less labor and materials. The method developed anonymously in the United States from the 1830s on. Later, American builders pioneered in the use of iron, ferroconcrete, and plywood, all of which also combined lightness with strength. These experiments culminated in the American invention of the skyscraper, which is a sort of urban, steel-and-glass version of the balloon-frame house.

The outstanding example of durability in the American vernacular is the Model T Ford, whose design was established in 1909. Unlike most automobiles of that era, the Model T was an undisguised machine with no pretentions to being a coach or carriage. It was available in any color as long as it was black. The market for the Model T was, in Henry Ford's words, "the 95 percent of the population" who could afford only a "completely utilitarian" means of transportation, without costly and extraneous ornaments. Its parts were interchangeable not only among all cars of one model but also among similar parts on all cars Ford had produced. Above all, the Model T was made to last. Ford explained,

> It is considered good manufacturing practice, and not bad ethics, occasionally to change designs so that old models will become obsolete and new ones will have to be bought. . . Our principle of business is precisely to the contrary. We cannot conceive how to serve the customer unless we make for him something that, as far as we can provide, will last forever.

Ford wrote this in 1923, the year Alfred P. Sloan became president of General Motors and initiated a sales strategy based on frequent technological and stylistic changes. At a 1925 sales meeting, Sloan explained that

> the entire automobile industry has been built up by and around people of mechanical and technical characteristics, rather than commercial, and I think we are just beginning to realize the great importance of the commercial side of the business.

Soon Sloan's emphasis on "continuous, eternal change" seriously cut into Ford's share of the market. Ford held out stubbornly in favor of his own ideas of good manufacturing practice and ethics, but finally, in 1927, his company stopped producing the Model T. The next model year, Ford introduced the Model A, available in many colors, and thereafter imitated GM's annual model changes. Any democratic instincts for simplicity, stability, and equality expressed in the American vernacular were losing out to elitist desires for novelty, ornamentation, and status.

In the 1920s and 1930s, corporate managers waged an intensive campaign to convince buyers that continual change was not just good for business but a necessary part of life itself. General Motors published articles in magazines like the *Saturday Evening Post* to defend frequent product changes. The articles spoke of growth, evolution, and Darwinism. "Nature is never satisfied with existing forms," GM asserted. In these decades, businesses established research laboratories to provide a reliable, institutionalized source of technological change; Charles F. Kettering, GM director of research, praised them as "departments of discontent." Also in the 1920s and 1930s, the profession of industrial design was established to provide a never-failing source of stylistic changes. Advertising became a major industry. The invention of "consumer engineering" was based on the premise that buyers should be reminded of their desires and needs and should be made to feel uncomfortable with out-of-date goods. Durability was criticized publicly as an obstacle to social progress. Christine Frederick, a home economist who published *Selling Mrs. Consumer* in 1929, enthused:

> America's triumphs and rapidity of progress are based on *progressive obsolescence*. . . as a ladder by which to climb to greater human satisfactions through the purchase of more of the fascinating and thrilling range of goods and services being offered today. We obtain a sense of speed and progress and increased fulness of life as a result.

The Futurists could hardly have said it better.

Planned obsolescence

Whether expressed by Futurist artists or business executives, planned obsolescence (a phrase coined by an industrial designer in 1940) is most disturbing not for what it says about goods but for what it says about people. If the role of human beings is to react to technological change, then people are part of the technological process: they become machines themselves. Then they too are disposable if they become outmoded obstacles to "progress." This is one of the revelations of Arthur Miller's play *Death of a Salesman* (1949), a moving requiem not just to the aging salesman Willy Loman but to a whole society committed to planned obsolescence. Willy Loman understands the material consequences of that commitment. When the refrigerator breaks down again, Willy explodes:

> Once in my life I would like to own something outright before it's broken! I'm always in a race with the junkyard! I just finished paying for the car and it's on its last legs. The refrigerator consumes belts like a goddamn maniac. They time those things. They time them so when you finally paid for them, they're used up.

Jonathan Atkin

Mothballed B-52s, part of a grounded air force of 4,000 planes sitting in the desert outside of Tucson, Arizona.

Poor investments

The most flagrant affront to durability is the modern military establishment. If their weapons are used, they are the most potent destroyers of durability imaginable, although proponents of "limited nuclear war" suggest that rebuilding would be rapid and that nothing irreplaceable would be lost. Even if modern weaponry is not used, it represents a staggering investment in planned obsolescence. As one general remarked, "If it works, it's obsolete."

ROSALIND WILLIAMS

What Willy never really understands is how the same philosophy applies to him. When he is through paying for himself, when he is "used up" as a salesman, he too is thrown into the junkyard. At the age of 63, he is fired by the young president of the company, who fiddles with a new wire recorder ("the most terrific machine I ever saw in my life") as he gives Willy the bad news. "Business is business," Willy is told, and the tragedy is that Willy himself partly accepts that sense of values. He has been so sold himself on the go-getter gospel, on the ideology of change and moving on, that he cannot stop dreaming of another commercial conquest.

But there is another side to Willy too, the fix-it-up side. He has spent hours puttering around the house, finishing the cellar, adding on a new porch, an extra bathroom, putting up a garage. "All the cement, the lumber, the reconstruction I put in this house!" he brags. "There ain't a crack to be found in it any more." His son Biff remarks that Willy's real happiness came from these projects, not from his salesman's dreams: "There's more of him in that front stoop than in all the sales he ever made." But Willy loses his job when he is just about to own outright the one seemingly solid, reliable thing in his life. Under this stress he begins to consider himself more disposable than the house. If he kills himself, his life-insurance money will pay off the house at last and may also, he dreams, let his son make a fortune mining diamonds. Willy junks himself and his car in a deliberate accident. At the end of the play, Willy's widow weeps over his grave: "I made the last payment on the house today. Today, dear. And there'll be nobody home."

Death of a Salesman is supremely prophetic in questioning the human consequences of planned obsolescence, and other voices began to question this ideology. Vance Packard's book *The Waste Makers* (1960) turned "planned obsolescence" into a dirty phrase; it disappeared from corporate vocabulary. Consumer resistance became well organized only after Ralph Nader charged in *Unsafe at Any Speed* (1966) that American automobiles not only self-destructed but also tended to destroy their passengers. Nader and his associates proceeded to create consumer organizations to pressure industry and government for higher safety and quality standards in a whole range of products. In 1980, the state of Indiana brought criminal charges against the Ford Motor Company for marketing an allegedly dangerous car, establishing that corporations are just as accountable for their actions as individuals.

The consumer movement born in the 1960s has been one significant factor in reviving concern about durability. Another is the environmental movement. As awareness of the finiteness of the earth's resources has grown, so has awareness that building things to last is a form of conservation. The ethic of durability has thereby been enlarged to include loyalty not only to the human past but also to the future of the natural world. But this new ethical awareness has yet to be translated into basic changes in the way we do business. Corporations may deny knowledge of planned obsolescence, but the economic forces encouraging a rapid turnover of goods are still as powerful as ever. "Business is business," and too much durability may hinder business—and many times this is equated with standing in the way of progress, as the term is most often used. However, we must first ask whether progress and business are really the same thing; we must ask how much progress is material and how much social or moral, and whether product improvements and novelties necessarily constitute genuine progress. To make the world safe for durability, we must first decide what we mean by progress and then restructure economic institutions: the two tasks are inseparable.

But these are tasks for a generation, or even generations. In the meantime, the new consciousness of durability is most likely to find expression on a private, noninstitutional level by individuals who try to live by the old Yankee adage, "Use it up, wear it out, make it do, do without."

The concern for durability threatens to go no deeper than a novel flavor of life-style for an elite few: the preference for durability can be degraded into a sort of calculated, obviously expensive simplicity that takes the form of chunky sofas, plain wooden toys, and indestructible cottons (see "Dressing down tastefully: an elegy for Design Research," p. 219). Even the durability of machinery has been promoted as the High-Tech look.

So we consumers try to probe our own motives for preferring durability. For us is it *only* a fashion? Is our preference for it an honest expression of personal values and needs, or an unconscious submission to the latest commercial trend? Is our preference rooted in social consciousness, or merely self-consciousness?

ROSALIND WILLIAMS

I am indebted to Theodore M. Brown, professor of the history of art at Cornell University, for allowing me to draw upon his unpublished manuscript, "Whatever Happened to Planned Obsolescence?" and to William M. Reddy, professor of history at Duke University, for his paper, "The Spinning Jenny in France: Popular Complaints and Elite Misconceptions on the Eve of the Revolution," which appeared in the 1981 *Proceedings of the Consortium on Revolutionary Europe*.—R.W.

A durable agriculture

On an organic farm, nature is the farmer's capital. Decisions are made with a mind to preserving this capital—the soil—or building it up if necessary. Treated this way, a farm should be infinitely durable, living beyond each tenant in turn.

According to the USDA's *Report and Recommendations on Organic Farming*, farmers switch to organic methods for several far-sighted reasons. They foresee an increasing vulnerability of an agriculture heavily dependent on petroleum for machinery and chemical fertilizers. They observe an ongoing decline in soil productivity caused by reliance on chemical fertilizers, which do not involve a living soil. They recognize the harm done to the environment by erosion and by agricultural chemicals in the water supply. They appreciate the hazards of pesticides to workers and animals and to those who eat the tainted food. They want to preserve the family farm and a localized marketing system.

These are admirable motivations, but the organic farmer faces the day-to-day responsibility of more hours in the field to raise the same amount of crops. Rather than make a pass or two over the field with herbicide, the organic farmer controls weeds by crop rotation, tillage, mowing, and even hand weeding. Crop rotation also serves to build up the soil after growing a nitrogen-demanding crop such as corn, sorghum, or wheat.

The organic farmer faces a lower economic return above variable costs because some land is set aside each year to be built up by nitrogen-building legumous crops. Pest control is more delicate, relying at least in part on natural predators and parasites.

So it is in any area covered by this book: the greater, long-term gain is earned by an investment today in time and purpose. Whether it's a long-life car or a successful organic farm, the equation must include a person who cares.

WHY THINGS DON'T LAST

(An open letter from an angry designer)

(We asked J. Baldwin, of CoEvolution Quarterly *and the New Alchemy Institute, to write a field guide to durable products, one that talked of weight, simplicity, materials, and brand names as clues. Impossible, said Baldwin. He wrote us to explain that even in the unlikely event a durable product could be found, the consumer would need an engineering degree to recognize its superiority.)*

I think the problem is clear: there is not a sufficient market for good stuff to make it profitable. Most new cars do not have grease fittings in the front end. It is well known among mechanics that cars without grease zerks won't last as long as those with zerks—if you grease them. But most people *don't* grease their cars, and so in the long run, for the majority, the "permanently" lubed front ends will last longer. Another example is carburetors. There aren't any mechanics around who can overhaul one anymore, so the automakers make them to be junked rather than overhauled. This isn't only the fault of the corporations, it's our fault too.

There are two general ways to have a long-life device: make it so it doesn't wear very fast; and make it so the wear can be taken up. But this information may not be much help to someone shopping for a car. When I go to buy a car, I check to see if the carb wear can be taken up. What do I look for? What if this car is the best available, but the carb is a throwaway type? Do I write the car company and say, "If the carb was adjustable, I'd buy your car, and in the meantime you can stuff it"? Would that help? They'd write back and say that the high cost of fixing cars, which is what we are talking about, would be even higher if the mechanic had to take the whole morning to diagnose and disassemble the carb to repair it. In the long run, for my pocketbook, it is going to be cheaper merely to replace the faulty one because of the high cost of skilled labor. Therefore, I am inclined to assert that unfixable assemblies are the direct result of an affluent society that pays its menials so much.

It is well to keep in mind that in a free market *any* manufactured item is made as shoddily as it can be and still sell, and that has *always been the case.* The free, unregulated market slowly brings quality down to the lowest level that'll still get by. It has to be this way. No matter what pride old-time workmen took in their work, they still had to compete. As soon as things got widely distributed, as for instance "store-bought" clothes, so that the local craftsman was not the sole source, then cutthroat competition forced quality reduction. Yet it can be argued (and was argued in that time) that store-bought clothes greatly reduced the drudgery of housewifery. At the time, housewives spent about *one-third* of their waking hours making clothes and/or yarn. What they made was mostly good quality of course, so they didn't have to do it again, but given their druthers, they *chose* store-bought. Now that phenomenon has taken a new twist: you can't buy cloth cheaply enough to make your own clothes at a reasonable price. Recently I priced 13-ounce denim and found that I could not make a pair of Levi's as cheaply as I could buy a pair, assuming that I paid myself nothing for labor!

This is part of a plot, of course. Another aspect of this sort of thing is apparent when you see for sale in "professional" catalogs so-called industrial-grade glue. That means that you *can* get the good stuff, but only if you're a manufacturer.

Then there's the matter of a manufacturer's incentive to take quality out of a product. For instance, if an auto manufacturer makes 3 million cars a year, saving a dime on the ashtray handle means the manufacturer makes a significant wad of money. In fact, automakers order bids figured out to the mil! For another example, a few pence worth of rustproofing oil on shock-absorber bolts would save countless thousands of folks much frustrating labor when it comes time to replace the shocks. Yet those few pence of oil are not applied, even on expensive cars. It makes sense for the manufacturer to save that money because oiled shock-absorber bolts will not help sell the car, and since people think (have been trained, that is, to think) that shock bolts are always a pain in the ass anyway, there is just no point in oiling them at the factory. There are lots of things that work this way. Ask yourself—would *you* oil the bolts?

Let good things be

Over and over, the urge to make "new" models leads to dropping a very good old one for no gain to the consumer or the manufacturer. The original Dodge Dart is an example. It went from being the best American car to being the dreadful Aspen model, which smirched Chrysler's reputation so badly they nearly lost the game. The Aspen offered few improvements over the old model and succeeded in losing the old model's reliability in the process. The heavy Skillsaw Model 77 is another case. Used ones bring more than the new version.

Manufacturers who have taken a different tack have generally not fared well. For instance, Citroen is virtually the only automaker willing to expend much money on exotic engineering. To pay for that effort, they make the same models year after year: the 2 CV since 1946, the DS from 1955 to 1973, and the still-in-production, best all-around car made, the GSA wagon. But they are in trouble financially despite the fact that their cars are the state of the art. Problem: they can't be "all new" every 3 years. It is very ironic. The '82 Toyota Corolla is essentially the same car as it was 10 years ago as far as comfort and performance go. Yet it sells well. When my Citroen DS finally wore out after 14 years (in 1980), it was *still* dramatically better than any 1980 model! In this case, I think that the problem with Citroen arose from an ineffective advertising campaign—the public was not shown what was what. One reason for this, though, is that the auto magazines, all of them with the exception of the excellent British *Car*, castigated the Citroen for presenting "about the same as last year's," while extolling the new models. Explanation is easy: the car mags need the advertising revenue. (*Car*, by the way, always greatly praises Citroen, and many of their staff drive them). Most magazines treated the Citroen as a freak, and only mentioned the fact that you could make the car go up and down hydraulically. The fact that the balanced suspension didn't permit dramatic wheelspin while leaving Kentucky Fried Chicken turned them off, and the reviews were also sneering or condescending.

What does this all mean? The ossification of mind and nerve caused by huge capital outlays for tooling means the big basic features can't be changed into "new" models without prohibitively expensive tooling changes, so frippery is stressed instead. In automobiles, they stress dashboard coin trays and velour seats and don't mention brakes and handling, for instance.

Since the business of business is to make a profit, and the best way to make a profit selling artifacts is to make those items as sleazily as possible and still have people buy them, the only way to change any of this is to get people to boycott poor quality. But the layman can't tell what's good. How the hell can I tell if the steel in a chisel is good?

I don't think a lay person can determine quality without expertise. There are some dreadful dichotomies around, including my beloved Citroen Corporation, which makes the world's most advanced, safest, most economical, most comfortable cars and then doesn't rustproof them. For many products, you could use the "apartment" metaphor: in any apartment, there is *something* lousy. Either the landlord is a crook, or there is a lot of street noise, or there is no place to park. There is no peace for the living! So it is with just about all products.

Quite often there are aspects of a certain product that are only known to a few. Take my humble abode, the Silver Turd, an Airstream trailer. Everyone says, "Oh wow, the Cadillac of trailers." Well, how many know that the handsome aluminum body is bolted to a steel chassis, and without any sort of dielectric pads to prevent disastrous rust under the floor? How many know that Airstream uses a body-sealer caulk that turns to little dry crumbs after about six years? And, how many care?

Durability in disguise

Brand name is most certainly *not* a good indication of durability, though it is better than nothing. Did you know, for instance, that "reputable" manufacturers of large appliances make especially low-quality versions for use in furnished mobile homes? Or, worse, woe and alas—what about the Chevy Vega and its meltdown motor? Or the Pinto Barbeque? Neither of these well-publicized turkeys suffered any drastic sales slippage because of their problems. And Pinto finally added a $10 part to reduce explosions. And Vega changed the name of the engine to something like "Dura-built" and lowered the temperature at which the overheat light comes on. The public not only ignores low quality or bad design, they may even make a fetish of it! Witness the growing popularity of the criminally dangerous Corvair as a used car and collector's piece. Even the vile VW Beetle lost no sales until thoroughly outclassed.

The traditional solid-door-slam test is 100 percent due to how many pounds of sound-deadening putty is in there, not how much strength there is. Indeed, some cars with good-sounding doors rust out faster because the deadener attracts water. Manufacturers give the *appearance* of quality, and they furnish the *symbols*, as with the Caddy having more fake wood than a Chevy.

Most brand names have a bad year now and then, and lately even big names are reneging on guarantees, cutting quality, and generally behaving badly. There *is* a difference between a Chevy engine and an Olds. The more expensive cars supposedly have a finer selection of parts, or at least they did at one time.

Weight has little to do with durability. One of the reasons Americans are energy pigs has been that we tend to replace clever design with excess iron: "Make the table out of 12 × 12s so the mother'll never fall apart." There is little correlation between strength and weight. Aircrafts and boats bear this out. There is also a tendency to equate weight with durability, when the opposite is the case. Do you think that the 250-pound door on a T-Bird lasts longer than a VW door?

> *"While the planting of a field crop . . . may be looked upon as a 'short-term investment,' the planting of a chestnut tree is a covenant of faith."*
>
> WENDELL BERRY, *A Continuous Harmony* (Harcourt Brace Jovanovich, 1972)

Does it protect the passenger better? (No, it's still only one layer of steel between you and the enemy car.) Much better is the huge sidebeam of the chassis of the Citroen DS, which puts the main frame of the car between you and the enemy, yet the Citroen weighs just a few pounds more than a Pinto. While it may be true that a Schwinn Varsity weighing 30 pounds may last longer in the hands of a 12-year-old than, say, a Colnago at 20 pounds, that is still not proof one way or the other. Weight is the *cheap* way to strength—so far, but not for long in this day of expensive energy and metal. Would a cast-iron, 5-pound flyswatter be more durable? I do not doubt that there are places where weight removal has cheapened the product and made it worse. But you're on thin ice if you champion heaviness as a virtue.

Size is not a good indicator of durability, either. There is no evidence whatever that a Lincoln will outlast a Citroen 2 CV. At 1,100 pounds, the 2 CV is certainly the all-time champ for retaining resale value in any country where it is available. Industrial-tool lines are built to a higher standard, but this is often not related to size or weight. Witness Milwaukee tools. Their ¼-inch drill, for instance, is no bigger or heavier than a Sears, but it has twice the torque (on less electricity, too) and must have ten times the life span. Moreover, the Milwaukee is easily overhauled for a second and third lifetime. In this case, "industrial grade" means good bearings, heat-treated parts, expensive insulation on the windings, and good quality control, none of which weighs more or is bigger.

Needless complexity can shorten life span. It is often merely the result of ineptitude rather than even manufacturing ease. I once went over a standard Jeep to simplify it. I quit my analysis after removing more than 1,000 unneeded parts! For example, the return spring on the clutch pedal is attached to the chassis by means of a cast fitting that is bolted onto the frame with two bolts, nuts, and lockwashers. That's 7 parts. They could have hooked the end of the spring in a hole in the chassis, meaning no parts, less weight, less inventory for the dealer, less to fall off, less to make. The whole Jeep is full of such things. None of them makes it stronger, more reliable, or better in any way.

J. BALDWIN

Entropy and you

Entropy is a 75¢ word that appears to be graduating from a law of thermodynamics to a household word. It pops up in writings and conversations about the bad things we're doing to our planet.

Entropy is the index of the relative amount of bound energy (energy not available to us to do work) to energy we still can use. We humans accelerate this effect in making our lives.

Even if we swore off cars and plastics today in one great global spasm of consciousness, entropy would wear on without us. It is a one-way process. Order runs to disorder, heat flows from the warmer body to the cooler body. Even if not turned to ash in a woodstove, a tree must gradually degrade into useless energy.

Humans are able to evade entropic degradation for a time, by borrowing energy in the form of a sandwich or firewood. That's why our bodies and minds are quite durable, relative to most of our possessions or a road kill. We maintain ourselves by speeding up entropy, but that's not our fault; any organism does its share. But our elaboration on survival needs—here's the reason for guilt, hopefully for concern. While other animals live on renewable solar energy, we alone dip into the earth's natural, finite dowry. As entropy theorist Nicholas Georgescu-Roengen puts it, "Everything man has done during the last two hundred years puts him in the position of a fantastic spendthrift."

RY

A REHAB CENTER FOR JUNK

Better design and manufacture contribute to durability, of course, but in a society that values novelty and change as much as durability and reliable service, things tend to be retired before their time.

A wall is taken out and a gate installed. The back porch is remodeled into a solar greenhouse. Someone breaks the lid of the toilet, which leads to a decision to remodel the bathroom with all new fixtures.

What happens to the materials that are displaced? Various cuts are made. Valuable things are given to friends or relatives, or sold through garage sales. But there are inevitably leftovers, and they find their way to the nearest dump.

A visitor to the town dump is impressed with the sheer chaos and disorganization of it all. A giant mixing operation is taking place there. But with a little mental sorting of the familiar from the strange, one can make out various subflows of material. In one area, we see parts of houses being dumped—windows and doors with their

Christie C. Tito

hardware intact, bathtubs, toilets, and shower doors, and wainscoting, molding, flooring, and structural lumber. Elsewhere, someone is pushing the fenders and hood of an old car into the pit. Bright clothing bursts forth from overloaded cardboard boxes. One wonders what treasure might hide in plastic garbage bags. Less mysterious is the compostable treasure of brush, leaves, and grass clippings.

Salvaging is the art and science of intercepting these materials before they are irretrievably lost; a salvage yard diverts them for productive reuse or recycling. Materials must be sorted, tested, repaired, or marketed, and these processes require a skill one can learn through experience. Salvaging demands imagination of the yard workers and customers. Always there is the possibility for surprise within the odd mixtures of time and effect.

Artists and artisans are among those who frequent the dumps. Gardeners may be found there as well, gleaning the mulches and composts, the wire fencing, the garden lumber and live plants and containers. There is an astounding diversity of materials and objects to be had, both old and new.

Most communities attempt to restrict or regulate salvaging at dumpsites. Some prohibit it, while others contract salvaging to a business or individual.

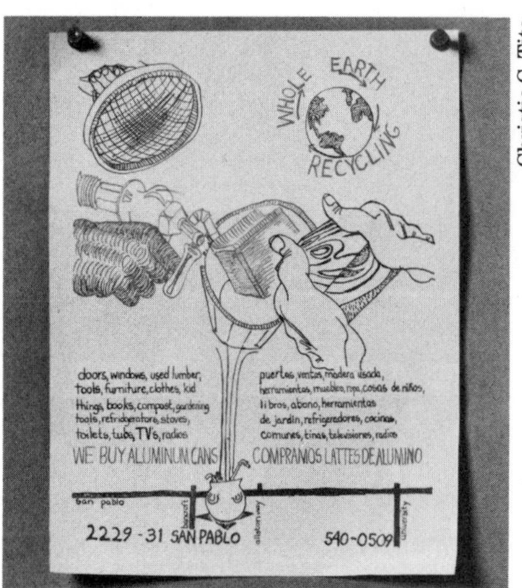

Christie C. Tito

Whole Earth Recycling's bilingual poster.

Dan Knapp

Everything under the sun *including* the kitchen sink.

Mary Lou Van Deventer

Doors are racked up according to type and size.

I helped start a company whose primary economic activity is salvaging from the waste stream at the city dump and selling the recovered material to a diversity of markets. While the typical dump is based on chaos, our approach has been to restore order to as much of the solid-waste stream as possible. One of the names for what we do is "highgrading," which involves cleaning, separating, and sorting materials into categories based on the principle of highest and best use.

We began by salvaging metals, because metals have existing markets that are predictable and strong. But we did not just throw the metals all together in one container; instead we set up a processing function, and using simple hand tools, we separated the metals into categories—about 20 to begin with—which we sold to several different metals buyers.

Scrap quickly became a category of last resort when we discovered that merely by accumulating materials in one place and organizing them, we were attracting eager buyers from among the hundreds of haulers and householders that use the dump. However, for the most part, our buyers were flea-market dealers, and they were primarily interested in smaller things that they could carry away in their cars.

Mary Lou Van Deventer

Whole Earth gets a load of aluminum.

Our prices were too low to keep the business healthy. So, we began looking for a place out in the community where we could sell the things flea-market dealers would not buy. We found a location on a main thoroughfare through town and stocked it with building materials from our collection. The buyers were ready for what we had to offer; pipe, doors, windows, lumber, and bathroom fixtures began to move through our materials-recovery system about as fast as they were coming to us.

A slippery idea

Do we have a right to expect durability in the things we buy? Or is durability some sort of esoteric nonsense? Durability is a slippery idea to get ahold of. We can't measure it until it's gone. We're not sure who's responsible for it, and we usually don't know how much of it is possible or worthwhile.

Rapid social or technological change can make durability less attractive. The resale value of a gas-guzzling automobile has plummeted, independent of its durability. A refrigerator that uses too much energy is virtually worthless today no matter how durably it was built. Rapid change in computer science shrinks the useful life of many computer products. But there are things that each of us can do. An energy-inefficient refrigerator or water heater can be given a new life by merely increasing its insulation or turning off its automatic defrost features. Durability in children's clothes or women's maternity wear may seem uneconomical because you don't use those things long enough to wear them out, but that's why used-clothing stores are good ideas; a revolving stockpile of comfortable, good-quality clothes can be had for a fraction of the economic dollar cost of throwaways. Second-hand outlets give economic incentive to purchase better-quality products and to treat them well to preserve their value.

TOM BENDER

The success of the new marketplace meant that the landfill surface could be kept cleaner; and fill space was not wasted on useful, saleable things.

At the salvage yard, doors and windows are racked up according to type and size. Lumber, too, is sorted. Contractors, apartment-house managers, and students are attracted to the always-changing cast of unusual and one-of-a-kind items—things like a wire wheel set for an old motorcycle, complete with inflated 20-year-old tires in new condition; a set of iron-filigreed drawer pulls with a patent stamp 95 years old; and an antique gas water heater with a massive copper coil inside and nine lions' heads cast into the thick metal of its skin. Thus, a salvage yard can extend the life of all sorts of objects by matching a discarded item with a new user.

But a salvage yard does more than recover and restore materials. Labor, both skilled and unskilled, is required to repair, install, paint, clean, and resell. The community is enlivened, and people's wants and needs are satisfied.

Here is a story to show how it can work.

Several bicycle rebuilders pay regular visits to the salvage yard to shop from our collection of bent and incomplete bicycles. I was building a new window rack one day when one of them walked through the gate and strode purposefully to the bike parts. Soon I heard steel clanking against steel as he assembled his purchase. When he had finished, we negotiated a price and the money was paid. We were carrying the parts out to his car when he said, "You know, building these bicycles has made all the difference in the world to me. I retired a couple of years ago, and I have a good pension. I don't really need anything, except something to do. I didn't even know I needed something to do until I had been retired for a while and started having trouble with my heart. I started rebuilding bicycles from parts about three months ago, and it's made all the difference, it really has. First I have to find the parts, and that gets me out and about, believe me. Then I sand and paint the frames, clean all the spokes and true the wheels, get the rust off, go through the bearings to make sure they're all there and everything is working smoothly. Sometimes I get a complete bike to disassemble, but more often it's just a collection of parts that I put together from scratch. It's interesting—never the same.

"I get up in the mornings instead of sleeping. I watch less television, eat not from boredom but because I really need the food. I don't sit around so much. I'm meeting people instead of being alone with nothing to do. I also get paid for my time, though money is not the reason that I rebuild bikes. My prices are low anyway—$65 is the most I've ever asked. I make adjustments sometimes if someone just can't come up with the money.

"I just finished my favorite job, a bike that will be ridden to South America. I've got a customer—he's a young German boy—who told me he wanted a bike that could make it all the way down there. I told him I could build it. So I did. He has it now, riding it every day, getting in shape for the trip. I told him I'd tune it up for him before he leaves.

"In fact," said the bike builder as he closed the trunk lid on his purchase, "the set of fenders that I just bought here will be installed on that bike. He will be going through a lot of mud and rain; he'll need fenders."

So the salvage yard is now part of this man's life, just as he and his work are part of ours. The exchange is mediated by currency, regulated and taxed and legal—a practical symbiosis between the salvage yard, as provider of parts and supplies, and the craftspeople, contractors, property managers, and inventors who purchase and use them.

Jøtul wood-burning stove

1973 $300
1981 $300

John Hamel

Norwegian Jøtul stoves hold their value better than most stoves made in America these days, said Bill Hauk, a New England inventor and wood-stove expert. "Stove-making is a lost art in America," Hauk told us. "In the early 1900s, Sears sold stoves for $19.95. Those same stoves today would be worth about $1,000 apiece. That's not all antique value, either. They made good stoves back then, and they looked good too."

Building materials

For the sake of illustration, I will use glass and windows to suggest that this waste stream constantly presents the opportunity for constructive action in the face of fossil-fuel shortages and higher prices for conventional energy supplies.

Window glass, wood, and insulation are among the materials that come to rest in a salvage yard, and they're about all that's needed to construct a rudimentary solar collector.

Volkswagen Beetle convertible
1977 $4,795
1981 $4,150

Volkswagen of America

Volkswagen's 1977 Beetle convertible held 86.5 percent of its price over the four years since leaving the showroom, according to the National Automobile Dealers Association's *Official Used Car Guide*, with the $22,000 Mercedes-Benz 450SL and the $16,000 Porsche 911S coming through nearly as well. "Foreign cars are doing best of all, retaining 60 percent of their original value," reported *Money* magazine in August, 1981.

Harley-Davidson Duo-Glide
1960 $2,800
1981 $4,000

Jon Gerber

A Harley-Davidson Duo-Glide motorcycle that sold for $2,800 in 1960 could bring about $4,000 in 1981, a spokesperson for *Easyrider* magazine told us. Look for a Harley made before 1968, the year AMF bought the company.

The glass lets the sunlight through and traps it as it degrades to heat. The wood and insulation define the space that is to concentrate the energy. With these basic elements, almost all of the current family of thermal-collection technologies can be constructed.

One can also work the other way using single elements—installing insulation and plugging air leaks, or adding a second layer of glass to existing single-pane windows to create a dead-air space.

Windows are plentiful in the waste stream; they are brought to the disposal area in dropboxes, dumpsters, trucks, and cars. It is not uncommon to see a whole truckload of good windows slide into the disposal pit.

Why are so many windows being thrown away? Partly because of the availability of tax credits or deductions for energy conservation and solar retrofitting. Double-hung and casement windows with frames made of wood are prime candidates for replacement. Also, many doors with window glass are replaced because they are not considered secure against intruders. Meanwhile, building restorers, weekend builders, greenhouse enthusiasts, and repair-and-remodel contractors are searching for old windows. Salvaging, weatherization, and solar retrofitting go hand in hand. Many examples and illustrations come to mind.

- One of the best sales we made in the first critical weeks after opening our yard was more than 400 2-by-4-foot fiberglass insulation batts. A big steel-truss building in our city had collapsed suddenly a few days previously, and trucks loaded with insulation pulled from the wreckage soon rolled into the landfill. Alert workers from our salvage business loaded the insulation directly onto trucks and brought it to the sales yard. We were just heading into winter, and it turned out that nearly everyone who entered the yard wanted some of that material. All of it was sold in two days.

- A man came in with a sash frame from an older home. The glass had been broken by his dog, he said. The dog jumped through the glass while defending the man from a burglar. Going through the sorted windows in stock, he found an exact replacement in minutes, for less than one-fourth the cost of a new custom-built replacement.
- One of my steady window customers is a woman carpenter who is currently building a meditation house for her garden. Her most recent purchase was eight matching three-light casements. Building in her spare time, with secondhand materials for the most part, she made an apartment in her home and has it rented. She maintains a regular circuit of the salvage yards in the area.
- One fellow came in recently and purchased 16 large double-hung sashes, 8 uppers and 8 lowers. He said he planned to trim them so they were identical in width and height, then fashion a structural system so they could be maintained as the vertical wall of a south-facing solar greenhouse. He said he expects to gain some of his home heating from the addition. This particular scene, with individual variations, has recurred many times since the yard opened.

Salvaging economy

One of the disconcerting things about our business is that our merchandise does not arrive with a price printed on it. Prices are set on the spot when a purchase is made, and the final exchange is an amalgam of many considerations.

Much of the time, price is set by custom. Materials that sell dependably tend to set their own price levels; but for one-of-a-kind items, price is mostly based on an educated guess. Bidding is entirely

---

Leica M-2 rangefinder camera

1959 $216
1981 $575

Simplicity of design, ruggedness, and small production runs are responsible for this camera's appreciation, according to a spokesperson for the manufacturer, E. Leitz, Inc.

***The Adirondack Reader*, by Paul Jamieson**

1971 $10
1981 $27.50

This out-of-print book collects the best of four centuries' writing on America's largest park. At Wildwood, a shop in the Adirondack town of Old Forge, a good copy brings nearly three times the price Macmillan asked for it a decade earlier.

Fender Stratocaster electric guitar
1955 $200
1981 $3,000

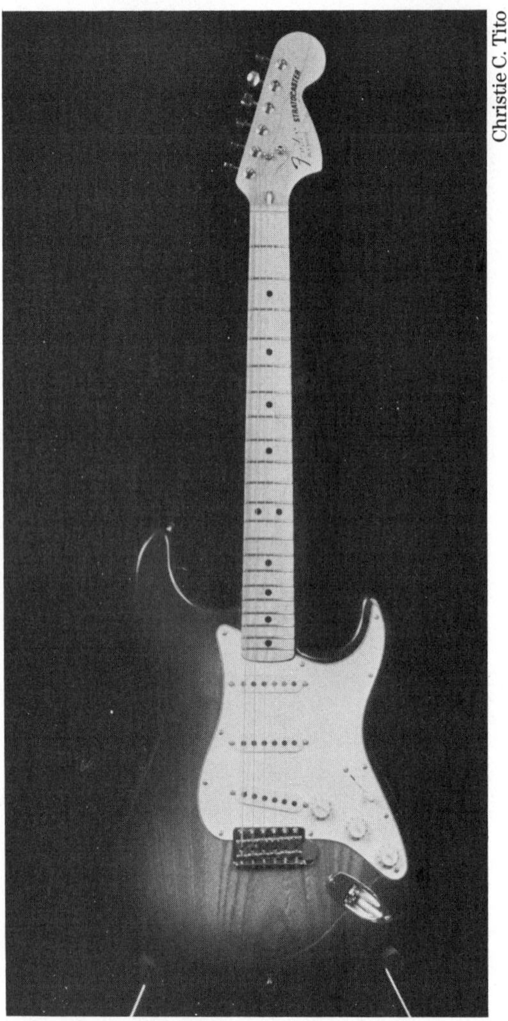
Christie C. Tito

"Stratocasters from the mid-'50s that then sold for $200 or so fetch up to $3,000 now," reported *Money* magazine in August, 1981. Look for a "pre-CBS" Stratocaster, one that was made before January, 1965, when the Columbia Broadcasting System bought Fender. Roger Rohrs, publisher of the Orion *Professional Sound Reference Guide* (the "blue book" of the musical equipment industry), recommended searching for a Strat that has a low serial number, looks clean and undamaged, and has its original parts.

appropriate in either case, since there are many subjective factors that may seem important in the transaction. If a bid is rejected, the buyer can up the ante by adding another item to the stack of material being considered. The seller tends to drop individual prices out or to concede a disputed bid when large-lot purchases are made. This is especially true for salvage yards that, like ours, are tied into the solid-waste stream. The problem here is essentially how to reuse productively a vast supply of varied materials.

Beyond cash lies the large and uncharted territory of barter, wherein services may be traded for things, or things exchanged directly. There are a lot of advantages to barter; above all, it is simple, and most salvage yards engage in it to a degree. Barter opens up an enormous range of possibilities.

For example, I traded $150 in materials for a charming little outbuilding, which we now use as the salvage-yard office. Part of the trade, in this instance, was the service of removing the building from the owner's yard. The weight and bulk of the building required us to use cash to purchase equipment and an operator's time to lift the building and get it safely to the yard. In this instance, the economic impact of the barter transaction extended into the mainstream economy: money as well as things changed hands.

It is tempting to conclude that the salvage-yard economy is more varied and flexible in the ways of trade than the new-products economy. At a yard, people find it satisfying that there are more ways of reaching agreement than just matching a published price. Agreement is the lubricant of free trade, and free trade—appropriately matching supply and demand—is the goal of any market economy.

As a locally oriented marketplace, the salvage yard tends to stabilize and prop up the value of our currency, even as it is under attack in the world economy. The salvage yard—and other similar institutions such as farmer's markets, craft fairs, flea markets, and garage sales—does this by extending money's "residence time" in the local exchange system. Money passes from person to person, instead of from person to large corporation.

For years, our money and credit have been used to purchase replacement goods manufactured from ever-scarcer virgin materials. Meanwhile, the excess has been disposed of as cheaply as possible, usually by burial. This characteristic channeling of currency and credit has subsidized the continuing search for the last cuttable tree, mineable deposit, or dammable stream. Through this mechanism, the cycle of overproduction and waste renews itself.

But at the salvage yard, prices are closer to those prevailing 20 years ago than today. The currency we use now is the same as that used in the hyperinflationary economy that is all around us, but it is a simple fact that a dollar buys more material at the salvage yard—which leads me to suspect that in a truly conservative economy based on recycling and reuse, it might be possible to "reflate" the currency to something like its former value.

So please patronize the locally oriented market system. Don't be afraid to bargain and bid; the give-and-take is all part of the fun. By so doing, you will be plugging your money into the *local* economy, paying for work that must be done for us to live successfully together. You will also be encouraging the flow of a resource that would otherwise become garbage.

DAN KNAPP

Martin D-28 steel string guitar

1960 $310
1981 $1,000

Christie C. Tito

Martin guitars are famous for both their good sound and their resale value. For years, Martin guitars were sold with a lifetime guarantee, but times have changed and with them the guarantee to five years. Fred Oster, who as owner of Vintage Instruments in Philadelphia advises investors, recommends Martin guitars. "Look for an old Martin," Oster told us. "If you look around, you can deal and get a good bargain."

Steinway Model-A grand piano

1909 $1,100
1981 $3,000 to $7,000

Christie C. Tito

We asked several piano dealers to estimate the value of our 1909 Steinway and got figures ranging from $3,000 to $7,000. The man stating the lowest number was anxious to come over and buy the instrument.

Record jointer plane

1960 $25
1981 $60 to $70

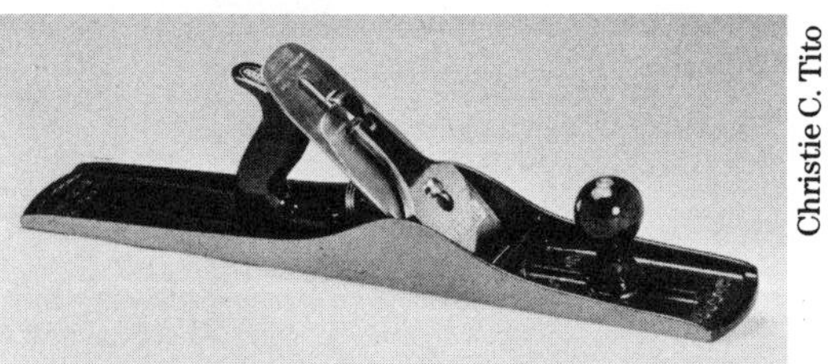

Christie C. Tito

Good tools not only get the job done but often increase in value. The Record jointer plane pictured here sold for about $25 in 1960. Twenty-one years later it costs $78 new, and an old one might bring $60 or $70 on the used-tool market, according to the people at Garrett Wade in New York City.

HOW LONGER PRODUCT LIVES CAN SAVE RESOURCES AND SPARE WASTE

Keep a car or appliance or shirt for ten years instead of five, and you stand to save money. That much is clear, but the good news goes beyond the household, in ways that aren't so apparent.

A family purchases a clothes dryer for $299.99. The dryer is installed in the basement, where over the years it extracts the water and coaxes the wrinkles from several tons of family wash. One day the dryer refuses to spin, and a service person is called. He makes a familiar pronouncement: for what it would cost to fix this antique, you could buy a new one. The family buys a new dryer, and the spent appliance is trucked to a landfill site. That's the end of the story, as most of us see things.

Taking a wider view—an ecological view—the story begins long before the purchase and never really has an end. The old dryer will either rust away in a landfill or be melted back down into an ingot. Even so humble an act as consuming a dryer sets off waves of consequences in what is increasingly regarded as a delicately balanced world. A popular conceit likens our environment to a great web of which we are but one strand.

If it's mentally exhausting to be forever sensitive to the consequences of our acts both large and seemingly insignificant, we can at least buy products with potentially long lives and maintain them solicitously. The American's style of consumption gives the environmental web a good hard shake: the U.S. Bureau of Mines estimates that each man and woman and child in the United States is responsible for unearthing 40,000 pounds of minerals annually.

Focusing for a moment on dryers and other major appliances, in 1982 they will answer for 106,551 tons of aluminum, 222,564 tons of plastic, and 1,757,355 tons of steel, shipped inside 90 square miles of packaging. Complicating matters is the fact that the flow of resources is increasingly international. The United States imports at least 50 percent of its needs for 20 crucial minerals and runs the risk of a politically triggered minerals crisis that could rival the impact of the energy crisis.

Scarcity a hoax?

Still, some people say that resource depletion is a hoax created by private interests to maximize their profits. For the present, the question is clouded by the fact that resource availability is as much a question of economics as of actual geological reserves. If it is technologically feasible to extract a resource but economically unattractive to do so, the resource stays in the ground. But as demand for the resource rises, we find ourselves tapping into lower-grade ores and deeper wells. Thus, the supply of resources is somewhat elastic, and the true limits are unknown. Our supply projections are based on extrapolations from known reserves or even mere speculation, unsupported by solid geological evidence. We place ourselves in a precarious position by clinging to the hope that new technologies will be discovered in time to avert serious resource crises. And there are those who see the earth as a finite place with foreseeable limits; to them, relying on technology to save the day would eventually result in total depletion and severe environmental damage. They worry that advanced technology will buy us time, but only at the price of exotic chemical and nuclear wastes.

Marantz 7T preamp

1968 $285
1981 $311

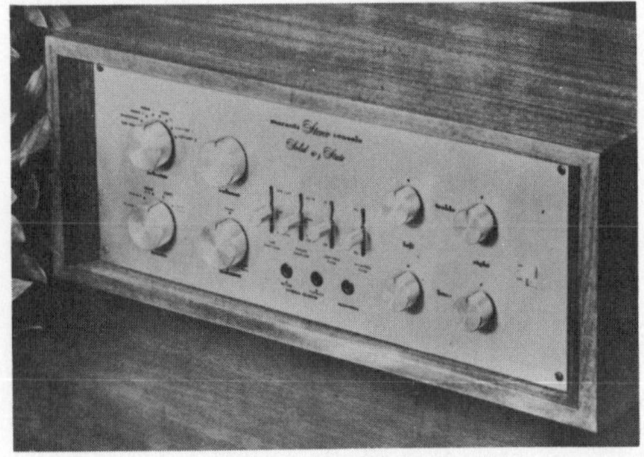

The Marantz tube 7T preamp is one of those few pieces of stereo equipment that appreciate with time, according to the *1981 Audio Reference Guide*. Need an amplifier to match with the preamp? A McIntosh MC-75 tube amp, retailing for $230 in 1964, could be expected to bring $325 in 1981. These amps have a mystique about them, due in part to the so-called warm sound of tube equipment.

"By pursuing his own interest [every individual] frequently promotes that of the society more effectually than when he really intends to promote it. I have never known much good done by those who affected to trade for the public good. It is an affectation, indeed, not very common among merchants, and very few words need to be employed in dissuading them from it."

ADAM SMITH, *The Wealth of Nations*

Semidwarf apple tree

1981 $12
2001 $728 worth of apples over 20 years

Patti Seip

A semidwarf apple tree bought for $12 in 1981 could yield $728 worth of fruit in 20 years, estimated orchardist Tim White of Alburtis, Pennsylvania. The tree begins to bear fruit in 3 years and pays for itself in 5 years. Taking into account several bad harvests caused by frosts, drought, and one winter ice storm, White calculates that a semidwarf apple tree will produce 105 bushels of fruit over 20 years, worth $844 at the 1981 price. After 20 years, the grower will have spent about $116 for supplies—such as an insecticide sprayer, fertilizer, and mulch—and about 157 hours of time caring for the tree. Subtracting expenses, after 20 years the grower will net $728 worth of apples or $4.64 for each hour spent orcharding, "and that's not bad for a job where you're your own boss, producing quality food, and having a minimal impact on the ecosystem," White says.

Ninety percent of the United States' aluminum ore comes from Jamaica, Australia, Surinam, and Guinea. Many of the auxiliary metals essential for making steel are largely imported: cobalt, nickel, and columbium are obtained primarily from Third World countries; nearly 100 percent of our manganese is imported from South Africa and Gabon; and 90 percent of our chromium comes from South Africa and the U.S.S.R. (it is ironic and potentially very discomforting that these two countries, with whom we are politically and ideologically uneasy, happen to be the world's most richly endowed with mineral resources).

Wresting minerals from the earth tends to be a violent process. Waste generated during mineral extraction and production can amount to hundreds or thousands of times the volume of the finished product, pound for pound.

Then there's the energy devoted to mining, refining, and transporting materials, termed "embodied energy." Energy used by private homes and automobiles accounts for only a third of our energy use. The bulk is consumed in the production and marketing of our goods and services.

The local dump is a rich repository of materials, receiving 30 percent of the major materials we produce, including in a year 27.7 billion pounds of iron and steel, 2.2 billion of aluminum, 12.1 billion of plastic, 6 billion of rubber, 5.4 billion of textiles, and 12.2 billion of wood.

All that junk takes up plenty of space—in the decade ending in 1988, the United States will have devoted 1,400 square miles to burying it all.

While recycling is important to some industries–in making cars and aluminum cans, for example–only certain materials are considered worth recycling, and then only when in quantities large enough to bother with. The typical car built in the United States in 1979 contains 2,000 pounds of steel, 492 of iron, 129 of plastic, 84 of glass, 85 of zinc, 28 of copper, and 143 of rubber–but only ferrous metals are currently separated out on a large scale, while landfills end up with most of the rest. Even with steel, recyclers run into problems caused by increasingly sophisticated metallurgy. For example, high-strength steels may be alloyed with columbium, manganese, aluminum, vanadium, molybdenum, titanium, phosphorus, and the rare earth cerium silicide.

Plastics are difficult or impossible to recycle, especially hybrid and composite materials reinforced with glass or minerals. The auto industry's use of plastics increases yearly in the pursuit of lower weight and increased mileage; a further advantage is that plastic does not corrode. But these economies eventually may be undone by the fact that little is recycled. Aluminum too is increasingly important to car manufacturers, again with the advantages of avoiding corrosion and trimming weight. But refining aluminum is highly energy intensive, and it has been argued that this works against the savings in gas and resources that a light, all-aluminum car might offer over its long, rust-free life.

Electronic components are expected to represent 10 percent of a car's selling price by the 1990s, and this promises to discourage recycling–these components contain silver, gold, and platinum in quantities too small to encourage recycling.

Farmland

1960 $116 per acre
1981 $796 per acre

T. L. Gettings

The average price of an acre of farmland in America increased almost 700 percent in the 21 years following 1960, according to the USDA. The government's price estimates include the cost of houses and outbuildings sold with the land.

Previously owned house

1968 $20,000
1981 $62,000

The National Association of Realtors reports that the median selling price of previously owned houses tripled in the dozen years following 1968.

Pie safe
1975 $350
1981 $750

Christie C. Tito

Fine wooden furniture has always appreciated. The antique Pennsylvania Dutch pie safe pictured here was purchased in 1975 for $350. Its owner, Ron Bortz, who collects wooden furniture as a hobby, says he could sell the pie safe for $750 in 1981. It's vital to know which furniture to buy—and which to avoid. How did Ron Bortz learn about wooden furniture? He befriended an antique dealer who gave him free advice.

What's to be done? This book explores ways of extending product life. Salvage yards and second-hand outlets (such as flea markets and yard sales) keep alive many products that might otherwise be thrown out or quietly abandoned to rust and mildew. Retired products that aren't saleable can be rebuilt. This is done widely with major car components—alternators, starters, engine blocks—but to date there hasn't been sufficient economic incentive to rebuild many electronic products or appliances. As manufacturing costs go up, remanufacture may appear more feasible, and parts could be standardized to facilitate this. But collecting, rebuilding, and distributing are labor intensive, and the cost of labor is going up, too.

When a product can't be resold or remanufactured, a just end is recycling—isolating the materials and converting them for resale. The Environmental Protection Agency (EPA) estimates that the 50 tons of municipal waste generated in the United States each year could yield 40 percent of manufacturers' needs for metal, glass, plastic, fiber, and rubber. Recycling also spares the pollution generated and energy used in the extraction and processing of virgin ores. By recycling aluminum scrap rather than refining the metal from ore, air and water pollution (as well as energy use) are cut by 95 percent.

Unfortunately, recycling is still held back by a variety of technical, economic, and governmental restraints. As mentioned above, metals and plastics are fabricated in hundreds of grades, many of which are incompatible; the resulting low-grade "mongrels" are of limited usefulness, and the market for them is understandably small.

Another major problem is that tax laws and freight rates favor virgin materials over recycled materials. It costs 20 percent more to ship a ton of recycled ore than a ton of primary material. The U.S. government is considering a variety of legislative alternatives to encourage recycling and other forms of materials conservation. A first step would be to remove the depletion allowance, a subsidy paid to mining interests for the extraction of virgin ores. We also could require a minimum percentage of recycled materials in certain goods. One legislative tool gaining steam is a tax levied on products made from virgin materials. Those made substantially from recycled materials would be exempt. A recent piece of legislation would grant a 10 percent tax credit on recycling equipment.

Oriental or Persian rug, 9 by 12 feet

1960 $4,000
1980 $15,000

"Yes, Oriental and Persian rugs have increased substantially in value," says an advertisement for Safavieh Carpets of New York City. "Yes, we live in inflationary times. Yes, you probably will sell your rugs for a profit in the future. But the first reason for buying a fine rug is for enjoyment. . . . The increase in value should not be your only motivation." A Safavieh spokesperson estimates that a 9-by-12-foot Oriental or Persian rug bought in 1960 for $4,000 could have fetched as much as $15,000 in 1980, and likely would have another six decades of wear left in it.

BK

Dear Sir:

I am a cement finisher and while breaking up some sidewalk, my Zippo lighter fell from my shirt pocket and was struck with a sledge hammer.

I was told by several people your guarantee would replace it.

All Zippo photos, T. L. Gettings

Each chapter of this book closes with a tale of how one Zippo lighter met its maker. The manufacturer mailed a free replacement to each of those who wrote to tell Zippo their woes. **See the Zippo story on p. 208.**

THE LONG-LIFE CAR

2

You might expect a book on the durability of consumer products to reveal the name of a freakishly long-lived car, an obscure marque known only to a coterie of automotive engineers.

That car does not exist. Or, if it does, they don't make them anymore. Tales of past models that are immune to friction and rust are common among people who fancy cars, but most of the talk has to be discounted as folklore in the making. While Hudson, Studebaker, Volvo, Models A and T, and others have their champions, for a bonafide 250,000-mile car you'll have to look to the future.

Right now, the state of the art in automotive design is expressed in the sophistication and close tolerances of racing cars and in the common sense of commercial vehicles. The engine of a racing car may eat itself up in an afternoon of sport, but if such materials and engineering were lavished on the engines of passenger cars, unheard of mileages might become normal; the cost would be prohibitive, however. Stainless-steel railroad coaches, sleepers, and diners go decades with little care and still look new. Truck and locomotive engines are periodically torn down and rebuilt, rather than being trashed when a bearing wears out. According to the Environmental Protection Agency (EPA), the average heavy-duty diesel truck engine undergoes at least one overhaul before the vehicle is scrapped, and railroad locomotives serve an average of 22 years.

Planned obsolescence?

With all the advances in technology of the past few decades, you might guess that today's cars are holding up longer than they used to. They certainly cost more, even the tiny ones, but in fact they last no longer than those of 25 years ago—about 10 years.

Why? Consumer advocates claim they smell planned obsolescence. The long-life materials are here today—aluminum bodies, stainless-steel exhausts, heavy-duty batteries, chrome piston rings, and so on. They just haven't been assembled into a production passenger car. Heavy-duty components and durable materials cost more, prohibitively so unless a lot of cars can be sold. Here is the industry's best defense. Dale Johnson, executive director of field product testing for General Motors' corporate engineering staff, says that while the company could come out with a super-durable car, it would sell in such small numbers that the price would be enormous. So it is that proponents of long-lived cars discuss not only the problem of building them but also the problem of making them attractive to the public.

All photos, courtesy of Henry Ford Museum/The Edison Institute

Extra passengers could hitch a ride on the wide running boards.

A Model T touring car splashes through a flooded rural road.

On the farm.

Bogged down in Alaska. The hip-booted drivers are well prepared, with two spare tires, tow rope, and other gear lashed to the running boards.

In the interests of maximizing profits while keeping prices competitive, automakers typically build in only as much durability as they perceive a new-car buyer will pay for. Whether or not this qualifies as a gross misuse of resources or just plain good business sense is the real question here.

The spectre of planned obsolescence has been haunting Detroit, among other industrial towns, since the term was coined in the 1940s, despite the best attempts of corporations to chase it away with image-building ads and pointed remarks about the American consumer's lust for junk and novelty. In the words of James Hillier, an executive vice-president for research and engineering at RCA, "Our wives are not being merely frivolous when we find them constantly moving from one fad and fashion to another. Perhaps they know better than we that change is a psychological necessity of the human condition."

Corporate heads seem to defend themselves with words rather than statistics, perhaps because the numbers wouldn't help their case. "The inference that any large, responsible manufacturer would knowingly permit potentially hazardous defects to exist in its products as a cost-saving measure," said Hillier, "is incredibly naive." This was uttered a couple of years after the Automobile Association of Missouri reported to a Senate investigating subcommittee that of the 10,000 recently purchased cars it had examined, 45 percent turned up with safety defects. Since 1966, 86 million cars have been involved in recall campaigns for safety-related defects.

Guilty or not, the auto industry has a special reason to be tempted to make cars that won't hold up more than a decade. It has to do with the fully matured nature of the car market—that is, the United States is pretty well saturated with cars, now that half of all households that own them have at least two. So, most new cars go to replace ones that wore out. Because that doesn't provide for much sales growth, automakers are acutely sensitive to something called the scrappage rate, the pace at which cars wear out. Going into the 1980s, it's 7.60 percent, up from 7.09 in the 1970s but off the prosperous-1960s rate of 8.15.

As the scrappage rate goes, so goes the industry's health. In its article "A Comeback Decade for the American Car," *Fortune* magazine pointed out that "the scrappage rate can vary by a percentage point or so, and that variation, applied to the 100 million cars now on the road, has a very large effect on sales." Lawrence J. White studied the industry's statistics for evidence of built-in impermanence, and in *The Auto Industry Since 1945* (Harvard University Press, 1971), he took this line of reasoning a bit further: "In a market in which replacement demand is the dominant element, there are always great incentives to try to speed up the pace of the replacement cycle." He found that between 1955 and 1967 the percentage of seven-, eight-, and nine-year-old cars still on the road dropped from 93, 85, and 70 respectively, to 84, 74, and 56. (Looking at the figures for 1979, they've shifted to 80, 67, and 70. Judging by that high 70 percent of 1970 cars still on the road as of 1979, '70 must have been a *very* good year.)

But White admits that shorter life spans don't necessarily point the finger at industry. They could mean that as incomes go up, people decide to scrap their old cars sooner. On the other hand, growing incomes have led to two- and three-car families, so that each car has less of a burden and could be expected to last longer.

White shies away from damning conclusions but notes that "perhaps the most striking thing about automotive technology in the postwar years has been the lack of fundamental change or advance." Most technological advancements are first applied to commercial vehicles because truck and bus buyers are technically more sophisticated than car buyers and relatively more interested in performance than in style and status. Power brakes, automatic transmissions, and power steering are cases in point. Long-life aluminum bodies are found on Grumman vans, and stainless steel is the material of choice for bus and passenger-car bodies, but neither has found its way to an American production auto.

Durable dogs

Manufacturers claim such improvements don't find their way into cars because consumers, no matter their gripes to the constant polls on the declining quality of American goods, won't invest in a more durable product, whether it's a 50¢ pen or a $10,000 car. This claim is not without substance. A study by Canada's Office of Energy Conservation found many manufacturers who rationalize shoddy goods with the conviction that most things are discarded before their time anyway: one vacuum cleaner manufacturer claims in its defense that it placed an ultradurable vacuum on the market only to have it bomb; when one Detroit automaker offered a package of safety options back in the 1950s, few consumers voted for this innovation with their dollars, and the package was dropped; Steve Kimball, managing editor of *Cycle World* magazine, recalls an unusually durable and inexpensive motorcycle that bankrupted its maker.

People want toys, not tools. Although they complain to pollsters that they're just sick about the decline of quality, the poll that counts is the marketplace, and here the cheapest product with the most gimmicks is often the winner.

When Ford brought out its Pinto in 1972, it didn't crow that here was a car for the ages. The Pinto was designed to weigh less than 2,000 pounds and to cost less than $2,000. Mileage, handling, performance, comfort, and safety took a back seat to that low sticker price, and no one complained loudly until an Indiana public prosecutor took Ford to court for criminal negligence, citing the company's knowledge of safety hazards inherent in the car's design. The media paid close attention to the ensuing trial, and Ford received a lot of bad press, but a very different sentiment was abuilding among the jurors and other residents of the small Hoosier town in which the 19-month trial was conducted. As told in *Reckless Homicide?* (And Books, 1980), an account of the trial by Lee Patrick Strobel, the citizens of Winimac, Indiana, sided with the defense, and "one prankster reflected the community's mood" by rearranging letters on a motel's outdoor sign into a message telling the prosecutor to "Go Directly to Hell; Do Not Pass Go." Interviewed after the verdict of not guilty, two jurors said that although the Pinto might be less safe than other cars, Americans nevertheless should have the choice of buying them; consumers weren't forced to buy an unsafe car. As one juror said of his own Pinto, "I have to have the gas mileage to live and support my family. . . . I'm stuck with it."

In other words, if durability costs more, then durability is in a bad way. Even a couple of percent added to the purchase price may sour the deal for the majority of car shoppers. B. B. Hundy has calculated that a car's life could be extended three years—or 30 percent—with simple body treatments adding only 2 or 3 percent to the retail price.

How to find a workhorse among the wimps

Is there much hope for a long-life car? A few automakers apparently are trying their best to produce a safe and durable car within the restraints of cost. One clue to identifying them is to look at the rocker panels and fender wells of five- and six-year-old cars. To confirm what you've seen, check resale values in the National Automobile Dealers Association's blue book (the guide for older car prices is $17, but friendly car dealers may let you look at their current copy or give you an old one) and in *Money* magazine's annual tally of how much four-year-old cars will currently bring. An excellent source of information on which cars are holding up is *Consumer Reports'* annual survey on the quarter-million cars of its readers.

The most reasonable conclusion is that planned obsolescence exists, but that the term is misleading. Any manufacturer, from a cobbler to an automaker, plans with the life spans of components in mind. The first *could* craft a heavy lifetime sole, but it would pull the walker's knee out of its socket; similarly, automakers acknowledge that a million-mile car is not beyond the technological means of the industry, but ask rhetorically if anyone would pay a hundred thousand dollars for it. General Motors' Dale Johnson admits that his company will build only as much durability into a car as the new-car buyers will pay for. To give them more service life would mean charging more, driving them to cheaper cars by other manufacturers.

An automaker knows full well that new-car buyers aren't very concerned with repairs six or seven years down the road, because most don't hold onto their cars that long. That's why cars don't have stainless-steel exhaust systems or proper rustproofing or lifetime batteries. On average, a new car is passed on in four years, and it's no coincidence that the average life span of many components is just a trifle longer. In its survey of some 25,000 cars, the British magazine *Motoring Which* discovered three patterns of mechanical failure. As the first graph shows, some components are subject to random failure over time; suspensions and steering systems aren't that much more likely to give out later than now.

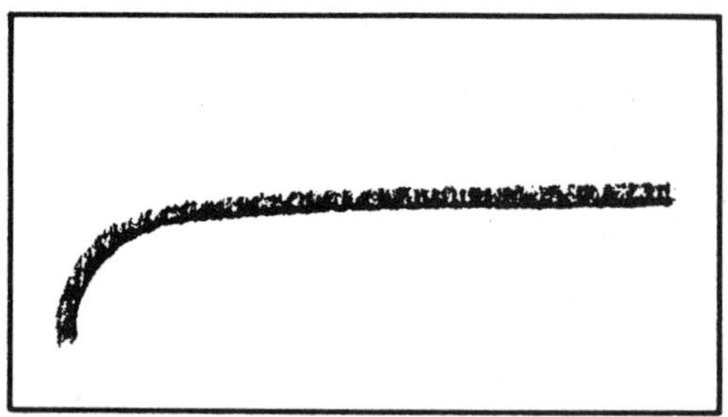

The second graph describes the failure rate of exhaust systems and batteries. Few failures are expected at first, but you can expect to replace the muffler every three years or so and the battery every four. There's an old joke about the rich fat cat who trades in his cars as soon as the ashtrays are full, and the humor is in exaggeration of a real-life pattern—getting rid of a car before the muffler falls off and the spent battery leaves you stranded somewhere.

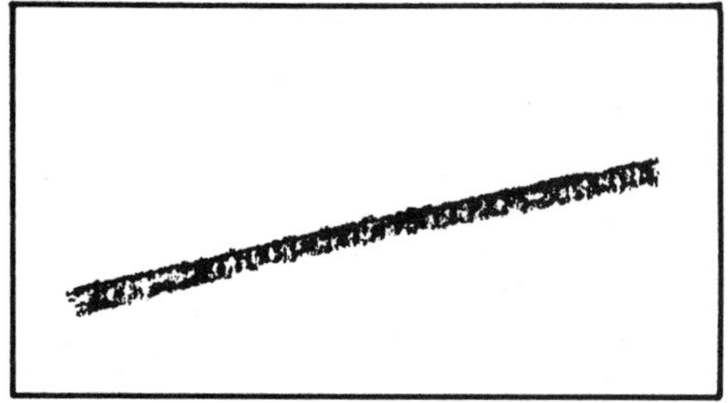

Most devastating are those components with a failure rate that is low early on, then increases dramatically with age, as shown in the third graph. Here are the heavy-duty repairs costing hundreds of dollars—engine failure and body rust. These wear-out patterns are especially crucial in determining a car's life span. When the owner feels he is about to invest more in an older car than he'll get back out of it, through either use or resale, the car is dead.

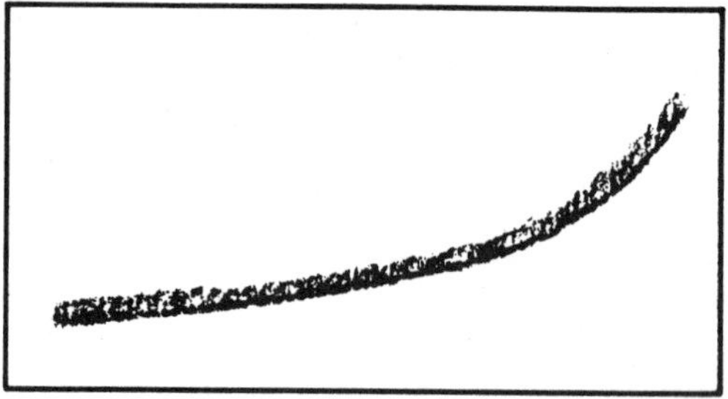

Clearly, manufacturers have an incentive to give the *first* owner the best possible car for his money—providing he passes it on soon enough. The victim is the person hit with repairs that typically begin at a car's midlife.

In time, the owners of older cars will make their pleasure or disappointment known. Their experiences are reflected in depreciation figures, those annual percentages closely monitored by manufacturers, car dealers, and smart buyers. These numbers may be the closest thing a car maker has to a report card. How well did each company read the minds of its buyers, and how closely did its cars meet the buyers' expectations?

In recent years, foreign cars have kept their value much better than domestic models, the main reasons being superior gas mileage and the public's perception of quality. A 1980 survey of the American Society for Quality Control found that more than a third of the 7,000 respondents believed domestic cars were poorly made, and three-quarters thought foreign products were as good as, or better than,

American. Another survey in that year by the Motor and Equipment Manufacturers Association found that 51 percent of 10,000 consumers favored the engineering of Japanese cars, followed by 21 percent for small American models.

So it is that we have little Detroit cars mimicking Hondas and Datsuns and Toyotas in a sort of protective coloration strategy. Appearances can be deceptive, and it is the responsibility of highly paid stylists and marketing people to see to it that appearances *are* deceptive.

20 years and 175,000 miles

Admirable statistics, these. They're the goals set by Porsche engineers in a long-life car study. Porsche's research was inspired by the Club of Rome's work, reported in *Limits to Growth* (Universe Books and NAL, 1974) and *World Dynamics* (MIT Press, 1973). The engineers studied not only the technical challenges of building such a car, but also the impact on society in terms of both energy and resource conservation, and the health of the industry itself. The project was supported by the German Federal Ministry for Research and Technology, and has had its friends and foes.

According to Ernst Fuhrmann, a Porsche engineer, an aluminum-bodied car could be expected to last 18 to 25 years and would cost about 30 percent more. The car might have a large-displacement, low-RPM engine, top-quality shock absorbers, and an electronic ignition. Most important is a corrosion-resistant body that could carry the vehicle into its third decade. The study estimated that a doubling of the average life span to 20 years would approximately halve the industry's consumption of manufacturing energy and raw materials. In West Germany alone, that would mean sparing enough energy to supply the 6 million inhabitants of Hamburg, Munich, Cologne, Essen, Dusseldorf, and Stuttgart. Roughly 1.3 million tons of steel and iron would be saved, 50,000 tons of aluminum, 25,000

Estimated materials consumption in a typical 1980 U.S.-built car

Material	**Weight (in pounds)**
High-strength steel	175
Aluminum	130
Plastics	195
Glass	83
Copper	28
Zinc die castings	20
Rubber	131
Lead	23
Stainless steel	28
Iron	484
Plain carbon steel	1,737
Fluids, lubricants	178
Other alloy steel, cloth, cardboard, etc.	151
Total	**3,363**

From *Ward's Automotive Yearbook.*

Two views of Porsche's model for a long-life car.

tons of copper, and 70,000 tons of plastics. Then there is the energy conserved by virtue of having fewer cars to recycle, and the pollution avoided by not having to generate all that energy in the first place. And the landscape would be less ravaged by mines and power lines. And so on. Clearly, a lot is riding on the average life span of the automobile.

An early step in the study was to determine those body parts that deteriorate soonest, and a survey of 741 mid-sized cars (registered in West Germany) yielded the accompanying graph. It shows the extent of deterioration over ten model years. (Note that brakes are kept in relatively good repair; that's because they're crucial to a car's safe operation.) The West German study ranked components by their vulnerability and identified the worst as the wheel arches, bumpers, and front floor panels.

Fuhrmann points out a not-so-apparent problem with corrosion. A car loses more than its good looks as it rusts—its structure is weakened as well, and West German collision tests showed that a car with a far-gone body offers less protection in a crash. "The lower deceleration level of a strongly corroded car, which might appear desirable because it reduces the loads on the occupants, proves in fact to be a drawback: it results in increased deformation and thus an unacceptable reduction of the passengers' survival space."

Fuhrmann gives a simple rule for durable design: if a part cannot be made to last, then it should be made easy to replace. He names clutches and exhaust systems as particularly deserving of attention. It's a rare automaker that's thoughtful enough to install an exhaust system with stainless-steel fasteners, rather than parts that corrode into shapeless blobs of rust that won't respond to any tool but a chisel or saw.

More expensive than aluminum would be a body of stainless steel. Again, this alternative is not unknown to automakers. From time to time, Rolls Royces have been fashioned of it, stainless-steel Jeeps are status symbols in the Philippines, and the new Irish-built DeLorean (the work of former General Motors vice-president John Z. DeLorean) is the one current production car made of the material. Cars made of stainless back in the 1930s have gone up to 25 years and 375,000 miles without significant deterioration.

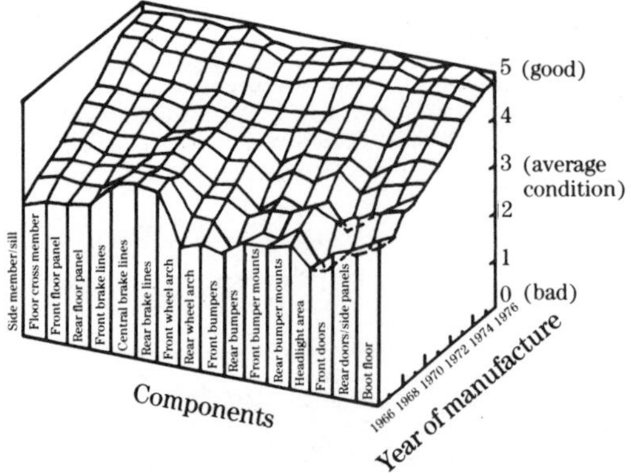

The deterioration of components in the European medium-size car.

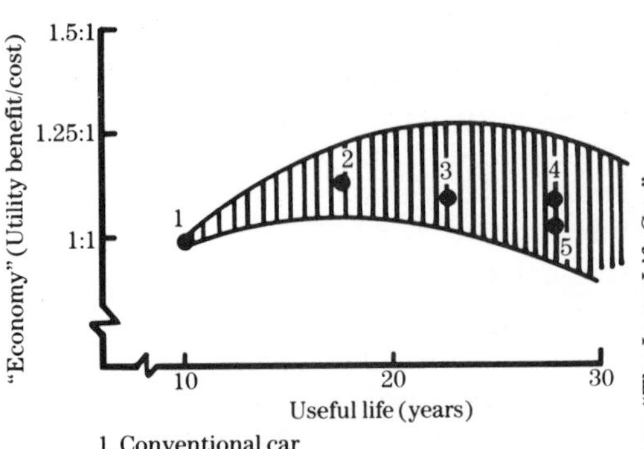

A cost-benefit analysis for four possible long-life cars.

Adapted from "The Long-Life Car," by Ernst Fuhrmann, *Futures*, June, 1979.

The fiberglass Corvette, introduced in 1954, has proven the practicality of this material. The three-wheel Free-Way, recently introduced and now in limited production, is of fiberglass-reinforced plastic, top and bottom. The steel frame is completely enclosed, enabling the manufacturer to guarantee it confidently for five years against rust.

Proponents of the long-life car believe that 25 years is the maximum practical life span. The costs of keeping a car alive past that become prohibitively expensive. Then, too, there is the risk of technical obsolescence, which could be expected to catch up to a car of great age, although the pace of major engineering changes in the industry has slackened and style changes are less frequent and less dramatic of late.

The Corvette has had a fiberglass body since 1954 and currently enjoys the lowest depreciation rate of any U.S. car.

The opposition heard from

The long-life car study has come into its share of criticism since introduced in the early 1970s. The advantages claimed for the car by Porsche's Fuhrmann are refuted by Professor Dr. Hans Joachim Förster of Daimler-Benz, who detects unreasonable optimism in the study's assumptions. The benefits of a 300,000-kilometer, 20-year car are exaggerated because they are compared with an unrealistically short life assumed for standard cars. Förster also argues that the fuel savings of a lightweight car are overstated, and calculates they would amount to but 6 percent, and even then only if Fuhrmann's assumptions about future energy and refining costs are realistically pessimistic. Savings of materials, claimed by Fuhrmann to exceed 50 percent, would in fact be minimal, the Daimler-Benz engineer believes, because almost all of a junked car is recycled.

While not discounting the importance of durability, Förster concludes that "even if the average life expectancy of the complete car and estate car [station wagon] population can be considerably prolonged, it is not safe to suppose that this would result in savings of energy or raw materials."

This line coincides with that of Ford's David J. Barrett, who says that "vehicle and component durability improvements over the last decade or so do not appear to have had a major effect on actual vehicle life." He explains that "today's chassis and drive-train components are already designed to have a potential life that significantly exceeds the time the vehicle is likely in service."

It may be in a manufacturer's interest to discredit the idea of a long-life car: with markets already saturated, the doubling of service life certainly would dampen business. Governments too can be expected to resist, as low production would mean unemployment and less growth.

Other critics have pointed out that the benefits of the long-life car would be reduced by the high percentage of cars lost to accidents. The British report, "A Bird's-eye View of Prolonged Car Life" (Intermediate Technology Publications), says that in the United Kingdom this figure is 30 percent over the current life expectancy of 10 years. If the average life could be stretched to 30 years, eight out of ten cars would be wrecked prematurely and a full 100 percent at 40 years. After citing these interesting statistics, the report recommends an optimum life of 20 years but cautions that "the extension of average-life has surprisingly little effect on motoring costs, with much of the depreciation gain being lost through higher interest charges and higher maintenance costs. Consequently there is little incentive from annual savings to offset the marketing problem of a higher first cost product."

A way around this would be to lease cars and provide a maintenance contract: the high purchase price is thereby absorbed and the leasing company could be expected to maintain their cars solicitously. (Through leasing, drivers would be spared the unpredictable bad news of car trouble—an especially vulnerable point for used-car buyers.)

The prospects for a long-life car are further downplayed by Intermediate Technology's John D. Davis. He suggests that only 10 percent of new-car purchasers would be interested in paying 20 percent more for a long-life car and concludes that such a limited production run wouldn't be economical. He recommends instead that cars be given two rustproofing treatments and be subjected to strict inspections. This could be expected to grant an additional ten years to a car's life, for less money. Such treatments are only a fifth the cost of galvanized steel or aluminum construction.

Making the best of today's cars

Until a long-life car comes along in your price range, you'll have to pamper the one you've got. Almost any car can be coaxed to more than 100,000 miles, but not without some attention along the way.

The great majority of cars are made out of a material that is highly vulnerable to moisture and salt, and because the benefits of responsible rustproofing may be negligible for at least six years, many automakers have been irresponsible. Knick the protective layer of paint or undercoating, and the exposed steel becomes a tiny battery, corroding away the sheet metal. You can do your part by touching up scratches with paint as soon as you spot them, and by flushing the car's vulnerable parts with water. (Britain's Automobile Association found that cars in low-rainfall areas seem to fare worse, as the bodies are not flushed as frequently in wet-weather driving.) These Achilles tendons vary from model to model but most often include the front fenders, sills, lower part of the doors, suspension mountings, subframe, and the floor's structural reinforcements. Wet cars shouldn't be shut up in warm, closed garages.

Of course, aftermarket fixes and desperate washing aren't the smartest ways to get around rust. It's as if *our* maker had provided for *us* to be a species of albinos, forced to cower from the sun's rays lest we be burned. The best rust prevention lies with the manufacturer, and some have gone to great pains and expense to combat corrosion. Many talk about their ambitious rustproofing procedures in ads and press releases, but the best way to make certain who's doing the job right is to look at older cars. One company that deserves at least an honorable mention is Mercedes-Benz. They've even published a booklet ("Mercedes-Benz Car-Body Treatment Techniques") that details exactly what steps they've taken on the owner's behalf, in unseen nooks and crannies and sealed chambers. All of this extra attention costs money, and the expense is ultimately borne by the owner, of course, but Mercedes owners enjoy one of the highest resale values of any current model. In Sweden, where a car lasts four more years on average than in the United States, Britain, or West Germany, the domestic Saab and Volvo both take their rustproofing seriously: Saab uses smooth fender liners to discourage the buildup of salt and mud, and Volvos last an impressive 18.7 years on their home turf. In Britain, the lowest depreciators are the Rolls, of legendary durability, and the plastic-bodied Lotus Elan. Of American cars, it's the fiberglass Corvette.

Looking to the near future

These are turbulent times for the auto industry, with all stops pulled in order to adapt to a world market. Some innovations have meant less pollution, more mileage, and simpler maintenance. Others have not been unqualified successes, suggesting caution on your part if you're intrigued by an unproven model. For example, General Motors, hardly lacking funds for product testing, has fallen down rather badly with three recent innovations. Its Olds diesel, the first U.S. oil-burner, has serious bugs; in a poll of 1978 owners, three-quarters reported one or more engine problems. The novel V8-6-4 Cadillac engine, able to shut down one or two pairs of cylinders when not needed, has been withdrawn from the market just a year after its introduction. And GM's downsized X-cars have been trouble-prone, according to early evidence on some 9,000 cars compiled by *Consumer Reports.* Not that a car company should be expected to pull off a flawless performance with radically different cars, but before you invest a big chunk of money in one, consider that even multibillion-dollar firms improve with practice. Detroit used to design an engine with the expectation that it would be made for at least 20 years; today, few people can confidently predict what the automobile will have evolved into 20 years hence. Another awkward period for the U.S. auto industry ran from 1971 to 1974, when Detroit was forced to move quickly on government emissions standards. These cars tend to be balky and fuel wasting, and little attention was given to corrosion protection—all evidenced today by a higher-than-usual scrap rate. It follows that those models most often lauded for their longevity were produced for a number of years, including the VW Beetle, Citroen 2 CV, BMW 2002, Volvo, Mercedes, and Chevy Nova (although the Nova nameplate was kept on after the car was completely redone).

Alternatives to rusty auto bodies

	+	–
Stainless steel		
	Bodies have lasted 25 years and over 375,000 miles	Heavier than aluminum and nonmetal materials
	Suited to recycling	Dependent on a source of nickel at reasonable price
	Good energy absorption in a crash	Material cost is five times that of steel
		Difficult to draw and weld panels
Aluminum		
	Proven in car bodies since the beginning of the century, including more than a million Land-Rovers	Material cost is nearly twice that of steel (energy costs are high)
	Lightweight	Difficult to draw and weld panels
	Corrosion-resistant	
	Suited to recycling and more attractive as scrap than standard auto bodies	
	Energy absorption per unit of weight is greater than for steel, of advantage in a crash	
	Raw materials appear in good supply	
Fiberglass (glass-reinforced plastic)		
	Proven by Chevrolet Corvette	Not easily recycled
	Lightweight	Plastic dependent on supply of petroleum
	Less capital investment required for production machinery	Exposes workers to harmful products
		Material cost is 35 percent above that of steel

Compiled largely from 1974 paper, "Long-life Car Research Project Study," by R. Schaefer of F. Porsche Aktiengesellschaft.

At the other extreme are models—and manufacturers—who suddenly cease to exist, leaving thousands of owners in something of a lurch. A dozen or so U.S. car makers went out of business in the decade following World War II; now Chrysler is in bad shape, and Renault owns most of AMC. Many foreign makes have ceased to be imported to the United States, which may enhance value in the romantic eyes of a collector but does not auger well for an owner faced with finding parts and knowledgeable mechanics. In the 1970s alone, 34 motorcycle manufacturers disappeared from the U.S. market. The ensuing problems can be imagined.

Most cars are losing weight so that they'll go farther on a gallon of the EPA's gas, and you might wonder if anything important is being taken out. A popular clue to durability is the heft, the density of a product, automobiles no exception. As explained in a following piece (see "One in 37," p. 63), lighter cars are generally more vulnerable in head-on collisions, with notable exceptions. And lightweight bodies, engines, and transmissions are designed "closer to the limit," according to GM's Dale Johnson, although he believes stronger materials will compensate for the metal trimmed away.

RY

Business, big and little

Can we expect corporations to produce sensible, long-lasting products for a conserver society? A large national corporation offered recently to buy out Smith & Hawken, the small importer of quality garden tools. If a deal were to go through, it could mean a large-scale commitment to quality production. Or, it could lead to the stifling of a durable alternative to short-lived tools.

The commercialism of the natural-foods market is a good indication of the odds against a more enlightened approach by business. People who wanted healthier, cheaper breakfast food started making granola at home. Small companies brought out cereals for the still-modest demand. Eventually, the big cereal companies came out with their own formulations—all "natural," of course, with 26 percent (natural) sugar content, (natural) preservatives, (natural) refined grains, and an extra (naturally) price premium.

Great size is not enough to automatically condemn a business. Both good and bad products are made and sold by both big and little companies. Big companies tend to have more momentum and resources, small ones more incentive and responsibility. You as a consumer can encourage the worthy producers by praising and purchasing what is good, and cursing and boycotting what is bad. The recent flush of decentralized alternative businesses shows that the desire for durable products left unfulfilled by big business can provide excellent opportunities for small firms. Cooperatives, collectives, partnerships, and community corporations have sprung up in housing, food, clothing, transportation, and a variety of other fields.

Again, small size is no assurance of quality or durability. Such alternative businesses exist because they tap new markets missed by bigger, centralized firms. The new small-scale decentralized businesses will likely form the backbone of a new economy, one in which producers feel directly their responsibility to serve the local market with durable goods. Every step toward closing the gap between producer and consumer strengthens the responsiveness of one to the other.

By itself, durability is not a particularly important goal. But it can be a means of redirecting our attention to more direct routes to happiness, achievement, and fulfillment. It's hard to ask more of any good idea.

TOM BENDER

PICKING A CHERRY FROM THE LEMONS

Each year, *Consumer Reports* magazine publishes its "Frequency-of-Repair records," an extensive tally of reader experiences with (as of the 1982 issue) 360,000 cars. The results are presented graphically, using a code of dots so that a car's merit or naughtiness can be judged at a glance. These records look something like the charts for your uppers and lowers at the dentist's office: certain cars with consistently below-average marks look like a mouth riddled with cavities. Just as dramatic are those dozen or so models with shining records.

Buyers who take the time to scan these automotive case histories will find clear, objective information on models of the recent past. To an extent, the marks can be applied to current models. The magazine also calculates each car's "cost index," a rating that compares the average maintenance-and-repair costs of each car with the average derived from those of all cars of the same model year.

Below we cull the best and the worst of the lot, taken from CR's 1976-through-1981 survey and reprinted here with their permission.

Unfortunately a book can't spontaneously regenerate updated material as it ages. The picks and pans and figures we give here are the latest available, but they will grow old quickly. You are referred to the annual issue of *Consumer Reports* (published by the nonprofit Consumers Union) for their fair, critical studies of cars and the invaluable annual Frequency-of-Repair records.

Consumer Reports' trouble index

Those models with at least three "much better than average" trouble index ratings over the six years of the survey.

TROUBLE SPOTS	Datsun 210,B210 '76	'77	'78	'79	'80	'81	Datsun 280Z, 280ZX '76	'77	'78	'79	'80	'81
Air-conditioning	○	•	◦	•	•	◦	○	•	○	⊕	⊕	○
Body exterior (paint)	•	○	⊕	●	●	⊕	•	◦	⊕	⊕	●	⊕
Body exterior (rust)	•	◦	○	⊕	○	○	○	•	◦	⊕	○	○
Body hardware	⊕	⊕	⊕	●	●	⊕	⊕	⊕	●	●	●	⊕
Body integrity	○	⊕	●	●	●	●	●	●	●	●	●	●
Brakes	○	◦	•	○	○	○	○	⊕	○	○	○	○
Clutch	○	⊕	⊕	○	⊕	○	⊕	⊕	⊕	⊕	⊕	○
Driveline	⊕	⊕	⊕	○	○	○	○	⊕	⊕	○	○	○
Electrical system (chassis)	⊕	●	●	●	●	●	⊕	⊕	⊕	○	●	○
Engine cooling	○	○	○	⊕	○	○	◦	○	◦	•	○	○
Engine mechanical	○	⊕	⊕	●	⊕	○	●	⊕	●	⊕	⊕	○
Exhaust system	○	○	•	⊕	○	○	●	●	●	⊕	○	○
Fuel system	●	⊕	●	●	⊕	⊕	⊕	○	⊕	⊕	●	●
Ignition system	⊕	○	○	⊕	⊕	○	●	●	⊕	⊕	○	○
Suspension	●	●	●	⊕	⊕	○	⊕	●	⊕	⊕	○	○
Transmission (manual)	⊕	⊕	⊕	⊕	⊕	○	⊕	⊕	○	⊕	⊕	○
Transmission (automatic)	○	⊕	⊕	⊕	⊕	○	⊕	⊕	⊕	⊕	⊕	○
TROUBLE INDEX	○	⊕	⊕	●	●	●	⊕	⊕	●	●	●	●
COST INDEX	⊕	⊕	⊕	⊕	⊕		○	○	○	○	○	

TROUBLE SPOTS	Dodge Colt (except front-wheel drive) '76	'77	'78	'79	'80	'81	Dodge Colt Hatchback (front-wheel drive) '76	'77	'78	'79	'80	'81
Air-conditioning	○	⊕	○	○	Insufficient data					•	•	○
Body exterior (paint)	○	⊕	●	●						●	●	⊕
Body exterior (rust)	⊕	⊕	●	○						⊕	○	○
Body hardware	⊕	●	●	⊕						●	●	●
Body integrity	⊕	●	●	●						⊕	●	○
Brakes	○	●	●	○						⊕	○	○
Clutch	●	●	●	⊕						●	⊕	○
Driveline	⊕	○	○	⊕						⊕	○	○
Electrical system (chassis)	⊕	⊕	●	●						●	●	●
Engine cooling	⊕	⊕	●	⊕						●	⊕	○
Engine mechanical	○	○	○	⊕						⊕	⊕	⊕
Exhaust system	⊕	○	⊕	○						○	•	○
Fuel system	⊕	○	⊕	⊕						⊕	⊕	○
Ignition system	○	○	○	○						○	○	○
Suspension	○	●	⊕	○						●	⊕	○
Transmission (manual)	⊕	⊕	⊕	⊕						○	⊕	○
Transmission (automatic)	◦	○	○	○							⊕	○
TROUBLE INDEX	⊕	●	●	●						●	●	●
COST INDEX	⊕	⊕	⊕	●						●	●	

● Much better than average ⊕ Better than average ○ Average

◦ Worse than average • Much worse than average * Insufficient cost data

TROUBLE SPOTS	Honda Accord '76	'77	'78	'79	'80	'81	Honda Prelude '76	'77	'78	'79	'80	'81
Air-conditioning	●	●	⊕	●	⊕	○				⊕	○	○
Body exterior (paint)	◦	○	⊕	●	●	⊕				○	●	⊕
Body exterior (rust)	•	•	○	○	○	○				•	○	○
Body hardware	●	●	●	●	●	●				●	●	●
Body integrity	●	●	●	●	●	●				⊕	●	●
Brakes	⊕	⊕	○	○	•	○				●	○	○
Clutch	⊕	⊕	⊕	⊕	●	○				●	⊕	○
Driveline	⊕	⊕	⊕	⊕	○	○				⊕	○	○
Electrical system (chassis)	●	⊕	⊕	●	●	●				●	●	●
Engine cooling	○	○	○	•	⊕	○				○	○	○
Engine mechanical	•	◦	•	⊕	⊕	○				●	●	⊕
Exhaust system	○	◦	•	○	○	○				⊕	○	○
Fuel system	●	●	⊕	○	◦	●				⊕	⊕	●
Ignition system	●	●	⊕	⊕	○	○				○	○	○
Suspension	●	●	●	●	⊕	○				●	⊕	○
Transmission (manual)	○	○	○	⊕	●	⊕				○	⊕	⊕
Transmission (automatic)	○	○	○	○	⊕	⊕				○	○	○
TROUBLE INDEX	⊕	⊕	⊕	●	●	●				●	●	●
COST INDEX	○	○	○	⊕	⊕					⊕	⊕	

TROUBLE SPOTS	Mazda 626 '76	'77	'78	'79	'80	'81	Mazda GLC (rear-wheel drive) '76	'77	'78	'79	'80	'81
Air-conditioning				○	•	○	Insufficient data	○	○	•	◦	○
Body exterior (paint)				⊕	●	⊕		○	○	●	●	⊕
Body exterior (rust)				⊕	⊕	○		○	○	●	○	○
Body hardware				●	●	⊕		○	○	●	●	○
Body integrity				●	●	⊕		○	○	⊕	●	○
Brakes				◦	○	○		○	○	⊕	○	○
Clutch				⊕	⊕	○		⊕	●	●	⊕	○
Driveline				⊕	○	○		○	○	○	○	○
Electrical system (chassis)				●	●	⊕		○	●	●	●	⊕
Engine cooling				●	⊕	○		○	●	●	○	○
Engine mechanical				⊕	⊕	○		○	●	●	⊕	○
Exhaust system				○	○	○		○	○	○	○	○
Fuel system				●	●	⊕		○	⊕	●	⊕	⊕
Ignition system				●	⊕	○		○	⊕	⊕	⊕	○
Suspension				◦	⊕	○		⊕	●	●	●	○
Transmission (manual)				○	●	○		○	○	⊕	●	○
Transmission (automatic)				○	⊕	⊕		⊕	○	⊕	●	○
TROUBLE INDEX				●	●	●		⊕	⊕	●	●	●
COST INDEX				⊕	●			*	●	●	●	

TROUBLE SPOTS	Mazda RX-7 '76	'77	'78	'79	'80	'81	Mercedes-Benz 240D 4 (diesel) '76	'77	'78	'79	'80	'81
Air-conditioning				○	○	○	●	⊕	⊕	⊕	○	Insufficient data
Body exterior (paint)				⊕	⊕	⊕	●	●	●	⊕	⊕	
Body exterior (rust)				●	⊕	○	●	●	⊕	⊕	⊕	
Body hardware				●	●	⊕	⊕	⊕	⊕	●	●	
Body integrity				●	●	⊕	●	●	●	●	●	
Brakes				○	○	○	○	⊕	○	○	⊕	
Clutch				⊕	○	○	⊕	⊕	⊕	○	○	
Driveline				○	○	○	○	⊕	○	⊕	○	
Electrical system (chassis)				⊕	●	○	○	○	⊕	●	●	
Engine cooling				○	⊕	○	○	⊕	⊕	⊕	○	
Engine mechanical				●	⊕	○	○	○	⊕	⊕	○	
Exhaust system				⊕	○	○	⊕	●	⊕	⊕	○	
Fuel system				⊕	⊕	⊕	●	⊕	⊕	○	⊕	
Ignition system				○	⊕	○	●	●	⊕	⊕	⊕	
Suspension				⊕	●	○	⊕	●	⊕	⊕	⊕	
Transmission (manual)				⊕	●	○	○	○	○	○	⊕	
Transmission (automatic)				⊕	⊕	○	○	⊕	⊕	⊕	○	
TROUBLE INDEX				●	●	●	●	●	●	●	●	
COST INDEX				○	○		•	◦	*	•	◦	

TROUBLE SPOTS	Mercedes-Benz 300D 5 (diesel) '76	'77	'78	'79	'80	'81	Plymouth Champ '76	'77	'78	'79	'80	'81
Air-conditioning	○	○	○	○	○	Insufficient data				•	•	○
Body exterior (paint)	●	●	⊕	⊕	○					●	●	⊕
Body exterior (rust)	●	●	●	⊕	⊕					⊕	○	○
Body hardware	⊕	⊕	⊕	⊕	●					●	●	●
Body integrity	●	●	●	●	●					⊕	●	○
Brakes	○	○	○	○	○					⊕	○	○
Clutch										●	⊕	○
Driveline	○	⊕	⊕	⊕	⊕					⊕	○	○
Electrical system (chassis)	●	○	⊕	○	○					●	●	●
Engine cooling	⊕	○	○	⊕	○					●	⊕	○
Engine mechanical	○	○	○	○	○					⊕	⊕	⊕
Exhaust system	●	●	●	⊕	○					○	•	○
Fuel system	●	⊕	⊕	○	⊕					⊕	⊕	○
Ignition system	●	⊕	●	○	⊕					○	○	○
Suspension	⊕	⊕	○	○	○					●	⊕	○
Transmission (manual)										○	⊕	○
Transmission (automatic)	⊕	⊕	●	○	○						⊕	○
TROUBLE INDEX	●	●	●	●	●					●	●	●
COST INDEX	◦	•	•	•	•					●	●	

● Much better than average ⊕ Better than average ○ Average

◦ Worse than average • Much worse than average * Insufficient cost data

TROUBLE SPOTS	Subaru (except 4WD)						Subaru (4WD)						Toyota Celica						Toyota Corolla (except Tercel)					
	'76	'77	'78	'79	'80	'81	'76	'77	'78	'79	'80	'81	'76	'77	'78	'79	'80	'81	'76	'77	'78	'79	'80	'81
Air-conditioning	○	○	○	◦	◦	○	Insufficient data	○	○	•	•	○	⊕	●	●	●	●	○	●	●	●	●	●	○
Body exterior (paint)	○	○	⊕	●	●	⊕		○	⊕	●	●	●	⊕	⊕	●	⊕	●	⊕	●	●	●	●	●	⊕
Body exterior (rust)	•	•	○	⊕	○	○		○	○	⊕	⊕	○	●	⊕	●	●	⊕	○	⊕	●	⊕	⊕	⊕	○
Body hardware	○	●	⊕	●	●	⊕		○	⊕	●	●	●	⊕	⊕	●	●	●	⊕	●	●	●	●	●	⊕
Body integrity	○	○	●	●	●	●		○	⊕	⊕	●	⊕	⊕	●	⊕	●	●	●	●	●	●	●	●	⊕
Brakes	•	◦	•	○	◦	○		○	○	○	○	○	⊕	●	●	●	⊕	○	⊕	⊕	●	⊕	◦	○
Clutch	⊕	○	●	⊕	⊕	○		⊕	⊕	⊕	⊕	○	●	●	●	●	⊕	○	●	●	●	●	⊕	○
Driveline	⊕	⊕	○	○	○	○		○	○	○	○	○	⊕	⊕	⊕	○	○	○	⊕	⊕	⊕	⊕	○	○
Electrical system (chassis)	○	⊕	●	●	●	●		⊕	●	●	●	●	○	●	●	●	●	●	●	●	●	●	●	●
Engine cooling	•	●	⊕	●	○	○		⊕	⊕	⊕	○	○	●	⊕	○	⊕	⊕	○	●	⊕	●	⊕	○	○
Engine mechanical	•	◦	○	○	⊕	○		○	◦	○	⊕	⊕	○	●	⊕	●	⊕	○	●	●	●	●	⊕	○
Exhaust system	●	⊕	●	⊕	○	○		◦	•	○	○	○	⊕	⊕	⊕	⊕	○	○	⊕	⊕	●	⊕	○	○
Fuel system	○	○	⊕	●	⊕	○		⊕	●	●	⊕	•	●	●	●	●	●	●	⊕	●	●	●	●	●
Ignition system	○	○	⊕	⊕	⊕	○		○	○	⊕	⊕	○	⊕	●	●	●	⊕	○	⊕	●	●	●	⊕	○
Suspension	⊕	●	●	●	⊕	○		⊕	⊕	⊕	⊕	○	⊕	●	●	⊕	⊕	○	●	●	●	●	⊕	○
Transmission (manual)	○	○	○	○	⊕	○		○	○	○	⊕	○	○	⊕	⊕	⊕	⊕	⊕	⊕	⊕	⊕	⊕	⊕	⊕
Transmission (automatic)	◦	○	○	○	○	○							⊕	●	●	⊕	●	⊕	●	●	●	●	●	⊕
TROUBLE INDEX	○	⊕	⊕	●	●	●		⊕	⊕	●	●	●	⊕	●	●	●	●	●	●	●	●	●	●	●
COST INDEX	○	⊕	⊕	⊕	⊕			*	○	⊕	⊕		⊕	⊕	●	⊕	⊕		●	●	●	●	⊕	

TROUBLE SPOTS	Toyota Corona						Toyota Cressida						Toyota pickup truck (2WD)						Volvo 240 series					
	'76	'77	'78	'79	'80	'81	'76	'77	'78	'79	'80	'81	'76	'77	'78	'79	'80	'81	'76	'77	'78	'79	'80	'81
Air-conditioning	⊕	●	●	●	⊕	○			●	⊕	⊕	○	⊕	⊕	○	⊕	○	○	⊕	○	○	○	•	○
Body exterior (paint)	⊕	●	●	●	⊕	⊕			⊕	○	●	⊕	○	⊕	⊕	○	●	⊕	●	●	●	⊕	⊕	⊕
Body exterior (rust)	⊕	●	⊕	●	○	○			●	⊕	○	○	○	⊕	•	○	○	○	●	●	●	●	⊕	○
Body hardware	●	●	●	●	●	●			●	●	●	⊕	●	●	●	●	●	⊕	⊕	⊕	⊕	⊕	⊕	○
Body integrity	●	●	●	●	●	●			●	●	●	●	⊕	●	⊕	●	●	⊕	●	●	●	●	●	●
Brakes	⊕	○	⊕	⊕	○	○			⊕	○	○	○	●	●	●	●	○	○	○	○	⊕	⊕	⊕	○
Clutch	●	●	●	⊕	⊕	○							●	●	●	●	●	○	●	○	●	⊕	○	○
Driveline	⊕	⊕	⊕	⊕	○	○			○	○	○	○	⊕	⊕	⊕	⊕	○	○	⊕	⊕	⊕	○	○	○
Electrical system (chassis)	⊕	●	●	●	●	⊕			●	●	●	○	●	●	●	●	●	⊕	○	⊕	○	○	⊕	○
Engine cooling	●	⊕	⊕	⊕	○	○			○	⊕	⊕	○	●	⊕	⊕	●	⊕	○	⊕	⊕	⊕	⊕	○	○
Engine mechanical	⊕	●	●	●	⊕	○			●	⊕	⊕	⊕	○	⊕	○	●	⊕	○	⊕	⊕	●	⊕	⊕	○
Exhaust system	⊕	⊕	⊕	⊕	○	○			○	○	○	○	○	⊕	⊕	○	○	○	◦	•	•	◦	○	○
Fuel system	⊕	●	●	●	●	●			●	●	●	●	●	●	●	●	●	●	○	⊕	●	●	●	⊕
Ignition system	●	●	●	⊕	⊕	○			⊕	⊕	⊕	○	⊕	●	●	⊕	⊕	○	⊕	⊕	●	⊕	○	○
Suspension	●	●	⊕	●	⊕	○			⊕	⊕	⊕	○	○	●	⊕	•	⊕	○	⊕	●	●	●	●	○
Transmission (manual)	○	○	○	⊕	⊕	○							•	○	○	⊕	●	○	○	○	○	○	○	○
Transmission (automatic)	⊕	●	●	●	●	⊕			○	⊕	⊕	⊕							○	⊕	⊕	⊕	●	○
TROUBLE INDEX	●	●	●	●	●	●			●	●	●	●	●	●	●	●	●	●	⊕	●	●	●	●	●
COST INDEX	⊕	⊕	●	●	⊕				⊕	●	○		⊕	●	●	●	⊕		◦	○	○	○	◦	

Those models with at least two "much worse than average" trouble index ratings over the six years of the survey.

TROUBLE SPOTS	AMC Pacer 6 '76	'77	'78	'79	'80	'81
Air-conditioning	○	⊕	○			
Body exterior (paint)	⊕	●	⊕			
Body exterior (rust)	○	○	○			
Body hardware	•	•	○			
Body integrity	•	•	○			
Brakes	○	•	○			
Clutch	○	○	○			
Driveline	○	○	○			
Electrical system (chassis)	•	•	◦	Insufficient data	Insufficient data	
Engine cooling	•	○	○			
Engine mechanical	○	○	○			
Exhaust system	•	•	○			
Fuel system	•	•	○			
Ignition system	•	•	○			
Suspension	•	•	○			
Transmission (manual)	○	○	○			
Transmission (automatic)	•	•	○			
TROUBLE INDEX	•	•	◦			
COST INDEX	○	○	*			

TROUBLE SPOTS	Cadillac Eldorado V8 (gasoline) '76	'77	'78	'79	'80	'81
Air-conditioning	○		○	○	◦	○
Body exterior (paint)	○		○	○	○	○
Body exterior (rust)	○		◦	○	○	○
Body hardware	○		○	○	○	○
Body integrity	○		○	○	◦	○
Brakes	○		○	•	○	○
Clutch						○
Driveline	○		○	○	○	○
Electrical system (chassis)	○	Insufficient data	○	•	•	◦
Engine cooling	○		○	○	○	○
Engine mechanical	○		○	⊕	○	◦
Exhaust system	○		○	○	○	○
Fuel system	○		○	•	•	◦
Ignition system	○		○	◦	•	○
Suspension	○		○	○	○	○
Transmission (manual)						○
Transmission (automatic)	○		○	○	○	○
TROUBLE INDEX	○		○	◦	•	•
COST INDEX	*		*	•	•	

TROUBLE SPOTS	Chevrolet Corvette '76	'77	'78	'79	'80	'81
Air-conditioning	○	◦	◦	•	○	
Body exterior (paint)	○	○	◦	•	•	
Body exterior (rust)	●	●	⊕	⊕	○	
Body hardware	○	◦	•	•	•	
Body integrity	○	◦	◦	•	•	
Brakes	○	○	○	◦	○	
Clutch	○	○	○	○	•	
Driveline	○	•	•	•	○	
Electrical system (chassis)	○	○	•	•	◦	Insufficient data
Engine cooling	○	○	○	◦	○	
Engine mechanical	⊕	○	○	○	○	
Exhaust system	○	○	○	○	○	
Fuel system	⊕	⊕	○	⊕	○	
Ignition system	⊕	○	○	◦	○	
Suspension	○	○	○	○	○	
Transmission (manual)	○	○	○	○	○	
Transmission (automatic)	○	○	○	○	○	
TROUBLE INDEX	⊕	○	◦	•	•	
COST INDEX	*	*	*	•	*	

TROUBLE SPOTS	Chevrolet Monte Carlo V6 (except turbo) '76	'77	'78	'79	'80	'81
Air-conditioning			◦	○	○	○
Body exterior (paint)			•	◦	◦	◦
Body exterior (rust)			○	○	○	○
Body hardware			○	○	•	○
Body integrity			○	•	•	•
Brakes			○	○	○	○
Clutch						
Driveline			○	○	◦	○
Electrical system (chassis)			○	○	◦	○
Engine cooling			○	○	○	○
Engine mechanical			○	○	○	◦
Exhaust system			○	○	◦	◦
Fuel system			○	◦	◦	•
Ignition system			○	○	○	◦
Suspension			○	◦	•	○
Transmission (manual)						
Transmission (automatic)			○	○	◦	○
TROUBLE INDEX			○	○	•	•
COST INDEX			⊕	⊕	⊕	

TROUBLE SPOTS	Chevrolet Monza 4 '76	'77	'78	'79	'80	'81
Air-conditioning	◦	•	◦	○	○	
Body exterior (paint)	◦	•	•	•	◦	
Body exterior (rust)	◦	○	•	◦	○	
Body hardware	•	◦	•	•	○	
Body integrity	•	•	•	•	◦	
Brakes	○	○	○	◦	◦	
Clutch	•	◦	◦	◦	◦	
Driveline	○	○	○	◦	○	
Electrical system (chassis)	○	◦	◦	○	○	
Engine cooling	◦	◦	•	•	•	
Engine mechanical	○	•	○	○	•	
Exhaust system	•	○	•	◦	○	
Fuel system	•	•	○	○	◦	
Ignition system	○	•	○	◦	◦	
Suspension	○	○	•	•	◦	
Transmission (manual)	○	◦	◦	•	◦	
Transmission (automatic)	•	◦	○	◦	○	
TROUBLE INDEX	•	•	•	•	•	
COST INDEX	○	○	○	○	○	

TROUBLE SPOTS	Chevrolet Monza V6 '76	'77	'78	'79	'80	'81
Air-conditioning			○	○	◦	
Body exterior (paint)			•	•	◦	
Body exterior (rust)			○	◦	○	
Body hardware			•	•	◦	
Body integrity			•	•	•	
Brakes			◦	•	○	
Clutch			◦	•	◦	
Driveline			○	○	○	
Electrical system (chassis)			◦	○	○	
Engine cooling			•	◦	•	
Engine mechanical			○	○	○	
Exhaust system			○	•	○	
Fuel system			◦	•	○	
Ignition system			○	•	○	
Suspension			◦	•	○	
Transmission (manual)			○	○	○	
Transmission (automatic)			○	○	○	
TROUBLE INDEX			•	•	•	
COST INDEX			○	○	*	

TROUBLE SPOTS	Dodge Aspen 6 '76	'77	'78	'79	'80	'81
Air-conditioning	○	⊕	●	⊕	○	
Body exterior (paint)	○	○	○	○	○	
Body exterior (rust)	•	•	•	◦	○	
Body hardware	•	•	•	○	○	
Body integrity	•	•	•	•	○	
Brakes	◦	•	•	•	○	
Clutch	◦	•	◦		○	
Driveline	○	○	◦	○	○	
Electrical system (chassis)	◦	•	•	○	○	
Engine cooling	⊕	●	⊕	⊕	○	
Engine mechanical	⊕	⊕	○	○	○	
Exhaust system	⊕	◦	◦	○	○	
Fuel system	•	•	•	•	•	
Ignition system	◦	•	•	○	○	
Suspension	•	◦	•	◦	○	
Transmission (manual)	•	•	•		○	
Transmission (automatic)	○	○	○	◦	○	
TROUBLE INDEX	◦	•	•	◦	○	
COST INDEX	⊕	○	○	○	○	

TROUBLE SPOTS	Dodge Sportsman Wagon (van) V8 '76	'77	'78	'79	'80	'81
Air-conditioning	○	⊕	○	•	○	
Body exterior (paint)	○	⊕	○	○	○	
Body exterior (rust)	○	○	◦	•	○	
Body hardware	○	•	◦	•	•	
Body integrity	•	•	•	•	•	
Brakes	○	○	◦	○	○	
Clutch	◦	•	◦		◦	
Driveline	•	•	◦	◦	○	
Electrical system (chassis)	•	◦	○	◦	○	Insufficient data
Engine cooling	○	●	○	⊕	○	
Engine mechanical	○	○	◦	○	○	
Exhaust system	○	○	○	○	○	
Fuel system	•	•	•	◦	○	
Ignition system	◦	•	•	◦	•	
Suspension	○	•	•	•	◦	
Transmission (manual)	◦	◦	◦		○	
Transmission (automatic)	○	◦	○	○	○	
TROUBLE INDEX	◦	•	•	•	•	
COST INDEX	○	○	○	○	*	

● Much better than average ⊕ Better than average ○ Average

◦ Worse than average • Much worse than average * Insufficient cost data

Fiat 131, Brava

TROUBLE SPOTS	'76	'77	'78	'79	'80	'81
Air-conditioning	•	Insufficient data	○	○	Insufficient data	Insufficient data
Body exterior (paint)	◦		○	○		
Body exterior (rust)	◦		•	◦		
Body hardware	•		◦	•		
Body integrity	•		○	◦		
Brakes	•		•	•		
Clutch	○		○	○		
Driveline	◦		○	○		
Electrical system (chassis)	•		○	○		
Engine cooling	○		○	◦		
Engine mechanical	•		◦	○		
Exhaust system	•		•	•		
Fuel system	○		○	○		
Ignition system	•		○	○		
Suspension	◦		○	○		
Transmission (manual)	○		○	○		
Transmission (automatic)	○		○	○		
TROUBLE INDEX	•		•	•		
COST INDEX	◦		*	*		

Ford Mustang 6, V6

TROUBLE SPOTS	'76	'77	'78	'79	'80	'81
Air-conditioning				⊕	○	○
Body exterior (paint)				○	○	○
Body exterior (rust)				⊕	○	○
Body hardware				○	◦	○
Body integrity				•	•	○
Brakes				○	○	○
Clutch				○	•	○
Driveline				○	○	○
Electrical system (chassis)				•	○	○
Engine cooling				•	○	○
Engine mechanical				•	◦	○
Exhaust system				○	○	○
Fuel system				•	•	○
Ignition system				◦	◦	○
Suspension				○	○	○
Transmission (manual)				◦	•	○
Transmission (automatic)				○	○	○
TROUBLE INDEX				•	•	○
COST INDEX				○	○	

Mercury Capri V6

TROUBLE SPOTS	'76	'77	'78	'79	'80	'81
Air-conditioning				⊕	○	○
Body exterior (paint)				○	○	○
Body exterior (rust)				⊕	○	○
Body hardware				○	◦	○
Body integrity				•	•	○
Brakes				○	○	○
Clutch				○	•	○
Driveline				○	○	○
Electrical system (chassis)				•	○	○
Engine cooling				•	○	○
Engine mechanical				•	◦	○
Exhaust system				○	○	○
Fuel system				•	•	○
Ignition system				◦	◦	○
Suspension				○	○	○
Transmission (manual)				◦	•	○
Transmission (automatic)				○	○	○
TROUBLE INDEX				•	•	○
COST INDEX				○	○	

Oldsmobile Omega 4

TROUBLE SPOTS	'76	'77	'78	'79	'80	'81
Air-conditioning					○	◦
Body exterior (paint)					•	•
Body exterior (rust)					○	○
Body hardware					○	•
Body integrity					○	○
Brakes					◦	○
Clutch					•	◦
Driveline					○	○
Electrical system (chassis)					○	•
Engine cooling					◦	○
Engine mechanical					•	◦
Exhaust system					○	○
Fuel system					•	○
Ignition system					◦	○
Suspension					○	○
Transmission (manual)					•	•
Transmission (automatic)					◦	○
TROUBLE INDEX					•	•
COST INDEX					⊕	

Oldsmobile Omega V6

TROUBLE SPOTS	'76	'77	'78	'79	'80	'81
Air-conditioning					○	○
Body exterior (paint)					•	◦
Body exterior (rust)					○	○
Body hardware					◦	○
Body integrity					○	○
Brakes					○	○
Clutch					○	○
Driveline					○	○
Electrical system (chassis)					○	◦
Engine cooling					•	◦
Engine mechanical					○	○
Exhaust system					○	○
Fuel system					•	◦
Ignition system					○	○
Suspension					○	○
Transmission (manual)					•	◦
Transmission (automatic)					◦	○
TROUBLE INDEX					•	•
COST INDEX					○	

Plymouth Volare 6

TROUBLE SPOTS	'76	'77	'78	'79	'80	'81
Air-conditioning	○	⊕	●	⊕	○	
Body exterior (paint)	○	○	○	○	○	
Body exterior (rust)	•	•	•	◦	○	
Body hardware	•	•	•	○	○	
Body integrity	•	•	•	•	○	
Brakes	◦	•	•	•	○	
Clutch	◦	•	◦		○	
Driveline	○	○	◦	○	○	
Electrical system (chassis)	◦	•	•	○	○	
Engine cooling	⊕	●	⊕	⊕	○	
Engine mechanical	⊕	⊕	○	○	○	
Exhaust system	⊕	◦	◦	○	○	
Fuel system	•	•	•	•	•	
Ignition system	◦	•	•	○	○	
Suspension	•	◦	•	◦	○	
Transmission (manual)	•	•	•		○	
Transmission (automatic)	○	○	○	◦	○	
TROUBLE INDEX	◦	•	•	◦	○	
COST INDEX	⊕	○	○	○	○	

Pontiac Firebird V8

TROUBLE SPOTS	'76	'77	'78	'79	'80	'81
Air-conditioning	○	○	○	○	○	Insufficient data
Body exterior (paint)	•	•	•	•	•	
Body exterior (rust)	•	•	•	○	○	
Body hardware	○	◦	•	•	•	
Body integrity	◦	•	•	•	•	
Brakes	○	○	○	○	○	
Clutch	◦	◦	○	◦		
Driveline	⊕	○	○	◦	○	
Electrical system (chassis)	○	○	○	◦	•	
Engine cooling	○	○	◦	○	•	
Engine mechanical	○	○	○	○	○	
Exhaust system	○	○	○	◦	○	
Fuel system	○	⊕	○	○	○	
Ignition system	○	⊕	○	○	○	
Suspension	○	○	○	○	◦	
Transmission (manual)	○	○	○	○		
Transmission (automatic)	○	○	○	○	○	
TROUBLE INDEX	○	○	•	•	•	
COST INDEX	*	○	○	○	*	

Pontiac Phoenix V6

TROUBLE SPOTS	'76	'77	'78	'79	'80	'81
Air-conditioning					○	◦
Body exterior (paint)					•	◦
Body exterior (rust)					◦	○
Body hardware					○	○
Body integrity					○	○
Brakes					○	○
Clutch					•	○
Driveline					○	○
Electrical system (chassis)					•	•
Engine cooling					•	◦
Engine mechanical					◦	○
Exhaust system					○	○
Fuel system					•	○
Ignition system					◦	○
Suspension					○	○
Transmission (manual)					•	•
Transmission (automatic)					○	○
TROUBLE INDEX					•	•
COST INDEX					○	

Pontiac Sunbird 4

TROUBLE SPOTS	'76	'77	'78	'79	'80	'81
Air-conditioning	Insufficient data	○	○	○	○	
Body exterior (paint)		○	○	○	○	
Body exterior (rust)		◦	•	◦	○	
Body hardware		•	•	•	◦	
Body integrity		◦	•	•	•	
Brakes		○	◦	◦	◦	
Clutch		◦	◦	•	•	
Driveline		○	○	◦	○	
Electrical system (chassis)		○	•	○	○	
Engine cooling		○	○	•	○	
Engine mechanical		○	○	◦	◦	
Exhaust system		•	•	◦	○	
Fuel system		○	○	○	◦	
Ignition system		○	○	○	○	
Suspension		◦	•	•	•	
Transmission (manual)		•	○	○	◦	
Transmission (automatic)		○	○	○	◦	
TROUBLE INDEX		•	•	•	•	
COST INDEX		*	○	○	○	

In presenting the following lists of good bets and cars to avoid (from its April, 1981, issue), *Consumer Reports* commented that models on the recommended list should be better risks than other used models: the list is derived from their Frequency-of-Repair data, which in turn is based on their readers' recent experiences with more than 360,000 cars.

Recommended used cars aren't guaranteed to be trouble-free, but none of them has had significant numbers of serious mechanical problems, according to the magazine's readers. Similarly, a model on the list of used cars to avoid isn't necessarily a clunker. It's just more likely than other cars to have problems during its life.

Consumer Reports' list of recommended used cars includes models that go back only to 1975. Cars older than that have been on the road so long that they may be nearing the end of their useful life. Even when a car is only four or five years old, the condition of the individual car is usually much more important than its Frequency-of-Repair record.

> *". . . The automobile is the most postponable consumer purchase there is. With a paint job, a new battery, and a little fixing,* [*a*] *car can last six or seven years."*
>
> ELLIOTT M. ESTES,
> chairman and chief executive officer,
> General Motors Corporation,
> quoted in the *New Yorker*

Recommended used cars by price

$1000–$1500
- 1975 Plymouth Fury V8
- 1975 Pontiac Catalina, Bonneville

$1500–$2000
- 1975 Chevrolet Chevelle, Malibu 6 and V8
- 1976 Ford Torino
- 1975 Mercury Cougar XR-7
- 1975 Mercury Marquis
- 1976 Mercury Montego V8
- 1975 Pontiac Ventura V8
- 1975 Toyota Corolla

$2000–$2500
- 1976 Ford Elite
- 1977 Mazda GLC
- 1976 Mercury Marquis
- 1976 Oldsmobile 88 V8
- 1976 Pontiac Catalina, Bonneville
- 1976 Pontiac Le Mans V8
- 1975 Toyota Celica
- 1976 Toyota Corolla
- 1975 Toyota Corona

$2500–$3000
- 1976 Buick Century, Regal V6
- 1976 Buick Skylark V6
- 1977 Chevrolet Caprice, Impala 6
- 1977 Dodge Colt
- 1976 Ford Thunderbird
- 1977 Mercury Marquis
- 1976 Oldsmobile Cutlass V8
- 1975 Peugeot 504 (diesel)
- 1977 Pontiac Catalina, Bonneville V8
- 1976 Pontiac Ventura 6
- 1977 Toyota Corolla
- 1976 Toyota Corona

$3000–$3500
- 1977 Buick Le Sabre V6 and V8
- 1978 Datsun B210
- 1978 Dodge Colt
- 1979 Dodge Colt Hatchback (front-wheel drive)
- 1978 Mazda GLC
- 1977 Oldsmobile 88 V6 and V8
- 1977 Oldsmobile Cutlass V8
- 1979 Renault Le Car
- 1978 Subaru
- 1976 Toyota Celica
- 1977 Toyota Corona
- 1977 Volkswagen Rabbit (diesel)

$3500–$4000
- 1977 Buick Electra, Electra 225 V8
- 1978 Chevrolet Caprice, Impala 6 and V8
- 1979 Dodge Colt (rear-wheel drive)
- 1979 Mazda GLC
- 1978 Mercury Monarch V8
- 1978 Oldsmobile 88 V6
- 1978 Oldsmobile Cutlass Salon
- 1978 Plymouth Arrow
- 1978 Pontiac Catalina, Bonneville V8
- 1978 Subaru (4-wheel drive)
- 1979 Subaru
- 1977 Toyota Celica
- 1978 Toyota Corolla
- 1978 Toyota Corona

$4000–$4500
- 1978 Buick Le Sabre V8
- 1979 Datsun 210
- 1979 Datsun 310
- 1979 Datsun 510
- 1978 Dodge Challenger
- 1979 Honda Civic, Civic CVCC
- 1979 Mercury Cougar XR-7
- 1979 Plymouth Arrow
- 1979 Plymouth Champ
- 1978 Plymouth Sapporo
- 1978 Pontiac Grand Prix
- 1978 Toyota Celica
- 1979 Toyota Corolla
- 1979 Toyota Corona

$4500–$5000
- 1979 Buick Le Sabre V8
- 1979 Chevrolet Caprice, Impala 6 and V8
- 1978 Honda Accord
- 1979 Mazda 626
- 1979 Oldsmobile 88 V6 and V8 (gasoline)
- 1978 Oldsmobile 98 (gasoline)
- 1978 Oldsmobile Cutlass Supreme, Calais V6
- 1979 Pontiac Le Mans V8
- 1979 Subaru (4-wheel drive)
- 1978 Toyota Cressida

1956 Ford Fairlane

"My car is a 1956 Ford Fairlane with a Thunderbird engine. I never cared for a blue car but when my husband drove this one into the yard I thought is was the most beautiful car I had ever seen.

"Everywhere I go, someone wants to buy it. It is not for sale. My son has it spoken for when and if I do not use it anymore. It is getting harder to find repair parts, though. Right now, I need a new fuel gauge but cannot find one."

LILLIAN D. STEWART
Loughman, Florida

$5000–$6000
- 1978 Buick Electra, Electra 225 V8
- 1979 Datsun 810
- 1979 Honda Accord
- 1979 Honda Prelude
- 1978 Oldsmobile Cutlass Supreme, Calais V8
- 1979 Toyota Celica
- 1979 Toyota Cressida
- 1978 Volvo 240 series

$6000–$8000
- 1975 Mercedes-Benz 240D (diesel)
- 1979 Oldsmobile 98 (gasoline)
- 1979 Peugeot 504 (diesel)
- 1979 Toyota Celica Supra
- 1979 Volvo 240 series

Some used-car models to avoid

AMC Eagle, 1980
AMC Gremlin 6, 1975–77
AMC Hornet, Concord 6, 1975–77
AMC Matador V8, 1975
AMC Pacer 6, 1975–78

Audi 100, 1975–77
Audi Fox, 1975–77

BMW 530i, 1976

Buick Opel Isuzu, 1976–77
Buick Riviera (turbo), 1979
Buick Skyhawk V6, 1975–79
Buick Skylark 4 and V6 (front-wheel drive), 1980
Buick Skylark V6, 1975, 1978

Cadillac Eldorado (gasoline), 1979–80
Cadillac Eldorado (diesel), 1979
Cadillac Seville (gasoline), 1980
Cadillac Seville (diesel), 1979

Chevrolet Camaro 6 and V8, 1975–79
Chevrolet Chevette, 1976–77, 1979
Chevrolet Citation 4 and V6, 1980
Chevrolet Corvette, 1978–80
Chevrolet Malibu V6, 1978–79
Chevrolet Monte Carlo V6, 1979
Chevrolet Monte Carlo V8, 1979–80
Chevrolet Monza 4, 1975–80
Chevrolet Monza V6, 1978–79
Chevrolet Nova 6, 1975–79
Chevrolet Nova V8, 1975, 1978
Chevrolet Vega, 1975–77

Chrysler Cordoba V8, 1976–79
Chrysler Le Baron V8, 1977, 1979
Chrysler Newport, New Yorker, 1976–79

Datsun 200-SX, 1978
Datsun B210, 1975–76
Datsun F-10, 1976–77

Dodge Aspen 6, 1976–80
Dodge Aspen V8, 1976–78
Dodge Coronet, Charger V8, 1976–77
Dodge Dart 6, 1975–76
Dodge Dart V8, 1975
Dodge Diplomat V8, 1977–78
Dodge Magnum XE, 1978
Dodge Monaco V8, 1977–78
Dodge Omni, 1978–79
Dodge Royal Monaco, 1977

Fiat 128, 1975–76
Fiat 131, Brava, 1975–76, 1979
Fiat Sport Coupe, Spider, 1976–79
Fiat Strada, 1979

Ford Fairmont 4, 6, and V8, 1978
Ford Granada 6, 1976–77
Ford Granada V8, 1975, 1978–79
Ford Maverick 6, 1977
Ford Mustang 4, 6, and V6, 1979–80
Ford Mustang V8, 1979
Ford Mustang II 4 and V6, 1975–78
Ford Mustang II V8, 1975, 1977
Ford Pinto 4, 1975–76
Ford Pinto V6, 1975, 1977–78

Honda Accord, 1976
Honda Civic, 1976
Honda Civic CVCC, 1976–77

Lincoln Continental Mark VI, 1980

Mercury Bobcat 4, 1975–76
Mercury Capri 4, 6, and V8, 1979
Mercury Capri II V6 (imported), 1976
Mercury Cougar XR-7, 1978

Recall hotline

You can check for recalls on your car by calling the National Highway Traffic Safety Administration Recall Hotline, (800) 424-9393.

Mercury Marquis, 1979
Mercury Monarch 6, 1975, 1977
Mercury Monarch V8, 1975
Mercury Zephyr 4, 6, and V8, 1978

Oldsmobile 88 (diesel), 1978–80
Oldsmobile 98 (diesel), 1978–79
Oldsmobile Cutlass V6, 1977
Oldsmobile Cutlass V8 (diesel), 1979
Oldsmobile Omega 4 and V6 (front-wheel drive), 1980
Oldsmobile Omega V6, 1977
Oldsmobile Starfire V6, 1975–77
Oldsmobile Toronado (gasoline), 1978
Oldsmobile Toronado (diesel), 1979

Plymouth Fury V8, 1976–78
Plymouth Gran Fury V8, 1975, 1977
Plymouth Horizon, 1978–79
Plymouth Valiant, Duster, Scamp 6, 1975–76
Plymouth Volare 6, 1976–80
Plymouth Volare V8, 1976–78

Pontiac Astre, 1975–77
Pontiac Firebird V8, 1975–79
Pontiac Le Mans V6, 1979
Pontiac Phoenix 4 and V6 (front-wheel drive), 1980
Pontiac Phoenix, Ventura V6, 1977–78
Pontiac Sunbird 4, 1976–80
Pontiac Sunbird V6, 1976–79

Porsche 924, 1977–78

Renault Le Car, 1978

Saab 99, 1975–76

Subaru, 1976

Volkswagen Bus, 1975
Volkswagen Dasher, 1975–77
Volkswagen Rabbit (gasoline), 1975–77
Volkswagen Scirocco, 1975–77

One in 37

The Citation before.

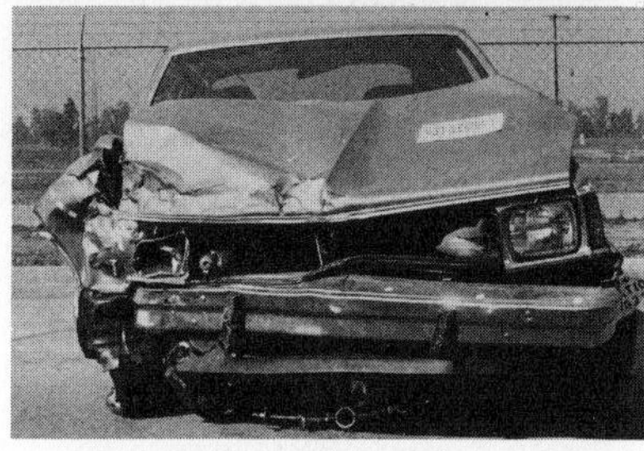

The Citation after. Both driver and passenger would have survived this crash test.

In 1980, 1,986,000 Americans died. The good news is that you weren't one of them. The scary news is that 53,000 of them were killed in car accidents, suggesting that your chances of going for a ride one day and never coming back are 1 in 37.

According to crash tests conducted by the National Highway Traffic Safety Administration, your chances of survival are significantly better in a heavy car—at least twice as good in a two-ton car as in a one-ton subcompact. The fatality rate for full-size American cars is lowest, followed by intermediates, then compacts, and finally subcompacts.

As these statistics are publicized, some people are expected to try to strike a compromise between safety and gas mileage by moving to heavier cars. This remains to be seen. But structural integrity is something to think about, given another statistic: we are subjected to a serious accident, on average, at least every ten years.

The crash-team reports were printed in *The Car Book*, distributed free of charge, but this has been withdrawn by the Reagan administration in response to industry criticism of its name-brand reports on safety, fuel economy, and operating costs. Crash-test results likely will continue to be reported and analyzed by *Consumer Reports*. Although the magazine doesn't have sufficient confidence in the tests to warrant down-rating a car they think highly of, they believe the crash ratings deserve a careful look by consumers in shopping for a car.

Notes from a *Consumer Reports* test-driver

Bob Knoll owns a Datsun, a Toyota, and a Mazda. He says he chose these cars on the basis of the tests run by *Consumer Reports* magazine, which in recent years has rated Japanese automobiles highly. Knoll takes these tests seriously: he directs the nine-person staff that test-drives cars for the magazine.

Knoll has test-driven cars for *Consumer Reports* since 1964. In those years he has seen Japanese cars get better, American cars shrink in size, and, he hopes, consumers grow smarter. "When I started working for this magazine, there were about 600,000 readers," says Knoll. "Today we have just under 3 million readers. To me that indicates we've done something right in attracting people to the idea of being good consumers."

Knoll has witnessed many automotive trends come and go. He remembers with nostalgia the hoopla that surrounded the Wankel engine when it was introduced (and the disappointment that soon followed); the excitement generated by Detroit's first small cars, including the Chevrolet Vega and Ford Pinto (the Vega quickly proved to be notoriously unrugged, while the Pinto had a nasty habit of exploding when hit from behind); and more recently, the promises of improved gas mileage claimed by Cadillac for its computer-governed V8-6-4 engine (which had so many mechanical problems that it wasn't very economical, after all). But the most important trend Knoll says he's seen is a change in the attitude of American car buyers. The American romance with the automobile is on the rocks.

"It's pretty hard to have a romance when there's no longer a need for a romance," Knoll says. "Today, people want reliable, low-cost transportation. I think the biggest indication of how much times have changed is the way the 1982 cars were introduced. This year the automakers merely announced that their new cars had been introduced. That was it. I remember years ago how they introduced new cars. It was a very big deal. The car was on a revolving stage and a curtain dropped. Not any more."

Detroit car makers recently have been advertising the durability and quality of their cars, but Knoll says he is not fooled by such Madison Avenue slogans as, "At Ford, Quality is Job 1," or, "GM is working to make cars better and better."

"My philosophy has always been that if you want to find out the weaknesses of a car, it's usually the weaknesses that are advertised," he says. "Right now, American car makers are having problems with quality, but instead of doing something about it, they change their advertising slogans."

Knoll points out that it is often hard to spot a good car in a showroom. He offers this advice: "First, you should know what it is you're looking for in a car. Do you want to go fast, or do you want to save gas? Then you should look at the car's fit and trim. If the car was carefully put together on the outside, chances are it was carefully put together on the inside, too." He says he does not believe in kicking tires or slamming doors, but, as should be expected, he highly recommends reading *Consumer Reports*, particularly the magazine's Frequency-of-Repair records.

"Our drivers test a car for performance," explains *Consumer Reports*' associate technical director, Conrad Harris. "From time to time we hold onto a car and see how well it lasts, but that's something we really rely on our Frequency-of-Repair records to do. We survey our readership and determine how well our readers' cars have held up. It's impossible to test-drive a car for 300 hours like we do and determine from that its long-term durability."

Consumer Reports' car-testing techniques have changed little over the years. A car is purchased at a local dealership near Knoll's Connecticut office. The car dealership knows it is selling to *Consumer Reports*, but Knoll says the magazine receives no special treatment. "In fact," Knoll says, "we've been sold cars that are barely functional. What comes to mind first is a Dodge St. Regis we bought in 1979. Chrysler had introduced its first big car at exactly the time everybody else was finally selling smaller cars. That car had so many problems we couldn't even test it."

Knoll's staff carefully inspects each new car to see that things like the radio, heater, and door locks work properly. They check the engine fluid levels, take note of any cosmetic imperfections in the car's finish, and measure the vehicle's dimensions. Bumpers are smashed with a bumper basher that simulates a 5-mile-per-hour collision. Each automobile is broken in for at least 2,000 miles before the real testing begins. Finally the cars are driven over a 195-mile test trip that includes both highway and back-road driving. Each car is steered through an obstacle course, and comments are recorded concerning the automobile's comfort. The staff members also take turns using each vehicle as a personal car, switching off daily. When all the data have been collected, Knoll and his team are ready to report to consumers.

"I spend most of my time behind the desk at my typewriter," Knoll says.

After the staff tests the cars, *Consumer Reports* sells them, mostly to people who live near the magazine's offices. "There's usually a long waiting list for the cars we've tested," says Knoll.

Each year, *Consumer Reports* tests more than 35 cars. Because its tests are geared to judge performance and not durability, occasionally a car that is not very rugged is recommended to the readers.

"The Fiat 128 tested out real well," remembers Knoll. "It had lots of things we liked, such as front-wheel drive, so we recommended it. Well, it turned out that car wasn't very durable."

Durability should be the concern of the car maker and not the car buyer, Knoll insists. "You shouldn't be able to misuse an automobile," he says. "Now, you might put a rake on your driveway and run over it again and again just to see what happens, but most people don't treat their cars like that. They just get in and drive them. Why should something go wrong?" Even so, he's pragmatic enough to realize that no car lasts forever. "Any object has to have a half-life," he says.

Knoll is encouraged by some of the innovations he's seen on cars he has test-driven recently. He says he's glad more cars are equipped with front-wheel drive these days. Electronic circuitry also has a place in today's automobile, he says. "Electronics are good if they work, though they're hard to diagnose and hard to fix when something goes wrong. Electronics are also the best way to meet stringent air-quality standards. My fear is that the Reagan administration will ease the tough standards, enabling automakers to revert to old, 1979 technology."

Other federal standards appear in jeopardy. He cites the cancellation of the U.S. Department of Transportation's outspoken consumer guide, *The Car Book*, and the possibility that tiremakers may no longer be required to grade tires for treadwear and traction as evidence of backsliding.

"There are two reasons why tires should be graded for treadwear and traction," he says, his voice rising in indignation. "First, it's badly needed information. Second, it was ordered by Congress. There's no reason why that information shouldn't be made available to the public. The information exists, so why shouldn't consumers see it? I believe consumers have a right to that information. I guess you could say I'm in the information business."

BK

Cars that keep their value best

As new car prices zoom out of sight, used-car sales could hardly be stronger. Both U.S. and foreign autos are retaining more of their value than at any time in recent years. "There's a buyer for practically anything that runs," says James H. Lawrence, editor of the National Automobile Dealers Association's *Official Used Car Guide.*

The table printed here compares the original prices for 1977 models with their average trade-in values during June of 1981. As in past years, foreign cars are doing best of all, retaining close to 60 percent of their original value. But Detroit's autos are catching up. Four-year-old U.S. subcompacts and compacts are worth an average of 55 percent of their original prices, 6 percentage points better than in 1980. Detroit's mid-size cars have held onto 52 percent of their original values, compared with only 39 percent in 1980. But domestic full-size and luxury cars made the biggest improvement by far. Their retained worth increased by more than 17 percentage points in a year, to 48 percent, largely because gasoline supplies are ample and, notes Lawrence, "people are getting used to $1.50-per-gallon gasoline."

The cars in the table are each model's best-selling versions. Those with similar body types—for example, the Buick Century Regal and Chevrolet Monte Carlo—tend to be worth about the same, though racy options can sometimes account for a big difference in retained value, as is the case with the Chevrolet Camaro and Pontiac Firebird Trans Am. Original prices include typical dealer discounts and, in most cases, automatic transmissions, air conditioning, and radios. The 1981 values represent the trade-in prices reported in the National Automobile Dealers Association price guide. Where a 1977 model has been renamed or replaced—for example, Volkswagen now makes Rabbits instead of Beetles—the new name appears in parentheses.

ED HENRY

Resale values, foreign and domestic cars

Foreign Median value retained: 59.3%	**1977 price**	**1981 value**	**Percentage of value retained**
VW Beetle convertible (Rabbit)	$4,795	$4,150	86.5%
Mercedes-Benz 450SL	22,601	19,200	85.0
Porsche 911S	16,105	13,000	80.7
BMW 3201	8,375	6,350	75.8
Honda Accord	4,645	3,475	74.8
Mercedes-Benz 300D	16,590	11,450	69.0
VW Rabbit	4,510	2,950	65.4
Toyota Celica	5,254	3,425	65.2
Datsun 280Z	8,314	5,400	65.0
Datsun 200-SX	4,854	3,100	63.9
VW Scirocco	5,955	3,725	62.6
Datsun B210	3,829	2,325	60.7
Honda Civic	4,144	2,500	60.3
Plymouth Arrow (Champ)	4,100	2,450	59.8
VW Dasher	5,864	3,450	58.8
Toyota Corolla	4,138	2,425	58.6
BMW 530i	12,495	7,225	57.8
Toyota Corona	4,239	2,400	56.6
Datsun 810	5,724	3,200	55.9
Dodge Colt	4,159	2,275	54.7
Fiat Spider	6,240	3,400	54.5
Audi Fox (4000)	5,890	2,975	50.5
Volvo 244	7,995	4,025	50.3
Subaru wagon	4,761	2,375	49.9
Fiat 128 (Strada)	3,407	1,550	45.5

U.S. Compact/subcompact Median value retained: 55.4%	1977 price	1981 value	Percentage of value retained
Chevrolet Corvette	$8,890	$7,275	81.8%
Chevrolet Camaro	4,654	3,325	71.4
Chevrolet Chevette	3,574	2,250	63.0
Pontiac Firebird Trans Am	6,074	3,800	62.6
Ford Mustang II	4,530	2,775	61.3
Chevrolet Nova (Citation)	4,206	2,525	60.0
Chevrolet Monza (Cavalier)	4,227	2,475	58.6
Pontiac Sunbird (J-2000)	4,541	2,650	58.4
Pontiac Ventura (Phoenix)	4,495	2,600	57.8
Oldsmobile Omega	4,660	2,600	55.8
Ford Pinto (Escort)	4,239	2,350	55.4
Mercury Monarch	4,736	2,625	55.4
Buick Skylark	4,560	2,525	55.4
Ford Maverick (Fairmont)	4,217	2,325	55.1
AMC Hornet (Concord)	4,228	2,300	54.4
Ford Granada	4,756	2,525	53.1
Mercury Comet (Zephyr)	4,392	2,325	52.9
Mercury Bobcat (Lynx)	4,237	2,225	52.5
AMC Gremlin (Spirit)	4,121	2,125	51.6
Dodge Aspen (Aries)	4,405	2,175	49.4
Plymouth Volare (Reliant)	4,393	2,125	48.4
Dodge Diplomat	5,417	2,350	43.4

U.S. Mid-size Median value retained: 52.2%	1977 price	1981 value	Percentage of value retained
Oldsmobile Cutlass Supreme	$5,132	$3,300	64.3%
Buick Century Regal	5,248	3,025	57.6
Chevrolet Monte Carlo	5,130	2,825	55.1
Pontiac Le Mans	4,804	2,600	54.1
Ford Thunderbird	5,143	2,725	52.9
Mercury Cougar XR-7	5,457	2,850	52.2
Pontiac Grand Prix	5,324	2,700	50.7
Chrysler Le Baron	5,384	2,675	49.7
Chevrolet Malibu Classic	5,021	2,350	46.8
Chrysler Cordoba	5,562	2,375	42.7
Dodge Charger SE (Mirada)	5,275	2,250	42.7

U.S. Full-size/luxury Median value retained: 48.2%	1977 price	1981 value	Percentage of value retained
Cadillac Seville	$11,970	$6,700	56.0%
Oldsmobile Delta 88 Royale	5,270	2,850	54.1
Buick Le Sabre	5,008	2,700	53.9
Chevrolet Impala	4,768	2,525	53.0
Cadillac Coupe deVille	8,650	4,575	52.9
Oldsmobile 98 Regency	6,730	3,475	51.6
Buick Electra	6,492	3,300	50.8
Continental Mark V	10,211	4,975	48.7
Pontiac Bonneville	5,346	2,550	47.7
Buick Riviera	7,213	3,300	45.8
Ford LTD	4,991	2,000	40.1
Mercury Grand Marquis	6,619	2,625	39.7
Dodge Royal Monaco (St. Regis)	4,654	1,775	38.1
Oldsmobile Toronado	7,425	2,800	37.7
Chrysler New Yorker	7,110	2,400	33.8
Plymouth Gran Fury	4,620	1,525	33.0

From *Money* magazine.

THE JAPANESE LESSON IN QUALITY

The high quality of Japanese cars goes more than skin deep. It also involves greater reliability, achieved through innovative and cooperative approaches to design, manufacturing, and above all, management.

Until recently, American firms generally have not given product quality the high priority they reserve for other considerations such as cost reductions, prompt delivery, and production efficiency. But growing pressures from the consumer movement, the courts (through increased corporate liability for their products, and government (in regulations requiring companies to deal more openly with customers through such practices as publicly announced recalls and warranty disclosures) are forcing significant changes. In addition, the companies themselves are increasingly aware of the enormous costs and reduced productivity from not doing the job right the first time. An estimated one out of every ten workers in automobile assembly plants is engaged in repairing substandard items.

But the big factor stimulating interest in quality is the massive flow of Japanese products into the American marketplace. The Japanese have successfully used high product quality as a major marketing strategy—it can be converted into higher prices or market shares. They have recognized that marketing means not only systematic selling but also knowing what is valuable to the customer.

Simply a better car

It is now generally accepted that the quality of Japanese automobiles has surpassed that of American cars. But the U.S. automobile industry recognized its own deficiencies only after it suffered massive defections at the marketplace. Its own warranty-cost comparisons and consumer surveys revealed a growing gap between the essentially steady trouble frequency of American cars and the rapidly declining trouble frequency of Japanese cars. Whether this is simply a matter of fit and finish—finish of sheet metal and paint, and the accuracy with which parts fit together—is an issue of some debate. But design methods, engineering, management, and assembly processes clearly are involved.

American automobile quality hasn't been declining, as popularly believed: Japanese auto quality has been rapidly improving. Moreover, the car-buying public has become much more sensitive to quality. In one consumer survey, quality was cited most often as the basis for purchase decisions, ranking above fuel economy, price, and styling. In another survey, quality of assembly moved from a ranking of sixteenth to second after "value for the money" as the critical factor in consumers' choice of car models. Studies conducted at the Institute of Social Research at the University of Michigan report that public concern about auto quality doubled between 1968 and 1975. In a survey reported in *Design News*, Japanese cars stand well above American cars, while German cars score higher than either in public perceptions of quality, suggesting that high quality is not simply a result of cultural conditions unique to Japan.

Japanese cars are not superior to American cars in all respects: American cars appear to be safer and more corrosion-resistant, for example, than comparable Japanese cars. But by and large, the news about quality has been bad for American auto firms and for those who depend on the auto companies for their livelihood.

American auto firms have lagged considerably behind in attention to consumer needs. They have been so busy competing for maximum profits while accepting their current market share that they have tended to overlook users' needs. Too often, American manufacturers have used product quality as an advertising gimmick without delivering the substance. As long as a firm's product quality was at the same level as its domestic competitors', it didn't need to worry.

Stanley Pace, president of TRW (a major automobile supplier), recently referred to General Motors chairman Alfred Sloan's observation in the early 1920s that to gain market share against a competitor, it is not necessary to have greater-than-competitive quality. "For most of this century we have followed this dictum," Pace said, "using domestic competitors as the standard of quality, and viewing such goals as zero defects in manufacturing as excessively rigid, unrealistic, and puritanical, if not impossible. Surely a few percentage points of scrap is good enough for most purposes—and we can fix the bad apples at the end of the production line." It took the raised public concern with quality, stimulated above all by the Japanese import invasion, to bring American manufacturers back to the real bottom line.

1964 Chevelle Malibu convertible

"We recently celebrated its seventeenth birthday. It has 141,000 miles, has been going about 400 miles per week for the last few months, and averages about 22 MPG. The engine and transmission have never had any work done on them. It had its brakes relined only once, at 85,000 miles.

"An oil change with filter and lube twice a year, plus a tune-up every 12 to 15 months, is about all it has ever required. In its lifetime it has run through two exhaust systems, two carburetors, three batteries, a starter, a water pump, and a couple pairs of shocks."

DAVID B. GROSS
Morganville, New Jersey

Arthur Burns, former chairman of the Federal Reserve Bank, recently attributed the poor quality of American products to the loss of the American work ethic. This view is not uncommon. However, considering that the gap in quality between Japanese and American cars results almost entirely from the more rapid decline in the trouble frequency of Japanese cars, one can hardly attribute the Japanese improvements to a decline in the American work ethic.

In many automotive plants, production supervisors are under tremendous pressure from superiors to meet production quotas. All too often, employees are slapped on the wrist for poor quality but penalized severely for failing to meet quotas. This often leads workers to run substandard parts and let the final inspector or dealer worry about the resulting problems. It's no wonder that hourly employees are a little incredulous when the same supervisors mouth company quality slogans.

Some observers attribute Japan's success to superior automotive technology. Advanced technology, particularly automation, can clearly improve quality, and there are indications that Japanese management is more likely to automate for this reason than American auto management. But allegations of a Japanese lead in automotive technology are highly exaggerated.

Product quality is not simply the result of statistics, hard work, and advanced technology—it derives fundamentally from the application of specific management systems. Several practices in Japanese organizations have been instrumental in lifting Japan from a reputation for cheap, shoddy products to a position of world leadership in quality.

Interactive design

Perhaps the greatest sources of automotive failure lie in weaknesses in engineering design. Because product development and design often precede usage by several years, it is most important to discover weaknesses during the engineering design stage. As is apparent from the recent massive recalls by auto manufacturers, costs are multiplied tremendously if flaws are discovered in the field.

In Japanese manufacturing firms, the product-design process involves cooperative relationships throughout the organization, including production workers. All parties take high product quality as given, reconciling their differences via discussions before final specifications are set. In the words of one high-ranking Japanese manager, "We work hard to build an overlap of different departmental skills at an early stage rather than allowing a clash of departmental interests at a later stage."

The design department in U.S. automotive firms is assumed to be relatively self-sufficient. Accustomed to a relative monopoly on product specifications, the design department tends to produce drawings with exact manufacturing details, even though it is not necessarily best qualified to set parameters on reliability, maintenance, and users' costs. Feedback from other departments, although increasingly common, is often highly formal, infrequent, and too late. Moreover, quality-control personnel often lack the authority to veto engineering designs, making it unlikely that they will be able to resist pressures to meet other priorities at the expense of quality.

In U.S. auto firms, pressures to shorten the period from product conception to production are often so extreme that fitness for use is downplayed, but this results in high testing costs and many years of "production fixes." Of course, the Japanese also try to shorten production cycles, but they recognize that good design is the key to quality, which they will not trade off against short-term savings.

We tend to look for technological fixes rather than deal with human and organizational shortcomings. For example, computer-aided design might be expected to solve some design problems, but ironically, the technological mystique of computer-aided design can make it even more difficult for the manufacturing department to propose manufacturing alternatives. As one computer designer explained, "You have to give the designers the authority to make decisions and do what they want. Let the other department come back later and justify any changes."

Management of quality assurance

Organization of quality control is critical. Japanese line managers and production employees, rather than staff specialists, are primarily responsible for quality assurance. Training in quality assurance is company-wide, including statistical problem-solving methods for top management, which actively directs quality-control activities. Middle management is largely responsible for interdepartmental planning and coordination of quality activities, while staff quality-assurance specialists have only a limited role as consultants and trainers. Production managers and supervisors assume an important role in product and process planning, quality control, shop improvements, and quality-improvement programs for workers. Finally, production workers themselves, through "quality-control circles," are encouraged to inspect their own work and are trained to identify and solve shop problems.

At Toyota, workers who spot quality problems can halt assembly without consulting superiors, and help to pinpoint the exact cause. Doing the job right the first time is more than a slogan–it is built into the organizational structure. Reliance on worker self-inspection encourages attention to detail and preventive problem solving, reducing the costs of hiring full-time inspectors.

Thus, Japanese managers treat their employees as resources that, if cultivated, will yield economic returns to the firm. Firms invest in training for all employees and emphasize development of a labor force skilled in a variety of jobs. All workers are assumed to be capable and desirous of contributing to the firm and are made to feel like fully contributing members: production workers, for instance, are on monthly salary rather than hourly wage.

By comparison, U.S. automotive firms maintain separate and large staffs of quality specialists, including quality-control inspectors and reliability engineers with major responsibility for achieving quality. Indeed, the term "quality control" accurately suggests the image of police monitoring others' performance. This approach greatly emphasizes continuous training for managers and staff specialists and is quite effective in establishing a formal system of quality planning and practices. But there are also significant costs. In particular, available human resources are not fully utilized. As one senior U.S. automotive executive says, "We wrote off the workers as contributors to the organization in the 1930s when they unionized."

More heads are better than one

Perhaps the most publicized Japanese innovation in quality control is the effort to involve production employees in quality assurance through the so-called "quality circles." Developed in the early 1960s, this practice has become standard at most large manufacturing firms. For example, at Toyota, there are 4,200 quality-control circles for 47,000 employees, and at Nissan, 99 percent of eligible employees participate in 4,162 quality-control circles.

Circles averaging ten workers apiece, usually led by the supervisor or a senior worker, meet every week or two for an hour to analyze and solve shop problems. The circles are geared to small-scale but continuous improvements, and the overall results are impressive. Consider the following: General Motors receives an average of 0.84 suggestion per eligible employee each year, of which it adopts about 23 percent. Nissan Motors reported in 1979 a total of 9 suggestions per employee and an adoption rate of 85.7 percent, with more than 70 percent of these suggestions made by groups, most originating in the quality-control circles. In 1980, Toyota Motors reported 17.8 suggestions per employee, of which it adopted close to 90 percent.

Steps in the Eastern direction

As we have seen, the sources of the growing Japanese advantages in auto quality are varied. Foremost is the recognition that quality and productivity are not contradictory objectives but mutually supportive.

Improved quality is vital to the health of U.S. automakers, and they are now taking significant steps in the direction of the Japanese model. Whether these developments portend a basic change or whether they are only halfhearted efforts is open to question. There is enormous pressure for instant solutions, and management may not have the patience to continue with efforts that don't yield immediate results. In Japan, quality-control circles resulted from a long-range effort to upgrade quality and increase employee responsibility. But because many U.S. firms are introducing the circles with little preparation and coordination with other needed changes, we will probably see a large number of initial failures.

Learning from the Japanese and meeting their challenge is not a matter of blind emulation but rather of building on our existing practices and adapting Japanese approaches, where useful, just as the Japanese so successfully adapted ours.

ROBERT COLE

A GUIDE TO THE SYSTEMS

The automobile is the most complex of consumer items, with some 15,000 components, each one bounced over potholes, subjected to heat and cold, and occasionally bathed in corrosive salt water. Cars of the past few years are the most awesome, or awful if you're a weekend mechanic, thanks to the sophisticated technology used in controlling emissions and boosting mileage.

Ford vice-president John Betti told the *Wall Street Journal* that "we may have passed the day some time ago when an individual could work on his own car." Dale Johnson, of General Motors' corporate engineering staff, acknowledges the problem but points out that the company will still sell a shop manual to owners. Enrollment at Shade Tree owner maintenance courses has slackened off, an indication that fewer people have the confidence needed to wade into a modern car's jam-packed engine compartment with a wrench.

A key to comprehending the automobile is its systems. These are interdependent, and each is vital to the operation of the car. They include the engine, cooling system, electrical system, fuel system, drive train (with transmission), and the body.

A car lasts as long as its weakest system. Since most components of these systems are designed so that they can be replaced, a car theoretically could run forever.

The engine

The perfect engine would have machined-steel crankshafts and cams, with forged connecting rods and pistons, all balanced to a gnat's whisker, X-rayed for cracks, and shot-peined to relieve any internal stresses inside the metal itself. The perfect engine would have super-smooth intake and exhaust ports for high efficiency, capped by sodium-filled valves. A high-pressure, high-volume oil pump would provide excellent lubrication. Large

1950 Chevrolet pickup

"Chevy produced this style of pickup from 1947 through 1954, and with a slightly different body on through 1956, but its six-cylinder engine is the same from the early 1930s through the 1960s. These old pickups (one-half and three-quarter ton, three- or four-speed transmissions) were ruggedly and simply built, and were sold in huge quantities. Since they went unchanged for so long, parts were always easy to get. No later make or model could be put on 'auto pilot' for seeding: with manual throttle and low gear you could walk behind it in the pasture and seed, then get back behind the wheel without chasing it. Ten years on a tune-up isn't ususual. And when the cold weather hits, you see lots of old Chevy pickups in town with owners saying, 'Only thing that would start.'

"They're commonly sold from $200 to $500. Gas mileage is around 16 to 18, respectable for new pickups and better than anything in the 60s and 70s. Heavy metal and straightforward design allowed them to resist rust well, and there's very little plastic on them. Later years had plastic knobs, but my truck could boast only a plastic needle on the speedometer. When it broke off a few years ago, I took out the speedometer and replaced the needle with a nice red-painted toothpick!

"Many new parts are still available from old dealer stock, and all drive-train, brake, and engine parts are available new from parts houses. Old out-of-use but still usable trucks can be found sitting around, for parts or for fixing up. I recently bought a motor for $75, installed.

"Some years ago I had another old Chevy pickup, a '53 I was fixing up, plus bought another for parts, and then I was given two more. From these I pieced together two good trucks and two trailers. I sold a pickup and a trailer, gave away the other trailer, and a friend made a horse exerciser out of an extra rear end. I kept the best pickup and drove it to my wedding.

"As a family dedicated to voluntary simplicity, we find durable possessions are a way of life. I have learned that every extra feature beyond the minimal, functional product will raise purchase price and operation cost, will increase the likelihood of early failure, and may be too complicated for me to repair myself. Our income is low but our quality of life is high—we make few purchases because nothing wears out."

RON THUMA
Hartford, Kansas

bearings and chrome piston rings should ensure a long life. The cooling system would keep the engine temperate while pulling a freight car through Death Valley.

That engine is available today, at a cost of $35,000 or so. It's made by hand for racing cars and designed to withstand, in one afternoon's sport, the stress a passenger-car engine endures over years.

Cost isn't the only constraint on engine design. The politics of oil supply dictate that the big, slow-revving engine of stolid cast iron is a thing of the past. Most engines now are of aluminum, at least in part, because it takes precious gasoline to haul the traditionally massive cast-iron engine; and engines are smaller, doing their work with a half, or less, the displacement. So, new engines are made of a material that expands dramatically with heat, and they revolve faster by a third, causing some people to doubt their longevity.

A discussion of cast iron versus aluminum doesn't deserve much space here, because manufacturers don't give you a real choice. (The last time you could order heavy-duty internal engine parts ended with the short-lived muscle-car period of the 1960s.) But this much remains the same: whether it's aluminum or cast iron, domestic or foreign, an engine will respond to your attention. As manufacturers go to extended service intervals that mean less owner maintenance, some observers of the industry are skeptical–just how much protection can be expected from a can of oil?–and they disregard such claims, continuing to change oil and filters at frequent intervals. From time to time, magazine articles profile the owners of extraordinarily long-lived cars, and though the cars are all sizes and makes, some gleaming and some battered, they tend to have one thing in common: a generous supply of oil over the years.

The oil itself does not break down unless heated above 300°F, but its additives–included to control acid, reduce aeration and scuffing, and maintain viscosity–are used up no matter what the brand. Oils *are* getting better, as suggested by manufacturers' recommendations for oil changes over the past 30 years. In 1951, the interval was every 2,000 miles, and oil filters were often an option. Ten years later, the standard was new oil and new filter every 4,000 miles. By 1971, oil could be expected to last four months or 6,000 miles, and a filter 12,000 miles. By 1981, a typical recommendation was an oil change annually or every 7,500 miles and a new filter every 15,000 miles.

Still, many people have continued to grant their cars new oil and a new filter every 3,000 or 4,000 miles, or every three or four months, whichever comes first. The time limit recognizes that the acids caused by combustion may break down oil additives and corrode engine parts.

Beyond frequent oil and filter changes, you can treat your car to a higher grade of oil. Use two criteria for shopping. First, check the manufacturer's recommended viscosity (thickness)–SAE 30 or SAE 40 for a single-viscosity oil, or SAE 10W-40, 20W-40, or 20W-50 in a multiviscosity oil. Then, look at the top of the can. There'll be a coded set of letters there, such as SA. The S means "service," and the letters A through F tell you what grade of duty the oil is. SA is very light duty and is not used in cars. SF is very heavy duty oil and is specified for use in 1981 models. Cars from 1971 to 1980 need SE oil, 1968 to 1969 need SD, and 1964 to 1967 need at least SC oil. Note that these are minimum requirements, and it's cheap insurance to use a better grade than that called for by the manufacturer.

If you use quality oil, there's no need to pour in oil additives. They may even conflict with the additives already in the oil and leave you worse off than when you started. The highly touted benefits of synthetic oils are a matter of debate at this time. Their makers specify oil-change intervals of as long as 25,000 miles or two years–you would expect as much for $4

Checker Marathon

With its bumper-car styling and three tons of mass, you'd expect the Checker to roll on forever. They're most familiar as taxicabs, of course, but each year 200 or so (some 4 percent of total production) go to private individuals.

Who buys Checkers? According to a company spokesperson, they're doctors, large families, sportsmen, and people with bad backs. These owners "hold on to her an average of 10 to 12 years," estimates Checker Motors Sales Corporation of Long Island City, New York. The six-passenger model sells for $9,600 and the nine-passenger for $10,700. A GM diesel is now available in addition to Chevrolet gasoline engines. Heavy-duty options include a bigger radiator, transmission-oil cooler, firmer shocks, and rear helper springs.

The company's brochure says that while "some cars are tributes to conspicuous consumption . . . the Checker is a tribute to the common sense of its owner." Sounds like the very car to feature in a book pushing the durability of consumer products, but its practicality is not beyond question. True, Checker styling ranks as the most durable in autodom: the current design appeared in 1959, and although a company spokesperson allowed that their car "is not pretty in any sense of the term," no changes are planned. As for the life expectancy of that sheet metal, however, the company is cautious about making claims for the Checker's longevity. "They'll rust just like anything else," said the spokesperson, although the car's traditional full frame could be expected to give it an advantage over today's lightweight, unit-bodied models.

It takes plenty of gas to move all that metal around. "The Marathon gets the kind of gas mileage that oil-company executives don't like to think about," says the Checker brochure, a wildly extravagant boast in the face of EPA estimates of 16.9 MPG in city driving and 18.6 out on the highway for the smaller and less thirsty of the two gasoline engines. The Checker's disappointingly low trade-in value may reflect its poor mileage rather than impugn its longevity. In any event, the car does not seem to qualify as the lone champion of common sense that its stolid demeanor suggests. And, as we go to press, the manufacturer announced it will cease production in 1982.

or $5 a quart. Synthetic oils do provide better friction protection and can improve fuel economy. But drivers who expect a long and happy relationship with their cars continue to use conventional oil at frequent intervals. They monitor the oil level and keep the engine to the full mark on the dipstick rather than entrusting this task to the 1 pump jockey in 50 who will offer to check. A gas station may not have your brand anyway, and it's not good to mix. Some brands aren't compatible and may cause problems if mixed, such as jelling in the oil pan.

If you pull a trailer or drive hard in the heat of the South or Southwest, an oil cooler might profitably prolong oil life. Emission controls can raise engine temperature 20°F, and even an automatic transmission can add a few degrees. As oil temperatures in the engine approach the dread 300°F mark, the oil begins to oxidize and lose its lubricating ability, so an oil cooler, even one of modest size, can save an engine. Some auto manufacturers offer them as options; more often you'll have to go to an aftermarket supplier to get one. Most of the accessory companies that service sports and imported cars carry them. Expect to pay about $100. Be sure you get one with a thermostatic control: otherwise, the engine might be too cool

The obsolescence of style

While mechanical obsolescence is a difficult rap to pin on a manufacturer, the annual manipulation of sheet metal is an obvious tactic: styling serves to make the new look irresistible and to make the old look tacky. This innovation in marketing was pioneered by General Motors in the 1920s, and it hurt the sales of Henry Ford's staid, no-nonsense Model T.

Today we again see the triumph of sensible, lasting designs—as dramatized on these pages by two decades of VW Beetles and Cadillacs.

Annual model changes cost the manufacturers huge sums that are now invested in downsizing, and at any rate, the thrill of the fall's new models is gone, replaced by concern for reliability, economy, and a handsome resale value.

Cadillac.

1950

All photos, courtesy of Cadillac Div. of General Motors

Volkswagen.

1948

All photos, courtesy of Volkswagen of America

in winter when you want to bring some of the heat into the passenger compartment.

Finally, use a good grade of fuel. Many brands of cheap gas leave deposits on spark-plug electrodes and on valves, creating hot spots that are the cause of detonation, or "ping." Cheap gas, or gas with too low an octane rating, ignites too early, causing a wall of flame to smash against the piston. The ping isn't awe inspiring, but it should alert you that pistons and valves are under duress. Avoid the problem with a better grade of gas. For newer cars restricted to unleaded gas, buy premium rather than unleaded regular. If you own a higher-compression older car built to take leaded premium, a mixture of about 25 percent regular and 75 percent unleaded premium should boost octane enough to prevent damage.

RALPH KEYS

Diesel troubles

Diesel cars save fuel money—at today's prices, about $3,000 over the life of the car—but they can't be treated as casually as other cars. The diesel's differences remain misunderstood by both drivers and mechanics:

1952

1954

1952

1953

- The high-compression engine uses fuel injection instead of a carburetor, and does not need spark plugs to cause combustion.
- The engine uses diesel fuel instead of gasoline.
- Lubricating oil for a diesel must do things that lubricating oil for a gasoline engine can't do.

High compression requires that a diesel engine be sturdier than a gasoline engine. For example, the Olds diesel is sturdier and, contrary to popular belief, different from the gasoline V8 from which it is derived. Crankshaft mains and crankpins are ½ inch bigger on this diesel, 3 inches instead of 2½ inches. The crankcase is heavier, and the cylinder head is totally new and distinctly diesel. Piston pins are full floating, not pressed in like those on gas engines. But diesel passenger cars aren't necessarily designed to give the length of service of commercial diesel vehicles.

Why do truck diesels commonly last 300,000 to 500,000 miles and longer? Because of the way they're treated and the way they're made. Industrial engines receive skilled care and maintenance, undergo used-oil analyses, and have a skilled operator who uses the gears to keep engine RPM in a narrow range. The engines have such features as forged crankshafts, replaceable cylinder sleeves, special valve inserts, and super-quality bearing materials, which would make the engine cost more than the car itself.

One thing both the industrial and automotive diesel engines share is an expensive fuel-injection system. This

Cadillac.

1956

1958

Volkswagen.

1955

1958

includes a highly sophisticated fuel-injection pump, which causes precisely controlled amounts of fuel to shoot out of the injectors into the combustion chambers at precisely the right times. There are important and enormous differences between a carburetor and a fuel-injection pump that cannot be ignored if a long and trouble-free life is expected.

A carburetor is essentially a pot with a series of holes for the gasoline to flow through. Some carburetor parts do move, but very little and under very low pressure. About the worst that can happen is for a carburetor to get plugged with dirt so it has to be cleaned out.

But a diesel-engine injection pump has many moving parts. They are precisely fitted—some to a tenth of a thousandth of an inch—and work at a pressure of 1,500 to 2,000 pounds per square inch. Moreover, a diesel pump controls not only fuel quantity but also the all-important combustion timing. Diesel timing is much more critical than spark timing. Improper diesel timing, even by a few degrees, can cause extremely high peak combustion pressures and can quickly wreck the engine.

Dirt and water are common in diesel fuel for a variety of reasons, including the way the diesel fuel is made, stored, and transported. Diesel fuel is a much less standardized product than gasoline. The chemistry and characteristics vary according to refinery, refinery practices at the moment, crude source, and region of manufacture. Its cetane rating, for example, can vary significantly.

Cetane is a measure of a diesel fuel's ignitability. It has a profound influence on starting, noise, engine roughness,

1959

1962

1959

1962

deposits, and car performance. The minimum cetane is 40 for both no. 1 and no. 2 diesel fuel in American Society for Testing Materials (ASTM) standard D-975. Theoretically, all diesel-fuel products meet this standard. But there is no law compelling them to do so, and sometimes they don't.

Actually, 40 is quite low. Most small, high-speed diesels start and run much better on at least 50 cetane. Unfortunately, unlike octane rating for gasoline, you're not likely to find cetane rating posted on the fuel pump.

Another important aspect of diesel fuel is its cloud point—the temperature at which wax becomes visible in the fuel. Wax can plug filters and reduce an engine's performance. Olds says this will not happen if the fuel is properly winterized and if drivers follow their owner's manuals.

Here again, the fuel specifications are not written with the consumer in mind. The actual cloud-point temperature is not given in ASTM standards. According to ASTM D-975, "appropriate low-temperature operability should be agreed on between the supplier and the purchaser."

Perhaps the purchasing agent for a bus fleet can make such an agreement, but a car driver anxiously scanning roadside signs for a station selling diesel fuel certainly cannot.

What all this means is that an automotive diesel must have a very efficient filtration system to decrease its chances of being harmed by bad fuel. There must also be a means for the car owner to check for water and to drain it out of the fuel if necessary. The Olds diesel hasn't a fuel-system water drain. In contrast, Mercedes, VW, and Peugeot each have means of draining water from the filter. The VW and Peugeot injection pumps use a different pumping action but otherwise resemble the Olds pump in that 11 of their major controls are internal.

Mercedes, on the other hand, has an entirely different type of pump; it may be one of the reasons why the Mercedes diesel has somehow survived, often in some very rough environments, since 1936. The Mercedes pump is the same basic multiplunger pump that has been widely used in construction and industrial engines for 50 years. It's called a multiplunger pump because it has a separate plunger for each cylinder. The Olds pump has a single pair of plungers that must supply all eight cylinders. So, the Mercedes plungers get less work and wear.

On the Mercedes pump, the critically important timing-advance mechanism is massive. It's mounted on the pump driveshaft up in the engine gear cover, where it is lubricated by engine oil. This eliminates the potential for sticking because of water or fuel gum. The governor, too, so important in regulating the fuel that enters the combustion chamber, is a separate device, mounted on the back of the pump and lubricated by its own oil

Cadillac.

1970

Volkswagen.

1970

supply. And finally, the cams and lifters within the pump are also oil-lubricated by a reservoir in the bottom of the pump housing. In the Olds pump, these items are lubricated only by the fuel. True, the Bosch pump on the Mercedes is heavy and bulky, but it probably tolerates bad fuel better.

What happens when bad fuel isn't properly filtered? In a typical scenario, accumulated water goes from the tank into the injection pump. Perhaps the fuel is old and gummy. Maybe the owner doesn't drive for a day or two because the car sits in an airport lot.

In any case, governor, fuel-metering parts, and pumping plungers stick or corrode. Later, some of these parts hang up, perhaps only for seconds, but during that time too much fuel is injected and at the wrong time. For a brief moment, peak combustion pressures overcome the head-bolt tension or break down the head gasket. The owner may sense nothing but a momentary shudder or stumble and a cloud of black smoke, but a cascade effect is now at work. The damaged head gasket lets cooling water seep in above the piston. Being a diesel, the clearance between piston crown and cylinder head is close, and the incompressible water won't budge when the piston crosses top center. Something must give—perhaps the piston, perhaps the connecting rod, perhaps a crankpin yields in a hairline crack. Continued running makes ultimate engine destruction inevitable.

Many new diesel owners are amazed at how black the oil turns in just a few miles. The blackness comes from carbon and other combustion residues, and is not harmful if the oil is made for diesel service and is changed on schedule. But these residues can and do interact with oil additives, and one of the results is that they inhibit the effectiveness of the antiscuff additive. When this happens, the areas of concentrated load, especially the cam lobes and filters, can quickly scuff and wear away.

Another aspect is that unlike the closely tailored oil-performance specifications for passenger-car gasoline-engine oil, there are no passenger-car diesel-oil qualification tests.

Another problem is that most automobile mechanics aren't really qualified to work on diesels. In my talks with mechanics, I found none who knew how the primary fuel pressure, governor setting, fuel-delivery quantity, and cam advance really worked together in the Roosa injection pump. Some mechanics described efforts to smooth out roughness by adjusting injector release pressure—a distinct no-no. When I asked how they checked cam advance, I found none who knew or had the tools needed.

The usual answer was that if they had injection-pump trouble they replaced the pump or injectors and sent the ailing parts off to a diesel-specialist shop. The flaw in this is that the mechanic never makes a diagnosis of the real trouble, and whatever caused the initial loss of an expensive pump can happen again. There's no way that a pump repair person working on hundreds of pumps in a distant shop can relate his findings on a given unit back to a specific customer's car and its symptoms.

E. F. LINDSLEY

Cooling system

The cooling system on the typical auto consists of the radiator, hoses to carry water to the engine, a water pump to circulate the water, a thermostat, water passages inside the engine, a passenger compartment heater, and the belts that drive the water pump and cooling fan. If you have reason to fear overheating—from either climate or towing—you can order a trailer-towing package from some manufacturers, consisting of a larger radiator, a larger fan or auxiliary electric fan, and occasionally, an extra-capacity water pump. Air-conditioned cars normally come with extra-capacity cooling systems as part of the package.

Preventive maintenance on the cooling system is simple, since there's not much to go wrong. Change all hoses, including heater hoses, at least every two years or 24,000 miles, and change belts at the same time. It's a good idea to change antifreeze at that time also, but no less than once every three years or 36,000 miles. When you add new antifreeze, you can include a can of water pump lubricant to extend bearing life in the water pump. Between changes, keep belts adjusted to proper tension.

Since air-cooled engines have gone the way of the dinosaurs (except in the Porsche 911 and the VW Vanagon), we won't look at air-cooled engines except to say that the fan belt is all that stands between the engine and a meltdown. Plan your fan belt maintenance accordingly.

A number of newer cars are fitted with thermostatically controlled electric fans instead of the older belt-driven types. These electric fans are good for gas mileage, since they don't cause a direct drag on the engine. They're also pretty reliable, since they don't run all the time. A good way to check these fans is to leave the car idling and raise the hood to watch. As the idling car heats up, the fan should come on. If it doesn't, have the thermostatic control checked or do it yourself with a multimeter.

Electrical system

The engine electrical system consists of the alternator, battery, voltage regulator, starter, distributor, coil wires, and spark plugs. The distributor may be the old points-and-condenser type or the new solid-state type, which is controlled by electronic circuitry.

It's not generally known that some new cars are available with a heavy-duty battery and extra-capacity alternator. Many cars with the trailer-towing package are fitted with these components, as are most cars ordered with air conditioning, but a heavy-duty alternator and battery are valuable to any car, especially if you live in a northern climate where winters are long and cold. The combination of short days (with plenty of lights-on driving) and cold weather (the heater fan is used more, the engine is harder to turn over, and a battery is less powerful) taxes a battery and charging system to the utmost.

Alternators are rated in amperes or watts, depending on whether they are in American or foreign cars. Batteries are rated in ampere-hours. Neither a heavy-duty alternator nor a heavy-duty battery is necessarily any larger physically than the standard components; the difference is internal. Better alternators have more windings, and better batteries have more and larger plates.

You can fit a more powerful alternator on a car you already own, but that's a measure rarely taken. Buying a heavier battery is more practical. Get the most powerful one that will fit in the battery box. You can expect a battery to wear out in three to five years; it's common, and there's really nothing to do about it. Therefore, buy a lifetime-guaranteed battery if you can find one; the company will have to replace it for free after it has died. If you can't find such a battery, buy a top-of-the-line model with a 60-month guarantee, and the company will prorate the cost of a new one when your old one dies.

Electrical-system maintenance is simple. The same care applies to alternator belts as applies to water-pump belts; often the two components are run from the same belt. Keep the belt adjusted and replace it on a regular schedule. Battery clamps should be removed from the terminals annually and the terminals cleaned with a wire brush. A thin film of lead oxide often builds up between the terminal and the clamp and stops the flow of electricity to and from the battery. After cleaning the terminal and the inside of the clamp, replace the clamp tightly and coat the entire assembly with a thin film of grease or Vaseline.

Battery cables are critical. If insulation is cracked on the positive cable, replace the cable with one that has the clamp molded directly onto the end.

The traditional ignition system consists of the distributor with points and condenser. This breaker-points system is nearly as old as the internal-combustion engine and is proven and reliable. A periodic renewal of the points, condenser, and spark plugs restores the system to like-new performance and is the major component of an engine tune-up.

The more modern breakerless ignition system was developed to keep modern engines within emissions standards, and it employs such features as optical sensors or magnetic sensors instead of points. Some use a capacitive discharge system, while others use a stock coil such as the one on the breaker-points system. All have the benefits of making the car easier to start and keep in tune, and preserving spark plugs. Most of the bugs associated with the early units have been worked out, so that the units now fitted on most cars are reliable and durable. Tune-ups consist of keeping the plugs properly gapped and replacing them at specified intervals. Unlike the breaker-points system, performance doesn't degrade gradually over a period of time, but if the electronic ignition system fails, it usually fails totally and is *not* repairable on the roadside. Here is a price of sophistication: in exchange for fewer maintenance tasks, you forfeit the chance to come to the rescue with a screwdriver and string.

Exhaust system

When it comes time to replace your car's original muffler, go to a dealer who offers a lifetime guarantee. As with batteries, it is acknowledged that muffler systems will burn out after a few years, but the manufacturers bank on the probability that the car will be sold in the interim. Warranties apply only to the purchaser of the muffler and are not transferable, but if you hold onto your long-life car, you stand to recoup your initial investment several times over.

Transmission

Manual and automatic transmissions are virtually tied for longevity. Both should last the life of the car, given proper care. The manual usually has the edge when it comes to rebuilding, since most well-maintained manual transmissions would require only bearing and seal replacement. And automatic transmissions need preventive maintenance—regular oil and filter changes at or before the manufacturer's specified intervals, and band or clutch adjustment if your transmission is one that needs such service. This should be done annually or about every 12,000 miles, and is required for some of the same reasons you change oil in your engine: the heat in the transmission tends to make the oil begin to oxidize after a while, after which it loses its lubricating qualities. Additives in the automatic transmission fluid also begin to lose their effectiveness with time and use.

As with manual transmissions, automatics appreciate not being abused. Abuse means downshifting manually at high speeds, shifting to Reverse or Park before coming to a full stop, and relying on low ranges for high-performance driving or trailer towing.

Several modifications to the automatic transmission will make it last much longer. Heat causes internal seals to harden, crack, and leak, so anything you can do to combat this great enemy of automatics is all to the good. Automatic transmissions use an oil cooler built into the lower part of the car's radiator, but an auxiliary oil cooler, mounted in front of the car's radiator and taking the transmission fluid after it has gone through the standard cooler, will drop the automatic's temperature an additional 50°F, greatly increasing the chances of a long and trouble-free life, especially when towing a heavy-duty trailer or running in hot climates.

A reprogramming kit may minimize wear. If this device sounds computerese, it should. The automatic transmission is actually a hydraulically operated computer, monitoring engine speed, road speed of the car, and driver demand, and then selecting the correct gear range according to its input. Manufacturers usually program the transmission to shift softly between speed ranges, but to do this, they design-in a certain amount of overlap: while the transmission is shifting to a higher or lower range, it is actually engaged in two gears at once. By reducing the overlap, the kit eases the transmission's job. The kit isn't a job for most home mechanics and is best installed by a transmission specialist. Kits can be installed during a regular transmission oil and filter change.

Overdrive was dropped from most manufacturers' options lists for some years but is now again finding favor as a means of stretching mileage. Instead of the traditional add-on planetary gearbox, the modern overdrive is really a five-speed manual or four-speed automatic transmission. These enable the engine to turn slower for a given road speed, giving better gas mileage and, ultimately, longer engine life. Expect to see overdrive options become more common as gas prices rise.

Shocks

Standard shock absorbers are often too small in diameter for the loads they must carry, and consequently they don't last as long as they should. When it comes time to replace them, consider heavy-duty shocks. Some manufacturers offer a lifetime guarantee, including Sears and Midas. For trailer towing, you may want to go to extra-heavy duty shocks with a helper spring, made by Monroe and Gabriel, among others.

Brakes

Brakes are either one of two types. Disc brakes grasp a disc between two pucks of brake material, and drum brakes use expanding shoes to press against the inside of a drum. Discs are now standard on the front wheels of almost all makes, with drums on the back, save for sportier cars with discs all around.

Long brake life is encouraged by conservative driving. Sudden, harsh stops wear the brakes prematurely. Longevity is also enhanced by replacing brake fluid at least once a year. This is not a common practice. Few owner's manuals mention it, and yet it's known in the industry that brake fluid is one of the most hygroscopic (water-attracting) fluids you can find. Water collects in the brake system, primarily from condensation and from humidity in the air, and causes corrosion in the master cylinder and wheel cylinders, often shortening their lives. Once the pitted cylinder walls begin to leak, the cylinders must be replaced.

The body

Rust can be merely inconvenient and ugly, or outright dangerous. It has sidelined millions of cars that otherwise were in excellent health.

Everyone is aware that rust causes cosmetic damage, and millions are spent each year in new paint jobs and body putty. Not so apparent is the effect of rust on the car's structural integrity. Presently, few cars have a frame—Land-Rover and Checker are two present-day exceptions—and they rely instead on the collective strength of the several body sections.

Traditionally, a car was bolted upon a massive steel frame. The resulting body was heavy and sturdy. It used up a good deal of metal and required a good flow of gasoline to move it about. When a body panel was damaged, it could be unbolted from its neighbors and the frame, and a new one bolted in place.

In the interest of paring away metal and improving gas mileage, manufacturers have gone to unitized bodies. The body itself gives the modern car its rigidity, and the sections are welded together in such a manner that when one is smashed in or rusted out, it's not easily replaced. The manufacturer's solution thus becomes the repair person's problem.

If you are in the market for a used car, be highly suspicious of frameless cars that show signs of rust. Remember, there is no behind-the-scenes frame to keep it all together.

RALPH KEYS

Rust

The best word to describe car-body cancer? Insidious. The word, says Webster, means "operating in a slow or not easily apparent manner, and more dangerous than seems at first evident." If not diagnosed almost at the beginning, rust is nearly impossible to get rid of. By the time you see it, you might well be too late.

That's why body-shop managers hate bad rust cases worse than an overdue bill. They know the only guarantee they can honestly give is that rust will return—no matter how nice they make a car look for the present.

In defense of body men everywhere, unhappy paint-job patrons just don't understand the problem. Rust *treatment*, for the most part, is not rust prevention. Rust *prevention* must start before there is any rust. That usually means when the car is brand-new. It's too late after the car has been driven down a wet or salted road. As soon as salt, water, and steel get together, oxidation begins. Still, you see four-, five-, or six-year-old cars without a bit of rust. What do their owners know that so many others don't? The answer isn't dramatic—in simplest terms, they just plain care more than most car owners. They are among the small percentage who understand rust and who realize that rust prevention, if it is to work, is a never-ending task.

Both undercoating and rustproofing are recommended. Undercoating—about $65 and up—puts a protective coating on the cross-members, frame, and the underside of the fenders. It's a way to deaden road sound and reduce rust. But it's not a guarantee against corrosion. Undercoating can crack and flake off, leaving portions of the car unprotected or allowing water into cracks. Be sure to undercoat before you take delivery. Once you've driven around for a week and built up a coat of dirt, it's too late.

Rustproofing involves treating all areas particularly prone to rusting, including quarter panels, fender wells, exterior seams and moldings, wheelhouse areas, rocker panels, and headlight areas. Most new-car dealers and a number of franchise car-care centers offer rustproofing for around $150. Shop around—the extent of treatment and the warranty period will vary, as will cost.

If you're lucky enough to know a body-shop man, ask his advice. He's probably seen various treatments and can report on how well the surfaces have been covered.

For do-it-yourselfers, rustproofing kits are available from dealers and independent auto-supply shops. For $20 and a day's time, you can treat the inside of the body shell as well as exterior surfaces such as fender wells and the underside of floor and rocker panels. Success with the kits will depend on how carefully you approach the job. Take plenty of time, or you'll probably be disappointed.

One of the first trips to make with a new car should be to a car wash. Check the car for any body leaks and leaks around windows. Have them fixed immediately. Also, spray the underside and wheel wells with a pressure hose to make sure there are no openings that will let water seep under the carpeting or floor mats. Caulk any openings you find.

When should you wash your car? "Every time it needs it," says a friend who owns a mint-condition '76 Cutlass. It's never been rustproofed, but you couldn't find a trace of oxidation on it with a magnifying glass. He cleans his car often, preferring his own driveway or garage to the 75¢ pressurized do-it-yourself setups. If you like those types of car washes, be sure you get under the wheel openings and around all the moldings. Wash inside the doors, making sure you get around the rubber seals. Finally, use the sprayer for final washing and rinsing. Afterwards, let the doors hand open a while for better drainage.

Wax twice a year, at least. Spring and fall are traditional waxing times. But if you live in an area where lots of sand, salt, and calcium chloride are used on highways, a midwinter waxing is advised, in a warm garage. Wax-cleaner combinations are available, but separate cleaners and waxes are preferred by serious car-care buffs. A new three-step system from Turtle Wax, called Polyshell, gives semi-permanent protection. The first step, a cleaner-primer, cleans paint pores and provides a prime base. The second, a base-coat sealant, fills paint pores and locks in a glasslike layer of polymers. The third, a top-coat sealant, locks on additional protective polymers. The kit sells for about $25.

And you don't have to stop there. The friend with the rust-free '76 Cutlass doesn't just leave it at washing and waxing.

Mercedes-Benz of North America

"The era of the 'Kleenex' car, which you use and then throw away, is long past," says A. B. Shuman, manager of public relations for Mercedes-Benz of North America. The new S-Class sedans, the 300SD and 380SEL, rely on zinc-coated steel and more than 130 pounds of preservatives and coatings. The wheel wells have plastic liners to prevent corrosion, and the vulnerable lower sides of the body are protected by plastic trim.

A rust-free car for $3,360

Compared with standard passenger cars and even today's water-cooled multicylinder motorcycles, David Edmonson's Free-Way is refreshingly simple. The entire vehicle can be torn down and reassembled in a few hours. "Try to take the body off your automobile and see the kind of mess that results," challenges Edmonson.

America's most efficient car is made in Burnsville, Minnesota. It's also the smallest, carrying two in a squeeze and balancing them on three wheels. As Detroit moves from eight cylinders to six, and from six to four, the little Free-Way gets by with one. Free-Way president David Edmonson guarantees that his 346cc model will travel 100 miles on a gallon of gas at 40 mph; if it won't, he'll refund a buyer's money. That's better than most motorcycles, an apparent irony explained by the little car's low coefficient of drag, half or less than that of a cycle.

But this book is about durability. The Free-Way is something out of the ordinary in this regard, also. The body is of fiberglass-reinforced plastic and entirely encloses the frame, so that Edmonson is pretty safe in offering a five-year guarantee against rust. The mechanical warranty, on the other hand, is only 90 days, on the order of a lawn mower. Indeed, the engine is an air-cooled, single-cylinder Tecumseh, found on larger mowers and garden tractors (an electric model is also available). But Edmonson estimates the car won't require a $175 overhaul until 75,000 miles or so, and this job can be performed by 15,000 lawn-mower dealers throughout the U.S. and Canada. A new engine can be had for about $500, but the cast-iron design is meant to be rebored. Parts are available via UPS in just two or three days, and owners can handle the routine chores of replacing transmission belts (a half-hour job) and drive chain (taking only a couple of minutes).

Edmonson originally planned on establishing a dealer network, but now has second thoughts; dealers typically take a 20 percent commission, and the simplicity of the car obviates the need for factory-trained mechanics and a local parts inventory.

The Free-Way has its drawbacks. Although a couple motored in one from the Minnesota factory to New York, Edmonson seems to regard this as an admirable feat rather than a logical thing to do. Second, the three little wheels don't offer much traction on snow or ice. Finally, a 700-pound car can't be as safe in a collision as a car of two or three or four tons, and Edmonson is candid in pointing this out in his literature (available from H-M Vehicles, Inc., 1116 East Highway 13, Burnsville, MN 55337).

This three-wheeler obviously is not a car for all seasons or all drivers, but its simplicity and common sense have earned it a six-month backlog of orders.

Once a year he takes the moldings off the wheel openings, around the headlights, over the wiper mounts, and so on. He washes and waxes those areas, cleans the underside of the moldings, and remounts them. It's not an easy job, but the results are worth it to him.

If you leave your car in a parking lot all day or visit a lot of shopping malls, you can't avoid nicks and scratches from door bangs. Get a can of touch-up paint to match your finish and clean and paint any tiny areas that will allow rust to begin.

Thoroughly hose down the underside of the car at least twice a year if you live where sand and salts are used to cut highway ice. Wash out the inside or channels in the frame and cross-member components. Lay down a lawn sprinkler hose to form a series of "S's" in your driveway, and slowly drive over the hose to clean the underside. Keep open the drain holes in the bottoms of doors, frame, and under the hood. Store your car in the garage as much as possible, even if you have to move your junk to do so.

Before buying a used car, be especially alert for rust that might be weakening the frame or cross-members. Check the body and underside. Put the car on a hoist, if possible, for an eye-level view. While it's on the hoist, check for telltale signs of a quickie paint job done to disguise rusted areas. If you see paint that's been blown on the bottom curve of the body or the frame, or on the tops of side moldings, beware. Somebody may have hidden a lot of headaches that will show up again in a short time. If it's had a good professional repainting, on the other hand, you stand to benefit.

If you're buying a used station wagon, take out the spare tire and examine the tire well. Also, lift the mat on the floor in the third seat area and check for rust and metal weakness. In other cars, lift the mat in the trunk and the carpeting in the passenger area. Be suspicious of musty odors.

RON ROSS

Tires

Tires depend on owner maintenance more than almost any other component of the car. Studies have shown that most cars have two or more tires that have low air pressure, and low air pressure causes poor fuel mileage, poor handling, excessive wear, and a heat buildup that threatens early tire failure. Buy a good, dial-type tire gauge (they're not cheap, at $12 to $18), and try to remember to use it weekly. Proper air pressure and conservative driving can yield amazing tire longevity—mileages approaching 100,000 miles.

And while on the subject, it pays dividends in fuel mileage and longevity, not to mention handling, to use only radial tires on your car. Radial construction provides better gas mileage, longer tire life, and better road holding (especially in wet or snowy weather) than either bias-ply or bias-belted tires. It doesn't seem to make a great deal of difference whether you buy fabric-belted or steel-belted radials, at least for longevity, nor does it make a difference whether you buy tube-type or tubeless radials. Simply, radial tires save gas, last longer, and are safer.

European brands are currently the best. Michelin, Pirelli, Metzeler, and Continental, among others, have been building excellent radials for many years. American tiremakers have not held quality control to such consistently high standards.

Wheel balancing eliminates wheel hop, and thereby slows wear of both tires and shocks. Front suspension care includes keeping the front end in alignment and replacing any worn parts. Improper alignment or worn parts can cause the tire to be dragged sideways a total of 20 or 30 feet per mile, with the concomitant accelerated wear.

Tires are victims of bad press: they are simply one of many cogs that combine to form a working automobile, and like most products of this nature, they receive their share of publicity only when they fail. How many people say, "Hey, my tires really look great today"?

Instead, they remember pulling off the road with a flat tire, and if it still had tread on it, they're apt to feel cheated and angry. Never mind that the tire had 40,000 miles on it, or that it was impaled by a spike.

The older among us can help put things into perspective. In the early days of cars and highways, it was common practice to carry along two or three extra tires whenever venturing far from home. Tread life expectancy varied widely (there were once over 400 manufacturers of tires), but one thing is for certain—high mileage from these "cord" tires was not anywhere near what it is today.

The first tire offered as original equipment was BF Goodrich's 34 × 4 (34 inches tall and 4 inches wide) cord-design model. The year was 1896. These tires were high pressure (50 to 60 psi) and expensive. Considering that cars cost less than $1,000, it's astounding, in retrospect, that tires cost $35 to $50 apiece, with another $10 for the tube. And the price was even higher for heavier cars. Add to this the fact that tires were lasting 400 to 500 miles, and today's radials look like a bargain. Curiously, early tires were not black, but rather the off-white color of natural rubber. It wasn't until tire-company chemists learned carbon black gave resistance against cuts and tears that tires turned black. The designs were nothing like those we see today, what with tiremakers putting their names in the tread, leaving miles of free advertising in the muddy roads of the era. Imaginative tiremakers chose suction cups or tiny hearts to set their brand apart from the rest of the crowd. But in 1922, such gimmicks fell by the roadside with the arrival of an important innovation, the balloon tire.

The balloon tire was able to withstand bumps better than cord tires because of its lower pressure (28 psi), and its wide stance allowed greater flexing so that fewer cord plies were necessary to distribute weight evenly. Between 1910 and 1937, average tire life quadrupled, from nine months to three years. Later, rubber extenders were added to fight aging, oxidation, flex cracking, abrasions, and heat. But the tires of today—even radials—are simply improvements on this design.

When natural-rubber supplies from Malaysia were cut off in World War II, synthetic rubber was thrown into the marketplace. Because the traditional cotton cords couldn't withstand the increased heat generated in synthetic rubber tires, the industry turned to rayon. Its superior strength permitted lighter and thinner tires, and the cotton-cord tire had all but disappeared from the marketplace by the post-war years. Next came nylon-reinforced tires, offering still greater strength to match the heavy cars of the 1950s.

Michelin had success with radials in the 1950s (radial bicycle tires were used as early as 1890), and radials are now the mainstay of the tire industry.

Aggressive research has seen the trial of radically novel treads, including button-type treads and extensive use of grooving and siping (a sipe is a hook-shaped groove used in tire treads for extra traction). Tread researchers must contend with a trade-off between handling qualities and durability. The characteristic open blocks of high-traction designs generate more noise, wear quickly, and compromise handling. But with extensive testing, better compounding techniques, and much work with computers, new designs promise to balance the trade-offs.

Today, radial tires are used almost exclusively on new cars and make up about 56 percent of the replacement passenger-tire market, compared to 27 percent for bias tires and 17 percent for bias-belted tires. Radial sales figures will probably increase dramatically over the next few years as gasoline prices enhance their lower rolling resistance.

Decreased rolling resistance seems to be the main concern of the industry today. Some companies feel the narrower a tire, the less resistance with the ground. According to others, the lower the sidewall height, the less flexing, and flexing produces heat and generates a standing wave that is believed to increase tire drag. In order to obtain the lower sidewall height, a large cross section is necessary for the sake of ride and durability.

In this, the so-called age of consumerism, tire dealers find that the average consumer takes little interest in tires. James Krakower, owner of J.K.M. Tire and Wheel in Champaign, Illinois, says, "The typical consumer doesn't understand the technical jargon, not even his tire size." Dick Barbieri, owner of B & B Tire Company in Sacramento, California, says he sees "a high degree of consumerism in the public, but many of them are pseudo-experts who have read one book and they think they know everything about tires."

As a guide to help consumers purchase tires, the federal government, through the U.S. Department of Transportation, initiated a Uniform Tire Quality Grading (UTQG) program. The program requires tiremakers to rate their tires in terms of tread life, traction, and heat resistance. Many tiremakers have declared that the testing procedures do not reflect real life (see accompanying box, "The controversial tire-grading program").

The UTQG program has also been criticized because tire manufacturers, and not the government, choose the grade and, for the most part, grade their tires conservatively due to the penalties for overrating tires.

Roy Littlefield, of the National Tire Dealers and Retreaders Association, says that consumers can't depend on UTQG ratings because each tire manufacturer selects its own criteria for assigning a treadwear grade. "We want a more uniform, better test for grading tires," says Littlefield, "or we want the treadwear tests eliminated completely. We want a test which is meaningful or no test at all."

The National Highway Traffic Safety Administration of the U.S. Department of Transportation finds fault with this system. "Some manufacturers evaluated [treadwear] data by applying statistical procedures," they report in the *Federal Register*. "Other manufacturers did not use a statistical procedure, relying instead on business and engineering judgment in assignment of grades. These differing approaches and judgments give rise to a very real prospect of different grades to their tires. Clearly, such a result would reduce the value of the UTQG information to consumers."

Part of the problem with the current UTQG system is that tread life is projected from a road test of only 7,200 miles. Tread wears at a different rate at different times in a tire's life. Generally, the first couple of thirty-seconds of an inch go quickly; then, the wear rate slows down drastically, and finally accelerates again at the end of a tire's life. Not all tires work this way, though, and some companies maintain that their tires should be graded differently due to unique wear patterns.

At least one tire manufacturer, Uniroyal, approves of the present tire-rating system. Proclaims a company brochure, "At Uniroyal, we applaud [the] grading system. We believe grade labeling offers the consumer the opportunity to judge tires in a more objective light. We think this is the progressive, efficient way to buy tires." After assigning treadwear grades equivalent to 66,000 miles on some of its tires, Uniroyal began touting the UTQG system in its advertising.

In the accompanying box are listed some of the UTQG ratings. As a rule of thumb, you should expect 20,000 to 25,000 miles from a bias-ply tire; 30,000 to 35,000 miles from a bias-belted tire; and 35,000 to 50,000 miles from a radial tire. Retreads may last up to 20,000 miles.

The current crop of tires on the market represents the advancements of an industry that has been with us for more than a century. The cost per mile is far lower now than in the industry's infancy. But many consumers think no more of their tires than to pay for them and see how long they'll run. This attitude ruins tires. There are several practical measures you can take to extend tire life.

First and foremost, constantly monitor tire pressure. An underinflated tire builds up heat quickly, and heat is a killer of tires. (Also, a flabby tire has increased rolling resistance and unstable handling characteristics.) Note that if a tire is underinflated, there has to be a reason for it. In the case of steel-belted radials, a nail will permit water to seep in and rust the steel cords, ruining an otherwise perfect tire.

GREG SMITH, with RALPH KEYS

The controversial tire-grading program

In 1980, tire manufacturers were required by federal law to rate their tires for treadwear. Because the manufacturers graded their own tires, some said the ratings were exaggerated. But a spokesperson for Consumers Union, publishers of *Consumer Reports*, told us that the tire ratings were "valuable information that's helpful to people who are shopping for tires." Here we've arranged the manufacturer's treadwear information for radial tires on a graph that also compares prices. Tires within the graph's shaded area should provide an average amount of treadwear for their price. Above and below that area are tires with above- and below-average mileage per dollar: in other words, inexpensive tires with long-lasting tread rate highest. It's worth noting that tires with the best handling characteristics often have poor treadwear (racing tires, for example, provide exceptional driving control but must be changed often in the course of a race). There is a trade-off, then, between durability and handling. The prices on this graph were accurate as of January, 1981.

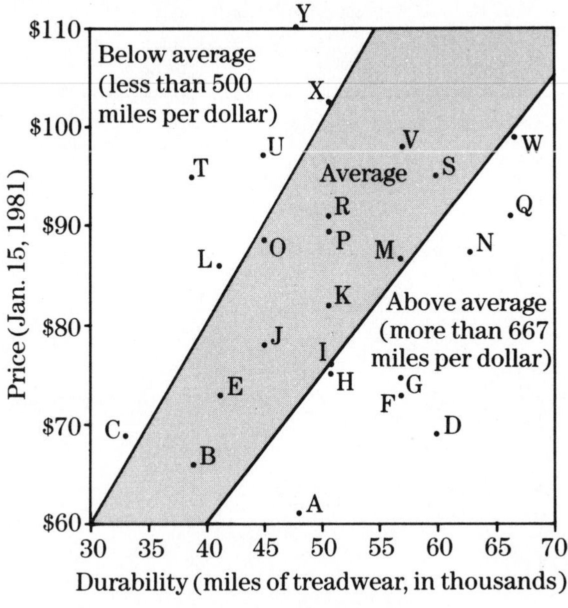

A sampling of best-selling radials

A. Goodrich Lifesaver All Season
B. Sears Weatherhandler
C. General VSR Radial
D. Goodrich The Advantage T/A
E. Firestone Deluxe Champion
F. Dunlop Gold Seal
G. Goodyear Tiempo
H. Firestone Trax 12
I. Goodrich Lifesaver XLM
J. General Jet Radial
K. Kelly Springfield
L. Michelin XWW
M. Kelly Springfield Supercharger
N. Dunlop Elite Seventy Radial
O. Sears Superguard
P. Sears Roadhandler GT 70
Q. Kelly Springfield Voyager
R. Firestone Steel Belted 721
S. General Grabber R60
T. Montgomery Ward Runabout All Season
U. Pirelli P77
V. Montgomery Ward Grappler All Season
W. Goodyear Arriva
X. Goodyear Custom Polysteel
Y. Montgomery Ward Grappler Elire

Land-Rover

"If they were no longer manufactured, Africa would sink like Atlantis into the sea," says Sandy Grice, president of the Rover Owners' Association of Virginia. The British Land-Rover enjoys a loyal following in the United States, all the more impressive considering that U.S. pollution standards have banned those made since 1968.

Grice is a real-estate appraiser whose work takes him into the rough country of western Virginia—aboard a 1972 Land-Rover, his only vehicle. Although he admits that it was not designed with speed or comfort in mind, he wouldn't own any other car.

What's the source of such loyalty? Land-Rover owners see their vehicles as unique in a world market awash with tinny, tricky-to-maintain junk.

Grice struggles to be objective. "I realize that other vehicles run as long or as well, such as million-mile Mercedes and the like. But how many of them go through their useful lives as tractors, snow plows, or log skidders? I have driven mine through four-foot-deep creeks, through snow as deep as the bonnet, and started it the first time on several −35°F mornings."

The Land-Rover is unique—the polar opposite of today's featherweight, facile, microchip-brained compacts, and here's a good bit of the car's appeal. While car manufacturers find themselves compromising between ride and handling, power and economy, solidity and good gas mileage, styling and engineering, Rover has not.

Rover is one of a very few British makes still with us. The company merged with Leyland Motors in the mid-1960s, was nationalized along with them in 1976, and Land-Rover Ltd. set out on its own in 1978.

Rather than comfort and speed, the Land-Rover offers an aluminum-alloy body (originally arrived at in steel-short, post–World War II Britain), box-sectioned ladder frame, and a cast-iron engine designed for owner maintenance. The engine was last redesigned in the late 1950s and hasn't changed much since (although a diesel and an aluminum V8 have been introduced). "There's not a lot of complex stuff on it," says Grice. He gaps the points with a matchbook cover. When the axle broke on his 120,000-mile Rover, Grice replaced it with the spare he carries, "in approximately a half hour, while wearing a three-piece suit, in a rather bad section of town!" Self-reliance is important to him, as he is contemplating a move to a mountain home that would serve as a refuge, come a holocaust of some sort.

If you're unhappy with mere convenience and compromise, look for a pre-1968 Land-Rover—that is, a model made before the Leyland takeover. Wheels, seals, gaskets, and brake parts are available at auto parts stores. Expect about 16 to 18 MPG in town and 25 on the highway.

As for new Rovers, fanatics have smuggled them in, one quasi-legally across the Canadian border as a "12-passenger bus." A West Coast car dealer told us one California firm is importing the more comfortable Range-Rover for $35,000, under the table.

Land-Rover models, top to bottom: truck cab, 10-seat station wagon, 12-seat station wagon, truck cab and canvas hood with windows, full-length canvas hood with windows, and metal hard-top with windows.

Through the Americas by Land-Rover

"Half a mile from the plinth, on the Panamanian side, we found a rusting red car, a sad reminder of the ill-fated Chevrolet expedition that had reached the frontier over ten years ago, and then turned back. Now it lay, a rotting hulk with trees growing up through the engine compartment and an ants' nest in the boot. As we poked sticks into the interior a venomous coral snake slithered from beneath the remains of the back seat and a large black spider emerged from the dashboard....

"Our sweat-soaked clothes rotted on us. Leather equipment grew mould, even the best jungle boots available began to fall apart. The mosquitoes, gnats and flies became a constant plague; there were inch-long black ants whose bite hurt like hell for hours, there were also stinging caterpillars and, in the rivers, electric eels. The heat and humidity were oppressive and even the nights brought little relief. Clusters of aggressive and vindictive hornets nested in hollow trees and swarmed out to meet anyone who disturbed them. I have never seen insects so vicious. Within seconds a well-ordered column could turn into chaos under attack from hornets. One of the girls became seriously ill when she developed an allergic reaction to one such assault. Inch-wide centipedes and black scorpions also took their toll, whilst spiders as large as dinner plates were fearsome to behold."

From "The Darien Breakthrough," the story of the Land-Rover-borne 1972 British Trans-Americas Expedition, by MAJOR J.N. BLASHFORD-SNELL, M.B.E., F.R.G.S., R.E.

The art of fording

"The maximum advisable fording depth is approximately 18 inches. Before fording, make sure the clutch housing drain plug is in position and if the water is deep, slacken off the fan belt. Avoid over speeding of the engine to prevent saturation of the electrical system and air intake. A low gear is desirable and sufficient throttle should be maintained at all times to avoid stalling if the exhaust pipe is under water. After being in water make sure the brakes are dried out immediately. This can be accomplished by driving a short distance with the foot brake applied. Tighten fan belt and remove the drain plug."

From a Land-Rover sales brochure

Jackson Square, in the French Quarter of New Orleans.

Skyline Drive, Shenandoah National Park, Virginia.

An electrician's van visits America

In the past 2½ years, this 1965 Ford Econoline van has taken my friend Susan Gross and I to more than 75 national parks, from wheatfield to bayou to desert to purple mountain's majesty, from sea to shining sea.

My van has a six-cylinder, 240-cubic-inch engine (its second) and is styled the same as every other Econoline van built between 1961 and 1967. What sets this one apart is its red-and-white paint job, for my van served an electrician near Philadelphia named William H. Ayers. It still bears his name, address, telephone number, and advertising slogan: "You phone us, we'll wire you!" We've dubbed the van *William*. On one cross-country trip, we visited Mr. Ayers. He is a friendly man who smiled often, pleased to see his old van back home. Apparently he is a good electrician, too: his ad in the Yellow Pages notes that he has served "over 20,000 satisfied customers in Delaware County."

I am of the school that believes "they don't make them like they used to," or, as I sometimes say to people, "This van was built before drugs invaded assembly lines." And proper maintenance, I'm sure, is one key to durability—an obvious answer, maybe, but the obvious often gets overlooked when the world moves so quickly.

The last few things I've had garages do for the van all had to be redone by Susan and myself. For peace of mind and proper satisfaction, don't trust anyone but yourself, once you're armed with the proper tools, a few gauges and timing lights, a repair manual, and maybe friends who have done it before.

That holds true whether you just drive to church once a week or drive around the U.S. in a home on wheels. We began slowly, checking and changing the oil, gapping spark plugs, putting in new points, rotor, and condenser. We haven't yet worked on the brakes, the gearing, or the valves, but one way or another, Susan and I eventually dealt with all other systems in the van.

So on we go, studying local customs and geography. Along with our log, I've created a photographic series, "The Electrician's Van Visits America," showing my home posing nicely with the White House, Old Faithful, Mount Rushmore, the Grand Coulee Dam, Manhattan's World Trade towers, Walden Pond, Fort McHenry, the Gulf of Mexico, Cape Hatteras, and other pieces of the great American puzzle. Our next step is to convert *William* somehow from fossil fuels to renewable energy and head for the twenty-first century.

RICHARD SASSAMAN

All photos, Richard Sassaman

On the Grand Coulee Dam, Washington.

At the Atlantic Ocean, Ormond Beach, Florida.

Walden Pond, near Concord, Massachusetts.

Gateway Arch, Jefferson National Expansion Memorial, St. Louis, Missouri.

Near the Continental Divide, I-70 in Colorado.

Reborn Citroens

John Bagley

Scott Curtin at work.

Scott Curtin wears a French hat and rebuilds only French Citroens, even though he works in Santa Clara, California. He considers the cars to be supremely durable and says that the discontinued DS model is good for 125,000 to 140,000 miles before needing an overhaul, with subsequent rebuilding every 200,000 miles or so. More than a dozen of his rebuilds have passed a million miles.

Citroen 2 CV

Some seasoned observers of cars consider the spartan Citroen 2 CV to be the world's most durable by virtue of its simplicity and unconventional design. No models newer than 1967 can be brought into the United States because they weren't modified to meet our emissions standards, but believers in this simple car continue to import old ones nevertheless. One dealer told us he'd bring over a pre-'67 2 CV (from Belgium, where he claims the best ones were made) for about $3,000, which includes his commission of $800 and a 30-day warranty.

REPAIR AND REMANUFACTURING

Hidden costs: parts and labor

A car is only as durable as its owner is willing and able to fix it. When car shopping you should consider a model's operating costs as well as its purchase price.

The U.S. Department of Transportation's *The Car Book*, published in 1981, lists maintenance costs for more than 80 domestic and foreign cars, including both preventive maintenance as specified by the manufacturer and repairs such as a brake job and a new transmission. The differences are dramatic, as a few examples will show. Among the intermediate-size cars, preventive maintenance costs range from $125 for the Mercury Zephyr to a burdensome $728 for the Peugeot diesel. Scanning the subcompacts, a new catalytic converter is a fairly inexpensive $117 for Subaru owners and $645 for Mazda GLC owners (most cars will need a replacement if they reach 100,000 miles). Comparing the cars by size turns up no real advantage for small-car owners. Generally, the most expensive cars to maintain are diesels and German makes. Among the compacts and subcompacts, American car parts are "considerably" cheaper than foreign car parts, and the accompanying labor charges are "somewhat" lower, in the words of the Motor and Equipment Manufacturers Association, who conducted *The Car Book's* survey. This conforms to the popular wisdom of the 1960s, when high-mileage foreign cars became a familiar sight on American highways: what the imports would spare you in gas money, it was said, you'd pay right back for parts and labor.

Note that the survey doesn't take into consideration the *frequency* of repair of the various models. Conceivably, the advantage of a low parts-and-labor charge could be undone by a high incidence of repair. For this information, consult *Consumer Reports'* annual survey of its readers' automotive woes.

The born-again car

A good, affordable car is hard to find, so much so that certain older models are being kept alive for extraordinary life spans with complete, bumper-to-bumper overhauls.

Some cars are more deserving of remanufacture than others. In Belvidere, New Jersey, Automotive Import Recycling (AIR) specializes in just three models, the Volvo 122 and 140 series (manufactured from 1963 to 1974) and the BMW 2002 (1968 to 1976). How did the company arrive at these candidates for immortality? People simply hate to give them up, said AIR's Peter Fuller, as evidenced by the conspicuous absence of Volvos and BMWs from junkyards. They are clearly perceived as more valuable–durable and safe and fun to drive–than cars with perennially low resale values. Also, the two makes are easier for AIR to work on because there were few body and mechanical changes over the years.

The remanufacturing process involves tearing down the body, interior, and engine, followed by a careful inspection for signs of aging, especially for a model's characteristic weaknesses–the Volvo's camshafts or lifters and the BMW's second-gear synchronizer, for instance. Specialization enables AIR to use some assembly-line techniques in putting the cars back together, such as scavenging parts from old cars and purchasing new parts in volume. In addition, the company equips Volvos with its own modified head, which is said to improve fuel consumption significantly.

AIR sells its remanufactured cars for about half the cost of equivalent new models. The Volvo sedan goes for \$4,750, a station wagon for \$5,250, a BMW 2002 for around \$6,000, and the rarer 2002ti for \$7,250. That's if the company supplies the "carcass." Bring in your own car and, depending on how far gone it is, the charge will run from \$2,500 to \$4,000. Rebuilt cars have a warranty of 12 months or 12,000 miles.

So far, the company has been able to come up with enough carcasses and enough drive-in customers, but they are considering expanding to diesel Mercedes, Saab, water-cooled VW, Jaguar XJ6, Triumph, or MGB.

Across the country, car owners are going to great expense to keep a trustworthy friend on the road. No horse enjoyed better treatment. One New York couple is having an entirely new frame custom-made for their 20-year-old Avanti, at a cost of almost \$10,000. That may sound sentimental rather than financially astute, but at today's prices (a typically equipped General Motors car now goes for \$10,000) and levels of depreciation (an average of 70 percent for full-size U.S. cars in just 4 years), dependable old cars are worthy of the care lavished upon them.

RY

Dear Sir:

The lighter I sent you was in an awful mangled shape, but for a good reason. I accidentally dropped the lighter into a silage chopper. I was riding the chopper and when I dropped it I had the tractor driver stop. We dug through the silage and I sent you all of the pieces we could find.

I hope something can be done about the lighter. Last Oct. 1st it was a birthday present from my wife.

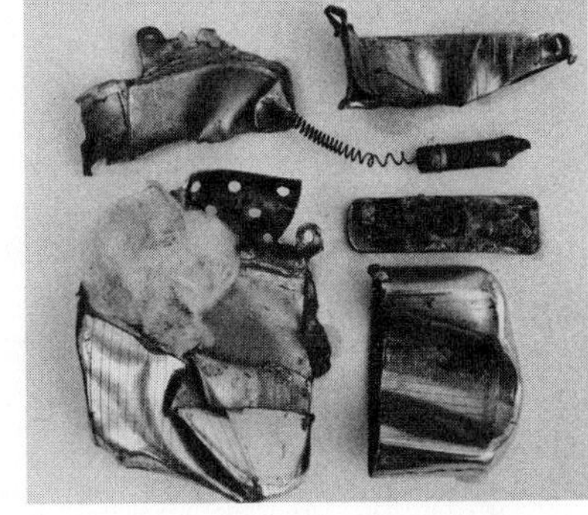

CYCLES, BIKES, AND A BOAT

3

Do fewer wheels mean fewer years? Motorcycles and bicycles don't seem to hold up as long as cars. Of course there's the enormous difference in weight between four- and two-wheeled vehicles, but it also matters that bikes and cycles have come to mean little more than recreation to most Americans. Because a toy doesn't tend to get the care that a tool would, our two-wheelers don't hold up as long as their practical counterparts in poorer countries. Ancient black BMW motorcycles are common on the island of Crete, even though they're used for primary transportation rather than treated as collector's items; in India, bicycles are used to transport freight and even livestock; and according to the Worldwatch Institute, bikes in the world's poor nations last an average of 75 years. In the United States, meanwhile, the makers of Huffy bikes admitted they had introduced a twelve-speed kid's bike to "obsolete" its ten-speed.

As fuel prices encourage Americans to turn to bikes and cycles for everyday transportation, expect to see both manufacturers and riders exercise more care with their machines. Just as affluence makes toys of tools, lean economic times return them to tools.

Christie C. Tito

A balloon-tired Schwinn from the 1930s.

MOTORCYCLES

The utilitarian motorcycle, and why it isn't on the market

"I can't fault the industry for obsolescence. The customers demand it."

An interview with Steve Kimball, managing editor of *Cycle World*

❝The motorcycle manufacturers who haven't changed their machinery, who have said, "Okay, this is a good, solid product," soon disappear. Hodaka, for instance, made a perfectly good, strong little trail bike. They came out with one model, they made sure that all parts were interchangeable, they kept the same model and just updated it each year. Here was a wonderful idea for a consumer product. The Hodaka was durable, carefree, performed its job well.

Hodaka went broke. People didn't want a durable, carefree bike. They wanted what's new—double overhead camshafts, electronic ignitions, and whatever the modern features are.

The manufacturers who make these changes readily admit that some are just for marketing reasons. One company added a six-speed transmission to its motorcycle, a small commuter bike, knowing that the performance didn't change a bit. I can't fault the industry for obsolescence—the customers demand it—but I still like the idea of a sensible, plain, utilitarian bike. Years ago somebody in our field referred to them as stone-axe motorcycles. In East Europe, they've got the Jawa and MC—low-performance, durable, inexpensive machines. They don't sell particularly well over there, and when they've been available over here, they haven't sold at all. Now whether a person could devise a marketing campaign for them, I don't know. Very few people ride motorcycles because it's a sensible, utilitarian thing to do. For the most part, it's just fun, not transportation. That's why, in the past, as soon as people could afford cars, they ditched their motorcycles. By the 1920s, Henry Ford was selling cars for $300, so there was no longer any point in driving an Indian or a Harley-Davidson or an Excelsior. Sales went down the tubes. Right after the Second World War, there was little money or car production through Europe, and a motorcycle was the first practical piece of transportation a person could get. As soon as their rotten, sniveling little cars became somewhat serviceable and people had the money to buy them, they traded in their Peugeot bikes to buy Renault Dauphines, and they were getting off their AJSs and Matchlesses and into Minis, and they were getting off their Moto Guzzis and into Fiats. The same thing is happening today in the Orient.

Today, a cycle is not simply practical transportation. The rider has to have a bike that suits his image of himself. A person who wants to tell the world, "Hey, I'm a stud, I'm tough, I'm fast," goes out and buys a Kawasaki 1000. The guy who doesn't want that image, would be embarrassed to be seen on such a bike, says, "Gosh, I want to tell the world that I don't care about performance and I'm sophisticated and I'm intelligent." He goes out and buys a BMW cycle. Then there are a number of Ma and Pa Kettles—"Well, I just been ridin' my Harley-Davidsons for 45 years now"—and it says something about them, that they're solid, middle Americans.

You are what you ride. The people who market automobiles have recognized this for years. Volvo's been selling the idea that if you want people to think you're intelligent, you buy a Volvo. It's worked very well: you go to any college town and look at the Volvos the professors drive.

Another person figures, "I can show I'm socially aware by driving a diesel Mercedes." Never mind that he spent $25,000 on a machine. He's showing that he really doesn't care about performance, he doesn't care about fad or fashion: "I'm showing the world I'm a sensitive person."

Perceived durability is a matter of price. Have you seen the billboard for Mercedes-Benz that says, "The $20,000 car"? The idea is, if you pay more you're obviously getting more. As for BMW cycles, they earned a reputation 30 years ago and they're still living on it. People who spend twice as much money for a BMW bike or a Mercedes have a certain emotional involvement, and they find a great need to defend the machine.

Durability is a matter of putting on a whole bunch of miles over a long period of time; *reliability* is not having to worry about the cycle breaking down somewhere along the way. To me, the Volkswagen Beetle was reliable, not durable. The Moto Guzzi is a cycle with durability greater than reliability—a switch may go bad, a lock may have a problem, but the basic engine is trouble-free and will last a long time.

Steve Kimball: "The Honda Gold Wing is a good, durable machine, although it's a lot bigger than it needs to be for sheer transportation. Honda figured that its engine life would be about 100,000 miles, and there are a number of them that have gone 130,000 or 140,000 miles without major work."

"Planned obsolescence? I think it's a crock. We like to think we're victims of a conspiracy. We all talk about how we want things to last, yet we've all got stuff in the closet we're sick of."

From an interview with ALLAN GIRDLER, editor of *Cycle World*

It used to be that after 20,000 miles the engine of a Japanese bike would be fine, but the clutch basket would rattle, the steering head bearings were pitted, the swing-arm bushings were shot. I know Honda, for one, is going through all their service records, finding which parts tend to fail in two or three years, and improving them. They are working on this because they don't want to have a reputation for making a two- or three-year motorcycle. Today, they have the Gold Wing. There are a number of them that have gone 130,000 or 140,000 miles without major work. But it wasn't always this way.

Back in the 1950s the BMW and the Harley-Davidson were considered the most reliable motorcycles. The English bikes were less so, and the only Japanese bikes anybody ever saw were pictures of funny-looking things that nobody would have ridden anyhow. Now we have a BMW that is no more reliable than it was then, a Harley-Davidson that is no more reliable than it was then, and there are no British bikes left except Triumph. But the Japanese bikes are far more reliable today. We've had a series of owner surveys, and the most reliable bikes have been Kawasakis and Suzukis, followed very closely by Hondas and BMWs.”

The BMW motorcycle: sophisticated simplicity

A survey of durable products is apt to overlook the motorcycle. Few two-wheeled, motorized machines can boast of any degree of longevity. That's unfortunate, especially in these energy-conscious days. The inherent economy of two-wheelers would otherwise look very sensible indeed. It can pay to know, then, that there's one motorcycle that has been built more sturdily than any other, even more sturdily than many cars: the BMW.

This is significant when one realizes just how dismal the durability record of most two-wheelers has been. Few mopeds, for instance, will run 10,000 miles before dying in the gutter, the victims of under-engineered and overstressed parts. Motor scooters and small-displacement motorcycles have a better performance record, but it's still unusual for one to make it past 25,000 or 30,000 miles without a major overhaul, which can be surprisingly expensive.

In contrast, it isn't unusual for a BMW motorcycle to go over 100,000 miles and occasionally as far as 200,000 with only normal maintenance—periodic tune-ups and frequent oil and filter changes. As late as the 1960s, before the current crop of large, well-built Japanese machines came on the market, the BMW was considered the world's only truly reliable motorcycle. It was chosen as a matter of course by long-haul touring motorcyclists, among them intrepid explorers who rode such jaunts as the Pan-American Highway from Alaska to the tip of South America, involving perhaps 40,000 miles of jungle trails, Andes mountain passes, and dirt roads. Other explorers have taken round-the-world tours, dashes

BMW Motorcycle Owners of America

The BMW 100RS, at $7,025, and its high-priced stablemates have inspired the U.S. ad writers to poetry: "For one long shining moment, stop compromising."

across the Sahara, and off-road excursions into Asian jungles or the African bush. In 1981, BMW motorcycles finished in first, fourth, and seventh places in the 20-day, 6,200-mile Paris-Dakar Race, an endurance race through deep Sahara sands and African jungles.

The BMW's longevity may be attributed to one fact: BMW motorcycles are designed and built by engineers. This may sound odd since every motorcycle manufacturer employs legions of engineers, but it's the relative importance of engineers in BMW's hierarchy that is unique. Most motorcycles are designed by a triumvirate of market analysts, stylists, and engineers, with the engineers relegated to obeying the other two.

At BMW, however, engineers permeate even upper-echelon management, and as a result, the company approaches problem-solving in the classical engineering tradition: first, define a goal, then define a machine to accomplish that goal, and finally, design the machine to do its job with utter efficiency and simplicity. You'd expect the product to be as angular as a tractor, as unexciting as the turbine room of a hydroelectric power station. But the resulting machines are elegant. Blending razor-sharp definition with sensuously swooping lines, the BMWs are undeniably beautiful, and yet they were not styled for beauty. Some models were designed in a wind tunnel to be as nearly aerodynamically perfect as a motorcycle can be, and the razor edges and swooping curves are there because air flows smoothly around them. The motorcycles are rigorously functional; no fillips were added, no chrome whistles or flashing lights to dazzle the masses. The design speaks to the educated eye with purpose and authority.

Besides style, another benefit of sound engineering is durability. The stiff, strong frames don't flex and therefore don't fatigue and crack. Strong, relatively slow-running engines are not overstressed. A driveshaft not only eliminates an oily mess but supplants the fastest-wearing component on a motorcycle (except for the tires)—the chain.

The engine, for simplicity, is a twin-cylinder design. Single-cylinder machines

Kieth Patchett

Kieth Patchett of Elmhurst, New York, and the 1976 BMW on which he rode over 170,000 miles before an overhaul. During the overhaul, Patchett found that the main bearings showed so little wear that he reused them.

BMW Motorcycle Owners of America

The craft-shop atmosphere of BMW's old factory in Munich.

A BMW en route to Afghanistan's capital.

Under the shade of a spreading cactus in Mexico.

"One comes through," says this German ad proclaiming the BMW's reliability and durability. The home-country ad campaign is markedly more concerned with the mechanics of getting from place to place than U.S. ads, which sell performance and style and prestige. These photos of BMWs in exotic places are from the company's German ad campaign.

Bogged down in Australian mud.

Bogged down in Australian sand.

Both photos, Jeff Dean

These 1951 models, in black and white pin stripes, express the company's straightforward approach to motorcycle styling and engineering. Over the intervening three decades, BMW has gone to colors and lightweight plastics, but the new machines have obvious genetic links with ancestors going back to the 1920s. The top cycle has the customary two cylinders; the lower cycle has but one, and modest power for its weight meant that single-cylinder BMWs never caught on in the U.S.

are limited in size and are rough running; engines with more than two cylinders become complex. The BMW's twin provides excellent low-end and mid-range torque, and can be made enormously strong without being unacceptably heavy. The BMW engine block is cast of aluminum alloy, as are the cylinder barrels and the heads. Pistons are forged, rather than of the more common, and weaker, cast construction. Beginning in 1981, all BMWs have cylinder walls of a super-hard silicone substance that reduces engine wear, increases heat dissipation, and prolongs engine life.

The engine is served by an automotive-type high-volume trochoidal oil pump. At 60 miles per hour, it delivers filtered oil to the bearing surfaces at a rate of over 212 gallons per hour, and the entire 2.5 quarts of the 1,000cc engine's oil supply is recirculated once every ten seconds, at a pressure of 60 to 74 psi. Because of this, tolerances can be kept within wide margins, reducing wear and ensuring that the engine won't seize during hot running. (Accessory manufacturers sell extra-capacity oil pans for added assurance.)

A motorcycle engine is fundamentally very different from an automobile engine, in one respect: it must be much more highly engineered because there's so much less of it.

In a car, the engine is very heavy, with relatively little thought given to refinement of the package so that it will weigh less. As a result, the modern V8 auto engine and transmission can be expected to weigh at least 700 pounds—about 260 pounds more than an entire 1,000cc BMW motorcycle.

The BMW's engine is placed in the frame with the cylinders sticking out, one on each side of the motorcycle. This 180-degree opposed cylinder layout is inherently smooth running; the cylinders are placed in the passing airstream for maximum cooling; the center of gravity is low for excellent cornering and stability; and the crankshaft is kept parallel to the longitudinal axis of the frame, giving an efficient, straight line of power transmission through the clutch, transmission, and driveshaft to the rear wheel. The BMW employs a single-plate dry clutch like that in a car, rather than the more complex multiplate oil-bath clutch of most motorcycles. The BMW transmission is strong, with massive machined gears. Its driveshaft and rear drive unit are sealed and bathed in oil for a long, trouble-free life.

The basic design is likely the oldest in continuous production. BMW first employed it in 1923. As good engineers will, the current crop of designers at BMW acknowledges the greatness of the past, while trying to make it better. This process of careful evolution results in motorcycles that become better, stronger, every year.*

Owners of older BMWs enjoy a surprising level of factory support; a full stock of parts is maintained for most models manufactured in 1955 or later. This is unusual among car manufacturers and is unheard of among makers of motorcycles.

Many of its owners find the BMW to be a happy introduction to the mysteries and delights of technology. Performing your own maintenance and repairs on a straightforward, logical machine, you are freed from the fears bred by lack of understanding. As you tighten bolts, adjust this, and tinker with that, your confidence builds until suddenly you find that even relatively complex machinery holds no terrors any longer. You're not utterly at the mercy of a repair person if things go wrong. The freedom brought on by self-reliance is well worth the time spent learning the basics of maintenance and repair. A BMW motorcycle makes the education all the more rewarding.

RALPH KEYS

*However, the next few years may bring the most radical revision ever of the traditional BMW concept. It may be a change the factory didn't want at all—a change to water-cooled engines from the traditional air-cooled engines, caused by ever-stricter limits on exhaust emissions and noise.

Commitment

Both photos, Jon Gerber

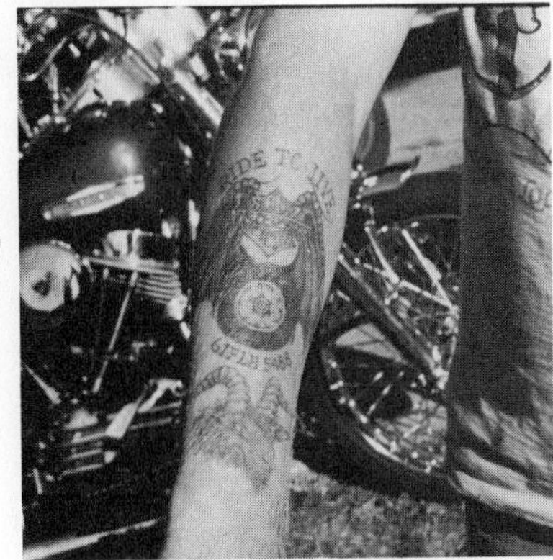

"Ride to live . . . 61 FLH 5488."

Virgil Courtwright aboard his Harley.

Virgil Courtwright of Eugene, Oregon, loves his 1961 74-cubic-inch Pan-Head Harley-Davidson so dearly that he tattooed the engine number on his right forearm.

"This bike is a keeper," Virgil says. "I'll own and ride it for the rest of my life." He is one of thousands of Harley owners who have branded themselves over the years.

The first Harley was built in 1903 inside a 10-by-15-foot shack in Mr. Davidson's backyard. That original Harley-Davidson was little more than a motorized bicycle, but it logged over 100,000 miles before it was put to rest in a museum. There have been many refinements over the years, but the basic design of the Harley V-Twin has remained the same for over 40 years. Many parts are interchangeable going back to 1937.

JON GERBER

BICYCLES

Keeping your bike on the road

There are 100 million bicycles in the United States—more bicycles than cars. But most of the bikes are gathering dust in garages and basements. What is keeping them off the road?

They likely as not are in a state of disrepair, and that's a sign that their riders aren't aware just how good an investment a bike—a working bike—can be.

Time after time, bicyclists have won cross-town races against cars and public transportation. That's because the bicycle travels door-to-door—no waiting for the bus, no looking for parking places, no walking. For short trips, a bicycle looks especially good, because a car's mileage suffers (one study shows that a car gets 15 percent of normal mileage on a one-mile trip), and its engine is more vulnerable to wear (90 percent of the wear to the engine is said to occur in the first 15 minutes of driving).

You shouldn't buy a bike that is more sophisticated than you need or can repair. Simplest is the one-speed *tank* or *cruiser* bicycle, with two-inch-wide tires, a heavy frame, flat handlebars, and usually a coaster brake. (For safety in traffic, it should have a front brake as well.) The tank bike is the least expensive and, if well made, the most durable. It is especially suited to off-road and dirt-road use. Prices range from $60 to $150, although more sophisticated versions with multi-speed gears, called clunkers or mountain bikes, have appeared recently at far higher prices.

The *internally geared utility bike* ($80 to $300) is typified by the English three-speed, with moderately wide (1⅜-inch) tires, handbrakes, flat handlebars, and fenders for wet-weather riding.

The *derailleur-geared, lightweight multispeed bike,* with dropped handlebars and narrow tires, is the most sophisticated. Materials and workmanship push its price from $100 to over $1,000.

The one- and three-speeds' advantages are their mechanical simplicity and lower cost. They are adequate for short commutes and shopping, and preferable if you need to lock your bicycle outdoors while you shop. The derailleur-geared bike, on the other hand, will allow you the full enjoyment of bicycling as an athletic activity. More important than the number of gears is the riding position, which, once you are used to it, will give you more control for maneuvering and let you use your body more efficiently to travel twice as far—50 to 100 miles in a day after a few months' practice—while still feeling good after climbing off the saddle.

Many bicyclists have learned that two or more bicycles are needed to suit different terrains and riding styles. For example, the avid cyclist's garage might hold a high-performance lightweight bike for recreational riding and perhaps commuting, and a sturdy, simple one-speed or three-speed bike, perhaps secondhand, for trips when it must be left locked outdoors. This "trashmo" bike is also suited to winter riding in salt, sand, and slush, because you're not rusting away a large investment.

Buy at a bike shop

Here's some solid advice. If you're buying a new bicycle, go to a full-service bike shop—not a department store, discount house, auto-parts store, or anywhere else. The people who work in a bike shop know bikes and can advise you on what to buy. They can see that the bicycle fits you properly, and this is important. They can set up the bicycle properly for you, and inspect it, switch parts, and add accessories to suit your needs. A full-service bike shop has trained mechanics and a large stock of spare parts for the bikes it sells, so that it can back up a guarantee. Not only that, but the shop will not likely sell poor-quality bicycles, as they're too much trouble to service and can hurt the business's reputation.

In the department store or discount house, things are very different. The usual sales tactic is to offer the lowest-priced, lowest-quality bicycle of any given type—say, $60 three-speeds and $89 ten-speeds. These are built to sell, not to ride. They appeal to people who are caught up with the image of a certain type of bicycle but who want to spend as little money as possible. Often the bicycles are sold unassembled, and the purchasers must put them together—perhaps correctly, perhaps not. It may take weeks to order parts for a broken bike, and even then the store may not have anyone who knows how to install them.

More important than brand names are the shop's quality of service, its attitude toward customers, and its supply of spare parts. Other bicyclists may lead you to such a shop. Visit two or three places before making a decision. As you shop, collect manufacturers' catalogs and compare features against the recommendations made here. Also, look through *Bicycling* magazine test reports for the past two or three years at your local library.

A bike shop is a good place to buy a used bike, too. If the machine carries a guarantee, it is probably as good as new. It may not look like new, but the quality of bike-shop overhauls is often better than that of factory assembly of *new* bicycles. If you buy a used bicycle from a private party, do not expect as much. But a low price may enable you to afford to have it overhauled at a bike shop. You can even assemble a complete bicycle from parts of two or more junked bicycles; for safety's sake, take your creation to a shop for a check-over.

The components

The *frame* is central to a bicycle's quality and durability. The largest stresses on the frame are at the joints. Better frames have reinforced joints. You can spot these: the line of one frame tube should either flow into the other tube, with a rounded, built-up contour, or there should be a reinforcing sleeve (called a lug) over each joint. Cheaper frames simply have one tube welded to the other; the sharp, unreinforced angle between the

All photos, Bill Keisling

A well-made frame with rounded contours.

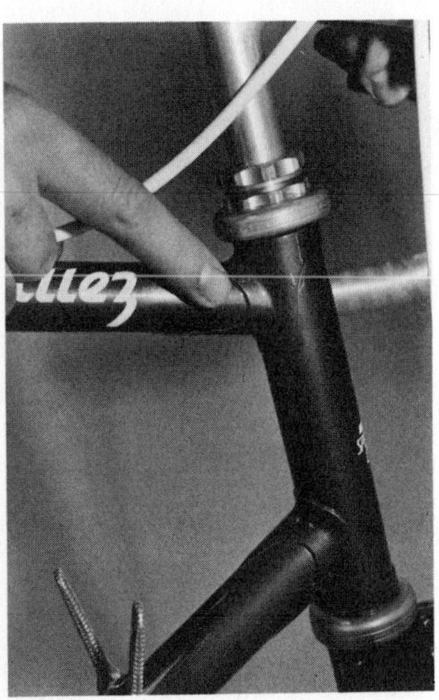

A good frame with reinforced, lugged joints.

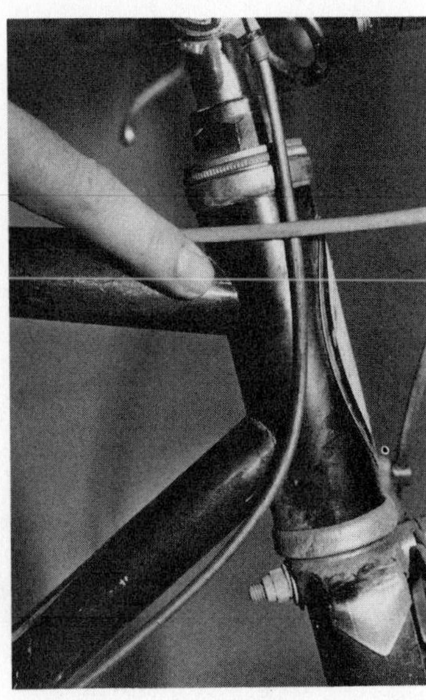

An inexpensive frame with one tube merely welded to another.

tubes concentrates stresses. Cheaper frames often break apart at the joints in a minor accident, even with the normal stresses of riding. Better frames, if damaged, will bend, not break; a good mechanic can often bend one back into shape.

The frame tubes that hold the rear wheel are stressed most highly at their forward ends, near the saddle and cranks. In better frames, these tubes are tapered—larger at the forward ends, smaller at the ends that are closer to the hub of the rear wheel. Notice how these tubes are attached near the hub: on cheaper frames, the ends of the tubes will be squashed flat against the sides of the metal plates (called dropouts) that hold the ends of the hub's axle; on better frames, the tubes will be slotted, rounded, and fitted to the dropouts.

The best frames have rear-wheel attachments that are tapered—larger at the forward end, smaller at the end closest to the hub—like the one pictured here.

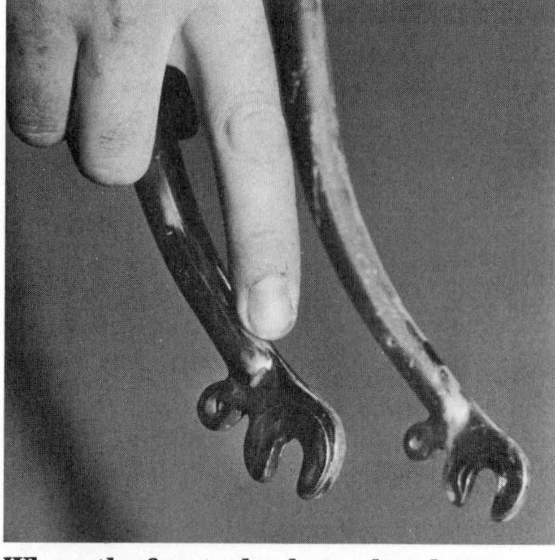

Where the front wheel attaches, better frames have dropout plates, like the one shown here.

On cheaper frames, the ends of the tubes where the rear wheel attaches will be squashed flat, denoting poor-quality workmanship.

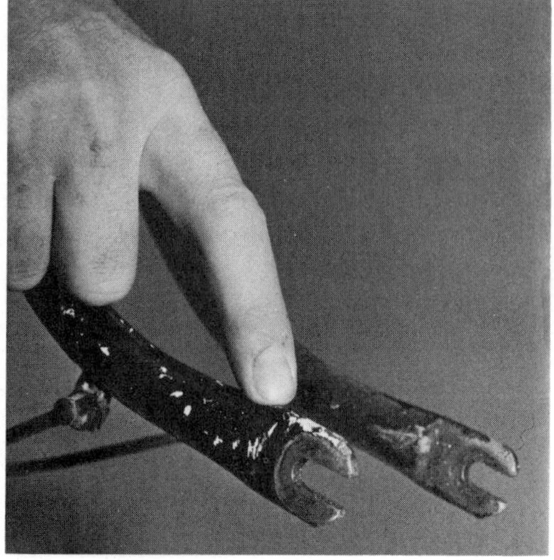

Cheaper frames have front fork tubes that are merely squashed flat and slotted to hold the ends of the axle.

Where the front wheel attaches, better frames have dropout plates. Cheaper ones have none—the front fork tubes are simply squashed flat and slotted to hold the ends of the axle.

Because of their higher quality of materials and construction, better frames are both lighter and stronger (although the lightest, double-butted frames are not worth the premium price for general use). Usually, frames of bicycles sold at bike shops are of decent quality.

The bicycle industry is unusual in that the frame is usually the only part of the bicycle made by the company under whose brand name it is sold. Raleigh, Schwinn, Peugeot, Atala, Fuji, and other makes buy parts such as brakes, hubs, rims, cranks, and handlebars (called components) from outside suppliers. Your choice between bicycles may depend more on the components than on the brand name. Some suppliers have better reputations than others. Here are some guidelines for evaluating components.

As for the *crankset* (cranks and front chainwheels), Sugino and Takagi are common, with parts widely available. T.A., Campagnolo, and Stronglight are common but more expensive. Some quality brands are less desirable because replacement parts are harder to find: S.R. (except models compatible with Sugino and Stronglight chainwheels), Shimano, and Nervar (except the steel three-arm Nervar crankset, which is very common).

Derailleurs are usually replaced rather than repaired, so parts availability is not a concern. SunTour and Shimano make highly regarded, inexpensive derailleurs, and there are too many other brands to list here. The model to use depends on the gear ratios on your bike. Consult a bike shop.

The sprockets in a *freewheel* (at the rear hub) can be replaced individually, and you can switch them if you need different gears. SunTour sprockets are very widely available. Regina and Atom are reasonably available and compatible with each other. Other brands may be hard to come by.

A good-quality Campagnolo side-pull brake.

A cheap side-pull brake found on a department-store bike.

Pedals are generally replaced rather than repaired, except for the most expensive ones. Avoid pedals with vulnerable reflectors that hang down.

Except in cases of accidental damage, only the friction pads of *brakes* usually need replacement. Most brands of aluminum brakes are of acceptable quality, if kept well adjusted. Stay away from bikes with steel brakes, except on three-speeds with reputable brand names.

Sturmey-Archer and SunTour three-speed *hubs* are reliable, and every bike shop has replacement parts. Avoid Shimano three-speed hubs. They have a reputation for breakdowns, and replacement parts are hard to get. Fichtel and Sachs are well designed and common in Europe, but parts are scarce in the United States.

As for front hubs, and rear hubs for derailleur-geared bicycles, Atom, Maillard, Normandy, Sanshin, and Campagnolo parts are widely available. Avoid unusual hubs and cheap steel hubs. If replacement bearing parts are not available, it may be necessary to respoke an entire wheel on a new hub—an expensive job.

To sum up, note the simplicity and economy of design of the highest-quality bicycles, the ones expert bicyclists choose. Your bicycle's components may be heavier and of slightly less refined design, but they should reflect the same principles. Some component manufacturers—notably Shimano—try to lure new customers by offering mechanical features that are claimed to make bicycling easier: special "positive-shifting" derailleurs, brake extension levers, airless tires that can't go flat, aerodynamic parts, and so forth. Such features are a trap. A so-called new model of positive-shift derailleur comes out every year as the old ones break down—and replacement parts are unavailable. Brake extension levers and stem-mounted shifters are hard to control. (If you can't reach normal brake levers, you just need a handlebar stem with a shorter forward extension. The stem is the L-shaped piece that clamps the handlebars at the center.) Airless tires quickly damage rims because they are solid and can't swallow bumps as air-filled tires do. Even the common kickstand can lead to a bent frame if the pedals back into it. Stick with what's tried and true.

How can you tell steel from aluminum in shopping for components? Steel often carries a mirrorlike chrome-plated finish, and it will attract a magnet. Steel components are usually built up of folded and riveted sheets of metal. Components made of aluminum (called *alloy* by bicyclists) have a softer, pearly gray finish and bulkier, sculptured contours. To achieve the same strength as steel, aluminum components must be bulkier—but they are nonetheless lighter in weight.

While components of fine quality may be made of either steel or aluminum, knowledgeable bicyclists demand light weight and consequently favor aluminum. Most steel components made for derailleur-geared bicycles are of the lowest quality and wear out quickly.

With three-speed and one-speed bicycles, the choice is not so clear. Since these are not intended for competitive or long-distance riding, weight matters less. As long as you stick with reputable brands sold through bike shops, steel components are likely to be of serviceable quality.

Aluminum has its greatest advantage in wheel rims. It increases maneuverability and acceleration. It adds to wet-weather safety, as brakes work much better on aluminum rims (although one- or three-speed bikes can rely on a hub brake). Bent aluminum rims can almost always be straightened, while steel rims must usually be replaced. Generally, only derailleur-equipped bicycles costing $250 or more are equipped with aluminum rims; but if you are buying a bicycle of this type for more than occasional use, you would be wise to spend this much.

Tires and rims of 27 inches and 700C are available in widths from 1¼ inches down to 1 inch and below. Unless you are enough of a bicycling expert that you do not need to be reading this, buy your derailleur-geared bicycle with 1¼-inch-wide tires. The tires and rims are the most abused and most easily damaged of bicycle parts. Extra-narrow tires give a slight increase in performance at the expense of a greater likelihood of flats and dented rims.

Long-term durability

As mentioned earlier, bike frames are largely standardized. When you take your bicycle in for an overhaul—next year or 20 years from now—you may have to replace entire components if small replacement parts are unavailable, but you will be able to keep your bike running indefinitely, unless the frame is damaged beyond repair. And even if you do have to scrap a bicycle, you can still salvage many useful parts, selling them or storing them away as replacements for your next bicycle. Because it is a collection of replaceable components, a bicycle is one of the most durable products you can buy. Still, entire bicycles are junked with perfectly serviceable parts still on them.

You can cut your maintenance expenses drastically by keeping a stock of parts. You can even take advantage of other people's mistakes by collecting the parts they have thrown out. Many riders will use these parts to upgrade their bikes instead of buying new ones.

A bicycle needs more maintenance than many machines because it is built lighter in the interest of self-propulsion. If designed to go five years without maintenance, like a washing machine or refrigerator, a bike would weigh so much you wouldn't want to ride it.

There are certain tools and supplies you should automatically buy with your bicycle: a frame-mounted pump, patch kit, and tire irons to repair flat tires; a tire-pressure gauge; a few small hand tools; and chain lubricant. The bike shop will probably be able to sell you the right tools for your bicycle in a convenient tool pouch you can carry with you when you ride.

Listen for rattles and squeaks. A bicycle in good condition is quiet, except for the ticking of the rear wheel when it is freewheeling. Experienced riders know that a sound means something either is about to fall off or is wearing and needs lubrication. Fortunately, the machinery of the bicycle can be seen and heard, and almost any problem will make itself known.

Children's bicycles

Because children's bicycles get plenty of abuse, they should be especially durable. A relatively new type of children's bicycle, the BMX (bicycle motocross), is rugged and widely available. Wide, deep tires protect the wheels from curbs and rocks. The frame is reinforced with steel plates, and the simple one-speed running gear is trouble-free.

Look for a children's bicycle with straight frame tubes and a small racing-type saddle. Curved tubes and a long "banana" saddle are typical of the earlier "high-riser" bicycle, which is less durable and less safe to ride. To withstand curb impacts, a one-piece steel "Ashtabula" crank, used on many brands, is best.

If your child wants to travel faster to keep up on longer, family trips, small three-speed and ten-speed bikes may be the best choice. Your example and participation will encourage your child to make good use of these less-durable bikes.

JOHN S. ALLEN

Bicycles for adults

"Kids are given bikes as toys, not as transportation. This childish attitude carries over into adulthood."

An interview with John Schubert

John Schubert is senior editor of *Bicycling* magazine. We interviewed him in *Bicycling's* testing shop, where a score of bicycles clutter the floor or hang dismembered from the ceiling. His legs were shaved clean ("These days most bike racers shave their legs," Schubert says, "because if you fall off your bike it's easier to clean and bandage a shaved leg, and you can also get a better leg massage"), and he wore a clinging pair of bicycle-racer's shorts.

BK

I'd say that a medium-priced bike, costing between $225 and $500, is probably going to be more durable than bikes costing more or less. Above that range, you'll pay extra money to get stuff like these skinny little tires that weigh less but get flats easily; there are lots of delicate parts like that on an expensive bike. When you pay less than $225 or so, you're getting something that isn't as well built. Millions of little details are made poorly on cheap bikes. Some cheaper derailleurs have parts mashed against each other with a rivet in between. That rivet is the pivot in that joint. You start to get slop in that joint (and all these little joints get slop in them), and all of a sudden the thing wobbles from side to side when you grab it. It won't last as long. Every component in a cheap bike is like that. But as an example of durability, take Campagnolo. Campy is irrelevant to most people, because their products are so expensive—but here is a Campagnolo derailleur that's almost ten years old and there's no slop in it at all. Try and twist that.

On the other hand, look at a Simplex derailleur, made in France. When the riveted-in pivots get slop in them, you throw the derailleur away. With the Campagnolo, you can buy replacement pivots and repair the derailleur. It'll work like new.

A bike is always one manufacturer's frame and other suppliers' components. So, a bike's manufacturer is only one of many companies responsible for the product. Most frames are guaranteed for life. Obviously, very few people collect on the guarantee. I've been wondering lately whether a bike frame can get deadened, like guitar strings, after much use. I've concluded that it can. When you stand on the pedals and stomp, the frame is less rigid and flexes more, which is very undesirable. There's nothing in metallurgy to support the notion that a frame will become less rigid and feel dead after it's been used for years, but bike riders know otherwise.

You can look at a department-store bike and see how crude the brakes are and how hard they'll be to adjust. Design defects are most often discovered by looking for poor workmanship. In general, bikes are not made like they used to be. The bikes that Captain Kangaroo used to talk about when we were kids were like tanks, and it's easy to make a bike like that durable. But how do you make a ten-speed durable? There's a lot more stuff on a ten-speed, and a lot less weight.

I haven't really done much work on inexpensive American ten-speed bikes, like Huffys, but every time I do, I find some poorly executed detail that bothers me. For example, the threads on the screws aren't cut very well, so when you go to fix something, the thread strips. The axles are low-quality steel. They bend. There are dozens of little details like this that a novice wouldn't check for. That's why a Schwinn Varsity costs $100 more than a Huffy that looks the same to the untrained eye. Schwinn spends more time and money to make its bikes durable.

Bill Keisling

John Schubert.

Parents would be better off buying their children a durable one-speed like Schwinn rather than a cheap ten-speed. There's lots of stuff on a ten-speed that a kid's not going to take care of. My neighbor has a ten-speed bike which I'm sure she can't maintain. I changed a flat tire for her the other day, and it was the first time she's ridden the thing with adequate air pressure. Her tires were like sponges. You could push your thumb all the way through to the rim. I had a pile of old tires in my basement, so I gave her two and pumped them up to 90 pounds of pressure each. The point is, that kind of casual neglect will cause lots of problems. She didn't oil the chain, so it'll get rusty and stretch and wear out. It's squeaky, annoying to use, and wears on the chainwheels. Aluminum chainwheels can get chewed up really fast, and they cost as much as $45 to replace.

That's why people finally throw their bikes away. Say you bought a bike for $150 a few years ago. It gets old and worn out and you take it to a bike shop, and they tell you both your rims are really bad and you have to buy two new wheels, tires, and tubes. Your rear derailleur is rusted. You have to replace your chain and your freewheel. That's more than $150. It's an economic decision to sell the bike. The bike still works, but it's not worth the money it would cost for repairs.

Maintaining a bike is real important. I guess I have a bias. I think being able to fix a bike is so easy that people who say they can't learn aren't being rational. Day-to-day preventative maintenance pays off handsomely, and it isn't very challenging. Get a good book and the right tools, and you'll see it's easy.

Kids own most of the bikes in America, and they treat them poorly. Go to a baseball field and look at the condition of the bikes there. Kids are given bikes as toys, not as transportation. This childish attitude carries over into adulthood.

There are adults who buy bikes the way they buy a Cuisinart food processor or a microwave oven. It's trendy and they have to have one. They'll spend a couple of grand on a single bike. They don't need a bike like that; they just want to own it for status. But most adults take their bikes seriously. They might not want to use toe clips and stuff like that—they might just buy a three-speed and ride sedately—but they'll take reasonable care of it.

What kind of a bike do I own? I own several. I have an old Motobecane touring bike. That's the bike I rode across the continent. I bought it in 1972 for $300. I have a cheap Peugeot racing bike in the car that cost me about $350. I also have a J. C. Higgins, which is a Sears three-speed, circa 1960. I got that at a flea market. And my touring tandem.

What kind of care do I take of my bikes? Very poor. My bikes could use some work. It's like they say: The cobbler's children go barefoot.”

A dozen bicycle tires compared

I've wanted to write a piece on bicycle tires for years. The problem was to develop a satisfactory method of testing tire performance.

In the summer of 1980, I got my answer in a phone call from Harlan Chapman, a Category II bike racer and a junior at the University of California, Santa Cruz. He was organizing a cross-country bicycle tour as a fund raiser for the Santa Cruz Hostel Society. Like most college bike racers, the tour group was short of cash. Could I help them and the Hostel Society by supplying tires and tubes?

The tour took 30 days and covered 3,000 miles. Each day, four riders pedaled and one drove the sagwagon; each morning, the riders switched wheels (and tires) on their bikes; each evening, they wrote down their feeling about the tires they'd ridden that day. The tires were switched in pairs. When a pair of tires had between 950 and 1,000 miles, it was replaced with the next set. Thus, by the end of the tour, each rider had ridden each of the 12 sets of tires two or three times for a total of about 250 miles.

The riders' opinions of tire performance were quite consistent. They found that wide (27 × 1¼) tires wear longer, ride more comfortably, get fewer flats, and are harder to pedal. Wide tires provide a safe, forgiving ride on all kinds of road surfaces. Narrow (27 × 1) tires feel more responsive, are easier to pedal, give a harsher ride, and get more flats. Narrow tires are the best choice for experienced riders on smooth pavement.

We were scrupulous about inflation pressure for this test. It was held exactly at the rating. Each tire was inflated with a Medai tank-type pump every morning before starting off. You, however, should experiment a bit with inflation pressure. Generally, heavy riders with heavy loads should try 5 or 10 extra psi, especially on the rear tire. Both over- and underinflation cause tires to wear out prematurely. (Reading through the riders' comments, I noticed many more "soft and soggy" comments than "harsh and hard." So I checked Harlan's Medai pump pressure gauge against three of my pressure gauges after the tour was over. It read about 8 psi low at 100 psi. I suspect that the mileage and performance evaluations were done with the tires inflated 6 or 7 psi under their maximum ratings.)

Tire mileage depends on tire design, weight on the tire, inflation pressure, and severity of service. Most of us get about three times as much wear from a front tire than from a rear. Obviously, mileage can't be predicted exactly.

At the conclusion of the tour, all of the rear tires were returned to me, and I approximated tread life as follows. First, I measured the average tread thickness on several new tires. Then I measured the average tread thickness on the worn 1,000-mile rear tire. The difference was the amount of treadwear in 1,000 miles. Then I took the worn tires and abraded away the tread with a wire brush until the cord just showed through. This difference—between 1,000-mile thickness and worn-out thickness—represented the treadwear remaining. The mileage in the table was calculated from the ratio of 1,000-mile tread to total tread.

As the tread wears from a tire, the "footprint" becomes wider, and (I suspect) the rate of treadwear per mile decreases. Most tires will probably give 10 percent or so more miles than my figures indicate.

Many riders, however, don't run their tires until the cord shows through. (Those who do will get a lot of extra punctures in the last few hundred miles.) So, all in all, I think that the table gives a reasonable estimate of the kind of wear the average rider can expect from a rear tire.

How a dozen bike tires compare

Make and model	Marked size	Inflation pressure (psi)	Estimated mileage	Performance (0-worst, 5-best) Smooth roads	Rough roads, gravel	Riders' comments
SBI Touring Turbo	27 × 1⅛	95	1,800	4.5	2.0	Minimum rolling resistance; very responsive; felt alive; firm, stiff ride
IRC Roadlite	27 × 1 × 1¼	100	2,200	4.1	2.0	Low rolling resistance; super-responsive; handles exceptionally well; corners well
Panasonic 100 (Racing Extra)	27 × 1¼ × 1	100	1,600	3.8	2.0	Little rolling resistance; light, responsive feel; handles well
Silver Star Trimline	27 × 1	95	1,400	3.7	2.0	Less responsive than Turbo; enjoyable, light; handles well
Michelin Chevron 50	27 × 1¼	90	2,100	3.5	4.0	Medium rolling resistance, very firm for this size tire; rugged and durable for rough roads
IRC Super HP	27 × 1⅛	100	1,600	3.3	3.0	Lively, but noticeable drop in performance from narrow tires; good handling; good in gravel
Michelin Elan TS	27 × 1	95	2,400	3.0	2.0	Little rolling resistance but mushy feel; fairly responsive; feels soft, comfortable
Schwinn HP LeTour	27 × 1¼	85	2,800	2.7	4.0	Medium rolling resistance; rides well; firm and positive; durable touring tire
Schwinn 250 Super Record	27 × 1⅛	90	1,300	2.3	3.0	More rolling resistance than the LeTour; rides well but feels heavy
SBI Touring X	27 × 1¼	95	2,500	2.0	5.0	Heavy, hard to push; not too responsive; good tire for heavy loads; good on rough roads
Hutchinson HP 22	27 × 1	100	2,300	1.5	2.0	Hard to pedal; feels soft on all road surfaces; feels mushy even with 100 psi
Panasonic 85 (Open Side)	27 × 1¼	85	3,000	1.4	4.0	Very safe and slow; high rolling resistance; makes hills seem steeper; good on rough roads

The testers kept close track of every puncture. I was surprised that they only had 12, about 1 puncture every 1,000 miles. I average about 3 punctures per 1,000 miles, so I must not be very careful in avoiding puncture hazards.

Because there were so few punctures, I haven't listed which tires got flats. The eight narrow, high-pressure tires got ten flats, and the four wide tires got two flats. I think that's significant. If you absolutely want to minimize flats, pick fat tires.

FRANK BERTO

All photos, courtesy of Adirondack Museum

Guideboats were built far lighter than their sea-going counterparts for one purpose—to ease the portages between the Adirondacks' navigable waterways.

How to minimize flats

1. Use a good rim tape. This is particularly important with the new box-section rims, because they have such big holes for the spokes. I find that two layers of fiberglass-reinforced strapping tape work well on these rims.
2. If you don't have box-section rims, grind or file off any spoke ends that protrude through the nipples.
3. Make sure that the inner-tube valve stem is bottomed on the rim. If you find a puncture right next to the valve stem, it probably means that the valve wasn't pulled all the way through the valve hole and the rubber was stretched. Note that you can't use tubes with bolted-on metal valves with the new narrow rims. There isn't room for the nut and washer in the rims' dropped center.
4. Always install your tubes with talcum powder.
5. Use a tube that matches the tire—smaller lightweight 27 × 1 tubes with the narrow tires and larger heavier 27 × 1¼ tubes with the fatter tires. The same size tubes fit both 27-inch and 700C tires.
6. When you fix a tire, always find and fix whatever caused the flat.
7. Install the tires with your hands, not with tire irons. If you have to use tire irons, your mounting technique is probably incorrect.

A BOAT

The Adirondack guideboat

Seventy-five or 100 years is nothing for a piece of fine furniture that remains under cover indoors, protected from the weather and accidental damage. But it is entirely different with boats that must endure scorching sun and drying winds, that are periodically soaked with rain and frozen in winter, buffeted and tossed about by waves, and sometimes hurled up on rocky shores. There is luck in it, true, but in the final analysis, such boats have lasted because they were intended to last.

The *Ghost*, on exhibit at the Adirondack Museum of Blue Mountain Lake, New York, is no disembodied spirit but a substantial 16-foot Adirondack guideboat. Built by H. Dwight Grant of Boonville in the winter of 1881-82, it is still sound and tight, and ready to be launched. This boat is by no means an exceptional case. Scores of well-preserved nineteenth-century guideboats continue to serve at camps and lodges throughout the Adirondacks. Their endurance is especially remarkable when you consider that guideboats are built of wood, a biodegradable material prone to decay, that they were very lightly constructed to keep down weight for portaging across wilderness carries, and that they are called upon to withstand hard use both in the water and on the carry.

In this effete age, when nearly everything produced wears out quickly because it is intended to wear out quickly, the longevity of these old boats is something to reflect upon. They have lasted because they were meant to last. They are the product of an era that demanded quality and abhorred waste of any sort. Such a thing as planned obsolescence had not then been thought of, but if it had, it would have had no appeal for guideboat builders. They would have rejected the idea as both dishonest and egregiously foolish.

As delicate as fine-boned bat wings, these newly built guideboats await their first touch of Adirondack water. Today, boats such as these from the old Hanmer boatshop in Saranac Lake, New York, will bring 10 to 50 times their original price.

Almost all the famous guideboat builders were North Woods guides who began by building boats for their own use. It frequently took a guide an entire winter to build his boat. Often the family helped out. Grandmothers and young children placed the thousands of tiny copper tacks, or sanded.

Material for North Woods boats came from the North Woods, and was selected with painstaking care. Only timber from the choicest well-grown trees would do. Stems and ribs were produced from the curving grain of huge, well-rooted red-spruce stumps—the strongest wood for its weight that grows on this continent. The $^5/_{16}$-inch planking was rift sawn, to minimize swell and shrinking, from the heartwood of mammoth butt logs of old-growth cork pine.

Guideboats are not the only small wooden craft that have lasted. There are planked-up cedar canoes still floating, staunch and tight and sleekly varnished, that came out of J. Henry Rushton's Canton, New York, boatshop nearly a century ago. Whitehalls, fan-tail launches, and St. Lawrence River skiffs, to name others, have also endured.

Nor should we overlook vintage yachts. Still sailing and winning races are those built and designed by L. Francis Herreshoff, the eminent designer, around the turn of the century and shortly after. Writing on yacht construction in his later years and after a lifetime of experience, Herreshoff admonished the young student who might have the opportunity to go aboard a well-preserved yacht 40 or 50 years old, "[Go with] eyes open, hat in hand, and head bowed in reverence, for here is the work of someone who understood wood." An old boat is the work of someone who built honestly and for the future, one who was a true builder and not a spoiler, a giver and not merely a taker.

Old boats become more than boats. In a deeper sense they are monuments to an ethic that abhors waste, to a practice that supports and extends the means for life, rather than exploiting and squandering them.

JOHN GARDNER

Warren Cole, the imposing guide and boatbuilder on the right in this view of the 1899 Sportsmen's Show in New York City, took seriously his summertime profession as guide. He apprehended a man known to have molested a woman vacationer while posing as a guide, and when the imposter tried to escape in a boat, Cole shot him. The Old Blue Giant, as Cole was known, once sawed down a monstrous white pine that was to provide him with enough planks for some eight years of boatbuilding. The tree cost him $10 and measured six feet through.

DEAR SIR,

AT LAST MY WIFE HAS FOUND A WAY TO PUT A ZIPPO OUT OF OPERATION. A SHORT TIME AGO SHE WAS TRIMMING THE LAWN WITH A POWER MOWER AND SHE DROPPED MY ZIPPO ON THE LAWN. SHE DID NOT MISS THE ZIPPO UNTIL THE LAWN MOWER CAME TO A SCREAMING HALT, AFTER WHICH SHE CALLED FOR ASSISTANCE. WHEN I DISCOVERED WHAT HAD HAPPENED I "BLEW MY TOP" BECAUSE I WAS OUT ONE DAMNED GOOD ZIPPO. SHE REPLIED, WITH GRIPING NAIVETE, "WHAT THE HELL ARE YOU YELPING ABOUT, ZIPPO GUARANTEES THEIR LIGHTERS!!!". I ANSWERED, WITH STUDIED CALM, "YES, ZIPPO DOES GUARANTEE THE LIGHTERS THEY MANUFACTURE BUT NOT AGAINST A FEMALE PLOW JOCKEY ABOARD A POWER MOWER!!!" (MY HEAD IS BETTER NOW).

AFTER SHE RETURNED FROM GOING "HOME TO MOTHER" SHE BOUGHT ME ANOTHER ZIPPO WITH THE PROVISO THAT I SEND HER "HANDIWORK" TO YOU SO THAT SHE CAN PROVE HER POINT ON ZIPPO'S GUARANTEE.

EVEN THOUGH SHE HAS BOUGHT ME ANOTHER ZIPPO I CAN'T BE SURE THAT I GAINED A DAMNED THING BECAUSE NOW SHE REFUSES TO COME WITHIN HAILING DISTANCE OF THE LAWN MOWER. IT TOOK ME TWO YEARS TO CONVINCE HER OF THE BENEFITS OF CUTTING THE LAWN (??) AND NOW SHE SAYS, IN ESSENCE, "CUT THE DAMNED LAWN YOURSELF AND YOU GET THE BENEFITS!"

THANKS FOR READING THIS, I APPRECIATE YOUR INTEREST.

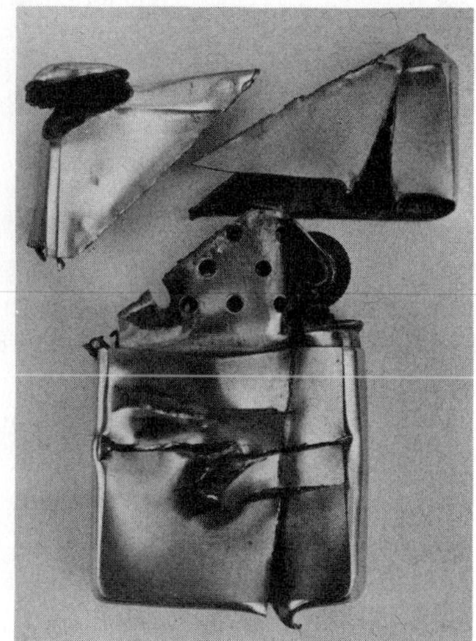

CLOTHING AS AN INVESTMENT

4

Beyond keeping us warm and modest, clothing makes a statement to the world, proclaiming our station in life, our values, our mood of the moment. While any of our possessions may be read for a message, clothes are more richly symbolic than the rest. In fashion we have not only an outlet for creativity, but the first phrase in any conversation, a boast or an apology. Even to dress in denial of fashion is, really, to make a statement: clothing is the flag of the eccentric, the shell of the wallflower.

Historically, clothing tends to be as practical as the wearer is poor, as elaborate as the wearer is well-off. That's because discretionary income, if there is any, goes toward padding the closet; the dozens of blouses and shirts, dresses and suits, shoes and accessories become a vocabulary. Carrying this burden of self-expression, our wardrobes are apt to change as frequently as we change our politics or our moods. Is durability appropriate here? After all, we don't trot out the same conversations season after season, or if we do, we are judged bores. How far are we to take durability?

For that majority of us who fall somewhere between poor and rich, clothes are both practical and fashionable, and as today's incomes wilt before inflated prices, practicality is taking precedence over style.

"The days of the fad garment are gone," Thomas Haas, vice-president at the Wool Bureau, has said. "Today, people are buying garments as they would a car." (And, it might be noted, they're buying cars as they would a house.)

Fortunately, the notion of a "classic" style comes to the rescue. Last seen on college campuses in the 1950s, the classic look has resurfaced in response to the need for a simple and serviceable fashion that won't be totally revamped each season. The elements of this style—cotton-knit Alligator-type and Oxford-cloth shirts, crew-neck sweaters, navy blazers, chinos, penny loafers and sneakers—offer a comfortable middle ground to both refugees from high-priced high fashion and graduates from the radical-chic, conspicuous-nonconsumption rags of the 1960s.

It is not coincidental that these clothes tend to be well constructed, of good materials; that lines are simple so that you won't tire of them; that colors are muted and don't advertise dirt and stains; that most are easily washed and maintained (and some are actually considered to look better with age, as is true of sneakers, blue jeans, leather garments, and even good haircuts).

Striking a comfortable truce between fashion and function

Classics come in vogue when money is tight, because cautious shoppers look for quality clothes they won't mind being seen in next year or the year after. They view their purchases as an investment, a hedge against lean times. While long fashion life should be matched by durable materials and construction, this isn't necessarily the case. As this book is written, the enduring classic, or so-called preppy, look is in fashion, and some apparel companies are exploiting the look without delivering the implied quality.

These classic "sports clothes" were originally designed to have some stamina, but the look has been appropriated by both cheap chain stores and prestigious designers, so that you can buy a "wool-look" blazer for under $40 or a designer edition for over $300. It's not easy to pick out the durable, reasonably priced items from the clones at either end of the price range. This chapter suggests how to check for a sturdy fabric that you can live with, carefully executed construction, and a proper fit. The search for the good stuff is made trickier by the complex structure of the apparel industry. Some labels carry the assurance of quality, some don't. A clothier may make all of its line (Woolrich), some of it (L. L. Bean), or none of it (most designer-label garments are farmed out to piece-rate factories here and abroad). Neither does the price tag necessarily tell you a great deal. A vastly expensive designer blouse is likely made on the same machine by the same worker to the same specifications as one costing a fraction as much. The fabric may or may not be better.

As sure as winter follows autumn, the tide of durability-chic will ebb. Venerable L. L. Bean, known for its line of durable outdoorsy clothes, has resisted expanding to meet the sudden demand for solid and sensible clothing because it sees the public's mood as fickle; within the near future, demand will return to

Springer/Bettmann Film Archive

Originating in World War I, the trench coat is still a standard item in a man's or woman's wardrobe. Here's Humphrey Bogart in the 1942 movie, *Casablanca*.

near its original level. Traditional, quality clothiers report that business is stable through good times and lean times. For J. Press, a New York men's store whose lapel widths have varied but a quarter inch over the past three decades, regular customers continue to come in at a time when the sales of cheaper clothing have fallen off.

Well-made clothes can be looked upon as a true investment, one that yields financial savings over the years as well as warmth and style. The all-wool suit lasts its owner an average of more than six years, according to a survey by the Cy Chaikin Research Group, whereas suits of a wool blend are kept for just over four years and polyester suits for three and a half. At average prices of $216, $175, and $137 respectively, the all-wool suit turns out to give the most wear for the money.

RY

FASHIONING A TEN-YEAR WARDROBE

Two hundred years ago, clothing for work, play, leisure, and sport were one and the same, except possibly in the case of aristocrats and the exceedingly wealthy. A Welsh coal miner of the 1830s lived and worked through the year in the same shirt. So did blacksmiths, coopers, merchants, farmers, surveyors, and indentured servants. Seamen and soldiers could not run to a post exchange for new issuances of clothing. Men and women lived for years on the Colonial American frontier without a fashionable haberdashery around the corner. Clothing had to last.

Examine a shirt of the period and you'll see why such clothing was so durable. The fabric was linen, wool, or both yarns woven together into what was called linsey-woolsey.

"You know, this is my oldest friend."

J. Monture-Knecht

Shown here is a week's worth of wages for a young man during the colonial period. Although the cost of clothing has gone down proportionately over the last two centuries, so has the quality of fabric, construction, and finishing.

Linen is an exceptionally strong fabric (even when wet), very absorbent, lint-free, cool to wear in the summer months, and characterized by an attractive natural luster. Wool is also a durable cloth, and one of the best natural insulators; warm and absorbent in the winter, it dries from the inside out. Linsey-woolsey combines an animal and a vegetable fiber to give the good qualities of both.

Assembly is crucial to durability, too; all sewing was performed by hand, using a variety of techniques ranging from the tight, nonraveling backstitch to the simple running stitch. The seams were usually flat felled, whereby one of the inside ragged edges was clipped and folded under to one side of the seam, and the other edge was sewn over so that there were no exposed raw edges of fabric to wear or fray. Each seam was essentially double stitched. Hems and linings were further reinforced by top-stitching–a line sewn around all edges, openings, cuffs, and collars to hold the layered fabric together. Shirts were designed to be full and blousy, with many pleats, and the resultant looseness insured minimal stress at seams and joints. Styles, especially in shirts, changed little from year to year, if at all (although in the upper classes fashion was a preoccupation).

Cotton was little used, except by the well-to-do, because it had to be imported from Egypt and India and was a luxury. But wool and linen were everywhere, in every garment worn by the noblest monarch and the lowliest pauper. Wool and linen lasted.

Yet, relative to today, the price paid for clothing seems outrageously high. Consider the plight of a British textile worker of the eighteenth century as an example. The English weaving industry of 1770 paid a typical salary of seven shillings to men (half that for women and still less for children) for a week of 60 to 80 hours. A yard of the cheapest fabric woven, wool broadcloth, cost nearly a quarter of this wage. The ten yards of fabric that went into a no-frills suit of men's clothing (including long coat, knee-length breeches, and short waistcoat) could consume two and a half weeks' salary.

Today, plant workers earn in the neighborhood of $200 to $300 per week on the starting level, more if unionized, and can purchase a very durable set of clothing for half that. But along with greater purchasing power has come a preoccupation with style. This point is made clearly

---

The polyester generation discovers cotton and wool

Inflation apparently has a positive effect on clothing durability, according to Joan Courtless, family economist with the USDA. Americans are buying fewer items, and they're consciously looking for styles and fabrics that last.

As long as inflation outsteps income, enduring and traditional designs should continue to find favor. Among these, says Courtless, are "Shetland wool crew- or V-neck sweaters, Oxford-cloth shirts, and blazers of madras or tartan plaids. Other plaids will be subtle or merged, including muted greens and blues." And although less-expensive grades of velour and terry saturated the market early on, "those of better quality are made mostly of cotton and are expected to retain their popularity. . . . Knitwear, which is warm and practical, will be fashionable with Argyle, jacquard, and intarsia patterns." The warmth and practicality of cashmere were responsible for a tripling of both demand for it and its price.

Still, many people are familiar only with synthetics, says Velda Rankin, national clothing and textile specialist with the USDA. "We have a generation of homemakers who haven't experienced wool, silk, and other natural fibers." And they haven't had access to top-quality construction, according to Jane Winge, clothing and textile specialist at North Dakota State University. Truly well made clothes were last seen in the 1940s and '50s. "Wool garments, in particular, had quality construction, and we have left them behind."

---

by the popularity of the $69 all-polyester suit, thrown together in Taiwan or Korea. Is our lot really much better than that of the 1770 British textile worker? On the surface, the prices he paid seem unthinkable, but then his clothing was functional, durable, and easily maintained. The fabrics were stout and the hand stitchery attested to quality. Seasonal styles did not compel him to buy a new suit before his own had worn out.

Although machines do not quite give us the quality possible through hand work, long-lasting clothes are still being made. Where do you look?

David Morgan, a clothier whose imported fashions reflect time-honored ethnic and domestic styling, says, "The integrity of the retailer, who's in a better position than the public to pick quality, should be the consumer's main concern when choosing clothing outlets." His mail-order offerings are obviously sturdy and functional, almost severely so, and include British North Sea sweaters, double-backed logging shirts, and Welsh welder's smocks. These tops are of a very full cut, reflecting a concern for function over style.

Eddie Bauer, Inc., is a manufacturer and retailer of expedition and sport clothing. The company works closely with mills to produce durable fabrics, and their research-and-development department conducts rigorous field tests of new or proposed garments. Bauer outfits expeditions, then studies each member's reactions and examines garments for flaws such as frozen zippers, failed seams, or fabric wear. Any problems that come to light are rectified before the garment is offered to the public. They're not a fashion-oriented company, explains Abbie Anderson, director of advertising. "Every product that we offer is designed to be functional, including leisure wear."

Brooks Brothers is a New York retailer distinguished by careful selection of fabrics, threads, linings, and interfacings, involving laboratory analysis for fabric wearability, hand finishing, color permanence, and definition. Their clothing selection is crafted primarily of wool-polyester, cotton-polyester, and linen-polyester blends, but offerings of top-quality woolens, worsteds, cottons, and silks expand their line. Durability at Brooks Brothers is the by-product of firm foundations in suits, careful fittings, and quality fabrics and threads (silk threads are used for resilience and seam strength in their top-of-the-line suit models). Equally important is the durability of style, characterized by natural shoulder tailoring (not boxy or padded), soft lines and comfortable fit, and an air of understatement that is an element of the so-called classic look. Their ties are 100 percent silk, lined with wool and chosen with a mind to

---

63 percent narrow lapels

Researchers from the University of Nevada at Reno recently alerted men to an inexpensive source of fashionable business wear.

The researchers have discovered the thrift shop. Sport coats and suits that end up there have been banished from the closets of style-conscious men, and as styles come full circle, the embarrassingly skinny lapels of yesteryear now look quite smart.

Designers haven't succeeded in getting men to pursue a new look each season—the only major style change in men's suit jackets in 40 years has been lapel width, and this grows and recedes with glacial slowness. Still, men are acutely sensitive to the width of these vestigial flaps. An extra quarter-inch of fabric can make a man look like a card shark or a bumpkin.

The Reno people examined the offerings at local thrift shops and found that 63 percent of the suit jackets and sport coats had satisfactorily narrow lapels.

---

lasting appeal. Their pure-cotton shirts are full cut from fine fabric and carefully sewn; the moderate collar lengths withstand the whims of fashion. "In choosing the basic wardrobe for business or weekend wear," says Mark Zoilo, vice-president of Brooks Brothers clothing division, "it should be timeless." That's a challenge, in the face of seasonal changes in lapel and tie widths, collar length, and colors. Zoilo points out that he still wears ten-year-old Brooks Brothers suits fashionably from season to season.

As this is written, the apparel industry witnesses a growing preference for natural fibers. Are synthetic fibers all bad, in all applications? A silky polyester or nylon shirt will not hold up as long as a cotton one, either in repeated washings, flame retardancy (the fabric will melt on the skin if ignited), seam strength, or styling. But a shirt made of a cotton-poly blend (65 percent cotton/35 percent polyester)–for instance, a white Oxford button-down made of stout broadcloth–should wear longer than all-cotton. The blend can be bleached whereas the polyester cannot, and it even saves you energy by requiring less drying and ironing than an all-cotton version. However, all-cotton garments are more comfortable against the body, absorb moisture, and insulate better than synthetic fabrics.

Woolens also have special qualities not duplicated by synthetics. Wool insulates the body even when the garment is wet. Manufacturers are beginning to mix synthetics in wool fabric, in blends such as 85 percent wool/15 percent nylon, or 70 percent wool/30 percent polyester; although the insulating properties are compromised somewhat, these blends permit gentle machine washing and tumble drying, and stabilize the garment's shape over time.

Wool on the rebound

Christie C. Tito

Old Pendleton shirts never die, they're just handed down. Bob Kneeland models a wool Pendleton his grandfather bought in the 1940s.

Pendleton Woolen Mills of Portland, Oregon, has been filling a demand for woolen classics since the 1800s. Pendleton developed its conservative designs for frontier buyers who demanded function over fashion in clothing. Today, the company still continues to offer quality woolens in the same timeless styles, although the 1970s were bad years for wool. Consumers turned to low-maintenance polyester knits, and the United States now shears fewer than half the sheep it did in the late 1960s. But today, the company is enjoying what Pendleton president Clarence Bishop describes in a *New York Times* interview as "a return to consumer identification with basic values compared to artificial ones."

"Our specialty is to provide quality and a long-term return on our customers' fashion investments," he says. Once again, the company finds the public is favoring function over seasonal styles.

Pictured here is a Pendleton handed down to Bob Kneeland of Schnecksville, Pennsylvania, by his grandfather, who bought it in the 1940s. A couple of buttons are missing, but the shirt is still in fine shape.

The old adage, "You get what you pay for," seems to apply here. At what price comes durability? Look through the catalog of a good mail-order firm, such as L. L. Bean, and you'll find the prices are certainly higher than those of the United States' number-one clothing retailer, K-Mart. And the prices are clearly lower than those asked by certain designer lines. If you pay either a lot or very little for an outfit of suit, shirt, tie, and shoes–say $800 or $150–you are apt to feel let down a year or two later. The stylish designer outfit will look dated; the discount-priced outfit is likely to tear or pill. But consider the middle course. For $350 or so, a prudent shopper with an eye for lasting construction and fashion can put together an outfit that will still wear well and look good after 5 years. Of course, clothes should be worn with their original function in mind. It would be ridiculous to expect a fine wool, satin-lapeled tuxedo to endure the same abuses applied to a karate uniform, and it should be expected, barring the whims of fashion, to be wearable for 20 years. By the same token, a pair of riveted Levi's blue jeans should last 5 or more years, but a crucible worker in a steel mill might expect only several months of wear from them.

J. MONTURE-KNECHT

New clothes from old

An often-overlooked source of good fabric is old clothes. A man's suit can be transformed into a tailored dress; a woman's skirt could become a child's coat. Men's clothing, especially business wear, is often made with superior fabric. It's a challenge to design around wear spots, make use of existing design lines, and incorporate old zippers and buttonholes. Pattern pieces should follow the grain line of the fabric to ensure that the new garment will hang correctly; to find the grain, follow a yarn or stripe in the fabric. The first step, once you've found an item to cannibalize, is to remove all major seams and separate the garment into pieces. Pull off loose threads and lint. Clean and press the pieces, being careful not to stretch the fabric out of shape. The illustration suggests how new clothes can literally rise from the bodies of would-be discards.

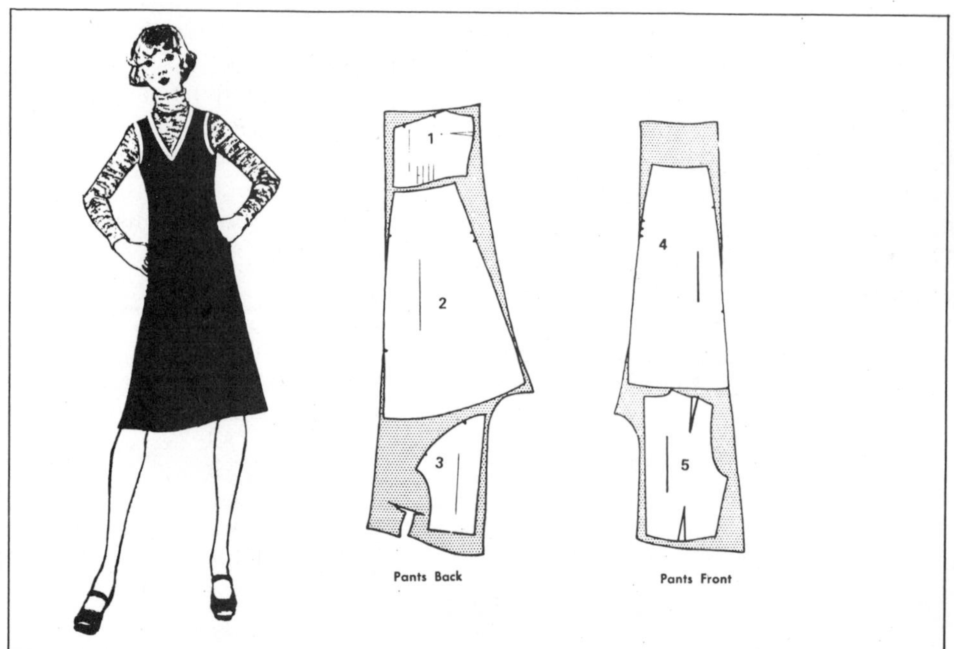

Oklahoma State University Extension

Making a jumper from a pair of men's pants. The pieces include lower-bodice front (1), skirt front (2), and upper-bodice front (3) from the pants back (pictured on the left), and skirt back (4) and bodice back (5) from the pants front (right).

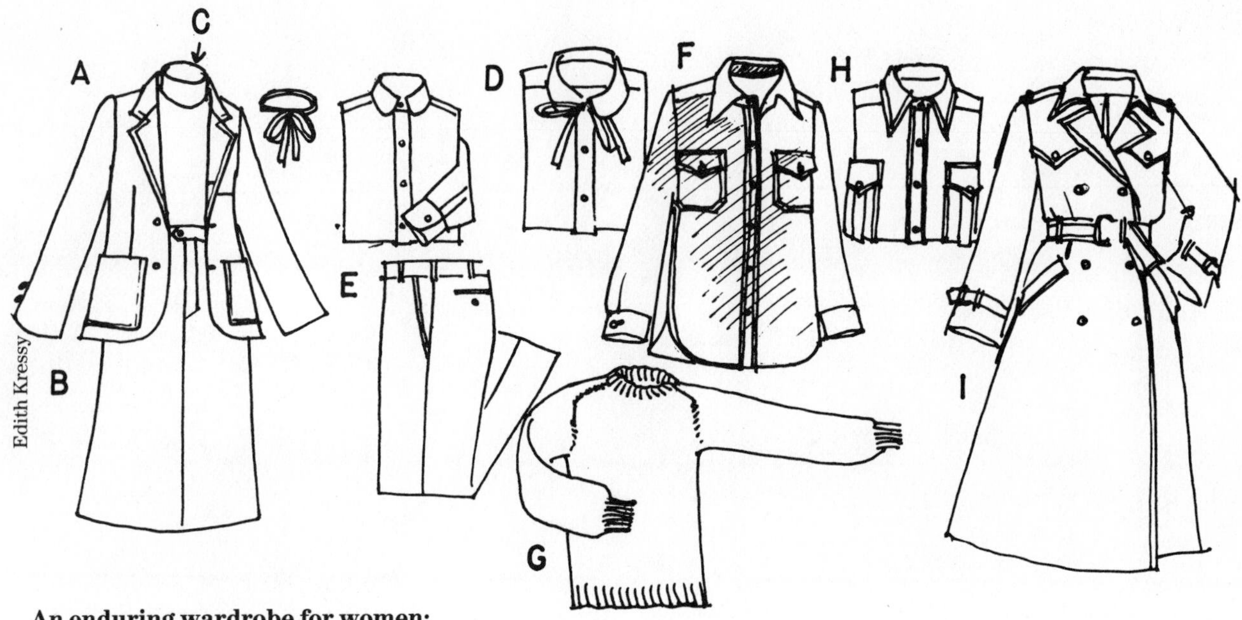

An enduring wardrobe for women:

- **A. Suit jacket, grey or brown herringbone tweed ($158)**
- **B. Matching skirt ($64)**
- **C. Turtleneck, all cotton ($13)**
- **D. Oxford shirt, with or without tie ($27)**
- **E. Trousers, corduroy ($34) or blue jeans ($20)**
- **F. Wool shirt/jacket ($32)**
- **G. Shetland-wool sweater ($30)**
- **H. Chamois shirt ($17)**
- **I. Classic trench coat with removable inner lining, for all seasons ($135)**

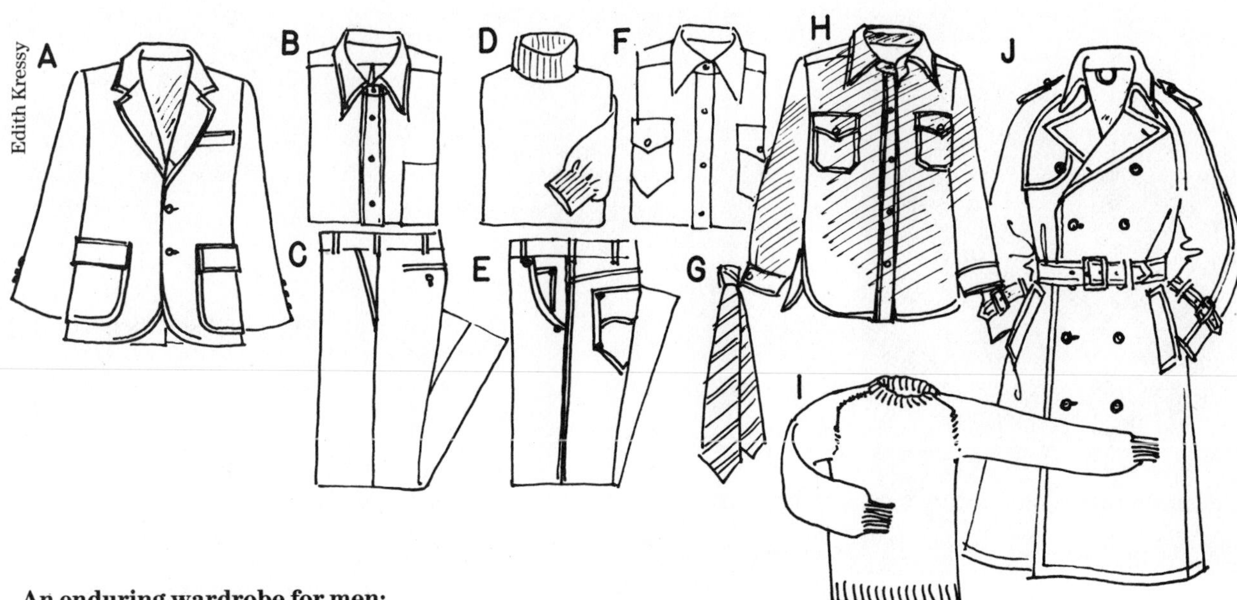

An enduring wardrobe for men:

- **A. Sport jacket, herringbone tweed or Shetland-wool blazer ($150)**
- **B. Oxford shirt, cotton ($16)**
- **C. Trousers, cavalry twill or worsted wool ($70)**
- **D. Turtleneck, all cotton ($13)**
- **E. Blue jeans ($20)**
- **F. Casual shirt, cotton chambray work shirt ($15) or chamois ($17)**
- **G. Tie knitted of wool and mohair ($9) or rep stripe of silk ($18)**
- **H. Wool shirt/jacket ($32)**
- **I. Shetland-wool sweater ($30)**
- **J. Trench coat with removable inner lining, for all seasons ($200)**

Please Note: these prices were taken from various mail-order catalogs and stores in 1981 and 1982.

Starting from scratch

J. Monture-Knecht

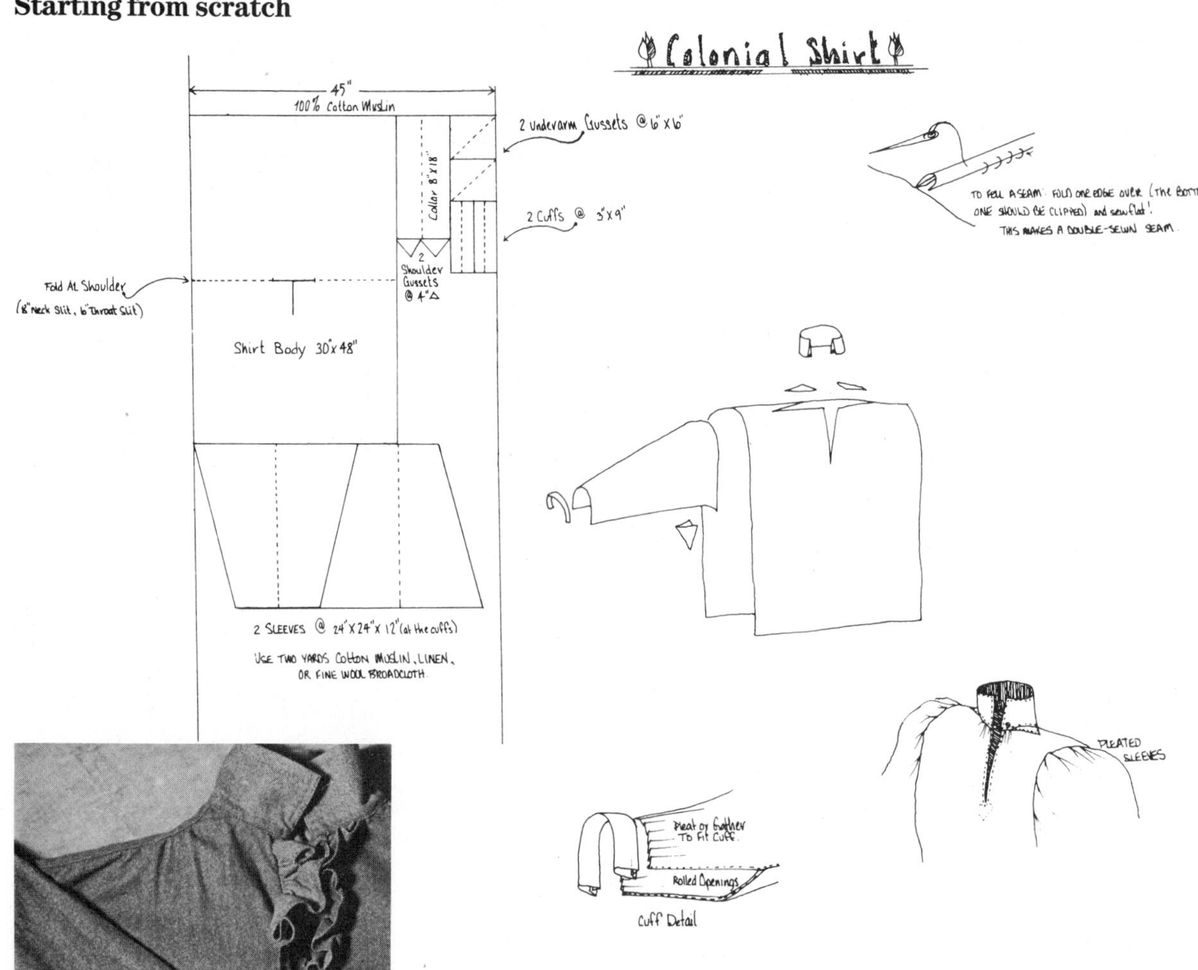

A fall-weight shirt of Pendleton wool.

You don't have to shop around for lasting clothes. Make your own and you have a wide fabric choice and can determine the level of quality that goes into them. You'll also feel confident repairing them. Some home sewers use ethnic or regional patterns because they're both functional and original. Although hand-sewn, pure-linen colonial shirts may not be just what you want to wear to the office or plant, they're suited for weekends working around the house.

1. **Prewash fabric to avoid shrinkage in finished shirt.**
2. **Use size 50 cotton thread, waxed with bee's wax.**
3. **Sew sleeves to shoulder, pleating as you go along so that the length is reduced from 24 inches to 18 inches.**
4. **Sew neck gussets in place, roll throat opening and hem.**
5. **Attach collar, gathering neck fabric to fit.**
6. **Closed sides of body and sleeves should remain open at armpit for gusset.**
7. **Add armpit gussets. Roll cuff slits along sleeve for 6 inches.**
8. **Pleat sleeves and inset into folded cuffs.**
9. **Add button and buttonhole to cuffs and collar.**
10. **Hem bottom of shirt.**
11. **Fell all inside seams to eliminate all raw edges of fabric.**

A New Hampshire clothes designer

"When I find a beautiful old cotton shirt, I can feel the life in the fabric."

An interview with Edith Kressy

A refugee from the fashion center of New York's Seventh Avenue, Edith Kressy now designs simple, serviceable clothing from her home in Plymouth, New Hampshire. She sells ready-to-sew kits by mail order, cutting the natural fabrics to the customer's measurements.

TK

“I never really fit in with the fashion world in New York. The main object of a designer there is to make more and more money; you've got to top last year's figures. A creative person isn't like a factory, but they expect you to produce constantly. And they're never satisfied. Competition is the name of the game. It's not a friendly business. If I had taken it seriously, I would have gone nuts.

The clothes I design now are a reflection of what I'm about. They're part of me. It's nice to give people something with care and thought in it. I find a challenge in seeing a piece of material evolve into something that hangs and moves. And I know it's going to hold up—it's not going to fall apart.

Fifty years ago, clothing was made with such care and thought. Today, clothing is meant to be eye catching and promotable. It's there to make a lot of money for somebody.

It's all a matter of dollars and cents. Every seam amounts to a dollar, so they put in the least amount of work possible. A garment can have very few seams and still cost a fortune.

Bob LaPree

Edith Kressy.

Today's fabrics are of poorer quality. We don't see a lot of pure wool fabrics like we used to. They're blended with polyester or some other synthetic. It's supposed to give the garment more durability, but I prefer pure wool myself. I love cotton because it's so gutsy. You can throw it in the washing machine, give it a pressing, and wear it over and over again. Unfortunately, the thread counts we see today are lighter than they used to be. I use drapery-lining cotton for blouses and dresses. It's really fabulously durable. Chintz is still pretty good, too.

I don't like the way synthetics cling, or the way they feel against the skin. They're marvelous if you just want to throw your clothes in the washer and dryer and put them on, but I think the old cotton clothes are still the best. When I find a beautiful old cotton shirt, I can feel the life in the fabric. That's why I tend to stay with 100 percent cotton. Occasionally I'll buy something with a little polyester in it, if I really love the style, but after I wear it for a while, I'm always disappointed because it just doesn't have the same feel as 100 percent cotton. And who said everything has to be straight and perfect, like it came out of a plastic box? It would be great if we all said wrinkled clothes were in. Style is everything. The armhole must be high, the armhole must be low; waists are in, waists are out. My idea is to get a few pieces that can be mixed and matched and changed with accessories. I say each person should find what looks good on him and stay with it.

Classic clothes offer comfort. They can move around, they can take wear and tear. You'll be going up and down stairs, sitting down, working in the garden, and your clothes must be able to move with you. Then they'll make you look and feel good.

Classic designs are simple and very clean. There are no gimmicks—no little tabs, ruffles, or lace, nothing that indicates a trend of the moment. You want to avoid trendy details like very deep pointed collars.

It's also important to get a good-quality fabric. Harris tweed is wonderful. My husband has a jacket that's 20 years old, and it's still beautiful. The more it's worn, the better it gets.

I love a lot of textures and natural colors in clothing. The key to a classic wardrobe is combining textures and colors with simple clean designs.99

The leisure look

"The changing [of] American lifestyle to a more casual attitude has greatly influenced men's clothing. . . . The leisure jacket, considered a revolution in menswear, resembles a shirt in styling and has less fit than a suit jacket. . . . Nylon sport shirts provide colorful patterns and textures for the casual look with a leisure suit."

From "Men's Clothing Guide," by MARLENE ODLE of the Texas A & M University System

Hats

All photos, Christie C. Tito; courtesy of Fashion Institute of Technology

1940s.
Cone-shaped hat in velvet.

1950s. A chicken hat.

1962. Black sea-urchin hat.

1942. Straw hat with black feathers.

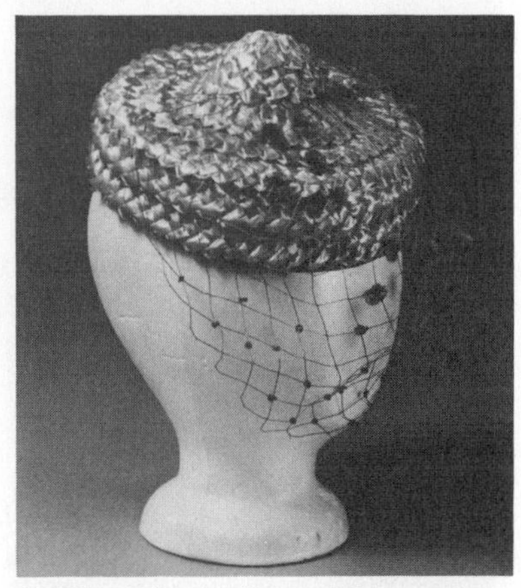

1955. Woven hat with netting.

1965. A sensible checked wool hat.

1950. A pink sack-shaped hat with pink plastic ribbon.

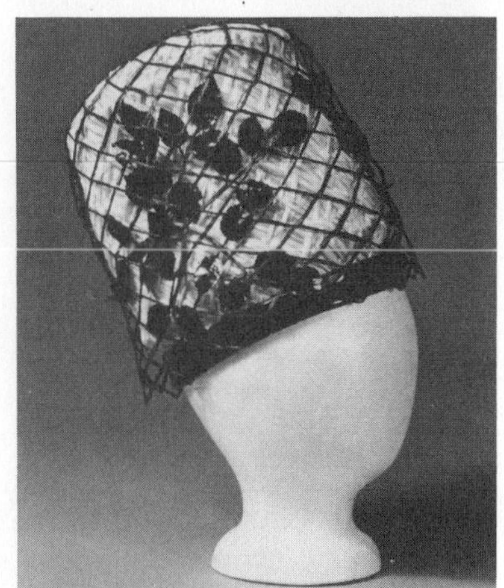

1960s. Pink plastic hat with black plastic leaves.

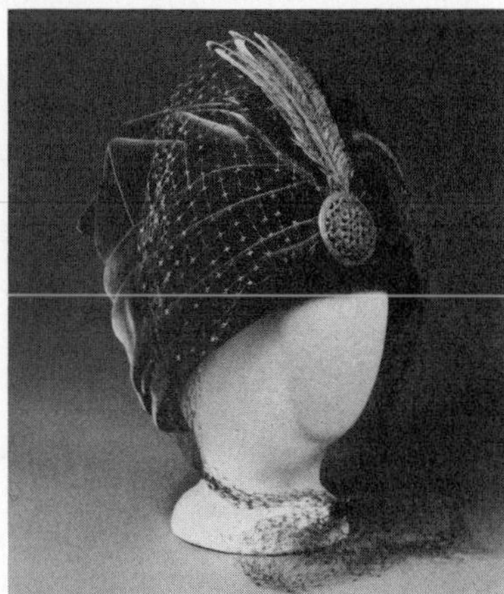

1975. A less-than-sensible hat of dark orange velvet with plume and netting.

The shirt

Both photos, Christie C. Tito

James McBride.

We asked James McBride, merchandising manager at J. C. Penney's in the Lehigh Valley Mall, Whitehall, Pennsylvania, to go over the fine points of shirt construction.

TK

"Proper fit is crucial to durability. If the shirt is too tight in the shoulders, it will wear out where the sleeve is joined to the body. If the collar is too tight, it will wear out and the buttons will come off. A shirt can be worn out in a couple of weeks just because of an improper shoulder or neckline. No matter how durable the seam, it can be pulled out if it doesn't fit properly."

"The looser the weave, the less durable the fabric. A loose-weave fabric should be reinforced with more stitching."

"Check all stitching for loops and loose threads. Look for nice tight stitching."

"Slide the collar between your fingers to check for interfacing. This is sewn in for stiffening, to make the collar stand up over repeated washings."

"Feel the cuff for the material inside. You can feel how much fabric is in there. In this shirt, it's at least ½ inch. We've also reinforced it with a double stitch."

"Check the hem for fraying. Loosened threads indicate that the hem could come out very easily. If you go along the seam at the bottom and find a section that wasn't attached, look for another shirt—the workmanship's not there."

"Check to see if the stitching at the armhole is reinforced. There should be at least a double row of stitching. Single-needle tailoring is a two-step operation found in quality men's shirts. They put one seam in from the inside and then take another stitch around the outside to reinforce the sleeve. This is important because the sleeve is the outstanding stress point on a shirt. Look for the exposed seam as a sign of durability."

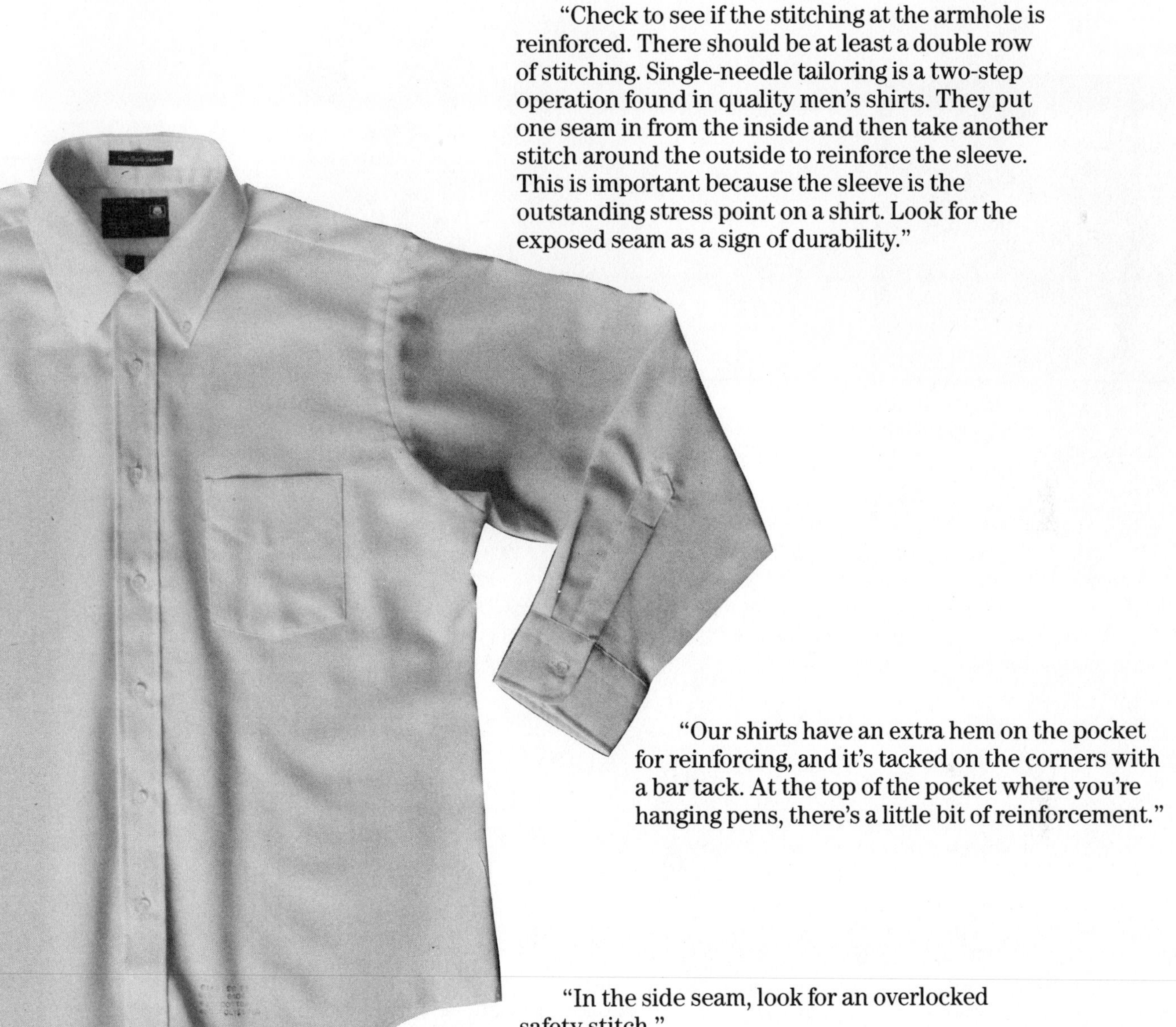

"Our shirts have an extra hem on the pocket for reinforcing, and it's tacked on the corners with a bar tack. At the top of the pocket where you're hanging pens, there's a little bit of reinforcement."

"In the side seam, look for an overlocked safety stitch."

"Buttonholes should be evenly spaced. With a proper fit, there are no gaps between buttons and quite a bit of tension on each. Pull on the buttons to be sure they are sewn securely to the fabric. Four holes are preferable to two. Stitching should be even on both sides of the buttonhole, not heavier on one side. See that the buttonholes aren't frayed."

The dress

All photos, Christie C. Tito

Pat Deem.

We asked Patricia Deem, merchandising manager with J. C. Penney, Lehigh Valley Mall, Whitehall, Pennsylvania, to point out the key features to look for in a well-made dress.

TK

"The basic dress is usually a solid, simple style, ideally of a woven fabric. If you're going to wear something to work and you're going to wear it hard, you don't want a soft fabric. You would not want chiffon or a soft rayon. That's not going to last. If you catch them on a desk or something, they'll be ruined."

"Take a garment and wrinkle it in your hand, then let it go. Come back after a few minutes and see what it looks like."

"A knit doesn't breathe. Your wools and cottons will be the most comfortable."

"There should be no raw seams. You need some kind of finish, either an overlock stitching or pinking, or it's going to ravel."

"You have to pull on the stitching to see if it is properly stitched. If you give it a little bit of tension and it breaks, you know that it's a poor sew job."

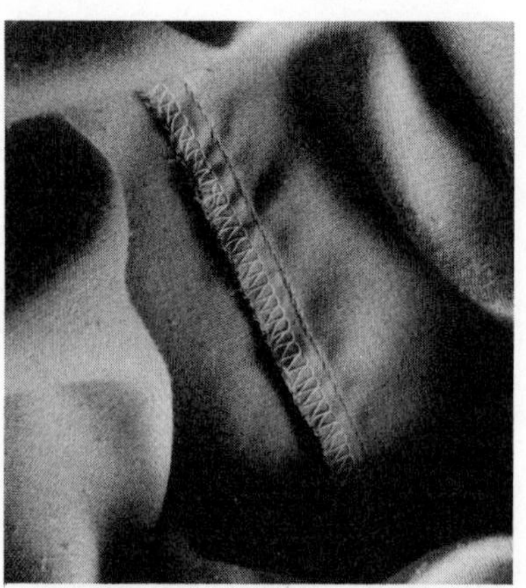

A true safety stitch consists of a straight locked stitch, and an overlock stitch. It is actually a double seam.

"The best thing as far as durability goes is the safety stitch. If it's put in properly, it's a sturdy seam. The overlock and the locked stitch together is called a safety stitch because if the first one were to break, you still have the overlock stitch. It's not going to come apart on you."

"If you're going to buy a knit, check the stitching, especially around a hem, to see if there are any little holes. A blunt needle will make little holes that will run."

"We prefer nylon zippers. On a woman's dress, it's smoother, so there's less chance that it's going to catch. A rough zipper is going to pull on soft fabrics."

"Fit wears out a garment faster than anything. Try clothes on. It's important to stretch and sit down. Many times a dress is designed on a mannequin, not a live model. If it doesn't fit properly, you're going to pull on the buttons and it's going to tear. Also, if a dress is too big, the armhole is down lower. When you move, it feels tight, and you're pulling on that seam."

"Look for a smooth, well-pressed dart. The threads should be caught at the ends."

"Look for bar tacks or back tacks at stress points. A bar tack is a line—a point of reinforced stitching. A back tack is where they back up the stitching so it won't unravel."

"There should be some type of reinforced stitching in the waist, especially if it's an elastic waist."

"Take a button and rub it against the fabric; if the color comes off, don't buy it. It will bleed onto the material."

Levi's jeans

Legend has it that 21-year-old Levi Strauss made it to California in 1850, close on the heels of the Forty-Niners. "Miners were digging a fortune in gold out of the California hills, but they couldn't buy a pair of pants sturdy enough to stand up to the work," reports a Levi's publicity sheet. "Until young Levi Strauss arrived to sell dry goods (including tent canvas) in San Francisco. He saved the day, and many a scraped knee, by making his canvas into pants. The miners called them Levi's."

In the 130 years since the canvas clothier met the gold miners, Strauss's original design has changed little. Today Levi Strauss & Company still makes the trousers its namesake designed. The company calls them Denim 501s.

"Those jeans have remained unchanged all these years, except rivets in the back pockets and a crotch rivet have been removed," explains Levi's publicist, Sally Brant.

Strauss and a Nevada tailor named Jacob Davis patented the use of copper rivets to reinforce pants pockets in 1873. "Davis had begun using rivets to repair the pockets his customers kept ripping by stuffing them too full," continues the company publicity sheet. "The rivets remained on Levi's until 1937 when they were concealed on back pockets because they were scratching school furniture and saddles. Later the back rivets were replaced by stitched bar tacking. Front pocket rivets are still in use. A crotch rivet was also used until the day a company executive crouched too long before a blazing campfire."

Pete Jacobi, Levi's vice-president of regular jeans, says, "Those 501s are the mainstay of the company. They're also the pants that are the basis of everybody else's designer jeans. Of course, we like to believe ours is the best product available. In a way, every customer designs his or her own pair of 501s. They're shrink-to-fit jeans, made of all-cotton fabric. The 501s will shrink about 10 percent when they're laundered. What some people like to do is put them on while they're still wet and they'll shrink as they dry, perfectly conforming to the wearer's individual figure. They become someone's own personal pair of jeans."

In the 1850s and '60s, reports the official company history, "Levi began substituting denim for canvas, insisting that it be dyed indigo blue for uniform color. (In the 1870s he dropped canvas altogether.) His denim jeans—he called them waist overalls—were guaranteed to shrink, wrinkle, and fade. San Francisco's miners, and the cowboys and farmers who followed them west, made each pair fit perfectly by putting them on and jumping into a watering trough; when they dried, they fit."

Today, Levi's makes several styles of jeans. Aside from the shrink-to-fit 501s, there are Saddleman Boot jeans and Straight Leg jeans. Each style is available preshrunk or not. Each pair of denim jeans is made from either 14-ounce cotton or a 14-ounce cotton-polyester blend.

The May, 1980, *Good Housekeeping* magazine reported that the cotton-polyester blend is slightly more long-lived than the all-cotton fabric. Technicians tested the different denim blends "by running them through numerous washings and by abrading samples with sandpaper to see how many rubs the fabrics could take before a hole developed," the magazine explained. The cotton-polyester blend could take 2,863 rubs, while the 14-ounce cotton was good for only 2,210. The least-rugged fabric *Good Housekeeping* tested was 12-ounce denim, a material that Levi's does not use.

As for Levi's competitors, company vice-president Jacobi points out that *Consumer Reports* magazine tested Levi's, Wrangler, Lee, and J. C. Penney Plain Pocket jeans in December, 1978, and Levi's came out on top. Since that time, a spate of designer jeans has entered the marketplace. From Jacobi's point of view, all these trousers are Levi's impersonators. And sometimes a manufacturer is brought to court for impersonating a Levi's.

"Our most valuable asset is the Levi's brand name and reputation," Jacobi explains. "We're most concerned when another manufacturer markets a pair of jeans with a name similar to Levi's. We don't want anybody to buy a bad pair of jeans incorrectly thinking they're Levi's, because that will hurt our reputation."

"Since the turn of the century," reads a company brochure, "Levi Strauss & Company has been dealing with trademark infringements (when a company uses a trademark other than its own for goods it manufactures) and counterfeits of its products around the world. In fact, at any given time, the company is involved in at least 50 such cases. The number began to soar dramatically after

Photos courtesy Levi Strauss & Co.

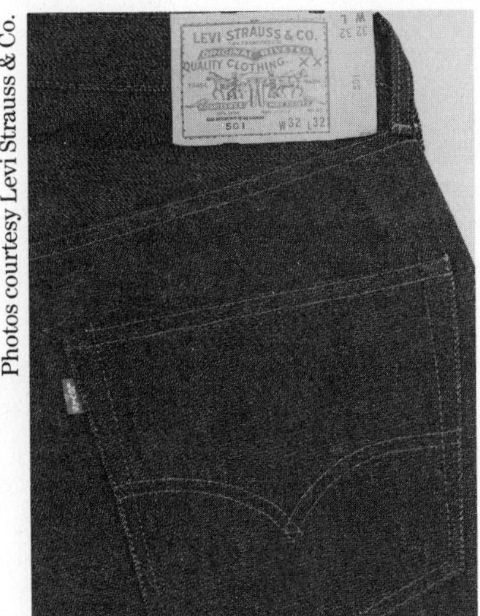

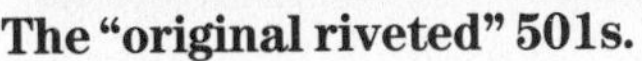

The "original riveted" 501s.

Gold miners pose in their Levi's.

World War II because of the new demand created by thousands of American Army and Navy personnel who were issued Levi's garments as working clothes. Local manufacturers soon found it easier and cheaper to supply this new demand with facsimiles rather than with the actual products."

The company also jealously guards the stitching pattern on the back pocket of its jeans. The pattern, shaped like a sea gull in flight, is called a "double arc arcuate," and the company claims it to be the oldest known American apparel trademark still in use.

Another Levi's trademark is the little tab that is sewn into the seam of every right-hand back pocket. Some tabs are orange and others are red. Sally Brant, the Levi's publicist, explains that the orange tabs denote jeans made with modern, automated techniques, while the red tabs signal jeans made a more traditional way, with less automation. "The red tabs are found on some of our sacred cows, like the 501s," says Brant. "Many people believe that red-tabbed jeans are best."

Levi's jeans are not only rugged and relatively inexpensive; they have also become a durable American institution. Pairs of Levi's jeans are on permanent display in the Smithsonian Institution. Synonymous not only with the old American West but also, in the eyes of many, with Western civilization itself, it is said a suitcase full of Levi's will fetch a high price in Leningrad.

BK

CLOTHING CONSTRUCTION AND CARE

Why is it difficult to find durable clothes in today's marketplace? In part, the problem stems from the structure of the apparel industry. Faced with growing labor costs, manufacturers design clothes suited for production-line assembly, with fewer pattern pieces and little inner construction. Hand tailoring is kept to a minimum, as speed is all-important.

Speed can mean sloppy construction. We talked to clothing and textile extension specialists and came up with a strategy for the wary shopper.

Joan Courtless, family economist with the U.S. Department of Agriculture (USDA), emphasizes checking seam construction. "As a general rule, cheaper garments have longer stitches. The longer the stitch, the more apt it is to break." Inspect all seams for unevenness, puckering, and missed or broken stitches. All seams should be finished in some way, unless the fabric is bonded or a very stable knit. Woven fabrics and loose knits should be pinked or overcast. Overcasting is preferable because pinked fabrics can still unravel if they are laundered frequently. Overcast seam allowances should be at least ⅜ inch; pinked seams should be more generous.

According to Harriet Tutterow, clothing specialist at North Carolina State University, "woven fabrics last longer than knitted fabrics. Knits are flexible so they wear snugly, but they snag and pill, which hampers longevity." Whether you decide on a knit or a weave, hold the fabric up to the light and look for tight yarn pattern. Check thoroughly for thin areas or flaws in the fabric.

Collars should set smoothly. If they don't, they can ruin the entire fit. To stand up to wear, collars should have some type of interfacing. Interlinings that are stitched in are preferable to those that are fused, because these may bubble and separate after repeated washings.

Tug on each button to be sure it is sewn on securely. Buttons should be sewn through at least two layers of fabric to handle the stress they're subjected to. Be sure buttonholes are securely stitched and not about to unravel.

Some formfitting garments have darts. Be sure that they come to a sharp point and that they are positioned properly for your body. A dart in the wrong place will distort the fit and stress on the fabric. That a good fit is crucial to durability may not be readily apparent, but the experts we talked to recommended bending, stretching, sitting, and reaching in a garment before buying it. Jane Winge, clothing specialist at North Dakota State University, adds that "better-quality garments have a better fit. Manufacturers of cheap garments will skimp on the amount of fabric used, in addition to the construction. Better-quality garments are more generous with fabric: the collar fits, the lining will give."

Fibers

The building blocks of textiles are the fibers from which they are made, and it is the fiber that determines a fabric's basic personality. Every garment is required by law to have a sewn-in label or hang tag that identifies the fibers present, by percentage. Each fiber is listed by its generic or family name and also by the trade name used by the manufacturer. The confusing array of fibers on the market today can be classified most simply as either natural or man-made. Natural fibers are obtained from plants or animals. Man-made fibers are created from petrochemical or cellulosic (as from wood chips or cotton wastes) solutions; these solutions are forced through tiny holes in discs called spinnerets, which extrude them into long strands that harden to become fiber filaments.

The following chart explains what you can expect from the common fibers on today's market.

Ply yarn.

The fibers compared

Fiber	Durability		Appearance		Comfort	Care
Generic name (trademark examples)	Abrasion resistance	Sunlight resistance	Pilling resistance	Wrinkle resistance	Absorbency	Check the permanent care label or bolt-end instructions. In addition:
Natural Fibers						
Cotton	Good	Good	If pilling occurs, garments do not become unsightly as pills often break off	Low unless finish applied	Good	Attacked by mildew, so protect stored items against dampness. Can withstand frequent hard laundering. Can be ironed at high temperatures. For best wear of linens, do not press sharp creases.
Linen (Flax)	Fair	Good		Low unless finish applied	Excellent	
Silk	Fair	Low		Good	Excellent	Handle carefully when washing since they are weaker wet than dry. Use neutral or slightly alkaline soap. Chlorine bleaches damage fiber. Wool is damaged by dry heat so use steam. Never wash wool in hot water.
Wool	Fair	Fair		Excellent	Excellent	
Synthetic fibers						
Acrylic (Acrilon, Creslan, Orlon)	Fair	Excellent	Fair	Good	Low	Remove oily stains before washing. Cool rinse before spinning to reduce wrinkling. Use moderate warm iron.
Nylon (Antron, Caprolan, Enkalure)	Excellent	Fair	Low	Very good	Low	Remove oily stains before washing. Cool rinse reduces wrinkling and fabric softener prevents static electricity. Use a commercial nylon whitener to maintain whiteness.
Olefin (Herculon, Marvess)	Excellent	Good	Fair	Good	Low	Do not iron 100 percent olefin fiber. Touch up blends with lowest setting.
Polyester (Dacron, Encron, Fortrel, Kodel, Trevira)	Good	Good	Low	Good to excellent	Low	Remove oily stains before washing. Cool rinse reduces wrinkling.
Rayon (Avril, Bemberg, Fortisan, Zantrel)	Fair	Good	Excellent	Low unless finished	Excellent	Launder carefully to prevent shrinkage or stretching. If in doubt about washability of garment, dry clean.
Tri-acetate (Arnel, Celanese)	Low	Low	Excellent	Very good	Low	Most can be machine washed and dried. If necessary, a hot iron can be used.

Courtesy University of Idaho Cooperative Extension Service.

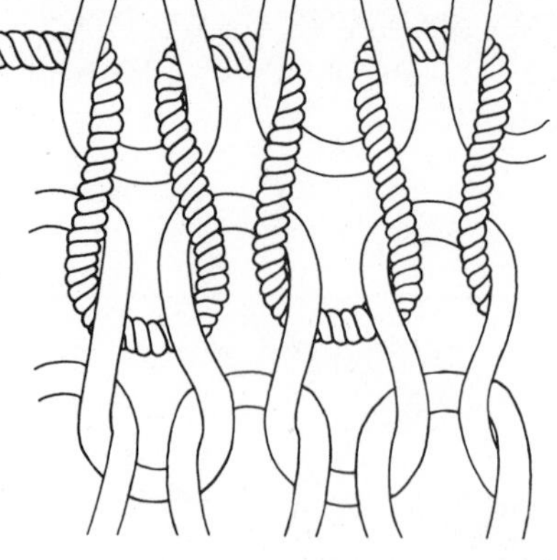
Knit.

Yarns

Yarns are the continuous strands of fiber that go into weaving looms and knitting machines to become fabric. The hundreds of fabrics on the market today are created from only two basic types of yarn—spun and filament.

Spun yarn is made by twisting together short fibers, known as staples. Staples can be natural fibers (cotton, linen, wool) or man-made. Before being spun into yarn, staples are taken through several steps of sorting, drawing, and combing. The longest strands are separated out and used for high-quality fabrics such as combed cotton and worsted wool.

Next, a process of continual twisting is used to bind the staples together. The amount of twist is a major factor in the appearance and strength of the yarn. A loosely twisted yarn will be used to make napped fabrics; a firmly twisted yarn will go into smooth, tough fabrics like gabardine. In general, the harder the twist, the more durable the yarn.

Filament yarns are produced from fine, slippery strands of fiber that can be several yards in length. A silkworm does this in its cocoon. Single filaments are used to make sheer fabrics, such as nylon for stockings, but usually two or more filaments are twisted together to form multifilaments, which produce stronger, more versatile fabrics. To give man-made fibers more bulk and texture, filaments are often heat-set into crimps, coils, or loops before being used to make fabric.

All photos, Christie C. Tito

1940s.

Knits

Knit fabrics are soft and stretchable, produced by shaping fibers into loops and linking them together into successive rows. The loops give knits elasticity because they behave like tiny springs when tension is applied to the fabric.

There are two major categories of knits: warp and weft. Warp knits have rows of loops that run in a lengthwise direction. They have very complex structures and can be made only by machine. The tricot knit is a common example. Such knits are usually smooth and flat and are found in dresses and lingerie. Double- and triple-warp tricots are stronger than the single-warp tricot and are also runproof.

Weft knits were originally hand knit and now are duplicated by machine. All weft knits are based on the simple knit and purl stitches, and are characterized by horizontal rows of loops. Since they are knit from only one yarn, a broken yarn will cause a vertical run.

Double knits are the product of two sets of needles interlocking two fabrics into one. The resulting double-layered weft knit is stronger than a single knit and has less of a tendency to sag and stretch out.

To find a durable knit, look for close, firm stitches. Loose knits will not be as durable and are more likely to lose their shape. Tightly twisted fibers will hold the yarn more securely and provide better wear.

In a sweater, look at the ribbing at the waist and wrists. Be sure it springs back readily after stretching. Sweater performance can also be improved by plying: two or more yarns are twisted together so that fibers are held down more permanently. You can't count the ply on a finished garment because you'd have to unravel the yarn, but the hang tag should tell if ply yarn is used.

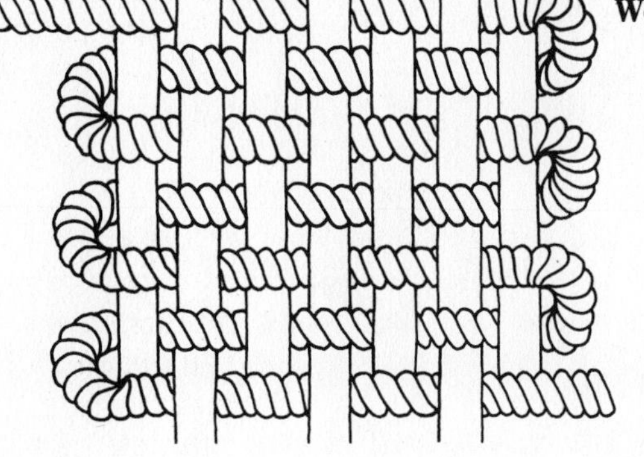
Weave.

Michael Radomski

Full-fashioned sweaters should keep their appearance longer because they're knit to shape. The seams have more elasticity and wear better than those of sweaters that are simply cut and sewn. You can tell a full-fashioned sweater by looking at the seams. The yarn angle should change and appear parallel to the seam. You should also see fashion marks (little dots) on the armholes, sleeves, and sides, which show where the stitches were increased or decreased to obtain a desired shape. Full fashioning is not as important in sweaters of man-made fibers because such materials can be heat-set into shape.

Weaves

Yarns are interlaced at right angles to each other to make weaves. Lengthwise yarns are referred to as the warp; crosswise yarns are the weft or filling. A fabric's durability is a function of both the strength of the yarn and the compactness of the weave. Dense weaves, made from tightly twisted yarns, are the toughest because they are the most resistant to abrasion and snagging.

When shopping, it is difficult to see how tightly the yarn is twisted, but you can compare fabrics by looking for those with the highest number of yarns per square inch. You can also hold garments up to the light to check the tightness of the weave.

There are three basic types of weaves: plain, twill, and satin. Plain, the simplest, alternates crosswise and lengthwise yarns in a one-to-one pattern. Muslin and percale are well-known examples. A common variation of the plain weave is the basket weave. Here, two or three strands of yarns are used in an alternating pattern. This weave is looser and less stable than the plain weave.

Fabric finishes

Fabric finishes may either extend or shorten the life of a garment. In fact, the finish may be more critical than the fabric itself.

Durable press makes nice, snappy creases and virtually eliminates ironing, but the process weakens cotton (a disadvantage that's less important in cotton/polyester blends) and makes fabrics more susceptible to oily stains. Cheerful creases give the impression your clothes were just ironed, but creases wear more quickly than surrounding fabric. You can counter this somewhat by washing durable-press clothes inside out.

Mothproofing may be applied to make wool less appetizing to moth larvae and carpet beetles. Mothproof finishes vary in their tolerances to laundering, so be sure to check the label for care instructions.

Mercerized cottons and linens are stronger and characteristically have a luster.

Blends

Fabric blends unite two or more fibers into a single yarn, combining the desirable characteristics and compensating for their weaknesses as well. Not all blends were designed to improve wear, comfort, or appearance: many exist because they look interesting. A synthetic is often added to natural fibers to make them more rugged and easier to care for. Just 10 or 15 percent of nylon will increase the strength and abrasion of wool and cotton. A fabric that's half or more synthetic may sacrifice the natural component's good qualities for the sake of economy or permanent pleats.

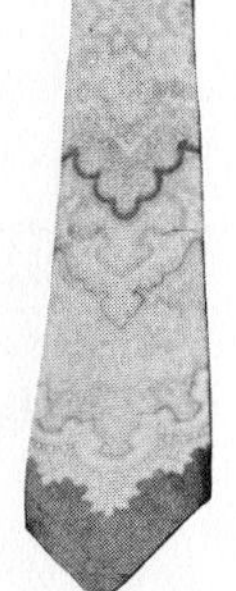
1950s.

In a twill, crosswise yarns pass over two to four lengthwise yarns, forming characteristic diagonal ridges that appear across the surface of the fabric. Twills are highly durable because yarns can be pulled very closely together. You can rate the tightness of a twill by looking at the diagonal ridges: the steeper the ridges, the tighter the twill. Denim is a good example of a tough, sturdy twill.

The least common weave is the satin weave, in which crosswise yarns are passed over four to eight lengthwise yarns. This pattern leaves a lot of yarn exposed on the surface of the fabric, making it very susceptible to snagging and pulling.

Here follow some durable woven fabrics.

- *Oxford cloth* was the shirt fabric popularly worn by undergraduates of Oxford University in England. It is a plain weave with a silky finish and comes in a variety of cotton blends. This soft, absorbent, sturdy, and washable material remains a classic cloth for men's and women's shirts.
- *Denim* first appeared in southern France as a sailcloth for transatlantic ships. A strong and serviceable cotton or cotton blend, this fabric is a dense twill that combines a tightly twisted indigo yarn with a soft undyed cotton.
- *Drill* is a sturdy twill weave created from tight, coarse cotton yarns. It has a wide variety of uses and can be found

---

Cotton vs. synthetic

Are natural fabrics more durable than synthetics? It all depends on your point of view.

Many people find garments made of natural fabrics more comfortable because they allow the skin to breathe and absorb perspiration. The pleasing feel of a cotton shirt makes it welcome on a hot summer day. In cold weather, wool keeps skin warm by insulating against the loss of body heat, even if the fabric gets soaking wet; also, wool absorbs moisture, is resistant to mildew, and does not soil easily. For practical, comfortable clothing you can't beat natural fibers.

If easy care is your main concern, you will probably be happiest with a blend of natural and synthetic fibers. Clothes of these blends can be washed at lower temperatures, require less time in the dryer, and can often be worn without ironing. They are also considered by clothing experts to be more durable than all-cotton or all-synthetic clothing: a recent three-year study concluded that 100 percent cotton shirts will last only two-thirds as long as shirts of a 65 percent polyester/35 percent cotton blend under typical laundering conditions. It can be argued, however, that since clothing made of natural fibers offers superior comfort, consumers take better care of these garments and thereby prolong their life. Also, natural fabrics age more gracefully and are therefore likely to be worn longer.

Special care is required for 100 percent wool garments. They should be dry-cleaned or hand washed, as machine washing can cause shrinkage or stretching. A blend of 85 to 90 percent wool with the remainder nylon will offer both the absorbency of wool and the durability of nylon, and it can withstand machine washing.

If you are concerned about the energy required to manufacture clothes, you'll be interested to know that it takes 25 percent more energy to make an all-synthetic-fiber shirt than to make an all-cotton one, and that cotton's initial savings can be undone by energy-intensive laundering, drying, and ironing. With just a few simple changes—using warm water instead of hot, line drying, and using the iron only for touch-ups or not at all—you can cut cotton's energy needs by 40 percent. These steps will also increase the wear life of your cotton garments.

TK

---

in everything from shirts and uniforms to mattress covers.

- *Chino* was the standard summer cloth worn by the British and American armies during World War I. It is a tough cotton or cotton-polyester twill, characterized by a slight sheen. Because it is very resistant to wear and tear, it is used today in work clothes.
- *Gabardine* is a smooth and extremely hard-wearing twill weave. It is so closely woven that it repels water. This fabric is created from cotton, silk, rayon, and a variety of blends.
- *Whipcord* is a rugged twill weave with a wiry texture. It is widely used for suits, overcoats, uniforms, and riding clothes.
- *Cavalry twill* is created from tightly twisted worsted wool and is characterized by double diagonal ridges. The name dates back to the First World War, when it was used for British military uniforms. Today it is found in jackets and trousers as well as uniforms.
- *Corduroy* was widely used for servants' clothing in the royal households of seventeenth- and eighteenth-century France. It can be either a plain or a twill weave. The characteristic ribs are created by adding an additional yarn to the warp, which is raised above the surface of the fabric to create a pile. It is not generally as durable as plain weaves or twills because the pile is subject to wear from abrasion.
- *Flannel* is usually created from cotton or wool and can be made from a plain or twill weave. The surface is brushed to create a soft nap. Chamois cloth is an all-cotton, heavyweight flannel that is very popular for outdoor shirts. A favorite feature is that it grows softer with each washing. British Viyella is a rich flannel made from 55 percent fine wool and 45 percent long-staple cotton.
- *Harris tweeds* are all-wool fabrics created by the cottage industry in Scotland's Outer Hebrides, mostly for men's and women's suits and coats.

Levi's jean jacket, 1960

"I have a Levi Strauss jean jacket that I bought in the spring of 1960 and have been wearing ever since. It's beginning to get just a little bit worn around the edges now, but I expect it's got at least another 20 years of wear still in it.

"I bought it in a farm-supply store in Barnsville, Minnesota. I don't remember exactly how much I paid for it, but I'm pretty sure it was less than $10. The denim in the jacket is especially heavy, much heavier than any that is now being made into the currently fashionable denim clothing. When it was new, the jacket was nearly as tough as a leather jacket of the kind motorcycle riders wore (à la Fonzie on TV). It has softened some, but not much, over the years since. In 1960 I was a silly teenager, and a genuine tomboy. I wanted the jacket more as a costume, a visual symbol of how 'cool' I was, than as practical clothing. But I did give it plenty of hard wear too, running around through the woods doing all the things kids tend to do.

"As I grew into a reasonably sensible adult, the jacket stayed with me. I continued to wear it whenever I was doing rough work and didn't want to have to worry about soiling my clothes. Now my husband also wears it for heavy work around the yard and garden–hauling in the wood and stuff like that. I think one reason the jacket has lasted so long is that since I don't worry about whether it's dirty or not I haven't ever washed it very often."

NEILA TILLMAN
Lansing, Michigan

1960s.

An afternoon at Blue Ridge Sportswear

"If the operator has a conscience and a heart... you know you're going to have a good garment."

An interview with Bernard Filler

Bernard Filler has been in the garment business for 32 years. He started by tying up parts in a cutting room, then moved on to running a small sewing room. After an education at the Fashion Institute of Technology, he worked as an engineer for a large manufacturer, then became assistant vice-president for another manufacturer. He now owns Blue Ridge Sportswear, a garment contract shop in Palmerton, Pennsylvania.

TK

Christie C. Tito

Bernard Filler.

"A manufacturer designs and sells a product. But a contractor actually sews the clothes. Most contract shops are small, with between 35 and 70 people. My function is a labor function. The manufacturers send me the piece goods and a specification sheet that gives me all the details of how the garment should look—seam allowances and so on. I cut and sew the material and send it back. Who gets them from that point on, I don't know. Some manufacturers have their own sewing plants, but more and more of them are getting away from that.

Today every manufacturer of any size is doing import work, because foreign labor is so cheap. There are two types of imports. One import is the package that comes in from overseas which is done on a jobbing basis. The other type has a label which says manufactured in the United States, but has actually been sewn together in another country. A number of manufacturers have opened cutting rooms in Miami. They cut the garments in Miami and send the pieces to the islands, Mexico, or South America where they can be made for $1 or $2 apiece, then bring them back to be pressed. This is a multimillion-dollar business, and the goods are labeled "Made in America," so they get around the import quotas.

Up until five or six years ago, domestic goods were much better quality than imports. There are still many garments coming from overseas that are not right, but the situation has largely improved. You probably imagine somebody sitting at home in Hong Kong making a garment or two, but the factories in Hong Kong and Taiwan have the most-modern equipment. As a matter of fact, I have mostly Juki machines in my sewing room. They're Japanese machines. All the factories over there had them before I did.

I am basically a blouse manufacturer. My average garment will have 32 distinctly different operations in it. I would guess that you're looking at 25 people handling each individual garment to put it together. Many years ago, each operator made a complete garment. But it's much faster if an operator just sets a collar. Quality depends on the operator: if she has a conscience and a heart, she's going to do it properly. You know you're going to have a good garment. If you've got an operator who doesn't have that kind of interest, every seam she puts in will be inferior. You can have two garments coming out of the same factory, one made with tender loving care and the other sewn poorly.

We are on a piece-rate system. The operator gets paid by the amount of pieces she does. That can give you quality problems. But my attitude is that if it's wrong, stop right there and fix it, because it takes twice as long to fix it over again, and you're going to get it back anyway. Many factories don't have that attitude. They get it out as fast as they can, so if it's not quite right, it's not quite right.

Labor prices are higher on designer items because they have smaller volume sales per garment. It costs me additional money to change over from one style to the next. For example, I'm making velour garments right now, and in four weeks you won't find a velour garment if you shake this place with a stick. In the higher price ranges, styles last for two weeks or a month, six weeks—very rarely more than that. We might make only 100 or 200 blouses that sell for $100, and then you're talking about changing styles every day.

Also, a style item has another cost factor built into it. What happens when it goes out of style? The store sells it off price, so you have to build in additional cost. You also have to compromise a little on quality—perhaps the weight of the fabric—but then because of the short-lived style, you're not going to wear it for three years. These clothes generally last as long as the style does.

In women's clothing, it's basically the designer name and fabric that create the cost. In a man's designer shirt, the fabric will be better. But you can put 50 percent more labor into it only by adding more stitches. Instead of 10 stitches per inch, you might find 22, but 22 stitches in an inch are not going to make that garment last any longer. It's just that you have to put *something* extra into a garment if you're going to charge $50 for it.

Christie C. Tito

The modern contract shop is really an assembly-line operation. Each operator performs only one specialized function—setting sleeves, closing side seams, attaching labels—and then the garment is passed to the next operator. In such shops, a typical garment is actually made by 30 to 40 people.

Look at the stitches. The true safety stitch is probably your best stitch. There are two types of safety stitch—the true safety and the mock safety. The mock safety stitch has four threads. If you look at it from the right side, it will look like an overlock plus another stitch. If you look at it from the wrong side, you'll see that the additional stitch is attached to the overlock. It is not a double seam. But it does have additional strength because it has four threads.

A chain stitch will ravel too. If you buy a garment which only has a chain stitch and you break the stitch in the wrong place, the whole thing will come apart. I would avoid anything with 100 percent chain stitch. Look for a garment which is made with a safety stitch or other locked stitch, and that won't happen.

1970s.

A true safety stitch has five threads. It has a three-thread overlock and a two-thread lock stitch. If one stitch breaks, it's locked into the next one and it will not ravel. It's sturdier than a mock safety and much sturdier than just an overlock. But it depends on the garment. You will very rarely see a true safety stitch in a knit garment because a true safety stitch doesn't have any give. Most knits have an overlock or a mock safety because they will stretch with the fabric.

At one time, clothing was made with felled seams. This is a double-wrapped seam where one ply of material is folded into another fold and stitched with two needles. Some jeans are still made this way. At one time you couldn't find a man's shirt that wasn't made this way. Today you won't find one that *is* made this way. A felled stitch requires more material and more thread, and today a properly sewn safety stitch will last just as long. The trouble is that it costs so much more for labor today that operators rush and aren't as careful. Another possible problem is the type of thread. The only thing a contractor provides for himself in most cases is thread. Some contractors use thread that can run or pop. But I would say that the biggest difference in durability today is not due to the stitch or the construction but the fabric. Quality control in the textile industry is not what it used to be. Damaged material comes through much more often these days. I've had fabric in here that you could tear with one good pull. Also, they're using lighter-weight fabrics today. The lighter the weight, the less expensive a garment is to make. You can have 140 threads per inch or 90 threads per inch, and they'll call them both a 65 cotton/35 poly blend.

Cotton is still your best value. It is easy to sew, and pucker-free. But the price of cotton has gotten so high that you have to combine it with other materials to keep the cost down. It's a compromise. Most people are going to accept a poorer quality for a lower price.

1980s.

Christie C. Tito

In contract shops, the fabric is usually cut by hand. Some large manufacturers have completely automated the process and use a laser for cutting.

Permanent-press materials never really look the same as cotton. They are stiffer and tend to pucker. You must press cotton, but when you do, it looks beautiful. Also, permanent press will not last as long as all-cotton. By building in creases and a nonwrinkle finish, you make the fabric stiffer. When you rub against something, it won't give. When permanent press first came out, men found that pant knees and seats started to wear. Today's version is much better, but still not as soft as 100 percent cotton.

For durable, classic clothing that doesn't cost a fortune, I would go to a chain that has a reputation to maintain, like Sears. When you're doing business with a discount chain, you know you're doing business with a company that buys imported goods as inexpensively as they can. There you have to examine what you buy, but not at Sears. Look for a chain that won't handle the cheapest merchandise or the best, but offers compromise goods. By compromise, I mean well-made clothing that is not high style.”

Don't throw out half your clothes with the wash water

Assuming that you wash your clothes, and that you wash them in a machine, half of the wear and tear on them is due to laundering. Modern washers are ruthless on dirt, and tough on fabric, dyes, and seams as well– especially if the care label is ignored. We were told by a merchandising manager that many manufacturers have started sewing "dry clean only" labels in clothes that could be machine washed because customers don't follow directions properly. Here's a list of tips to make wash day a little easier on your clothes.

Laundering

- Follow manufacturers' temperature recommendations for the washer, dryer, and iron. If care labels are unclear, set temperatures for the most heat-sensitive fiber in the garment.
- Don't stuff the washer beyond its capacity. Crowded clothes will take a beating and wear out faster.
- To reduce abrasion on edges and creases, turn garments wrong side out before washing and drying.
- Use the lowest agitation speed or shortest wash time possible to clean garments.
- Use cool rinse water in the washer both to maintain fabric finishes and to save energy.
- Don't let dry clothes spin in the dryer. Tumbling and excess heat can break down fabric fibers.
- Wash clothes as needed–dirt and sweat cause fabric to deteriorate.
- Don't iron dirty clothes. Heat can permanently set stains.
- Remove stains quickly. Fresh stains respond better to cleaning methods than old stains because dirt and soil become absorbed into fabric with time.

Hand washing

- Do not wring water out of clothes, but squeeze them.
- Rinse clothes until the water is clear. Leftover soap will attract oil and dirt.
- Button or zip sweaters and other knit garments before washing, to preserve their shape.

Storage

- Clean clothes before storing them for the off-season. Oil and dirt attract moths, carpet beetles, and other insects.
- Don't store clothes in plastic bags from the dry cleaner. Residual fumes can soften the plastic, damaging clothes.
- Store sweaters flat, because hanging can stretch them out of shape. If you get a snag in a sweater, pull the loop to the wrong side.
- Don't store cotton garments where it is damp. This fabric is particularly susceptible to mildew.
- Leather garments need to breathe, so store them in a well-ventilated area.
- After taking off your clothes, hang them up and let them air out before putting them back in the closet. This helps garments retain their shape and cuts down on the need for laundering.

The enduring Rooster tie.

Read the label

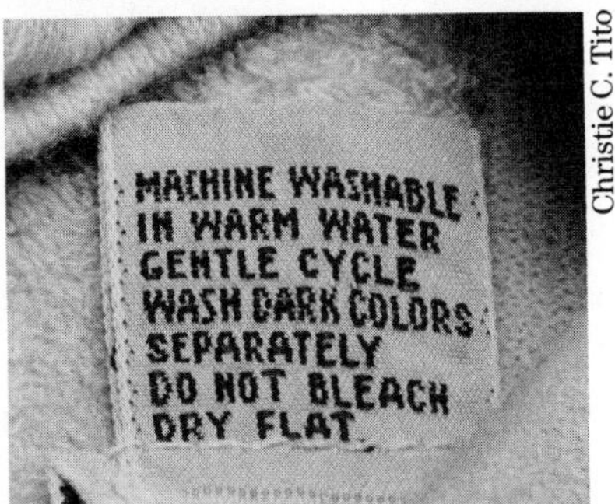

Christie C. Tito

A sewn-in care label.

When shopping for clothing, be sure to note hang tags and sewn-in labels. These labels offer valuable information on minimum garment life guarantees, special fabric finishes, fiber content, and proper methods of care.

The fiber-content label lists what fibers are present in the garment and in what percentages. Armed with this information, you can make conscious choices about which fabrics you wear. Fiber content is also a determining factor in choosing a method of care for a garment that insures the longest possible life. As a general rule, you should care for a garment in the manner befitting the most sensitive fabric present.

For further information on proper care, check the garment-care instructions that have been sewn in by the manufacturer. By law, the manufacturer is required to provide you with one method of care. Unfortunately, these instructions are often vague. Another problem is that manufacturers are often unnecessarily conservative in their recommendations. For instance, a label may say "dry-clean only" not because it is the only method of proper care, but because the manufacturer is afraid that the consumer will wash the garment in water that is too hot.

The Federal Trade Commission is currently backing legislation that would require manufacturers to produce more explicit garment-care labels. This may involve listing temperature settings for washers, dryers, and irons, as well as warnings about bleaches or dry-cleaning solvents that may damage the garment.

TK

Cashmere: durability for a price

Cashmere is a warm, woollike fiber obtained from the fleece of molting cashmere goats. It is perhaps the world's rarest fiber and also one of the most durable. It feels soft but is incredibly tough: a well-made cashmere sweater can last at least 20 years.

Demand for cashmere continues to rise, despite a threefold increase in price. A sweater of the stuff can cost in excess of $175, but people turn to it because of its fantastic warmth and long wear life.

Dawson International of Scotland is the world's largest buyer and processor of raw cashmere. They fashion functional, classic styles and have trouble keeping up with demand, especially now that political strife in Iran and Afghanistan make supplies uncertain. China is now putting more of its cashmere on the international market, which has eased the situation somewhat.

SECOND HAND ISN'T NECESSARILY SECOND BEST

"Once you start buying things used, there's just no going back. When you know you can buy a hand-smocked Polly Flinders dress for $8, it's like tearing skin off yourself to pay $32 for a new one."

PAT ZAZO, Twice As Nice children's used-clothing shop

Once a haven only for people in serious financial straits, the secondhand-clothing store now finds cutomers from every economic class. They're drawn by the bargains—stylish clothes of top quality for a fraction of the original price. There's the stigma of slipping into a garment that once held another body, but inflation is making people do all sorts of things they wouldn't have considered a few years ago.

Secondhand-clothing shops are thriving across the country. As we learned from our visits to several shops in eastern Pennsylvania, there are different shops for different clientele, but all serve a common purpose: to coax dormant clothes out of the closet and give them a second—or third or fourth—life.

ALICE NASS

The thrift shop

An interview with Barbara Bachman, director of the Encore Shop

The nonprofit shop exists to make money for charity. Prices are usually low for a fast turnover. Generally, the quality of the merchandise is less than perfect and not of the latest fashion, but exceptions to the rules draw a wealthier, style-conscious clientele. The successful thrift-shop shopper frequents stores on a regular basis; stock changes daily, and there's no telling when someone will drop off a treasure.

Interview photos, Christie C. Tito

Barbara Bachman (left) and the Encore Shop's manager, Mrs. John Seedorff.

Thrift shops accept all clothes, appliances, furniture, and books, no matter what the condition. Most donors request a tax receipt for the estimated value of the goods so they can write it off at the end of the year.

Usually, you'll find thrift shops where the rent is low, on a side street or in a basement.

At one of the busiest corners in Allentown, Pennsylvania, is a turn-of-the-century brick row house that's the home of the Encore Shop, a nonprofit organization operated by the Arthritis and Rheumatism Society of the Lehigh Valley.

Inside, volunteers work in the somewhat dimly lit rooms among tables of neatly stacked clothes. A few racks hold dresses, blouses, and coats.

Men's suits

1930.
Double-breasted, cuffs, and lapels that could send you aloft on a windy day.

Smithsonian Institution photos 74-9635; 74-9653; 74-9669; 74-9671; 74-9654, 74-9660

The shop doesn't turn down anything given to it, no matter what the condition. Volunteers wash items that come into the shop in a shabby state. Between overflowing cardboard boxes, little gray-haired women iron freshly laundered clothes. The clothes are held for one season. A half-price sale follows. Anything left goes toward the bag sale: for $2, customers can buy all the clothes they can stuff into a large supermarket bag. Anything that remains is sold by weight to a middleman who in turn ships them to underdeveloped countries.

Fashion is not the main consideration to the Encore Shop's regulars. Nor are labels. However, there are a few shoppers who come looking for the unique. Director Barbara Bachman told us that one of her best customers is a bank president's wife who can instantly spot better brands of clothing. Another regular customer comes hoping to find '40s nightgowns and wide-cuffed mink coats. For such style-conscious people, timing is everything.

Mrs. Bachman proudly showed us around the shop. She pointed out a classic paisley flannel dress and told us that she had no idea why anyone would bring in such a dress. "If it were mine, I'd wear it to death."

1945.
In a decade and a half, the lapels lose a fraction of an inch.

❝It surprises us how people don't take care of things anymore, how good things are discarded. It's easy come, easy go.

This is why manufacturers don't care. Poor quality may be the fault of the consumer as much as it is the producers. People are so conscious of style and fashion, whether it be clothing or refrigerators, that they don't want something that's going to last for years. We tend to blame the manufacturer: "Well, they don't make things the way they used to." Obviously, they don't. But the average person doesn't want to keep their refrigerator for more than five years anyway.

When you shop in a store like this, you must have time to look. It isn't like a retail store, where you can go right to a particular rack or counter and pick out what you want. But I think you can do much better in a place like this than in a second-rate store. Here, if you are lucky enough, you might get a good pair of pants in new condition. But you have to be willing to poke around.

A lot of people that you think might buy here, like public-assistance cases, would rather have new merchandise from K-Mart, even though it's not as good. They feel better if it's new. I suppose it's a matter of pride.

People want acrylics. They want clothes they can take care of themselves. With the exception of wool coats, they won't buy anything made with natural fibers, like men's all-cotton shirts, for example.

We can sell things that are very new and things that are very old. But the in-between things don't go. For example, we can't sell mini-skirts, but we can sell the shabbiest old fur coat. We can sell jeans regardless of the condition, even if a hem is out or they are fringed at the bottom or terribly faded.❞

Two consignment shops

The consignment shop closely resembles a retail store in both purpose and design. Clothes are in very good or excellent condition, in season and in style. Typically, the shop owner and consignor will share the profits on a 50-50 basis; merchandise is held for up to a set period, at which time they are either returned to the owner or given to charity. As with thrift shops, timing is everything if you are after something in particular.

Pat Knapp (left) and Pat Zazo of Twice As Nice.

An interview with Pat Zazo, co-owner of Twice As Nice, a children's used-clothing shop

Pat Zazo and Pat Knapp met at their children's bus stop a few years ago. Commiserating with each other on the rising cost of school clothes, they became friends. A business partnership formed, and Twice As Nice opened soon after.

Of the various types of used-clothing shops, those for children have the greatest turnover. Not only do children grow out of their clothes, but the prices tend to be more than reasonable. The owners of Twice As Nice price their clothes at a third of the original figure. The profits are shared 50-50 by the shop and the consignor.

They hold everything for two months. After the first month, there is a half-price markdown. At the end of the second month, the clothes are either picked up by the consignor or given to a local charity.

Only fashionable clothes in new condition are acceptable. The owners told us that children know what they want. If all the kids are wearing skinny-legged pants, mothers won't get away with buying wide-legged ones for their children.

Business is good. The reputation of Twice As Nice has gone beyond the immediate community, and customers bring in their out-of-town visitors.

“People are attracted to our store because of economics. Once you start buying things used, there's just no going back. When you know you can buy a hand-smocked Polly Flinders dress for $8, it's like tearing skin off yourself to pay $32 for a new one.

Many people bring in A-quality, beautiful things a few times without buying anything. Then they look around and their common sense takes over. It's just absurd to pay the price for new kids' clothes.

We aren't dealing with people who can't afford to buy new clothes, but people who are smart enough not to do it. For instance, our customers would much rather come here and pay $30 for a $100 Mighty-Mac jacket than buy something from K-Mart for $30. They know the jackets from an inexpensive store just won't wear as well—wash it once and the lining is likely to come out.

Basically, we have to be pretty choosy about what we take. We have over a thousand customers. We go out of our way to make the shop look as much like a regular store as we can. Some people come in and don't realize that the clothes are used until they really inspect things.

1950.
Single-breasted, and the lapels have shrunk.

I have two boys who really beat things up. When you have more than one child wearing the same thing, it's especially worthwhile buying something good. Weather Tamer, Mighty-Mac, and Pacific Trail, for example, are coats made to last. In boys' shirts, the two which last the best for me are Donmoor and Kaynee jerseys. You can wash them and rewash them, and they never shrink out of shape or pill. You might spend a couple dollars less for a Sears shirt which looks really good, but they shrink, come apart under the armholes, or unravel at the cuffs.

There are a million different name brands. People snatch the well-known brands up real fast. Billy the Kid is a good one. Oshkosh sells quickly. Health-Tex and Carter in the baby things hold up well. Buster Brown doesn't always hold its shape. Even when you take it out of the dryer immediately, it is very wrinkled and so requires a lot of maintenance. Sears double-kneed jeans sell real well.

Weather Tamer and London Fog are good name brands. But a name doesn't necessarily mean you're getting anything better. Izod's shirts are as good as Donmoor or Kaynee but you pay an extra $10 for the alligator. Polyester things are very hard to sell—blouses and even the pants. I don't blame people, I don't like them myself.

We recognize many things brought in for resale that were purchased here, particularly the little girls' good dresses. I know we have resold some of the same dresses at least two or three times since we opened.

1958.
Skinny lapels, skinny tie. This look would resurface late in the 1970s. If fashions continue to come and go as regularly as Halley's comet, expect this one to reappear around the turn of the millennium.

Here's a good example of recycling. My husband's sister bought a Pierre Cardin suit here for her son last year. It had really elaborate detailing and was just beautiful. She paid $30 for it. The original owner paid about $125. She just gave it back to me for resale. Since prices have gone up and it's still like new, we marked it for $35. When we sell it, she'll get $17 back. So that's not bad: the suit ended up costing her $14 instead of $125.

A woman from Scotland found a pretty little plaid kilt here. The tag on it even said "Made in Scotland." It was all wool and cost about $6. She mailed it to her sister in Scotland. Over there they would pay about $80 for the same skirt.

The kids don't seem to object to buying used things. My own kids won't look at anything new. It's got to be used. They find them to be softer and more comfortable. Baby things in particular are a lot nicer when they are soft and worn in. I think I've bought two new things for my sons since we've opened. Other than that, every stitch they have on, from their underwear to their overcoats, is used.

People actually spend $85 for a new little knitted name-brand outfit that can only be worn by a child a few times. To me there's no justification for paying prices like that. It infuriates me that people spend that kind of money on children's clothes. If I were a *millionaire* I never would.”

An interview with Sally McGovern, owner of Once Is Not Enuff

With its well-dressed mannequins in the large display window, you'd probably never guess Once Is Not Enuff is a used-clothing store. Even when you enter, the attractively displayed clothes might lead you to think you are in a women's boutique or a better dress shop. Located in a suburb of Allentown, it's somewhat off the beaten track for women's finery. The town's shops sell bakery goods, cheese, produce, meat, and fish to local customers, but women come from far and wide to seek out Once Is Not Enuff.

Sally McGovern, Once is Not Enuff.

You will never find owner Sally McGovern dressing in anything less than chic. The clothes in her store reflect her sophistication. In fact, just about everything she wears comes from the business, and her outfits make a statement: you can wear used clothing and still dress with panache. It's a message that she can't always get across in words. She says there's nothing like showing them. So she puts on fashion shows with clothes from her store. The women who attend are "fairly with-it and pay a decent amount of money for their clothes."

Once Is Not Enuff started out in a shop the size of a walk-in closet. Since then she has built up a considerable clientele. Some of her contacts send clothes from as far away as California and Boston, and she makes frequent trips into New York City to bring back clothes from metropolitan friends who've found they can do better selling their things in her store than in the city.

And then there are those who live in the vicinity of Allentown who are too embarrassed to be seen in a second-hand shop. For a select few with beautiful and very sellable clothing, she'll personally visit to pick up the things.

Only fashionable clothing, shoes, and purses are accepted. She's had to establish certain guidelines so that people don't come to her with the rejects from the back of their closets. Dresses must be at least 40 inches from the top of the zipper to the hem. Flared pants are unacceptable unless they are made of the finest-quality material, in which case customers who appreciate $80 pants will pay a few extra dollars to have the legs altered by a dressmaker.

“I never will forget this one woman who was bringing a few things in to sell. She lives in Executive Estates, plays golf and belongs to Lehigh Country Club, and she saw this real cute David Smith golf outfit hanging on display. She said, "That's so darling, what size is it?" I told her it was her size. "I would just be a fool not to try that on," she said, and it fit. I could just tell she was really wrestling with a decision. Finally she said to me, "Promise me, if I buy this will you swear never to tell anyone? My husband would kill me if he found out I was wearing something that was used."

In the early days, there wasn't much crossover between those who brought in things and those who purchased them. But today, because the economy is bad, people who never dreamed of shopping here before are regular customers. One woman who lives in this monstrous home

1972.
The turbulent 1960s had their liberating effect on men's fashion, with questionable benefit. Full-blown lapels, bells, and no fabric scrimped on the tie. Suit fabric by DuPont.

in the West End came in, and I was sure she was here only to bring in clothes. I kept waiting for her to say, "I have some clothes in the car," but finally she asked, "Where are your long dresses?" I walked over with her to the rack. She said to me, "You know, we have three children in college now." She ended up spending $150 and went out with six bags. She remarked that she just couldn't believe it. That gives me a good feeling.

Some of my customers are just super-rich bargain fanatics who could probably afford to buy the entire store. However, my typical customer is Mrs. Middle America. She has a big mortgage, a couple of car payments, and probably children in private school. Her husband is a young up-and-coming executive who wears $250 suits. They are paying for a country-club membership. Now where does that leave her? She wants to look nice and wear $120 silk shirts. It's possible she'll find the kinds of clothes she wants to look smart in right here.

Cashmere sells no matter what the condition. Another thing people love is silk. If I get a silk blouse in that has perspiration marks, I'll send it to the cleaners. If it comes back and they didn't quite come out, I'll still put it in stock with a note that it's been cleaned, and if it was a $75 blouse, I'll mark it really low, maybe for $15. Any normal blouse with perspiration marks I wouldn't even fool with. For everything I accept, I reject one. Some things just don't hold up well, like acrylic. You can wear acrylic one time and it will get pills on it.

1974.
A leisure suit for the man who will not be intimidated by tradition. Black-and-white photography cannot capture the vibrance of the red, white, and blue stripes. Designed by John Weitz.

Once is Not Enuff is a used-clothing shop that upper-class patrons can enter without embarrassment.

Several years ago, name-brand designer clothes held up better, but I don't think a label necessarily means quality anymore. I had to laugh when I saw Laneco [a discount chain] advertising Calvin Klein and Jordache. So big deal, what's a designer anymore? I've seen some things come in here with Calvin Klein on them and they are just garbage. Still, when you get into your top-of-the-line designers like Gallanos, the clothes look as good today as they did 25 years ago.

This shop is the product of unfortunate times. People are keeping just the things they like in their closets because they'd rather clear the rest out of there and have the cash. And as the economy has gotten worse, people like to see their things going to good use. They like to know that somebody, somewhere, is appreciating them.99

SHOPPING BY MAIL: GOOD CLOTHES COME IN LITTLE PACKAGES

Back around the turn of the century, the Sears, Roebuck catalog brought the shelves of a big-city department store to the village post office. Today, there's a second boom in mail-order catalogs, as you already know if the mailing list computers have your name. See one catalog and you'll soon see them all.

The disadvantages to ordering clothes by mail may be more obvious than the reasons for doing so. First, you can't try anything on or feel the weight and nap of the fabric. A few catalogs have yet to go to color, and many of venerable L. L. Bean's photographs still have a surreal, hand-tinted look about them.

Then there are the prices. Depending on where you shop, they'll strike you as reasonable or steep or preposterous—but not cheap. Catalogs as a rule must run good-quality items at a considerable price to suit the business of mail order. That's why you're not apt to find $1.29 flip-flops or run-of-the-mill socks and underwear. *Extravagantly* priced sandals, socks, and underwear—yes. (Early Winters offers the appropriately named Millionaire's Sock, which gets you a lifetime guarantee for $20 the pair.)

Now on to the reasons why catalog clothes shopping is so popular. Most mail-order companies offer a line that's a cut or two above the shopping-mall standard, in terms of both practicality and perpetuity of style. Copywriters come up with cloyingly quaint names in the attempt to suggest both qualities: Orvis sells a Game Keeper Oxford shirt; the identical red knit shirt is listed by L. L. Bean as a River Driver's shirt, by Lands' End as the Prospector, and by straightforward Cabela's as Scarlet Underwear. But it's true that many mail-order firms select styles that are all but immune to time. Years before the chain clothiers discovered them, the classic and preppy looks covered the pages of L. L. Bean, Eddie Bauer, and other purveyors of what were originally thought of as sporting clothes. Khaki and twill and denim and leather have become high fashion—as this is written, that is. Durability chic may be passé by the time the book gets to you.

Addresses

Here are the addresses of the mail-order merchants we mention. These aren't necessarily the best of the many, or even the most persistent, but just a sampling.

Eddie Bauer, Fifth and Union, P.O. Box 3700, Seattle, WA 98124
L. L. Bean, Freeport, ME 04033
Brooks Brothers, 346 Madison Avenue, New York, NY 10017
Cabela's, 812 13th Avenue, Sidney, NE 69162
Arnold Craven, 1119 Textile Place, P.O. Box 7408, High Point, NC 27264
Early Winters, 110 Prefontaine South, Seattle, WA 98104
EMS, Vose Farm Road, Peterborough, NH 03458
Esprit, 800 Minnesota Street, San Francisco, CA 94107
Gohn Bros., Box 111, Middlebury, IN 46540
Lands' End, Lands' End Lane, Dodgeville, WI 53533
David Morgan, P.O. Box 70190, Seattle, WA 98107
Orvis, Manchester, VT 05254
Talbots, 164 North Street, Hingham, MA 02043
Vanson Associates, 50 Thayer Street, Boston, MA 02118
White's Shoe Shop, West 430 Main at Stevens, Spokane, WA 99201

Dresses

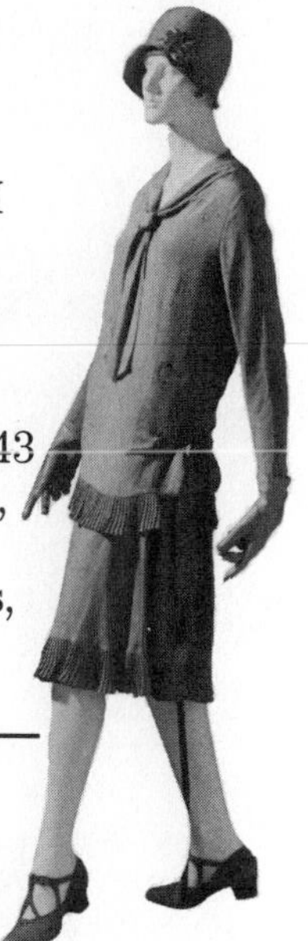

1924-28.
Dress of green silk crepe, with border of knife-pleated ruffles.

Smithsonian Institution photos 74-9629; 74-8627; 74-9631; 74-9633; 74-9617; 74-9665; 74-9662; 74-9664

The fashion of no-fashion

The current issue of *Vogue* contains a several-page ad for designer Ralph Lauren's "Rough Wear." The ad is highly peculiar. There is Ralph himself, leaning against what appears to be a scarred tractor, wearing a ripped, frayed denim shirt over a long-sleeved Wallace Beery undershirt. The copy reads, "Rough wear is an idea that evolved from a time when clothes were made for function and durability—not fashion. Today's rough wear is true to that spirit. It's crafted of strong, fine materials that work hard. It was made to be worn and weathered, and only gets better with age."

Ad copy with the nonacquisitiveness of a holy man: the fashion of no-fashion. It's inferred that here is Ralph Lauren's matured statement. He no longer will pull out novelties each season to obsolesce the wardrobes he pushed just months ago.

Can Ralph Lauren make a durable career out of durable styles? Next month's *Vogue* may tell. But it's certain that Bean and Bauer and company will continue to offer *their* rough wear. Practicality, as expressed in cotton and wool (perhaps toughened with a smidgen of synthetic fibers), is their stock in trade.

Another advantage of catalog shopping is the low-key, often informative sales pitch offered by the more established companies. Take for example this schoolteacherly lesson from the White's Shoe Shop catalog:

> LEATHER Soles are BEST of all for Strong Arch Support, for Superior shape holding qualities, for HEALTH and COMFORT.
>
> OIL PROOF COMPOSITION Soles are best for wear and are less slippery than leather.
>
> LEATHER Soles studded with ⅛-inch HUNGARIAN nails give good wear and non-slipping qualities. . . .

**1934.
One-piece dress with sash and false bolero jacket.**

**1942.
Brown-and-white check wool suit, slightly fitted jacket with padded shoulders.**

The cover from the tiny White's Shoe Shop catalog. The grizzly logo is in keeping with the company's no-nonsense boots for loggers, linemen, smoke jumpers, and hunters.

At the bottom of each page of this tiny 3⅜-by-5¾-inch catalog are finger-wagging mottos: "Good Grease Preserves Leather," "Clean Shoes Well Before Greasing," and "Undershot Heels Make Short Arches."

The Orvis catalog gives a short course on the proper construction of chino pants:

> Nothing fancy, no gimmicks, no flashy colors—just all-natural cotton, the chino you remember from years past. Very tightly woven, 100 percent long-staple Egyptian cotton. . . . All stress points have been bar-tacked, and the seams are double-stitched. . . . Swatches available.

All for $35. L. L. Bean has been selling its Bird Shooting Pants ($62) going on a half century and the catalog's sales pitch sounds like it's from another time.

> All new wool reversed whipcord—one of the hardest wearing wool fabrics. Briar resistant. It looks and feels like highest grade serge. Leather trimmed pockets are made of extra heavy drill.

Shoppers of the polyester generation likely will need to consult a dictionary or an older friend for definitions of whipcord, serge, and drill.

Gohn Bros.' catalog of Amish and plain clothing lacks pictures of any kind, and relies instead on the most reasonable sales copy (see the sample reproduced here).

Motorcyclists and others who appreciate the look and security of leather will find a considerate salesperson in Vanson's catalog of jackets, pants, chaps, and racing suits. To ensure the best-possible fit for the suits, the order form requests that men take 24 measurements and women 26. You are to indicate not only height and weight but also age, "Shoulder-Back" profile, customary riding position (touring/flattrack, café/medium tuck, tight tuck), and whether or not you expect to grow. Vanson offers two grades of leather and 11 colors in a near-infinite variety of schemes, and such racing-suit options as leather stars and diamonds, spine padding, pockets wherever you want them, and patches at likely points of contact with the pavement. This level of custom service is unheard of at most stores, and you probably wouldn't want a salesperson measuring your body 24 or 26 ways in the first place. Vanson's jackets run from $143 to $200, and the basic one-piece racing suit is $319.95, or about $75 less than the basic three-piece worsted suit in Brooks Brothers' catalog.

MADE TO ORDER AMISH SUITS

3-Pc. Frock suit (Mutzhe Style) **$189.00**
3-Pc. Coat suit (Vamus Style) **$169.00**
Single Trousers **$55.00**

Send for samples of our very fine 100% wool serges from which these suits are made. We will send you a measurement sheet that makes measuring very simple. We will also send you a question sheet that will give us all the information we need to make the suit exactly like you want it. These are true Amish style suits. Also if after you receive the suit there are any alterations necessary you may return the suit to us within 30 days and we will alter it for you free of charge and return it to you free of charge. These suits are made by the finest cutters and tailors.

Because these suits are made especially for you to your measurements, payment in full must accompany your order.

MEN'S BROADFALL WORK PANTS

No. 1190 10 oz. Sanf. Blue, 35% Dacron, Vat Dyed $11.98 pr.
No. 55 10 oz. Sanf. Blue Saddle Denim, 100% cotton . **$11.98 pr.**
No. 66 10 oz. Sanf. Grey Saddle Denim,
100% cotton, Vat Dyed .... **$11.98 pr.**

No. 66 and No. 55 are solid colors. No white in it. Dressier than regular denim, but make excellent work pants.
Size 28 waist available in 28, 30, 32 inseam only.
Size 44 in 30, 32 inseam only.
Sizes 29 to 42 waist available in 30, 32 or 34 inseam only.
Sizes 46, 48, 50 waist Broadfalls available at $1.50 per pair extra. (Oversize). Available in 32" inseam only.

For $2.00 per pair extra, we will make any longer length wanted.

Give both waist and inseam measures when ordering. These broadfalls are superior because:
1.—Buttons put on by machine fasteners. Will stay on for the life of the overall.
2.—Made from denim furnished by the country's best mills.
3.—Full cut for ease and comfort.
4.—Cut by outstanding cutters and made by skilled American seamstresses. **Not** made by **unskilled** sewers in a foreign country.
5.—Reinforced at points of stress.

These broadfalls are also available by so stating on your order:
1.—Without hip pockets.
2.—Without pliers pockets.
3.—Without buttons stamped on.

We will send you plastic buttons for you yourself to sew on. We do not sew buttons on here.

These Broadfalls can be made special with belt loops for 60c per pair of pants extra. Pants made with belt loops cannot be returned for any reason.

A couple of listings reproduced from Gohn Bros.' austere catalog.

Please circle Shoulder-Back picture which most accurately resembles you.

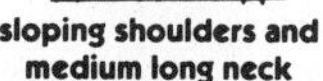

sloping shoulders and medium long neck

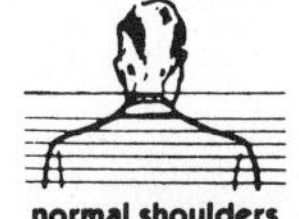

normal shoulders and medium neck

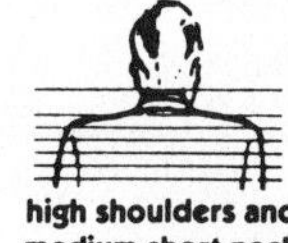

high shoulders and medium short neck

Before ordering a custom racing suit, Vanson asks that you classify yourself as a turtle, giraffe, or something in between.

1950. Dress of red-and-white check cotton, as recalled by reruns from television's Golden Age.

On opening day of trout season, the first eddy of a stream to yield a fish is soon crowded with anglers; similarly, once you place a catalog order, the unsolicited catalogs will start to pour in. Nibble at several and your mailbox will yield two or three each day. Soon you'll have a library of this literature, enabling you to comparison shop without leaving your chair. (In fact, a recently published book on sensible fashion, *Good Garb*, is little but a compilation of catalog photos and copy, packaged between soft covers for $8.95.) For example, if you're after khaki-colored trousers, you have a choice between Brooks Brothers' cotton-poly pants for $29; Lands' End's all-wool gabardines for $62 or their all-wool cavalry-twill pants for $77.50; Eddie Bauer's all-cotton chinos for $23.95 or Orvis's for $35 ($42 with flannel lining); Cabela's cotton-poly pants, chamois lined, for $17.99; three varieties of chinos from L. L. Bean, running from $14.75 to $22.50; $34 canvas pants from EMS; "authentic British khaki bush trousers," $34 from Arnold Craven; and for women, khakis "in the new jodhpur style," $45 from Esprit, and the invitation to "invest" in Talbots' $65 wool gabardine pants.

The list goes on but we won't. Suffice it to say that they do make them like they used to and that you do have an alternative—lots of them—to plastic pants that grow pills on the thighs and seat. You just have to ante up, and not all that much if you browse the literature.

No less important than practicality and sales information is the suspense of ordering by mail. The package from the UPS driver is like a dear friend's letter, only better—you never know exactly what's inside, and have probably forgotten what you ordered anyway.

RY

1957. A green knit two-piece dress with rib-knit straight skirt.

FIT SHOES

Worries about dwindling natural resources tend to center on petroleum, steel, and precious gems. Just as dramatic is the scarcity of animal hides. Leather is disappearing from the nation's feet. Fewer cattle are being slaughtered, and of those hides still available, some 70 percent are exported.

"For 200 years," laments Ralph Pleatman, a Cincinnati consultant involved with leather production, "the well-constructed shoe for both sexes was completely made of leather—upper, lining, sole, counter [the support at the back of the heel]. The sole was stitched to the upper and usually included a welting. Today I doubt if 3 percent of all shoes made in the United States are of this construction and material, since the price would be so high that 97 percent couldn't afford to buy them."

Christie C. Tito

Nevertheless, materials and construction are the keys to durability. A shoemaker could fashion a shoe that would last a hundred years, but it would be hell to walk in. The material should breathe and conform to the foot in time. In both categories, plastics lose out to leather. Given that good leather is costly, it behooves you to look for an inexpensive source. Ralph Pleatman explains why the local shoe store is not your cheapest option.

"Let's say that a good leather shoe costs $20 for labor and materials only.

One manufacturer has a national brand, well advertised, plenty of overhead, high costs, etc. He must add $15 for all of this, so his final selling price to the retailer is $35. Today, most retailers of shoes will operate on a 100 percent mark-up plus $1, so this shoe would retail for about $72.

"The same leather shoe—$20 labor and materials—is now being made by an unbranded, low-cost, no-advertising producer, and his costs add up to $7. This shoe would retail for $55, a big difference for the same intrinsic value." Pleatman mentions Hanover as a fine mail-order source of "terrific shoes for the money."

Uppers usually are joined to their sole by one of three methods. Welt construction is best in the long run because it allows shoes to be resoled. The welt is the strip between sole and upper through which both are stitched together. Unfortunately, the industry has gone to fake welts and fake stitching. You have to rely on a salesperson to tell them apart, unless you've studied a disassembled shoe.

Most shoes are now cement lasted, or vulcanized, as the trade calls the process: the upper is glued to the sole. Cheapest is the injection-molded shoe, in which the soles are molded to the uppers. The bargain shoes at discount chains are likely injection molded. Leather soles are easiest to repair and are more flexible than most synthetics, but they don't necessarily outlast crepe, polyurethane, or Neolite.

Researched by PAT DONAHUE

Leather shoes need a little help

No other apparel product is subject to the stress placed upon a pair of shoes. Every step exerts one and a half times the body weight on the shoe: a person weighing 150 pounds generates the force of 225 pounds per step, or 225 tons per mile. Running, jogging, or climbing doubles the stress; quick starts or sudden stops double it again. Shoes are expected to bear that stress day after day, for years, in every kind of weather, and still look presentable.

The price of a shoe is not an accurate measure of its durability. For example, an inexpensive work shoe made of heavy leather will outwear an extremely lightweight shoe with a thin leather sole and a fine kidskin upper that costs three times as much.

Upper materials of polyurethane have been perfected so that they are indistinguishable from leather, are water-resistant, scuff-proof, and easily cleaned. Leather still is the most desirable material for footwear—it breathes, molds to the foot, and offers the greatest comfort—and it will last long enough if you take these precautions:

- Rotate at least three pairs of shoes. Wearing shoes every third day will double their lives. Daily wear does not give a shoe a chance to air out; it encourages bacterial accumulation from perspiration and body acids, harming the lining and uppers of the shoe.
- Keep shoes clean and polished. The wax contained in polishes protects the surface from scuffing.
- Use shoe trees to keep shoes in shape.
- If leather shoes or boots get wet, stuff the toes with paper and permit them to dry away from heat.
- Replace run-down heels before the changed foot position can distort the counter, or back, of the shoe.
- Do not wear lightweight leather shoes or boots in rain or snow; they are not intended to resist the corrosive effects of water. In bad weather, choose heavier, weather-resistant footwear.
- Make sure you're properly fitted. Misfitted shoes not only create foot problems but wear out more quickly.

HAROLD GESSNER

1965. Black-and-blue tent dress, with matching stockings, designed by Rudi Gernreich.

1969. The 1960s expressed in this multicolored printed acetate mini-skirt and over-blouse.

Shoes renewed

"You can get two pairs of plastic shoes for $29 . . . but usually I can't repair them."

An interview with Jimmy Montalto

Jimmy Montalto is the owner of Jimmy's Shoe Repair Shop in Allentown, Pennsylvania. We interviewed him on a hot day in June as he pried the sole from a trampled shoe with a cobbler's pliers. Piles of shoes and boots filled the one-room shop. He pointed to two shelves crammed with shoes that he said must be repaired by the end of the next day. Through the interview, a mechanical shoe-shine machine whirled in the background.

BK

Both photos, Christie C. Tito

Jimmy Montalto.

"I've been repairing shoes since I was 9 years old. I'm 65 now. When I was a kid, we had to work after school. I started shoe shining. From shoe shining, I became an apprentice shoe repairer. While an apprentice during the depression, I had an opportunity to buy into a shoe-repair shop.

Shoes were more durable then. They were made better. You had all-leather shoes. Today, about 60 percent of shoes are made of plastic. Did you want to see a plastic shoe? Here, this lady's shoe is plastic. It's hard to tell the difference if you're not experienced. It looks like leather to you, don't it? I can tell it's plastic by the way it's made. It's hard to explain. I can tell by the feel that it's man-made material.

Leather breathes but plastic don't. Plastic has a tendency of making your foot hot. It'll crack and fall apart–the shoe, I mean, not your foot. A lot of plastic shoes that come in here have plastic soles and heels on them. I can't fix them. They're unrepairable. You wear most plastic shoes until there's a hole through them, and throw them out.

Plastic is the going thing right now. You can get two pairs of plastic shoes for $29. They look nice and everything like that. People who can't afford to pay $70 to $100 for a pair of shoes will buy plastic shoes at two pairs for $29.

But usually I can't repair them. I just had a fellow in here this morning who bought a pair of shoes, and he wanted me to fix the soles. I said, "I can't repair these, they're plastic." He said, "My God! I paid $32 for them two years ago!" I said, "Now they're not worth a dime." He said, "They're a good pair of shoes." I said, "No, they're plastic. I can't repair them." Lots of people are like that. They're surprised. A lot of them don't believe me. They think I don't want to do the work. But it's plastic and it can't be repaired.

I wear leather shoes. As you can see, I have holes in the toes of my shoes. These were a little short for me. They're expensive shoes, so instead of buying another pair, I cut the toes out. Of course, I only wear them inside to work. These shoes are Wright Arch Preservers. Being a shoemaker, I can't afford $100 to $110 for a pair of shoes. That's what good shoes cost these days. I had this old pair and they were a little bit small, so instead of spending a hundred bucks, I just cut the toes out. They'll last me another couple of years. I also put a whole new bottom on so they're nice and soft. I'll keep these shoes running maybe another four or five years. For a hundred bucks a pair, maybe I'll keep them running longer than that.

Because I take care of my shoes, each pair usually lasts eight to ten years. I have all my shoes stored on a shoe tree in the closet. They all look like new. Every time I go out, they're polished and cleaned up. When I come back, I put them right back on the shoe tree. The shoe tree keeps them in shape. Taking care of your shoes is important for getting long life out of them.

I've always been a Hanover Shoe man. That's a good, durable shoe for a working person. Hanover makes some of the greatest shoes in the country, and the best shoes in the country for the price. I can't explain why. I've been repairing Hanover Shoes for over 50 years, tearing their shoes apart. That's the only company I know that's always used leather all through their shoes. They still do. Of course, now they cost more. They used to cost $7.50. Now they're in the $35-to-$75 class. But that's still about the best shoe I would say you could buy today in the country. I'd be willing to prove that and put them against any shoe. Sometimes I'd put a Hanover Shoe against a $100 shoe.

Look at the shoe I'm repairing now. This guy wants heels put on. They were worn down pretty far. On the average, I can repair a shoe like this in 5 minutes. If you want to make a bet, I'll do it in 2½—not standing here gabbing like this, though. But I can do this job in 5 minutes.

I can tell a lot about people by looking at their shoes—the way their house looks and the kind of education they have, even their temperament. Most of the time I hit it. Looking at your shoes, I'd say you're just an average guy. I'd say you're a high school graduate, maybe a year or two of college. According to your shoes, you're medium about your home and keeping yourself neat and clean and everything like that. You're just about average. Nothing superior. Am I right on that?

Jimmy's shoes.

I had a guy from Finance America come in here and we got talking about this. He said, "Here's my daughter's shoe. Can you tell me something about her?" I look at the shoe and I said, "She's high-strung."

"My God!" he said. "How'd you know that? She *is* high-strung!" I could tell by the way she polished her shoes and kept them real neat that she was over-fussy with her shoes. She was *over*-fussy. That type of people usually are high-strung people. Every little thing bothers them. They're ready to jump at you.

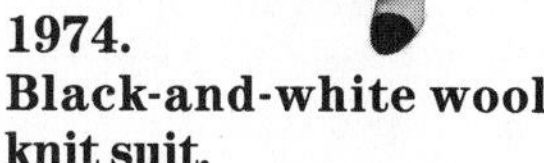

1974.
Black-and-white wool knit suit.

Some people want too much. I refuse to repair a lot of shoes, and then people get mad at me. But if I can't do them right, then I won't do them. People won't accept that. But if I do repair them, somebody's going to say, "Look at the lousy job that Jimmy the shoemaker did!" I'll lose my reputation if I do a bad job. I got a pretty good reputation in this town. My work is perfect, not semiperfect. Now, once in a while I'll slip up, but I don't know when I did last.

Shoe repairing used to be pretty nice. Now it's hard. This morning a woman brought an umbrella in here. Hell, I don't have time to work on an umbrella, putting a thingamabob on a thingamajig. My God, it's crazy! People come here and ask me to fix umbrellas, hats, trusses, handbags, luggage, and I could tell you about a few more things but I better not.

Look at this shoe. This guy came in and wanted a heel and a sole. He asked how much. During the Depression, I'd do this job for 69¢. Now I charge $13.95 for a half sole and heel. He said, "I want a *full* sole and heel." Now that's hard. It used to be that I could take the whole thing off and sew a new sole onto the welt. These you can't. It's triple the work the way they make shoes today. I must work three times as hard but charge the same price.

I told this guy I'd rather not fix his shoes. "It's too much work," I told him. "If you want to take your shoes somewhere else, it's okay with me." He said, "Why should I go somewhere else? You've been fixing my shoes for years." Then I had to fix them.

Will shoes be more or less durable in 20 years? I'd like to be around and find out myself.”

1976 Timberland boots

"They feel more supple than a boot that sturdy could possibly be, comfortable even to my hard-to-fit (size 6 and very wide) foot. They *are* scuffed but structurally are completely sound and the soles hardly worn. I expect them to last 10 full years at this rate, with only a little silicone each fall to spruce them up.

"The picture was taken during a bridge rescue. We live on a small creek, spanned only by a foot bridge that is lifted out of place whenever the water rises more than a foot. When this happens I wade across the creek and tie a rope to the bridge, and then my husband pulls the bridge back into place. This time the water was a bit over my boots. My pants got wet, but not my feet."

CATHERINE (MISSY) MINK
Brooktondale, New York

Missy retrieves the bridge.

Missy Mink's boots.

Death of the long-life sneaker

In 1980, I developed a simple and inexpensive idea for a long-life running shoe, a shoe that wouldn't wear out in 500 miles.

At five critical places where the sole abrades the quickest, I installed replaceable plugs of rubber. The plugs wore out instead of the sneakers. I reasoned that consumers would rather spend a nickel to replace a wearplug than buy a new pair of sneakers.

My idea ran into trouble. Many retailers told me that customers didn't care how long their running shoes last. And the company that marketed my design, Keds, decided to mark up the plugs from a cost of 2.8¢ each to 50¢—ten times the nickel price tag I had envisioned.

Keds dropped this innovative design before 6,000 pairs had been sold. The company's promotion was halfhearted. Here the plugs could easily double the life of a sneaker for pennies—a colleague got 2,000 miles out of his pair—but Keds came around to the retailers' belief that people aren't concerned with durability.

Not all the blame rests with the consumer. The antiquated shoe industry is comfortable doing things as it always has. Although superior materials and technology are now available, these new ideas are resisted. When I developed a cushioned air sole at Nike, I found only two people who were receptive—one of the boys who tested it and the company's president.

Even when this resistance is overcome, an innovation is apt to die because the out-of-date machinery can't handle it.

Running shoes suffer short lives for reasons other than design. Quality control often goes no further than merely weeding out the worst products. The percentage of defects then may be carefully manipulated to convince management that the manufacturing arm is doing a good job. Everyone congratulates everyone else, and once again the consumer loses. At both sport-shoe companies for which I worked, quality-control personnel reported to the production directors, which is a lot like students grading their own exams.

Quality control can be expensive. If a supplier botches a run of rubber worth $100,000, it will be tempted to pass the material on to a manufacturer with a reputation for inconsistent quality checks. The largest supplier of ethyl vinyl acetate (or EVA, a midsoling material) sells three densities of the material, but makes them to overlapping specifications that allow great inconsistencies from batch to batch. Much of the industry operates under such meaningless specifications, if specs are used at all.

Such shortcomings are hard for the consumer to spot, but you can tell a great deal by examining the outsoles, midsoles, and uppers, as well as the cementing and stitching.

Christie C. Tito

Skaja's revolutionary running shoe, with seven replaceable wearplugs. The sole was durable, but the manufacturer's convictions were not.

Outsoles

The outsole is the part of the sole that contacts the ground. Durability is crucial here—once the outsole wears through, the rest of the shoe can be expected to go quickly. Most runners wear down the rear outside heel first. Check to see that there is plenty of outsole material in this area. The type of material is as important as the quantity. The best are *synthetic* rubber and *polyester* polyurethane, as long as these materials are solid and not "blown" with microscopic air bubbles for the sake of lightness. Most of the highly marketed and hyped Vibram sole compounds, found on several of New Balance's shoes including the $70 730, are highly blown. This is a simple way of making a lighter shoe, but at the cost of drastically reducing outsole life.

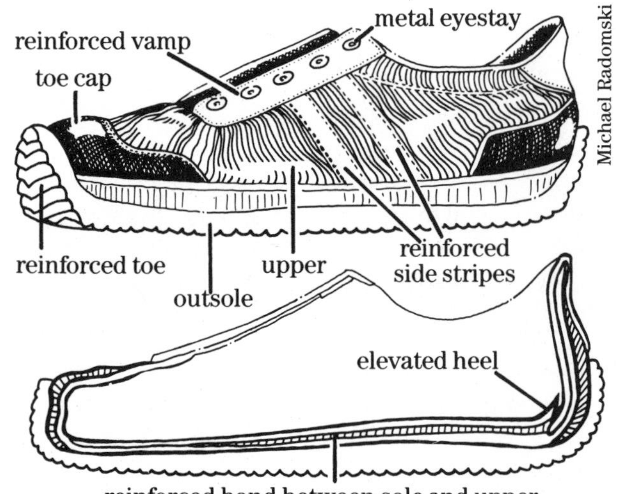

The cobbler's lexicon.

Less-durable outsole materials include polyvinyl chloride (PVC), polyester urethane, Crayton, EVA, and any that are blown with air. A material must be correctly formulated for long wear, and sneakers from Third-World countries have suffered in this respect. Because you can't judge formulations yourself, the manufacturer's reputation is an important indicator of ruggedness. (As a rule, if you spot any cracks or tears, or if you can abrade the outsole with your thumbnail, don't buy the shoe.)

Tread design, by the way, does not much affect durability, but influences traction and overall weight of the sneaker.

Midsoles

The midsole is that soft layer between the upper of the shoe and the outsole. All running shoes should have midsoles to cushion the foot from shock; better tennis shoes also have midsoles.

Uppers

A sport shoe is most stressed where the upper (the part that encases the foot) is attached to the sole. Only the best materials will hold up: full-grained leather, thick nylon mesh, and heavy nylon Oxford. Uppers are often reinforced along the bottom edge by extending the sole up the side, a technique called "foxing." In addition, uppers may be reinforced with suede strips on the outside, or nylon or canvas on the inside. Such reinforcement is important if you expect to treat your shoes roughly.

The runner's big toe may wear a hole right through the upper. If this has been a problem, look for a shoe with a reinforced toe area.

Eyestays tend to tear through, especially if the shoe holds a wide foot. Look for reinforcement between the eyestay and the vamp (the part of the sneaker that covers the tongue and through which the lace passes). You should be able to see the reinforcement material by lifting the edge of the eyestay. Metal eyelets add weight but make the strongest eyestay.

Of the materials used for uppers, full-grained leather conforms best to the foot, but it does not breathe well, may be heavy, and can crack if not cared for properly. Nylon Oxford is light but does not conform as well to the foot and also does not breathe well. Because nylon mesh is woven less tightly, the material breathes (as long as there is no foam backing it), and it conforms to the foot, but few meshes have sufficient tear strength for athletic use; only a very heavy mesh will stand up.

The cemented bond between upper and sole is apt to be a trouble spot. Cementing is the most unpredictable of operations in the manufacture of a sport shoe and has caused many a production supervisor to become unglued. Problems may be caused by a dusty room, operators with dirty hands, and incorrect temperatures. You should test the cemented bond with your fingernail before buying a pair of shoes, in particular the cement line between upper and lower sole. If you can part the materials, the sole will likely fail before long.

The best bonds are made by placing the still-liquid sole onto the upper, a process known as direct bottoming.

The stitching process requires more time and skilled labor than any other, and workers are pressured into making mistakes. If a stitcher is off by as little as 1/16 inch, the shoe may fit improperly and give out early on as a result.

Reject a shoe with loose or broken stitching, especially around the toe cap. Stitches should run roughly 9 to 11 per inch; more or less will yield insufficient strength.

Suede (or "split") is cowhide from which the top layer is removed, and for use in sport shoes it measures about 3/32 inch thick. Contrary to popular belief, suede is much weaker than nylon Oxford, nylon mesh, or canvas. Some suedes are stronger than others: those taken from the legs or underside will not hold up as well, and are used most often on the heel of the upper. Weak suede frays when sanded and will look very coarse.

"Ultra-marathoner Stan Cottrell runs coast-to-coast in Keds Millennium trainers.

"He ran 66 miles a day, 48 days in a row. He set a new world record. Ultra-marathoner Stan Cottrell kept up this blistering pace, without a blister, in just two pairs of Keds Millennium trainers. 3,168 miles in just 48 days without his Keds (or himself) wearing out once. That's durability.

"What makes this feat even more incredible is that Stan put over 2,000 miles on one pair of Keds. In fact, he probably could have gone the entire distance in just one pair of Millenniums had he not needed a spare dry pair to switch into when the going got wet.

"Keds created the first 2,000-mile running shoe by looking at runners' needs from a commonsense point of view.

"At Keds, we're determined to make technical innovations that will put us strides ahead in our field. It's going to be tough. But, like Stan Cottrell, we're not going to stop pushing ourselves until we succeed."

From an advertisement

If durability is your concern, don't buy a sport shoe made entirely of suede unless it is strongly reinforced with nylon or canvas. Suede tends to stretch out of fit. Because it is not easily made colorfast, feet and socks may become stained by, in many cases, toxic dyes.

You're likely to be on your own when shopping for sport shoes. Few salespeople can discuss a shoe's merits and weaknesses. If a shoe proves defective or was misrepresented by the retailer, return it to the store with your receipt. Every return is a clear message to the manufacturer, who eventually credits the retailer.

JOE SKAJA

Shoes, pedestrian and frivolous

Certain parts of the wardrobe have been singled out to proclaim our fashionability as boldly as flags. Unfortunately for the female foot, shoes are two of them.

Men choose to put up with a tie that nuzzles the Adam's apple and tampers with important veins, but they have not been hobbled by four-inch heels and foolishly engineered straps. Crippling shoes are a curious carry-over in this time of sensitivity to sexism in the media, in marriage, in the workplace.

The current revival of the classic look suggests that women's fashion can be more than contrived packaging, but shoes continue the centuries-old masquerade of disguising the woman's foot as something other than a callus-prone limb for moving about.

1932. Black pumps, gold high heels.

1946. Brown alligator pumps with cut-out toe.

1959. Black pumps with stiletto heels and pointy toes.

1940. This white satin platform shoe features gold Greek-god heads.

1950s. The classic penny loafer, now enjoying a revival.

1962. Gold brocade and spike heels.

1960s. These platform sandals give the wearer five inches at the heel, two at the toe.

All photos, Christie C. Tito; courtesy of Fashion Institute of Technology

Shoe fashion is as ephemeral and flighty as millinery, and also has the responsibility of supporting one or two hundred pounds of agitated mass. That responsibility has not always been taken seriously, as the pictures show.

1960s. A futile attempt to wed the fashionability of black patent-leather pumps with the practicality of gaiters.

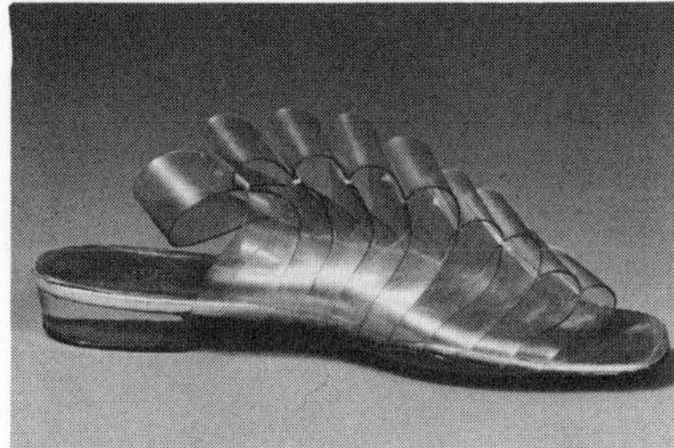

1965. Silver flats with beguiling loops of plastic.

1977. The classic look is on the way in, but the dumb shoe holds its turf.

1910. Black high-button shoes.

1940s. The deathless wing tip.

1960s. An upstart from the do-your-own-thing decade, executed in blue patent leather with red leather trim.

1970s. The wing tip revisited.

The march of time has been kind to men's footwear. Not surprisingly, the 1960s introduced a note of frivolity, but traditional loafers and wing tips and work boots have never been challenged seriously.

Sew your own

We make time for those things we truly enjoy, and one of the things I have come to love is sewing. Because I sew up just about everything I wear, except for shoes and underwear, I not only save a lot of cash for more affordable items, but I know they will last a good long time. Also, the process of finding a beautiful fabric and matching it to a great design is an exciting one. Every curve or line is tuned right into my feelings. When I was a designer in New York City, I learned to appreciate how exact a seam or curve must be with everything matched. I discovered how strategic that ⅛ inch was.

Sewing does take patience and practice. But if you have a good machine, you can endure the occasional frustrations and disappointments. Even at this stage, I sometimes find the left sleeve on the right armhole and have to rip it out. But if all goes well, I can complete, after cutting, a pair of pants in one or two hours, including inseam pockets. In the past, I've whipped up a coat two days before a trip to New York City. Everything around me goes to pot and I am totally in a frenzy, but nine times out of ten I have a lovely garment to take with me.

I am partial to a couple of the many mail-order fabric companies. Imaginations (Marble at Blandin, Framingham, MA 01701) sells year subscriptions of fashion-oriented fabrics that change with each season. A season's collection of color-coordinated, top-quality fabrics can run from 80 to 100 swatches. Owners Laurie Schecter and Jeanne Cowan enjoy close customer relations. If you're looking for a particular type of fabric, they'll try to accommodate you. Generally speaking, prices start at $4 a yard for domestic fabric and run up to $15 a yard for imported.

Sawyer Brook (Box 194, Orford, NH 03777) also offers a richly varied group of fine fabrics from here and abroad. As this is written, you can order a season's collection of color-coordinated swatches of linens, silks, wools, and cottons for $3.

Kit-sewn clothes save you half to two-thirds the cost of ready made, spare you the trouble of hunting down the right pattern and fabric, and assure you of sturdy construction.

Frostline Kits (12376 Frostline Circle, Denver, CO 80241) offers creative adventures in sewing precut down-filled outerwear for the whole family—from vests and jackets to mitts and booties. The kits use highest quality products and contain all necessary notions, such as heavy-duty thread, zips, and snaps. The instructions are illustrated.

Charing Cross Kits (Box 79960, Meredith, NH 03253) markets a durable collection of silk-screen-printed kit-form clothes for the whole family. The quick, easy kits include all necessary notions. The fabrics are machine-washable cotton.

My own Edith Kressy Designer Kits (RFD #1, Plymouth, NH 03264) offers seasonal brochures for women and girls with fabric swatches. The clothes are designed for machine washing and offer classic, easy-fitting country clothes. Items include 100 percent cotton, reversible calico quilted coats, jackets, skirts, Guatemalan cotton dresses, and separates. The kits are precut according to the customer's measurements.

EDITH KRESSY

PARKAS, BAGS, TENTS

Outdoor outerwear

The simpler the design, the less potential for failure: fewer seams provide less chance for abrasion; fewer zippers mean fewer zipper breaks; fewer pockets mean fewer strain points.

An exception, perhaps, is that any heavy-weather garment should have a fail-safe row of snaps to back up the more vulnerable zipper. Take time in the store to examine these points in detail. Avoid garments sewn with 5 or fewer stitches per inch—6 or more are stronger. More than 12 may weaken the fabric at the seam.

All main seams should be of the flat-fell variety, and sewn with lock stitching. Chain stitching is common in cheaper garments, and when a single thread is broken, the entire seam may unravel. Main seams should be double stitched on the heavier shell garments, such as those of 60/40 or 65/35 cloth, and on most single-layer nylon shells. However, you'll find single stitching on even the best of insulated garments, and this is acceptable if well done with an optimum number of stitches per inch.

Beware of stitches that wander all over a seam or even drift off it. Watch for stitching with too much or too little tension. Avoid garments with puckered or stretched seams. If you spot a line of stitching that has simply ended without backstitching, the seam is suspect.

Check for reinforcements at strain points such as the ends of zipper seams and the upper corners of pockets. You should find a bar tack or something similar. Snaps should be set through a tape backing, a heavy lamination of fabric, or through a zipper tape.

No artificial insulator has yet been devised that is as warm for its weight as prime goose down, but the containing fabric must be tightly woven or the fine down plumules will eventually leak out. When buying a down garment, try to find out what the air porosity value of the fabric is. Air porosity should be 3.5 cubic feet per minute or less to properly contain good down. Watch out for jackets that have tiny bits of down showing through fabric and seams. A few are all right, but many are a sign of trouble ahead.

Don't dry-clean a down garment, regardless of what the cleaner may say. Dry-cleaning is hard on the delicate down and often causes significant loss of loft. Wash the garment gently in a rotary machine with one of the special down cleaners now to be found in good outdoor stores, or with a very gentle laundry soap, and tumble it dry at a warm—not hot—setting in a large commercial dryer.

Sleeping bags

Few outdoor items have gone through as many variations in the last few years as sleeping bags. Not long ago, most bags were down filled. Now, synthetic fills command about half the market. Down prices have become awesome, and the finest downs are now hard to come by. Fabrics have gone from long-staple cottons to synthetics, and now some makers are offering coated nylon bags that keep you slightly clammy with perspiration but ensure that the insulation will stay dry. And there are bags of Gore-Tex, which, it is claimed, are waterproof but will still breathe.

Through it all, the criteria of durability remain quality materials, workmanship, and the care you invest in the bag. Quality of construction is difficult to detect. Most materials look the same, and much of the critical workmanship and all of the fill are sealed inside the bag where you can't evaluate them. For this reason, the most important criterion in selecting a durable bag must be the reputation of the manufacturer. You are at the manufacturer's mercy. And prices for good bags run high—there are few bargains.

Down bags have, surprisingly, a longer life than most synthetic fills if well cared for. Once you have located a down bag of a design and loft that suit you, ask about the air porosity of the fabric, a consideration important also with down-filled garments. If the salesperson can't answer you, try slapping the open bag firmly several times to see if any dust or down fragments escape through the fabric. If they do, move on. Don't be put off by an occasional bit of down showing through fabric or seam, but a dramatic exodus of fill suggests a short useful life.

Bathing suits

1925-27.
One-piece of black wool, with trunks attached to the waist.

Smithsonian Institution photos 74-8623; 74-9625; 74-9673; 74-9619

Down is kept from shifting and leaving thin spots by baffles of fine netting. While you can't see the baffles, you can get an idea of how well they are sewn by examining the many lines of stitching across the bag. If the stitching is good (as described in the discussion of insulated garments), things look bright. Optimum stitching for a sleeping bag is around 8 or 10 stitches to the inch, while 14 to 15 may weaken the fabric.

The care you give your bag will greatly affect its life span. Down bags should be stored uncompressed. When packing, don't roll a bag tightly, as this tears up the plumules, but stuff it gently. Wash or clean no more than about once a year. Commercial cleaners who claim special experience with down may be all right, but ask what fluid is used. If the answer is perchloroethylene, or if the cleaner doesn't know, steer clear. Only mild solvents such as Stoddard are suitable. Home washing can be done by hand in the bathtub with a down detergent or a mild soap such as Ivory Flakes. Press and knead the suds through the bag, and rinse the same way. *Never* hang a wet down bag unless it is supported from beneath, or its sodden weight will rip out fragile baffles. Press out extra water with your hands, let drain a while, and dry it at lowest heat in the biggest commercial rotating dryer available. Dry until the down is well fluffed: it takes nearly forever.

Synthetic bags should show the same good workmanship. On all bags, check for reinforcements at the ends of zippers, around snaps, and at ends of hood closures. Zippers should be heavy duty, preferably plastic, and bear a good name such as Talon or YKK. Well-designed bags often have stiffeners along the zipper to reduce the chances of jamming.

There are many good manufacturers, but not all models of a company will necessarily be long-lived. Generally, the top-of-the-line bags in any weight will be superior. Keep in mind that some small, little-known manufacturers do superb work—in fact, many top names started that way. Let local reputation among knowledgeable campers be your guide. A good bag is a big investment and well worth researching.

Tents

Durability is vital in a tent, more so than for most other outdoor gear. If your tent fails in a storm, you are left at the mercy of the elements, and because the fabrics and poles of modern backpacking tents are exceedingly light, materials and construction must be first-rate.

Car-camping tents, if used only in sheltered campgrounds, may be of less quality and still serve well. Here, the thrifty camper can often save by purchasing a tent of reasonable fabrics but less-than-optimum workmanship, and then beef it up on the home sewing machine by adding reinforcements, securing chain-stitched seams with a line of lock stitching, and adding multiple lines of stitching wherever this appears to be needed.

Although quality of nylon in a lightweight tent is hard to judge in the store, workmanship is not. Unroll a tent for a close inspection before buying. Pitch it, if possible, right in the store. Then go to work examining all seams carefully.

The best tents are built with doubled, lock-stitched seams throughout. Main seams should be of the flat-fell type, although there may be simple seams, heavily stitched, at zipper tapes. Chain stitching on major seams is an indication of rapid mass production. It is usually seen on floor seams and should not be used on the canopy or fly. If chain stitching is found only on the floor, you can run over that seam with a sewing machine and seal all threads with seam sealer to ensure a rugged shelter.

You should expect reinforcements in the form of doubled fabrics or added tape where guys attach, at pole ends, at the bases of stake loops, wherever grommets are set, and on tent flies wherever they fit over pole ends. Bar tacking or multiple stitching should secure the ends of zipper tapes.

Almost all backpacking tents are made of nylon *ripstops* and *taffetas*, and it is unusual to find a really poor-quality fabric in any but the cheapest tents, which are suspect anyway. Ripstop, identifiable by its crosshatched pattern, is light and tough and is best used for tent canopies. In its coated form, it is also used for flies. Ripstop is particularly good for these applications, since the regularly spaced double thread tends to keep tears from widening, and the material is light and breathable. However, ripstop is poor under abrasion and should not be used for tent floors even if coated, *unless* light weight is the overriding factor. Nylon taffeta is a simple smooth weave, generally a bit heavier than ripstop. It tears a little more easily but is more resistant to abrasion. Look for coated taffetas in tent floors and sometimes in flies. Nylon *Oxford*, another smooth weave, is sometimes used for heavy-duty floors.

Dacron looks much like nylon and is sometimes used for flies and canopies. It does not stretch as much as nylon, so a Dacron tent deforms less in the wind. (It also resists deterioration from ultraviolet rays in sunlight, which can cause nylon to weaken over a period of time; however, this minor weakness of nylon is hardly worth worrying about for the average backpacker.) All around, nylon remains the best material for the price.

Cotton is rarely used except in a few European makes. Although airy and breathable, it absorbs and holds water, rots and mildews easily, and can't approach the strength of synthetics.

Poles take far more stress under wind or snow loads than is generally recognized, and are often the first things to fail. Rigid poles, such as commonly used in I-pole or A-pole forms, are tubular aluminum alloy. The strongest appear to be 6061 T-6 and 6063 T-6 alloys; look for these numbers on the pole material. Avoid any pole that is softer or less tempered. Ordinary aluminum tubing is totally unsuitable.

Flexible poles, as are used for the ever more common dome and tunnel tents, are generally of solid or hollow fiberglass or of a very hard, springy aluminum alloy designated 7001 T-6. The engineering and metallurgy of these flexible poles is critical but not visually apparent. Here, the reputation of the manufacturer and the cost—usually high—are probably the best indicators of quality.

1943.
A perky one-piece suit in blue-and-white check seersucker, with an "evening-dress" back and skirt over pants.

Examine poles in the store for smooth and careful finish. Tubing ends should be smooth and rounded so there are no sharp or rough edges to abrade tent fabric or the shock cord, which is often found holding the segments together. The best poles have plastic or metal bushings in the male ends to protect the cords. Assemble the poles to be sure they fit snugly but with no tendency to jam.

Northface, Sierra Designs, Caribou, Jansport, Marmot Mountain Works, and Wilderness Experience are a few of many reputable manufacturers of durable tents.

Packs

Exterior-frame packs are still the standard for most backpackers. Kelty unquestionably did more for backpacking with the popularization of the contoured aluminum frame than anyone else before or since, and there have been few truly significant improvements on that basic design. Some of the best innovations have been well-padded, one-piece hip belts, more-durable strap padding, and more-adjustable harness arrangements. It is difficult to estimate frame durability from appearance, but here are things to watch for.

Aluminum frames should be one of the alloys used for tent poles: 6061 T-6, 6063 T-6, or 7001 T-6. If you can't find the designation on the tubing, ask the clerk or check the literature. Avoid softer or unknown alloys.

Frames may be joined by heli-arc welds, by plastic or metal fittings, or by nuts and bolts. Examine welds for neatness, finish, and completeness. There should be no "holidays," or unwelded spots. Fittings and nuts and bolts are harder to evaluate but often are not as strong as welds. Be sure that there is no chance of nuts being lost. Manufacturer's reputation is a good index here.

1954.
A black stretch-taffeta bathing suit with dramatic red taffeta rose and optional hook-on strap.

Check the finish of the frame. Sharp edges may abrade the pack fabric. Beware of any sharp bends in the tubing. These almost invariably are weak points.

Ask the clerk if he or she minds if you test the frame by resting one lower end on the floor and pushing down on the high end opposite. This diagonal pressure is the worst strain a frame can be subjected to, and it happens when a loaded pack is dropped on one corner. You can get an idea of the rigidity of a frame this way, but do it with caution. Generally, the more rigid the frame, the stronger—unless it is designed for flexibility, of course. For example, Coleman built an unusual one-piece frame for their Peak I of high-impact polypropylene. This has a good record for ruggedness, having been used successfully in severe cold and on Himalayan expeditions. It is also slightly flexible in spite of its strength, which endears it to the ski-tourer.

Pack bags take a lot of punishment, and must be well sewn and reinforced. There should be bar tacks or multiple stitching at all pocket corners, ends of zippers, strap attachments, and flap connections.

Zippers are usually the first thing to go. They should be of top quality (look for good brands, such as Talon and YKK), heavy duty, and well stitched in. Back-loading packs should have straps encircling the load to take the strain off the zippers.

Straps should hold a firm, flat shape rather than being soft and noodly. Tips should be sealed with a fitting or by fusing the end of the strap. (You can prevent a nylon strap from unraveling by holding the end of the strap over a candle flame until the surface of the nylon starts to melt and fuse together. This will create a hard coating of nylon on the tip of the strap, which will prevent it from unraveling.) Straps should be secured with multiple rows of stitching or with bar tacks.

Hiking boots

Perhaps the most noticeable trends in bootmaking have been the proliferation of injected-construction boots in the less-durable, lower-priced models, and the appearance of ever-larger and puffier "scree collars" or padded ankles. Neither do much for the hiker who wants long-lasting boots. Injected sole boots are almost impossible to resole. The foam-filled scree collars make the boot more comfortable initially but are usually the first things to go if gripped to pull the boot on. They also tend to close the boot tightly around the ankle, which is fine for keeping pebbles out, but also cuts down the air pumping through the boot, resulting in more perspiration.

Also fairly new on the scene are boots with uppers partially made of heavy nylon fabrics. These—mostly lightweights—are surprisingly durable if the design does not expose the fabric to abrasion.

For the present, leather in its various forms is king. When hides are cured, they are far too thick and must be split into layers. The outer or "hair-side" layer, called full grain or top grain, is denser, tougher, and more water repellent. The inner layers, or "split leathers," are softer, more absorbent, and much less rugged.

You may find top-grain boots in both smooth-out (skin surface out) and rough-out models. The relative durability is arguable. Rough-out fans claim the rougher split surface will absorb more wax, resist abrasion, and protect the water-resistant skin surface. Smooth-out aficionados claim that the water-resistant surface should be *outside* to be most effective. If your boot will be subject to much abrasion, rough-out may be better. If keeping dry is a greater problem, smooth-out may be better. Either way, top-grain leather is the main criterion.

Be cautious of a smooth-out appearance with a pebbled surface. While the graining may be applied merely to hide unsightly but harmless imperfections in otherwise excellent leather, it could also be a plastic- or lacquer-coated split masquerading as top-grain. Be suspicious if the boot is inexpensive.

Before purchasing a boot, determine the method of construction. There are five relatively common types of construction, listed below in order of sturdiness and longevity. The term "welt" refers to the manner in which the sole is fastened to the upper.

Norwegian-welt construction is generally acknowledged to be superior, when properly done. The leather of the upper is turned outward and sewn separately to both insole and midsole. The rubber lug sole is then cemented to the midsole. Since the stitching is visible, you can check that it is even, has no loose ends, and has at least four stitches per inch.

Littleway, or inside-stitched, construction is often used if a close-cropped sole is desirable, as for mountaineering. Here the stitching is *inside* the boot and catches the edge of the upper between the insole and the midsole. This has the advantage of protecting the stitching from abrasion and direct water, but you'll not find it easy to check the condition of the stitching. In a quality boot, assume it is excellent.

The *Goodyear welt* is not as durable as the preceding methods but holds up better than most injected or cemented types. Few repair shops have the machinery needed to replace the Goodyear welt, and it is more vulnerable to abrasion and water than other stitched types. Nevertheless, if most of your hiking is confined to easy trails, these boots may be quite satisfactory.

Injected-sole construction, the newest of the common techniques, involves injecting molten neoprene under pressure to form a midsole that simultaneously catches and welds the upper and insole. The result is similar to cemented boots. You are apt to find this construction used in light trail shoes of split leather, although a related technique is used in some mountain boots. Injected boots are almost impossible to resole and usually are worthless once the sole wears out.

1960.
Aquarian beach attire.

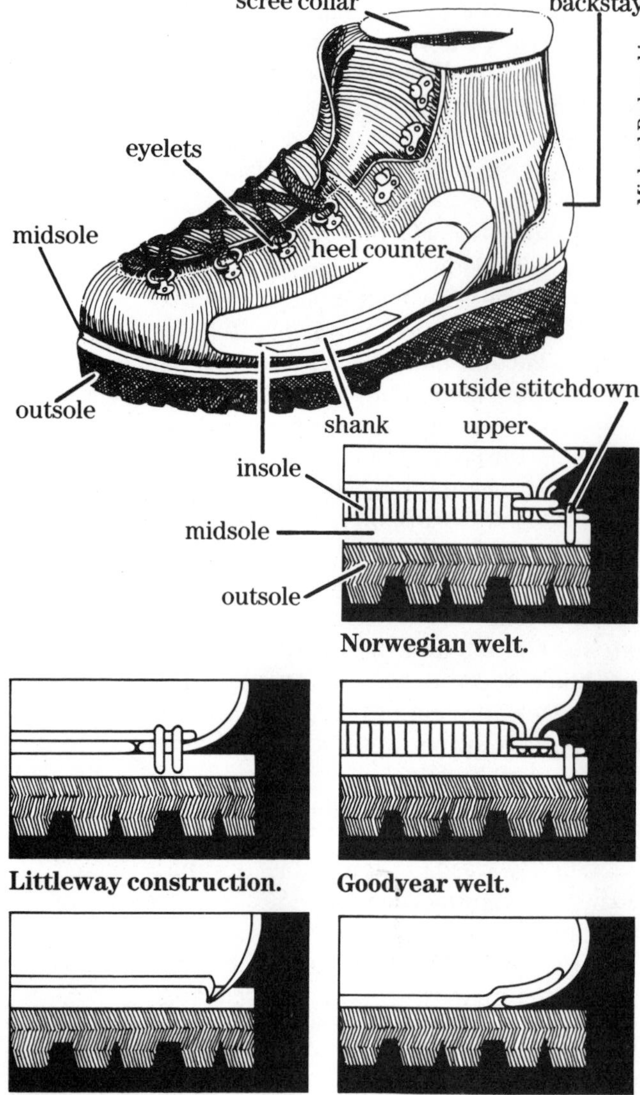

Norwegian welt.

Littleway construction.

Goodyear welt.

Injection molding.

Cemented welt.

Cemented-welt boots are among the cheapest and aren't suited for serious hiking. They offer little support and protection, as they are usually made of light splits. In sum, they don't last long and are often difficult to resole.

High-carbon neoprene rubber lug soles are the most durable and versatile now on the market. The vast majority found in North America are Vibram brand, and these are uniformly good. The most common varieties are the Montagna, which has a deep, sharp lug and is commonly seen on mountain boots; the Sestogrado, which is also quite thick but with a shallower tread; and the Roccia, which is light, flexible, and found on light hiking shoes and some rock-climbing shoes. Softer lug soles offered by other brands may provide a softer, springier walk at the sacrifice of long wear and a stable and protective platform underfoot.

Seams should be double stitched and protected from abrasion. The longest-lived and waterproof types have no seams above the sole except at the back and where the tongue is attached. Avoid exposed seams at sides or toe. Common work or hunting boots with a moccasin toe aren't sturdy enough to take rough and rocky terrain.

Simple eyelets are less convenient than D-rings or hook lacing but are more durable. Most hikers settle for eyelets or D-rings low on the boot and hooks near the top where they are not easily bent on rocks.

Rugged, chrome-tanned leathers are superior to softer tans but should be treated frequently with either wax or silicone-type water repellents (it is best not to mix them). Avoid boot oils, which may cause leather to stretch and are less effective as sealers. Chrome-tanned leather boots are generally harder and stiffer than softer tans, but it is difficult to spot chrome-tanned leathers in the store; ask the salesperson or read the boot manufacturer's literature.

Some of the better, readily available boots are made by Kastinger, Asolo, Vasque, Raichle, Fabiano, Pivetta, and Danner. There are many lesser-known brands as well. For the ultimate in fit and durability, go to a custom bootmaker.

Outdoor socks

Hiking socks have been greatly improved in recent years. You can now purchase socks that are actually guaranteed for one year or 1,000 miles, for two years, even for life. I'd have trouble swallowing this, except that almost nine years ago I bought a couple of pairs of thick, stretchy knicker socks of the Norwegian North Cape brand. I wore them on a 30-day, 300-mile ski trip. Then I wore them to teach cross-country skiing almost every day, all day, for two winters. And I have been wearing them ever since. They don't have any holes, have never been darned, and though the heels have worn a bit thinner, the socks will see more years of use.

The secret of super-long life seems to be a yarn of wool and nylon spun around a core of Spandex elastic. Proportions are usually around 80 percent preshrunk wool, 15 to 18 percent nylon, and 2 to 5 percent Spandex. The combination is not only astoundingly resistant to abrasion, but feels soft and luxurious, stretches to fit, and stays snug. You can wear these socks over other socks if you skin can't take the wool.

Guarantees? Marmot Mountain Works offers a two-year guarantee on their Toe-Toasters, regardless of mileage. They are around $14 a pair at this writing. Sports Accessories' Super Socks carry a one-year guarantee. Early Winters retails socks at two levels of durability: the Thousand Mile Sock is guaranteed for one year or 1,000 miles, and the Millionaire's Sock (appropriately named at a staggering $20) is guaranteed for life. I've had a pair for a year now, and there's no sign of wear in spite of heavy all-season use.

Less durable but still worth consideration are the less-boastful wool-synthetic mixes. Stretch socks seem to have the edge in both durability and comfort. Be sure to get socks you can machine wash. In this age, there's little point in hazarding ruinous shrinkage when there are plenty of makes you can toss in the machine with impunity.

WAYNE MERRY

Dear Sirs:

Enclosed you will find the remains of my Zippo lighter. I am sending it to you hoping that in some way possible you can replace it. I don't expect to receive one free, all I want is to be able to get one like it. I purchased it while serving aboard the U.S.S Thuban AKA-19 four years ago.

I had just had it serviced by your repair department and was very pleased with the job that was done, it was returned to me like a new one. Now you can see how one looks after it falls in a garbage disposal.

Thank you for your time and trouble. I will be looking forward to hearing from you.

APPLIANCES

5

"You can talk all you want about durability," Walter Bennett of General Electric told us, "but who wants to own a refrigerator for more than 15 years?"

Taking this line a bit further, Sears, Roebuck's governmental and technical liaison, N. R. Pugh, says that many products last too long, and their longevity actually should be decreased: a "more nearly optimum design would use many less expensive components and materials, with reduced, but still adequate, reliability and durability. . . . There are a lot of ranges in excellent condition which are quite obsolete in comparison to the self-cleaning oven, the microwave oven, the smooth-top range, and induction cooking, for today's homemaker. In retrospect, consumers might ask, 'Why were ranges made that lasted so long?' "

Bennett and Pugh seem to be unaware of consumers' growing dissatisfaction with the service their appliances give, as pointed out by the industry's own trade magazine, *Appliance Manufacturer*. In its 1980 survey of 1,000 consumers, the magazine found that 39 percent thought the reliability of major appliances had declined in recent years. Only 22 percent thought reliability had improved. Consumers complained about cheaper components, poor-quality materials, and shoddy workmanship. The magazine summarized the results of its survey by cautioning manufacturers, "Perhaps [it] is possible to go too far in shaving costs and the industry may be nearing a danger point in this area."

Several appliance makers have responded to such public opinion by claiming that consumers imagine a decline in durability, when in fact, the products are as long-lived as ever. "Our grandparents thought nothing of lifting a 90-pound vacuum cleaner," says Harry Kennedy, Hoover's national service manager. "Today's product is more lightweight, so people think it's not as good as it used to be." Stephen Upton, vice-president of consumer affairs for Whirlpool, believes that "as we make shots to the moon and electronics take a bigger part of our lives, we tend to forget what we had ten years ago."

As with other areas of consumer products, the decline in durability is the shared responsibility of user and manufacturer. This was the opinion of one washer repair person, who, when asked to explain, told us, "You're opening up a real can of worms there. There ain't no simple answers." Not only don't the manufacturers make them like they used to, but consumers don't take care of them like they used to, he said. They misuse their washing machines by overloading them, and they don't maintain them.

It's interesting to note that laundromat washers, while nearly identical mechanically to home models, often last three times as long. This is because laundromat proprietors take better care of their equipment than do home owners. When it breaks, a commercially owned washer is more likely to be repaired rather than junked.

This chapter attempts to help you sleuth the most durable washing machines, refrigerators, vacuum cleaners, and other household appliances. While reading, keep in mind the conclusion drawn by the repair person who told us, "The durability of a washing machine depends more on its owner and the care he gives the appliance than it depends on the brand name of the washer."

If major appliances were coaxed to last just a third longer, says Robert Lund of the Massachusetts Institute of Technology, consumers could save $4.5 billion annually, and the nation would be spared $35 million a year in municipal waste-collection expenses. One study estimated that 70 percent of all major appliances will sooner or later make their home in a landfill.

COOKWARE COMPARED

Cookware has evolved from the one-quart cast-iron pot, first made in America in 1642, to the gourmet lines of today, from a purely functional tool to one that is both functional and fashionable. Consumers in today's marketplace are bombarded with choices in their search for durable cookware. There is no ideal material, as each has its own set of characteristics, good and not-so-good.

Aluminum

Aluminum is a good conductor of heat vertically and horizontally, meaning that heat spreads quickly and evenly without hot spots. It is lightweight and will not rust, but may be discolored by hard water and detergents. And dark, pinhead-sized craters may be formed on the interior surface of the pan by acidic foods (such as tomatoes) and salty foods that have been allowed to stand in the pan. Pitting does not harm the food, but in time a thin-gauged pan may leak. The heavier the gauge or thickness, the more durable (and probably the more expensive) the utensil.

You can extend the life of aluminumware by proper cleaning. To remove burned-on foods, soak the utensil in warm water or simmer over low heat, scraping occasionally with a wooden spoon, or scour with a plastic scouring pad or soap-filled steel-wool pad. Remove stains by boiling for five to ten minutes a solution of two tablespoons cream of tartar, lemon juice, or vinegar to each quart of water. Cooking acid foods will have the same effect, but aluminum may end up in your food. To restore the shine, lightly scour with a soap-filled pad.

Stainless steel

Stainless steel is durable, easy to clean, strong, attractive, and resistant to pitting by food acids and alkalies. However, it is an uneven conductor of heat. Food tends to stick on hot spots. To remedy this problem, manufacturers place a thin sheet of copper or aluminum on the bottom of the pan exterior, or sandwich a metal core between the outside and inside bottom surfaces. Better yet are three-ply stainless-steel utensils, using a core of copper, carbon steel, or aluminum.

To remove burned-on foods from stainless-steel utensils, use the procedure described above for aluminum. A commercial stainless-steel cleaner will remove the rainbowlike discoloration caused by high heat. When copper-clad bottoms discolor with exposure to the air or to heat, polish them with commercial copper cleaner, a mixture of vinegar and flour, or vinegar and salt. Then wash in sudsy water, rinse, and wipe dry.

Cast iron

Cast-iron utensils are still popular after thousands of years because they retain heat well for long, slow cooking. On the debit side, cast iron is heavy, may break if dropped onto a hard surface, and rusts if not treated properly. If cast iron is not preseasoned before purchase, it should be coated on the inside with unsalted fat or oil and placed in the oven for about two hours at 250° to 300°F. Then remove the utensil and wipe off excess grease. If you wash a cast-iron pot with harsh detergents or in the diswasher, it will require reseasoning. Some cast-iron cookware is coated with porcelain enamel and does not require seasoning.

Glass

A wire grid should always be placed between an electric heating element and a glass utensil. Heat-resistant glass is not affected by food acids or alkalies.

Glass-ceramic has become popular because it withstands quick changes of temperature without breaking and therefore can be used for cooking, serving, and storing. It does not warp, crack, or craze but it is somewhat heavy and will break if dropped. Avoid using metal scouring pads on glass-ceramic cookware. You can use plastic scouring pads to remove gray marks made by metal tools.

Tin

Tin is a finish used over steel, and when new, the coating is shiny and a good reflector of heat, giving results similar to those with aluminum pans. Thus, crusts of baked goods brown only slightly. However, the tin coating darkens with heat, and baking time or temperature must be decreased to obtain the same results. The tin coating wears off easily, and as it does so the base metal is exposed and will rust.

The tin coating is damaged by scouring with a steel-wool pad and scraping with a sharp object. To remove burned-on food, soak in water to which baking soda has been added, two tablespoons per quart of water. Always thoroughly dry worn or scratched pans to keep them from rusting.

Anodized aluminum

This finish is applied by placing the utensil in a bath of aluminum oxide, through which electric current flows. The surface resists stains and corrosion and lasts indefinitely. It absorbs color easily, but the color is susceptible to heat.

Clean as for aluminumware, and avoid abrasive cleaners. Colored anodized aluminum will fade in the heat of a dishwasher.

Porcelain enamel

Porcelain enamel is durable, colorful, easy to clean, resists alkalies and acids, and is dishwasher safe. It can be chipped by sharp impact, and may craze with a sudden change in temperature. To clean these utensils, soak them in warm sudsy water or use a nonabrasive scrubbing pad.

ROSEMARY GOSS

The simple kitchen

"The simpler, the more durable."

An interview with Tom Ney, director of food services at Rodale Press

BK

The four-star Sabatier knife with carbon-steel blade.

Interview photos, Christie C. Tito

There's little this arsenal can accomplish that a good knife can't.

"Simplicity is the key to durability. A lot of stuff is being brought into the kitchen these days that wasn't there for centuries. We should be reverting back to the simple, manual kitchen tools because they do the job and they're proven. They're tried and true. All these gadgets are just more moving parts.

As far as electric kitchen equipment is concerned, you can certainly get by with just a refrigerator-freezer, a range-oven, a blender, a hand-held electric mixer, and maybe a toaster-oven.

You don't need a food processor. You don't even need a blender. You can do everything with a whisk, a French knife, and a hand grinder. It would be better to learn how to use a knife properly—a good $40 French knife—than to spend $200 on an electric food processor. You should have two sizes of French knives—a utility knife and a large knife for big jobs. I like a blade containing stainless steel mixed with carbon steel. Carbon will discolor, but it's the easiest to sharpen because it's soft metal. The more stainless steel in a blade, the harder it is to get an edge, but it'll hold the edge longer. I have a carbon-steel Sabatier knife at home that I used to sharpen every single day for two years, five or six days a week. As the quality goes down, the more stainless steel, generally. Cheaper knives are completely stainless steel.

You don't even need a portable mixer. I prefer using a whisk. People should learn to use these hand tools. I think they're easier. There's less to clean; if what you're mixing with a portable electric mixer splashes up onto the plastic housing of the mixer, you have to clean that and you have to clean two beaters.

One thing to remember when shopping for hand tools is that you should feel for weight. A heavy hand tool is going to do half the work for you. If you're doing a lot of chopping, for instance, it's better to have a heavy knife, because that's what's doing the work; you're just guiding the knife. A good, sturdy whisk needs practically only your guidance around the bowl.

Heaviness is a good clue for durability. These days, they're bringing commercial-grade equipment into the domestic market.

Each appliance has its talents but demands storage space and upkeep.

A Le Creuset enameled cast-iron pot can do the work of the seven appliances to the left.

In commercial cookware there are different grades. The top grade, which of course you're going to pay more money for, is extremely heavy-duty and will be an institutional model. That's used if you're feeding 2,000 people. An average home owner shouldn't buy an institutional-grade oven. But you could probably get a real nice restaurant-grade range for not much more than you would pay for a flimsier domestic range. The restaurant-grade range won't have a clock and it won't have a timer, but you don't need all those fancy things. A restaurant-grade range merely has four burners, an oven and a broiler. If you do a lot of cooking, the investment in a restaurant-grade range is probably worth it. If you cook for just two people, then it probably wouldn't be worth it.

You're also better off going to a restaurant-supply house and buying a commercial blender, because you don't need all those buttons on a domestic one. There's less to go wrong with a commercial blender. They're more expensive, but the money is put into durability rather than all those buttons. How often, when you're working on a recipe, do you read, "liquify this?" You end up just going buzz, *buzz*, BZZZ, *BUZZ!* You're either going to liquify your dinner or chop it to pieces. Commercial blenders are the blenders bartenders use. They use them a hundred times a night, three hundred nights a year. They'll last forever.

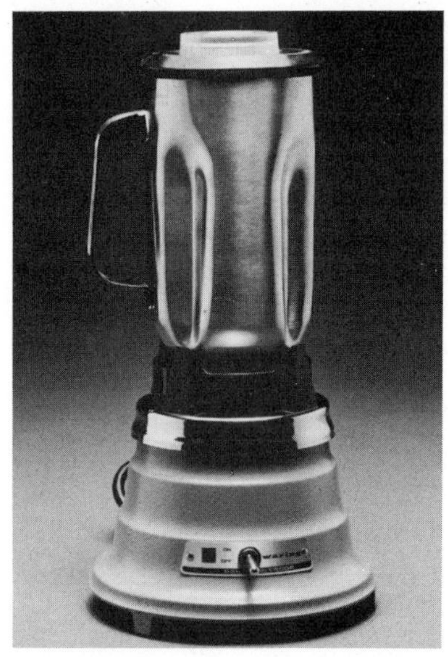

The Waring bar blender, with a stainless-steel jar.

These days, people can buy pots and pans with nonstick surfaces such as Teflon or SilverStone. I would recommend buying

The Melitta coffee maker: "The simpler, the more durable."

the same pots without the nonstick coating because the pot will last a lot longer than the coating, no matter what the manufacturer says.

The longest-living pot material–cast iron–has been around for a long time. The next most durable material for pots and pans is probably enameled cast iron. My favorite pot at home is a Le Creuset enameled cast-iron pot. I also have a bunch of copper pots. They're solid. The thing against a lot of the heavier pots, which are better-cooking pots, is that my wife doesn't like to use them because of the weight.

I don't like spot-welded handles on pots. Once they fall off, I can't fix them at home. There's more of a tendency for a welded handle to fall off a pot than a handle with two or three solid rivets. And a pot's handle should be metal. You have to use hot pads. Everybody has a hot pad or a towel in their kitchen. Whenever you attach a piece of plastic or wood to a pot's handle, it's just another piece to fall off.

The simpler, the more durable.”

Thermax toaster (before 1905)

"I remember my mother saying she got five dollars for a birthday gift and used it to buy the toaster. It is a functional upright appliance about eight inches high and some six inches wide. The heating element is three strips of mica held in place by wire and wrapped with wire. The bread is placed on hinged holders which are held upright by a strong spring. After a few pieces of toast are made the holder gets extremely hot and unless care is taken you can get branded with U-shaped burns.

"My brother married during the 1920s and borrowed the toaster when they started housekeeping, as we did, later, after World War II. It still makes excellent toast, and is the only toaster we have.

"I believe such appliances last so long because they were made of good material, with pride in workmanship. Also, all of them predate plastics."

MRS. ALICE WALKER
Kooskia, Idaho

A repair person's perspective

"I used to jam my old toaster, but no more: now I take it easy going down."

Frank Adesso.

An interview with Frank Adesso

The Culinary Institute of America has been training chefs and bakers since 1946. The institute is located in Hyde Park, New York, on the site of a former Jesuit seminary. We thought it would be worthwhile to interview Frank Adesso, who repairs the institute's kitchen equipment. We found him to be an affable man in his thirties, born and raised in New York City. He spoke with us from his desk in the institute's busy workshop.

RICH KLINE

"We're trying to stay away from plastics because our equipment is not only used, it's abused. We just have too many students using the equipment. Metal holds up better.

Take a piece of metal: it'll bend. You can reshape it. Take a piece of plastic: you can melt it, but you can't bend it. It'll just crack on you. That's true with the plastic tops on blenders. So out comes the Crazy Glue. Hopefully that'll do the trick. But if that blender was made of a piece of machined metal, it wouldn't break.

One of the chefs came across a Hamilton Beach blender, an old one. That thing dates back over 20 years. Every soda fountain had one, for malteds. It's a collector's item. But it was making sparks, arcing, and the chef was afraid to plug it in anymore. I just put in new brushes, and it works like brand new. That's the way with the old ones: just a little contact cleaner, a little WD-40, new brushes, and she'll just keep going. Hamilton Beach still makes it, and it's still a good blender. There's nothing fancy about it. I believe in simplicity. The simpler the better. I worked as an electrician for 15 years, and I've seen manufacturers adding, adding, adding, this feature and that feature. There's so much more that can break.

The selector switches are not made the way they used to be. They burn out constantly. Switches from ten years ago were made a lot stronger. You start taking the metal out of the switch, and your durability will drop. Manufacturers go that route because most people won't spend the extra money. If you want to spend a pot of money, you can buy commercial grade, like the coffee machines we have here. Our commercial-type coffee machines last a lot longer than those plastic models you buy for the home. Mr. Coffee—I can't tell you how many times I've had my hands on a Mr. Coffee to repair. Norelco, too. They really don't last. We also have commercial Hobart mixers, big 10-quart and 20-quart mixers. They get abused, but they hold up real well.

Some appliances simply can't be repaired. We have an icemaker that constantly broke down, thanks to a printed circuit board. When something blew in it, the circuit board melted. That kind of sophistication is no help. I could see it in a computer that doesn't generate a lot of heat. But you get a printed circuit board on an icemaker with 110 volts running through it, and the board acts like a fuse element. You can only repair it so many times. We got fed up with it. It'd be better to go with a fuse. You can replace one for a dollar, as opposed to a printed circuit board that costs as much as $25.

I also avoid pop rivets. Screws and nuts are sturdier, and repairable. I find I can keep repairing my friend's toaster because it's got screws and nuts, not rivets. I can take it apart, like an Erector set. Everything was so beautiful in those days. Today it's all computer chips.

I find that when I use equipment these days—appliances, my chain saw, my TV—I'm handling it more delicately than I do older equipment. I think unconsciously we're all doing it. Years ago, you used to take the TV tuner and zap it and zip it around and go crazy with it. Today, you have to be careful with it or the knobs will break. When I use my toaster, I don't jam it down. I used to jam my old toaster, but no more: now I take it easy going down.99

1884 Conservo steam cooker

"The Conservo didn't come into the Gardner family until 1944, when my mother-in-law got it from her grandmother's estate. Bob, my husband, remembers that Conservo very well. The year we were married, 1971, he bought a second one at an auction for $15. Inside was the original instruction book, with the date of purchase, 1932. Over the past nine years I've preserved 300 quarts or more a year. One year I did 150 quarts of green beans in two weeks.

"On September 16, 1979, we were making vegetable juice. We each have certain jobs to do, even the children. We began around 10 AM and by 8:53 PM we had 98 quarts of juice and one healthy 7 pound, 14 ounce baby girl—we left for the hospital at 6:30 PM, leaving the children and grandma and grandpa to finish the last quarts and clean up the mess."

KATHY GARDNER
Cambridge, Illinois

Boxwood

Jeff Glancz

The name boxwood is used for several heavy woods with pale yellow color. European box, occurring from Britain through Southern Europe to Turkey and Iran, is among the finest-textured of commercial woods. The grain is straight or, more often, irregular. It is heavy and will only just float in water. Box is durable by reason of this high density. To a large extent, box has been superseded by cheaper woods or synthetics–it has excellent turning properties for both plain and ornamental work and is the traditional material for engravers' blocks, rulers, and scales–but box is still used in small turned items like chessmen and corkscrews.

Spoons furnished courtesy of Murray Johnson, H.A. Mack & Co., Inc., Boston, Massachusetts.

Olivewood

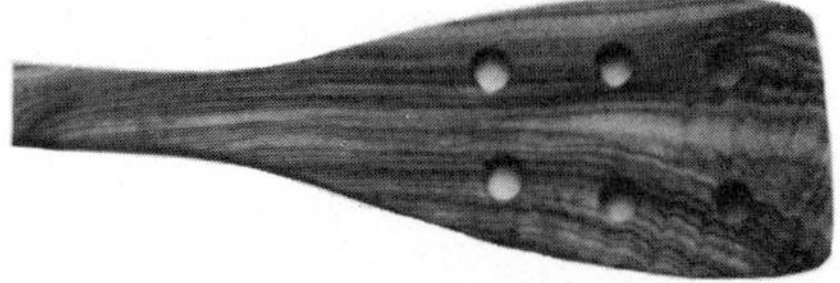

Olivewood is obtained from the olive tree, grown in the Mediterranean mainly for its fruit and oil. The wood has a distinctive appearance: pale brown to medium brown, with darker gray or brown markings in an often-irregular grain. With a high density and low porosity, olivewood is noted for its resistance to abrasion. It works well with hand or machine tools and can be finished to a very smooth surface. European olive is used mainly for small turned and carved items. The wood is so expensive that it is sold by the kilo instead of by the foot. Utensil handles should be fairly thick, since the wood has a tendency to split.

Woodenware

In early days, before there were lumber mills, wood products were carved straight from the tree. The main section of the trunk provided simple furniture, while other parts were used for domestic vessels and implements. Larger portions of the boughs were fashioned into bowls and platters; the smaller sections were hollowed out for cups and ladles, and the scrap was whittled into spoons. Hardwoods like sycamore, maple, and beech were used extensively to handcraft these articles, collectively known as "treen," an old English word meaning "of trees."

With the invention of the pole-lathe in the Middle Ages, the manufacture of treen became an important part of the woodturner's trade, but wood-carvers continued to make a variety of domestic and agricultural implements. Kitchen articles such as pestles and mortars, skimmers, and vegetable choppers were made by both amateur and professional carvers, but it was the amateur who produced most of the treen that survives today.

In his spare time, the husband made clothes pegs, cheese scoops, or simple nutcrackers for his home. Young men courting expressed their feelings through love tokens painstakingly whittled from odd pieces of wood. The term "spooning," in fact, originated with Welshmen, who, for more than three centuries, made declarations of love by carving spoons with intricate symbols. A wheel, for instance, meant "I will work for you," and spectacles meant "I want to see you."

Treen became less common after 1830, as machine-made articles began to predominate. Nevertheless, collectors can still find a wide range of these handcrafted domestic wares. One such collector, Murray Johnson, displays an unusual selection of butter prints, graters, gingerbread and cookie molds, ladles, spatulas, and spoons along the walls of his office. As the owner

Christopher Borne

Murray Johnson.

Birch

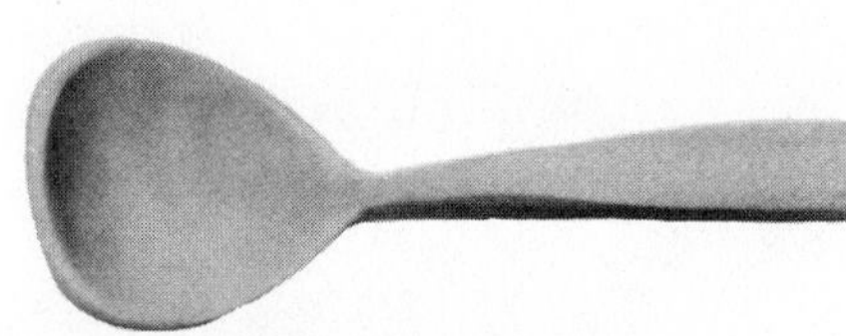

Birch is normally a fairly straight-grained, fine-textured wood of plain appearance. The wood is normally white, though yellow birch has a brownish heart. It is moderately heavy but is an excellent wood for turning. Birch is useful as a general-utility wood, having high strength and good working and finishing properties. Available in small sizes, it is largely used for turning brooms, small-tool handles, and small kitchen items.

Walnut

European walnut is gray-brown, with nearly black streaks. The grain is straight or occasionally wavy; texture medium; and weight a little less than beech. Walnut is one of the world's outstanding decorative woods, long used for cabinetwork. Walnut's moderate density, good working and finishing properties, toughness, and resistance to splitting have made it a popular wood for bowls and other turned kitchen items.

of H. A. Mack & Company, a Boston-based importer of gourmet cooking utensils, Johnson has traveled the world for more than 20 years buying merchandise. Along the way, he has also acquired an uncommon understanding of wood, as well as his personal collection of fine, crafted implements.

A fit, silver-haired man in his early sixties, Johnson is able to tell where a spoon was made simply by looking at the shape. He says round-bowled spoons are usually German; oval ones are Swedish or French unless they have flat ends, and in that case they're Danish. Spoons that resemble pipes—the handle is on the bottom of the bowl—are Moroccan, and those with the handle at the middle of the oval bowl are Japanese.

Reaching for one of the spoons lining the shelves of his showroom, Johnson talked about craftsmanship. He turned the spoon over in his hands and explained that fine utensils like this require a lot of hand working. "In Portugal, many two-man shops produce these pieces individually. You can't afford to buy that kind of workmanship in this country. It would cost a fortune, so Americans compromise quality by using automatic lathes and shapers. That's why I go on three-week buying trips, visiting small shops and production facilities all over the world."

Hornbeam

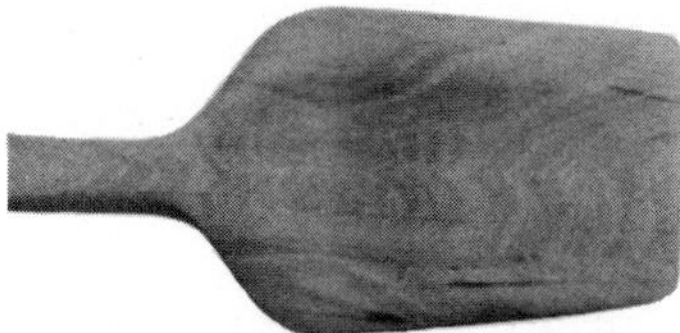

Hornbeam is outstanding among European hardwoods for its combination of high density, strength, toughness, and resistance to splitting. The wood is white and has a fine texture and almost featureless appearance. Its grain may be irregular and may show undulating growth rings. In many respects, hornbeam is like a dense beech. In strength, it compares well with beech. But because of its weight, hornbeam is very difficult to work except when turned on a lathe. When dry, it will take a fine finish. With supplies limited, hornbeam is a special-purpose wood used for handles, mallets, and kitchen utensils if great strength is required.

Beech

Beech is one of the most important hardwoods of Western and Central Europe. It is a general-utility wood of plain appearance, straight grain, and fine, even texture. White or pale brown in color, it is sometimes steamed to a pinkish color. Beech is strong but works easily. For mass-production, where ease of working is the main consideration, softer beech from Central and Southern Europe is often preferred. Its superior strength properties, combined with moderate weight, good working qualities, and clean appearance, make beech a popular wood for a wide range of turned items, including spoons.

Today, so many fine wood utensils are manufactured in Spain and Portugal because the poor people of those countries still use wood implements at the table as well as in the kitchen, according to Johnson. But in the Orient, where the people use chopsticks, wood utensils are made primarily for export, and they're often poorly made in low-grade wood.

H. A. Mack imports finished wood articles from Morocco, Turkey, Madagascar, Japan, and the Philippines, as well as most European countries. When buying utensils, Johnson carefully looks at the wood used to fashion each item. There are differences in grain, figure, texture, weight, and strength that affect the appearance and function of the finished product. To understand these differences, it is necessary to understand the terms.

Grain. The direction or orientation of the actual wood cells. Often it is more or less straight, but occasionally wavy or irregular. In many tropical woods, the grain spirals in alternate directions. Woods with interlocking grain are usually the toughest and most resistent to splitting.

Figure. The decorative appearance of the wood caused by structural features such as rays, growth rings, grain, and color variations. The figure changes depending on the sawcut used to expose the wood surface.

Texture. The evenness of the wood surface. In softwoods (cone-bearing trees), it is often influenced by the contrast between early and late wood. In hardwoods (broad-leaved trees), texture is determined by the size and distribution of the pores. (Pores are a cross section of the vessels which carry sap from the roots to the leaves). Where the pores are large, the texture is coarse, but where there are many fine pores, the texture is also fine.

Weight. Varies considerably between species. It is affected by the amount of water retained and by the wood's density. Hardwoods vary from the light balsa to the heavy box- or olivewood.

Johnson goes on to explain how these characteristics affect the function of finished wood products. "When buying kitchen utensils, I first look at the figure of the wood to see if it is pleasing. Then I check the texture, looking for a wood that has fine pores rather than large ones. The higher a wood's porosity, the more moisture the wood absorbs and the greater the chance it will swell and stain.

"Mahogany, for instance, is fairly porous, and when lacquered on the outside, the wood swells, forcing the lacquer to break off. Pine is another wood with relatively high porosity, so most pine utensils absorb moisture and rapidly stain black. These woods are only good for kitchen use if they have been properly treated with lacquer or oil. The Portuguese have developed a successful lacquering method, for instance. They spray it under high pressure, so the lacquer is actually absorbed into the wood."

Depending on their porosity, hardwoods absorb a certain amount of moisture. But, if properly cared for, most wood can be kept free of harmful bacteria. Salad bowls should be thoroughly washed after each use, according to Johnson.

Woods with low porosity are usually the denser woods as well. And the denser a wood, the less likely it is that the fibers will separate. When the fibers do separate, it is called furring, because the wood takes on a woolly appearance. Furring usually occurs after a wood absorbs moisture, but with light, tropical woods, the fibers may separate when dry. Johnson realizes full well that this is a lot for the novice to comprehend and recommends *Know Your Woods*, by Albert Constantine, for a more detailed discussion.

Of the 30 or more commercial woods used to make kitchenware, boxwood and olivewood are most desirable because they have the lowest porosity and the highest

Alder

The common alder is found widely in Europe. The freshly cut wood is pale but turns a bright orange-brown on exposure. It has a fine texture, and the cut wood is characterized by lines and streaks like pencil marks and scattered rust-colored flecks. Alder is comparable to poplar in most of its strength properties and is of medium density. It works well and is used in crafts and in small industry for such purposes as broom backs and handles.

Ramin

Ramin is almost white, moderately even in texture, and generally straight grained. The wood has a tendency to split and discolor, especially in thicker sizes. Lighter than beech, ramin is not so tough and splits more readily. The wood's straighter grain makes it popular for machine turning. It is widely used in inexpensive, mass-produced utensils imported from the Far East.

Plane

In color and texture, plane resembles beech but is easily distinguished by the numerous dark rays. The European plane, the common urban landscape tree, is about 15 percent lighter than beech and has a fine, even texture and straight grain. It has only moderate strength, so it is often used for handles and nonstriking implements.

Maple/sycamore

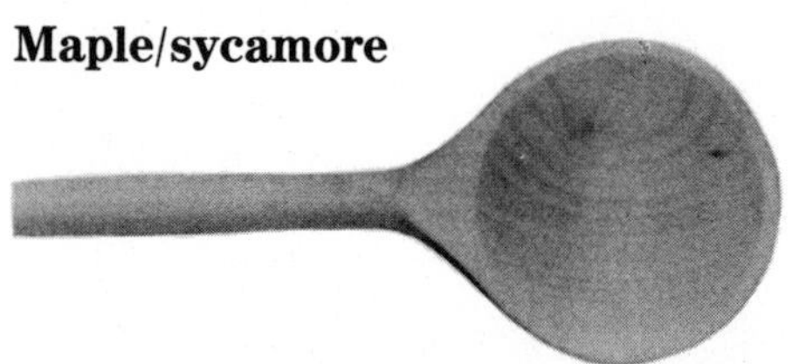

Maple is a pale wood and is normally straight grained, but the European sycamore has a wavy grain. The soft maples are about 25 percent lighter than beech. Sycamores and soft maples are used for kitchen implements and rollers, while the wavy-grained sycamore is the traditional wood for violins.

density. Both are considered special-purpose woods, however, because supplies are limited and the cost is often prohibitive. Beech, a fine-textured wood of moderate weight, is more common and more affordable than box- or olivewood. For these reasons, it is the major wood used to produce kitchen utensils in Europe. Beech is closely followed by plane, sycamore, maple, alder, poplar, birch, and willow.

Because tropical trees grow year-round, they have large vessels for transporting sap to their leaves. This makes tropical woods like ramin and jelutong very porous, light, and, according to Johnson, "practically worthless for kitchen use. These woods swell, absorb too much stain and oil, and quickly turn black," he says. "Still, most inexpensive kitchenware imported from Taiwan is made of jelutong and ramin. And many wholesalers and retailers sell these woods without knowing it. They pass them off as pine, or simply say they're 'strong hardwoods.' "

Care of woodenware

Learning to care for woodenware is crucial to those who want products to hold up after many uses. Woodenware can warp, crack, and splinter if it isn't properly cleaned and seasoned.

The first rule is that woodenware should never be soaked in water. Even if immediately dried, soaked pieces will crack. A piece may be washed lightly with a mild soap, rinsed quickly, and then thoroughly dried. Extreme hot and cold temperatures in water may also cause cracking. Seasoning is important. Most suppliers advocate the use of mineral oil for this. Linseed and vegetable oil are poor agents in seasoning. Oil should be liberally applied, allowed to soak in, and then wiped dry. Oil may be reapplied if dryness appears.

After use, a damp sponge may be used to wipe out salad bowls or clean off cutting boards. Seasoning helps to prevent staining and odors, and lemon juice will generally lift stains. No woodenware is truly dishwasher-proof.

The best woods for kitchen use are obviously those that are attractive and have low porosity and high density. Then, depending on a particular utensil's function, the wood's tensile strength may be taken into account. Tensile strength is based on whether the wood grain is interlocking. If so, the wood resists splitting and is good for items, like spatulas, that must accept a certain amount of pressure. Hornbeam, a European specialty wood, is outstanding among hardwoods because of its combination of strength, toughness, and resistance to splitting. This wood is a favorite for tool handles, mallets, spatulas, and other kitchen implements for which great tensile strength is required.

Olivewood, which is superior in every other respect, is very brittle and tends to split across the grain. So olivewood handles should be very thick if the utensil is to be durable. Pine is also weak, so most utensils fashioned from this wood are made with separate handles.

Because many of the woods used in kitchen articles are white or light-colored, subtle differences are not readily apparent. Such woods may need to be moistened or dyed with a food such as grape jelly to make these variations visible. If a wood cannot be identified, send a section to the U.S. Department of Agriculture, Forest Products Division, Madison, WI 53706, for positive identification.

MARY ANN BACHER

Jelutong

This Southeast Asian timber is found in Malaysia and Indonesia and is exported as sawn wood or finished items. The wood is plain and straw-colored with occasional, and sometimes abundant, horizontal cavities. Jelutong lacks any distinctive figure. It is very light in weight, usually weak, and dents easily. If drying is delayed, jelutong quickly discolors. It is difficult to obtain wood free of cavities, so most jelutong is used in Taiwan to make inexpensive kitchen items for export.

Poplar

Poplar is white, sometimes with pink or brown tint. It is generally a straight-grained wood with a fine, even texture. Light in weight but surprisingly tough, poplar does not easily split or splinter. It saws and works easily but with a tendency to a woolly surface. The wood is used for boxes and crates and for many small domestic articles such as wooden shoes and kitchen implements.

Willow

This timber is typically straight grained with a fine, even texture. Willow looks like poplar. The wood is light and soft and not particularly strong except for its toughness. Willow tends to dent rather than split under rough usage. It is easy to work but requires sharp tools for a smooth finish. Willow is used for sieve rims and other kitchen utensils, as well as cricket bats.

REFRIGERATORS

Compared to other appliances, large and small, the refrigerator is long-lived. Over the years, USDA surveys have indicated an average life of around 15 years.

The refrigerator ages gracefully because it is so simple—not much more than an insulated closet with a thermostatically controlled compressor at the floor and a system of tubes to carry off the heat. Or so it was until recently. Today's models are nearly all frost-free, and can be loaded with such options as icemakers, cold-water spigots, and heated butter dishes. How will increasing complexity affect service life?

That's a matter for debate. Predictably, industry spokespeople say things are looking up. Walter Bennett of General Electric points out that fewer refrigerators are breaking down during the warranty period these days, and he is supported by a report of Massachusetts Institute of Technology's Center for Policy Alternatives. According to senior research associate Robert Lund, "Refrigerator warranty expense today [1974] is approximately $57 million per year which represents less than a half of 1 percent of total sales. This has been a fairly constant record over the years in spite of rising labor costs, because of the emphasis placed on reducing the first-year service-incidence rate by the manufacturer. . . . [and] in spite of the fact that the newer refrigerators have greater complexity as industry strives to introduce technological innovations into the product. The record substantiates that manufacturers have placed emphasis on increasing reliability of the various parts and components in today's refrigerators."

Curiously, 19 of the 25 refrigerator repair people we talked to think that today's refrigerators are not holding up as long as they used to. (Only 3 said current models should give *more* years of service.) Overall, they consistently cited a declining quality of both parts and labor as the reason for their pessimism. Several pointed out that an otherwise sound refrigerator must often be discarded because the shelving breaks, and they suggested buying refrigerators with a porcelain interior lining and metal shelving, rather than plastic lining and shelving.

Complexity is the enemy of long and reliable service, in refrigerators as in other appliances and machines. Unfortunately, the family-sized refrigerator without a frost-free system is a rarity these days, and today's popular add-on features carry with them the potential for trouble.

"The simpler things last longer," says GE's Bennett, and he suggests that the fancier models may be earning for refrigerators a reputation for declining durability. "The refrigeration system may work perfectly, but if the icemaker keeps breaking or if the exterior trim falls off, the consumer is left with the impression that the refrigerator is falling to pieces."

Smaller iceboxes, of up to 14 or 15 cubic feet, can be had with manual defrost, and one retailer suggested that larger ones can be special-ordered. James Scism, of Residential Refrigerator Repair

What our repair people said: refrigerators

Brand, model, price	Average life-span estimates, years
Frigidaire, FPE-17TJ, $729	13.23
Whirlpool, EHT181AK, $595	11.77
Sears Kenmore, 46A61716N, $500	11.66
General Electric, TBF17LB, $500	11.42
Amana, ESRFC-16E, $665	11.39
Hotpoint, CTF17PA, $500	10.84
Gibson, RT17F-3, $579	10.78
Kelvinator, TPK170SN, $538	10.50
Westinghouse, RB188A, $715	9.94

We telephoned 25 Pennsylvania refrigerator repair people in March, 1981, and asked them to estimate the average life span of the nine refrigerators listed above, assuming that each refrigerator was given "reasonable" care by its owner. The model numbers above refer to 17-cubic-foot, "no-frills" refrigerators with white exteriors. The prices and model numbers shown were current at the time of the survey but are subject to change.

in Poughkeepsie, New York, advises, "If I was a consumer going out to buy a new refrigerator, I would buy a standard unit–with no timers, no heater, no defrost thermostats, and all that crap–as simple as I could get it. But you've got to order it. You used to have to order self-defrost; today you have to order standard." He has found that as a rule, the more expensive the refrigerator, the more likely it will break down. "The compressor is continuously running in a self-defrost. It has to in order to keep cold, because you've got heaters that are going on every defrost cycle. The most common parts that go are the timer and the defrost heater, and the condenser and evaporator and fan motors. In a standard model, the thermostat is the most common thing to go wrong, or a relay–not the compressor."

You might come to the conclusion that a used manual-defrost refrigerator will give you superior service for the money. "Nowadays," says James Scism, "you're better off buying an older, used unit. They're putting out more garbage now than they were five years ago. Every year it's getting worse. More of my service calls are for new units."

Whether you buy a new or used icebox, you still have to pick a brand, and this matter has been clouded by the recent spate of brand takeovers. "Frigidaire always was considered the Cadillac of refrigerators," Arnold Johnson, a Philadelphia repair person, tells us. "But that was because General Motors made Frigidaires." In our survey of 25 repair people, this brand was rated most durable, but these opinions were based largely on refrigerators made before White Consolidated Industries bought the troubled Frigidaire appliance division from GM in 1979. Today, White also manufactures boxes bearing the name of Westinghouse, Kelvinator, and Gibson. Are the four appreciably different from one another? Jim Hughey, of Frigidaire's marketing department, won't say whether White's four brands are now produced on the same manufacturing

1942 Frigidaire refrigerator

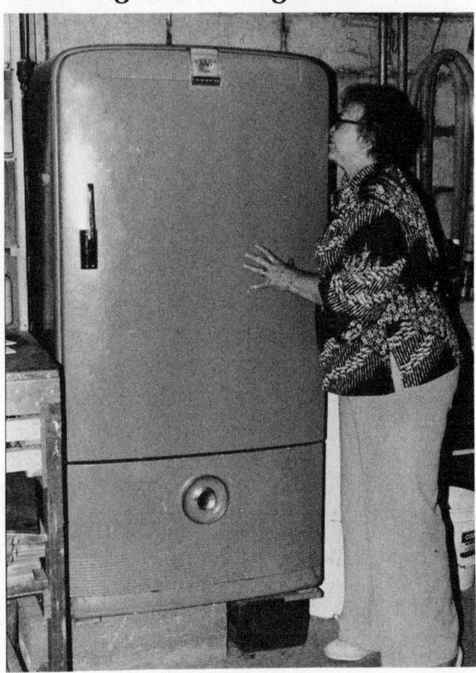

"My friend Kathy took the picture. I hope it conveys our feeling of trust and affection for that 1942 refrigerator. The interior is of steel construction with a porcelain finish, sturdy as all get out. The shelves are of heavy metal, as are the shelf supports. Outside of a broken glass cover over the vegetable crisper, it is in perfect condition. Ice cubes and ice cream are made as fast as when the refrigerator was new.

"We were given a newer Frigidaire for our basement. To say I was shocked at the difference in quality is putting it mildly. The interior is of plastic, broken where articles have been dropped. The shelf supports are of plastic, and many of them are broken with no way of repairing them. The shelves are flimsy aluminum and are not strong enough to support much weight. This is truly a product of today's planned obsolescence. We pitched it out to the scrap heap. Isn't it tragic that, due to planned obsolescence, our nation's garbage heaps grow by leaps and bounds, while our natural resources are being exhausted? We are living in a plastic society, and it goes against the grain to put out hard-earned dollars for such shoddy, short-lived equipment. So, we treasure 'Old Faithful' and say a prayer that it will last many more years and continue to give such good service."

GERTRUDE E. JOHNSON
Lamont, Washington

1950 Westinghouse refrigerator

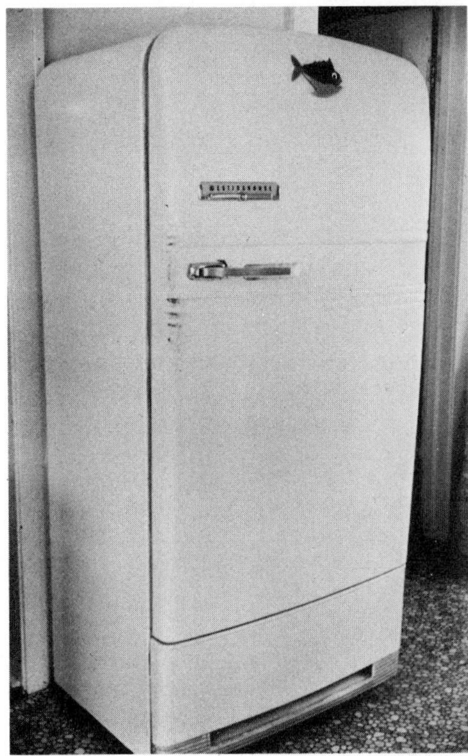

"My mother and father were married in 1911, and this was the first refrigerator my mother ever had. Prior to that, she had only an 'ice box' to keep food cool in summer, and a cupboard on a porch to preserve food in the winter. The only repairs in all these years have been the replacement of the gasket around the door and the light bulb that comes on when the door is opened. It is a product made to last, in contrast with the current built-in obsolescence syndrome which seems to prevail in these times."

ROSE PITTERLE
Freeport, Illinois

line, but he allows that they "share some common components and perform the same basic function."

It's hard to know just what you're getting behind the name plate. *Appliance* magazine admits that "the private brand business is so broad and so comprehensive that it would require volumes just to list who makes what for whom." One thing is clear—the consumer is not served by the manufacturer's name games. A name is thus reduced to a marketing tool and may not be a guide to how long a particular refrigerator can be expected to hold up. General Electric makes GE, Hotpoint, and J. C. Penney; Admiral makes Montgomery Ward, Norge, Roper, Tappan, and Western Auto, among others; Whirlpool makes some Sears models, as do Sanyo and White.

Many of the repair people we interviewed told us that Whirlpool-made Sears Kenmore refrigerators are virtually the same as Whirlpool. General Electric and Hotpoint iceboxes come off the same assembly line and are "different in terms of features and styling but the durability and quality are the same," according to GE's Walter Bennett. In defense of the industry's name game, Bennett said that "a GE appliance dealer might get angry if another GE dealer opened across the street at a busy city intersection, but he won't care if a Hotpoint dealer opens up next door."

In our survey of service people, Frigidaire came out as most durable, but, again, they have been working on pre-White refrigerators. Whirlpool, Sears Kenmore, GE, and Amana followed in a group. *Consumer Reports* names the first two of these as "least apt to break down," basing their opinion on an owner survey. *Appliance Manufacturer*'s owner survey turned up Whirlpool as the cheapest to service, with the lowest average number of service calls of five brands.

What can you do to prolong the life of a refrigerator? The repair people we talked with recommend that you vacuum the condenser coils located at the back or bottom, because dust interferes with heat dispersion. Coils at the back should be vacuumed every six months or so, and those at the bottom twice as often. And if you have so far resisted the convenience of a frost-free model, take care that you don't puncture the cooling tubes when attacking the ice.

If you find yourself in need of a gasket, switch, or other hardware, you might consider ordering it from a parts firm before calling a repair person. The prices are reasonable and the replacement job may be within your ability. See the Appendix for a list of parts suppliers.

BK, with DOUGLAS C. SMYTH

Appliance Manufacturer owner survey: refrigerators

	All brands	Sears Kenmore	General Electric	Frigidaire	Whirlpool	Hotpoint
Average number of service calls	2.1	2.3	2.2	2.2	1.7	1.9
Average total cost of service	\$57.64	\$68.26	\$66.67	\$59.76	\$41.00	\$52.40

Appliance Manufacturer magazine surveyed 1,135 refrigerator owners in 1980. Note that the average number of service calls could be inflated if many owners of a make have service contracts; this should be kept in mind in looking at these figures, we were cautioned by Kenneth W. Yee, electronic engineer at the National Bureau of Standards.

A manufacturer's own DIY repair system

General Electric has come out with an ambitious program to help consumers repair their own GE products. They would have done so sooner if their consumer researchers hadn't underestimated how many people attempted home repairs.

Forty percent of all major appliance repairs are performed by the consumer—not 20, as GE originally thought—and a quarter of the amateur repair people are women. Consumers take repairs into their own hands, not only to save money but to get the job done right.

For these 40 percent, GE has established its Quick Fix System, involving five \$6.95 instruction manuals with diagnostic charts and plenty of illustrations, and a stock of 94 parts in color-coded boxes (out of a total of some 45,000 parts). Each part carton is labeled with the estimated time needed for the repair.

The new EnergyGuide labels and what they mean

Home energy use accounts for 20 percent of all the energy consumed in this country. To encourage people to consider the energy needs of appliances and heating and cooling units, the Federal Trade Commission (FTC) and the Department of Energy (DOE) have implemented the EnergyGuide labeling program.

EnergyGuide labels suggest the true cost of owning an appliance by estimating yearly operating costs. Energy costs may in time add up to as much or more than the purchase price. Many of us don't realize how much operating expenses actually add to the cost of owning an appliance. EnergyGuide labels permit shoppers to compare the operating costs of brands and models, so that they can save money and energy in the long run. Did you know that the cost of running a refrigerator for its average lifetime of 15 years can surpass the original purchase price?

Bright yellow-and-black EnergyGuide labels can be found on furnaces, refrigerators, freezers, water heaters, clothes washers, dishwashers, and room air conditioners. Together, these appliances account for 73 percent of all the energy consumed in American homes. Central air conditioners and heat pumps eventually will have labels too. Why have many appliances been omitted? Kitchen ranges and ovens, televisions, clothes dryers, humidifiers and dehumidifiers, and heating equipment other than furnaces were all considered for the original program, but research revealed that energy use doesn't vary considerably between brands and models of these items. And you won't find labels on small appliances such as toasters, blenders, or hair dryers, as they use relatively little energy and a labeling program for them was not considered cost-effective.

The energy labels that appear on appliances are basically of three types. The energy-cost label provides the estimated cost of running an appliance for one year at an average electricity rate (or gas rate); this cost is put in perspective by displaying the lowest and highest energy costs found among brands. The label on room air conditioners provides an energy-efficiency rating for the appliance (the higher the rating, the more efficient the appliance). Furnaces are labeled with information on home energy conservation, and on how to obtain efficiency ratings from your heating-system dealer or contractor.

As you go about pricing appliances, you will notice that products that are more energy efficient often cost a bit more, due to the expense of features such as improved insulation or better motors and compressors. But an investment in an energy-efficient appliance pays back the extra expense over time through energy savings—often in two to five years. And the savings continue, making the energy-efficient appliance a better buy in the long run.

(Name of Corporation)
Model(s) AH503, AH504, AH507
Type of Defrost: Full Automatic

Refrigerator-Freezer
Capacity: 17 Cubic Feet

ENERGYGUIDE

Estimates on the scale are based on a national average electric rate of 4.97¢ per kilowatt hour.

Only models with 16.5 to 18.4 cubic feet are compared in the scale.

Model with lowest energy cost **$45**

$60

THIS MODEL

Model with highest energy cost **$88**

Estimated yearly energy cost

Your cost will vary depending on your local energy rate and how you use the product. This energy cost is based on U.S. Government standard tests

How much will this model cost you to run yearly?

		Yearly cost Estimated yearly $ cost shown below
Cost per kilowatt hour	**2¢**	$24
	4¢	$48
	6¢	$72
	8¢	$96
	10¢	$120
	12¢	$144

Ask your salesperson or local utility for the energy rate (cost per kilowatt hour) in your area.

Important Removal of this label before consumer purchase is a violation of federal law (42 U.S.C. 6302)

(Part No. 371026)

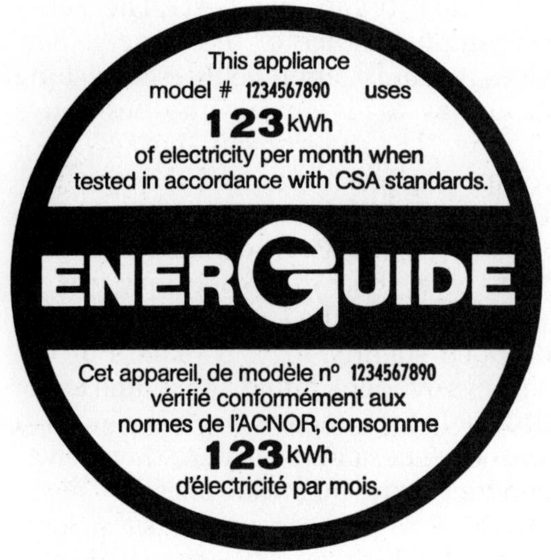

The appearance of energy labels should not only encourage energy conservation by consumers choosing between models but also spur manufacturers to build more efficient appliances.

Appliance energy conservation efforts are not stopping with labels. The DOE hopes to phase in minimum energy-efficiency standards for eight major home appliances over a five-year period beginning in July, 1981. If these standards go into practice, DOE estimates that literally billions of barrels of oil and millions of consumer dollars could be saved.

Canada's energy labeling program extends to refrigerators, freezers, dishwashers, clothes washers and dryers, and ranges. Future plans may include hot-water heaters, heat pumps, and incandescent lights. Displayed on each label are the model number and energy consumption in kilowatt hours of electricity per month. Further information is available in directories published by the Canadian Standards Association for each product category. These directories are available free of charge from regional offices of Consumer and Corporate Affairs Canada.

TK

Sources for appliance parts and service

- *Small appliances.* The National Appliance Service Association can supply you with the names of authorized centers that service small appliances in your area. They recommend that you check your Yellow Pages first, however. NASA-member service centers will sell small-appliance parts to individuals, but the national office stresses that it does not encourage do-it-yourselfers to undertake what it considers potentially dangerous repair jobs. For authorized centers in your area, write: National Appliance Service Association, 1308 Pennsylvania, Kansas City, MO 64105.
- *Large appliances.* The members of the Appliance Parts Distributors Association are happy to sell large-appliance parts to individuals. Members listed in the Appendix may be able to provide you with a local parts source. We do not list all stores due to space limitations.

Repair manuals and parts catalogs are available from some service centers. See the Appendix for a list of appliance-parts firms. Whirlpool has a toll-free number for do-it-yourselfers with repair problems; in 1980, 187,000 people called in for help. The number is (800) 253-1301.

"When a $20 item costs $30 to repair, you throw it out."

JAY WAYMAN, Electronic Industries Assoc., quoted in the *Wall Street Journal*

WASHING MACHINES

Our search for the longest-lived washing machines turned up two maxims that hold for many other product lines as well: the simpler, the more durable; and, durability comes at a slightly higher sticker price.

According to our interviews with 25 washer repair people, the bare-bones wringer washer lasts longer than conventional automatics, with an estimated average of 14.8 years. Front-loading automatics cost more than the more common top loaders of the same make, and hold less; but the front loaders' average life span came to 11 years, as compared to only 8.5 for top loaders, which must sling roughly twice as much water to get the cleaning done and use expensive transmissions rather than the simple belts found on front loaders. Because a new transmission can cost up to half the purchase price, an ailing top loader is likely to be scrapped rather than repaired.

The most attractive things about compact machines are their smaller size and smaller price. But on average, they appear to be the least durable of models, at 6.7 years, according to our survey. People tend to overload them, and the small-scale components can't handle the abuse.

Which brands are best? The Federal Supply Service of the General Services Administration field-tests washing machines to determine the best buys for the U.S. government—but will not release its test data. In 1957, the U.S. Department of Agriculture (USDA) surveyed 17,500 households and determined that the average life expectancy was 11 years; by 1972, the USDA's estimate had dropped slightly, to 10.8 years. But the surveys overlook brand names and are of little help for someone out shopping for a washer. The manufacturers themselves conduct tests, but "that does not mean anything to the consumer," says Steve Sizer of Whirlpool. "We simply do not talk about these things. No intelligent manufacturer does." Spokespeople for Kelvinator, General Electric, Hotpoint, Sears, Frigidaire, and White-Westinghouse also declined to estimate the life expectancies of their products. "It's like cars," says Jim Ellis of Speed Queen. "There's some people who drive a car into the ground in a week. It's the same with washing machines." Only the spokesperson for Montgomery Ward would give an unqualified estimate of his machine's life span: "Norge manufactures Montgomery Ward's top-loading washers," he says,

Appliance Manufacturer owner survey: washers

	All brands	Sears Kenmore	Maytag	General Electric	Hotpoint	Frigidaire
Average number of service calls	0.82	1.12	0.70	0.72	0.71	1.13
Average total cost of service	$52.69	$52.94	$52.58	$38.79	$44.71	$61.73

Appliance Manufacturer magazine surveyed 904 owners of washing machines in 1981. The magazine determined the average number of service calls and the average cost of repairs for five leading brands of washers.

"and we specify that Norge make our machines to last 15 years. Period." (Our survey of repair people suggested a Ward's top loader would last just half that long).

The average life-span estimates of the repair people ranged from only 5 to 6 years for several compact models to a top end of 15.1 and 18 years for two traditional wringer washers. More-conventional machines fall in between.

Of our 25 informants, 11 named Maytag the most durable washing machine. Whirlpool trailed a distant second, with 5 votes, and White-Westinghouse front loaders got 3. (Only 2 repair people had no comment.) In 1980, Maytag was also *Consumer Reports'* top-rated machine overall, as well as the most reliable in that magazine's four-year survey (Speed Queen had the worst service record).

Christie C. Tito

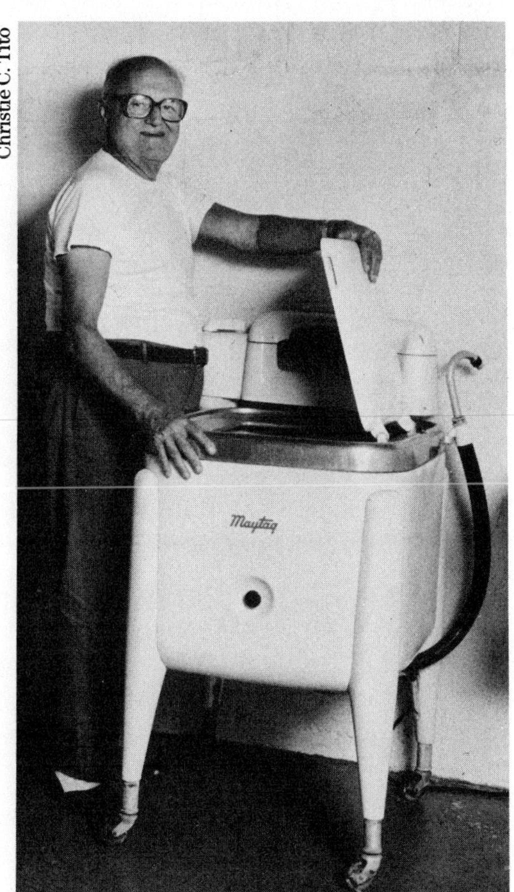

The basement durability champ, Maytag's wringer.

What our repair people said: washers

Brand, type, model, price	Average life-span estimates, years
Maytag wringer, E2L, $389	18.00
Speed Queen wringer, FW3092, $316	15.09
Wards wringer, 890, $270	13.79
Gibson wringer, WW279PI, $295	12.36
Maytag automatic, A710, $539	11.65
Westinghouse front-loading, LT570A, $469	11.36
Gibson front-loading, WS14M6, $530	10.86
Wards front-loading, 6508, $470	10.65
Whirlpool automatic, LHA7680, $387	10.00
GE automatic, WWA8350V, $399	9.23
Speed Queen automatic, HA6450, $384	9.07
Hotpoint automatic, WLW4700A, $369	8.83
Sears automatic, 20801, $420	8.64
Westinghouse automatic, LA570A, $379	8.23
Frigidaire automatic, WIJ, $460	7.91
Wards automatic, 6329, $330	7.42
Maytag compact, A50, $298	7.17
Westinghouse compact, LC600A, $379	7.09
Gibson automatic, WA18D3WL, $399	7.07
Norge automatic, LWA7120S, $389	7.02
Wards compact, 7068, $250	7.00
Whirlpool compact, LHC4900, $420	6.88
Kelvinator automatic, AW1830P, $400	6.70
GE compact, WWP1150V, $349	6.67
Sears compact, 40901, $320	6.15
Gibson compact, WA10P4WL, $355	5.75

We telephoned 25 East Coast washer repair people in February, 1981, and asked them to estimate the average life span of the 26 washers listed above, assuming that each machine was given "reasonable" care by its owner. The prices and model numbers shown were current at the time of the survey but are subject to change.

Maytag top-loading washer

Christie C. Tito

The redoubtable Maytag automatic.

Averaging the life-span estimates from our 25 washing-machine repair people, we found that the Maytag top-loading washer came out on top at 11.65 years—3 years longer than the average top loader. But you'll pay for that durability: a Maytag costs up to $200 more than other top-loading washing machines.

Arnold Schnoebelen, a spokesperson for Maytag, said a time-tested drive mechanism was one reason Maytag washers last so long. And when something does go wrong there's a 25-year parts inventory.

A repair person from Norristown, Pennsylvania, Stanley Pomilio, told us that if you "take the front off washing machines in the showroom and look for heavy-duty components and motors, you can see for yourself that Maytags have better components and are made to last."

Throughout the industry, durability seems to be eroded by indifferent craftsmanship and a move to cheaper materials—thinner metal and plastics, aluminum rather than copper windings in motors, and bearings of cheaper alloys. Of our 25 repair people, 16 said today's machines are less durable, 4 said they're more durable, and 5 had noticed no change.

The repair people were nearly unanimous in discouraging owner repairs. It seems a good deal of their business is generated by tinkerers who end up making matters worse. We also learned that there isn't much a shopper can do to judge the durability of a washer on the showroom floor. (Only one repair person said you could actually see durability in a machine: peer behind the front panel of a Maytag, we were told, and you'll find the heavy-duty parts that make this brand the longest-lived.) Repair people suggest that you rely on brand-name reputations and the advice of trustworthy salespeople.

In general, you can expect fewer problems from the simpler machines. The wringers are the extreme case in point, while automatics with modest control panels give a compromise between convenience and reliability.

Energy cost will become increasingly important in determining how long a washer is kept in service, and it is worth repeating here *Consumer Reports'* information that the White-Westinghouse front loaders need less hot or warm water for a wash than conventional models, and that Maytags run on roughly half as much electricity as the competition.

Interviews and survey by BK

Good words for Maytag

"Rust is the biggest factor."

An interview with Ray Stein

Washer repair people often are leery about being interviewed. One recalled fixing a machine with a shotgun at his head; another's truck was stripped of parts. When first approached for an interview, Ray Stein of Poughkeepsie, New York, told us he only worked on the books, although his repair truck was just outside the door.

DOUGLAS C. SMYTH

"People abuse washers and dryers. They put three pairs of sneakers in there and let them bounce around until they jam between the agitator and the tub and stop it like a brick. The motor's spinning, and it's turning the clutch and transmission, but nothing can go. The weakest part's going to break. In Maytags, it's the belt; in other machines, it could be something more expensive.

Maytag's drive belt also acts like a clutch. If you put 40 pounds of clothes in another machine and jam up the agitator, the transmission or drive will break, something will burn up, but in the Maytag, only the belt will go, and it only costs about $6 to replace. If you get something in the Maytag's pump—a sock or something—it'll burn up the pump belt, but the pump will be fine. Maytags will outlast anything on the market.

But you can't predict just how long a washing machine will last. It depends on the person using the machine. Some people wash conservative amounts of clothes; if they've got an 18-pound-capacity washer, they'll put 18 pounds in it; some people'll shove 28 pounds of clothes in it, constantly. Another factor is where you place the machine. There's more vibration on a wooden floor, which is no good for the machine. Or the dampness—that's the most important thing.

Check your laundromats and you'll find Maytag and Speed Queen, or occasionally Westinghouse because it's a much less expensive machine and it's a front loader. Some people prefer a front loader.

Some laundromats dispose of machines every 8 to 10 years, not because they wouldn't last longer, but because the cycles will be obsolete and the machines will look bad. I have commercial machines out there that are 20 years old.

At home, washers are thrown out because people get tired of them and because they rust. The tank of your washer sweats in the summer, just like the back of your toilet tank, and all that water drips down inside the cabinet of the machine. When you fill the washer with cold water in the summer or hot water in the winter, it sweats.

A lot of people will take a machine and stick it in a wet basement with an inch of water on the floor most of the year, and expect it to last 15 years. Well, after 4 or 5 years, the whole bottom of the machine will be rusted. If you have to change a part, you'll have to break it to get it off. But if the machine is in a dry spot, and it's taken care of, and the owner doesn't dump bleach all over the machine instead of in the tub, it might last a good while.

As far as durability goes, it really doesn't make any difference what features a washing machine has. There's only a difference in the number of switches on the control panel. The parts doing the work are still the same—same motors, same pumps, same transmissions. But if I were looking for a washing machine, I'd look for something simple to work on."

CLOTHES DRYERS

The USDA's 1957 survey of 17,500 American households concluded that the average electric clothes dryer should last 14 years. In 1972, a similar USDA survey reported that the service life of electric clothes dryers had been reduced by a fraction, to 13.7 years.*

*Our February, 1981, survey indicates an average life of 10.4 years; gas clothes dryers, we were told, last slightly less due to a more complicated design.

What our repair people said: dryers

Brand, type, model, price	Average life-span estimates, years
Maytag full-sized, DE410, $359	13.52
Speed Queen full-sized, HE6434, $384	11.86
Whirlpool full-sized, LHE5800, $327	11.72
General Electric full-sized, DDE8200V, $329	11.59
Sears full-sized, 69741, $290	10.94
Hotpoint full-sized, DLB2880A, $339	10.64
Maytag compact, DE50, $224	10.38
Gibson full-sized, DE18A3WL, $319	10.03
Westinghouse full-sized, DE570, $289	9.69
Frigidaire full-sized, DEIJ, $340	9.48
Norge full-sized, DDE7120S, $329	8.55
Kelvinator full-sized, D61830, $300	8.50
Wards full-sized, 7339, $250	8.38
Whirlpool compact, LHE4900, $305	8.35
Sears compact, 80901, $220	7.83
Westinghouse compact, DC600A, $275	7.31
General Electric compact, DD120V, $249	7.17
Gibson compact, DE10PLWL, $265	6.75
Wards compact, 7068, $250	6.64

We telephoned 25 East Coast clothes-dryer repair people in February, 1981, and asked them to estimate the average life span of the 19 electric clothes dryers listed above, assuming that each dryer was given "reasonable" care by its owner. The prices and model numbers shown were current at the time of the survey but are subject to change.

As is the case with washing machines, these government estimates assume that one brand of clothes dryer is as good as the next. Hoping to sleuth out the most durable brands of clothes dryers, we telephoned 25 laundry-equipment repair people asking about 19 models. We learned that clothes dryers generally last longer than washing machines because dryers do not slop around a basketful of hot water and are simpler machines, with fewer moving parts.

For our dryer survey, we interviewed a different set of 25 repair people than for our washing-machine survey, but Maytag still came out on top: 12 of 25 said Maytag makes the most durable clothes dryer, while 7 preferred Whirlpool models (compare this to 11 votes for Maytag and 5 for Whirlpool in our washer survey of 25 service people). Like their washers, Maytag's dryers came out on top, at an average of 13.5 years. They also are the most expensive, at $359 for the DE410—$33 and just under two years more than the next-best Whirlpool LHE5800.

Fifteen of our 25 said that clothes dryers aren't as durable as they used to be. They told us manufacturers have been devaluing their components in an effort to maintain prices in the face of inflation. Only 5 said that dryers were *more* durable. Curiously, they attributed this to technological innovations such as lightweight metals and space-age electronics, the same factors blamed by service people for shorter life spans. Four respondents said durability hadn't gained or suffered, and one had no opinion.

The repair people we interviewed also indicated that compact dryers, on the average, last almost three years less than full-size models because scaled-down components can't stand the frequent overloading. On top of this, fewer compact dryers are sold. Some cost more than full-size models. You get less for more.

Most of our repair people advised against tinkering with an ailing dryer. They're simpler inside than a washer, but many run on 220 volts rather than 110, compounding the consequence of forgetting to pull the plug.

Still, in our limited experience with home repairs, there was little work involved in replacing a faulty $10 thermostat and a broken belt.

BK

Appliance Manufacturer owner survey: dryers

	All brands	Sears Kenmore	Whirlpool	General Electric	Maytag	Frigidaire
Average number of service calls	0.53	0.66	0.46	0.43	0.61	0.39
Average total cost of service	$46.20	$40.25	$46.50	$26.90	$51.47	$42.00

Appliance Manufacturer magazine surveyed 796 owners of clothes dryers in 1981. The magazine determined the average number of service calls and the average cost of repairs for five leading brands of dryers.

Hand mill, 1918

"My father sent for the mill from Montgomery Ward in Chicago. I was ten years of age at the time. We had to go to the railroad station in Byesville, Ohio, to get it. The mill can be adjusted to grind anything from cracked corn to flour.

"The reason it is still in good condition is that years ago manufacturers put quality in their products. Today, everything we buy is high priced, highly advertised, with lots of eye appeal on the outside and junk on the inside."

WALTER VELOVITCH
Canton, Ohio

Gene Logsdon

1939 Hoover sweeper

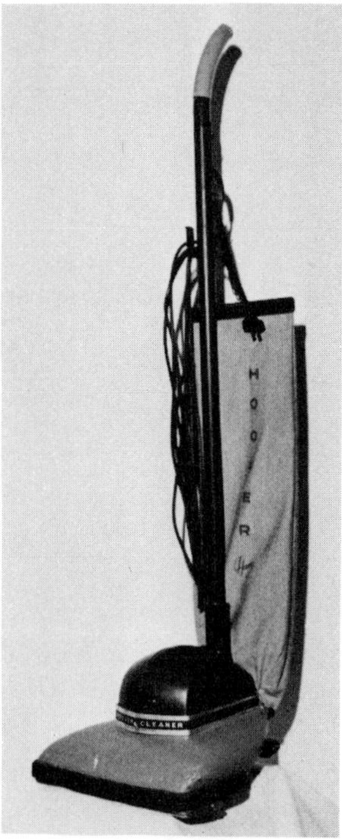

"Our Hoover sweeper has served us well for 42 years. We've had no problems with it and very little expense—just a servicing, a new bag, and new brushes several times. It has been used every week through four children, two dogs, two cats, and 25 automobiles!"

PATRICIA DAVIS
Bloomington, Indiana

VACUUM CLEANERS

If you're in the market for a vacuum, consider a used, reconditioned model: 18 of the 25 repair people we surveyed told us they don't make them like they used to. Our respondents put the blame on manufacturers' substitution of metal parts with plastic. Uprights tend to last a couple of years longer, on average, than canister models. Power nozzles may be ruthless on dirt, but they're one more feature to break down, said many repair people.

Which brands are best? The Kirby Classic III upright scored highest in our survey, with an average estimated life expectancy of nearly 18 years, but the extra years of service come at a price—the Kirby costs $500. The Electrolux Super J canister can be expected to last 14 years, and again, longevity has its price, at about $300. The Eureka upright should give at least 11 years of service, our survey told us, and it costs only $200. If you don't have a large area to clean, or aren't very fastidious, you might be pleased to get about 8.5 years out of the $65 Eureka canister vacuum. All told, Eurekas seem to be good investments for the money, with Hoover vacuums consistently rating somewhat less durable. Sears was rated least durable by our service people, and many of them said the company has a poor service network.

***Appliance Manufacturer* owner survey: vacuums**

	All brands	Hoover	Eureka	Sears Kenmore	Electrolux	Kirby
Average number of service calls	2.0	2.1	1.6	2.1	1.7	2.1
Average total cost of service	$33.74	$32.50	$18.93	$23.33	$35.86	$39.48

Appliance Manufacturer magazine surveyed 1,182 owners of vacuum cleaners in 1980. The magazine determined the average number of service calls and the average cost of repairs for five leading brands of vacuums.

Appliance Manufacturer magazine's 1980 poll of 1,182 vacuum-cleaner owners tends to support our findings: "Eureka owners got a better deal not only as price and quality-expected relate but in service, too."

Eureka vacuum cleaners were subject to an average of 1.6 service calls, the magazine reported, the lowest of any brand. Electrolux finished a close second, with an average of 1.7 service calls (but remember that Electrolux costs almost 2.5 times more, on the average, than Eureka vacuum cleaners). Hoover, Sears Kenmore, and Kirby vacuum cleaners each required an average of 2.1 service calls.

According to *Appliance Manufacturer's* poll, an average service call to fix a Eureka vacuum cleaner cost $18.93, the lowest of any brand. Sears Kenmore service calls, on the average, cost $23.33; Hoover, $32.50; Electrolux, $35.86; and Kirby, $39.48.

BK

What our people said: vacuums

Brand, type, model, price	Average life-span estimate, years
Kirby Classic III upright, 2CB, $459	17.91
Electrolux Super J canister, $274	14.39
Electrolux L power nozzle, $326	12.98
Electrolux heavy-duty upright, $230	11.27
Eureka upright, 4040A, $200	11.22
Hoover upright, J3101, $280	11.20
Eureka canister, 3220B, $65	8.43
Eureka power nozzle, 1277D, $220	8.13
Hoover canister, 2120, $85	7.82
Hoover power nozzle, S3061-030, $265	7.65
Sears canister, 2060C, $95	6.60
Sears upright, 3886, $175	6.25
Sears power nozzle, 2197, $300	6.00

We telephoned 25 East Coast vacuum-cleaner repair people in April, 1981, and asked them to estimate the average life span of the 13 vacuums listed above, assuming that each cleaner was given "reasonable" care by its owner. The prices and model numbers shown were current at the time of the survey but are subject to change.

1928 General Electric vacuum cleaner

"I bought the G.E. vacuum with my first income from teaching. It is easier to lift about than my 1950 long-cylinder model with all of its tubes, rods, and various attachments. The original electric cord needs a little repair, but we still use the vacuum."

AMELIA JO WIER
Sevierville, Tennessee

The big sweep

"Durability depends more on the owner than the price tag. Remember, you can tear up a fan in a $500 vacuum cleaner just as quickly as you can tear up the fan in a $60 vacuum."

An interview with Dave Odenwelder

Dave Odenwelder is the owner of Dave's Vacuum Cleaner Service in Allentown, Pennsylvania. The front room of his shop is cluttered with shiny new models, but much of his business is in repairs. While Odenwelder spoke with us, we were distracted by a steady stream of customers as they banged through the store with their vacuum cleaners, trailing snakelike vacuum cleaner hoses.

BK

Christie C. Tito

Dave Oldenwelder.

"This is the age of plastic. Plastics are hard to get away from. Today, because of plastic, vacuum cleaners are less durable than they used to be. Once vacuum cleaners were all metal, and some of them are 30 or 40 years old and still going, still running. I'm sure the average vacuum cleaner that's made today isn't going to run 30 years from now.

We've had a few plastic parts melt. Today, most all of the hoses on vacuum cleaners are made of plastic, when, yesteryear, hoses were made of a clothlike material. I've had several cases, in the winter months, where people laid a hose against a radiator or by a hot-air duct and the hose melted. The big problem with plastics is people dropping the vacuum; the plastic breaks.

Manufacturers have cut back. Today, 99 percent of all vacuum cleaners are using a paper bag, whereas they once used cloth dump bags. A lot of today's manufacturers are using sealed bearings instead of ball bearings. A sealed bearing will keep out dirt and foreign objects, but the grease in there will dry out and the bearing will have to be replaced.

Different sales people and manufacturers I've spoken with have told me that the average life of a vacuum cleaner these days is considered to be 7 years. If you're going to abuse a cleaner, it might only last 2 or 3 years. If you treat it with kid gloves, you may get 15 or 20 years out of it. Durability depends on the owner, rather than the price tag on the vacuum. Still, the more expensive vacuum cleaners will last longer. They'll also draw out the deeper-embedded dirt. I would say in the long run it is better to buy a good piece of equipment. You can buy vacuums today between about $49.95 and $700. Some people have a theory that they can buy four or five $100 vacuums, and they'll do as good a job as a vacuum costing $400 or $500, and last as long. I'd say, don't buy the most expensive vacuum or the least expensive: try to hit a happy medium. Get something in the $150-to-$200 price range. You can buy a vacuum in the $250-to-$550 price range which would be more durable, yes, but not two or three times more durable.

Being in the business, I probably take better care of my vacuum cleaners than most people do. It's not only that they'll last longer, but they'll also perform much better. By cleaning out the fan chamber and making sure the paper bags are clean and empty, there'll be less friction in the cleaner. The less friction, the longer the vacuum's going to last, and the better it's going to perform.

Upright vs. canister

When you're using an upright vacuum cleaner, you're using it in the dirt. When you pick up dust and dirt, hair and what have you, it gets in the motor, it gets in the bearings, it gets into the fan chamber. It blocks up a vacuum over a period of time. For this reason, all uprights should be periodically torn down, cleaned, and greased. Manufacturers used to say that should be done once a year. I would say an average upright vacuum cleaner should be serviced every other year. A canister, on the other hand, with its paper bag assembly, has much less dirt going through the motor. The dirt's in the bag before it reaches the motor, so, consequently, you don't have quite as much dirt getting into the motor, and they don't have to be greased and cleaned quite so often. I would say a canister vacuum cleaner should be checked every third or fourth year.

These days, lots of people buy a canister vacuum with a power nozzle. A motor in the power head runs a beater bar, to get the beating action on the carpet. For cleaning carpets, you need a beater bar, but an upright—with one motor—will probably hold up a little better than a two-motor canister with a power nozzle.

Filtration makes a big difference in the durability of a vacuum. Some vacuum cleaners have triple filters in them. For example, they'll have a cloth bag with a paper insert, and a fiber-type filter in front of the motor. This will help prevent dust and dirt from getting into the motor and tearing up the fans or bearings. But some vacuum cleaners—in fact, most today—have only a paper bag. People will pick up a foreign object, a tack or a nail or a piece of grit, and it may tear the paper bag. Without realizing it, you may vacuum for several days or even weeks, and if your bag is torn, you can suck all that dirt from it right into the motor.

Keep your ears open when running your vacuum, listening to loose things. If you're hitting something, or if something's rubbing, then get it repaired. Quite often, people will pick up a coin in the rug, and they'll break the fan. Then it really rumbles. They'll say, "Yeah, it does make more noise," but they tell themselves, "It's still running; I'll let it go." Next thing you know, the broken fan will throw the motor off balance and tear it up. It pays to have it repaired right away. Or, a vacuum will start making noise when the bearing goes bad. And with this bearing being tight, it binds up on the shaft of the motor. Next thing you know, you short out the motor.

It boils down to preventive maintenance. When a vacuum cleaner is brought in to me for service, I'll find a loose nut, a screw or something, and I'll tighten it. It may cost you $10 to repair today, but if you let it go, it'll cost lots more to replace the vacuum.

Overall, I would say Kirby makes the most durable vacuum cleaners. That's an old company. Kirby makes a decent vacuum cleaner. The old Eurekas were good. The old Hoovers were good. Royal still makes a very good vacuum—that's still an all-metal cleaner. But the whole market, just about, has switched to plastic.”

The longest-burning light bulb

Livermore Fire Department

The longest-burning light bulb in the world.

From the ceiling of the Livermore Fire Department's Station #1 hangs the longest-burning light bulb in the world.

Experts from "Ripley's Believe It or Not," *Guinness Book of World Records*, and General Electric have concluded that the bulb has been burning since 1901 (with exceptions for power failures and three times for moving it to another station). General Electric representatives determined that the bulb was manufactured by the Shelby Electric Company and was hand blown with a carbide filament.

According to Mrs. Zylpha Bernal Beck (born 1884), the bulb was donated to the fire department by her father, Dennis Bernal, in 1901.

There is widespread interest in the light bulb, and not only have letters from all over the world been received, but also visitors from as far away as New York and Florida have stopped to view it.

From a press release of the Livermore Fire Department, Livermore, California

Light bulbs

"We sat and looked, and the lamp continued to burn, and the longer it burned the more fascinated we were. None of us could go to bed, and there was no sleep for any of us for 40 hours. We sat and just watched it with anxiety growing into elation. It has lasted about 45 hours, and then I said, 'If it will burn that number of hours now, I know I can make it burn a hundred.' "

That was how Thomas Edison remembered the invention of the light bulb. Other inventors had tinkered together a globe that would glow for several seconds or even a minute or two, but it was the Wizard of Menlo Park who perfected the durable light bulb.

Few consumer products have been scrutinized so closely from the standpoint of durability. Some people even argue that today's bulbs burn out sooner than those of Edison's time. A California fire station claims to own the world's longest-burning bulb, a hand-blown globe made by the Shelby Electric Company in 1901 (see accompanying box, "The longest-burning light bulb"). Few light bulbs made today can be expected to light the darkness in the 2060s.

In 1933, according to Scot Morris's *Book of Strange Facts and Useless Information*, most American light bulbs were rated for 1,000 hours of service; now the majority are rated for 750 hours.

"It has often been suggested," wrote economist S. J. Prais in 1974, "that a longer length of life has not been chosen because light-bulb manufacturers would lose in sales; and that manufacturers have been in a position to fix a shorter life as a result of national and international agreements."

Actually, there is no light-bulb conspiracy. To make a bulb burn longer, its filament must merely be made sturdier; but a thicker filament uses more electricity. It's a trade-off, then, between energy efficiency and durability.

Consumer Research magazine tested light bulbs and concluded that a Hungarian bulb, sold in America as the Action Tungsram Safe-T, burned longer than famous-name American bulbs. Imported by Action Industries, of Cheswick, Pennsylvania, the 1,000-hour-rated bulb proved to last 1,085 hours. European bulbs typically burn longer than American bulbs, but there's a drawback–they make less efficient use of electricity. (*Consumer Research* magazine also found that there is not much difference between the major brands of American bulbs.)

"We made a light bulb that will burn a million hours," Larry Muelhing, a spokesperson for General Electric, told us. "We take it with us on exhibits sometimes. People say, 'Gee whiz, a million-hour bulb! Why can't I buy one for my home?' The answer is because it's too expensive to own a million-hour light bulb. Nobody'd want it. That's really an inefficient light bulb."

On the other side of the spectrum are camera flashbulbs, which burn only a fraction of a second. If you've ever closely examined a photographic flashbulb, you know that the bulb is filled with a long, thin filament that burns up in an instant with a tiny electrical charge. That's excellent efficiency. In general, the *less* efficient the incandescent light bulb, the *more* durable it is.

You can switch to fluorescent lights in your home or workplace for longer life. *Popular Science* reports that a fluorescent light left to burn continuously should last 38,000 hours; if allowed to burn for 8 hours and switched off and on every 3 hours, simulating office working conditions, it should last 22,000 hours. But some people are turned off by fluorescents' glaring light.

Manufacturers recently introduced metal halide bulbs that are rated to last 5,000 to 7,000 hours. These bulbs cost about $15 and GE is "having trouble getting consumers to understand that they can actually save money by spending $15 on a light bulb," admits GE's Muelhing. "We have a real marketing problem. These bulbs have a lower life-cycle cost, but people don't understand that. When people go to the store and see one bulb selling for 79¢ and another selling for $15, they're going to buy the 79¢ bulb, no matter how long it lasts."

But halide bulbs might not be for everyone. Shopping-mall parking lots are illuminated by metal halide bulbs. A spokesperson for GTE Sylvania says its halide bulb produces "harder light than that produced by an incandescent bulb." Even so, Sylvania ballyhoos that its halide bulb will save about $30 in electricity and replacement costs over the life of the bulb.

BK

1946 Hamilton Beach mixer

"Over the years, it has successfully mixed 5,000 loaves of bread and in 1955 alone it mixed over 300 dozen lefse, a Norwegian delicacy. Today, four sets of beaters and two paint jobs later, it is still running without service."

VICKIE CARTER
Nashua, New Hampshire

Zippo took on the throwaway match and now challenges the throwaway lighter

In an age of disposable products, the Zippo Manufacturing Company of Bradford, Pennsylvania, continues to thrive on a cigarette lighter that is made to last. Most modern lighters are made to be discarded when their fuel is exhausted, but every Zippo is guaranteed to work forever, regardless of age or condition, or it will be fixed or replaced at no cost.

"It's the best lighter in the world," boasts Bob Galey, president of Zippo. "It works. If you've got flint and lighter fluid, it'll work forever or we'll fix it free. And that's a fact."

According to the company, Zippo lighters have worked after undergoing all sorts of traumas—everything from being pierced by bullets to being dropped from airplanes, from being run over by buses to being swallowed by fish. If the damage proves irreparable, the customer gets a new Zippo for free.

The company has flourished since George Blaisdell set up shop a half century ago, weathering such ill winds as the Surgeon General's warning about the possible harm of smoking, a wave of cheap imitation imports, and the arrival of disposable butane lighters.

"Every year is better than the last. Last year was our best ever. We hope next year tops that," says Galey, whose tie is emblazoned with the word Zippo. "Our only down year was in 1964, the year the Surgeon General's warning came out. We've grown ever since."

In an average year, about 300,000 come back in various stages of disrepair, the most common ailment being a worn-out hinge. The company's goal is to fix a lighter and mail it back to the customer, postage paid, within 48 hours of verifying that it is a Zippo.

The basic Zippo costs $5.95.

"Without that guarantee, we'd be nothing. We'd be just another lighter company," Galey says. "There are lots of good lighters. That guarantee makes us unique."

The unconditional guarantee was born soon after Blaisdell, who died in 1978 at age 83, began manufacturing lighters in an unplastered loft above a service station in this town in north-central Pennsylvania. When a customer had a hinge on his lighter repaired and asked for his bill, Blaisdell replied, "If I can't make them better than that, I don't deserve to be in business. I'll guarantee these lighters will work or I'll fix them free."

No one has paid a penny for repairs since, except for an anonymous customer in Lincoln, Nebraska, who felt guilty about having his Zippo fixed three times without charge. "I want you to know I appreciate your policy of free servicing, but I don't think you can go on doing this forever," the customer wrote in an unsigned letter sent in 1949. He included a dollar bill. And ten years later, he sent another dollar. Both bills and the letters are in a display case at the company. Mutilated lighters are exhibited in a separate display as a testimonial to the guarantee.

Blaisdell got the idea for the Zippo after seeing a friend's awkward, two-piece Austrian lighter. He modified the Austrian lighter's design, adding a hinge that allowed the lighter to be used with one hand and a chimney that ensured lots of flame, even in the wind.

He named it Zippo because he was intrigued with a clothing fastener called a zipper that had just been invented by the Talon Company in Meadville, Pennsylvania. The original Zippo sold for $2 when postcards cost a penny and $550 bought a new Ford automobile. Today's standard Zippo costs $5.95.

Zippo got a big boost from World War II. Soldiers needed a source for tobacco ignition that would work under the most adverse conditions, and Zippos provided that service from the beaches of the Pacific to the hedgerows of Europe. "There's no question that World War II exposed Zippo lighters to more people under the worst use conditions possible," Galey says. "The war proved the lighter's dependability and reliability."

Zippo faced its first threat in the 1950s when the Japanese flooded the American market with cheap copies. But the imposters were not guaranteed. The real Zippo, meanwhile, became a status symbol in Japan, and the company now peddles a substantial chunk of its products in the Far East. Not even the advent of the disposable butane lighter dented Zippo's business. In fact, company officials contend the disposables ultimately enhanced Zippo's sales.

"It was the throwaways that got individuals who were using matches to use lighters," says Howard Fesenmyer, vice-president and sales manager. "When they discovered they had to buy several throwaways a year, they switched to a Zippo. It lasts forever.

BOB DVORCHAK

Dear Sir:
I received your "Zippo" as a Christmas gift. The lighter was damaged by an ice crusher by accident.

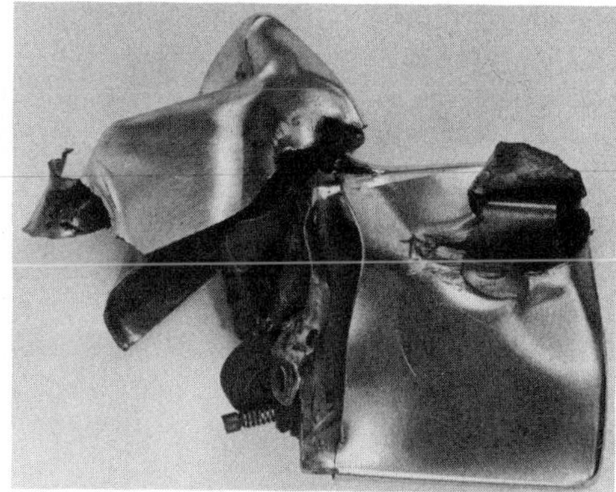

THE CONSUMABLE HOUSE

6

This is not the golden age of residential construction. It well might have been, considering the building materials and techniques introduced over the past few decades. But along with innovation came inflation, rising costs of labor and materials and money, and perhaps most damaging, the death of the notion that a house should be built for future generations as well as today's.

Before World War II, America had not yet seen the man-produced development house. Plaster walls and hardwood floors were the norm. Housing was still closely tied to log cabins and Georgian mansions. Post-war construction got off on the right foot—although often maligned, the Levitt houses of the 1950s were more solid than those in today's tracts—but that decade saw the beginning of the end for the rambling middle-class mansion.

Residential building started on a downward spiral in the 1960s and now is in a frantic whirlpool that by the end of the century may swallow up the ideal of the single-family home. In its place are forecasted 300-square-foot apartments, Pullman kitchens, possibly even communal kitchens and bathrooms.

Not that durability can be had for cheap. A long-life tile roof may cost six times as much as a standard asphalt shingle roof, and considering the nomadic ways of our society, the average family won't hang around long enough to take full benefit from first-rate materials. The mobile home is an expression of this mentality: people shop for housing as they do for such consumables as stereos and sneakers.

Contrast today's housing with the Gothic cathedrals of Europe. A magnificent 800-year-old cathedral has been used and loved by some 25 generations for less cost per year than the shabbiest structures we toss up today.

The economist E. F. Schumacher warns us about confusing what he calls *ephemeral* and *eternal* goods: ephemeral goods, like food, entertainment, and travel, are meant to be used up; other things, like bridges and buildings and works of art, are of greater value the longer they last. We've also produced disposable goods made to standards of refinement and luxury as if they were meant to last forever—like hamburgers in individual insulated and nondegradable "houses." At the same time, we make flimsy houses, tools, and clothing that may not outlast their finance payments.

If the economics of durability are so good, why haven't people insisted upon it and home builders fallen over each other trying to provide it?

The period of rapid economic growth that our country has just passed through is peculiar in placing a high value on impermanence. That attitude was appropriate to frontier construction on a new continent. Immediate needs were served until there was time to do a better job—time and energy were in shorter supply than materials. As a new country, we were rich in the found wealth of virgin forests, minerals, and fossil fuels.

Obsolescence of old, drafty housing is often given as an excuse for making shoddy, short-lived products. By underestimating the adaptability of what we already have, we destroy or abandon huge investments of love, effort, and resources. Victorian houses and rambling glass-walled suburban ranch houses alike can be retrofitted with insulation to cozy, affordable snugness. It all depends on recognizing the value in what we already have rather than throwing up our hands and starting over again. Today's real-estate depreciation laws are no encouragement, permitting each subsequent owner of a building to depreciate, or write off, its value in a few years—while the true value of the building is probably actually increasing. Such laws give incentive to build short-lived buildings rather than durable buildings whose long-run economic cost is far lower.

TOM BENDER

The tyranny of the new

Americans have come to buy and sell their dwellings as they do stereos and sneakers. Each home is traded in for a larger, newer, more prestigious model. Or, if a family is stuck in its old "starter home" for a time, the facade at least can be updated with no-fuss plastic siding, perhaps a touch of brick. This impatience for the new and improved can be seen on the faces of houses across the country.

Local wood and foundation stone, roof slates from a nearby quarry, and idiosyncratic style mark this house as built for the ages—or a century at least.

The same house a century later. Rather than rejoice in the character of their old, sturdy homes, today's owners often perform a quickie face-lift.

THE DISMANTLING OF THE SINGLE-FAMILY HOME

Think of how durability would benefit if it weren't for the constraints of time and money.

Sure, productivity would suffer. You wouldn't be able to put together 50 carburetors a day on the assembly line. But if you had that day to assemble just 1, to get it just right, to fiddle and finesse, check and recheck, you would have a product that serves long and well. It wouldn't require servicing after 1,000 miles, and 5,000 miles, and again and again until the warranty expired and the mechanic finally got it right.

Well, in the real world of 40-year mortgages, of 2 × 4s that measure 1½ by 3½, of heating-oil costs that seem to increase while the delivery truck is en route, you can't find this kind of durability at any price—unless you build your own place from scratch. Professional home builders today seem more preoccupied with making them cheaper than making them better.

While we home buyers understand this kind of economic pressure—we experience it in supermarkets and gas stations every day—the inferior structures come up short of our expectations. Why? Because in the back of our minds there is a message about that pyramid, and the Parthenon and the Roman aqueducts. The fact that they have survived centuries speaks well of their builders. Such lasting things become symbols of civilization, of how things should be, of a faith in the future.

Even in these economic hard times, when more and more households have two wage earners, there is something inescapably alluring about the idea of building a home to last. Maybe it is a basic human feeling common to all ages: I exist, I am important, I belong here, and therefore my shelter should be permanent. What's more, housing is an investment. But durability is not served by today's mass production and mechanical complexity. A telltale indicator of durability is simplicity—a Shaker rocking chair, for instance, uses appropriate materials in a straightforward structural design to offer maximum utility and length of service. And that is the way home building began in the Colonies.

The way it was

The first plans were minimal, single-room houses with massive chimneys at one end—just the kind of design you would expect from a new community preoccupied with survival. But as the colonists began to manage the environment instead of merely reacting to it, the basic oak frame was expanded.

In describing these early Colonial houses, it is customary to single out the massive fire column as the heart of the house. It was the source of heat, of baked bread, of venison-steak dinners, of a warm nightshirt in the evening, of dry boots in the morning. But the real heart of the house, the part that everything else depended on, the element that has allowed many of them to survive 300 hot summers and freezing winters, was the frame.

Frames that last so long took a long time to assemble. As early as 1633, precut, prefitted frames were shipped from Plymouth to virgin settlements in Connecticut to minimize assembly time in a new, untamed environment. Frames that were this strong, that included 6½-by-10-inch sills and 8-by-12-inch chimney girts, had to be hewn from large trees individually cut and hauled to the building site.

After the logs were debarked, they were dogged to wood support blocks, and a chalk line was snapped to mark the boundaries of the beam in the rough tree. Then, standing on the log, a carpenter used a felling axe to make scoring cuts of equal depth on the sides. Working on the ground with a broad axe (many had a slightly crooked handle to minimize busted knuckles), the carpenter hewed to the depth of the scoring cuts.

Every stick in the frame was handmade from scratch and joined to the frame with an array of interlocking dovetail or mortise-and-tenon cuts secured with pegs. These frames were exceptionally strong and so heavy that communities gathered to raise one wall section at a time. The carpentry was so precise that compound cuts at critical corner posts fell into place like the tumblers on a bank safe. They were difficult to put together, and almost impossible to pull apart.

Construction materials and methods have changed dramatically in three centuries, and so have our housing priorities and perceptions of what is important in a home. Today, the structural guts of a house are invisible, buried beneath layers of plywood and wallboard and wood-grained vinyl siding.

Those shopping for a house today won't find the frame mentioned in the list of sale points. The contract for a new home does not specify grade or allowable moisture content of the studs. No one tells you if the floor frame of the second story deck is tacked to the siding with tenpenny nails (in which case the deck may fall, as some have, when crowded with people) or securely tied to the framing of the house with heavy lag screws. The writer Calvin Trillin has a satirical law which states that an author's cash advance must be larger than the bill for lunch at which the book contract is signed. Home buyers should be protected by a similar if more sobering law, that the structural core of a house should stay intact longer than the term of the mortgage that financed it. Frequently it may not.

How have we strayed so far from the simple, utilitarian Colonial house?

Until roughly 1720, survival needs were the formative influence on house design and construction. This date can be taken as a signpost of stabilization, of relative security brought about by growing settlements, productive trade, and a sense of permanence.

From 1720 to the end of the Civil War in 1865, an array of architectural styles flourished and faded, from Georgian and Federal to Classic and Gothic Revival.

Style was paramount, but not at the expense of structural solidity. Some knowledge of architecture and the Palladian orders of classical style was considered an essential part of any gentleman's education. But houses were still built by hand, stick by stick, and made to last. The leisurely era of piece-by-piece building and handcrafted details might have continued indefinitely had it not been swallowed up in an explosion of American industry and technology.

Enter the machine

An early technological boon was the circular saw, invented in the early nineteenth century by Tabitha Babbitt, a Shaker Sister in the Harvard, Massachusetts, settlement. She made the first one after watching the back-and-forth motion of Shaker Brothers sawing timbers from trees. She determined that half their work (the noncutting back stroke) was wasted, and demonstrated the principles of her invention by notching the edges of a sheet of tin and attaching it to her spinning wheel.

In the 1850s, there was another radical departure from traditional building. Midwestern builders experimented with a new construction system called balloon framing. In it, the size of each timber was greatly reduced while their number was increased. The system used machine-made, mass-produced lumber and nails. Dovetails and mortise-and-tenon joints were done away with. Small 2-by-4-inch studs were set between the sill and the roof rafters. Such structures could be erected by relatively unskilled labor in less time for less money.

But with efficiency came a sacrifice in quality, as defined by durability and aesthetics. Frank Lloyd Wright, the first prominent American architect to synthesize the ideals embodied in early Colonial homes with the prospects of modern materials and building procedures, described Chicago (and American cities in general) as an ugly expression of life. He asserted "... that all this magnificent resource of machine-power and superior material has brought us, so far, is degradation." By incorporating modern materials into functional residential designs, Wright both improved the strength of American housing and humanized technology.

Thomas Edison experimented with an all-concrete house, formed and poured in one shot. But advanced building technology was still reserved for industry. And just as the style and layout of a home alters the way you live, industrial architecture continued to alter the way goods were produced. In 1913, Albert Kahn's single-roof, single-level plant for Ford in Detroit started pumping out mass-produced Model Ts. But houses were still framed board by board, plastered, trimmed, and painted.

In the 1920s, Art Deco was in and the Bauhaus functional philosophy of "less is more" was still experimental. Bauhaus architects and craftsmen like Walter Gropius, Marcel Breuer, and Mies van der Rohe simplified houses inside and out. Simplicity of design meant less material had to be used. This meant that less time was needed for construction, costing less money and requiring less maintenance. Fewer ornamental frills, such as molding, dental-toothed cornices, and the like, were thereafter used in American housing.

When Dustin Hoffman returned home from college in *The Graduate*, he meandered through a patio full of people until one of his father's friends laid out the future for him in a memorable, whispered message: "Plastics." He was several generations too late. Plastics and aluminum entered the home in the 1930s and gave new importance to industrial designers. High-tension plate-glass doors were introduced at the 1936 New York World's Fair. Walls were insulated. Affordable, factory-fabricated houses were introduced with 15-year financing allowing monthly payments of less than $50. The factory-built housing of the 1930s never did catch on, however, and is still not widespread.

Kit or panelized houses of the 1950s also never caught on, although there were attempts at aluminum-skinned homes, trailer homes stocked with initial supplies of food, and sectioned masonry blocks that could be nailed in place. The kit homes of the 1950s were like most construction of that time, before material and labor costs soared—pretty solid, and certainly better built than today's tract houses.

Without the constraints of time and money that severely influence building today, builders worked from custom, individualized layouts. Strip-oak flooring was laid board by board and cut to fit. Baths and kitchens were customarily proportioned so that tiles had to be custom-cut squares at the edges of the rooms. Labor was still cheap, which meant that construction, by today's standards, was thorough.

In the 1950s, the Nautilus was launched, Bikini Atoll was deadened with H-bomb tests, and Sputnik and Explorer made banner headlines. But this amazing and often alarming advance was not reflected in the housing industry. The prefab house never found its predicted popularity; neither did modern building materials. Today's house presents an irony: a flimsy package made of traditional framing and nails, containing a wealth of space-age electric gadgets and energy-saving features.

Generally, the waves of the future evaporated. In 1952, one how-to encyclopedia reported that "radiators are threatened with extinction since the appearance of radiant panel-heating," and for a time this technology was popular in low-cost, concrete-slab construction. Until recently, one U.S. wallboard manufacturer still carried a slightly dusty stock of gypsum panels with built-in electrical-resistance heating grids. Plastic pipe, another post-war innovation, was desperately fought by unions and is still not code approved in many areas.

If you discount the newest high-energy oil burner heads, the most recent solar technology, and other mechanical-energy-related equipment, there is little in today's home that was not in use 25 or 30 or even 40 years ago.

Production first, quality second

Balloon framing has given way to western or platform systems (studded and decked one story at a time) due to both speed and the cost of producing lumber in long lengths. In the 1950s, studs dwindled from a full 2 by 4 inches to 1⅝ by 3⅝, and today's homes use studs measuring 1½ by 3½. Lumber mills used to sell the shavings produced by this dressing process for the equivalent of hauling costs. Now, shavings are scooped up and turned into flakeboard. Similarly, tongue-and-groove sheathing and decking has been replaced by plywood that covers more area with less wood for less money–altogether an irrestible combination from a profit-making point of view.

Today, the message from the bankers to the developers to the builders to the contractors and even down to the union apprentice programs has become production first, quality second. This can only hurt the durability of housing. It takes just a generation or two of new construction blood for the workers to collectively forget many high-class tricks of the trade. When times are tough financially, corners are cut: concrete is cured more quickly, foundations are not waterproofed, termite shields are forgotten. Builders now feel the incentive for minimal frames, fragile roof trusses, and thin subfloors, along with fast-paced construction that may not allow time to achieve high quality or correct inevitable mistakes. New home owners are routinely faced with wet basements due to skimpy foundation waterproofing, popping wallboard nails due to wet studs, or excessive settling because of undersized footings on inadequately prepared soil.

Structural systems may be buried beneath Colonial or modern decor. But a substandard system will rear its head. Baseboard trim will pull away from the floor. Mitered door and window moldings will open at the joints. Four-foot-centered seams in wallboard will darken and crack. Sixteen-inch-centered nailheads in the wall will pop through the spackle. The even margins between doors and jambs will become uneven.

The 1974 recession (it started in 1973 for the housing industry) put a lot of builders out of business. And it scared the hell out of many contractors and developers who carried the taxes on unsold homes because buyers wouldn't or couldn't get financing. That single economic shock, which had been building for years, effectively dismantled the affordable, single-family house. Its basic nature has changed more in the wake of new economic constraints than in decades of mechanical advances and architectural influences.

MICHAEL MCCLINTOCK

THE ROOF

Three types of roofing cover an estimated 99 percent of all homes in this country: asphalt shingles, cedar shingles, and slate. Their cost in application labor and material are very roughly in the following ratios: 1:2:4. Thus, if a new asphalt-shingle roof will cost $1,000, the same roof made of cedar shingles will cost $2,000, and a slate roof will cost at least $4,000. The life expectancies of these roofing materials follow the same rough ratios. You can expect 15 to 25 years from a properly applied asphalt-shingle roof. A cedar-shingle roof will last 50 years without trying. A slate roof can last almost forever, as it will not deteriorate in the ordinary sense of the word. It is the slate's fastenings and supports that give way first.

Of the remaining 1 percent, some are covered with material such as tile or tin. Tile is as durable as slate but more expensive. Gusts of wind can terrorize tile, and tile roofs are not often seen in windy areas.

Tin (and other metallic roofing material, such as copper-plated iron) is generally two or three times as expensive as asphalt shingles; tin roofs are more durable than asphalt-covered roofs but less durable than slate. All-copper roofs should last 35 years or more.

Asphalt shingles

Asphalt roofing is made from asphalt, various fibers, stabilizing chemicals, and fine pieces of stone, pressed into a sheet and cut into shapes. Asphalt roofing is fire resistant, meaning that it is not easily ignited and will not readily burn by itself. But it will burn, with varying degrees of resistance. Modern asphalt shingles are wind resistant to some extent. Shingles that carry the UL label for wind resistance can withstand winds of up to 60 miles per hour for two hours or more without lifting. They have a line of cement lengthwise across the center of their surfaces. When the shingles are fastened in place and warmed by the sun, the cement locks each shingle to the one above.

Craig Markcrow, Vermont Structural Slate Co., Fair Haven, Vermont.

A Vermont roof of Vermont slate.

These shingles are manufactured in different weights and sold by the "square," or the number of shingles necessary to properly cover 100 square feet of roof surface. The weight of sufficient shingles for one square varies from as little as 180 pounds to as much as 390 pounds. If you purchase lightweight shingles, you will find you have only three bundles of shingles per square; if you purchase heavyweight shingles you will have five bundles.

Bear in mind that the materials used to manufacture the entire range of shingle weights is alike. This means that the difference in shingle weights translates into differences in shingle thicknesses. Obviously, the thicker the shingle, the longer it will last. Generally, the very lightweight shingles can be expected to last no more than 15 years. The heavy shingles will provide good service for 25 years or more. One point of caution: shingles that have textured surfaces and edges weigh more than flat shingles, but this extra weight does not provide additional life. Therefore, when seeking maximum shingle life, you should select the heaviest shingles exclusive of the added-on texture weight.

Dressing down tastefully: an elegy for Design Research

Design Research, the store that initiated a revolution in interior design, has succumbed to bankruptcy.

Founded in the early 1950s in Cambridge, Massachusetts, DR came of age along with the New Frontier and the Great Society, with urban renewal and Medicare, with peaceniks and protesters, with all the liberal causes for which it provided a visual expression. DR was a protest song in birch and cotton, a March on Washington in wine glasses and floor lamps. The store sold not just merchandise but merchandise that made a statement—what the '70s would call a life-style. This life-style was compatible for consumers who were relatively well educated and affluent, who were concerned about the poverty-stricken "other America" but clearly not part of it. As consumers, this group faced a dilemma. Out of the question were the decorative banalities of wall-to-wall carpeting and cushioned Barcaloungers, which, as much as the Pentagon or General Motors, symbolized mainstream capitalism. DR's customers wanted to feel the bare, hard surfaces of reality, not sink into plushy piles of comfort.

DR provided a way of dressing down tastefully. The right angles and well-fitted joints of the furniture, the forthright colors of the fabrics, the sturdy toys that parents adored and children tolerated, the shaggy honesty of the rugs—all this spoke of resistance to the avocado rococo of the Sears, Roebuck. DR items were returns to simplicity, honesty, and utility, but relatively expensive ones that would never be confused with the simple and honest utility of poverty.

In the 1970s, the crowd discovered life-style and forgot about politics. Branches were opened. The Cambridge store moved from its cramped but quaint frame house to a spectacular glass box across the street, a building that was an advertisement in architecture because the entire store became a display window for itself. The firm gained floor space but lost the quality of being somewhat off the beaten track of commerce. Competitors began to carry merchandise that was not always of DR quality, but which provided a reasonable facsimile at a considerably more reasonable price. The masses flooded in, and the sense of making a cultural statement in buying the DR style was drowned in the democratic tide.

What happened to the aspiring young professionals who had been DR's customers? They fell away, but not just for the snobbish reason that teak tables and Finnish fabrics were defiled by the common touch. The expectations of this group were thwarted as academic and other professional salaries stagnated. DR's type of customer is now refinishing turn-of-the-century oak dressers and gluing together broken pieces of family china; he affirms his simultaneous sympathy for and distinction from the less privileged by restoring an old house very much like the one DR vacated to move into the glass box. Gone is the zest for urban renewal—throwing out all the old junk, cleaning up, scrapping deteriorating old things for new well-designed things—which had been the motivation behind city planning and DR decorating alike in the flush 1960s. Renewal is too expensive now: rehabilitation can be done on the pay-as-you-can-afford-it plan.

Meanwhile, the glass box on Brattle Street became a place for visitors to examine examples of the classics: DR turned into an institution rather than a thriving business. Its series of futile attempts to find a new aesthetic culminated in the promotion of High Tech—hard rock in interior design. The manufactured look was an obvious attempt to manufacture new customers: any faint signs of integrity in the aesthetic ideal were buried under the sales pitch. A blatant example of radical chic, High Tech deservedly failed to salvage DR.

Today, DR's influence is seen not in homes but in offices all over the country, where bright colors and functional form have become the common idiom of decoration. Corporations have bought up the very aesthetic ideology that originally protested mainstream capitalism. They can afford the prices that young people can't.

Mixed with our disgust at this irony is nostalgia at seeing the brave glass box turn into a tombstone, one more monument in the cemetery of a decade so rich in ideas and good intentions.

In the meantime, Sears survives.

ROSALIND WILLIAMS

A good portion of the cost of a new roof is the cost of labor. Because the difference in labor involved between applying light and heavy shingles is negligible, it is shortsighted to install the less expensive lightweight roofing in place of the heavier, especially when the heavier may last twice as long. A good portion of the service life of an asphalt-shingle roof depends upon the quality of installation. Proper installation is not a matter of positioning the shingles in neat, straight rows and lines. Neatness is nice, but unimportant in terms of durability. The key is proper exposure of the shingles. Examine the top surface of an asphalt shingle and you will see that it is not entirely covered with crushed stone, but that a portion is smooth and bare. When the shingle is properly applied, none of the bare surface is exposed, and a fraction of the mineralized surface must be covered by the shingle above. The proper width of the exposed mineralized surface–its exposure–varies from four to six inches, maximum, as specified on the wrapping of each package of shingles. Exposing more than this specified width will shorten the life of the roof. As you can see, stretching the most out of each shingle would reduce the number of shingles needed and reduce the labor involved, but obviously this is bad practice.

Asphalt shingles should be installed upon a layer of 15-pound roofing felt. The felt should be overlapped five or more inches and held in place with a few roofing nails. Thicker felt should not be used, as it tends to fold and crease.

Slots, surface texture, and edge indentations have no effect upon the life of the shingle, but color does. Black and very dark shingles do not last longer than light-colored shingles, but as a shingle ages, it loses its mineral coating, and a light coating will reveal the underlying black asphalt much more quickly.

Flashing is the metal or asphalt felt used to close a joint between a roof and a chimney or a roof and a vertical wall. The best flashing is of copper. The next best is aluminum. Ninety-pound mineralized felt is also satisfactory, but not as long-lasting as the metals. Least desirable is metallized kraft paper, which is vulnerable to scratches.

You may need to gauge the potential life in an asphalt-shingle roof when buying a house. First examine the ridge of the roof to see if there are one or two layers of roofing. If there is only one, you can, if need be, place a second layer of asphalt roofing shingles directly on top. If there are already two layers, reroofing will mean removing all the old, existing roofing down to the deck.

Examine the lower edges of the shingles. Do they lie flat or do they curl upward at the edges? Look closely at the surface of the shingles. Can you see the shingle itself? Is all the mineral coating intact? Do the shingles lie flat? Consistent color means there are no spots bare of minerals; if there are more bald spots than mineralized area, the shingles are on their last years.

Cedar shingles

Cedar shingles are made by splitting short logs of cedar into long wedges of wood, either by machine or by hand. Cedar is ideal for this purpose because it both splits easily and resists decay. Evidence indicates that cedar can remain on wet soil for 250 years without rotting. The wood is light, filled with millions of air spaces that are responsible for making it a good insulator. When fresh, it has a pleasant aroma.

Cedar shingles do not require a solid roof deck but can be laid down on open sheathing–in other words, there can be wide spaces between the roofing boards.

On the negative side, cedar shingles may become a garden of moss and ferns, and if your roof is heavily shaded, you will have difficulty keeping it clear of this growth. Most building codes prohibit the use of cedar shingles for a roof when the structure includes a wood-burning fireplace.

Cedar shingles vary from blonde to red-brown in color, but they darken with time, especially near a city. Darkening does not affect the life of the wood shingle, and you can paint them if you wish, but they do absorb loads of paint.

Red cedar shingles are manufactured in grades and sizes. The best is No. 1 Blue Label. It is all heartwood and clear. No. 2 Red Label is partially clear and may have some flat grain. No. 3 Black Label is a utility grade; a much smaller portion of these shingles are clear than are those of the previous grade. No. 4 Under Coursing has large knots and should be used only beneath another shingle. No. 1 and No. 2 Rebutted-Rejointed are similar to the previously mentioned No. 1 and No. 2, but are machine trimmed. With the exception of grade No. 4, all the grades come in lengths of either 16, 18, or 24 inches. More of the longer, better grades can be exposed, which means you need fewer of the 24-inch No. 1 Blue Label or the No. 1 Rebutted shingles than of the 16-inch No. 3 Black Label to cover the same roof area. The difference can be at least two to one—that is, on a roof with a pitch of 4 inches in 12 or more, you can expose 3½ inches of the Black Label 16-inch shingle, or 7½ inches of the 24-inch Blue Label. But don't assume the longest, best grade of shingles is your best buy.

More skill is required to apply wood shingles than asphalt shingles, and three times as much labor. You cannot simply cut wood shingles with a razor knife, but must use a hatchet and then smooth the edges with a plane. Care must be taken to see that no two joints are in line (one above the other), or the roof will leak. To finish ridges, the shingles must be cut to form a tight angle, whereas asphalt shingles are merely bent over the ridge and nailed.

MAX ALTH

Slate

Slate endures. It is the choice of architects designing expensive houses and commercial, public, and college buildings. In parts of California particularly vulnerable to fires, insurance companies want fireproof roofing of slate or tile. Among most home owners and contractors interested in the short term, the slate roof has fallen out of favor.

According to John Lee of the Structural Slate Company in Pen Argyl, Pennsylvania (named for the slate-mining city of Argyle, Scotland), "It'd be safe to say a slate roof will last 75 to 100 years." Warranties were once given for the life of the building, but in recent years acid rain has hastened slate's deterioration.

Slate roofs are expensive. Slate goes for about $250 per square for ordinary Pennsylvania blue-gray slate, more for Vermont colored slate. Red slate is especially expensive, now running close to $1,000 a square. Man-made roofing is a third the cost but can be counted on for only 15 to 20 years of life for asphalt of average price or for fiberglass shingles.

Beyond its durability, slate offers unique advantages. A roof of stone offers not only physical security but an emotional feeling of well-being. A square of slate weighs from 650 to 750 pounds at its standard thickness of about 3/16 inch. Slate allows for aesthetic treatment because of its subtle variations in color and its graceful aging. Slates of different shades can be combined for effect, in either predominantly warm or cool tones. Slates called "permanent" by the trade are of an unvarying color, while "weathering" slates will fade attractively with time and exposure. The variety of shadings is approximated by manufacturers of asphalt shingles, but the effect cannot be duplicated.

You may have seen elaborate designs defined in multicolored roofing slates. Maine produced a black slate, New York's Granville quarries a red, California a green, and Vermont slates of green, purple, and a mottled purple and green.

Slates are still split and nail holes still punched with manual treadle machines dating back to the late 1800s. In Pennsylvania's slate belt, operators work in little shacks heated by pot-bellied stoves. This labor intensiveness is partly responsible for the higher cost of slate. Shipping is more costly as well. Another mark against slate is that replacing slates as they come loose is a tricky job, and you may have trouble finding a roofer willing to take it on. *Old House Journal* has written that slate-roof owners likely will have to "fight off hordes of roofing contractors who will tell you that it is impossible to repair slate and who instead want to sing the praises of the line of asphalt shingles they are pushing this month." You can take care of repairs yourself; tools and information are available from the Structural Slate Company, 222 East Main Street, Pen Argyl, PA 18072.

A house of slate, top and sides.

THE SKIN

As the exterior surface of a wood-frame house, siding may be considered the building's face. But siding does more than present an appearance; it can strengthen the house's frame and protect its innards from wind, rain, and temperature changes.

Of the many materials that are currently used for residential siding, no one provides the best of everything at the least cost in material and labor. Each material has its own advantages and limitations.

The life expectancy of a material is likely to be considered in the context of cost. But pricing siding is complicated by the fact that not all of it is sold by the square foot. For example, assume you opt to apply 8-inch bevel wood siding. This must be overlapped, usually by 1 inch. Therefore, you are going to need 15 percent more 8-inch siding than ordinary measurement of the area would indicate. And this figure only accounts for width loss. Since none of the boards you purchase will be the correct length, you can expect to waste from 5 to 10 percent because of cutting to size. Assume you opt for 6-inch drop siding. This siding has a shiplap (whereby one board edge overlaps another) of close to an inch, so you will need 20 percent more siding than the measured area called for. On the other hand, if you elect to utilize 4-by-8-foot plywood panels with narrow board battens covering the joints, and the reach from sill to fascia is exactly 8 feet, you will only suffer waste at the windows and other fenestrations.

The price of siding varies greatly according to the quality of the material that is used. Some wood sidings, such as cedar, cost more than most aluminum or vinyl sidings, while single-layer hardboard can be less expensive. Other factors, such as the need for a layer of insulation beneath vinyl or aluminum siding, make it difficult to compare costs.

Clapboard

Clapboard, the name given to traditional wood siding, is applied horizontally over sheathing. It comes in a variety of styles and widths and in several grades. The best is made from cedar. The next best is made from clear pine. The last on the list is made from No. 2 pine, which means it has small, tight knots. With some care, you can cut this knotty siding near or at the knots. When this is not possible, the knots are given a coat of varnish, so that when the siding is painted, it looks as good and lasts as long as the other two sidings.

Clapboard, however, is tedious to apply and requires a measure of skill. All board ends are butted against each other and against the frames of doors and windows. These joints must be square and tight.

If painted every four years or so, clapboard siding has the proven ability to last for hundreds of years, as witnessed by the pre-Revolutionary homes still standing.

Board and batten

Board-and-batten siding is applied vertically over sheathing or over an open frame on which a number of horizontal stops have been positioned between the studs and the frame otherwise braced.

Since the boards are applied vertically, with the battens covering and hiding the vertical joints, little skill is needed, and application is rapid. There is also little waste, as the boards cut out for the windows can often be used beneath the doors and elsewhere. Board widths are not full. The width of all finished boards is a full ½ inch less than their nominal widths. Thus the 8-inch board is only 7½ inches wide.

Cost is low, since you can use almost any grade of lumber—even the rough sawn, which is full width. However, if you elect to purchase aged barn-side boards, the cost can be very high. As with other woods, board and batten can last indefinitely if painted properly.

Plywood

Plywood is used in large sheets without supporting sheathing. The sheets are made in thicknesses of ⅜ inch to 1⁄32 inch and in panel sizes of 4 by 8, 9, or 10 feet. The joints can be shiplapped or covered by battens. In any case, there are two immediate savings here. The large boards go up very fast, and, depending upon local building codes and the thickness of the panels, you can space the studs 24 inches on center instead of the usual 16 inches.

Any number of different surface plies are offered, including redwood, cedar, fir, and MDO. The latter indicates a medium-density layer of wood that has been permanently bonded and sealed with resin. In addition to the many species of surface woods available, a variety of surface treatments are offered, including rough sawn, V-groove, board and batten, and channel groove.

Panel costs vary with thickness, surface ply, and treatment. When making your selection, bear in mind that panels of equal thickness are equally strong. If you are going to paint and don't mind a little raised grain, the fir-topped panels are your best bet.

Plywood, of course, is a wood, and if you keep it painted it can last for centuries. However, if you give it a clear finish, you have to sand and revarnish the wood every year or it will become dark and stained. The durability of plywood often depends on the purpose for which it was made. Maine plywood, for example, will not rot underwater. Most plywood, though, will rot if not properly treated; generally, you should regard plywood as a way of buying a wide board at a good price.

Hardboard

Hardboard is made by reducing wood to its fibers and then molding the fibers along with glue into a board. Hardboard siding is manufactured in 16-foot strips of 6, 8, or 9 inches in width; it also comes in panels of 4 by 8 or 9 feet. Thicknesses range from ⅜ through $^9/_{16}$ inch.

Hardboard siding strips and panels are sold unpainted, just primed, and painted in a number of colors. The paint is guaranteed on a prorated basis for five years. The board itself is similarly guaranteed for 25 years.

Shingles and shakes

The difference between the two is only surface texture. Shakes are rough, while shingles have a much smoother surface. Either can be used for either roofing or siding.

Compared to other siding materials, application is very slow and requires some skill in cutting and fitting. Bare or primed No. 2 Rebutted-Rejointed shingles, 24 inches long, have machine-cut sides and require less hand fitting. Used on walls, shingles and shakes can be exposed 25 percent or so beyond the width recommended for roofing application.

Several solutions to the same problem: aging.

Aluminum

Aluminum siding is fireproof, rotproof, and corrosionproof for all purposes. Some brands carry 40-year paint warranties.

The panels are cut with a hacksaw or tin snips. Panel ends fit into each other or into channels. The panels themselves hang from nails. Panel application is relatively fast. Covering the house trim takes time, however, and a metal forming brake and some skill. But all in all, formed strip aluminum siding goes up much faster than wood shingles.

The horizontal panels are made in 8-inch and double-4-inch widths simulating clapboard siding. Panels are usually 12½ or 13 feet long and come in two thicknesses, with or without insulation. Financially, your best bet is the thin metal panel with the backer board. The backer insulation gives the panel the stiffness necessary to allow one person to handle it. Together, metal and board have an R (insulating value) rating of 1.5. The metal itself has a rating of no more than 0.6. When used as residing, it is customary and wise to apply the siding over a layer of insulation. Doing so can bring the total insulation factor of the siding up to R-6.

MAX ALTH

Vinyl

Initially, vinyl siding is cheaper than aluminum siding and has the advantage of resisting dents. It may crack rather than give in very cold weather. Vinyl siding is fire resistant but can burn to produce dangerous fumes. Colors are solid through vinyl siding but do tend to fade with time. In very warm climates, panels tend to sag a little with the heat.

Dimensions and application are similar to those for aluminum siding, but vinyl cannot take a sharp bend around trim, and the trim is either left uncovered or is done with aluminum bent to shape from colored stock.

"New is not necessarily better. For example, aluminum siding is widely promoted as an improvement over painting. But experience is showing that after 10 to 15 years, the aluminum siding begins to look pretty ratty and requires—yes—painting! In the meantime, the siding contractor may have destroyed significant architectural detail during installation. And the aluminum siding may be masking dangerous rot and/or termite conditions. This is a case where 'new' does not mean 'improved.'"

From the *Old-House Journal*

Neither aluminum nor vinyl siding adds anything to the strength or the rigidity of the house. They must be applied over a fully sheathed house frame.

If you aren't particular about the appearance of the house, aluminum and vinyl sidings can go on indefinitely without maintenance (although if aluminum or vinyl siding panels are bent, broken, or blown, they must quickly be replaced to protect the house's underlayer of sheathing from the weather). Over a decade or so, aluminum siding loses its luster and needs paint to restore its original appearance. Once the siding's original paint fades, you can expect to repaint every two or three years because, unlike wood, aluminum has no pores to absorb and hold fresh layers of paint. The original, factory-applied paint on aluminum siding is anodized to the metal. After several coats, it will be necessary to remove old layers of paint with a blowtorch before priming and painting again. Vinyl siding should look fresh for six or seven years. It usually cannot be repainted because of the difficulty paint has adhering to it. If you find that your vinyl siding needs a face-lift, you may have to rough up the surface with sandpaper before painting.

Unlike aluminum and vinyl, wood siding must be painted periodically or it will eventually rot and fall to the ground. Bob Holcombe, a spokesperson for the National Forest Products Association, says unpainted wood that is exposed to weather will deteriorate at an average rate of a quarter inch per century, but "wood that is painted and properly protected from rot should last several centuries."

The walls of George Washington's Mount Vernon homestead, covered with pine-board siding that is beveled to simulate stone, are expected to last indefinitely, says Ellen McCallister, Mount Vernon's librarian. McCallister says that Mount Vernon is protected with paint mixed with sand—a formula used by Washington—and "the wood is somewhat buried under layers of paint." Open to the public since 1858, Mount Vernon is one of America's best-known wooden structures. "Many, many offers from publicity-seeking companies like Sears have been made to paint Mount Vernon," McCallister reports, "but we still treat the wood siding the same way Washington did, though surely Washington didn't paint as often as we do. I guess Mount Vernon is overmaintained these days. Even so, we would never consider covering George Washington's house with aluminum siding to reduce our maintenance costs. Aluminum siding would be much scorned."

Which type of siding is most durable? No conclusive test comparing the durability of wood, aluminum, and vinyl siding has been conducted, but several years ago, an engineer working for the National Association of Home Builders fired golf-ball-sized ice balls from a nitrogen-powered gun at aluminum, steel, and vinyl siding to simulate a hailstorm. Aluminum and steel sidings dented the most (about equally), while vinyl siding hardly dented at all, says Hugh Angleton, the engineer who conducted the simulated-hailstorm test. Though wood siding was not tested, Angleton says he believes wood is more susceptible to hailstorm damage than vinyl but should dent less than metal sidings. Angleton, who lives in an aluminum-sided house, says aluminum has "better lasting quality" than wood or vinyl siding. "My neighbors have wood siding, and it's my own personal opinion that after six or seven years wood looks lousy," says Angleton. "I prefer aluminum siding because vinyl can crack in cold weather and is also damaged by the sun's ultraviolet radiation."

BK

In a style that could be called Disneyland Revival, the owners of this century-old brick house spruced up the walls with stones of aluminum paint. Similarly, older commercial buildings are often brought up to date with a jaunty tack-on mansard roof of rough shakes, rather than allowed to age gracefully.

PAINT

The effectiveness of paint as a protective medium is evidenced by carefully painted, pre-Revolutionary homes that are still in good condition today.

Paint's second function is visual. Without paint, our homes would look like a collection of different-colored boards pierced by many nails dripping rust stains. Paint gives a structure visual unity.

The durability of paint depends on its chemical composition, exposure, the condition of the surface to which it was applied, how it was applied, and what is expected of the paint. Paint protected from the elements can last for centuries; witness the oil paintings of the old masters in our museums. However, certain colors are fugitive: they tend to fade. Purples, violets, and pinks containing a little blue tend to fade more quickly than other colors.

Outdoors, the useful life of paint varies with its geography. Paints last a bit longer in cool, dry climates than in hot, damp climates. Paint lasts longer amidst green farmland than on the sides of a beach house or in a desert area where the wind may carry abrasive particles. Paints exposed to industrial fumes do not last long either. Generally, a good grade of exterior paint will last three to four years, assuming a benign atmosphere.

The durability of a paint also depends greatly on the proper preparation of the surface to which it is applied. Different types of paints require somewhat different preparations, but a few basic rules obtain.

For proper adhesion, remove dust, dirt, and the chalkiness of chalking paint with sandpaper or a steel brush. If the surface has been previously varnished or coated with glossy, semigloss, or enamel paint, the surface must be given "tooth," which means it must be roughened. This can be done by rubbing the surface with fine steel wool, fine sandpaper, or a preparatory solution sold under a variety of trade names such as Will-Bond. If this is not done, the paint will not adhere properly, and it will pull away and form cracks and wrinkles. Eaves and soffits should be hosed down to remove any salts that may have accumulated there.

Paint must not be allowed to build up in successive coats. Allow at least two years to pass before repainting a house. When exterior wall paint is too thick, it may crack or peel. But note that the paint does not wear evenly on all exterior surfaces. It disintegrates more quickly on windowsills, porches, and steps than on side walls because the sun strikes a horizontal surface directly and remains on it much longer than on a vertical surface.

On bare wood, knots and sap streaks must first be given a coat of shellac so that resin won't bleed through the paint. On new work, the general practice is to give the wood a priming coat of paint, then set and putty the nails, and finally apply the second or final coat.

The present and future moisture content of the wood also has a great influence on the durability of the paint you apply. Not only must the surface you are going to paint be dry, the wood must also remain dry. External moisture is avoidable by not painting when it is raining or foggy or damp. Internal moisture depends on the construction of the house and on its occupants. If a moisture barrier has not been installed within the walls of the dwelling, moisture in the house may seep through the walls, permeate the wood and literally drive the paint from its surface. No paint will adhere to wet wood. The house walls can be ventilated by any of a number of small vents made for the purpose. The house itself can be vented by keeping at least one window partially open. You can help further by seeing to it that all cooking pots are covered.

Application also plays a part in the longevity of paint. The paint should be spread over the surface in two directions, but there is no need to rub it in. Two coats of moderate thickness are always better than a single coat of equal thickness. The optimum coating thickness is between four and five mil, which means that the average gallon of paint on a nonporous surface should cover 300 to 400 square feet.

While primers can be used at temperatures down to 40°F, and paints formulated for final coats can be used down to freezing, it is inadvisable to do so. In order to make the paint workable, thinners have to be added. The result is that you apply less paint than you believe you do. Drying is slowed down tremendously, encouraging dust to adhere to the paint.

Types of paint

Paint consists of a pigment suspended in a liquid called a vehicle. Most often, the pigment consists of an oxide of metal that has been ground into a powder. When spread over a surface, the vehicle oxidizes and otherwise changes chemically to form a tough, permanent film that locks the pigment in place.

Primitive peoples made paints from colored earths mixed with animal greases. Some of this artwork can still be seen on the walls of caves in Spain and France. Eventually, humans learned that linseed oil, pressed from the seeds of the flax plant, worked much better than animal grease. Linseed-oil paint is still in use today. In many ways, it is still the best interior and exterior paint we have, but it has some drawbacks, as we shall see.

Paints commonly used in and around the home can be grouped into three general types: oil base, alkyd, and emulsion (which includes latex).

Oil-base paint consists of a pigment suspended in linseed oil and a dryer. Oil-base paint probably lasts a bit longer than other paints. It can be had in flat, semigloss, and enamel (which is regular paint with a great deal more vehicle mixed in). The creamy consistency makes it easy to apply. It holds color well and is easy to touch up.

On the other hand, oil-base paint costs more than the other types (except catalytic) and requires either turpentine or mineral spirits for thinning. Cleaning a large brush or roller in turpentine or mineral spirits is both a nuisance and expensive. The pure white tends to turn a pale yellow after a time. A final disadvantage is that oil-base paint dries very slowly, giving off a strong smell as it does. A minimum of 12 hours must pass between coats, even longer on cool days.

Many paint shops call *alkyd* paint an oil paint without realizing the difference. Alkyd-paint vehicle is usually linseed-castor modified soya alkyd resin. In a sense it is an oil, requiring turpentine or a similar mineral spirit for thinning and brush cleaning. On the plus side, alkyd costs somewhat less than linseed oil-base paint and dries more rapidly. Alkyd takes color well, though it tends to pale a little after it has been spread. It dries to a hard, tough, nonyellowing surface that can be washed like oil-base paint.

On the negative side is the expense and trouble of thinning and cleaning up with turpentine or mineral spirits. While alkyd has no smell, it produces toxic vapors and rooms must be well ventilated for interior paint jobs. In addition, touch-up is difficult. If too much time elapses before you go back to a missed spot, your touch-up will be noticeable, even though the paint came from the same can. Alkyd adheres best to itself or to a primer on a new surface.

Emulsion paints are made from an emulsion of chemicals in water. Spread over a surface, the water evaporates, and the chemicals go through a transformation to produce a tough, waterproof film. Generally, the paint is called by the chemical which is present in the greatest quantity, such as latex, vinyl, or acrylic resin. Their qualities are more or less alike, so we will not differentiate between them.

Emulsion paints cost less than the first two paints and can be thinned with water. Brushes and rollers clean easily with soap and water. The water vehicle means drying times are short; often you can apply the second coat in less than an hour. Emulsion paints can be applied over damp surfaces without peeling or blistering because they are somewhat permeable.

Emulsion paints tend to hold color better than alkyd paints and are easily touched up. There is no visible demarcation if you return to a missed spot within a reasonable length of time.

On the negative side, emulsion paints supposedly do not withstand the weather as well as alkyd and oil base. A primer should be used on all bare wood surfaces before applying an emulsion paint. Because they are not waterproof immediately upon drying, they should cure for several weeks before being washed.

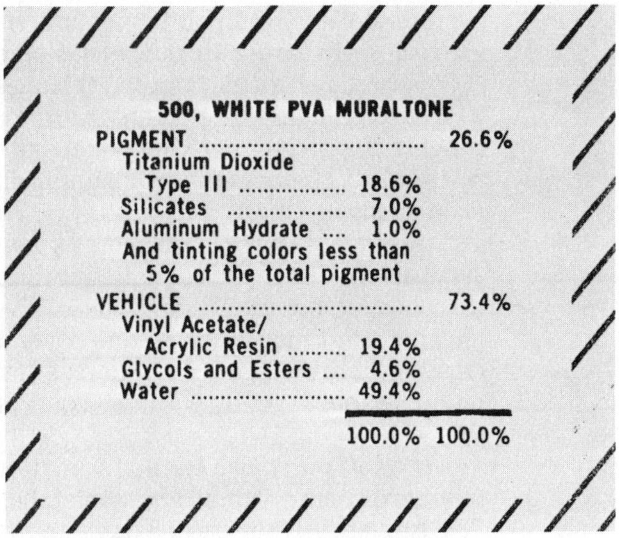

500, WHITE PVA MURALTONE

PIGMENT		26.6%
Titanium Dioxide Type III	18.6%	
Silicates	7.0%	
Aluminum Hydrate	1.0%	
And tinting colors less than 5% of the total pigment		
VEHICLE		73.4%
Vinyl Acetate/ Acrylic Resin	19.4%	
Glycols and Esters	4.6%	
Water	49.4%	
	100.0%	100.0%

Contents label from a can of Muralo PVA, an exterior-interior, water-base emulsion paint. This is a relatively inexpensive paint manufactured by a local company. Note the percentage of pigment.

Selecting a paint

Durability of a paint, and its hiding power, depends mainly on the percentage of pigment it contains. The higher the percentage of pigment, the greater its hiding power and the longer the paint will last. For example, linseed oil will not last more than a few months alone, but when mixed with pigment, the resultant paint will last for years. Generally, the more expensive the paint, the more pigment it contains.

The two contents labels shown here illustrate this point. The label taken from a gallon can of white Muralo PVA, an emulsion paint, indicates that only 26.6 percent of the can's content is pigment and that of the pigment only 18.6 percent is the all-important metal oxide, in this case titanium dioxide. Different colors of paint contain different tinting metals; for example, iron oxide is found in red paint.

The second label, taken from a can of white alkyd paint manufactured by Benjamin Moore & Company, indicates that the pigment accounts for 56.6 percent of the volume and that 30.4 percent of the pigment is titanium dioxide.

Both photos, Christie C. Tito

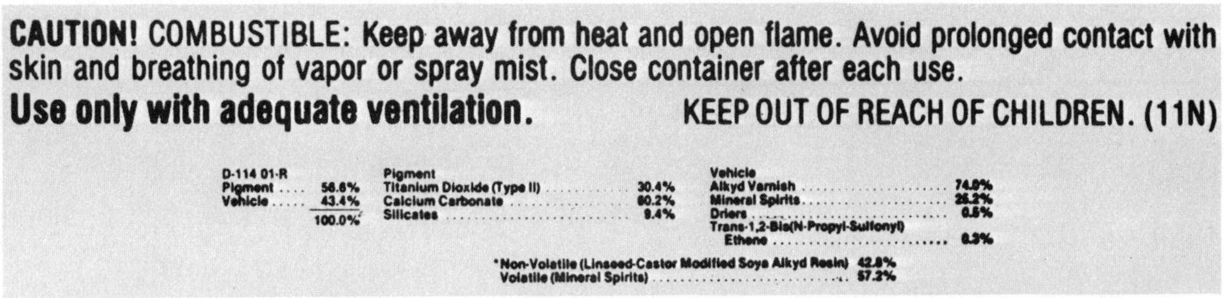

CAUTION! COMBUSTIBLE: Keep away from heat and open flame. Avoid prolonged contact with skin and breathing of vapor or spray mist. Close container after each use.
Use only with adequate ventilation. KEEP OUT OF REACH OF CHILDREN. (11N)

D-114 01-R

Pigment	56.6%
Vehicle	43.4%
	100.0%

Pigment	
Titanium Dioxide (Type II)	30.4%
Calcium Carbonate	60.2%
Silicates	9.4%

Vehicle	
Alkyd Varnish	74.0%
Mineral Spirits	25.2%
Driers	0.5%
Trans-1,2-Bis(N-Propyl-Sulfonyl) Ethene	0.3%

*Non-Volatile (Linseed-Castor Modified Soya Alkyd Resin)	42.8%
Volatile (Mineral Spirits)	57.2%

This label from a can of relatively expensive Benjamin Moore & Co. alkyd-base exterior paint notes a higher percentage of pigment, with a considerable amount of metal oxide, than the cheaper Muralo PVA.

Muralo is a local paint company. Its PVA paint sells for $12.10. Benjamin Moore & Company is a national brand and charges $17.10, or roughly 30 percent more for roughly 30 percent more life on an exterior surface. (Indoors the two paints will last equally as long.)

One point in favor of the more expensive paint is that it will cover better than the cheaper brand. Three coats of the cheaper paint may be needed to cover a dark color with a light color, whereas you might be able to get by with two coats of the better paint.

Do not purchase paint, no matter how inexpensive, without a contents label. You cannot judge a can of paint by its weight or consistency. Good paint is thick and heavy, but poor paint can easily be made thick and heavy.

"Durability? We believe in it. But we also believe that there's a value that can be found in these durable objects that goes beyond their functional capabilities. This may sound corny, but it warms my heart to sew on Mama's machine and grind my chicken livers with her meat grinder and knead bread dough on Grandma's board. And if I ever get the chance, I'd like to teach *our* children to cook and sew and make music with the same instruments on which I was taught. Durable objects, especially ones that prompt family memories, are a reminder of the cycles of nature in a way.

"Oh gosh, armchair philosophic mediocrity rears its ugly head!"

BARBARA JEAN ROGERS
Nashville, Tennessee

Do not purchase old, leftover cans of paint unless you intend to do no more than paint a shed's interior. Time induces chemical changes, and chances are the old paint will not go on properly nor behave properly.

Do not purchase military paints unless you know exactly the type of paint you are purchasing and have a need for that special paint. The most expensive paint in the world can be useless if it doesn't meet your needs.

Untreated wood can be beautiful, and a clear finish is fine if you are willing to put up with the work involved. Application is easy enough—easier than paint. Simply apply a good grade of spar varnish with brush, roller, pad, or spray. Then come back in six months and sand over the cracks and breaks in the varnish and revarnish these areas.

Wood expands and contracts with temperature and moisture changes. Paint gives a little, and when cracks appear, they are tiny. Varnish is not as flexible. It cracks more readily, permitting moisture to discolor an area in and around the opening. Slight stains can be removed by sanding, but deep ones are difficult to remove and sometimes will only respond to bleaching. When you revarnish the building, you have to provide a roughened surface for the second coat, or it will not adhere properly. Varnish is relatively slow drying and may attract dust and other airborne particles. Polyurethane coatings cost about the same as varnish and last about as long, with the added advantage of not yellowing.

MAX ALTH

MOBILE HOMES

"I think there are many misconceptions about mobile homes," says George Alexander of the U.S. Veteran's Administration (VA). "Today's mobile homes are extremely well built and represent good housing for the dollar. People who can't afford so-called conventional housing can buy a mobile home." Alexander estimates that 5 percent of all VA housing loans processed in 1981 will be spent on mobile homes. "We're very high on mobile homes," he says.

Gary Mitchell, who lives in a mobile home outside of Harrisburg, Pennsylvania, doesn't go along with Alexander's assessment. He recalls a wind storm in 1980 that almost did in his dwelling. "The whole trailer was shaking, and then suddenly I could feel the thing lift several inches off the ground. It was scary. If the trailer hadn't been anchored to the ground, I'm sure it would have blown away." Mitchell says he would never move into another mobile home. "Not just because I think they're unsafe," he says, "but because they're shoddily built. The walls are just two inches thick and are no more than paneling and Styrofoam stapled onto aluminum. Everything's stapled—they don't use nails. You can actually push the walls out of shape with your hands—the walls bend. The doors are so thin, just vinyl and Styrofoam and a little bit of cardboard, that our dog actually ran right through one. I believe that a home should be solid, not so terribly flimsy. Even the floors of my mobile home are wavy and bent out of shape."

A spokesperson for the Federal Housing Administration (FHA), Stanley Pohutsky, says that people may perceive mobile homes as being flimsy, "but they're actually more durable today than they've ever been. This is primarily because of standards adopted by the federal government in 1976."

An early model.

Tougher government standards are also cited by Holt Blomgren of the National Manufactured Housing Federation, an industry lobbying group, as one reason why mobile homes are perceived as being more durable than ever before. Perceptions are important to the mobile home industry. Blomgren ruffles as he explains that these days mobile homes are properly called manufactured housing. Most people in the industry seem to want to forget the days when mobile homes were called trailers and looked like oversized sardine cans. Even so, Blomgren admits that most mobile-home manufacturers guarantee their products for only one year.

Jim Carroll of Skyline mobile homes, the nation's largest maker of manufactured housing, says that mobile homes are now "perceived as having more intrinsic quality, mostly because the 1976 government standards brought a greater degree of uniformity to the industry. It would be a mistake, however, to believe that all mobile homes made before 1976 were flimsy." Skyline has been manufacturing mobile homes for 30 years, Carroll says, and "some of those first mobile homes are still in use, though they were a very basic product. Of course, today's manufactured housing is much more durable and should last 30 years, beyond question. We're all the time conducting tests to improve the durability of our products. We use copper water pipes only, for instance, while builders of conventional homes rely more and more on plastic piping. In fact, I can take you to construction sites and show you the poor-quality lumber many conventional builders are using these days. I know most conventional builders aren't using the high grade of lumber that we use." While the quality of conventional housing is generally perceived as declining, Carroll says, the quality and durability of mobile homes have steadily increased: "The proof that mobile homes are more durable than ever is that their value has begun to appreciate for the first time. Progress can and will be made. Marketplace factors compel the industry to continuously upgrade construction standards. What we don't need is more government regulations."

A regulator at the U.S. Department of Housing and Urban Development's (HUD) Mobile Home Standards Division was willing to talk with us but asked not to be identified by name, apparently because these are not good times for outspoken regulators. "More mobile homes are sold now than conventional homes," the regulator says, "primarily because conventional housing is now priced out of the reach of the average American. Mobile homes have traditionally been regarded as low-income housing. You must remember that the mobile-home industry grew out of the automobile industry. Historically, a mobile home was bought like a car and paid for in carlike installments. These days, a single mobile home can be financed by a 15-year mortgage. A double-wide mobile home can be financed up to 20 years. We're trying to improve the durability of mobile homes so that they can be paid for over 30 years. The trouble with financing one of today's mobile homes is that after 30 years, there's nothing left of the mobile home; there's nothing left but a piece of paper on which is printed the mortgage agreement."

Marty Luke, of Percy Wilson, Inc., a Chicago-based finance company, explains that 30-year financing is available for mobile-home buyers—if the purchaser owns a piece of land that can be used for collateral. Holt Blomgren, the industry lobbyist, adds that another condition usually attached to a 30-year mobile-home mortgage is that the structure must only be moved once—from the dealer's lot to the purchaser's site.

Explains the HUD regulator: "The problems with a mobile home's durability start with the transportation of the home. Transporting a mobile home invariably weakens the structure; therefore, the less a mobile home is moved, the longer it will last." Transportation is not the only threat to mobile-home durability. "If a mobile home is sited improperly and the earth beneath it settles, the structure will bend and weaken. As well, after a few years, the floor begins to bend beneath the weight of the refrigerator or piano. A big party, with lots of people, can also warp the floor of a mobile home."

The federal government has studied ways of improving the durability and fire safety of mobile homes, but a conservative political climate will probably prohibit any substantive new regulations from being enacted. A report prepared for HUD in the late 1970s determined that twice as many people die each year in mobile home fires as in conventional one- or two-family homes; further, the very young (one to four years old) account for more than one-fourth of all mobile-home deaths.

A mobile-home fire can spread quickly. Writing in *New Shelter* magazine, Roger Rawlings describes such a blaze. "One afternoon my wife was sitting on our back porch when she noticed a wisp of smoke curl up from a nearby mobile home. Within a very brief period, the mobile was ablaze. After ten minutes, by my wife's estimate, it was completely destroyed. When I drove home that evening, all that remained of the mobile was its heavy metal chassis which had been twisted by the intensity of the fire."

"We would like to improve the safety and durability of mobile homes," says the HUD regulator, "but times prohibit us from doing so."

"Right now, mobile homes are safe and durable," counters Jim Carroll of Skyline. "If the industry is forced to spend more money to comply with needless regulations, the price of the mobile home will increase, and manufactured housing will no longer be low cost." In 1980, Foremost Insurance Company, a mobile-home insurer, estimated that the average income of a mobile-home owner was about $9,500; the average price of a new mobile home that year was $18,500, as opposed to almost $70,000 for a new single-family house.

BK

A happy owner

Christie C. Tito

Judith New and her mobile home.

"Before I moved into mine, mobile-home owners always reminded me of gypsies," says Judith New, who has been living in this mobile home for 9 years near Allentown, Pennsylvania. "Then I saw mobile homes for what they are: good, cheap living." New says her home still has more than 20 years of life in it, "if it's not moved and it's taken care of." Aside from a slight creaking sound in the floor whenever she walks in the kitchen, her mobile home has not deteriorated.

Just the opposite. "I bought my home for $5,000, and I think I can sell it for $7,500, which is a better investment than if I'd been paying rent for nine years."

New says she hopes to move soon into a bigger mobile home.

"A trouble light comes in handy. Run it through a heavy-duty cord with a three-pronged plug for the ground–not a string of ten-foot cords that you use for stringing up Christmas-tree lights."

"For the home owner, a ¼-inch electric drill is fine; for more power, go to a ⅜-inch drill. Variable speed is a handy option for putting in screws with a screwdriver bit."

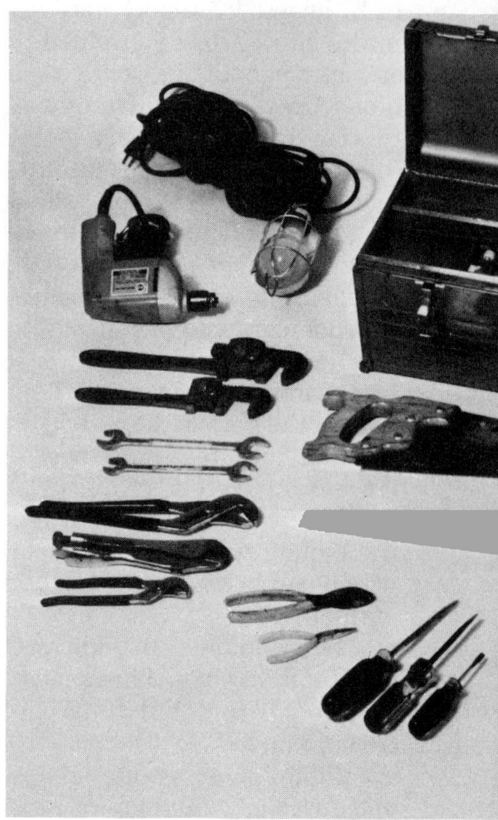

"For plumbing, you'll need large, medium-size, and small monkey wrenches, plus a pair of Vise-Grips and a pair of Channellocks. With two sizes of Channellocks, you can take apart anything that's threaded together. I always use open-end wrenches on copper and brass fittings, because these strip easily if not turned the right way."

"For electrical repairs, you need pliers and cutters. Only use tools with insulated handles. More people are killed by 110-volt lines than 220, simply because most people think 110 can't really hurt you. They work on the live wires and get zapped. One bit of advice: don't take anyone's word that the electrical supply has been shut off; check it yourself, and then test that particular outlet or system with a circuit tester. You can get a tester from Sears for $1.39."

"Craftsman screwdrivers are good. It's better to look for a dependable name-brand screwdriver than a countertop special. Work up to an assortment of about six screwdrivers–three each of common and Phillips, in different sizes–and you'll be able to handle any job around the house."

Home toolbox

Robert Mitchell, Jr., manages his own construction company. We asked him to recommend tools a person would need to keep an apartment or house in good repair.

Interview by ROGER MOYER

"You can build your own toolbox of wood or buy a metal one. It's good to keep tools in one place so you'll know where to find them when the need comes up. We use leather tool aprons, and they can do as a toolbox, but they're now about $50. They have four separate pouches for nails and a place for a tape measure, pocket square, pencils, knives, a hammer, pliers, screwdrivers, snips, and chisels. A simple cloth tool apron will work all right, and sometimes you can get them free at a lumberyard, or for a buck."

Christie C. Tito

"On the job we use the commercial-grade Rockwell 315 circular saw, which runs about $110. I wouldn't recommend that for working around the house; more appropriate would be a $40 to $50 saw with a five-inch blade. These are sturdy enough so that you could make all the cuts you need for the next ten years."

"Two planes will suffice for work around the home. You can use a large plane, one with a blade width of 2 to 2½ inches, to shave down a sticking door, and a smaller plane with a width of 1 to 1½ inches on cabinet doors."

"The tool kit should include a tape measure."

"I suggest having two saws, one an 8- to 10-point, the other a 12-point. The points are the number of teeth per inch. The first is used for rough-cutting and ripping, the second for finer cuts."

"Buy a hammer with the flattest head you can find. If you plan on having two hammers, one should have a straight claw to pull out nails that are in awkward positions, like tight against the wall or in a corner; a curved claw head gives a little more leverage."

UPHOLSTERED FURNITURE

"They'll put a good piece of material on a piece of junk furniture. As long as it looks good, most people don't care."

An interview with Anthony Baumann

On Long Island's north shore, Anthony Baumann has built, rebuilt, and refurbished furniture for a third of a century. Through his small shop in Mt. Sinai, New York, have traveled both furniture that lasts and furniture that doesn't.

When we visited Baumann, he had just finished rebuilding an armchair that he estimated to be at least 50 years old. As we admired the chair, he explained what makes some chairs last longer than others.

RICH KLINE

"Why'd this chair last? First of all, of course, the wood wasn't green. Nowadays the wood is cut, and they make things out of it right away. And instead of using a coil spring on the seats, they use zig-zag springs, and they stretch them from front to back. When the wood is green and still drying out, the zigzag spring gets so much tension on it that it pulls the wood all out of shape. Years ago, they done it the way it was supposed to be done: they put webbing on it, they put springs on it, then they tied the whole schmier. But they can't afford to do that anymore.

I do all my own work. I won't even hire anybody. I used to hire people, but nowadays there isn't an upholsterer anywhere on Long Island—anywhere at all, in fact—who does hire apprentices. These younger fellows don't want to do a good job, they just want to make money. I had one young fellow here, all he wanted to do was learn enough about the trade to see how much money he could make at it. I fired him.

Myself, I went to school. After World War II, I went to upholsterer's school, more than 30 years ago. There are some schools still around. Matter of fact, I even gave a course at Port Jefferson High School, adult education, for people who wanted to do their own furniture. And actually, if you teach it the way you're supposed to, it's a snap. But there isn't an upholstery school that's doing a good job today anywhere. They can do a good job—they just don't want to. Instead of that chair taking two days, they teach you to do it in a day. It took me two full days. I don't do any butchering because I have all my own customers. A lot of upholsterers do contract work. They'll cut all kinds of corners, leave the old material on it, all kinds of things. That's why I won't hire anybody.

What you got to look for in a chair is construction—if it's got a solid bottom. In other words, if there's webbing on the bottom, and coil springs beneath it, you got a guarantee it's a good chair. Then you look for staples on it. If they used a staple gun to reupholster the chair, nine out of ten times, it's a quickie. Everybody else uses staples, but I won't. I've been too long in this line to go changing over to modern ways. I don't have to.

The average chair now, people tell me, runs $500. I'll make chairs every day for $500! And yet so many chairs are poorly made, most people don't even know the difference.

Your best upholstery material used to be 100 percent cotton tapestry. Cotton is actually a lightweight fabric, but cotton tapestry is a heavyweight fabric and one of your best covers. The tighter the weave, the better the wearability.

These days, all these new synthetics are starting to come into the picture. I know for a fact that Herculon, if you're in a room with no sun, will wear like iron, but if you have the sun beating on it for three months, you might as well forget it. Now they're putting rayon in tapestry. It cheapens the fabric. Rayon, when it's mixed with something else, is fine, but 100 percent rayon is no good. If people want it, I give it to them, but I tell them it's not going to last. You can feel it.

As far as wearability of furniture, the new stuff is no good. Years ago, people had a parlor, and the chairs sat in the parlor with covers on them. On Sunday, they'd turn the heat on in the room, take the sheets off, and the family would go sit in the parlor. Today, people live in their parlor, and watch TV. Right now, you're doing good if you get 8 years out of your furniture. How do you get 20 years out of your furniture? By not using it.

But if you sit in your chair and it wears out, get the best material and the best construction you can afford. Nine out of ten times they won't even retie the springs. I'm one of the damn fools that insists on doing a good job.

Here's a tip: if you can pick up a big chair yourself, I guarantee it's cheaply made. Naturally, if it's light, the wood is thin. There's no heavy construction underneath it. And zigzags are lighter than coil springs.

Another thing–if you've got a chair with hair in it, then you know you've got a good chair. Right now, nobody's using hair. Everything is done to make the job take less time. You tear a chair apart and there's moss dust all over the place. Moss was a cheaper job.

Same thing with cushions. If you find a chair with a down cushion, you know you've got a good piece of furniture. Down is so expensive, only the good pieces have it. Down lasts longer. Even if I get a down cushion 25, 30 years old, all flattened out and so on, I put it out in the sun to dry and beat the hell out of it, and it'll be as good as new.

There's a lot of things that signify a good piece of furniture. Feel the wood. If the wood is thick, you've got a good chair. If the wood is thin like cardboard, you've got a piece of junk.

They didn't always make good furniture years ago. Some places used to sweep up floors and use the sweepings for stuffing.

I stopped making new furniture. It got too expensive. I'd hate to price a bag of hair right now. I always had a bag around to freshen something up. People'd say, "Why you using that hair? That costs money." But it added something to the quality of the job.

These two chairs here are well over a hundred years old. They lasted because they've got good wood and, second, good construction. A stitched edge lasts almost indefinitely. You stitch it and you tie the springs properly, it'll last indefinitely. When that stitched edge goes, you're not going to find too many guys who can do it over again. The average upholsterer wouldn't stitch it.

Some sofas cost $1,200 today. If you pay less, you're probably getting junk. But spending a lot of money doesn't mean you're getting good quality, either. You see, they'll put a good piece of material on a piece of junk furniture. As long as it looks good, most people don't care. Nowadays, everybody is cutting corners. If I had to do a chair right, I'd have to charge $500 for it, but all I can get for it is $250. How do I compensate for that? Cut corners. I won't retie the springs in the seat, I won't tighten the frame up. I'll leave the material on and save another hour or so. That's the only way I can earn a living nowadays.

You see, most people don't buy things to last. They're not satisfied with the same things all the time. I make furniture, but my sister-in-law goes out and buys hers at Macy's. They change every three years, and they don't pay cheap prices, either. But in three years, they're tired of the colonial sofa. They don't like colonial anymore, so they take it out and throw it in their bungalow. Now they want a more modern piece of furniture. Then it's French provincial. Disposable, like Pampers.”

THE ENDURING STOVE

What makes some woodstoves last longer than others? We might imagine stoves as lasting indefinitely, like the Pyramids. Massive, solid, and confined to one place, they are not subject to the forces of motion or the vagaries of chance that govern the useful life of an automobile, nor to the inexorable forces of wind and rain that might destroy a house. Yet while some stoves may perform for over a century, others burn out in only a few years. Why? Stoves are really no different from many other objects in our daily lives in that their useful life span is determined by the materials that they are made of, the extent to which longevity was considered in their design, the quality of construction, and their treatment and maintenance. Care is the watchword—in design, manufacturing, and use.

A $10.25 Montgomery Ward stove, from their 1895 catalog.

Materials

In terms of materials, the choice in stoves is limited to iron, steel, and masonry. Among stove buffs, there is an ongoing controversy concerning iron vs. steel. Both have their advantages and drawbacks, yet neither is clearly superior. Since the oil embargo of 1974 began the modern stove boom, more stoves have been made of steel than of iron because steel plate is readily available and steel stoves can be assembled by any welding shop. Foundries, which are needed to produce cast-iron plates, have become extremely expensive to establish. Iron was the traditional favorite, largely because steel plate was expensive in the last century and welding didn't exist.

The thermal properties of heat transfer and heat-holding capacity are similar for iron and steel, since they are, after all, related materials. Whether of iron or steel, a stove that is operated red-hot for extended periods of time will not last long. Moreover, steel and iron both have their drawbacks; steel tends to oxidize and scale more rapidly than iron, and a steel plate may burn out more quickly than an iron plate of equal thickness. Steel plates may warp at elevated temperatures, sometimes with sufficient force to break a weld. Warpage is quite common, however, and there is no evidence to suggest that this deformation in itself shortens a stove's useful life.

Unlike steel, iron can be surprisingly brittle and may break under rough treatment, as when a heavy log is slammed into a broad back plate. Iron is also subject to breakage by thermal shock, so cast-iron stoves should be warmed gradually. Large kindling fires may crack a cold stove.

"Stove-plate" iron is the cheapest grade and lacks the tensile strength of the more expensive structural grades. Modern foundries test each batch of iron before the pour is made, but the range of impurities that they allow in stove plate is relatively wide. In this regard, American and

European foundries are more fastidious than the Taiwanese, and extra care is reflected in the price of the product. Whether of iron or steel, a stove should have thick plates, $^{3}/_{16}$ inch or thicker, for long life. Seek to get the most metal for your money.

The firebox of the woodstove can contain what's known as an "aggressive" atmosphere, with temperatures up to 1,800°F and streams of flame and hot ash. Coal burners are subject to even greater heat. Many manufacturers line fireboxes with firebrick, or plates of iron and steel, to protect the exterior plates from actual contact with the coals. This contact could cause plates to crack as could the physical abuse of overzealous fueling. Thin-gauge steel plates, in particular, must be protected with firebox liners to prevent warpage and rapid burnout. Some manufacturers have resorted to specialized steels for liners, such as the aluminized steel used by Riteway in their popular 2000 and 37 heaters, or high-strength, low-corrosion steels like U.S. Steel's Cor-Ten, used in some boilers and furnaces.

Liners also insulate exterior plates from the punishment of direct and intense radiation, but they can insulate the consumer from those warming rays, too. You may find yourself with a durable stove that does not deliver adequate heat. Due to the trade-off between durability and heat transfer, many manufacturers line the firebox only where coals are likely to contact the exterior plates, and leave the rest uninsulated. It would make even more sense for manufacturers who use iron or steel liners to perforate them with small holes that would keep the coals at bay and allow more of the exterior surface to "see" the fire. Such a design modification has recently been undertaken by the innovative Cawley Stove Company in their huge iron box stoves.

In the past few years, massive masonry heaters, sometimes called Russian fireplaces, have gained popularity, particularly in northern New England, where a growing number of adventurous young masons have learned to build them. These stoves strike me as the most efficient way to heat with wood or any other type of solid fuel. They offer optimum combustion and heat-transfer efficiencies and several tons of brick, stone, or tile for heat storage.

This is how they work. The owner builds one or two small, hot fires daily in a firebox lined with firebrick. Convoluted flue passages capture most of the exhaust heat and store it in the masonry mass, from which it is slowly released into the living space. Since there is no attempt to throttle combustion, air pollution is minimal. These stoves offer a large warm surface rather than a small hot one, and emit gentle radiant heat that is very pleasant to live with. They are also quite durable: a well-made one may last indefinitely. Masonry heaters are expensive, costing thousands of dollars, although skilled amateurs have built excellent ones for much less.

Design

In the past century, durability was probably the prime consideration of the designer, and so there are many well-maintained antique heaters still in use today. But in the early part of the modern postembargo stove boom, durability was rarely the primary consideration of the stove designer, who was generally preoccupied with bottom-line costs, as well as ease of operation, efficiency, appearance, and other more readily marketable factors. The stove market has been so competitive, however, that manufacturers were eventually forced to offer some sort of guarantee on their products. Having a stove returned on warranty, known in the trade as "eating it for breakfast," was so expensive that manufacturers began to design more durability into their products. This did not result in an overall level of design that was more sophisticated, nor in increased quality. Most manufacturers responded to the durability problem merely by making everything heavier, so that today there is just as much ugly, poorly designed garbage on the market as ever, except that it is now *heavy-duty* garbage, likely to be with us for a longer time. The increased cost of heavier materials, of course, has been passed along to the consumer.

Christie C. Tito

Vermont Castings' Vigilant.

Beyond the reflex responses of insulating the firebox and beefing up the various plates, a designer can strive for durability in more sophisticated ways. By prototyping and thorough testing, he can determine where thermal stress occurs and reinforce those points. Warpage, for instance, can be largely eliminated by using curved plates, which distribute thermal stress into their curve.

At this point, it would be instructive for us to compare two stoves of similar size, materials, and configuration. Take, for example, Vermont Castings' Vigilant and the Portland Stove Foundry's Atlantic 228, both handsome American iron fireplace stoves of remarkably similar appearance, with power output in the range of 40,000 BTUs per hour. The Vigilant is a popular stove and a successful piece of design; the Atlantic 228 has been less successful, plagued by design flaws. Iron stoves are assembled from separate plates with interlocking joints, sealed with refractory putty and held together by bolts. A poorly designed joint may spread when the plates are heated, causing an air leak that may result in a runaway fire and serious overheating. Such was the major design flaw of the 228. This could easily have been prevented by designing the joints so that thermal stress pulled them more tightly together, as in the Vigilant, rather than spreading them apart.

Another illustrative failure in the recent history of the industry was the Ram Tile Stove, a heavy steel box stove with decorative ceramic tiles fitted in tracks on the sides and top, made by the Ram Forge Company of Maine. These tiles insulated the stove from the outside and caused considerable warpage in the side plates, which in turn broke the tiles. A prototype had been made, but for some reason it was never fired, and the model was released untested onto the market. Many damaged stoves were returned, and the financial burden of honoring its warranties helped force the company into bankruptcy in 1980.

Martin Industries' popular Ashley line has also had several design problems. The most notable was an interior door latch that closed in an upward direction and could be knocked down by a falling log inside the firebox. This design flaw was rectified, but Martin Industries has been sued by consumers who alleged that it caused fires that destroyed their homes. Increased safety testing in the industry, which is now mandatory in many states, should halt most such disastrous design mistakes before they appear on the market.

How can the naive consumer distinguish a durable design from an expensive throwaway? One way is to avoid new models: buy a stove that has been on the market for a few years and has a sound reputation. Chances are that two or three years in the marketplace will shake many of the bugs out of a new design. The better manufacturers are constantly making improvements.

Shopping for a stove

The care used in constructing a stove affects its durability as much as any of the variables we have discussed thus far. Unfortunately, stove sales are seasonal, and stove dealers are notorious for withholding their orders until the last possible moment and then expecting immediate shipment from the manufacturer. Speed of construction becomes essential, particularly in the late summer and fall, when stove dealers put on the pressure for fast deliveries. In the panic that ensues, mistakes can be made. Quality control may be poor, and at the very least, the fit and finish may be hurried. In this regard, you may do well to buy in the off-season. (You can also take advantage of inventory-clearance sales.) The prospective stove buyer should shop at reputable dealers' showrooms and avoid bargain stoves at hardware stores. Also be wary of dealers who handle only one or two brands.

When considering a stove, examine it carefully. Bring a flashlight along to check the interior for missing or damaged liners, inadequate or missing welds, or signs of cracked plates. All joints should be tight and thoroughly sealed. The more a stove is handled, the greater the chance of breakage; double-check imported stoves, which are particularly susceptible to shipping damage. Point the flashlight at each individual surface and close the door. If a light shows through a joint of an iron stove, it means there is a large air leak.

Sources

High-temperature paints

Thurmalox, Dampney Co., 85 Paris Street, Everett, MA 02149

F.C.C. Stove Paint, Freedom Coatings Co., P.O. Box 196, Franklin, MA 02038

Pyromark (black only), Tempil Div., Big Three Ind., South Plainfield, NJ 07080

Thermosetting plastic putty (for stove joints)

Stove Mate, Industrial Gasket and Shim Co., P.O. Box 368, Meadow Lands, PA 15347

Door-gasket kits

Bentley Harris, 241 Welsh Pool Road, Lionville, PA 19353

Stove types and brands

Woodstove Directory, Energy Communications Press, 105 West Merrimack Street, Manchester, NH 03108

That alone may not be grounds for rejecting the stove, but you should insist that it be properly sealed before you buy it. A leak in the welded joint of a steel stove will probably be beyond the ability of a dealer to repair, but any welding shop should be able to fix it.

A flashlight can also illuminate a leaky door gasket. The door should seal tightly and latch securely, and the gasketing should be firmly glued in place.

A little surface rust in the interior is nothing to worry about, but on the exterior, it is a sign of an inadequate paint job. See that the dealer knows what brand of paint was used, and that he can supply a can for touch-ups.

Other than evaluating the physical condition of your purchase, be sure to shop for a stove that is the right size for your needs. Try to match the stove's rated power output to the heating requirements of your house. A stove that is too small will run hot, need frequent tending, burn out more quickly, and probably fail to provide efficient heating. On the other hand, a stove that is too large for the job will be operated at low power with smouldering fires, generating a lot of smelly and corrosive creosote. Most stoves are capable of a fairly wide range of power output and function best in the middle of their range.

The more knowledgeable manufacturers rate their products in terms of power in BTUs per hour for a six- to eight-hour overnight burn using seasoned hardwood. European stoves are rated in watts (1 watt = 3.4 BTUs per hour). Most manufacturers, however, rate their stoves in terms of the amount of space that they will adequately heat, a nonsensical rating that fails to account for the heat loss in that space. A tight, insulated modern home in a mild climate will obviously require much less power than a drafty, uninsulated home in northern Minnesota or Maine. The best indicator of power capability is the size of the firebox. For example, a stove with three cubic feet of firebox capacity will typically be rated at around 45,000 BTUs per hour. This translates to 15,000 BTUs per hour for every cubic foot. Smaller heaters will put out somewhat less than this ratio, while larger stoves put out a bit more.

Treatment and maintenance

The consumer is the greatest variable in a stove's durability. A high-quality heater that is abused will have a short life, but even a stove of indifferent quality can endure for many years if well treated and properly maintained.

Damage and wear to the interior of a stove usually occur when the stove is in use, from overheating, dripping pyroligneous acids that dry into creosote, or overzealous stoking. The off-season, however, is the time when the exterior of a stove suffers. Summertime brings hot, humid air, which will condense moisture on cool stove plates, causing rust. A touch-up of paint or blacking should be applied in the spring before muggy weather sets in. If the paint is not the same brand as that used by the manufacturer, the old paint first must be removed with a wire brush and steel wool. Several high-temperature paints have appeared on the market in the last ten years, some of which have won acceptance in the industry. A few are available to the consumer in spray cans. Steel stoves typically rust somewhat faster than iron stoves and require more frequent repainting, but both eventually deteriorate from moisture. Small surface pits become larger until a considerable amount of metal is gone. If a stove is stored in the off-season, it should be kept in a dry, well-ventilated place. If it must be covered, use an old sheet or a tarp, not plastic, so that condensed moisture can evaporate.

The hidden effects of moisture can be devastating. Bolts, which hold iron plates together, can expand dramatically as they rust, creating enough force to crack a plate. To keep moisture out, caulk the joints of an iron stove in the spring. A well-sealed joint in an iron stove is essential to its durability, not only to keep out moisture but to prevent air leaks that can cause hot spots in areas not designed to withstand excess heat. Most iron stoves will need to be completely torn apart, wire-brushed, recaulked, and reassembled about every ten years, depending on the design of the joints. Also, damaged liners and tattered door gaskets should be replaced.

WILLIAM HAUK

DEAR SIR:

THESE TWO LIGHTERS WERE IN MY HOUSE WHEN IT BURNED AND I LOST EVERYTHING. I DID MANAGE TO SALVAGE THESE, THE SLIM ONE WAS MY WIFE'S, THE REGULAR WAS MINE. THE ZIPPO LIGHTER IS THE BEST I HAVE EVER USED, THEY NEVER FAIL TO LIGHT. I AM SORRY THEY WERE IN SO BAD OF REPAIR.

HOME ELECTRONICS AND CAMERAS

7

EVOLVING ELECTRONICS

Electronics excites mixed emotions in both fans and critics of technology, in both people who buy the stuff and those who fix it. The issue goes beyond electronic hardware—stereos and computers and such. Every sort of consumer product is evolving a microchip brain, or ganglia at least.

Watches, car dashboards, appliances, tools, even man-made internal organs are now driven by the silent pulse of microcircuitry. What does this mean for durability? Clearly, the microchip does not invite the fingers and wrenches of would-be do-it-yourselfers. In their tininess and sophistication, such parts are inscrutable to all but a few. If the old-fashioned vacuum tube was also something of a mystery, at least it put out a sanguine glow when healthy and could be tested at the drugstore when ailing. A replacement was nearly as easy to install as a light bulb. And if all else failed, a tube device might be brought into line with a good slap.

Solid-state components will have none of it. Even repair people have trouble doing their work. Far from being invulnerable to their environment, these components may be bollixed up by greasy fingertips or the heat of a soldering iron. To diagnose the problem may take an oscilloscope. Often, repair means tossing out an entire panel of components. That's wasteful, obviously, but a lot simpler than hunting down the faulty part. Some electronic hardware tells where it hurts with lights so that the layperson can yank the offending panel and plug in a replacement. The pennies of plastic and metal thusly wasted are more than made up for by avoiding a $25 or $50 bill for the repair person's time.

Solid state does away with people—in production, assembly, and repair. At this point in time and economics, a person's time is far more costly than an ounce or two of material. Until this relationship is reversed, you will continue to see the wane of accessible parts, of understandable assembly, of mechanisms that move and throw off heat when they work, and grow cold and still when they fail.

The most lovable of machines was likely the steam locomotive, for the reason that it was so nearly animate. Panting and sweating, its ligaments bared, this now-extinct beast seems an ice age removed from the cool and remote circuitry of today.

Electronic hardware

Perhaps nothing determines the durability of electronic equipment as much as the failure rate of its individual electronic components. The accepted reference failure rate for electronic components is 2 percent. In plain terms, this means that for every 10,000 integrated circuits used by a manufacturer, 200 can be expected to fail. Some will fail when the finished product is tested at the end of the manufacturer's assembly line, some will fail during the warranty period when it costs the consumer nothing but trouble to have the repair done, and others will fail after the warranty expires.

Essentially, 2 percent is the failure rate under optimum conditions, and it can only go downhill. If the manufacturer's design causes the component to operate toward its upper limit of heat dissipation, the component might fail earlier than expected. It will be less likely to fail in a more conservative design: a manufacturer consciously building durability into a product might employ a design that distributes the heat load among several individual components, all operating at low capacity, rather than attempt to push a single component to handle the entire load. For example, an electronic function might be distributed between two or three transistors rather than having it all done by a single transistor. Naturally, the final undiscounted selling price, or price point, will partially determine which tactic is chosen.

Few engineers can judge the adequacy of a particular product outside of his area of expertise or interest. So, the notion of a manufacturer's track record comes into play. Some companies have in time acquired a reputation for durability. A few examples will illustrate the point.

In the late 1940s, at the dawn of the modern age of television, RCA introduced its 630 television-receiver circuit. A design of outstanding reliability, the circuit was used for many years by other manufacturers. Even consumers with no understanding of electronic circuits were familiar with the 630 designation—they claimed the 630 gave the best TV picture and the least repair expense. The term "RCA 630" became synonymous with quality and reliability.

Another example is the Garrard brand of record changers and turntables. Back in the early 1950s, when high fidelity was getting out of the hobbyist's basement and into the general marketplace, Garrard was the one reliable brand of automatic record changer suitable for what was considered high-fidelity sound in the early '50s. A Garrard record changer was built like a battleship and almost never needed repair. Long after the appearance of other automatic record players of equal or even better performance and durability, consumers still associated the Garrard brand with the standard of reference for record players and turntables.

Hunting for long-lived brands has been complicated by the fact that many well-known names bear no relationship to the original company. The founders, management, and even the engineers and technicians might be long gone. Mergers are sometimes brought about by conglomerates interested only in the name of the company, or a registered brand it owns. Or, there might be some financial advantage, such as a tax-loss carry-over from previous years that might offset the profits of the conglomerate. Whatever the reason, the original company exists only as a name on paper.

An example of what can happen to a company with a previous history of quality, performance, and reliability is Marantz, a name brand well known to high-fidelity enthusiasts. Marantz was founded by Sol Marantz, an engineer of outstanding reputation. His products were superior for their time, and even some ten years later, original Marantz designs and equipment were as good as, if not better than, much of the contemporary equipment. The Marantz company was purchased by one of the other better-known names in high fidelity, which soon introduced a lesser-quality line of equipment under the Marantz marque. The name was the same, but the quality was not. Where formerly only the highest-quality equipment was sold under the Marantz label, now there was a broad line of equipment manufactured to price points.

In the end, durability comes down to using whatever technical knowledge you possess (regardless of how little), what little knowledge the manufacturers allow to leak out to the general public, your own powers of observation, and common sense in applying everything you know about a product and a company. In the sections that follow, we'll show you specifically what to look for in order to get the most durability for your money.

Television

TV is often the largest "general-equipment" family expense because the majority of families own more than one TV set, with at least one likely to be a relatively expensive color receiver. Until recent years, color TV, and to some extent black and white (B&W), not only represented an expensive initial expense, but repair and service were often so substantial a cost as to be factored into the monthly budget. At that time, a service contract might run upwards of $100 a year in the days when $100 was a week's net salary.

The basic durability problem was threefold: heat, mechanical failure, and the color picture tube. Heat is probably the primary cause of component failure. Until the mid-1970s, virtually all color and most B&W TVs used the vacuum tube, which is really a miniature electric heater in a closed cabinet. A 20- to 25-inch color TV using vacuum tubes will use approximately 500 to 750 watts of energy, to be dissipated as heat within the cabinet. (This is the same as sticking an electric heater in the cabinet; in fact, rooms with large tube-type color TVs often require less heating in the winter because the color TV serves as a 500- to 750-watt heater.) The heat both shortens the life of the components, and as we'll see below, it draws in dust. Of course, such problems created a new industry—tuner repair.

Until recent years, virtually all lower channels (numbers 2 through 13, called the VHF channels) were tuned through a selector that moves a multicontact switch or turret whose contacts "self-wipe" as the selector is rotated. The contacts are normally made of a springlike metal material, which eventually—from thousands of motions in and out—loses its tension, creating intermittent electrical connections. At one time or another, you have probably experienced an "intermittent tuner," one that requires moving the channel selector back and forth in order to secure a stable picture. Often, the channel selector must be precisely positioned, else the slightest vibration, perhaps caused by a single footstep on the floor, will cause the picture to "tear" and go out of sync.

It's also the job of the self-wiping action of the contacts to remove any dirt that might interfere with the electrical connections. How does dirt get on the tuner contacts? Through heat. The tuner contacts are within a metal turret, which, among other things, serves as a dirt shield. But the turret is not hermetically sealed. There are openings near the bottom and top of the cabinet for air circulation. As warm air flows from the bottom to the top of the cabinet, airborne dust is pulled inside the cabinet and deposited on the TV chassis, tuner, and tuner contacts. It is not unusual for tube-type color TV sets some five years old to have a half inch of dust on the chassis, and while dust usually does no harm, it spells disaster on a tuner's contacts, causing intermittent tuning.

So, a tuner that might otherwise be electrically perfect requires an overhaul or replacement in order to produce a stable picture. Because labor charges have come to make up the big part of any repair charge, it's now common practice to replace the tuner rather than repair it. A tuner replacement at a manufacturer's service center (meaning you carry the set in) costs nominally $75 plus sales tax in 1980—equal to or close to the original cost of some B&W TV sets.

Finally, we come to the picture tube. All picture tubes eventually require replacement unless, as often happens with B&W TVs, the set wears out first. Color picture tubes are something else. Through the early 1970s, color-tube replacement was frequent and expensive—so expensive that "picture-tube insurance" was also sold in addition to a service contract for color TVs. A basic service contract might or might not include the picture tube. Two unrelated circumstances, however, have sharply improved the durability of color picture tubes. The first is simply better materials and techniques. In addition, the transition from vacuum tubes to transistors and integrated circuits has reduced the heat load of color sets from almost 750 watts to less than 100 watts (in many instances), and internal heat is no longer literally cooking the components inside the cabinet. It is not unusual for color TVs some five years of age or older to be running on the original tube.

Of course, as with anything else, there is always the possibility a picture tube will fail early in life, but you can't shop for a more durable tube: one is not necessarily longer-lived than any other.

To our knowledge, all modern TV sets are solid-state, but tube models (in particular B&W portables) still appear from time to time as if found in some long-forgotten warehouse, and these are often advertised at special prices. Remember that tube sets are apt to suffer mechanical failure. Also, you may come upon periodic sales of refurbished tube-type color TVs formerly used in hotels and motels. Though the price might seem attractive at first glance, bear in mind that repairs might well undo the bargain, not to mention the inconvenience of having the set tied up at the service shop.

Though the inherent heat of the solid-state TV is well below that of tube models, for maximum durability it should be dissipated over a relatively broad area, not in hot spots. The easiest way to test for broad heat dissipation is to shop at one of those stores that have shelves, or banks, of TVs all running at the same time for viewer comparison. Pass your hand along the top and rear of the set in which you're interested, and then along the top and back of other models. In particular, a hot spot above or behind the channel selector could mean the somewhat sensitive tuner is being baked.

Though the majority of tuners used on both B&W and color TVs are still mechanically switched, many color sets in the intermediate to higher price range feature electronic tuning with no sensitive moving contacts to go bad. Touching a channel-selector button either on the TV or on a remote controller causes a minute electric current to electrically adjust the tuner to the desired channel. Other than the button being pressed, everything is electronic; there are no moving parts. While there are a greater number of electronic components in an electronic tuning system, thereby increasing the possibility of a defective component, over the long haul this system will prove more reliable than a mechanical tuner.

If there are problems with electronic tuning, it will most likely be in the channel-selector touch-buttons, where more attention is given to styling than mechanical reliability. As a general rule, a "tactile" touch-button will last longer because the user applies less effort. A tactile button creates a "click" or "pop" when depressed. The click or pop might have absolutely no relationship to what is actually taking place electrically. Often, it's built into the touch-button solely to instill confidence in the user that the switch really was depressed. When there is no tactile sensation—it might even be an audible tone "chirp" from the TV's loudspeaker—a person is apt to use damaging force in punching buttons.

As much expense as possible has gone into making a TV look like a million dollars to a particular type of consumer, while the electronics may be the cheapest the manufacturer can get away with. Since external appearance represents the manufacturer's best effort, it may be a good guide to overall quality and durability. If you're buying a portable TV, you'll probably be moving it around. Will the telescopic antenna built into the set stand constant handling? Try it. Does it slide in and out easily? Can it be rotated from side to side without using undue force? Is the antenna in a sturdy mount?

If the set has a conventional channel selector, is the control a dainty bit of molded plastic certain to crack if given a sharp twist by a child, or is it adult size, with enough heft to stand rough handling? Remember, a cracked tuning control often leads to a damaged tuner because tuners were not intended to be adjusted with pliers.

If you're purchasing a console cabinet TV, check the chassis number. A TV manufacturer has only a limited number of electronic models, which are put into different cabinets. While a "natural woodgrain cabinet with brushed-gold-tone front panel" might look as if it was intended for some king's castle, the actual electronics might not be the top of the line. All TVs indicate the chassis number. Find out from the dealer which are the best, intermediate, and bare-bones models, and then make certain you get the quality you pay for. Never assume that the most expensive TV is the best.

Always bear in mind that the dealer is out to sell you the model on which he makes the most profit, and durability does not generally go hand in hand with maximum profit. So you're on your own: consider the manufacturer's track record, the experiences of friends and neighbors, and of course your own common sense. One final tip: anything rugged enough to take several months of hard knocks and rough handling on a showroom floor is more than likely to prove reliable in your home.

We have devoted considerable coverage to conventional TVs because they represent a substantial family investment and because other kinds of consumer electronic equipment are often evaluated by the same considerations applied to the purchase of a TV.

We have not spoken of projection TVs because they are too new to have a service record worth commenting on. Because they are highly complex devices requiring precision adjustment through their lifetime, your first consideration should be the reputation of the local authorized service agency. You might also get a list of nearby people who own the model you're considering and visit them. That may seem a bit extreme, but you'll learn about serviceability firsthand.

Video recording

Though there is always talk of some new and better video recording system, only two systems have survived in the marketplace as of this writing: the Beta, originated by Sony, and the VHS, originated by JVC (a subsidiary of Matsushita, which is better known in this country through its Panasonic marque). Several companies are licensed to manufacture Beta recorders. Except for the JVC VHS recorder, which is an original design, all VHS models to date are manufactured by Matsushita and are essentially identical except for the panel appearance and control arrangement. While upgradings have been too frequent to permit comment on durability, the overall record of the known-brand models has been unusually good. An important point is that when a video recorder breaks down (fortunately, early in the warranty period, as a general rule), it is too heavy to ship by mail or United Parcel Service. You must find a local authorized repair facility to which you can physically carry the machine—and not a mere retail outlet but a service facility that stocks a full line of replacement parts. Once you have decided on the particular recording system you want—Beta or VHS—pick the machine for which there is a local service facility. Also, because of the unusually high cost of replacement recording heads, this is one of the few consumer appliances for which you should seriously consider a service contract.

The same thoughts apply to video cameras. The best advice is to stick with the camera made specifically as an accessory for your recorder. This way, if you have problems, you can deliver both to the repair facility.

The videodisc systems, of which there are three noncompatible types, are so new that no one has any idea which will eventually survive in the marketplace. While manufacturers claim little wear takes place, one importer of replacement videodisc laser and capacitance pickups is already bringing stock into the country because he says the heads wear after several hundred hours. Beware of paying several hundred dollars for a model that doesn't survive in the marketplace, and for which there will be no reasonably priced replacement parts, service, or programs.

High-fidelity equipment

Most of our suggestions on how to determine a durable TV also apply to hi-fi equipment, with one additional principal caveat. With rare exception, once a major brand has made a reputation with superior-quality equipment of exceptional durability, it follows with a line of lesser quality at a lesser price.

The manufacturers of high-fidelity equipment have developed packaging into an art—they can make nylon look like 24-karat gold, and paper-thin plastic look like a solid block of steel. They can take an ordinary volume control and give it the damped feel of a $200 level attenuator found on sound-recording consoles. They add on winking red and green lights that look sophisticated but convey no useful information. Virtually all hi-fi components, except for the bottom-of-the-line loss leaders, appear to the eye and touch as if they will last a lifetime and then some.

Underneath the packaging, high-fidelity equipment has been upgraded slowly and constantly over the years. The hi-fi industry upgrades even more frequently than the camera manufacturers. If your purchases are confined to the better-known brands, or those rated highly by the *Stereo Review* and *High Fidelity* magazines, you'll probably end up with equipment of exceptional durability. As with all products, lemons do come along, but as a general rule, when it comes to the all-electronic high-fidelity equipment the odds are in your favor.

About the only user check you can make is for heat in power amplifiers and receivers. The best models dissipate the heat evenly through a large heat sink on which the output transistors are installed. This runs across most or all of the rear of the cabinet or along the sides. After the amplifier has at a high sound level for some 15 to 30 minutes, place your hand on the top of the cabinet. If you find a particular area that's unusually hot compared to the rest of the cover, it means something inside the cabinet has a concentrated heat pocket. FM tuners subject to unusually high ambient heat can develop "drift"—the tuning wanders from the desired station during the first 30 to 60 minutes of operation, as the receiver warms up.

Electromechanical hi-fi devices are a different situation because even the best of intentions can go bad. As an example, I came across a highly thought of record player that suddenly died after a few years of operation. The motor wouldn't turn. The repair was simple enough: I installed a new, though somewhat expensive, motor. As it turned out, the motors weren't defective, but a small bit of grease used on the bearings solidified into clayey material virtually overnight. (The record-player manufacturer had actually purchased what he believed was premium grease.)

Another illustration of electromechanical problems affecting durability concerns one of the highest-rated players. The problem manifested itself as intermittent sound drop-out after several years of use. It eventually turned out that the connections between the phone pickup and the tone-arm wiring were made through contact springs that simply had lost their tension. Even when sharply bent to make contact with the tone-arm connecting pins, the springs eventually just dropped down and intermittently broke the connection.

Here's a final illustration of how the most unsuspected things can go wrong with electromechanical devices. One of the most outstanding names in high-performance, high-fidelity tape-recorder equipment is Revox. Their model A-77 has long been the standard of reference to which other recorders are compared.

Electronic kits

Legend has it that kit-built electronic equipment is more reliable and longer-lasting than mass-produced goods. In fact, the legend was true for many years. During the era of the vacuum tube and point-to-point wiring, when components were actually connected by lengths of wire, do-it-yourselfers could assemble a superior stereo, color TV, or radio, for two reasons: first, the larger kit manufacturers—in particular, Heathkit—often employed the most modern, up-to-date circuits; second, someone assembling and soldering point-to-point wiring on the kitchen table would likely take more care, and make better connections and a more precise alignment, than assembly-line employees working for just-better-than-minimum wages.

But times have changed. Not only have transistors and integrated circuits replaced vacuum tubes, but circuit assembly of consumer-grade equipment is now done almost entirely on a printed circuit board; and more often than not, insertion of the components on the board is done by automated machine. Many consumer circuits are never touched by the human hand. Also, soldering is automatic, and except in rare instances, the job is better than if done by hand.

In terms of the circuit's function and performance, a kit can—and often does—prove superior, but rarely can it match factory assembly in terms of durability if the components and design are of the same quality and reliability.

Of course, the direct savings represented by "sweat equity" can more than offset any potential reduction in durability, but that's a personal decision that only you can make.

But a few years after the A-77 was introduced, owners found that the reel brakes wouldn't release. It turned out that the adhesive used on the brake bands—which were worth just a few cents—would bleed and lock the reels. Revox provided replacement brakes for just about the mailing costs and changed the bands on all subsequent production. But the point is that, again, even the best of intentions may be undone by mechanical gremlins.

While it might be logical to assume that one of the modern computer-controlled direct-drive turntables would have greater durability than the old-fashioned AC-motor drive, this is not necessarily the case. The AC-motor turntable has only the drive motor and perhaps a drive belt or drive wheel. On the other hand, the computerized turntable is jam-packed with components. By the law of averages, a computerized turntable should fail first.

Virtually all variable-pitch turntables and players have a strobe or digital device to indicate proper calibration of 33 and 45 RPM. When trying out turntables in a showroom, place a record on the platter, calibrate the strobe or whatever is used to indicate proper speed, and come back to the machine in 15 or 20 minutes. Check the speed indicator: if it's off, if the turntable requires speed recalibration, figure that it can only get worse over the months and years you'll use it. For durability, the turntable should be able to hold its speed in the showroom. Don't be influenced by the claim that "the showroom creates unusual wear." Showroom wear is the best test. If it can't play a few hours a day in the showroom and stay in decent condition, how long will it last in your home?

The motor and mechanism of a record-changer turntable does a lot of extra work because it must also simultaneously drive the tone-arm return and the changer mechanism. Few of the intermediate- to higher-quality changers have problems with the extra load. In some high-performance models, the extra load is handled by a second motor that serves only to drive the changer mechanism. Budget and loss leader models, however, often have a motor barely large enough to drive the platter, let alone the changer mechanism. You can test these by loading the maximum number of 12-inch LPs specified for the machine, letting three or four drop, then observing how the remaining records are cycled. If the platter slows down perceptively during the change cycle, or if you hear the mechanism grinding, or if the tone-arm cycles from the end of the record toward its rest with a jerky, intermittent motion, then you can assume the motor and/or the mechanism is working at its maximum potential and will suffer with time.

For reel-to-reel recorders, about the only reliable indicator of durability is the number of motors. A recorder can work well with just a single motor that provides the drive source for play/record tape motion, fast forward, and fast rewind. Problem is, a single motor generally provides power through rubber "pucks," or wheels, that wear or just go stale from lack of use. As a general rule, more reliable recorders have two motors, one for play/record and fast forward, the other for rewind. The most durable machines have three motors, one for play/record, one for fast forward, and one for rewind.

Cassette decks and recorders are in a class by themselves because there are so many places the manufacturer can skimp on components that directly affect long-term reliability. And all of them are buried deep inside the cabinet. First there's the motor. It can be a beefy, heavy-duty model that might last ten years, or a skimpy toy that'll barely hold out for a few years of heavy service. You cannot tell by looking at the cabinet or by working the controls.

As a general rule, among cassette equipment from the same manufacturer with the same general features and specified electrical performance, the higher the price, the better the durability. Here is one of the few areas in consumer products where price is usually directly related to long-term reliability.

Be extremely careful of unusual, cute ways to load the cassette itself. The most reliable, trouble-free loading is the one where the user simply inserts the cassette in the machine. Tricky loading systems that utilize a separate motor mechanism to insert a cassette from a drawer, or which slide the cassette in some convoluted fashion, are using a lot of hardware for no essential purpose, and have poor service records.

Eight-track tape equipment is no longer manufactured for high-fidelity use. Modern eight-track equipment is intended for car players and for cheap mass-merchandized stereo systems. With rare exception, eight-tracks are built for sale at specific price points, and you shouldn't expect them to hold up.

The high-fidelity phonograph pickup can last a lifetime, or at least until you're dissatisfied with the sound quality and feel it's time to retire it. Durability here is usually a matter of friction: the stylus wears with use. Or, the stylus damping material may dry out during a hot, humid summer, necessitating replacement. Because the overall sound quality of a hi-fi system is substantially dependent on the phono pickup, durability should not be the basis of choice.

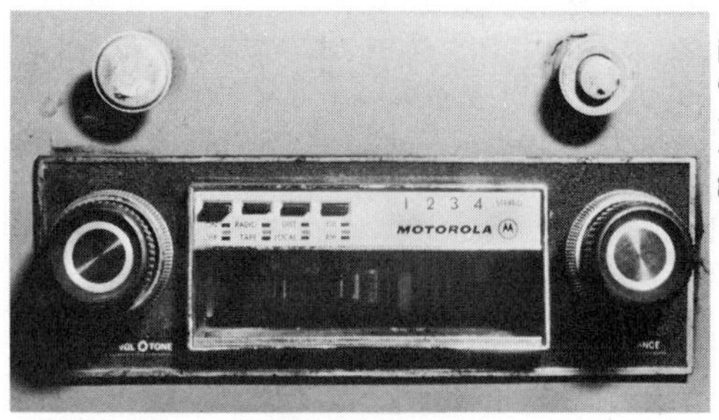

Christie C. Tito

On the way out: the eight-track tape player.

The same is more or less true of loudspeakers. They too can last a lifetime if not abused. Abuse is driving them with excessive output power from the amplifier (this can actually burn out a speaker component called the voice coil). True hi-fi speakers have a power rating, meaning the amount of output power they can safely handle. Driving speakers rated at 30 watts with, say, 100 watts, will eventually damage or destroy some part of the speaker system: the woofer, tweeter, honker (midrange speaker), or even part of the crossover network. Driving the same 30-watt speaker from a 300-watt amplifier operating at nearly full power output would result in an early, if not immediate, demise of the speaker system. This does not mean you cannot use a 100-watt amplifier with a speaker system rated for perhaps 30 or 50 watts, as long as volume levels are moderate. If the amplifier never delivers more than the speaker's rated power, there will be no abuse of the speaker. But to be on the safe side, the speaker system should be capable of handling at least 50 percent of the amplifier's maximum power.

Radios

A radio is a radio. They are manufactured almost entirely for specific price points, sensitivity (ability to receive very weak signals), and in some rare instances, for better sound quality. A single integrated circuit chip now can provide all the electronic circuits for an AM radio, while two or three chips are all that are needed for an FM or AM/FM radio. Many radios are simply the same chip circuit in different cabinets. There is almost no way to judge or estimate durability other than by brand name and track record. The better-known brands—Sony, General Electric, and Panasonic, among others—have good reputations, with price being somewhat an indicator of overall quality and reliability. Essentially, you pay your money and take your choice.

Home computers

Home computers, or personal computers as they are also known, have a history of myriad problems—everything from frequent breakdown of integrated circuits, to poor mechanical connections, to almost abysmal design of peripheral equipment. The problem is that many entrepreneurs saw computers as a road to instant wealth and rushed equipment to market before it was really ready for mass merchandising to the lay public. As one might expect, this gave personal computing a bad reputation. Fortunately, most of the bad names have been driven from the marketplace, and the major brands that remain—Apple, Commodore (PET), Heathkit/Zenith, Radio Shack—are now refined, debugged, and upgraded to dependability.

Because of the complexity of computer circuits and the unusually large number of components involved, there are going to be breakdowns. Generally, breakdowns tend to happen during the warranty period, and once the bugs are eliminated, a computer will usually prove reliable. But because you can expect trouble early on, you'd be wise to pick a brand for which there is either a local factory-authorized service facility or service close enough to justify using United Parcel Service (their weight limit is 50 pounds). The one thing you do not want to do is ship your computer back for repair by truck or the U.S. mail.

While it is possible to obtain peripheral equipment such as line printers and disc drives from "second sources," which might prove more durable and reliable than those of the computer manufacturer, bear in mind that you might have extreme difficulty in getting repairs if something breaks down. For example, assume you have a Brand AAA computer and a Brand ZZZ printer. If the printer fails to work, the problem might be either in the printer or in the computer, and the service shop might need to examine both items—but many authorized shops work only on certain brands. For the nontechnician, it is best that all equipment be of the same brand, or specifically approved by the computer manufacturer.

Calculators

As with high-fidelity equipment, calculator manufacturers have had time to refine their products. From the least to the most expensive models, they tend to give long-term reliability. More often than not, calculators fail because of mechanical damage. For example, those new business-card-sized calculators will bend very easily, just by jamming an eyeglass case alongside one in a shirt pocket. Usually, however, a tiny calculator will be lost before it breaks.

If larger portable and desk-top calculators don't break down during the warranty period, they'll probably last a lifetime, or until replaced by an upgraded model. Printing calculators using ribbons and standard paper seem destined to have long lives, but "heat" printers are something else. These print by applying heat, or an electric current, to a specially treated paper. They usually require some form of cleaning, generally when a new roll of paper is installed. Some models do not self-clean properly and eventually require factory service.

Perhaps the major caveat concerning calculators is to avoid models with nontactile keyboards. There should be a decided feel when a key is depressed—a click, a pop, or even an audible beep. Past experience has shown that people, particularly children, tend to exert excess pressure on nontactile keys to be certain they really are pressed, and this may damage the machine.

HERB FRIEDMAN

The death of the tube

"Solid state was originally said to be less troublesome—longer life without repairs. I haven't exactly found that to be true."

An interview with Earl Fenstermacher

Earl Fenstermacher owns Fensty's TV Service in Emmaus, Pennsylvania. His shop is filled with television sets waiting for repair. We spoke with Fenstermacher at his workbench in the back of the shop. During the interview, a man with a thick Pennsylvania Dutch accent wandered in with a garage-door opener that was on the fritz. "It don't vork wery vell," said the customer, leaving the device. Fenstermacher is a country doctor to all kinds of hinterland electronic gizmos.

Toward the end of the interview, a woman telephoned to say that her TV was flashing like there was a thunderstorm outside. But it was a sunny day with no thunderstorms in sight. The woman asked Fenstermacher to fix the set so she could get back to the soap operas.

"Tell me," said Fenstermacher to the woman, "do you know what ozone smells like? Well, ozone is in the air, and your clothes sometimes smell like it after they've been out on the line. Some manufacturers even put an ozone lamp in clothes dryers to make clothes smell like they've been hung outside. Here's what I want you to do: smell the back of the set. If you smell ozone, that means something's probably burned out."

Fenstermacher held the phone while the woman went to smell her television set. She returned and said that it smelled like dust.

BK

"I carried a rifle in the Army during World War II. When I got out of the service, I was like a lot of other guys. I had no idea what I wanted to do, no goal or anything. There was an advertisement in the newspaper where they were starting classes for radio and television servicing. With a little prodding from my parents, I decided to look into it.

People mostly had radios at that time. The largest television screen was ten inches. That was a monster then. You hardly ever saw them that big. The chassis that it operated with was a big old monstrosity. It weighed a ton and a half, I think.

Lately, I've had a number of old-time sets with small screens brought in here. I had one not too long ago. It was an Admiral. It was different from what we use now. The deflection, or the method of scanning the beam across the screen, was using an electrostatic field rather than electromagnetic. This old Admiral had one of those types of tubes. It needed a new tube. The picture was no good in it. But the tube was unavailable. I couldn't find anyone who'd even agree to attempt rebuilding it. Nobody had the internal components. Those people wound up with a television set that was useless.

These days, I favor Zenith television sets. I have for a long time. Zeniths have quite good picture quality and the serviceability of the set is generally decent. I favor the American brands. It's sort of nationalistic, I guess you might say. Also, you have more difficulty getting components for some of these imports.

The Japanese did get out ahead of everybody else using solid-state circuitry. Solid state was originally said to be less troublesome—longer life without repairs. I haven't exactly found that to be true. We have as many repairs, at least, as we had before, and they're more involved because of the complexity of the circuit. They have circuits interconnected with other circuits. A malfunction in one area could damage components in a completely separate circuit.

Bill Keisling

Earl Fenstermacher.

We wind up taking more televisions out of the home and into the shop than we used to. In the old days, you pulled a tube out, stuck in another one, and you had things going again. If there was a problem with your repair, you wouldn't blow the tube out right away. You could safely put a tube in, and if you saw that the tube was overheating slightly, you knew there must be something else wrong. Now, with transistors, if you haven't located the source of the problem, the instant power enters that circuit, the new transistor will be blown out again. A lot of the transistors are soldered fast, making things worse. You can't unsolder them unless you're reasonably sure it's necessary to replace them because if you unsolder a transistor, you're liable to damage it from the heat. In solid-state circuitry, almost every repair job involves a certain degree of test procedures with meters and so forth in order to localize the problem. And, more often than not these days, that means taking a TV into the shop. In fact, Zenith has a circuit board now that the company highly recommends not repairing in the field.

Things change quick in this business. Tuners, for instance, are no longer fully mechanical. It used to be a switch. You'd rotate the switch to different positions in order to select a different channel. Now this is done by computer circuitry.

There will always, I think, be a certain amount of local repairs. But what they could do right now—and it sounds like something out of Buck Rogers—is manufacture modules, sealed into a package, with a plug-in system much like a tube. It would be fairly simple to incorporate light-emitting diodes—LEDs—to give an indication of function or no function. When the set quits, the customer could look at the lights, pull out the corresponding module, and plug in another. No repairman, no volt meter, no oscilloscope.

It's technologically possible to do that now. But if they had, I'd probably be out of business.”

Component resale value

Resale value is largely dependent on the type of component in question. The highest values and longest market life generally fall to separate audio electronics: preamps, power and integrated amps, tuners, and signal processors. Speakers survive with somewhat less vigor, according to the Orion *Audio Reference Guide*, but many dealers report that such well-known lines as Advent, Klipsch, and EPI rival electronics in resale and trade value.

Depreciating the most rapidly are mechanical components, where significant wear is likely. Thus, turntables and open-reel tape decks, even from top manufacturers, can be expected to yield only a fraction of their original value. Cassette decks, especially in the lower price regions, will likewise bring disappointing trade-in bids. An exception is high-end cassette decks, which hold their value far better than other mechanical audio products. The *Guide* reflects dealers' reports of high trade-in and resale figures for high-demand units, such as Nakamichi's 1000 series.

If you stop into Harvey Sound on West Forty-fifth Street in Manhattan, you'll find Izzy Meyrowitz presiding over the store's used-equipment department. Harvey's secondhand gear is all carefully checked and reconditioned and demands top dollar. Prices for some of the equipment pictured above are: from left to right, front row, McIntosh XR-5 speaker, $799 per pair, B&O M-70 speaker, $440 per pair, KEF 105, $1,400 per pair; on the shelf behind Izzy a GAS Thaedra preamp, $550, sits atop of GAS Ampzilla 2 power amp, $650; to the right, an Audio Research SP-6A preamp $1,000, is stacked on an Audio Research D-76A power amp, $1,000.

Don't be seduced into thinking that the mere presence of tubes guarantees the kind of prices associated with prestige classics. A well-maintained McIntosh 2205 power amp or a Marantz 10B tuner will command bullish bids, but not most tube models from Fisher or Scott or Bogen.

With lower-priced new gear rivaling the performance of much more expensive models available just a few years ago, the market for used equipment is pretty soft right now. After all, why buy a two-year-old tuner for $100 when a new one will give you better performance (and a warranty) for $50 to $75 more? Along with that, of course, goes the assumption that even the new equipment you purchase today may be improved upon next year without a substantial price increase. So the second-hand market focuses primarily on high-end gear, which are rarely heavily discounted and therefore can be counted on to maintain both value and an aura of quality.

Dave Adams, whose Rebuy Hi-Fi operation in Santa Clara, California, devotes some 90 percent of its business to used gear, notes that most of his customers are interested in trades or purchases of individual components rather than full systems. But he adds that even high-rated, "esoteric" equipment can present problems. Not every esoteric line will find a market. "One of the things that's very frustrating about working in this business," he says, "is that it's very hard to sing the praises of a piece of gear from a company that was only in business for two years and has since shut down." Equipment orphaned by the bankruptcy or closure of its manufacturer can thus prove an albatross for its owner. On the

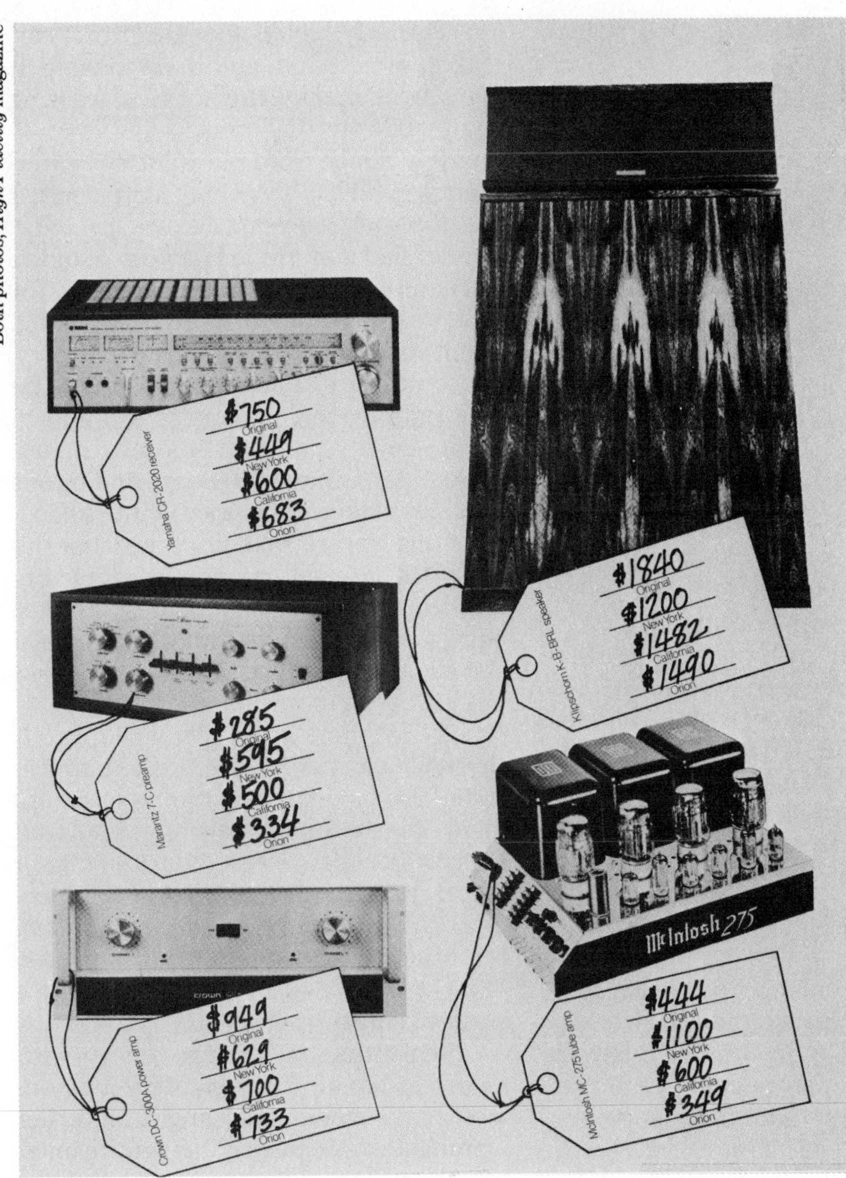

Prices for used audio gear vary widely across the country. To help us, we contacted Dave Wasserman of Audio Exchange in Manhattan and Dave Adams of Rebuy Hi-Fi in Santa Clara, California, for their opinions on the mint-condition market value of each component pictured here. The used value cited in Orion's 1980 *Audio Reference Guide* and the model's original retail price are also given.

Both photos, *High Fidelity* magazine

other hand, it can represent a real bargain for the buyer—provided he knows the specific model and has already addressed the questions of service and parts replacement.

At the same time, even gear from full-line, nonesoteric manufacturers can sometimes hold its value, if cut-rate prices are not available at retail. According to the Orion *Guide*, some recent Yamaha products, for instance, command up to 85 percent of their original price at resale and more than 50 percent at trade-in.

SAM SUTHERLAND

Shopping for stereo equipment

"The nouveau riche want something that's going to wangle-dangle their friends. They couldn't care less how long the thing's going to last."

An interview with Roger Rohrs

From his offices in San Luis Obispo, California, Roger Rohrs compiles the trade-in values of stereo equipment and publishes the figures in the annual *Audio Reference Guide*, a $75 hardcover used by retailers to set prices on used speakers, receivers, amps, and tape recorders. Over the nine years he's been collecting prices from around the country, Rohrs has found that solid-state equipment generally has fewer problems than tube (although some esoteric tube amps have appreciated over the years); turntables enjoy a greater resale value than changers because the changer has more parts to go awry; and certain technologies, such as eight-track and quadrophonic, are rapidly going the way of the 78.

RY

"Some of the older products are definitely coming into demand, for two reasons. One is that tube amplifiers have a sound that's unique: people claim that they hear a "warm" sound not apparent with transistors. The McIntosh is a classic example, and Audio Research. Second, I don't think you'll find a lot of deterioration in these esoteric, quality products. They're doing their best to hold the quality instead of keeping the price, and it's very difficult in these times.

The larger companies are hitting, say, a $200 price point, and then, to make it even worse, they are mass marketing things, discounting them as low as $150. So, they could have put a lot more into their product if they had more limited distribution. Ten years ago, we had what they called fair trade. Dealers couldn't sell equipment below a certain price. But that was determined to be price fixing, and it's not allowed any longer.

A number of stores throughout the country now deal with nothing but used equipment. And their success if just incredible, because people are finding out that—let's take a $100 price point—a good, new receiver at that price just doesn't exist. But a used one at $100 probably retailed around $300, a quality piece of equipment you couldn't afford otherwise. But some people have a prejudice against buying used components.

Today, there aren't many people out there who can afford the tube. Manufacturers are modularizing transistor equipment. If something goes wrong, you send back the old card—a modularized circuit board—and they'll supply you with a new one. This doesn't mean owner servicing is on the way, because it's not worth the $200 or so it would cost you to carry a stock of cards.

Five years ago, Yamaha came up with a new design for the front of their equipment, and when that caught on, other manufacturers changed their entire lines, too. These companies didn't *plan* to make their own units look obsolete, they just wanted to keep up with the times. Right now, it's the same with Marantz: they've got the gold look. They don't really want to go with that, but their entire marketing plan is built around the slogan, "We have a gold mine," and the products are restyled to support it.

Some people care about durability when shopping for stereo equipment. But the nouveau riche want something that's going to wangle-dangle their friends. They couldn't care less how long the thing's going to last.

Quadrophonic sound was an idea that fizzled, and I think the reason is that there were too many systems. Do you want to go the SQ method, do you want to go discrete, do you want to go this guy's method, that guy's method? The record manufacturers really weren't behind any one a hundred percent, so there wasn't a great amount of software for any one method. And I see a similar thing happening now with the videodisc market.

Cassette has taken over from eight-track because the cassette's transport is closer to that used in the reel-to-reel format. The eight-track works on a friction principal; a drag is inherent in this system so that the chance of binding is much greater. And it's impossible to rewind an eight-track tape, once something goes wrong.

Looking into the future, I would say that both vinyl discs and the new laser discs will be completely obsolete 10 or 15 years down the line. Instead, you'll have something that closely resembles a credit card with a magnetic strip on it. You'll insert this card into a special phone, and you'll call and say, "Hey, I'd like to have Country Joe and the Fish," and they'll say, "Fine, give us your account number," and bamm-o, all of a sudden that card's got Country Joe and the Fish on it. The card'll be digital, it'll be a hundred-percent accuracy. The technology is there now to do it, but they're working on a way to stop counterfeiters, because it's like a computer: once you have that digital information on the card, you can transfer it as many times as you wish, without any loss or degradation.99

Rock and roll is here to stay, but not at 33 1/3

Chances are you have at least a shelf of them at home: well-worn cardboard jackets, containing 12-inch black vinyl discs, long-playing records you have been accumulating ever since you graduated from 45s. It is hard to imagine life without them; they are as full of memories as they are music. They are also teetering at the brink of obsolescence.

Rapid advances in audio technology have far outdistanced improvements in the LP, making its sonic deficiencies starkly apparent. Each consumer who buys expensive new equipment becomes more sophisticated and more demanding about sound quality, and those who have heard true digital sound are less likely to be satisfied with the LPs' limited dynamic range and abundant surface noise. Many of the industry's recent ills, from slumping sales to home taping, can be traced to consumer dissatisfaction with the quality of records and prerecorded tapes.

Nostalgia aside, this is good news. Within a few years, an affordable home sound system will be able to reproduce the concert-hall sound that audio manufacturers have been talking about since the dawn of stereo a quarter century ago. But it is good news with a catch: some of the systems will probably shrivel on the vine, and most of them are incompatible with one another. So for the next few years, audio (and video) equipment buyers must take care that the machines they buy have the greatest chance for a long, useful life and are not likely to quickly become outmoded.

This is not a signal to trash your stereo or melt down your records for fuel. Turntables that play LPs and 45s will be manufactured for a long time to come, since millions of people are still buying records and will continue to need machines on which to play them. Record companies, too, have a great stake in the LP in the form of pressing and plating equipment, and they'll probably continue to offer LPs as a secondary configuration (like eight-track tapes in today's market) as long as people will buy them. Finally, the makers of new recording technologies want the public to accept their product as quickly as possible and are making every effort to see that their inventions fit snugly into existing home systems.

All of which will make the LP, with its dynamic range of 60 to 65 decibels, seem woebegone. New audio systems will offer 80- to 85-decibel digital sound, or its rough equivalent, in ways that the conventional vinyl record cannot. More and more discs are being made from digital master tapes and have digital trumpeted across their covers, but the records themselves are no more digital than a grapefruit. The 70- to 75-decibel "audiophile" LPs on the market use a higher-grade vinyl and are mastered and pressed more carefully to provide better sound, they're not digital, and they cost seven or eight dollars more than the standard LP list price that manufacturers say they will charge for the truly digital records that are on their way.

A quick recap of digital recording—computerized sound—may be in order. A digital recorder "listens" to a piece of music and assigns a number to each tiny particle of sound, which is then printed on magnetic tape much as words are printed on paper. Like most computers, digital recorders use a binary number code, all zeros and ones, and the number given a particular sound is usually 14 or 16 digits long. Because there are thousands of possible number combinations, the digital "alphabet" can tell the difference between, say, a snare-drum beat and one that follows it, even though the two beats may sound the same to the ear.

On the other hand, in conventional analog recording, a machine tries to reproduce on tape or disc a picture of the sound wave it is recording. The picture, with all its peaks and valleys, is never exact and becomes even less distinct when a copy is made of the original, and a copy is made of the copy, and so on. The string of numbers on a digital tape can, by comparison, be duplicated by any machine that can scan and reprint the numbers, so the 10,000th copy should sound the same as the first.

Digital vinyl discs, which are smaller than LPs, are the basis of two highly touted new audio systems. The smallest of all, the compact disc developed jointly by Philips and Sony, is 4½ inches in diameter, carries up to an hour of music, has no grooves, and is played from the inside out on only one side. Its digital code takes the form of microscopic pits and flat areas along a 2½-mile track. The disc is inserted face down in a player the size of a cassette machine and scanned by a miniature laser mounted on a movable arm underneath the record. As the record spins, it slows down from 500 to 215 RPM while the laser beam moves toward the outer edge of the record. Discs for the system should cost about $8.98, or whatever the standard list price may be two years from now when they are introduced. The player, which will plug into a standard amplifier, will cost roughly the same as a top-of-the-line turntable.

JVC's digital discs will be ten inches in diameter, the same size as JVC videodiscs, and both will use the same player. This system, which JVC calls VHD/AHD (for video and audio high-density) will be on the market, at least in part, by January, 1982. The 900-RPM player, which uses a diamond stylus, will come first, along with a number of videodisc titles. Panasonic, Quasar, General Electric, and Sharp are expected to manufacture machines using this technology. But JVC has not set a date for international distribution of the AHD system, which requires a new piece of equipment—an adapter that plugs into an amplifier to decode the digital signal. List price for the player should fall between $500 and $750; no prices for the video and audio software or the adapter have been set.

No one expects both of these systems to thrive, just as no one expects the public to support all incompatible video systems now struggling for acceptance. It is still too early to predict which will survive, but record companies are preparing for the day when one wins out. "The marketplace will make the demands on us," says Robert Summer, president of RCA Records. "Ultimately, the public tells the industry what their preference is, and I believe that is what will happen here."

While all these new systems are taking shape (or taking a dive), the record industry will probably continue to sell millions of LPs, tapes, and even 45s. So far, their most serious response to all this new technology has been the introduction this past May of CBS's Compatible Expansion (CX) system, which greatly reduces the surface noise of a conventional LP and expands its dynamic range by 20 decibels. CX encodes the quieter passages in a piece of music and raises them above the level of the record's surface noise. When played through a CX decoder, the soft passages are brought back to their original level, but in the process the surface noise (and the tape hiss from the master) is greatly reduced. The decoder plugs into the tape-monitor position on a home amplifier and costs less than $100. When decoders are built into amplifiers, as CBS hopes they soon will be, they will add perhaps $10 to the machine's price tag. "A CX-encoded record would supposedly offer the same benefits as a digital disc," says Al Teller, vice-president of operations for the CBS Records Group. "I say supposedly only because the digital disc is in the discussion stage, whereas we have this technology available today."

The CX encoding process limits the dynamic range of the music, but does it subtly enough, CBS says, that CX records played back without a decoder will sound the same as conventional LPs. CBS has therefore begun to make CX records, even though the decoders (which will be made by other companies under license from CBS) will not be available for some time.

"It's an advantage for the consumer," Teller says. "He will get a quieter record with a wider dynamic range for the same price as a conventional record." It's also an advantage for CBS because CX will allow the company to keep its current pressing plants and equipment in operation while it waits to see who wins the battle for audio supremacy. CBS will also license the CX system to other record companies, whose response, Teller says, "has been extremely enthusiastic," although no deals have been announced.

CX might help keep the LP healthy throughout the 1980s, yet it will probably not fend off the digital onslaught forever. "It offers an extension to current technologies," RCA's Summer says, "but it doesn't take the leap into the twenty-first century that some of the other developing technologies do."

"We wouldn't close out the possibility [of making digital discs] any more than we'd say we aren't interested in new technology," Teller adds. "But again, the digital disc is not a reality today. We can improve our product today with the CX system, and that is our intention."

The LP's future, then, is probably a limited one, but the long-awaited arrival of improved records (and cassettes—as high-quality tape gets cheaper, prerecorded tapes should get better) will probably soften the loss. Like Edison's waxed cylinders and 78s before them, LPs will ultimately take their place in the attic, the basement, or the scrap heap, and that—no matter how fine the new recordings sound—must make any child of the LP generation a little sad.

MARC KIRKEBY

How to get more life from your records

Unless you live in a pristine, dust-free environment, you've undoubtedly heard the sonic consequences of dirty records. Nobody should be surprised by the statement that keeping discs clean is vital to the durability of phonograph records, but the market abounds with such a variety of brushes, pads, liquids, and gadgets dedicated to vinyl hygiene that selecting the right cleaning method and product is far from simple.

To ease your path somewhat, I conducted an informal survey of the available devices and their relative merits. In my investigation, I did not employ a microscope for intense scrutiny of tiny accumulations of dust, nor did I attempt to quantify the reduction in clicks and pops afforded by each cleaner. Instead, I conducted my tests under real-world conditions. The test environment was an apartment in New York City, and the instruments were my eyes and ears. All cleaning operations were performed on new LPs that had been left out on a table for 24 hours; the abundance of particulate matter in the air, combined with a very low ambient humidity, made for extremely dusty records.

All photos, *High Fidelity* magazine

Decca-Zero Ohms Record Brush.

I searched the market for a representative sampling of nonmotorized record cleaners, weeding out the inexpensive knockoffs of nationally advertised brands. The devices fall into four main categories: conductive brushes, pad/fluid combinations, tracking brushes mounted on their own "tone arms," and what might be called adhesive picker-uppers.

The various conductive brushes on the market are similar in design and concept. Several thousand carbon-fiber bristles are bound to a metallic handle. When you lower the brush onto a rotating record, the fibers bleed off static charges, reducing the attraction between disc and dust. You then sweep the loosened dust either toward the center of the record or out past the edge bead. I tried the Empire Dust Eliminator ($19.95), the Decca-Zero Ohms Record Brush ($18.95), the Goldring Exstatic ($20), and the Reference Statibrush ($19.95).

Each of the brushes performed reasonably well in removing deposits of dust. Without grease solvents, they had no impact on fingerprints, of course. And all shared one fault: shedding. Due to either the brittleness of the carbon fibers or poor bonding to the handle, records emerged covered with tiny pieces of the bristles the first time I used each brush; less shedding occurred with subsequent use, but the fibers still had a tendency to loosen if too much pressure was exerted on them. The brushes must be cleaned after each use or dust will be transferred to the next record.

A more satisfactory method of cleaning, in my opinion, involves velvet pad/fluid combinations, which remove both dust and fingerprints. The systems I tested were the Discwasher ($15), the Watts Parastatic Disc Preener ($7.65), the Keith Monks Record Care Kit ($7.60), the Robins Whiskee ($4.85), the Audio-Technica Rotary Disc Cleaner ($12.95), the Sound Guard Record Cleaner Kit ($9.95), and the Transcriber Classic One ($15). All but one is sold with a proprietary cleaning fluid; Watts suggests plain water for the Disc Preener.

Attached to the Discwasher's walnut handle is a curved velvet pad whose fibers are all slanted in one direction; an arrow embossed in the handle points in the direction of the nap. A small brush is supplied to clean accumulated dust from the pad, and a bottle of D3 cleaning fluid completes the system. You apply a small amount of the fluid to the leading edge of the pad and bring it down onto the surface of a rotating disc—a revolution or two will moisten it sufficiently. Then you rock the handle back so that the dry trailing edge of the pad mops up the moisture and debris. Overall, results were excellent with the Discwasher. I could see no remaining specs of dust on the record. Removing fingerprints took a bit more pressure on the pad, but to my eyes and ears the Discwasher cannot be faulted.

The Transcriber Classic One looks similar to the Discwasher, but the concept is quite different. The velvet pad is flat and much smoother, and moistness is maintained by fluid from a reservoir in the handle, refilled via a cap at the top. Dubbed Micro Stor, the reservoir is made up of a core of densely packed tiny glass beads that mete out small quantities of the supplied humectant/cleaner. The Classic One removed dust quite nicely, though fingerprints required that fluid be applied directly to the pad. I wonder, however, about long-term storage of the system; according to Transcriber, it should be stored face down in its molded plastic case to prevent evaporation. Considering the accumulations of organic material that the pad may harbor after several record cleanings, wet storage seems a likely environment for growth of mold and mildew.

Audio-Technica's Rotary Disc Cleaner has a unique design that permits the disc-shaped velvet pad to rotate freely when you hold it by the top-mounted knob, minimizing arm twisting. I obtained good results in both dust and fingerprint removal, though I did have some difficulty manipulating the pad so as to lift off all the dust at the end of the cleaning operation.

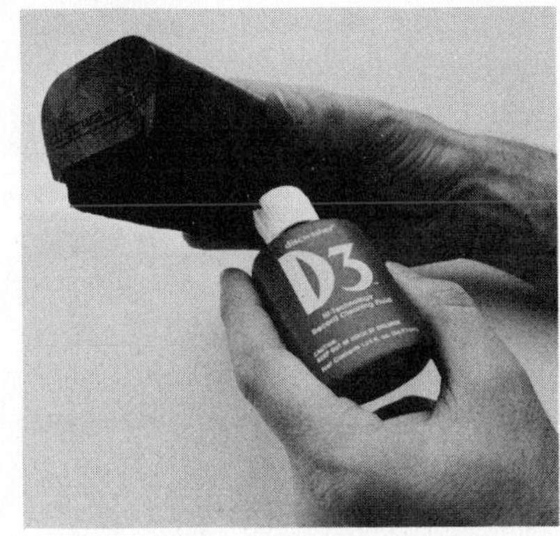

Discwasher.

The Monks Record Care Kit also includes cleaning fluid, velvet pad, and pad-cleaning brush. You moisten the pad by applying the fluid to four holes atop its handle. The surface of the pad is extremely narrow but long enough to cover the full radius of an LP. Performance with dust and fingerprints generally was on a par with the rest—but once again I wonder about long-term storage of a moist pad.

The Whiskee, by Robins, proved to be the least effective of the group, although not a complete dud. The kit comes with a velvet roller (instead of a pad), a stylus brush, and cleaning fluid. I found two problems: the velvet sheds, and the revolving of the roller makes it difficult to lift the dust off the record.

This last point is important in using any of these cleaners, especially if you opt not to use a moistened pad. I found that a sharp twist of the wrist, making a sort of scooping motion, worked best. Moisture aids the process, both by reducing the static charge that binds the dust to the record and by imparting an adhesive quality to the pad.

The Watts Disc Preener is a velvet roller with a moisture-retaining wick in the center. The directions say the wick contains an "ionic compound" that is activated by the tap water you are instructed to moisten it with. I found handling the device a bit awkward, and I have strong reservations about the use of tap water—at least in New York, where the concentration of particulate matter and dissolved minerals seems to leave a residue on records.

Of all the wet cleaners, the Sound Guard Record Cleaner Kit takes the most direct route, instructing the user to spray the supplied fluid onto the surface of the disc—for heavily soiled records—and warning that the record must be removed from the turntable lest the moisture damage it. You should wait for 15 to 30 seconds before mopping up the fluid with a small cellulose sponge and then dry the record with a velvet buffing pad. The system consistently produced good results, but it takes more time than the other methods.

Two products combine brushes and velvet pads. The Goldring Super Exstatic ($30) has two rows of carbon fibers mounted on either side of a pad; no liquid is included. Again, shedding gave the pad more material to pick up. The Watts Manual Parastat ($20.85), which does come with a liquid, consists of two pads on either side of a nylon brush. Using the liquid in the quantity and manner stipulated by Watts didn't do a lot to loosen the dust.

Next we come to the brushes mounted at the end of a pivoted arm. They are intended to provide constant dust removal while you're playing the record rather than heavy-duty cleaning. The classic of the genre is the venerable Watts Dust Bug ($9.85). Unlike all the other models I used, it employs a fluid (rather than a ground line) to bleed off static charges. And unlike most, it combines a nylon roller with a brush. The Dust Bug has a loyal following, but I found the nylon bristles so stiff that the roller simply floated above the record surface, accomplishing little within the grooves. The brush, however, managed to sweep off a good deal of dust.

The Reference Staticleaner ($39.90), which has a carbon-fiber brush attached to an all-metal arm and base, worked very well. A ground wire plugs into the base and can be attached to any nearby ground. The only problem I found with the Staticleaner's otherwise smooth operation was a great deal of initial fiber shedding.

The brush with the Decca Record Cleaner ($16.95) shed less, but I found it difficult to raise the carrying arm high enough to track on my Technics turntable. Even the supplementary base, supplied to add arm height where necessary, could not raise the record cleaner high enough, causing the brush to zip across the record without pausing to clean. I had to add a homemade wedge.

The Keith Monks Pivot Sweeper ($23.70) uses an animal-hair brush with a few short copper strands mingled in to conduct static to the base and thence, through the wire provided, to the ground. Height is adjusted by turning the screw base, and it easily mated with the Technics. Tracking and dust removal were quite good.

Audio-Technica calls its arm-mounted brush the Autocleanica ($12.95), and this velvet roller and carbon-fiber brush combination did a fine job. It also has a ground wire and a well-designed arm rest.

Finally, there are the "adhesives." I hadn't expected much from the Pixoff ($17.50), a device that looks like a clothing lint remover, but it turned out to be one of the most effective dust removers I tested. It does nothing for or against static and fingerprints, but records were apparently spotless after a thorough cleaning with the device.

Also very effective but less convenient is Empire's Discofilm ($14.95 for enough to clean 22 records), a gooey fluid that you spread around on the disc. An applicator sponge is built into the bottle, and the cap doubles as a support for the record you're cleaning. The liquid dries (in an hour, to play it safe) to a film that peels off, taking the dust and debris with it. If this "facial" is to come off intact, you must apply a very thick coat; if small patches of film stay on the record, you'll have to use tweezers to remove them. Discofilm is quite expensive—about 75¢ to clean both sides of a record.

I also tried one of Falcon's Dust-Off aerosol cans of compressed gas, which come in various sizes ($17.85, $3.85, $1.98). I couldn't detect any residue left by the chlorofluorocarbon gas. Whatever the relationship between fluorocarbons and the ozone layer, Dust-Off seems no better than old-fashioned (and free) lung power.

There's one more cleaning method that I should mention, simply because it has cropped up so often in the past: soap and water. Perhaps that solution made sense years ago, when the commercial alternatives generally were treated cloths (which picked up grit and scratched the records they purported to protect) or "antistatic cleaning sprays" (which often were so loaded with silicone that they gummed up the grooves something fierce). It should be clear from the discussion of vinyl technology (see accompanying box, "What price cleaning?") that there has been a lot of research into the subject since those days, and our alternatives have become more sophisticated, if not necessarily clear cut.

There are, however, some general guidelines for choosing a cleaning system. First, avoid immersing your records in anything if you want them to last. This rules out soap and water and the more arcane (and, I'm told, even worse) use of wetting agents like Kodak Photoflo: they won't do anything good for polymer stability and probably will speed up vinyl disintegration. But do be willing to use moist systems; you won't get rid of contaminants like fingerprints with any of the dry systems I've tried, and if the moisture is limited, so is the potential polymer leaching.

Discofilm.

Until the day arrives when record-care solutions have to carry a list of ingredients, as canned foods do, you're left guessing about their properties and the possible harmful effects they may have. Cecil Watts, who died in 1956, was almost alone in his investigations into the chemistry of these cleaning fluids. Much more research has been done recently, most notably by Dr. Bruce Maier, founder of Discwasher. But between the carefully conceived and researched products of such well-known specialists and the obvious quick-buck copies that seem to be backed by no research there lies a host of cleaners that can vary from effective to harmful. With no information on formulations available, the consumer must ultimately depend on his own empirical findings and on brand names. The bigger the manufacturer, the more it has at stake should it produce an inferior or deleterious formulation, and that's your only guarantee of quality.

At least part of the best cure, of course, is prevention. Store and handle your records so that contamination will be kept to a minimum. When they do need cleaning, give them no more than they need. A laundering just before storage, to prevent dust from becoming embedded and to inhibit mildew and such, is a good idea. But, for precisely that reason, be sure the records are totally dry before you put them away.

MYRON BERGER

What price cleaning?

During the past few years, the possible long-term deleterious effects of fluids on record vinyl has been a subject of considerable debate—and often outright prejudice. We were not surprised to learn, however, that the issues are anything but new and that audiophiles are not the only ones concerned with this topic. Back in the 1950s, the Library of Congress commissioned a study to determine the factors that could degrade the quality of the phonograph records in its extensive collection. The report, published in 1959 as "Preservation and Storage of Sound Recordings" by A. G. Pickett and M. M. Lemcoe, outlines in part the issues involved in wet cleaning.

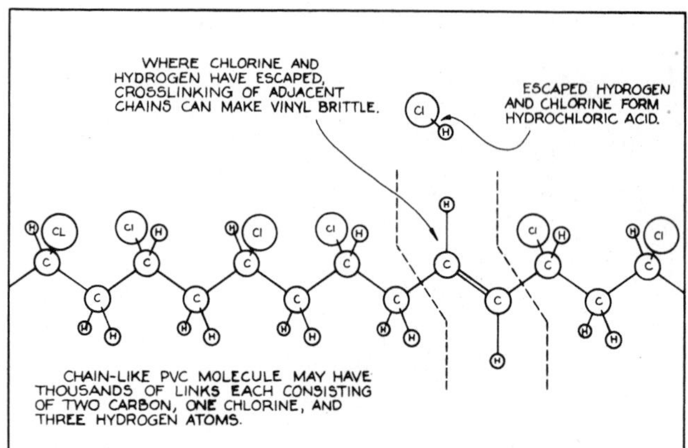

The molecular structure of record vinyl.

Record vinyl is composed chiefly of polyvinyl chloride (PVC). Its molecular structure (visualized here) is formed of three basic elements: carbon, hydrogen, and chlorine. As with other polymers, the central carbon atom of each molecule binds to another carbon atom, creating long chains of randomly oriented, curled molecules. The complete PVC molecule, however, is somewhat unstable; in the presence of pressure, heat, or ultraviolet radiation, the atoms of chlorine and hydrogen tend to break loose and recombine as hydrochloric acid, which acts to further degrade the integrity of the vinyl. To slow down the formation of hydrochloric acid, small amounts of chemical stabilizers (usually lead) are added to the vinyl to bind the hydrogen and chlorine atoms in a chemically inert form.

One of the conclusions of the report is that "the potential life of a disc can be assumed equivalent to the life of the stabilizer . . . ," though under good storage conditions "chemical degradation of a vinyl disc should not occur in less than a century." The issue, then, becomes the effect of cleaning solutions on vinyl stabilizers—that is, how much stabilizer will a liquid actually pull from the vinyl? No manufacturer supplies a chemical breakdown of its cleaning fluid, and reliable figures as to the amount of stabilizer removed by each is simply not available. Even Bruce Maier of Discwasher, who is responsible for the airing of this debate, states that any fluid cleaner will pull out some stabilizer, but that a properly buffered solution will have a minimal effect. Other manufacturers give similar replies, and just about all of them warn of the pulling effects of homemade cleaning solutions—namely, soap and water.

Use of wet cleaners, therefore, is a necessary compromise, and their *proper* use becomes paramount, especially the drying operation. That same report warns of the danger of fungal growth spurred by dampness and nourished by surface contaminants, paper liners, and record labels. A growing fungal colony, because of the acidity of its metabolic by-products, will permanently etch the vinyl surface. If you are in the habit of cleaning records after playing, make sure that their surfaces are perfectly dry before replacing them in their protective sleeves.

The editors of *High Fidelity* magazine

CAMERAS, PLAIN AND CREAM FILLED

You can expose film nicely by affixing a sheet of it to the back of a sealed cardboard box and allowing light to enter a pinhole made in the opposite side. Some of the finest, most expensive cameras today do no more than this, in principle. They leave you to guess or measure the light, select a lens opening, select a shutter speed.

Curiously, cameras designed for mass consumption are more complex by far. One by one, the amateur photographer's responsibilities have been shouldered by the camera's tiny but uncanny mind. This encroaching complexity has upset many a serious photographer. In the camera more than almost any other product, technology has been challenged as being superfluous, an interference, a liability. Here follow interviews with three men of a similar mind on this issue. They want tools, not toys.

1954 Canon II F camera

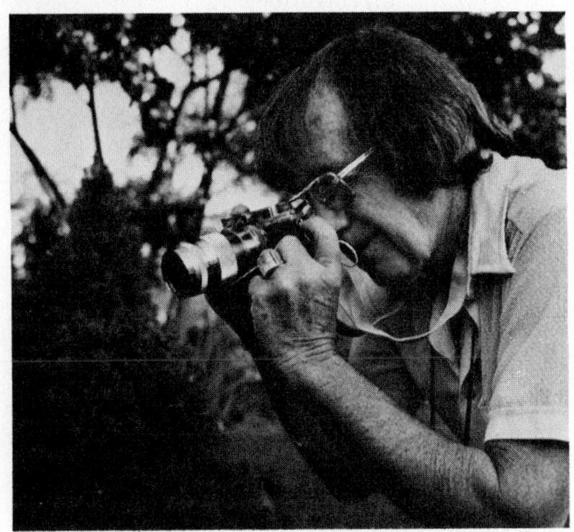

"I purchased it in Tokyo in May, 1954. This camera travelled with us for 26 years. It's had no malfunctions, and still does a marvelous job. I believe the Japanese had copied the German Leica camera, not only the Leica's design but also quality of materials and workmanship."

ROBERT SHOTLIFF
Missoula, Montana

1934 Kodak Brownie Junior camera

T. L. Gettings

"I received it for Christmas in 1934. It's the only camera I have ever had and I love to take pictures. I have raised five children, who all used it, and it takes pictures just as well (or better, because of the film) than it did when new. One of the mirrors came loose once but my husband was able to put it back and it was fine."

GRACE BARBEE
Veneta, Oregon

Cameras as tools

"Make tools, not toys: that's what I've been telling the manufacturers to do."

An interview with Marty Forcher

As head of the Professional Camera Repair Service in New York City, Marty Forcher services equipment used by some of the finest professional photographers in the world. In the past few years, he has heard more than enough complaints about what he calls "the fragile, elegant toys" many photographers have come to distrust. In a widely quoted speech before a 1979 seminar of industrial photographers, Forcher called for a return to durability and simplicity in 35-millimeter cameras, both consumer and professional models.

RICH KLINE

"I don't want to be identified as a drag, a stick-in-the-mud, somebody who's opposed to technological change. But change for change alone doesn't interest me. We saw a lot of medium-priced, highly sophisticated cameras with a lot of features for the dollar. But the guy who wants the top-of-the-line camera that'll last for years has been sold down the river. The cameras I like from the past I call hockey pucks, because they'll tolerate lots of abuse.

The hockey pucks were the old M-series Leicas, the early Nikon Fs, F2s, the Canon Fl—all of those mechanical cameras are classic cameras. You've got to do an awful lot of research to understand what's happened to the camera market. In the past, maybe a hundred thousand top-of-the-line cameras sold a year. Now there's a potential market in the millions. That has its positive and negative aspects. If they made cameras today in the same way that they made cameras in the past, very few people could afford them.

But now, finally, I think we're beginning to see a trend back toward durability. For instance, NASA was finally willing to accept an electronic camera: a Nikon F3. As I understand it, it is essentially the same camera that the average person can buy on the market. That to me is a very good indication that electronic cameras are becoming more durable. There was a time when NASA's philosophy was, if you have a problem, solve it mechanically, and if you can't solve it mechanically, solve it electro-mechanically, and if you can't solve it electro-mechanically, then solve it electronically but make sure you have several backup systems.

In the early stages of the electronic development, they incorporated computer technology into cameras, and we all know that in the world of computer technology, environmental influences are very important. That's why if you go into a place that depends on computers, you'll find it air-conditioned, humidity controlled, temperature controlled. I think there is a shakedown period for the use of this kind of technology in photographic equipment. We have to see where the breakdowns occur, what the shortcomings are, as they are related to use and environment. Obviously, a camera is exposed to a lot more abuse than a computer in somebody's office. But I have no doubt that all of these problems will be overcome.

If you buy a good $400 mechanical camera with a matched-needle exposure feature, in my judgment you would get more durability than if you bought a $400 camera with automatic exposure function. That doesn't mean you're getting more or less for your money, it means you're getting different value for your money. The more of the $400 goes into complicated technology, the less goes into durable construction.

You increase the odds of buying a durable camera if you buy something that you know was made ten years ago and is still in good condition. For instance, we have people coming in with Leica cameras that were made in 1938, 1939. Except for the fact that they've made contemporary cameras much easier to operate—the viewfinders are bigger and brighter, and so forth—old cameras perform the same function. And the damn things are indestructible.

The twin-lens Rolleiflex, for example, was made like a brick. For somebody who wants to shoot a 2¼-inch format, that camera will last a lifetime. But there are relatively few people who seek out real quality.

Talk about planned obsolescence to the manufacturer's face, and he'll say, "We're building as good a product as we can within the price range." And yet, what rolls off the production line might be called "unplanned obsolescence."

Lately, though, there have been some voices from the wilderness who have been saying that there's an untapped market out there of people who are interested in high-quality cameras.

Premium-priced cameras are improving. For a time, all the manufacturers went small. But you can't go small without making some compromises. I think that's borne out by the fact that later, when those manufacturers came out with their top-of-the-line, sophisticated, high-technology cameras, they were no longer compact or quite as light as they were. So, when you ask the manufacturers how come they don't make them as small as the ones they were pushing so hard a couple years ago, the answer, if you read between the lines, is, "You need a little room if you want to put in some guts."

If you go to a hardware store for a circular saw, the guy'll say, "Do you want a home craft tool or a professional tool?" The difference is that the professional tool is engineered to stand up to rugged use. Make tools, not toys: that's what I've been telling the manufacturers to do.

If you examine the photographic equipment of the great professional photographers, whether it's David Douglas Duncan or Ansel Adams, it is pretty simple. And there's a reason for it: they have more faith in their own judgment than in light meters.”

"Shop for the simplest camera in the highest price range you can justify."

An interview with T. L. Gettings, director of photography at Rodale Press

BK

“Cameras today are convenient. It's an electronic convenience, where circuitry takes the place of manual override. Lights light up in the viewfinder, flashing numbers come on, and it says, "Yes" or "No." It does, through its light meter, just about everything that you used to do manually by adjusting lenses, shutter speeds, and so forth.

Americans love gimmicks, and manufacturers are trying to out-gimmick each other now. Cameras will probably be talking to you before long. They'll say, "Don't take this photograph!" I don't know what's next. Whatever happens, they'll try to do more for you before they try to do less again. And when cameras did less, they were better. If you want a durable camera, shop for the simplest camera in the highest price range you can justify.

You don't have to buy a professional-quality Nikon to get good photographs. If you take good care of a camera, you may not need the durability of a $600 camera. I'd look for the simplest and most inexpensive camera that'll get the job done. If you use your camera once a week, then maybe you can justify a $600 camera. That's about $10 a week over a year, and that's an affordable hobby. But if you'll only use the camera once or twice in a year, a $600 camera will cost you $300 both times you take it out. That's a ridiculous amount of money to spend on a hobby—that's a trip to the Bahamas.

There are some good-quality, inexpensive cameras for occasional use. For example, you can buy a Polaroid camera for $29.95. It does just as fine a job as a Polaroid SX-70 Sonar camera that costs $225. You get the same photograph. The cheaper model doesn't have a sonar beam on it that focuses it—you have to focus it yourself—and you also have to wait a minute to get the photograph, but the photographic image is the same. I bought a simple camera for my daughter. It has few moving parts—just a shutter. It goes "click" and that's it. When it breaks—and the camera I bought my daughter probably won't break—you just fix the shutter. I'd hate to see the inside of an SX-70 with its sonar tone.

Here at the Rodale photo lab we buy used Nikon F2s. They were produced up until 1978 or '79. A Nikon F2 is standard among professional photographers. You can throw it down a flight of stairs and pick it up and still use it. If the battery doesn't work and the light meter doesn't work, you don't have anything to override. You're always in control of the camera.

In the late 1970s, the camera manufacturers decided that the big money is with the amateurs and began making cameras for them. The F2 was too expensive—it cost about $750 new—so Nikon made a camera that is more automatic, of cheaper

T. L. Gettings.

quality, to sell to a market that can afford to pay $350. Along with these cheaper automatic EM and FE cameras, they began to produce an $800 camera, the F3, into which they incorporated the electronics. But professionals are buying used F2s. They don't accept the F3. As a result, a used Nikon F2 costs as much today as a new one did. F2s are not losing their value. If you can find a used Nikon F2, buy it. You can't go wrong.

Manufacturers are trying to make a camera think for you so you can be unthinking. But if you learn the process of working a camera, it'll never fade from you. It's like riding a bicycle. I was a Big Brother once, and I taught an eight-year-old how to use the basic lens opening-shutter speed-light meter triangle of information.

The Nikon F2.

You change one measurement to match the other, and through the combination you make the light right inside the camera. You move two things to make the third thing–the light coming into the camera–correct. That's not a particularly bright eight-year-old I taught, but he learned how to use a camera in three hours. With proper instruction, anyone can learn how to use a camera. You'll never again have to worry about blinking lights or "Yes's" and "No's" or automatic overrides.

I think of cameras as tools. A carpenter needs a good hammer: a hammer is a means for him to complete his task, to pound a nail into a board. The best tool is one that doesn't get in your way but is an extension of you. A camera should be an extension of your eye, like a hammer is an extension of your hand. A camera is just a tool for a photographer. It's a means for getting an image that a photographer sees onto a piece of film. With all those lights going on in the viewfinder, you forget to look through the lens. You're not composing photographs anymore, you're a manipulator of a machine.

Cameras used to be designed for the professional photographer and then those advancements filtered down to the amateur photographer. Now it's the other way around. Cameras today are made for the amateur, and the professional is being left high and dry. I see no movement toward the construction of durable, reliable cameras.❞

"The more gadgets you have on a camera, the more likely something'll go wrong."

An interview with Dick Weaver

Dick Weaver is owner of the largest camera-repair shop in the Philadelphia area. In the shop's crowded quarters, his crew does some 30,000 repairs a year on cameras that come in from over 200 dealers in the area as well as from the walk-in amateur and professional. His truck route covers an area 100 miles north, south, and east of the shop, and at least twice as far west.

PAT DONAHUE

❝Very few cameras aren't electronic anymore. They're all made on assembly line. In fact, a lot of it's done with no hands even, all automation. The more gadgets, the more people seem to like them. They beep at you now, they whistle at you. Light shows, that's what the people want.

The pros are upset. They want heavy-duty, solid cameras, but the industry is going for the lights, for what the public wants. The pro's camera is a big, healthy camera, it's heavy, the gears are husky, everything is strong and solid, it'll take a lot of wear and tear. Today, everybody wants smaller, lightweight cameras, but materials have to be sacrificed in order to get the small camera with all these gadgets. It will still last, for people who don't expect to use it much. But for the professional who shoots dozens of rolls a day?

The Nikon F1 and F2 are the best ever built. That's what the pros want. You can buy them used, but they don't manufacture them anymore. Other brands? Again, we're going back to the old breed of cameras, the Nikkormats, the old Canons, the old Minoltas–they're going to outlive everything.

The more gadgets you have on a camera, the more likely something'll go wrong. There are more parts you have to remove to repair it. With the mechanical things, if you had a good eye, you could work it and watch it, find the problem. But the electronics require a whole new way of testing. You have to follow the schematics, use test equipment. It takes more time.

Leaving the batteries in for a long period of time and not using the camera is one of the worst things you can do. You can virtually ruin some cameras by doing that. If the batteries leak and run along the wires up to the circuit board on top, the camera's ruined.

You should try to keep the camera clean. Dirt, dust, and sand are really hard on cameras. You can get a lens filter to protect the lens, and when you store the camera, use those silica bags to keep the moisture out.

The biggest thing–read the owner's manual. You'd be surprised how many people just do not read the manual when they buy a piece of equipment. They come in here, with all kinds of complaints about the camera, and there's nothing wrong with the equipment. You ask them, "Did you read the owner's manual?" No, they just go by what the guy in the store told them and they think that's enough. The problem's usually something very simple, like loading the film. They say, "Well, I've been using 35-millimeter cameras for ten years, I know I can't be loading it wrong." You ask them to load it, and they load it wrong.

A camera is like a body: if it lays in bed for a long time, it's going to get bed sores and the muscles stiffen up. If the camera's going to sit for a long time, take it out and exercise it to keep the lubricants from getting solid.99

The fading image: how to preserve color pictures

"Since color dyes may in time change, this film will not be replaced for, or otherwise warranted against, any change in color." So says the disclaimer that appears in every box of Kodak color film. We have all been told, from the earliest days of color photography, that dyes will fade, that no color image is permanent, that the subtle shades of our most beloved ancestor's image will eventually fade away.

Forewarned is not necessarily forearmed, however. It always comes as a shock when one of our favorite slides, or an exhibition color print or portrait–lovingly made or expensively purchased–begins, inexorably, to change.

The process is as inalterable as human aging. Dyes, whether in films, fabrics, or fine oil paintings, do gradually fade under the bombardment of visible and invisible radiation, chemical reactions among their own constituents, and atmospheric pollutants.

How fast? An accurate timetable is almost impossible to set up, except in the broadest sense–so much depends on storage conditions, particularly temperature and humidity. In addition, the amount of light present and its UV (ultraviolet) content, the color material itself, and how your particular batch was processed all affect the ultimate stability of a color image. But, in the tables below, we attempt to classify some popular films of today and yesterday in terms of their staying power in dark storage and in the projector.

Until recently, the only hope for really long-term preservation of color photographs was to get them onto black-and-white film stocks, which are known for their long-term stability. What was involved here was making separation negatives through tri-color filters to a very accurate density and contrast values in a procedure that is basic to the dye-transfer process and color lithography. This process is complicated, critical, and requires proofing or dye-transfer printing to confirm its accuracy. Since black-and-white sheet films are involved, the material cost is low, but unfortunately, your black-and-white separations may prove embarrassing to deal with for some future technician who has no idea of your original color image's appearance. Very complete and careful records of your procedure would have to accompany the separations for the original colors to be accurately reconstituted.

Fortunately, color materials have improved gradually, and continuing research—particularly in electronics—promises further improvement. We feel quite confident that economical and practical techniques will be unearthed in the next decade to preserve whatever color pictures we cherish or need. So our present task will be to hold the fort for the next ten years.

Much credit must be given to the Eastman Kodak Company. Kodachrome films, almost since their inception in 1935, have been the most durable transparency films in general use. The new E-6 Ektachrome films are greatly improved; their estimated dark storage life under normal temperature and humidity conditions approaches 50 years, a remarkable achievement for a chromagenic (the color dyes are formed in processing) film. The dyes in Kodachrome are added to the film during its extremely involved process cycle and are, consequently, inherently more durable. Perhaps the most important recent development has been the production of E-6 Ektachrome Slide Duplicating Film, an easy-to-use, premium-quality duplicating material with the same durability as the other E-stocks. This film gives us a stable tool to preserve our transparencies—if we act in time.

Color negative materials are more difficult to assess in terms of durability. Even Kodak finds them intrinsically less durable than slide films, yet some of their

Relative stability of 35mm color films

(Class 1 is best, 5 is worst)

- Class 1
  - Kodachrome 25
  - Kodachrome 64
  - Kodachrome 40, Type A
- Class 2
  - Ektachrome Dupe Film (E-6)
  - Ektachrome 64
  - Ektachrome 200
  - Ektachrome 400
  - Ektachrome 50T
  - Ektachrome 160T
  - Kodachrome II
  - Kodachrome X
  - Kodachrome II, Type A
  - Fujichrome 100 (E-6)
- Class 3
  - High-speed Ektachrome (E-4)
  - Ektachrome X
  - Fujichrome R100 (E-4)
- Class 4
  - Agfachrome 64*
  - Agfachrome 100*
  - GAF color slide films*
  - All color negative stocks by Kodak
- Class 5
  - Ektachrome E1
  - Ektachrome E2
  - Ektachrome E-3 sheet film
  - Ektachrome E-4 dupe film

*Agfa and GAF films are particularly sensitive to high relative humidity. Their lives can be greatly extended by storing them at low (30 to 45 percent) relative humidity.

Dark keeping rankings are based on tests performed by Henry Wilhelm as outlined in ANSI PH 1.42-1969, *Method for Comparing the Color Stability of Photographs*, modified to use 45 to 76 percent relative humidity with the results averaged. Color negative stability is based on estimated printability. Copyright 1980 by Henry Wilhelm. Adapted from the forthcoming book, *The History and Preservation of Contemporary Color Materials* (Preservation Publishing Co., Box 775, Grinnell, IA 50112).

Estimated time before perceptible color change in dark storage, in years

Current Kodachromes–100-plus
E-6 Ektachromes–up to 50
Earlier Kodachromes–up to 50
High-speed Ektrachrome E-4–about 20
Ektachrome E-3 sheet film–about 6
Vericolor II–2-5
Cibachrome–100-plus
Dye transfer prints–100-plus
Ektacolor 74, 78 paper–7-10

Dark fading time at 70°F, 40 percent relative humidity, from Eastman Kodak publications.

Relative fading in slide projection

(Class 1 is best, 3 is worst)

Class 1
- Ektachrome 64 (E-6)
- Ektachrome 200
- Ektachrome 400
- Ektachrome 50T
- Ektachrome 160T
- Fujichrome 100

Class 2
- Kodachrome 25
- Kodachrome 64
- Kodachrome 40, Type A
- Agfachrome 64
- Agfachrome 100

Class 3
- All GAF color slide films

From Wilhelm, *The History and Preservation of Contemporary Color Materials*, copyright 1980. For the typical amateur photographer, the light-fading stability of most 35mm color slide films is adequate for the usually limited total times a projection (periods longer than a minute at a time or more than 45 minutes total to be avoided). Dark keeping stability is generally the most important consideration for amateur applications. If prolonged projection is expected, duplicate slides should be made for projection. Not applicable to color negatives. Enlarging light exposure in printing is minimal in effect.

time-wrought color changes can be compensated for in printing. Their usable lifetimes would also appear to depend on the colors in the scenes photographed and whether they changed or bleached away with time. Critical users would be well advised to plan on refrigerating color negatives of special importance after five or ten years. Once this is done, however, new prints or display transparencies can be generated as needed. New York's Museum of Modern Art now photographs its priceless art on Vericolor films and files the negatives under refrigeration. Large transparencies for reproduction, quantity 35-millimeter slides for projection, and black-and-white prints can be made as needed.

Kodachrome's 100-year-life expectancy and Ektachrome E-6's 50-plus-years predicted life represent a great leap forward and point the way toward easier solutions for the preservation of today's color photography.

Current state-of-the-art in stable color prints is Cibachrome. Its dye-bleach print materials incorporate durable dyes right from the start, etching away unwanted color to make the image. The non-RC glossy prints may even be more durable than routine black-and-white, in dark storage.

Hard-to-answer questions

Before we can decide what to do with our collections of images, we must ask ourselves a few questions that may be difficult to answer. "Do I really care whether my pictures last beyond my generation? Will the kids give a damn what grandma and grandpa looked like or wore when they sat around the throwaway wooden Christmas tree in their quaint split-level ranch house? Which of my pictures, if any, will stand the test of time aesthetically?" Some pictures will be cherished; others we'd all just as soon forget right away.

The easy, and conservative, answer is to say, "Save everything." But, as we will see, this isn't so easy to do. And it can be fairly expensive. Some compromises in film and print stock may have to be made.

On the other hand, we must admit that the itinerant pros and hard-working amateurs who struggled with the primitive black-and-white processes of yesteryear had no inkling that their snapshots, family bibles, cartes des visites, and other photographic leavings would have any interest for future generations. Now they are a pictorial treasure trove for historical researchers and sentimental searchers after the genuine image of "the good old days." And every year they become more valuable.

In future generations, it may not be so. The wave of color photography is still cresting. *The Wolfman Report on the Photographic Industry in the United States* showed, in its 1980 edition, an increase in the percentage of color photographs taken by amateurs from 71 percent in 1968 to 92 percent in 1978, while the total number of exposures increased from slightly over 4 billion to over 10 billion. Of the 9.65 billion exposures made in color in 1978, over 82 percent were taken on color negative films, the less durable medium. Pros, by comparison, exposed 700 million black-and-white negs, 565 million color negs, and 635 million transparencies in 1978—a much more even, and potentially more durable, output. While our black-and-whites and color transparencies may persist, color negative/positive photography is presently a "one-lifetime" record only under ideal processing and storage conditions.

A program for today

Here are some easy, and not so easy, steps you can take to save the color images you love, or need.

Don't forget black-and-white films. Their capacity for creative image simplification makes them the perennial favorite of many photographers who prefer them to the excessively literal rendition of color photographs. And the results are perennial, too—silver-image black-and-white films have a potential life expectancy of close to 1,000 years when properly fixed, washed, and stored. Even routinely processed, commercially finished black-and-white negatives have lasted 50 to 100 years by now, in actual practice. While the best-conceived accelerated-aging tests of color films produce results that are, to some degree, conjectural, you can't argue with the proven capacity of black-and-white to preserve the goods.

In color, shoot Kodachrome for keeps. Even conservative Kodak now claims a 100-year life expectancy from current Kodachromes under *average* storage conditions. Current Ektachromes and Fuji E-6 stocks should last over 50 years under the same conditions and will be your choice for higher film speeds, softer renditions, or color-slide duplication.

If your major interest is in color prints, consider the color transparency/Cibachrome route for maximum stability or be prepared to refrigerate your most valuable negatives and reprint periodically when existing prints fade. Steady improvements are being made to Ektacolor papers so that the images will last long enough for nonarchival purposes if properly displayed. Refrigeration is a small price to pay to assure the durability of really important negatives.

For black-and-white, there are well-documented procedures that give us near-permanent negatives and prints. The production of durable negatives is routinely achievable using fresh fix, a hypo neutralizer, and adequate washing. There's no reason, except carelessness, for black-and-white negatives not lasting. Good print washers and well-documented procedures for print finishing have been available for years. There are easy and accurate tests for fixation and washing effectiveness.

In color photography, there's little we can do to evaluate the quality of processing by test. With transparencies, we can eyeball the slide for gross errors. If your color balance and speed are varying all over the map, it's doubtful that the bleaching, fixing, washing, and stabilizing are up to snuff either. But make sure that such errors are not caused by a defective camera or your own mistakes.

How good is photofinishing?

Large photofinishing installations are sophisticated and very expensive. They are generally well maintained to ensure continuous production and good profitability. Still, to be perfectly safe, we'd recommend going to the lab maintained by the only other party that cares whether your picture lasts, the company that made the film. Its future also rests on your satisfaction with its materials. Smaller labs doing custom or wedding processing may or may not be zealous about their housekeeping. Watch for visible signs of negligence: dust, dirt, scratching, sloppy trimming. An operation of borderline profitability *may* be tempted to cut back on replenishment and washes to save water and money—and ruin your pictures some years hence.

With color negative films, it's even harder to keep track of the effects of bad processing. We rarely look at the negatives at all unless we do our own color printing. Again, look for visible defects.

It doesn't matter what you've got to preserve if you're foolish enough to store it in the steam room of the local Y or a damp basement, so let's define ideal storage conditions.

The deterioration of photographs is greatly accelerated by high heat and humidity, improper filing enclosures, air pollution, hungry bugs, sloppy handling techniques, and a host of other factors. For medium-long (10 to 20 years) storage, black-and-white film and color materials, and people, do well in moderately cool (68°F), relatively dry (40 percent relative humidity) rooms, air-conditioned if necessary. Avoid the constantly cycling temperature and humidity of air-conditioned spaces where systems are turned off at 5:00 P.M. and on at 9:00 A.M., particularly if you're storing resin-coated black-and-white or color prints. The emulsion can crack or delaminate.

Filing and storage

Avoid PVC (plastic) slide-storage pages for long-term keeping, especially in humid locations, and avoid stacking films or slides, or cramming them in drawers. The resultant high pressure may cause them to contact filing enclosures, producing "ferrotyped" glossy surfaces and possible physical adhesion. Good circulation of air is to be preferred.

Refrigerated storage, even deep freezing will extend the life of most photographic materials beyond a century. The problem is twofold: inconvenient accessibility to the images, and the need for maintaining controlled humidity around the film so that it becomes neither moldy nor brittle. Kodak recommends the use of (and supplies) Kodak Storage Envelopes, Cat. No. 148-6398, for cold storage of processed films. They should look familiar. They're the same laminated foil and plastic envelopes that sheet films come in. The cost is nominal, \$5.20 for 50 4 × 5 envelopes and \$7.40 for 50 8 × 10s. Slides or films in acetate sleeves, or without interleaving materials, should be preconditioned in a 70°F room at 25 to 30 percent relative humidity for one hour, inserted in small quantities into the envelopes, and then heat-sealed at the flap with an electric iron set for cotton. Store the filled envelope, not under extreme pressure, and protected from puncturing, in a refrigerator or freezer. When removing them, *do not break the seal* until they have warmed to room temperature, to prevent damaging moisture condensation. Even your household refrigerator or deep freezer will do the job, though a separate unit will maintain domestic tranquility.

Up to now, we've been talking mainly about dark storage problems. Overexposure to light causes a phenomenon called light-fading. If processed color materials are exposed to bright light for long periods, color and density shifts can result quite rapidly. Ektachrome films, interestingly, are more durable in projection than Kodachromes, so AV and other users needing long projection times make E-6 dupes of their originals. Do not leave color prints, negatives, or transparencies exposed to sunlight, bright fluorescents, or light tables.

PETER MOORE

DEAR SIR —
I AM A U.S. NAVY DEEP SEA
DIVER, AND LOST THIS LIGHTER
LAST FALL. FOUND IT LAST
WEEK. PLEASE TRY TO REPAIR IT.

TYPEWRITERS, PENS, AND WATCHES

8

TYPEWRITERS

"The extra care . . . has disappeared."

An interview with Martin Tytell

In the shadow of New York's World Trade Center, on the second floor of 116 Fulton Street, are the cluttered offices of Martin Tytell. Here, Tytell has spent a lifetime studying, repairing, and building typewriters. A consequence of his self-admitted obsession is that mail has reached him addressed only "Mr. Typewriter, New York."

His vocation got off to an early start when he dismantled a typewriter in school, but the 550 pieces frightened him and a repair person had to be called. Next day, Tytell again went at the machine, and again the repairman was called. On his third trip to the school, the repairman took the boy aside. "Look, kid," he said. "If you can't keep from tearing them apart, you better learn to put them back again."

Tytell specializes in converting American typewriters to any one of 145 languages. "What do you need?" Tytell asks rhetorically. "I have Arabic, Hebrew, Yiddish, Japanese, Korean, Portuguese, Polish, Spanish, Greek, Armenian. You need a Hindidevanagari machine? That's Indian. We got it. We got Cyrillic, Georgian. I even have Bulgarian. I didn't do well with Siamese, or Thai, which was popular until two years ago. Now nobody's buying. You want one cheap? I'm building machines now for the language Jesus Christ allegedly used. There's a Lebanese church that still uses that language for regular services."

Over the years, Tytell and his wife Pearl (he lured her away from a competitor in 1938 with the promise that he'd marry her) have acquired an astounding knowledge of typewriters and typefaces that makes them valuable to law keepers. Martin testified as a typeface and documents expert at the Alger Hiss perjury trial, "the trial which first brought mass attention to typewriter identification," Tytell explains. Government agencies now regularly ask Martin and Pearl to testify in court; the Tytells' son, Peter, has also become a typeface identification expert.

Martin Tytell is a friendly, white-haired man authoritatively dressed in a laboratory robe and bow tie. His offices house a typeface identification lab ("one of the best in the world," Tytell says), a showroom piled high with foreign-language type and typewriters of every conceivable make and vintage, a machine shop, typewriter washing and cleaning apparatus, and a "typewriter morgue" full of typewriter carcasses that have proved to be not so durable. This morgue holds

the earthly remains of practically every American typewriter model with the notable exception of the one machine Tytell cites as his personal durability favorite–the Underwood 5.

BK

Bill Keisling

Martin Tytell.

“One of the early typewriters I worked with, and there were many of those– hundreds, thousands, actually–was the Underwood 5, and that's one machine I could take apart and put together practically with my eyes closed. I love the Underwood 5 because when I was a youngster I used to practice taking the machine apart and assembling it blindfolded.

My most popular typewriter through the years has been the Royal Magic Margin. I'd say I've sold more Royal Magic Margin machines than any other model; then would be the Underwood 5. I still have thousands of people who come in and have us keep those Royal Magic Margin machines going; some of them go back over 40 years. Those machines are heavy, but you'd be amazed how people don't seem to mind lugging them in here. On Saturdays, I'll have 20 people bringing in old machines just for me to change a ribbon for them.

They lug the machines in. I have some old ladies of 70 who somehow manage to lug the machines in on Saturdays. You've got to witness this to believe it. I often think I'm in Wonderland when all these old people come in with their machines. I had a man in here just yesterday; he must have bought this machine 50 years ago, and he just barely managed to lug up this old typewriter here to change the ribbon. He loves the machine and doesn't let anybody else come near it. All I really have to do is wipe the type off, wash down the roller, and put a ribbon in, which I've been doing for 50 years as a courtesy.

Today, typewriters are not made to last as long as they once were. When you bought a manual machine, it was for half a century. When you buy an electric typewriter today, maybe it's got a five-year life. Why is that? I think old machines were built with a little bit of love and attention. Today, typewriters are made to be what they call “adequate,” just so they'll pass the customer's initial typing, and after that they really don't care. I don't regard “adequate” as really being adequate. Every machine we unpack these days (and we sell a lot of machines here–every day I sell a few typewriters), we have to spend anywhere from a half hour to two hours when we take the typewriter out of the carton, to be sure the alignment is right, to be sure the ribbon reverses, that the tabulation works. In many cases, the ribbon doesn't reverse. In many cases, the motion–that's the upper- and lower-case meeting on a given line–is out. Certain letters will strike heavier than others. We touch them up, and that takes time. On the electric machines, you'll here “dig, dig, dig,” where the motor pulley belts are not perfectly aligned. We adjust those. Every typewriter coming out of a carton has to be adjusted today. Although you're supposed to be able to remove it from the carton and give it to the customer, it just does not work.

For example, here's a machine that just came in. It's a Smith-Corona with a Ukrainian keyboard. I'll have to spend two hours checking the alignment of this machine. The alignment's going to stink on this typewriter, I know that. Whoever aligns Russian or Ukrainian keyboards doesn't know or doesn't care. So it comes through "adequate." I have to finish that. Some machines are so badly made to start with that it's hopeless. I have learned the hard way—I send the typewriters back and the manufacturers think I'm a nut—not to even bother with some machines. I carry a very limited number of models and designs of different manufacturers because I don't have the time to complete work they should have done in their factory.

The old typewriters were checked by final inspectors. For instance, a few years ago the Olympia typewriter company had a graduate engineer check each machine, who then would sign his name on the final sheet that went with the typewriter to the customer. Today, they have inexperienced people doing the same job, and they may be thinking about last night's date or tonight's date, and they'll pass many obvious flaws that they should not be permitted to pass. So, even Olympia, which started out as making a fine machine that was perfectly aligned and so forth, today is a little bit of a hit or miss. I'm merely trying to point out that the extra care, which, in my opinion, is extremely important, has disappeared.

Recently, I received an offer from a manufacturer for a batch of machines at a ridiculously low price. These were typewriters that department stores had returned, and the manufacturer had refixed them, allegedly, at the factory. They offered these typewriters to me at such a ridiculously low price that I could have made a lot of money selling them. I thought about it for two minutes, then decided I didn't want to get involved. It just wasn't worth the effort. I know what a piece of junk they had made, and what a mistake it was for them even to have gotten started on that particular design. You see, this manufacturer is trying to get rid of its inventory rather than junk it. I know manufacturers, by the way, that have junked hundreds of machines—destroyed them—because they realized there was a foul-up and that they should never have produced those machines. These are the manufacturers who want to protect their name. Other manufacturers hope they can get away with it.

Most manufacturers, however, try to make a better product and design it so it's going to stand up. They're not looking for any problem. Of course, there are human frailties—some engineering is better than others—but I don't think anyone deliberately sets out to give you an inferior product. They're simply incompetent. Furthermore, many manufacturers believe—and they are correct—that the average guy doesn't want a machine to be absolutely perfect, doesn't know the difference, or doesn't care. So, why should the manufacturer spend more money making a better product? For that small percentage of people who are super-critical, they would have to increase their price. What difference would it make if the machine lasted another year or two if you have to double the price? Then they would probably get out of the market.

Most people are not interested in durability. This is rather a shock to you, isn't it? They want a typewriter which will perform with ease, which will have nice copy. They couldn't care less if the machine will last 20 years or 10 years. Many typewriter buyers have a son or daughter who is going to college. They want a typewriter that the student can take through school. After college, they really don't care what happens to the machine. When the student goes to graduate school, he or she can come in and get another machine. The American doesn't mind spending more money for another machine later on.

It seems that the American consumer has a throwaway nature. This is best exemplified by the little calculators they're selling these days—it's cheaper to throw them out when the batteries run down and buy another. This attitude carries over to more-expensive products.

Personal standards of quality

I have observed that certain companies use a lesser inspection standard for American typewriters than for those going to the European market. It's the psychology of the American, who either doesn't care, or doesn't know any better, that's causing this trend. My customers are very fussy. They come in here and expect the machine to work perfectly. Sometimes I get real fusspots, but I appreciate that they want the machine to perform properly. I will tell them when the machine they are selecting is one that they're going to be unhappy with because it cannot live up to their expectations. I explain to them that they should go to a better-built or more costly machine. In many instances, they will listen to me and buy the better machine, and they're happy with it.

Fortunately for the consumer with limited resources, more money does not mean more durability. A consumer today can buy a good electric machine for $400

30 Jan 1981

Dear Mr Keisling

A neat, precisely typed letter creates a good impression on the person who receives it. That's one reason I like my Underwood 5.

Reasoner says my typewriter is an affectation. My answer to that is, a writer needs all the affectations he can get to distract him from the heartbreak of not being able to say it the way he wants.

I like my Underwood 5 for other reasons: 1) It is the same age I am, 60. 2)Unlike an IBM Selectric, it is not any smarter than I am and is not ready to go before I have anything to say 3) It works and I sit down at it with perfect confidence that it, at least, is one thing I'm not going to have any trouble with.

Sincerely,

Andrew A Rooney

I have about 18 Underwood 5s now. I buy one everytime I find one because theyve stopped making typewriters I can work on and I have this dread of running out of typewriters before I run out of things to say.

ISAAC ASIMOV
10 WEST 66th ST. 33-A • NEW YORK, NY 10023

19 February 1981

Bill Keisling
Rodale Press, Inc.
Organic Park
Emmaus, Pa., 18049

Dear Mr. Keisling,

My wife and I, between us, have four Selectrics. We each use one and have one in reserve.

I can use my typewriter perfectly because it is not computerized so I just have to hit the keys with the letters or numbers on it in order to get those letters or numbers.

It hardly every breaks down, but when it does I am utterly helpless to fix it. However, a call to IBM gets it fixed within twenty-four hours---and I also have the reserve to fall back on.

Isaac Asimov

Two recommendations.

that will last as long as any $1,000 typewriter. The criteria for durability is not only how well a machine is made originally, but how the individual uses it. Some people abuse machines. I have typewriters coming in here I sold 20 years ago that are as clean and neat and sharp as though the guy just walked out with it. Other people have a machine for six months and they bring it in and you would never believe it. I have one guy who thinks that the typewriter is an erasing basket. He must go through enough erasers to keep them in business. Erasure is ground glass and rubber. It's the same with emory. If you fill your typewriter with emory dust, of course you're going to wear it down.

How typewriters have changed

Old Royals and Underwoods were made of cast iron. After World War II, they went to various alloys that combine zinc, aluminum, and other metals. The alloys are just as durable as cast iron. In fact, when you dropped the cast-iron machines, invariably the backs would break. If you dropped the alloy typewriters, they would bend and give. Today, plastics are being used because they are less costly. Whenever you can mold something instead of machine it, costs are reduced. A lot of people are under the mistaken idea that they want a typewriter that's all metal. It really isn't necessary. The plastic parts are found only on the outside cover; the internal parts of the machine are still metal. In fact, plastic covers are more durable because you don't have to paint plastic–it comes in that color, so paint won't chip off.

As I mentioned, today's typewriters are not made to last as long as they once did. Today's electrics have circuitry that's going to wear out. If there's a short circuit in the machine, or the power goes off, or the on-and-off switch fails, or any part of the electric mechanism stops, the machine dies. Whereas, if a part quits on a manual machine, you still have the rest of the typewriter to work with. If your backspacer doesn't work, or your tabulator doesn't work, or your right margin doesn't lock, you still can type. That's the nature of the animal. But electric typewriters are here to stay. There's no question that the IBM Selectric Two is a better performer than any manual typewriter, once you've mastered it. It would be silly to say that an old manual will match the ease of operation of an IBM Selectric, but there are some people who don't care about ease of operation. They are more comfortable with the machine that Daddy used, and there are so many of those people it's amazing. Some people only want the kind of machine they were using 25 years ago.

How do I tell a good typewriter from a poor typewriter? It's no mystery. I sit down at the machine and type out a line or two. If the type looks good, crisp, and clear, it's a good machine. If the type looks fuzzy and crooked, it's a poor machine. I also notice the touch of the machine, what it feels like to *me*. People laugh when I say typewriters talk back to you and behave as you treat them, but it's a fact that you can develop a friendship with a machine.

You see, I love typewriters. They're my friends. Maybe I'm queer for typewriters. All right, I am.”

Typewriters and top secrets

My trusty IBM Selectric served me well for years. It cranked out many crisp pages a day until the instant when the thing surrendered its ghost, reducing me to a Galahad without his sword. I could not suspect when I began shopping for a new typewriter that I would end up battling the government of the United States.

My private consumer's crusade started innocently enough. I wanted a good electric typewriter, so I went to an office-supply store. The sales clerk led me across the showroom. Five brands of typewriters—IBM, Olivetti, Royal, Facit, and Remington—were perched on the shelf. Price tags dangling from the typewriters proclaimed that each machine sold for about $1,000—sinfully expensive, considering writers are shamefully poor, so I had to choose my typewriter carefully, weighing not only purchase price but on-going expenses as well. I quizzed the salesperson as to how much electricity they'd use, and the relative frequency of breakdowns and repair costs.

That information doesn't exist, I was told.

I suspected that the manufacturers *must* have a good idea of these and other so-called life-cycle costs. How else could a manufacturer know to guarantee its typewriter for three years, for example, instead of five? I returned empty-handed from the office-supply store and telephoned the manufacturers. A spokesperson for IBM told me that, yes, the company regularly pulled typewriters from the production line at its factory in Lexington, Kentucky, and tested them for durability and reliability, among other things.

"Would IBM make its testing information available to me so I could compare its typewriters with other brands?" I asked the spokesperson.

I received a concise reply. "No."

Next I telephoned Remington, and was told by Denny Smith, a quality-control expert, "Remington tests its typewriters, but we don't do it for the public. The results of our product tests are confidential information that is used to make improvements in our products."

I decided to take a less direct approach when I telephoned Olivetti. "What would happen if a potential Olivetti customer asked to see the company's product-testing information?" I asked an Olivetti publicist.

"We wouldn't give them a definite answer," replied the publicist.

I consoled myself that I at least had proved the typewriter sales clerk wrong: life-cycle cost information did exist for each of the brands of typewriters. The problem was that the manufacturers did not want consumers to see the information.

Several weeks passed. I needed a typewriter badly, but I didn't want to buy a second-rate machine. Then, quite by accident, I happened to read in an office-products magazine that the U.S. government's General Services Administration (GSA) had recently conducted life-cycle tests on electric typewriters. The magazine reported that every year the GSA buys $50 million worth of typewriters for the government, in the same chancy way the government buys most things—bids are solicited, and the supplier submitting the lowest bid is awarded the contract. But someone at the GSA had decided that every typewriter it considered should be tested to come up with life-cycle costs that were as clear and easy to understand as a price tag. The agency invited manufacturers to provide sample typewriters, and in 1980, IBM, Olivetti, Royal, Facit, and Remington responded. Each company shipped four electric typewriters to Washington, D.C., for testing.

Testing typewriters in Washington, D.C.

Public employees fastened the typewriters to robot typists. The robots pecked each typewriter 21 million times, which is equivalent of seven years' use, the period of time the government keeps a typewriter. The testers kept track of how many times each machine broke and tallied repair costs, compensation for "downtime," electricity consumed, and ribbons and correction tapes each used. I telephoned the GSA and asked to see the data. "No," I was told. "That's confidential information." I was told I could file a Freedom of Information Act request, but shouldn't expect much success.

Since the dawn of the Atomic Age, secrecy has been a growth industry in American government. One writer recently estimated that 17,500 federal employees are empowered to declare various information "secret." In 1967, Congress passed the Freedom of Information Act to help private citizens unearth those secrets.

I filed a Freedom of Information Act request with the GSA on January 30, 1981, asking for the results of the government's typewriter test. Since I have no formal training in jurisprudence, my request was worded simply. "I believe these test results should be made available to the American public so consumers can make intelligent decisions before a purchase is made," I wrote.

The government wasn't cooperative. According to the law, my letter should have been answered within ten days. But ten days passed and no word from Uncle Sam. A month went by and still no word.

I telephoned my contact at the GSA. He apologized. There had been an "administrative error," I was told.

On the first day of March, 1981, a letter came confirming my telephone conversation. "We apologize again for the administrative error which delayed our providing you with a timely response," the letter read. "The material you request should be available next week."

The next week I got a letter from Herbert McCarthy, Commissioner of the GSA, but it held a bill for $98.50 in photocopying fees for 85 pages of material. "Upon receipt of your check, the information will be sent to you," wrote McCarthy. But there was a catch: I would only receive data concerning the bid-winning typewriter, and I would not be permitted to see the complete results. I could not compare the different brands.

Ninety-eight dollars and fifty cents is a lot of money to pay for worthless information, I thought, and I said as much in a letter to Commissioner McCarthy. I again asked for the complete results of the government's test.

Two weeks later, McCarthy wrote back, "Test results are generally expressed in technical terms, and there is serious question as to any reasonable public benefit these would serve, or the degree to which they could be presented to the public in any meaningful form . . . . [Also], many corporations, for a variety of sound business reasons, do not participate in government procurement programs. Therefore, publication of test results of products bought by the government will not be valid as a comparative tool and might cause injury to products not included."

McCarthy enclosed the life-cycle cost data for the model—an Olivetti— that won the contract. I found the information straightforward and easy to understand. After seven years, the owner of an Olivetti typewriter could expect to have paid $89.54 for "lost productivity and downtime," $57.87 for "service and parts costs," $110.60 for ribbons, $115.20 for correction tapes, and $16.42 for electricity, for a total operating cost of $389.63. Added to the purchase price (the government was quoted a price of $686.76), the seven-year life-cycle cost of the Olivetti typewriter came to $1,076.39.

Again I wrote McCarthy, informing him that I found the information he sent of interest. I restated my request. I also asked to whom I could appeal his reply should it be negative.

Again I was turned down. "Your futher request for any similar information collected while testing other brands of typewriters must be denied," wrote McCarthy. "We released the information on the Olivetti test results because that firm was the successful bidder and the awarded contract is public information. However, the information regarding the product of the unsuccessful bidders constitutes proprietary information furnished to the government voluntarily, with the understanding that it would be kept confidential if no contract was awarded. The basis for our decision to withhold this information from disclosure is set forth in 5 U.S.C. (b) (4). That section exempts from disclosure documents which are 'trade secrets and commercial or financial information obtained from a person and privileged or confidential.' It has been held that the government may invoke [this exemption] on behalf of a person who has submitted commercial or financial information where it can be shown that disclosure is likely to cause substantial harm to his competitive position. The interest of the government is to enable it to obtain necessary information through purely voluntary cooperation in the future." If I wished to appeal McCarthy's decision, I could do so by writing the GSA's director of information.

I was angry. As I read McCarthy's letter, the life-cycle costs of typewriters became less important to me. What seemed more important was the way the government and the manufacturers cooperated to keep their testing information secret. Everybody seemed to know the life-cycle costs of typewriters but consumers, who would benefit most from the information. No doubt consumers would have just as much trouble finding test data on washing machines, refrigerators, or automobiles, I thought.

I replied to the GSA that the life-cycle cost information I sought did not constitute trade secrets, as Commissioner McCarthy maintained, because government employees collected this data during government-financed tests while using government-owned equipment. Further, I argued that release of the GSA's typewriter testing data would not prove demonstrably harmful to the government or the GSA.

"I believe that this government-produced testing data can be useful to the public," I wrote. "The spirit (if not the letter) of the Freedom of Information Act has been violated by refusing me this information."

A month later, the government wrote to say it had reconsidered and would release the data. Six months after I first wrote the GSA, I received the complete typewriter test results in the mail.

The results were surprising. Some brands of typewriters are two or three times as expensive as others to own and maintain, as the following table shows.

Typewriter operating-cost breakdown

	Olivetti	Royal	IBM	Facit	Remington
Lost productivity and downtime	$ 89.54	$ 98.86	$ 56.83	$ 72.69	$133.51
Service and parts	57.87	24.70	20.65	55.21	75.85
Ribbons and ribbon replacement	110.60	103.72	113.27	165.36	129.83
Correction tapes and replacement	115.20	50.89	87.48	83.25	74.20
Energy	16.42	12.87	28.46	11.82	34.15
Extra equipment	0.00	1.00	0.00	0.00	-43.35
Total operating cost	389.63	292.05	306.69	388.33	404.20
Bid price	686.76	814.08	864.00	783.34	818.57
Life-cycle cost	**1076.39**	**1106.13**	**1170.69**	**1171.67**	**1222.77**

Remington electric typewriters experienced the most costly breakdowns of any of the five brands tested by the government. Understandably, the company was not pleased that the results had been made public.

"We're protesting the government's life-cycle cost tests right now," Remington's Denny Smith told me. He disputed the government's conclusion that Remington typewriters are more expensive to own than the four other brands tested. "I don't know how you got the government data," Smith told me. "Those test results were supposed to be confidential."

This story has an interesting postscript. Remington's in-house attorney, Phillip Seaton, rang me up to say that the company had filed a legal challenge against the GSA that would prevent the government from buying typewriters based on the results of its life-cycle cost test. The government's test was "unscientific" and "ridiculous," Seaton said, and if I would care to visit Remington's corporate headquarters in New Jersey, I would be permitted to see the company's own test results, which, said Seaton, would prove the inaccuracy of the government's findings.

I did not bother telling Seaton that months before, when I was shopping for a typewriter, Denny Smith, Remington's quality-control spokesperson, had refused to let me see the same test results because they were "confidential information." Instead, I explained to that attorney that I was no longer interested in the testing data; I said I was very concerned, however, that the information was unavailable to consumers.

"We would be glad to share our product-testing information with the public." All a consumer has to do to see Remington's product-testing information is to visit the company's offices in Princeton, New Jersey.

The attorney even gave me directions. "You take a train to Philadelphia. Our corporate headquarters are right off U.S. 1. Just go to the reception desk and ask for me. We'd be glad to show you our product-testing information."

BILL KEISLING

PENS FOR A LIFETIME

"In the long run, the best route to go—the most thrifty—is to buy the finest fountain pen you can afford and then maintain it. The point should be solid gold."

An interview with John Sullivan

For years, it was known as Fahrney's Fountain Pen Hospital, the place where the lawyers, diplomats, and office workers of Washington, D.C., took their prized but ailing writing instruments. Today, it's simply called Fahrney's, and although there's a new branch over in Alexandria as well as a thriving mail-order business with a computerized customer list of 30,000 names, the store retains the commitment to service and personal attention that has characterized it since Ed Fahrney bought the business in 1928.

The current owner, John Sullivan, is a former stockbroker who was attracted to the business as much by an interest in working with his hands as by the economic potential. When he bought Fahrney's, he threw himself into pen repair under the guidance of a staff that has a total of some 70 years of experience working with pens. The approach paid off, because Fahrney's—one of less than a dozen stores in the country that service the pens they sell—has prospered despite competition from drug stores and discount houses selling cheap, throwaway pens by the thousands.

JOHN BLACKFORD

❝You can give a ballpoint pen to a chimpanzee and it's going to work, but not a fountain pen. A fountain pen does not travel well on a plane; it requires refilling and attention. But a fountain pen in the hands of a person who enjoys writing or who writes professionally becomes almost as addictive as coffee in the morning. The person just can't function without that pen.

Some of our customers are professional writers who, if their pen is out of action, are literally out of action themselves. One in particular, a noted news columnist, uses the Mont Blanc Diplomat. If that pen is damaged or dropped, he'll send a messenger or bring it in himself right away. He doesn't keep a spare—he should. But a spare isn't the same. No two pens are exactly alike, even though they are manufactured to very tight specifications.

Our customers cut across all economic lines, but there's no question that if they had a good pen, they will pay almost anything to get it repaired. Yet our charges for repair average only about $7. As a source of profit, pen repair is insignificant to our business. When we sell a pen, it's like putting in a foundation. We want to keep that foundation solid with good service. We feel that in the long run it pays off in additional sales and loyalty.

There are only a handful of retailers repairing pens now, and the manufacturers won't repair the older pens after about 20 years because they run out of parts. We stock quite a few parts, so in some cases we can service pens the manufacturers won't touch. We buy parts from Parker, Shaffer, Mont Blanc, and a few from Lamy. If a customer brings in a foreign brand that we don't buy parts for, we just take some pens and tear them down for the parts. At our downtown store, we have four or five large cabinets with little drawers, all full of parts. We have an unbelievable amount of money tied up in parts. I'd be afraid to even look, I really would. For Parker 51s, which are no longer manufactured, we must have accumulated a hundred of those little solid-gold points. I don't think anybody could go into the parts-and-repair business today, the way we're into it. It would not pay. There are a few independents around who repair pens, but they are dying off. We knew of a gal out in the Midwest who was in her eighties and had a *lot* of valuable parts. But they were valuable to only one or two people, ourselves in particular. She wanted like $8,000 for them. I was going to fly out and look at them. And she died. The estate got hold of them. They took all the gold points and had them weighed and sold them for scrap. It's criminal, but that's what's happened with this big run-up in gold. A lot of good parts went down the tubes that way.

Cross pens and pencils

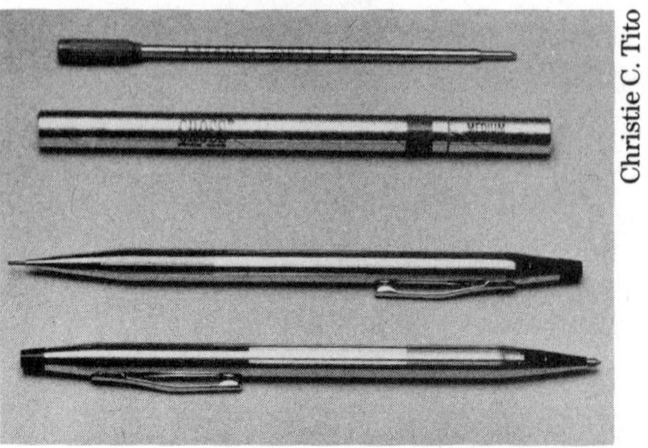

Christie C. Tito

Cross offers a "full perpetual" warranty on its writing instruments, not including refills, pencil leads, and erasers, of course. These may be purchased direct from the company in Lincoln, Rhode Island, thereby encouraging the owner of a Cross pen or pencil to hold onto it. This level of quality assurance doesn't come cheap. A 14-karat gold-filled pen is $30; refills are $1 each.

One reason for the pen's trouble-free service is that there are no springs and just two moving parts—the top, which you twist to make the point appear or retract, and the ball of the refill.

We bust our fannies to provide service and expertise. I think that's basically how the independent merchant and the specialty store have survived the onslaught of the discounters and the department stores and the mass marketing. Today, you're shocked when you have a merchant who takes a personal interest in you. I mean, shocked—you may think there's an ulterior motive. "The guy is going to stick it to me."

We don't want to change the way a customer writes. We want to give him a pen that is best for the way he is writing. First, we find out what he can afford to spend, and next we see if he has a heavy hand or a light touch. But, the main thing in selecting a pen is that the customer is comfortable with it. He can buy the best pen possible, and if it's not comfortable, then it's not worth a damn to him. We encourage the customer to use one for a few days, and if it's not right, bring it back. That's what we tell them. I've even had customers ask *me* to try out a pen for a few days and tell them whether it's a good one. And I'll do it, because if I can't make a judgment on a product, then I have no business doing what I'm doing. I encourage the people who work for us to pick up every single pen they sell and try it. That's the only way they are going to be able to tell a customer what it's like.

Materials and workmanship

In the long run, the best route to go—the most thrifty—is to buy the finest pen you can afford and then maintain it. The point should be solid gold. The gold is much smoother. Actually, you're not writing on the gold, you're writing on the tip, which is iridium, a very hard material. But the gold is flexible, so the point will flex a little bit, yet come back to its original shape. A steel point won't do that. Gold feels softer, lighter to the touch. It tends to take on more of the peculiarities of your hand. It's more accommodating.

The feed should be hard rubber rather than plastic. The filling system—both the feed and the point—should be as simple as possible, repairable and cleanable.

In most cases, these qualities are exhibited by products that go back to the 1920s and '30s. The fountain pen, when you get right down to it, hasn't advanced technologically in recent years. There are really no fountain pens more advanced than the Parker 51 of the late 1940s, which is the most famous fountain pen Parker ever made. They stopped making it a couple of years ago, and yet we still have numerous requests for it. We ordered a couple of hundred of them when we knew it was going out of production, but we only got 60. When Parker stopped producing them, I think they were about $20, with a solid-gold point. You couldn't get an equal pen today for $50, whereas the Mont Blanc Diplomat costs $210. The Diplomat is reminiscent in design and workmanship to pens that were made 40 or 50 years ago in this country, although there have been compromises for the purpose of manufacturing them at a more rapid rate.

Older pens are easier to work on than the newer ones because of the simplicity of the way they are put together. New fountain pens are designed for ease of manufacture, not for function. To cut down on labor costs, a design consists of maybe three or four components. The nib and the feed are mated together so that they can't be taken apart or cleaned. If a nib goes bad, you throw it away, put a new one in. In a used pen, look for Parker, Sheaffer, Eversharp. They will be writing for another 50 years. The workmanship on some of the Watermans, the tip, is just absolutely superb. They last, and the nibs were probably the best ever made, in terms of the feel and flexibility. Older pens that don't work often just have a cracked filler bulb. The charge for replacement is about $6 or $8.

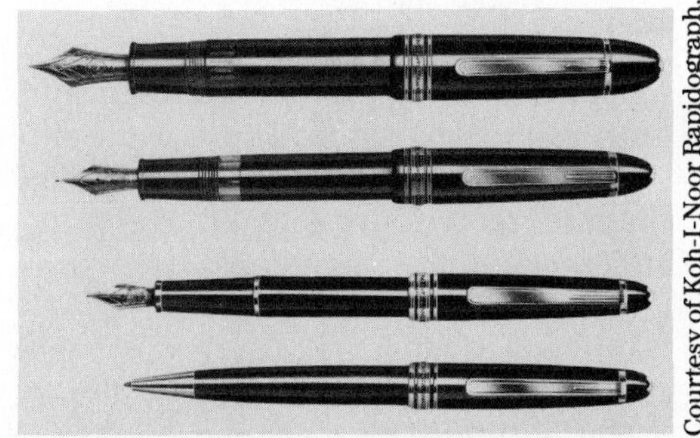

Courtesy of Koh-I-Noor Rapidograph, Inc., Bloomsbury, New Jersey

The Mont Blanc lineup. From top to bottom, the piston-filled, cigar-sized Diplomat with etched facing; the piston-filled 146; the 144 cartridge model; and a matching ballpoint with a giant-sized refill.

People let a fountain pen sit, and the ink hardens in it. Rather than throw the point away (which runs from a minimum of $30 on up to $60, or $100 for the Diplomat), we can tear that thing down and clean it out, which is a very simple operation, taking 20 minutes.

Still, there are very good pens being made today. The Japanese are making some fine products. Sheaffer, in the U.S., has been doing great things with its new Targa line. Some of them are gold-tipped, some are steel. It's been a resounding success.

Today, throwaway products are not nearly as cheap as they used to be. And they are not nearly as good because of the skyrocketing cost of plastics. I think people are becoming aware of that. They are stepping up from throwaways to inexpensive refillable pens. The rolling-writer design is extremely popular. It's a hybrid between a ballpoint and a fountain pen: it uses a ball like a ball pen, and liquid ink, like a fountain pen. But at best, like any hybrid, it is a compromise. It's horribly expensive to use because of the ink costs. You almost could buy the most expensive pen available for the cost of roller writers you'd use up over the course of two or three years.”

WATCHES

Until recently, it was simple to shop for a good wristwatch. There were only two types to choose from—mechanical timepieces with jeweled movements, and mechanical timepieces with pin-lever movements.

Into this simple set of trade-offs comes the electronic watch, a radically different machine. While a mechanical watch is powered by a mainspring and necessarily exerts tremendous stress throughout the timepiece, an electronic watch has few moving parts; an analog watch retains hands and the standard clock face, and a digital watch relies on an electronic display. In both, timekeeping is the function of a quartz crystal. It would seem that electronic watches stand to hold up longer by virtue of their simpler innards. An analog timepiece has a small electric motor that advances its hands upon receiving a 1/100th-of-a-second pulse from the quartz circuitry. Whereas a mechanically powered watch's movement is always in motion, an analog's electric motor rests 99/100th of a second, every second. A digital electronic watch, with no moving parts, theoretically should last longest of all. But in practice, the electronic innards are vulnerable to the hazards of daily use. The crystal is not as rugged as you might guess, and it may malfunction if the watch is dropped or hit sharply. Batteries must be replaced, and they may leak and corrode the works. A digital watch's electronic display, like its quartz crystal, may be damaged if dropped onto a hard surface or immersed in water. The biggest factor affecting the durability of an electronic watch, however, is the reliability of its labyrinthine electronic circuitry. While mechanical watch technology has been refined and perfected over the centuries, electronic circuitry is relatively new; it's still too early to predict how today's circuitry will endure 40 or 50 years from now.

An advantage to owning an electronic watch is that its guts can be readily and inexpensively removed and replaced. For that matter, its case can also be replaced. If a manufacturer guaranteed an electronic watch for, say, 100 years, then faithfully replaced its innards and case every 20 years, at the end of a century there still would exist a watch, though nothing remained of the original timepiece. (We are reminded of a woman who reported that an axe had been in her family for generations; aside from being refitted with several new handles and several new axe heads, the woman related, the axe performed reliably for years.)

If the works of an electronic watch are easily replaced, they're not easily repaired, and here is an advantage of a mechanical watch. If it quits ticking, it can probably be fixed by a local watch repairer. But few neighborhood watch repairers can do much more than ship an ailing electronic watch back to the manufacturer or replace the entire electronic module.

One man who can fix electronic watches, Charles Goshman of the Watch Repair Shop in Madison, Wisconsin, says he had to invest between $4,000 and $5,000 in equipment to repair electronic watches and that he must continually attend seminars and take university courses just to keep up with the technology. "Theoretically, electronic watches are more durable," Goshman says, "but, let's put it bluntly: the durability of electronic circuitry is unknown." Even so, Goshman put away his mechanical watch three or four years ago and wears an analog. He believes that electronic watches are the timekeepers of the future.

Michael Jenner, president of Media Digital Corporation of Media, Pennsylvania, a concern that trains repairers of electronic watches, agrees. "I'm a firm believer that electronics have changed the course of watchmaking forever," Jenner says. "There's no turning back." Though electronic watches are "designed to last a lifetime," says Jenner, "push buttons in most electronic watches provide avenues for moisture and crud to work into the watch, limiting its life span. If an electronic watch is displayed in a dust-free museum, it could last indefinitely. Worn on a wrist, an electronic watch should last 20 to 25 years."

"Electronic watches are more accurate than mechanical watches," observes Jayne Barrick, who is the managing editor of *Watch and Clock Review*. "An electronic watch usually is accurate to within three seconds a month, but frankly I don't need that much accuracy." Barrick owns a 20-year-old Longines mechanical watch. "The cheaper electronic watches are probably not as durable as similarly priced mechanicals—more can go wrong. In my opinion, a $50 electronic Timex is just as durable as a $500 electronic Seiko La Salle. Remember that there are no secrets in electronics these days; everyone uses the same electronic modules. Some manufacturers claim that their electronic modules have more quality than their competitors', but to me, they look pretty much alike: generally, a high price tag on an electronic watch indicates a more expensive case, not a more durable electronic module. It's like anything else; the price of a watch depends more upon the market the manufacturer is targeting than on the quality of the watch. And regardless of the price of the watch, it is usually cheaper to throw away the electronic module than to repair it."

Can the watch that ticks and pings continue to compete with the $20 electronic throwaway? That remains to be seen. With periodic cleaning and care, even a $30 jeweled mechanical watch can be expected to serve a century or more, a feat that electronics technology would do well to match.

And suppose a digital or analog did manage to hum its way to a hundredth birthday—what would be the likelihood of finding a battery? No doubt you'd stand a better chance of scaring up a watchmaker, tending to the enduring device of mainspring and escapement.

BK

The mechanical watch

Both photos, Christie C. Tito

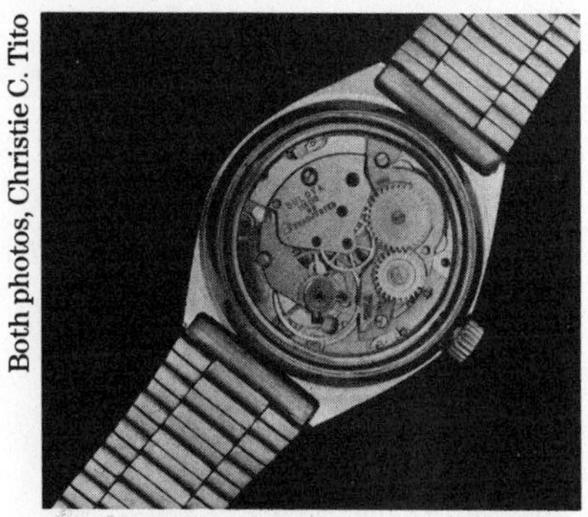

An inexpensive 17-jeweled Bulova, inside and out.

There is surprisingly little difference in durability between a $30 17-jewel movement watch and a $1,000 17-jewel movement watch, says Herb Novick of the Bulova Watch Company. "The $1,000 watch will probably have an extremely thin movement and will probably be hand finished," Novick says. "The expensive watch will also be subjected to more quality-control inspections. But the $30 watch and the $1,000 watch both contain identical imitation ruby jewels and have nearly identical movements. The durability of a watch depends largely upon its case. People should always look for a waterproof case. The less humidity, dust, and dirt that gets into a watch movement, the longer the watch will last. Protection of the movement is what counts."

A clockmaker looks back and forward

"There will always be a market for the mechanicals."

An interview with Victor Stoltz

The watch industry within the last 10 years has seen changes that have shaken it right down to its mainsprings. Manufacturers have seen a product that evolved over 300 years—the mechanical watch—eclipsed almost overnight by electronic watches controlled by a quartz crystal and a silicon chip. The chip wiped out the slide-rule industry—who would buy one when a calculator will do more, more cheaply and more accurately? The watch industry didn't fare that badly, though. There remains a place for the mechanical watch, largely because electronic watches don't offer an absolute superiority over their mechanical predecessors. Still, the changes have been dramatic:

- Up to 80 percent of all watches produced by Swiss watch companies will soon be electronic.
- No mechanical watches are currently manufactured in the United States.
- The dozens of watchmaking schools that flourished only a couple of decades ago in America have dwindled to three.
- Although there seems to be plenty of work for skilled watch repairers, employers are having trouble paying them good wages, and consequently, many are leaving the profession.

Should the consumer mourn these changes as yet another example of how unprofitable it has become to manufacture quality goods, or welcome the new technology as both cheaper and better? To find out, we talked to Victor Stoltz of Bowman's jewelry store in Lancaster, Pennsylvania. Stoltz has been with Bowman's for 35 years, first as a watchmaker and clockmaker (that's what people who do repair are called in the idiom of the trade), and more recently as an appraiser, overseer, and purchasing agent. He was trained in watch and clock repair at Bowman's Technical School—separate from the store but under the same ownership. The school is the oldest and largest of its kind in the country and, many feel, also the best.

Christie C. Tito

Victor Stoltz.

Lancaster itself is a watch town, the home of Hamilton Watch Company, which was one of the last firms to manufacture complete watches in the United States, instead of just assembling foreign-made components. Bowman's has been in business there for 103 years. It's not a run-of-the-mill store, with high ceilings, walls hung with venerable clocks, and expensive watches set in display counters worn smooth by years of use. All lend an air of eminence and stability that seems to belie the transformation that has overtaken the watch industry.

Christie C. Tito

"There's always enough work for a good watchmaker . . ."

Stoltz's desk faces toward the very end of the long, narrow store. He wears a jeweler's eyepiece around his neck, ready for use when someone wants his appraisal of a ring offered for sale or advice on repairing a wayward watch. His spectacles are fitted with a tiny magnifying glass that he pivots down with practiced ease when he needs a closer look at some tiny part. Next to his desk, a rickety staircase leads up to the clock-repair room. The technical school used to be located there before it moved to larger quarters, and the thousands of students who plied up and down over the years nearly finished off the stairs. Whenever someone ventures up, conversation with Stoltz is obliterated by an astounding range of creaks and crashes.

JOHN BLACKFORD

"I've been in this business for the past 50 years. I started out working in a jewelry store in Cleveland, Ohio, then went to the Bowman Technical School and got my training right here as a watchmaker and clockmaker. Bowman's developed the concept of individual training and shortened the period of apprenticeship from 7 years down to a year and a half, and got just as good a training. I personally don't do much repair work at all anymore. We have two jewelers and three watchmakers. I'm overall coordinator and purchasing agent; I do appraising and estimating. It's been about 20 years since I did major repairs; minor repairs I'm still doing. I love it. It's a great business.

When you're working on a mechanical watch, you know from past experience why it won't work properly—it's much easier than an electronic watch. Basically, mechanical watches are pretty much the same—five wheels in an ordinary watch, and the parts are practically the same.

There is practically no wear at all in a well-made mechanical watch. It can last anywhere from 30 to 150 years. Good watches are fully jeweled. By jewels I mean bearings—everything that moves has a bearing around it. Barring falls and drops and so forth, there is no reason why, with periodic cleaning, a watch shouldn't run 100 to 150 years. There are watches 150 years old still running and keeping good time. And mechanical watches are developed to a point right now where they are almost completely shock-resistant. They will take a tremendous amount of beating.

The electronic watches are more of an unknown factor, but I can assure you that they won't run nearly as long. Dehydration of the display plates, dropping the plates and cracking them, all take their toll. If you drop a watch with a liquid crystal display, that will just about finish it off. And the liquid crystal display will fade over time. We've also found many of them with leaks between the sandwich material. There are a lot of bugs that have to be ironed out, and as a result, the digital is just not going to hold up as well as the mechanical. So at the top end of the spectrum of watches, you're actually getting less durability with the digital types.

Christie C. Tito

Melanie L. Parkhurst behind the counter at Ezra F. Bowman.

The watch of the future

The greatest work is now being done with what are called analog watches, which have conventional watch faces but electronic components inside, rather than the liquid crystal or the red glass numerical displays, both of which are passing by the way. The analog watch, I believe, is the watch of the future for the average individual. It is here to stay, definitely. The analogs are as reliable as the digitals, but they still can't be repaired by a small watch-repair shop because only the hands and the dial train move—otherwise its a small motor, what they call a step motor. That's the only mechanical function. All the rest is electronic, and extremely accurate. An analog uses quartz crystals to produce a very accurate signal.

From the manufacturing standpoint, the analog watch is cheaper to make than the mechanical. However, I would say that the moderately priced 17-jewel would outlast either the digital or the analog.

You can't argue against the electronic watch, because the price is there and the accuracy is there, but the longevity of that watch is an unknown factor. The buyer is taking a little bit of a risk, purchasing practicality and economy for a little bit less assurance in the long run.

We do come across a good many of them that are not repairable. In most cases, it doesn't pay to repair the digital, so the companies will put a complete new unit inside—a new watch in your old case. It's almost an interchangeable thing, and the replacement cost is quite moderate. But the average watchmaker is in no position to have test equipment for this. It's much harder for the average watchmaker to repair. The equipment that you'd need to service every watch would be fantastically expensive. And even then, it would not be a matter of repairing watches, you'd be replacing components. It's highly advisable to send them back to the factory or the importer for repair, unless it's minor work that's involved.

Since we can't do very much with electronic watches in repair, we do a lot of changing of batteries. We do have some of the equipment for timing, but it's very expensive, so few stores have even that. Practically all the instruments are in a state of development. What's new today would be obsolete tomorrow. I'm not saying that in the future prices of the service instruments won't reach a point that individual shops can afford them. But for the present, nearly all work on electronic watches is done by the manufacturer or importer.

Although there's been a considerable change in the repair field with the advent of the electronic watch, there's always enough work for a good watchmaker in fine mechanical watches. The attrition in the clock and watch field is great. The old-timers are dying off, so new people are needed. At one time, there were dozens of schools, but that's no longer the case. Bowman's is the largest of them all, with an enrollment that varies between 65 and 110.

Although the industry will eventually go to analog watches, there will always be a market for the mechanicals. The lesser companies are going by the way, but the fine companies are still commanding high prices for their watches. Some of the better ones are Patek Philippe, Vacheron & Constantin, and you could even include Omega in that field, or the moderately priced watches such as Piguet. Vacheron & Constantin and the better watch companies will always have a mechanical watch. Many of them are also starting to have their own electronic watches, but they continue their regular lines. Omega is making a fairly decent electronic watch, an analog. Concord makes an excellent one, too.

But, let's put it this way. You can buy an electronic watch for $29, accuracy within minutes a year. That's the answer. And it's simple because you can put an untrained person on making circuit boards and so forth, someone who doesn't have to have any background or mechanical knowledge.

You can buy a Timex for $14 and get two years, three years, four years of wear out of it. There are some electronic watches that are selling for $150, there are some of them selling for seven, eight, nine hundred, most of it in the quality of the case. But for somebody who wants a quality watch that's going to hold up for years and years, look for a mechanical watch in the $100-to-$200 range.”

Dear Sir:
I am very proud to have received a letter from you, concerning my Zippo light. I will be proud to tell you how it happened.

I have been using my Zippo lighter for the past five years, and this is the first time that I have sent one to you to be repaired in all that time. To begin with I am a farmer and at the time I damaged my lighter I was driving a tractor, and was trying to light a cigarette and I dropped it into a weedcutter behind the tractor. And I will remain an unsatisfied customer until I get a repair on my lighter.

TOOLS

9

In many regions of North America, the only obvious artifacts left of the native civilization are tools. Worked pieces of flint and chert and obsidian turn up in fields after spring plowing and emerge from the soil after heavy rains. These tools are beautiful, are collected even by small children because their purpose can be read easily in the simple design. Arrowheads look like missiles or birds. A stone for pounding grain fits in the hand so well that the hand is invited to pick it up, over and over again.

You won't find any stone implements in Garrett Wade's $3 catalog of woodworking tools, other than grinding stones, but like Indian artifacts, these tools of brass and steel and hardwoods ask to be picked up, hefted, put to work. A good hardware store, too, will display tools that beg to be owned and loved, if not necessarily used. Most of us have been liberated from the necessity of using tools. In the meantime, tools degenerated, as will a disused limb, into flabby "consumer-grade" products—much to the distress of serious woodworkers and carpenters.

You can still find three or more grades of most tools, hand and powered. If your hardware store doesn't stock them, try Garrett Wade (161 Avenue of the Americas, New York, NY 10013), U.S. General (100 Commercial Street, Plainview, NY 11803), or the Yellow Pages.

Unlike many other top-of-the-line consumer products, the better tools are so ruthlessly handsome and honest that a weekend tinkerer finds himself compelled to buy *more* durability than he needs. Don't overlook the broad midrange between rosewood-handled collectibles and hardware countertop specials.

WOODWORKING TOOLS

Perhaps the best advice I've ever had about buying tools was that of a kind-hearted retailer. He talked me out of buying a beautifully made specialty plane that I'd have been happy to take home. But I recall only one or two times in the past several years when I really could have used it. Because the retailer was also a producing craftsman, he had the good grace to dampen my enthusiasm.

Back then, I was making the transition from amateur to professional tradesman, so his words came at a good time. They distinguished tool collecting from tool use, elegance from practicality, and occasional convenience from cost-effectiveness. The chisel he sold me that day has repaid me well and has been a pleasure to use ever since.

My infatuation over tools is a common ailment. The other extreme, that of buying the tool just good enough to serve the present need, is probably more common. Both approaches overlook the best role that tools can play, as modest but thoroughly reliable friends, owned because of the job they'll do.

There is no separating the ability of the user from the tool. It is an unhappy fact that the many excellent products on the market generally outrun the skillfulness of their owners. Still, the wide availability of good tools invites us to develop the satisfying manual skills and thought processes that make for the best results.

When it comes to hand tools of simple construction, much can be told just by comparing appearances. These are large-volume products, made by many competing manufacturers. Because there are relatively few steps involved in their production, the only sure ways to reduce the price are to cut labor cost, eliminate steps, or use cheaper, often less adequate material. While the shortfalls in appearance may be the factor that puts you off initially, the qualities apt to disappoint you are invisible. Examples of this are the use of cast rather than forged metal in stress-bearing parts, and inadequate heat treatment.

Appearances are often deceiving, but they may be a good indicator of the thoroughness of the manufacturing process. In a subtle way, good appearance and clean design can also encourage the owner to care properly for tools.

In the case of specialty tools (cabinetmaker's tools are especially guilty), appearance is sometimes taken to absurd lengths. An old friend who is a furniture restorer remarked to me that this class of tool is "just too nice to use."

He submits that the right appearance is an acquired one, earned with the patina of sweat on the handle and the minor nicks and scratches of everyday use.

Christie C. Tito

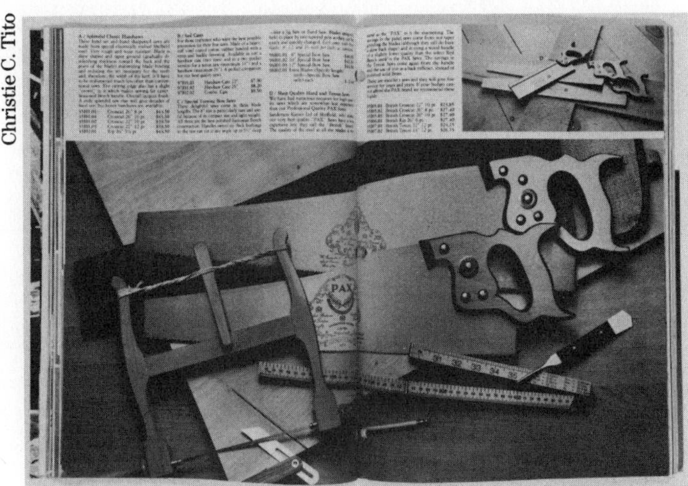

A sampling from Garrett Wade's sumptuous catalog.

Used tools

Naturally, looks count for little if you acquire your tools second-hand. The market is awash with excellent material at modest cost if you are willing to do a minimum of buffing and regrinding, or to replace an occasional handle. If you appreciate worth over looks and can exercise good patience and discretion in your choices, there is no more economic route, and you also may be the beneficiary of a bygone level of metallurgical care (Barton chisels, long off the market, are a good example) now prohibitively expensive because of today's high labor costs.

Tradesmen's estate auctions are a good source of quality merchandise if you are willing to pay a fair secondhand price. There is substance to the rumor that table saws and the like were built more heavily 25 years ago. With a judicious eye and a little research into the classic makes (the names Delta and Walker-Turner come to mind), real gems can occasionally be had for reasonable cost at auctions.

Garage sales are the cheapest recourse, all told, but the quality tends to be second-rate or worse. It's well to remember that poor-quality tools have always been with us, and that a handyman's castoffs tend toward that category. This is not to deny the excellent buys that have a way of cropping up among the thorns.

You might also contact a reputable antique-tool dealer. You should make it plain that you are a user rather than a collector. A dealer may be delighted to part company with the perfectly good but not-quite-antique tools he acquired in the same lot as the real collector's item he was after—and at a surprisingly fair price.

Unless you have a ready source of three-phase power and are dead certain you won't be moving soon, avoid really large equipment. There is an abundance of fine old industrial machinery (as well as a good deal needing major repair) on the market at deceptively low cost. In shopping around, consider the rigging costs involved in relocating the equipment, the unparalleled floor space such a monster will consume, and the high cost of conversion to single-phase. Be sure to ask yourself how much capacity you need. Finally, consider that the same complications you encounter setting up this class of equipment eventually will make resale difficult.

Since it is rare for any used tool to come with a guarantee, be thorough in your inspection. This applies especially to power tools, whose faults are least visible. Many lack important safety features incorporated into newer designs, and replacement parts and accessories may also prove unobtainable. By all means, insist on a test run played to a sharp ear, and manipulate all adjustments through their full range.

Grades of tools

Tools are deliberately offered in several durability grades, ranging from the shabbier discount varieties to lines carried by merchants who deal primarily with tradesmen. The former remind me of a child's toolkit panel saw I once got for Christmas; for a long time I was convinced that panel saws as a whole were worthless. If you are a rabid impulse buyer, ask yourself how much care the grocery or drugstore puts in the line of tools it carries.

Tool metallurgy

The type and grade of metals used in the construction of hand tools have an obvious relationship to durability. There are several key factors that affect tool life, discussed here.

Impact strength is the ability to withstand sudden shocks—they are usually much more destructive than gradual loads. This is a critical factor in the housing or main body of many tools. It is the measure of the tool's response to being struck or dropped. Tools with good impact strength are usually labeled "impact-resistant" or "shock-proof," though this term is sometimes stretched. Look for this label particularly where light die-castings, thin stampings, or plastic housings are involved.

Toughness can be defined as the capacity of a material to absorb repeated impacts (such as hammer blows) without fracturing. Toughness is related to ductility. A tough material will deform, rather than crack, under the energy of regular impacts, but the deformation is limited. As an example, the ideal toughness of the head of a cold chisel is a play-off between resistance to chipping and excessive deformation (seen as mushrooming of the head).

Toughness is directly related to metal-grain structure, which in turn is influenced by the presence of alloying elements. Like case hardening, toughness is ordinarily the result of carefully controlled heat treatment. The blades of good shovels, for example, are composed of a grain structure called bainite, a special phase of steel that combines maximum toughness with very high yield strength. This is expensive to produce because a high-alloy steel must first be fully hardened, then tempered in a slow and tightly controlled manner. The result is superb durability.

Yield strength is the ability of a material to return to original shape after being flexed or deformed. This quality is related to flexibility. Spring metal, by definition, has very high yield strength. Thin sections can be bent significantly before they reach their elastic limit; beyond this point, permanent bends occur. High yield strength is an important feature of flexible rules and putty-knife blades, to name some instances. In heavier sections, metals with high yield strength can withstand considerable bending pressures (torque) without damage.

Hot-forged, high-alloy steels have excellent yield strength and are used extensively for mechanic's wrenches, leverage tools, mason's chisels, and screwdriver blades. In the hot forging process, the stresses created by forging (which would make the metal harder but more fragile) are canceled out by maintaining the fresh forging at high temperature until it has recrystallized into a relaxed, fine-grained structure. Ideally, after the required machining is complete, a separate heat treatment is then given to certain parts for the appropriate case- or through-hardness. Finish grinding and plating are the last steps in the process.

The durability of a forged part depends more on the characteristics of the particular steel and its heat treatment than on the quality of the finish. Craftsman tools, marketed by Sears, serve as a good example here: the external appearance is not always good, but the material used justifies Sears' unqualified warranty. Snap-on produces forged wrenches which are virtually flawless in appearance, but this comes at a premium price.

1955 20-ounce Estwing hammer

T. L. Gettings

"Twenty-five years ago I began a summer job as a framing carpenter. At that time, I bought a 20-ounce Estwing straight-claw, metal-shank hammer. It was used vigorously on my summer jobs, all the way through high school, college, and part of medical school. It then joined my traveling tool kit until three years ago when I purchased a ranch. It has since stretched and stapled fence, chipped and pried and occasionally even served those purposes for which it was designed."

NORMAN J. SCHAFER, M.D.
Cottage Grove, Oregon

Ultimate strength can be loosely defined as the maximum shear, bending, or tensile load a part will bear before it breaks. Yield strength, a lower value than ultimate strength, is of primary importance with tools, since permanent damage begins at this point. In cast-metal parts (as in many, but certainly not all, molded plastics) there is often very little separation between yield and ultimate strengths. In other words, the part breaks shortly after it begins to bend.

Malleable and ductile (nodular) cast irons are exceptions to this rule. Parts cast from these high-strength alloys will be plainly labeled as a selling point. In ordinary cast iron (often called gray iron, because it machines to a grayish finish), the metal grain is interspersed with minute graphite flakes that look something like miniature cornflakes. "Close-grained" is a common term applied to iron castings in which particular care has been taken to keep the size of those flakes small, and to limit the physical size of the casting's metal grains. Both factors contribute to a stronger iron casting.

Even when the metal grain is fine and porosity and sand inclusions are at a minimum, ordinary gray cast iron has poorer ultimate strength than mild steel because the flakes act as natural starting points for cracks. But the same flakes are accountable for cast iron's excellent machining qualities. Its special flake structure and inherent mass also result in significant vibration dampening in stationary tools.

Low vibration not only makes a power tool safer to use; it also inhibits the loosening of screws that hold the tool together, and to some extent reduces wear and fatigue on the moving parts.

In fairness, though, light zinc and aluminum-alloy castings can be used very effectively to quiet vibration. Very close ribs and a material whose natural resonance is directly opposed to the cutter vibration are combined to obtain this effect. The Inca 10¼-inch jointer/thickness planer is the best example of this I've seen. At less than 80 pounds, it is as quiet as many 800-pound cast-iron monsters. Mounting your stationary tools onto the floor through rubber or urethane pads (isolation mounts) will also help in many cases.

Ordinary cast iron has good strength for most purposes when the sectional thickness is adequate (0.25 inch or better). Malleable and ductile cast irons have excellent strength, by contrast, because the free graphite is converted into small spheres within the iron, either by special inoculation or heat treatment after casting. These treated irons are the material of choice for C-clamps and other stress-bearing cast parts. Ordinary gray iron is best by far for stationary tool working surfaces, trunnion brackets, and bearing and spindle housings. In recent years, some stationary tools have been produced using stiff aluminum castings capped with stainless-steel wear surfaces. This is also a very good combination, especially in damp environments.

Aluminum (with a little silicon), zinc-aluminum alloys, bronzes, and magnesium can also be cast very well into elaborate forms of reasonable strength, given adequate thickness. Because they melt at fairly low temperatures, they are usually cast against either plaster-investment or permanent steel molds. The result is a lower factor of contamination and a smoother finish than with sand casting. You can easily see this difference in finish.

Resistance to wear can be accomplished by selecting intrinsically hard materials, or by further enhancing hardness by case- or through-hardening.

Case-hardened steel tools usually have a hardness of Rockwell C-scale 60 to 65 (R_c 60 to 65)* in their outer skin, to a depth of 0.03 to 0.06 inch. A softer core provides greater toughness and impact resistance. Some nonferrous metals, like nickel, cadmium, and chrome, are inherently wear resistant; others have certain alloys that can be hardened either by heat treatment or aging. Practically none

*There are actually several Rockwell hardness scales, corresponding to different ranges of hardness and methods of testing. The most common is the Rockwell C-scale (R_c), applied mainly to steels and carbide materials. An R_c 25 measurement would indicate a very mild steel, while R_c 68 is about the practical maximum that can be obtained from high-alloy tool steel. This maximum might be appropriate for the surface of a file, for instance. The Brinell hardness scale and the Rockwell B-scale are the usual measures for softer materials like cast iron, brass, or aluminum. The wider range of these scales makes finer distinctions possible among soft metals.

One carpenter's tool hall of fame

"I am a carpenter. My occupation requires that I own a couple thousand dollars worth of tools that must, of necessity, be of factory make. I must say that if I had the money, I would buy the fine handmade planes and chisels and such that are made on a cottage-industry scale in the United States, England, Japan, and elsewhere; but if I had that kind of money, I wouldn't be busting ass five and six days a week. It's a sad and worn cliché by now, but American factory-made goods have declined drastically in quality, so much that when I walk into the hardware store for a tool, most times I am so disgusted with what I see that I usually walk out empty-handed. I don't blame factory workers—I know that they simply can't produce quality goods when they are forced to produce more and more in a shorter time. It is factory owners who are responsible, as I see it, for they have ultimate control over quality.

"My ire is directed primarily toward the hand- and power-tool companies, which of late have directed their marketing to the home-owner-hobbyist—the same person who expects toasters, TVs, and station wagons to give up after shorter and shorter life spans. Last month, I heard the statistic that these people buy two-thirds of hand power tools sold. Quality has deteriorated incredibly in the last 20 years, still worse in the last 5.

"Nevertheless, I have come across tools worthy of placing in the factory-goods hall of fame. Some are not made at all anymore, to my knowledge, and some, alas, aren't made like they used to be.

"Here's my list of durable tools:

- *Stiletto* carpenter's hammers. I have one that must be 80 years old, which was my grandpa's, and another that I found gathering dust in an old hardware store. Nothing like 'em.
- *Stanley* planes and chisels. Only the old ones are worth owning. They can be found in flea markets, older than your mother and in better shape.
- *Disston* saws. The old ones are of better steel. I have one of my grandpa's.

Bob Stahl with his Bosch variable-speed jigsaw.

- *Klein* tools. Tools for linemen and electricians, they're high quality, constantly improved upon. Great pliers.
- *General* tools. A good line of carpenter's tools.
- *Indestro.* The best wrenches and sockets; no one else comes close.
- *Bosch.* Their best product is a hand jig-saw with variable speed and varying degrees of reciprocation (for wood, plastic, or metal). Light, runs like a sewing machine, well and thoughtfully crafted. I've had one for years and expect it to last my lifetime.
- *Milwaukee.* Best drills.
- *Dietzgen.* The drafting tools I have were made to last. Some must be 60 years old.
- *Wetzler.* Their clamps are of amazing quality and sturdiness.

"At least one-third of my tools are from the local flea market. I don't have the satisfaction (transitory at best) of being the original owner, but can pick and choose the best of the oldies, inspecting each carefully without being foiled by a plastic blister card or brightly colored advertising hype."

BOB STAHL
Point Reyes Station, California

of these is comparable to a hardened steel surface. Certain metallic oxides, borides, nitrides, and carbides exceed hardened steel, but their uses are mainly confined to grinding wheels and special cutting tips.

Edge-holding quality is simply a tool's ability to hold a keen cutting edge under normal working conditions. Most metals will take a keen edge initially, but only a few alloys hold that edge well. High-carbon steel, for instance, traps carbon molecules in its crystal structure when it is heated to high temperature then quenched suddenly in a cooler medium. This hardened steel is called martensite. Small quantities of other metals, like chromium, vanadium, and molybdenum, as well as some nonmetallic ingredients, may be added to carbon steel to give the martensite good wear and corrosion resistance. Martensitic steel is a stiff, brittle structure that is highly resistant to deformation.

Anyone who has snapped a file will realize that maximum hardness also means brittleness. Usually, hardened steels are mildly reheated (tempered) to relieve the stresses introduced by quenching, sacrificing some edge-holding quality in exchange for higher ultimate strength. Chisels used for wood are tempered for shorter periods and at lower temperatures than those meant for brick (a brick chisel might have an edge hardness of R_c 50 to 55). So while the edge-holding quality of wood chisels is better, the edges themselves are easier to chip. A wider bevel angle on a blade will also reduce the chance of serious chipping.

Edge tools require hollow grinding from time to time, and thus a hardened case would quickly be passed through. Consequently, good chisels are through-hardened over the working length of their blades for maximum service life. Overheating during grinding can soften local areas of the cutting edge by further tempering the martensitic grain. Because of this, frequent cooling in water or oil is advisable during grinding.

If you should ever attempt to harden steel on your own (the procedure is not so difficult), be sure to select a steel with a carbon content of 0.60 to 0.80 percent. Mild steels, like 1018 (0.18 percent) or 1020 (0.20 percent) have far too little carbon to produce a martensitic structure. If the carbon content is over 1 percent, the excess carbon will form iron carbide (Fe_3C), which makes the result exceedingly brittle.

Tungsten carbide is commonly used as a blade-tip material on wood-, plastic-, and metal-cutting tools where edge hardnesses of R_c 70+ are desirable. Since most carbides are very brittle in any thickness, the tips are made by powder-metal process. This involves compacting a mixture of powdered tungsten, tantalum, or titanium carbide with cobalt powder or another binding material or relatively low melting temperature. The combination is then recompacted (sintered) at higher pressure with heat applied, melting the binding element, which acts as a cement for the carbide crystals. By this means, a combination of maximum hardness and reasonable impact strength is obtained.

Carbide tips are brazed or silver-soldered into supporting notches cut into a tempered-steel bit or blade. Either technique of attachment is acceptable if performed properly. A higher-priced carbide tool usually received more attention in this quarter, as well as better finish grinding and inspection.

Carbide tools are important if you deal extensively with abrasive materials, and an 8- to 12-point carbide saw blade is an asset if you intend to do remodeling work, where you are liable to hit concealed nails. But the more economic method for most uses is to learn to sharpen hardened-steel blades correctly. Carbide tips require grinding on special wheels not ordinarily found in home workshops. Also, poor carbide blades are dangerous because of the potential of the tip to take flight.

Corrosion resistance may or may not be important, depending on the conditions of use. Steels intended for indoor use are often just spray-lacquered or lightly oiled after manufacture. Wider-range applications call for nickel or chrome plating, or the use of stainless steel. While aluminum is a highly reactive metal, it is quite acceptable in exposed parts because it develops an oxide film that protects the metal from further corrosion. Under extreme conditions, some pitting may be the result. Certain alloys, both ferrous and nonferrous, also have a greater inherent corrosion resistance.

Cast metal parts (especially sand- or plaster-investment castings, which are allowed to cool slowly) are in general more corrosion resistant than forged or stamped parts, because the metal finds its own equilibrium as it crystallizes. Most forgings are also calm because they have been stress relieved. If steel is either cold forged or cold rolled, though, the stress within the metal will encourage the object to corrode. Welded joints trap stresses also, because the weld cools so quickly. For this reason, the joint corrodes rapidly compared to the unaffected areas away from the joint. Thus, paint is a must on welded steel joints. Nonferrous welds and brazes are less severely affected.

Several thin layers of paint or lacquer are, of course, a perfectly good means of controlling corrosion on nonmachined surfaces. You can do wonders by applying a thin layer of machine oil on occasion.

Note that used tools with excellent basic durability are often comdemned or overlooked at auctions because of mild surface corrosion, which often can be corrected with a little naval jelly, a fine wire brush, and a buffing wheel.

Structural plastics

Probably no related subject arouses as much bias and confusion as the use of plastics on tools. Part of the difficulty is that there are so many plastics, with wildly different qualities. Another part is the rejection of plastic on aesthetic grounds. This perception is a conditioned one that is becoming less and less valid from a practical standpoint.

In the broadest terms, plastics offer these potential advantages:

- Good overall moisture resistance. (Contrary to popular opinion, some plastics will absorb significant amounts of moisture, swelling in the process; nylon is one offender.)
- Complete resistance to oxidation, as well as resistance to chemicals.
- Perfect electrical insulation.
- Excellent molding properties.
- High potential strengths and impact resistance, especially when reinforced with glass or carbon fiber. (Carbon fiber has become affordable for common use recently and will as much as triple the strength of many plastics.)
- Good flexibility and fatigue resistance where needed (as with cords).
- Reasonable resistance to heat, with certain materials.

Because most manufacturers fail to advertise the plastics used for their tool components (except where the choice is especially rugged), you can only look for prominent words in the catalog description that specify high strength or impact resistance. Even if the plastics used are identified, it may take a specialist to distinguish whether the choice was a good one. But like any other quality material, a good plastic will add something to the price of the tool. If you are inclined to buy tools at a price that doesn't allow for good manufacture, you will get what naturally follows.

Handles and adjustment knobs

Though wood is hardly the most durable material for handles, its excellent feel and shock-absorbing quality makes it a good choice for many hand tools. Hard maple, walnut, rosewood, boxwood, and beech are satisfactory for the handles of planes, screwdrivers, files, and a variety of knives and scrapers. Solid birch plywood, or any dense hardwood reinforced with a dowel passing at right angles through its short grain, is also adequate for saw handles. Boxwood and white ash have long been preferred as handle materials for wood chisels because of their superior toughness. Ash chisel handles should have their ends hooped with steel rings if any significant pounding is intended. A beech, maple, or lignum vitae mallet is the proper instrument for striking a wooden-handled chisel. Hickory is the wood of choice for hammer handles, though it is no match in strength for tubular steel, fiberglass, or integrally forged steel. Similarly, fiberglass handles are far more durable than hickory for the handles of axes, sledgehammers, or splitting mauls, though they are considerably more expensive.

In recent years, plastic handles with excellent impact resistance largely have replaced those of wood. Some have steel pounding inserts in their ends. This is actually a redundancy because of the quality of the synthetics, which will take fierce pounding with an ordinary hammer without significant damage. Some chisels have heavy tangs with an integral cone-shaped ferrule to accept the handle. This is an excellent design.

Heat- and impact-resistant plastics are the material of choice for power-tool handles because they can be readily molded to very comfortable contours, they insulate perfectly, and they will accept most abuse without ill effect.

The same class of synthetics is often the best choice for large adjustment knobs, when tapped steel sleeves (barbed on their outside) are inserted to bear the stresses of tightening. In this way, a larger, more workable knob can be made from a good synthetic than an equal weight of metal. Handwheels on stationary tools are another story; the classic cast-iron versions are still best, though a few good synthetic examples may be found. However, weight is no limitation in this special case.

Thumbscrews and wing nuts of cast bronze, plated iron, or cast zinc are far superior to stamped metal versions and are usually more durable than the best plastic equivalents. Threaded wood adjustments and thumbscrews should be avoided at all cost because of their low strength and their habit of swelling tight with changes in humidity.

Fasteners

Fine-threaded steel machine screws of moderate hardness (R_c 30 to 45) are the long-time best choice for tool assembly. They should be set into secure metal inserts if used on plastic housing parts, or passed through both mating pieces and fixed with a lockwasher and nut, or self-locking nut. Sometimes good tools are assembled with soft machine screws made deliberately long so they will stretch slightly when they are torqued down. A self-locking preload is the outcome. Although it is widespread practice to fasten plastic parts to one another with self-tapping screws, this method sets up stresses in the plastic that invite breakage.

In static constructions, steel or brass rivets are acceptable if they are peined over well and are snug in their clearance holes. Generally speaking, the more rivets and the larger their diameter, the better the resulting impact resistance. Hardened pins fixed with C-retainers (external retaining rings) are a good bet if occasional disassembly is desirable, or if the pin acts as a pivot for a moving part. A stiff spring washer beneath the retainer eliminates slop between the parts (as in tin snips or scissors). Various kinds of self-locking nuts will also do this job well. Compounds like Locktite or epoxy may also be applied to fix the fastener almost permanently. A panel saw should have the best possible fastening system because its handle goes through repeated screw-loosening motions.

It is a long-established point that good fastenings can do their best work only when accompanied by close-tolerance machining. Some stamped-metal or molded-plastic parts lack that precision.

Adjusting mechanisms and scales

On light power tools, adjusting mechanisms—angular adjustments, for instance—are often constructed of light stamped steel of the cheapest variety and lack both precision and rigidity. The accompanying scales are commonly inaccurate and provide no means of truing. Shocks to the sole of the tool will pass directly through these adjustments, so they are especially susceptible to damage. Heavier die-cast constructions, well-supported by the main housing and firmly attached to the sole, are the better choice. Depth adjustments that run within machined dovetail housings are strongest and most accurate. The best in this category have a steel plate bearing against the inside of the dovetail. In this arrangement, the machine screw that the knob engages will be seated permanently in the steel plate. A larger clamping surface will improve the hold of the adjustment. Tightening stresses will also be distributed more safely over larger clamping surfaces.

Many inexpensive table saws rely upon light threaded rod, running through a pivoting captive nut, to produce angular and height adjustments. This is a poor substitute for the greater strength and accuracy of worm gear adjustments found on all good models. The same saws substitute common light hinges of stamped steel for heavier steel pivots housed in cast iron or heavy cast zinc. In an equal vein, the trunnions (angle adjustments) on these saws are often made of a very light cast zinc without the benefit of any machining, as contrasted to the large, precisely machined iron brackets on the better models. In certain cases, the trunnion mechanism is dispensed with entirely, replaced by another flimsy common hinge. The results are predictable in terms of vibration, accuracy, and life expectancy.

Scales are best when deeply engraved. They should be heavily plated if there is any chance of corrosion and should have notches filled with contrasting lacquer for visibility. Ordinary steel carpenter's squares, for example, become very difficult to use after a short time because they lack adequate plating. The recent stainless-steel-and-aluminum versions are designed to cancel that shortcoming. They are preferable to plated models because plating will peel off if the tool is repeatedly flexed. Similarly, all good tape rules are coated with mylar or epoxy to prevent wear and corrosion on their surfaces. Some try squares are still treated with gun-bluing or black penetrant as a corrosion inhibitor, though this method has its limitations where conditions of use are adverse.

Many good power tools have their scales cast directly into the adjustment parts. If the casting is accurate, this is a good arrangement. Separate scales, lithographed or engraved onto light steel or aluminum then riveted onto the tool, are proper on stationary tools since they can be located very accurately during assembly. They are not as welcome on light power tools, which generally receive rougher treatment. Decal scales and labels are poor practice on any tool.

Soles, fences, and weight-bearing parts

Choice of material and sectional thickness are important here. Thin stampings may be corrugated to have acceptable strength, but a heavier stamping is almost always preferable. Light flanges along the edges will stiffen a sole and help prevent marring of the work. Plastic surfaces are good in the latter respect but are rarely a match for metal in terms of either wear resistance or impact strength, two important considerations. Clear plastic bases, like those on some routers, may be promoted on the basis of better working visibility, but most scratch—or even groove—so readily that this apparent advantage is quickly lost.

Any wooden surface that bears weight or receives direct wear should be of very dense hardwood and, better still, have metal inlay to accept the punishment. Good wooden marking gauges are equipped in this manner.

Fences on portable or stationary tools should be of heavy stamped steel or rigid cast metal. A few good stationary tools provide fences of extruded aluminum or magnesium, which are very resistant to warpage if corrugated and kinder to blades than steel or iron if accidentally nicked. Fences with replaceable hardwood faces protect both the blade and the work while providing an easy means of correction for wear.

Chucks

All good drills and braces use taper-adjusting chucks rather than the spring-loaded type found on the poorest examples. The bevel gearing on the chuck key and chuck should be as large as possible and properly case-hardened. It is not uncommon for inexpensive drills to be provided with 3/8- or 1/2-inch-capacity chucks, while the motor amperages are insufficient to support the resulting loads. This invites an early demise for the drill.

You can easily and permanently damage a chuck by carelessly tightening a bit off center or chucking an out-of-round bit. For safety, any drill with a ½-inch chuck should be provided with a side handle for added control.

Cutting bits and blades

Metallurgy is everything in this department. The alloying elements and the best heat treatment really make a difference.

Drill bits, for example, are commonly offered in two grades: high-carbon steel and high-speed steel. High-carbon steel is fine for soft materials, but it rapidly softens if used on metal, from the heat of contact. High-speed steels are made from specialty-tool steel, which will hold up to heat very well. Both sharpen well and hold their edges acceptably when used on unhardened metal. Similarly, brad-point or Forstner bits are very handy on woods of moderate density but are improper for hard materials. The life of cutting bits can be directly affected by how well they are resharpened. A little metal removed at just the right angle will usually do the job best.

Saw blade life depends not only on good material but also on proper sharpening and resetting. Good metal can almost always be revived in spite of abuse, though.

Bearings

Several distinct types of bearings are used on light power tools. Sticker price is directly related to the bearings' durability and accuracy. Here is a scale from worst to best.

Ferrous sleeve bearings are nothing more than a block of steel or iron, drilled and reamed to accept a shaft. Iron has a high coefficient of friction, so this arrangement is good only if the shaft is made of a slippery material like bronze (which is most unusual). A means of greasing the contact surfaces is a must, and proper use is confined to low RPM.

Plain journal bearings involve an inserted sleeve (sometimes split and provided with an oiling groove) made of a slippery metal like babbitt or bronze. The sleeve supports a steel shaft. This is fine for relatively low speeds with good lubrication. Plain bearings may score over time or seize if overheated.

Oilite bronze bearings are of powder-metal-formed bronze, with pores saturated with oil. Sometimes these are provided with oil-retaining seals, but not often. This type is very common and represents a moderate improvement over the plain journal bearing at speeds up to 2,000 RPM. Though often subjected to speeds up to 5,000 RPM in light tools, they will rapidly deteriorate with continuous use at these speeds. The user's clues to malfunction—smoke and an evil odor—generally come after the damage gains a foothold. If use will be intermittent and brief and you are obliged to buy a less expensive tool, then this bearing type is quite acceptable. Self-aligning types will help compensate for misalignment or housing distortion.

Even commercial grades of *plain ball bearings (radial contact)* can withstand high operating speeds. Precision grades are used if maximum tool accuracy and quietness are needed. Most ball bearings used today have their races permanently sealed to keep the grease in and the dust out. A good ball bearing will be packed with a premium grease for best service life. A good motor design will dissipate armature heat before it affects the bearings. Top-quality motors call for ball bearings whose parts have a superior micro-finish for quietest and tightest operation. "Sealed and permanently lubricated ball and roller bearings throughout" is a label convention that says something very important about drive-train durability.

Plain roller bearings are interchangeable with radial ball bearings in some power-tool applications. They're best for somewhat lower speeds and in situations that require the highest accuracy. Plain roller bearings are less tolerant of heat than ball bearings.

Angular-contact ball bearings find use in those situations where lengthwise (axial) thrust is anticipated or great stiffness is desired. Good drill-press spindles are provided with double-row angular-contact bearings to guarantee maximum precision.

Tapered roller bearings give the ultimate stiffness and strength for stationary equipment. They're as expensive as they are durable.

Lubrication

While permanently lubricated components are best, maintenance-free service is not always practicable (as with saber-saw plungers). If a grease fitting or oil hole is provided, by all means, honor its presence. An occasional film of oil or silicone spray is also essential on any ferrous parts that slide against each other.

Armature shafts, windings, and brushes

Armature brushes should be readily accessible for ease of inspection and replacement. The best type is self-limiting when the brush wears too short, avoiding possible shorts through the brush clip or wire.

A good motor will have a high-volume fan, solidly fixed on the armature shaft. Poor grades use plastic fans press-fitted onto the shaft; better models use a key or toothing for a positive grip.

Occasionally, circular saws and other high-risk tools are equipped with friction brakes to arrest blade movement immediately. Unless perfectly balanced, these are hard on both armature and bearings. Frictionless electric brakes overcome this problem, but expense limits their use to industrial machine tools.

You have an influence on tool manufacture

Some manufacturers are guilty of producing substandard products, but consumers are often coconspirators in that they ignore the essential relationship between durability and price.

Comparing the costs of the quality grades offered by the industry, it's quickly apparent that many best buys fall in the middle range. The economies of high-volume production are partly responsible, and market competition also plays a role in keeping prices down. These tools cost about twice as much as the lower consumer grade and half as much as professional grade.

Manufacturers of middle-range tools go to considerable lengths to outdo each other with safety features and convenient design. But since the target retail price of these power tools has been held fairly well in check, you well may wonder what was sacrificed to provide that additional fail-safe switch or quick-disconnect cord.

By contrast, professional-grade tools aren't as apt to adopt special features, emphasizing instead good structure, mechanical quality, and simplicity. Not everyone needs professional-quality tools, of course. Brief use and light applications produce very little heat in lower-amperage motor and drive train. But the weaker motor will lag when the load on the tool becomes too great (hardwood and metal are the usual villains). A portion of the incoming current then is converted to heat within the motor housing rather than doing the work of rotation, with predictable ill effects on bearings, brushes, and motor windings.

When do you need a professional-grade tool?

Professional- or industrial-grade tools are built, more and less successfully, to serve the needs of the tradesman. The emphasis is on the capacity and durability of the tool. Usually this means heavier structure, plus better motors and fans and bearings. The resulting tool may be much heavier, but this needn't be.

Most professional tools are capable of doing a full day's work without overheating. Accessories are usually of the same good quality as the tool itself, as is often not the case with less expensive models.

Professional tools suffer every test possible on the job, and professionals more often than not have strong opinions, which they are willing to share for the asking. This is a source of good entertainment as well as information.

Particular lines are repeatedly recommended—Milwaukee, S-K, Draftsman Industrial, Stanley Professional, Ridgid, Snap-on, Williams, Crescent, Estwing, and Starrett, to mention a few. What distinguishes these makers is the near absence of any substandard designs in their offerings, in some instances combined with a no-questions-asked warranty.

Professional tools are appropriate if you use them heavily or if you are a serious amateur and appreciate tools that work very well.

Christie C. Tito

A consumer-grade drill, right, and one of professional quality.

Home foundrywork: how to create your own metal castings

There are a few craftsmen who enjoy doing the whole job when they construct something, right down to the raw materials. A common instinct is shared by the cabinetmaker who makes his own hardware, the gunsmith who bores and rifles his own barrels, and the home builder who logs his own lumber.

Home foundrywork involves the same spirit. Here the object is to create a metal casting. This fundamental form may become the main structural element of a hand tool, an essential replacement part or accessory for a revivable piece of machinery—or pure art, if that's your desire. There is a reasonably simple set of techniques that make home metal casting feasible and affordable for the determined individual.

Metals are cast in a molten state into molds of heat-resisting materials. Sand and plaster mixtures are the most accessible and workable mold materials. Gas-fired furnaces of very simple design can be used to melt the required metal. These work very well for metal alloys with low to moderate melting points, like aluminum, leaded red brass, and phosphor bronze. Pellets or small ingots of these common alloys are readily available from raw-material distributors at reasonable cost.

A cast-bronze plane with the two cherrywood patterns used to make the molds for body and throatpiece. This is a unique tool, cast from scratch because it's not to be found in the marketplace.

A home foundry set

A home foundry can be set up quite inexpensively. A basic set sold by Pyramid Products (3736 South Seventh Avenue, Phoenix, AZ 85041) includes a furnace with lid, electric blower, crucible tongs, molding sand, silicon-carbide crucible, and instruction booklet. A set with a three-pound metal capacity goes for $155 plus shipping.

A metal casting is really a raw form awaiting completion. Even in the case of an art casting, a certain amount of cleanup and surface finishing is required. A tool or machine casting will, in addition, need to have some of its surfaces machined to serve its purpose. Light tool elements, cast from readily machineable materials like aluminum or red brass, often can be finished using nothing more exotic than a drill press and disk sander, fitted with a cloth-backed abrasive disk for metal finishing. Hand-plane bodies, for instance, can be completed with no more equipment than this.

If more complicated or precise machining will be called for to make your casting useful, the best recourse is to enroll in an evening machine-shop class. Should your time be too limited or your metalworking skills too basic for this, you might contact the nearest vocational school to see if they will do the work for you, as a training exercise for their more promising students; you'll need to prepare a clear, specific sketch of your requirements. If a large casting exceeds the capacity of vocational-school equipment, a commercial machine shop is the only alternative. This argues for keeping machining to the practical minimum. It is wise to talk in advance with the shop and to keep your design as straightforward as possible.

PAUL SUWIJN

A GUIDE TO GARDEN HAND TOOLS

Broadly speaking, the worth of a tool can be gauged by finding the answers to three questions: Who made it? What is it made of? How is it put together?

Whenever possible, buy recognized, name-brand tools from an established dealer or manufacturer in your own locality. Manufacturers and dealers who have been in business for any length of time have reputations to protect, and the buyer can expect greater satisfaction from concerns that back their products. Returning a tool directly to a retail store is much less trouble than having to ship back an unsatisfactory item with a letter. Complaining isn't much fun, but unless the manufacturer hears specifically what is wrong, it won't be able to be corrected.

Retail stores should have plenty of product literature on hand. This material isn't usually lying about on the counter, so the clerk will have to pop upstairs to the office to find it. Take advantage of this chance. High prices are inescapable, but investigating the differences between a good tool and a poor one can result in a sound investment instead of a disappointing purchase.

What is it made of?

Tool blades are commonly made of steel, stainless steel having the greatest resistance to rust, and the higher price. The better tools are made of so-called special-analysis steel, usually heat treated

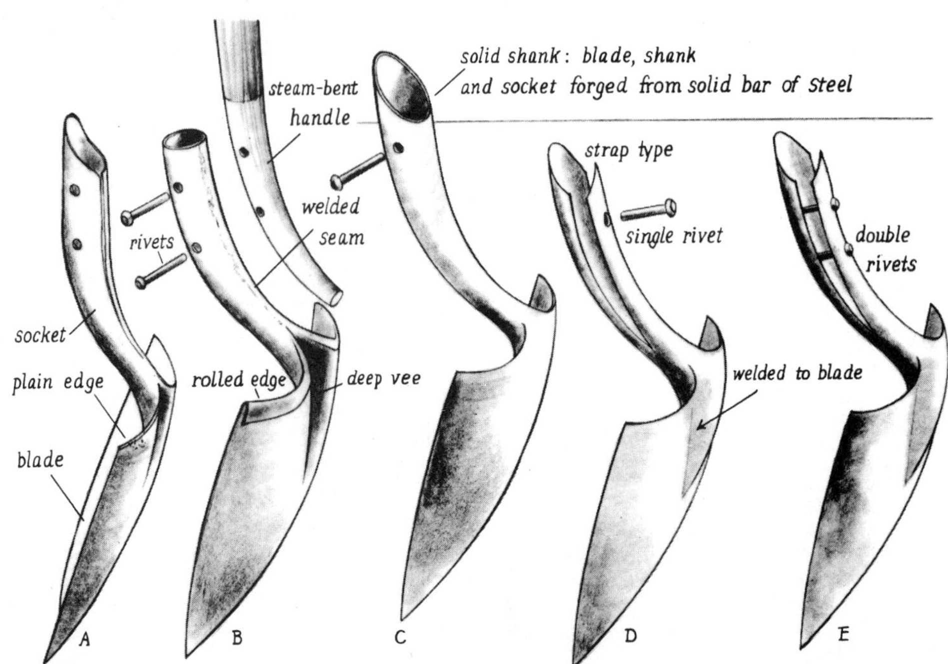

Five types of shovel construction: (A) Plain edge, shallow V-back with socket rolled from sheet steel; (B) similar but with deeper V, welded socket seam, and rolled-edge foot pads; (C) the so-called solid-shank version—blade, shank, and socket all forged from a solid bar of steel; (D) strap type; (E) strap type with double rivets.

The solid-shank model (C) is the strongest, and the most expensive. All have steam-bent wooden handles and most are fastened with just one rivet, although two would be better if spaced far enough apart. All these shovels are strong enough if properly used. Don't use a shovel as a crowbar—something will give, probably the handle just where it enters the socket.

for extra strength. Manufacturers who employ good production techniques generally advertise the fact by die stamping their tools with one or the other of these designations: forged steel, taper-forged, tempered steel, drop-forged, heat treated. These are specific and visible indicators that can be checked. At one time, the legend "Sheffield Steel" referred to a particularly fine alloy and as such was a sure sign of quality. It is well to remember, however, that Sheffield—a town in the heart of England's industrial Midlands—is home to more than a few toolmakers; stamping "Sheffield, England" or even "Sheffield Steel" on a tool is not necessarily a mark of superior metal any more than the legend "Pittsburgh Steel" would be.

Aside from those of the blade, a variety of materials are used in tool manufacture. Some handles are made of steel, while others are constructed of tubular aluminum—rustproof but with little elasticity. Plastics are being used more and more. A number of tools are assembled as a single unit—blade, handle, and grip all made from one piece—and there are tools welded or riveted together. Small hand tools of this type stand up well, as they are subjected to less leverage stress than the long-handled kind.

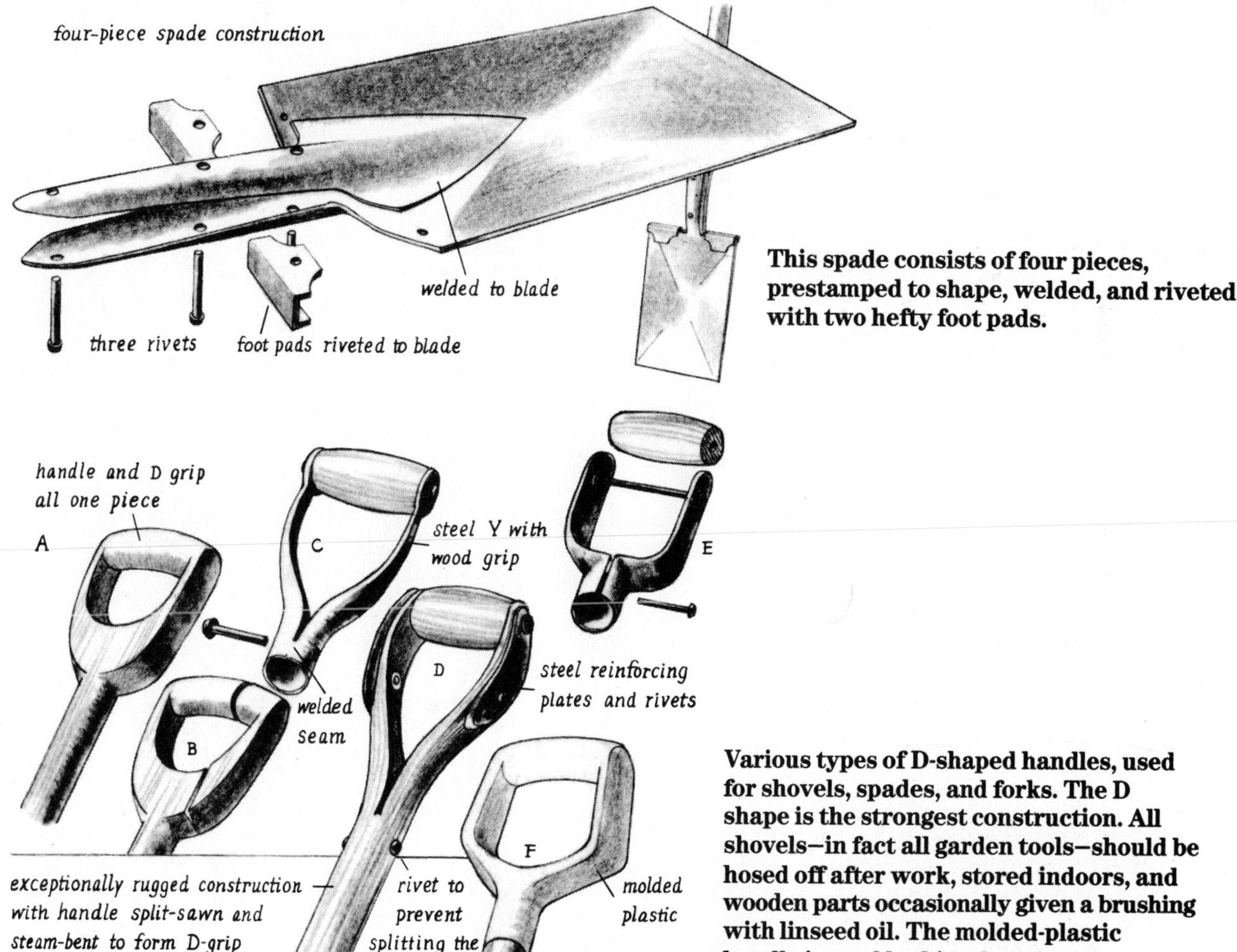

This spade consists of four pieces, prestamped to shape, welded, and riveted, with two hefty foot pads.

Various types of D-shaped handles, used for shovels, spades, and forks. The D shape is the strongest construction. All shovels—in fact all garden tools—should be hosed off after work, stored indoors, and wooden parts occasionally given a brushing with linseed oil. The molded-plastic handle is good looking, but there is no visible means of attachment.

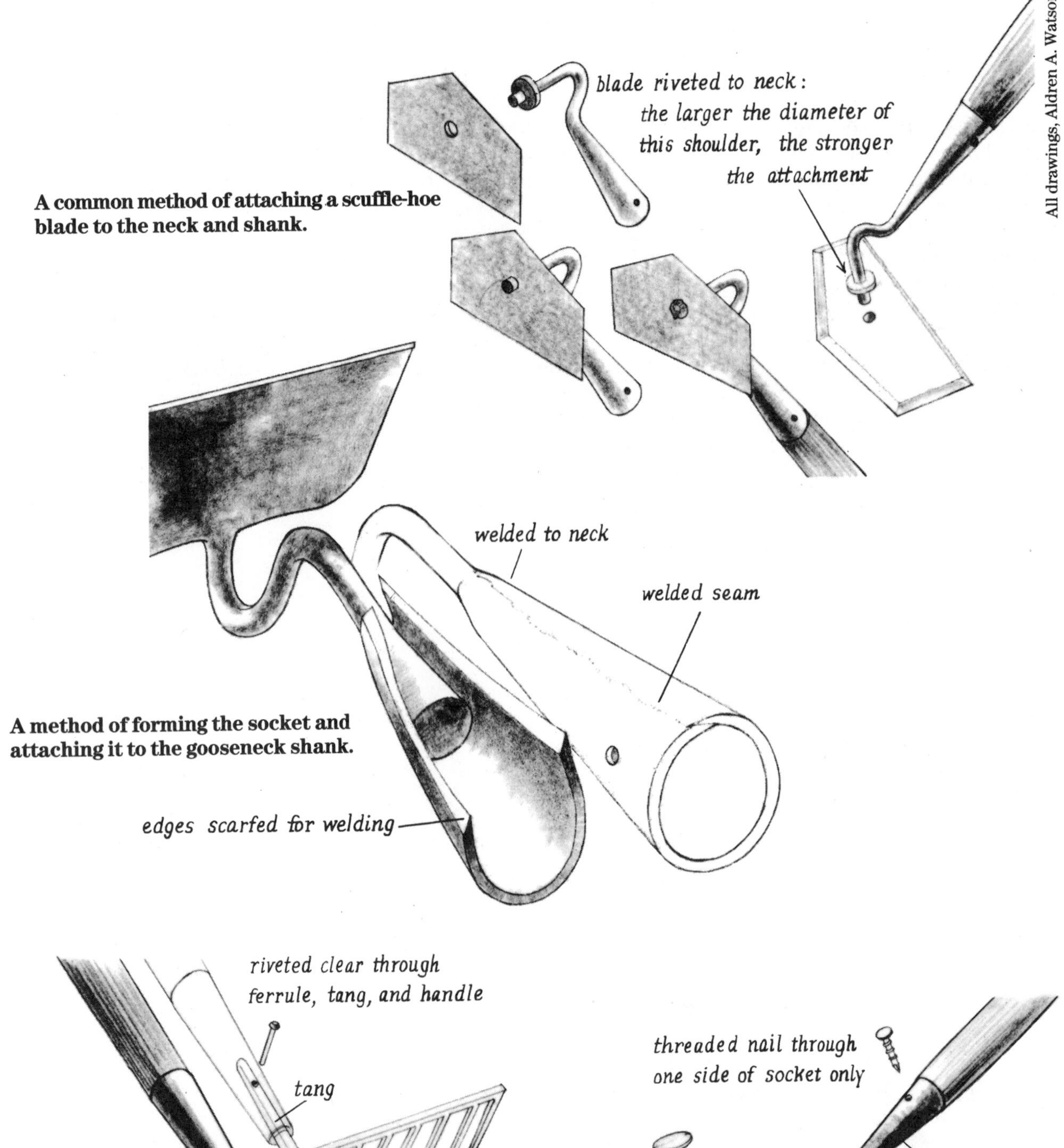

All drawings, Aldren A. Watson

A common method of attaching a scuffle-hoe blade to the neck and shank.

A method of forming the socket and attaching it to the gooseneck shank.

The well-made iron rake should have a forged head and a good long tang with a hole through which the rivet goes to unite head, ferrule, and handle.

A brand-new tool made this way looks very solid but will probably work loose. A clear-through rivet is much stronger than even a threaded nail.

With tools such as shovels, spades, rakes, and hoes, all-steel construction in itself is not a guarantee of durability. Back your car over a tubular-steel scuffle hoe and you will abruptly end its working days. Yet a white-ash handle abused in the same way will, nine times out of ten, bend dangerously and then spring back to shape. The inherent elasticity of wood allows it to give enormously before breaking.

Pound for pound, wood is still one of the toughest, least expensive, and most easily fabricated materials. White ash and hickory have long been the favored species—highly resistant to shock and weathering and renowned for flexibility and long wear. In general, the texture of wood provides a more comfortable and less slippery grip, and therefore, more precise hand control.

Beware of painted wood, for no matter how attractive the color, paint is often an inexpensive way to disguise inferior wood. Catalogs may use terms like "strong hardwood," or "American hardwood," and although it is true that ash and hickory are classified as hardwoods, the term is also technically correct for other species that are totally unsuitable for tool handles.

How is it put together?

Workmanship—the quality imparted to a thing in the making and so hard to describe—is a fine point in detection. The durability of a tool depends not only on quality materials, but also on how well they fit together and how securely they are fastened. Nails, screws, bolts, washers, rivets, special adhesives, and the welding process are variously used to join wood to wood, wood to metal, metal to metal, and, more frequently today, plastic to wood or metal. Each fastener has its own characteristics and its own failure point, which means that they are by no means interchangeable. A small brad is sufficient to secure the cross brace in the frame of a wheel cultivator, but it would be poor engineering to use the same brad to attach a shovel shank to the handle. Fortunately, all these fasteners are unmistakably visible and distinguishable. Look for them and learn to recognize each one's suitability for the application. Some tools are assembled simply with a tight push-fit and a bit of epoxy or a short metal ferrule without rivets. This kind of construction arouses the suspicion that the manufacturer may have gone too far down the road toward economy.

ALDREN A. WATSON

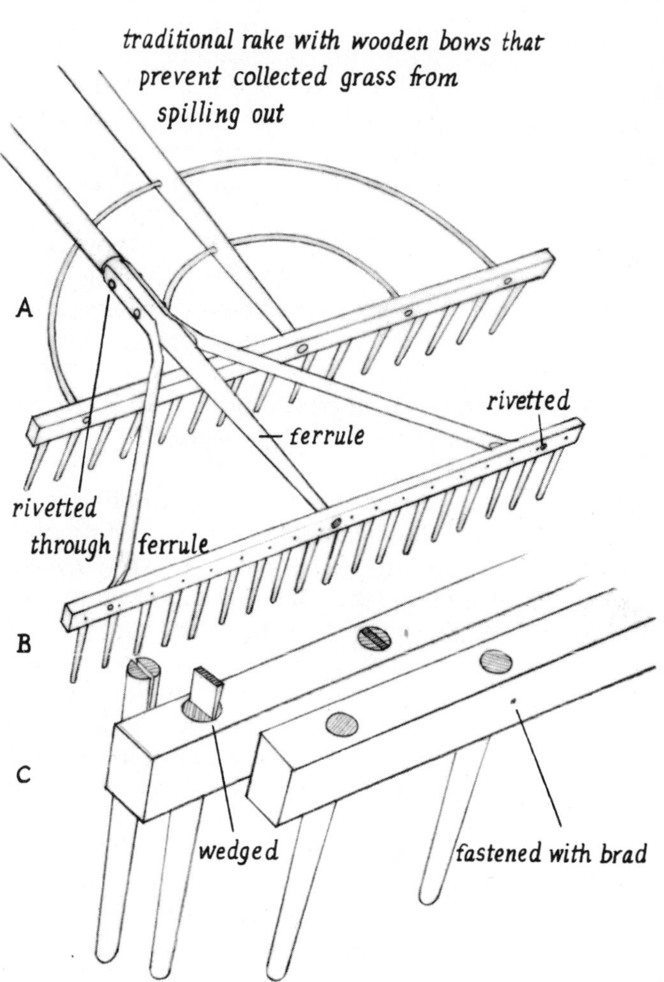

A farmer's rake can be repaired at home and will last almost indefinitely. In the best ones, the teeth are secured by cross wedging (C). The modern version (B) is braced with tubular steel arms and the teeth fastened with brads.

True Temper hoe, date unknown

"When you drop this hoe on a weed, that weed is in trouble.

"Its exact age is not known, but I first used it in 1916 when I was eight years old. The blade is six inches across the cutting edge and is of heavy metal. The handle has been replaced with a piece of Osage orange. Although heavier than hoes made today, this tool does not tire you out. Today's light hoes require much pressure to cut weeds or move soil, and I cannot find a hoe in the stores that will sharpen and hold a cutting edge."

HAROLD L. WRIGHT
Norborne, Missouri

Good toys

"We got into this business ten years ago to try to get the best quality toys we could find. So, there are many, many American toys that we don't carry for that reason, and a lot of European imports that we do carry for that reason.

"This has to do with the way Americans market things, the way we teach our M.B.A.s to do business—that is, to sell as many things as you can. And I think that's less the case with handmade American things or some of the things you get from small companies. I think it's a matter of growing to the size where advertising dollars are more important than anything else in selling a product. And when it gets to that point, it's really creating an image in the consumer's mind for a product rather than having an item that's genuinely terrific."

Interview with BOB JOY,
The Red Balloon toy shop,
Washington, D.C.

LAWN MOWERS

Lawn mowers come in a befuddling array of sizes, types, and (especially) prices. To further confuse matters, higher-priced mowers don't necessarily last longer.

All the mowers we surveyed were rotary cutters because, as Stu Kotchie of A-1 Lawnmower, Hopewell Junction, New York, put it, "reels cost a dollar an inch to sharpen and none to break. All you've got to do is hit one stone, and it's got to be sharpened again." Powered reel mowers are costly to maintain and thus suited to manicured estates. Rotary mowers are likely to last longer under the conditions home owners encounter.

Among rotary mowers, there are push mowers, self-propelled walk-behind mowers, and riding mowers. Push mowers are the least expensive, starting at well under $200 and approaching $300 at the top end. The average price of the four walk-behinds in our sample was $263. Self-propelled mowers we considered range from $218 for the Sears Eager 1 to twice that figure, with our sample of seven averaging $325.

The extra dollars invested in locomotion aren't apt to buy a longer service life. An interesting alternative is to invest in a commercial-grade mower, either walk-behind or self-propelled. You'll get more years out of these heavy-duty mowers (and likely less frustration) but not necessarily more years for your dollar. (The Gravely walk-behind mower is a notable exception—prices start at $1,469.) We found that durability *does* have some relation to price at the price extremes of this class of mowers. For example, repair people we questioned agreed that the cheaper Sears mowers were not built to last, and that the Gravely would last at least 6 or 7 years and perhaps 20 or more. Between these extremes, price is not a clear predictor of durability. We found little agreement among repair shops on best buys for durability, although Snapper and Gravely drew the most praise.

The power plants of lawn mowers under eight horsepower vary less between brands than between price classes, because most are powered either by Lawson-Tecumseh two-stroke engines or by Briggs and Stratton four-stroke engines. All the repair people had good words for Briggs and Stratton; parts are readily available, and they're easier (and therefore cheaper) to work on. For example, when points have to be replaced in a Tecumseh engine, it has to be timed as well, but the Briggs engine only needs to have the points set. Our repair people also pointed out that you have to remember to mix oil with the gas for two-stroke Tecumseh and Lawn-Boy engines. A good number of sorry owners have forgotten to do so, and the consequence is a burned-up engine. No matter what the make, the smaller and cheaper engines, like those used to power push mowers, are not apt to be durability champs. Note that the longer-lived models likely have an adjustable carburetor, several speeds, and moving parts of good-quality iron and steel instead of nylon, stamped metal, or pot-metal castings. Perhaps to maintain a competitive price, some makers have progressively down-graded models, resorting to cheaper components, and you might quiz a local repair person on a model you're about to buy.

Kohler and Honda power plants are sometimes found on walk-behind mowers. Our repair people weren't very familiar with the Honda engine but called it more sophisticated and less prone to vibration than other power plants. On the other hand, the Honda is tricky to work on, and parts can be difficult to get. It is too new for an assessment of its durability. The Kohler is a more expensive engine than the others and is commonly used on large mowers and small tractors. One repair person respectfully called it "the king, a cast-iron engine that lasts and lasts." However, within the class of walk-behind mowers, it is only used by Gravely, which helps to explain that mower's considerable price.

What our repair people said: lawn mowers

Brand, type, model, price	Average life-span estimates, years
Gravely, two-wheel tractor, 5200, $1,380	13.70
Sears, push mower, Craftsman, $80.00	11.89
Wheel Horse, garden tractor, C-85, $2,100	11.26
Toro, push mower (21″ blade), 16310, $280	10.30
Snapper, commercial self-propelled, $520	10.00
Snapper, commercial push mower, $410	9.77
Snapper, rider, 25063, $910	9.52
Wheel Horse, front-engine rider, B-115, $1,450	9.41
Ariens, lawn tractor, YT-11, $1,295	9.25
Toro, commercial self-propelled, 23158, $575	9.23
Wheel Horse, rear-engine rider, A-81, $779	8.29
Snapper, self-propelled (21″ blade), $374	7.83
Toro, front-engine rider, 57300, $1,800	7.75
Gilson, 11 h.p. rider (36″ blade), 52061, $1,900	7.50
Jacobsen, rear-wheel drive (cast-iron deck), 42236, $330	7.21
Lawn-Boy, self-propelled, Supreme 8237, $370	7.00
Lawn-Boy, push mower, Supreme 7229, $280	6.96
Toro, self-propelled, 20775, $430	6.48
Jacobsen, rear-wheel drive (steel deck), 42186, $220	6.17
Sears, push mower, Eager 1, 9A90788N, $259	5.12
Gilson, two-way push mower, 56018, $235	4.74
Gilson, self-propelled, 56020, $336	4.72
Sears, self-propelled, Craftsman, $210	4.53

We telephoned 25 Pennsylvania lawn mower repair people in January, 1981, and asked them to estimate the life span of the 23 mowers listed above, assuming that each mower was given "reasonable" care by its owner. The prices and model numbers shown were current at the time of the survey but are subject to change.

With the exception of the Gravely, riding mowers cost a good deal more than walk-behind models, but you get more than just a place to sit down for your money. Riding mowers are designed for heavier service, and therefore tend to be built with better, more expensive engines and durable frames. A good many of them have cast-iron engines, not cast-aluminum, since weight is not so critical. Cast-iron engines can be rebuilt more readily; we were told, "Get a score into an aluminum block, and it's shot, but a cast-iron block can be rebored a couple of times." Because rider frames are built to withstand more abuse, it may be worthwhile to replace an engine when it has worn out. We learned of a Wheel Horse riding mower that was 18 years old and had outlasted several engines. In our survey, the estimated life spans of riders began at about 8 years and for some makes stretched to 20 years and beyond.

Regardless of brand, certain parts of a mower are more vulnerable than others. Our service people mentioned the crankshaft. The longer the crankshaft (the greater the distance from shaft bearing to blade hub), the more likely that it will bend if you hit a rock or a log, requiring the considerable cost of replacement. The shorter the shaft, the more likely that the blade will break. And a further tip, expressed by one repair person: "Don't hit any immovable objects!"

Other vulnerable parts are the mower wheels and mower deck. Ball-bearing wheels are best. But we found some difference of opinion on whether cast- or sheet-metal decks are superior. One service person praised a cast-aluminum deck as virtually indestructible, and preferable to sheet metal, which bends and rusts. Another man felt that a sheet-metal deck is superior because it will only bend if hit by rocks, while a cast deck can break.

Push cultivator (purchased used, more than 40 years ago)

Margaret Smyser

"I have a push cultivator that I bought more than 40 years ago. It was considered worn out by its former owner. I took it home and rebushed the wheel, straightened the wheel spokes, painted the rest of it, and gave it proper housing. I cleaned and oiled it every time I used it and today it is still in good condition. I would not take the price of a new one for it, because I don't believe there is one on the market that is better than my old friend. By the way, the proper way to use these critters is to cultivate when the weeds have just sprouted. Make a few passes in the morning of a sunny day and you will have a clean garden."

PAUL E. HILTON
Angelica, New York

Christie C. Tito

A 1954 Gravely Model L.

Perhaps a cast deck is best used on lawns that are relatively innocent of stones. Cast iron may be more costly, as shown by two Jacobsen self-propelled mowers with decks of steel ($220) and cast iron ($330).

Because of its high engine speed, a mower is even more sensitive to lubrication than a car. The oil should be topped up each time a four-stroke mower is used and should be changed at recommended intervals or better. In addition, if your mower is to be retired for the winter, clean the air fins, drain the gas, and (if it has a pull-starter) pull the cord until the engine is in the compression cycle—that is, pulled until the engine begins to tug back.

Would it be wiser to buy an old mower? Some of the service people we interviewed felt that there had been some cheapening of their lines in the last five years, suggesting older mowers may be more solid. However, considering the indifferent showings of many cheaper models, as shown on the lawn mower table, used push or walk-behind mowers may well be suffering from old age. If a long-lived commercial mower comes on the market, beware: we learned that professionals as a rule either lavish care on their machines or run them into the ground. Rider mowers and the long-lasting Gravely, on the other hand, may still offer the second owner many years of service. A recent check of used machines on the market turned up a Gravely 5200 with a rebuilt engine for $400 and a 17-year-old Wheel Horse (equivalent to the C-81) with a 3-year-old engine for only $275.

Supposing your lawn is large enough to justify such a mower, buying a used model could make sense. Or, of course, you could let your lawn go to meadow, and be out only the legal fees for your defense against the charges of the local zoning board.

BK and DOUGLAS C. SMYTH

1947 Coremaster tiller

"When I moved here on my own 12 acres in 1947, I only had my wife and me but still made a garden big enough to feed the whole town, 1,000 feet by 100. It was a job to take care of this garden by hand so I had a salesman come and show me how to run a one-wheel Coremaster.

"Just as he got started my wife came up and said that he had a call on the telephone. So he told me to try the machine myself.

"After about an hour or so he still hadn't come back. I was finished with my garden work so I put the machine away in my garden shed. I came up to the house and my wife told me that the salesman had been called to his office.

"A week later he didn't come back. So again I used the one-wheeler, and then each week the whole summer. Late in the fall I saw the salesman in town and said that I wanted to buy it. He said, 'Give me $95 cash and the machine is yours.'

"This is a wonderful machine. It's too bad they don't make them any more. In 34 years I've never done anything to it outside of adding grease, oil, and gas—not even a new spark plug. The machine don't owe me one damn cent."

FRED C. WEISSE
Clinton, Connecticut

1926 Barker vegetable cultivator

"The day the Spirit of St. Louis with Lindbergh aboard was flying the Atlantic, my husband bought me a Barker cultivator. Pushed as fast as you want to walk, the Barker takes care of all weeds in its path. This morning I did my entire garden without tiring."

ELSIE KAISER
Waterloo, Iowa

Hibernation

Even when the grass is dormant and the lawn mower rests in the garage, harmful acids in the oil may attack metallic surfaces inside the engine. Once this corrosion begins, it cannot be reversed except by replacing the damaged parts. Change oil at least twice a year.

A mower that mows trees

If the test of a good lawn mower's mettle is its ability to level summer-old weeds, then the mark of the best might be success with small trees.

The Kenneth R. Hach family of Elkader, Iowa, has such a machine. It is the Roof VP-75 ($785), a curious thing perched on bicycle-type wheels. The cutting is done by a serious-looking blade that spins right out in the open. The VP-75 was built to handle weeds, but the Hachs say the mower "has done a lot more than tidy up fence rows–it has cleared land. It has cut down one- and two-inch saplings in stride and three- to four-inch saplings by letting it chop at their base. If it encounters an object that is immovable, such as a rock or post, the motor kills, eliminating broken shafts and burned-out motors. A pull of the starter rope and it's back in service. It easily mows roadside ditches, steep slopes, feedlots overgrown with horseweed, six-foot-tall thistle, slew grass, and many others. It has also served as a simple lawn mower when our regular one was broken down. One winter the mower got left in our timber where we were clearing a prospective site. The next spring it started right up and mowed as though it had the best of care."

Such testimony does not surprise Lowell Sidfrids, design engineer for Roof. The VP-75 and its stablemates express his no-frills approach, and the company's line shares a look that might be described as home-built–all of the pieces are there in plain sight and painted fire-engine red. As a concession to styling, the company has applied pinstriping to a couple of models, but Roofs are kept simple, with the commercial mower in mind.

The open-blade VP-75 has been around since 1945, but is a recent victim of Federal safety requirements. A similar model is the 400 Push-type ($475), cutting a 21-inch swatch with a five-horsepower engine. A small, pivoting front wheel supports the 21-inch rotary blade. There's a

The Roof VP-75 with a 30-inch lawn-shield unit.

The Roof 400.

handle-mounted clutch, and the pitch of the blade can be adjusted to handle especially tough jobs, a patented feature said to prolong engine life. The big semi-pneumatic tires ensure that the 400 is easy to push over rough terrain. Equipment-rental companies appreciate its longevity, and home owners with very large yards can put this model to good use.

Roof's 21-inch Commercial walk-behind rotary ($300) was originally designed to meet the near-fanatic specifications of the General Services Administration (GSA). This government procurement

1951 Howard Rotavator Gem

"I was in the landscape and nursery business and felt I needed a more substantial tiller than a general garden tool. After witnessing a dealer's demonstration, I decided to go ahead and buy the Gem despite what seemed to be a high price of $830. I was not to be disappointed.

"The tiller was made in England and has a one-cylinder, 600cc J.A.P. engine. I used it for seven years in the landscape and nursery business, under the less-than-favorable conditions imposed by the rocky soil common to northwestern New Jersey. During that period the forged steel blades were replaced twice, not because of breakage but due to wear.

"I left the landscaping business in 1959 but continued to use the Gem in the nursery and garden. In 1975, we decided that we would move west. We took inventory of our possessions and decided the quarter-ton tiller was not worth the moving expense, considering its age. However, that spring, following a whole winter's idleness, the engine started after only three turns of the crank and that changed my mind. Off we went to Montana with the tiller. I know that it was no mistake. With it, I cleared an acre of brushland for the garden and have used it ever since.

"I have never owned a piece of equipment that has given so much service with so little care. I doubt the Gem will ever die as long as I give it reasonable care. Who knows, it might even outlive me."

EUGENE E. GRAF
Whitefish, Montana

1945 Graham-Paige Rototiller

"I bought this tiller in 1946 after it had been used one season, and it has been in service each year since. It is the most rugged and durable machine I have ever seen, and does the best job of preparing soil of any I have ever seen. It is no longer manufactured, but still can be serviced by Frazer Farm Equipment Corp. in Auburn, Indiana."

VIRGIL E. GOOCH
Killen, Alabama

1927 ('28?) Buda stationary four-cylinder engine

"We bought this sawmill engine 15 years ago from a cousin who had used it on a sawmill for some 25 years, and it was second hand when *he* got it. The engine is in excellent condition, doesn't burn oil, and considering the load it handles it's not a heavy gas user."

MRS. ALICE WALKER
Kooskia, Idaho

branch told Sidfrids their run-of-the-mill mowers were holding up for only a couple of weeks. "We kind of wanted the contract real bad," he says, and came up with an "automotive quality," solid cast-iron engine with replaceable connecting rod bearings.

Although the machine held up far longer than conventional mowers, the fickle GSA later switched to a cheaper Sears model. The Roof walk-behind is still available, with a conventional Briggs and Stratton four-horsepower engine. The heavy-duty deck is of welded 10- and 12-gauge sheet metal. The wheels turn on sealed ball bearings with grease fittings, rather than on standard open bearings. Because the deck is shallower than on most mowers, the crankshaft is very short—¾ inch—and so not apt to bend when the blade connects with something immovable (the mower "comes through with flying colors in the solid-iron stake tests," says Sidfrids). Strength and simplicity come at the expense of convenience. You do have to push the 21-inch Commercial, and it's heavier than standard mowers. Also, the sturdy high-yield-tubing handle is innocent of choke or throttle levers.

Why the Briggs engine? "It's not us that picks it, it's the public," explains Sidfrids. The Briggs name is better known than Tecumseh, and service centers are easier to come by, but he rates the Tecumseh as just as good or a trifle better.

Roof distributors are not to be found in every shopping mall. If you have trouble locating a dealer, check with Roof Manufacturing Company, 1011 West Howard Street, Pontiac, IL 61764.

RY

1940 ('41?) Singer sewing machine

"My mother's sewing machine sits comfortably in the basement in the center of a maple-stained Queen Ann cabinet. The black enamel is scratched; the gold-leaf scrollwork chipped here and there. But it is threaded and ready to stitch at the touch of a foot pedal.

"My mother bought the machine, cabinet and all, in 1940 or '41 with her own money, hard-earned working as a registered nurse. She bought it to sew her "wedding clothes," and through the years she sewed her own clothes and mine and did countless jobs of mending. I learned to sew on it myself–tutored to my mother's strict standards. She last sewed clothes for my junior year at college. After her death, no one questioned the rightness of the machine's coming to me.

"I sewed on it my own wedding clothes. And in the ensuing 11 years of marriage, I have sewn my own clothes, infant sleepers, little girl dresses, little boy knit shirts (yes, you can do it without zig-zag!), shirts for my husband, and pieced many a quilt.

"The machine is a Singer, model AJ245381. She has a buttonhole maker that attaches with a variety of screws and clamps, and other assorted gadgets that I've never found a use for. I've bought her new needles, a new light bulb, a new drive belt once. I give her a few drops of oil every couple of years. She could probably use another overhaul like the one she had in 1971. But there's a quilt to be bound, flannel pajamas to sew up, a Christmas dress for my growing-taller, almost-eight-year-old daughter–maybe we'll have her worked on next spring."

ARDEN E. ATKINSON
East Lansing, Michigan

Dear Mr. McLane:

I received your letter asking me to explain the unusual condition of my lighter and can understand your curiosity not being acquainted with the facts. This is the third Zippo I have owned in the past 12 or 13 yrs and never had any trouble to speak of except losing them but the wheel stuck on the one you have now and caused it to fall from my hand into a piece of heavy machinery which was in operation at the time in the prison Tag plant. I have one finger missing and the top half of my right hand is numb caused from an injury so that explains why I didn't have a firm grip on it. The machine smashed my lighter so even that it looked like it may have been done deliberate but I assure that was not the case as it was a perfectly good lighter. I still haven't figured what made the wheel stick as it never did before and I had a good piece of flint in it. I wish I was able to pay the difference in the price I would ask you to exchange my lighter.

BOOKS AND TRAINS

10

SELF-DESTRUCTING BOOKS

No doubt you've bought a book, started in on the first chapter, and then heard a sickening crack as the binding split. In the wake of this small tragedy, the joy of reading is forgotten. You're apt to feel guilty, clumsy.

You should be angry. The mechanical requirements of reading seem to have been forgotten by many publishers. The book industry has grown remarkably in the past century: in 1880, about 2,000 different books were published in the United States, while last year's total was over 40,000, in editions ranging from a few thousand to a million or more copies. As publishing changed from a gentleman's profession into a multibillion-dollar industry ruled by enormous conglomerates, economic forces exerted a powerful pressure on the choice of production materials and methods. Costs have to be controlled. Speed in manufacture is crucial in a fickle marketplace hungry for the newest, the latest. Authors and readers have both benefited, as more people are reading more books. But the books themselves—as objects to be held, inscribed, and handed through generations—have suffered.

Every book consists of three basic components: the paper on which its words and illustrations are printed, the thread or glue that fastens the pages together, and the cover that forms a protective case around the first two. The development of cheaper, faster methods for the manufacture of all three has brought with it a marked decline in durability.

The paper

Paper was once laboriously made from cotton, linen, and other plant fibers, softened and separated by prolonged soaking and gentle beating into a slurry containing thousands of individual, flexible strands. A fine screen was lifted through this slurry and agitated by a skillful hand to achieve an even deposit. The moisture flowed away, leaving a mat of interlocking fibers, which, when dry, formed a seamless flexible sheet. Dried under pressure, the sheet would be quite flat; blotters of various textures determined the surface finish of the paper, and gelatine was applied to "size" it to make a smooth writing or printing surface. The Chinese apparently originated papermaking about 2,000 years ago, to be followed by Europeans 12 centuries later. Even today, a few specialty firms and individual craftspeople produce handmade papers. But hand processes are clearly inadequate for producing millions of books each year.

The nineteenth century brought with it many wondrous technological developments, not least of which were new techniques for the mass production of printing paper to satisfy a growing reading public. Wood chips supplemented, and soon almost replaced, rags as the fiber source. Beaters and mills chopped and ground them. The pulp was cooked with caustic agents to speed the fiber separation. Bleaches insured uniform color. Alum-rosin and aluminum sulphite compounds replaced externally applied sizes. The remarkable Fourdrinier machine, with long screen-and-felt belts passing through tanks and rollers and drying chambers, was able to feed yards and then miles of paper in a continuous ribbon onto huge rolls for use in high-speed printing presses.

But, chopped wood fibers are shorter than plant fibers, and thereby reduce the strength and flexibility of the page. Wood contains lignin, the powerful bonding agent that makes a tree rigid; broken down in a chemical slurry, lignin becomes a free agent, unstable and prone to reactions with other elements either within or surrounding the paper. The added bleaches, sizes, and caustic substances introduce acidic compounds, which are encouraged by a little heat, moisture, or direct light to attack the bonds within the paper, both the physical bonds holding one fiber to its neighbors and the chemical bonds within the molecules of each fiber. The paper darkens, becomes brittle, and finally crumbles to dust.

Many different kinds of paper are made today, as a quick comparison of several books, magazines, newspapers, and even the contents of the day's mail makes readily apparent. Ingredients and techniques vary widely from mill to mill, and from batch to batch. Some of this paper is very permanent (meaning, in paper talk, chemically stable) and some is durable (meaning strong and flexible). But much of it is rapidly self-destructing. Unfortunately for those who care about books, most of the book papers produced since the introduction of mass production around 1850 have been in the last category. Libraries are filled with nineteenth- and twentieth-century books whose paper literally shatters to the touch. Perhaps a third of the 19 million books in the Library of Congress are too far gone for circulation. Rebinding can rescue some library books; others are placed on microfilm. Books produced early in this century seem to have a life of about 50 years, while today's titles can be expected to last only 20 to 30.

Studies in the late 1950s identified acids as chief villains in the brittle-paper disaster, and several standards and specifications have been developed for the manufacture of "permanent/durable" paper. Industry acceptance has been slow, to put it mildly, in part because alkaline (the reverse of acidic) papers have been slightly more expensive to produce and also because few publishers were aware of their value and therefore never asked for them. Ironically, economics *might* turn the dismal tide. It seems that alkaline paper pulp corrodes machine parts much less rapidly than acidic pulp. The process consumes less energy. And environmental restrictions covering the disposal of waste water from paper plants are more cheaply met with alkaline processes. A few paper mills have switched all their production to alkaline papers, and perhaps a fifth of all book papers in the United States are currently of this type. The increasing demand from a small but growing number of enlightened publishers may stimulate greater production, thus keeping prices in balance. There is some reason for hope in the long run. Even now, almost 60 percent of European book paper is alkaline based. But thousands of books are still printed each year on paper that will not last, when we do have the potential to make paper with a potential life of two or three centuries.

The binding

Compounding the paper problem have been changes in the way the pages are fastened together to make a book. The traditional method involved printing on double pages, which were stacked in thin sections and folded into "signatures." Thread was laced through the center fold, around several horizontal bands or cords to which many signatures were attached to assemble the whole book. Special stitches over the top and bottom cords, often in color, formed the "headband." The square block of signatures was then rounded to produce the familiar convex spine essential to maintain the structure despite gravity and use. The result was a strong, flexible attachment that enabled each page to open fully and lie flat. But it wasn't a very fast process, even when a through-the-fold sewing machine took the place of hand sewing. New sewing machines appeared that ignored the folds and eliminated the need for signatures, stabbing through stacks of pages. Square-backed books began to appear, doing away with the skill and time needed for rounding. Then new adhesives eliminated sewing altogether. Speed meant economy—more books at modest prices for more people.

But a stab-sewn book doesn't open very easily and seldom lies flat unless the pages are very large and flexible. Unless inner margins are very wide, text may disappear under the sewing. Pressure may break the threads or, since they tend to be stronger than the paper, cause them to tear the pages. The needle holes alone can act as perforations so that, as the paper stiffens with age, pages tear out neatly along the sewing line. Square-backed books soon become concave, and pages may pull completely from the covers. If the adhesive applied to the flat back of a stack of pages (like the strip on top of a note pad) is well formulated to remain flexible, the book might open well, but

All photos, Christie C. Tito

A traditionally bound book, with sewn bundles of 16 pages, called signatures. Note the threads between the open pages. The striped headband is decorative and doesn't add to the strength of the binding.

the pages may pull out as easily as a sheet from a pad. If the adhesive is applied too thickly, or dries out, or was applied hot and becomes rigid when cool, the spine will not flex. It may crack all at once when opened, or one page after another may come loose.

There is some cause for hope about adhesives, since research-and-development people are busily formulating flexible, long-lasting adhesives that may be appropriate for books. Machines that fan pages slightly as the adhesive is applied offer a more secure bond, by attaching the pages to each other along the inner edge. The potential is certainly there: look at a large city phone directory or the Sears catalog, whose glued pages stay in place through countless uses. Can the technology be adapted to book manufacture? Probably so, *if* the economic incentive is powerful enough.

But even the best adhesive-bound volume is no match for a well-sewn book, and there are still a few publishers, some goaded by their authors and some recoiling from bad experiences with poor adhesive bindings, whose works are printed in signatures and sewn through the fold. Whether such quality can survive remains to be seen.

More and more often, a hardcover price buys you a paperback glued to cardboard wings. If anything, the book pictured here is flimsier than a less expensive paperback.

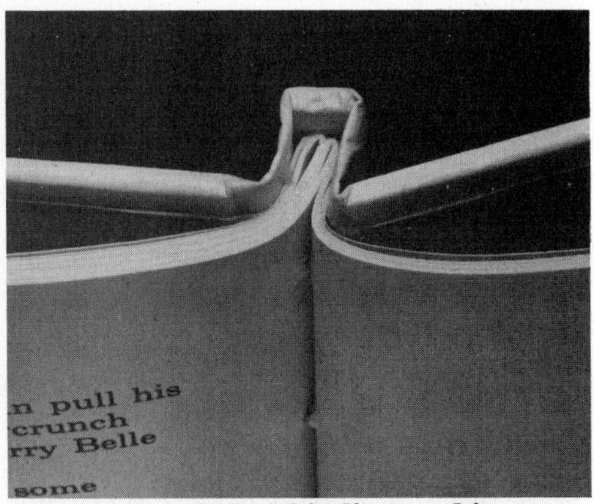

The saddle-stitched binding on this children's book isn't pretty, but it's tough.

A field guide to durable books

- *Cover (paperbacks).* The front and back covers should open easily. Make sure the covers are firmly attached to the block of pages. Is the spine smooth, or do lumps of glue bubble the surface?
- *Cover (hardcovers).* Check to see if the boards are covered with cloth, synthetic material, or paper. Does the surface feel smooth and moisture-repellent? Have the inside corners been folded and mitered neatly? Look for a gauze or cloth hinge under the paper. When a traditionally bound book is open, you can see through a hollow tube between inner and outer spine. The covers should extend evenly beyond the pages.
- *Page fastening.* Look at the top or bottom to see whether pages appear grouped in signatures. If so, open the book to the center of one and look for stitches down the center. Look carefully, because some volumes that look as though they have signatures have really been shaved and glued. If there are no vertical stitches, look for horizontal ones stabbed through the stack of pages, visible crossing the center margin. If no thread can be seen, the book is probably glued together. Telltale signs are streaks of adhesive across the top or bottom of several pages, or a glob that oozed inward to stick two pages together along the center margin.

  Does the book open easily without a cracking sound? Does it lie flat without being held? The pages should turn easily, one at a time, and should lie open so all the text is easily readable. If one illustration covers two facing pages, you should be able to see the center of it without forcing the two sides apart.
- *Paper.* The acid content of paper can only be determined by laboratory test. However, some publishers have begun placing a notice about the paper used in a book, usually on the copyright page, or sometimes on the last page. "Permanent/durable" is the term to look for, indicating that paper meets several specifications for chemical stability and ability to withstand handling. "Acid-free" or "neutral" are good, indicating permanence, though not necessarily durability; "100% rag" usually implies durability, but is not a guarantee of permanence; "recycled" is ecologically pleasing but may mean only that the fibers are one step closer to biodegrading.

  Paper that looks like newsprint is probably very short-lived, but in general, the aesthetic values of color, thickness, and texture are not good clues to potential longevity. Flexibility is crucial, since pages are moving parts in the book's structure. Look for waviness or warping along the center margin of the paper, signs that the text was printed against the grain. Such pages will seldom turn easily or lie flat, and will tend to crack along the flex line as they age.

The case

What of the third component, the cover or case which surrounds the block of pages? Here, too, there have been dramatic changes in production methods and materials. Originally, signatures were sewn onto tapes or cards that were glued to the "boards" forming the front and back covers. These strong, flexible hinges gave way to cloth or gauze strips pasted over the spine and extending onto the boards; and these gave way to narrow paper hinges glued along the edge of the board and the first and last pages. Even with these simplifications, assembly was still complex: boards were covered with cloth on the outside and paper on the inside, each cut to match and carefully put together, with a hollow tube between the binding edge and the outer spine for flexibility as the volume was opened. The traditional hardcover demanded many different materials, many steps, and much expense. Enter the paperback—no cloth, no boards, no rounding, no hollow spine. Just a stiff paper wrapper with an eye-catching design glued to the flat spine. More books at modest prices for more people. And now a great number of hardcover books have only a glued binding to show for their higher price.

The cover of a book is not just packaging to be discarded when the product is brought home from the store. It is an integral part of the structure, supporting and protecting the pages as they are handled, bearing some of the stresses, shielding paper from damp hands, protecting pages from abrasion through its overhanging edges. Paperbacks, even so-called "quality paperbacks," which may have a sewn binding under their paper covers, are intrinsically weaker and less durable than traditionally sewn hardcover books.

Technology promises little to improve the cover problem, though some synthetic fabrics appear to be as durable as cloth at less cost.

Finding and keeping a good book

What does this gloomy tale of technology mean for the consumer about to enter a bookstore? Many, many books are available, but few will stand the test of time—indeed, some will fall apart in a single reading. Unfortunately, the potential book buyer can do only a little comparison shopping, for books, unlike most consumer goods, are monopoly items: only Rodale publishes *The Durability Factor*, and if you're not satisfied with the quality of Rodale's product, you'll have to do without.

Sometimes there *are* choices—between mass-market and quality paperbacks and hardcovers, deluxe editions, or even between two books on the same subject. The accompanying box ("A field guide to durable books") suggests how to examine a book for long-life traits.

While the manufacturer, and hence the publisher, bears the major responsibility for the durability of a book, much also depends upon the way it is handled and the conditions under which it is stored after purchase. Care and common sense are the first principles for good handling. Even the best paper will tear if handled roughly, stain and warp if spilled on, discolor if exposed to strong sunlight for several days. The best-sewn binding may crack if opened much beyond 180 degrees, if sat on, or if closed with a pencil inside. The best cover will not ward off crayons or scissors in young fingers, support a heavy volume if dangled by one corner, or protect the pages if used as a doorstop.

Use caution when first opening a new book. If hinges seem stiff, flex them slowly several times, without forcing, to loosen. If pages don't fall open readily, lay the volume on a clean surface, holding the pages vertically while the covers lie flat. Working carefully from each end, separate a few pages at a time and press them down toward the cover, running your finger gently along the inner margin to shape the paper into a curve—not a crease—where it should flex. But beware: some adhesive-bound books, whether hardcover or paperback, will *never* lie open, and this treatment may hasten their cracking apart.

To maintain their shape and protect the basic structure, store average-sized books vertically on shelves with support from book ends. Books that lean on a half-full shelf become permanently distorted and may suffer hinge damage. Very tall and very fat books should be kept flat, or gravity will tend to pull their insides out.

Book papers and cover materials are extremely sensitive to extremes of heat, light, and moisture or dryness. They may warp, discolor, or mildew, and deteriorating chemical reactions are accelerated by increases in temperature and prolonged exposure to sunlight or fluorescent light. Ideally, books should be stored away from direct sunlight at 65°F, and 50 percent relative humidity. Short of the ideal, avoid storing books near heating pipes or vents, in attics or basements, or near south-facing windows. Use a portable dehumidifier to reduce the possibility of mildew if humidity remains above 70 percent for several days, and a humidifier to prevent warping and embrittlement if it drops much below 30 percent.

Under the best of circumstances—in their manufacture, use, and storage—books are not immortal. The shame of today's situation is that the Gutenberg *Bible* is in better shape after 500 years than most books published in our own century. Perhaps discriminating consumers can make a difference. Take the trouble to send a new book back to the publisher if its pages pop loose or its cover hinge breaks. You may get a better-made replacement, and if enough people reject that self-destructing book, the publisher's next one may be manufactured with reading as well as selling in mind.

PAMELA W. DARLING

Stitch your own

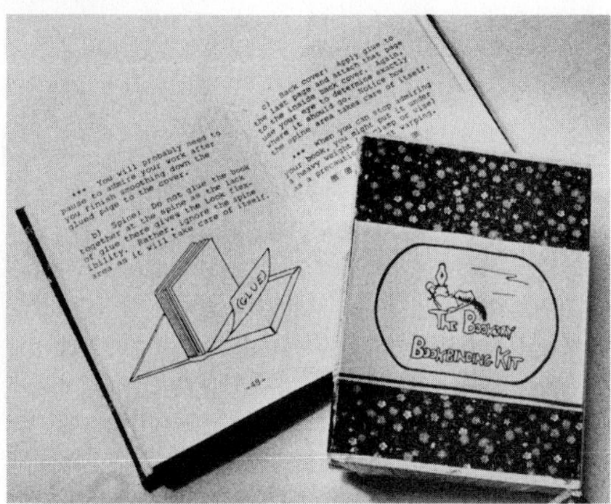

You can get a better idea of how a stitched book goes together by making your own. A kit for a 140-page, 4½ by 5¾-inch book is sold by The Bookery, P.O. Box 1036, Anderson, CA 96007. For $3.25 plus 75¢ postage, you receive instructions, prefolded signatures, fabric and cardboard for the covers, spine, and needle and thread.

An invisible impregnation

Maps last indefinitely if rolled up and tied with a ribbon, but curly maps don't cooperate. So, they find themselves folded and jammed into pockets, used as campfire hot pads and coasters. With this treatment, they soon turn to Kleenex along the seams.

Comes Stormproof, a mildew-resistant water repellent that sponges on and impregnates the paper rather than coating it. Treated maps should hold up much longer, for less than half the cost of a new topographic map. A one-pint container can be had for $7, postpaid, from Stormproof, Martensen Company, Inc., P.O. Box 261, Williamsburg, VA 23185.

Bound to stay bound

"If you want books that last, you have to know what you're buying. The first thing I'd do is take off the jacket and have a close look."

An interview with Fred Shihadeh

The building where Fred Shihadeh does his hand bookbinding is a gracious old house in a Philadelphia suburb, with flower and vegetable gardens in the yard as meticulously cared for as his collection of books.

To see the tools of his trade, one would suspect that Shihadeh would be just as much at home in the cottage of a fifteenth-century German bookbinder. As he himself says, the tools of the bookbinding craftsman haven't changed in the last 500 years, and Fred Shihadeh is definitely one of that disappearing breed.

"I'm an anachronism. I'm a hundred years out of date. There aren't too many who do what I do."

Shihadeh's craft grew out of his love of books, which led him to the shop of a German bookbinder while he was living in that country. "He was complaining that he couldn't get help because he couldn't pay much. So I said, 'Great, I'd like to learn.' I've always liked books and was curious as to how books are put together. I did all the dirty work, anything he said, I did—sweep floors, sew the books, all the tough jobs. Sewing all those books was the most monotonous. But I learned everything else from him too. I developed from there, and I also have a terrific library on bookbinding, every book there is on the subject, I think."

Interview photos, Christie C. Tito

How long can a book last? If you bring a book to Fred Shihadeh and he deacidifies all the pages, rebinds it with leather, the best that can be obtained today, and gives it the alkaline treatment, then puts on the proper oils, it should last 200 years. "Of course, we won't be around to measure it," says Shihadeh.

Since then, Shihadeh has bound books ranging from mass-produced editions of Ayn Rand novels to a twelfth-century Greek manuscript written on vellum, the specially treated animal skins used before paper was introduced. He does restoration work on rare books from Bryn Mawr, Swarthmore, and Haverford colleges and the University of Pennsylvania.

PAT DONAHUE

Paper is the main part of the book. Now, they can use papers today that'll last hundreds of years, but it costs a little bit more per book.

Since the Civil War, it's been a very bad period for paper. The residual acid isn't washed out. When you see books that turn yellow and get brittle, that's why.

I can show you old books, going back to the fifteenth century, where that paper is just as crisp as if it was made yesterday. But in the nineteenth century, it began going downhill. They started trying to get paper as white as possible, by bleaching, and when the acids remained in the paper, it deteriorated. The paper after 1850 just wasn't as good as before, didn't feel the same, didn't take the print as well, didn't take the colorings.

What's the date on this book, 1726? This spotting is acid absorbed from the atmosphere. But if we took this book apart and washed it, and properly maintained it, the paper will last indefinitely. Two hundred years from now, you might want to do something else with it, but it'll still be around.

Look at this paper—isn't it beautiful? It's handmade paper, made in 1688. It's beautiful, white, crisp. You know how they make paper? They heat up pulp in a big tub where the pulp sort of floats around very loosely, like a soup with little flecks of paper. So they take what looks like a window screen and dip it in, and then the water runs off and the lint settles. That's the paper.

Most papers today are made of wood. There's some rag, but not much. Some people think the more rag the better the paper as far as longevity. Not necessarily. There's acid in cheap rag as well as wood. But they can make wood paper now that will last 300, 400, 500 years. They print some of your more expensive books on it now, but Dover paperbacks use it as well.

Instead of having a thousand lousy paperbacks, wouldn't it be better to have a few nicely done books? But we're living in a different age, we like quantity instead of quality. People who buy books really are not concerned with the book itself. They're more interested in the material, the contents. But I still think the main ingredient is the paper. If they would produce a book on good paper, it wouldn't even have to be sewn, just glued and then taken apart to be rebound. As long as the paper is good, everything else can be crumbling.

Then there's the binding. Books were always bound in leather or paper or both up until about 1830. That's when cloth started coming in. The early cloth is all right, that held up well. But leather and animal skins—I can show you a sixteenth-century book with the leather still good. The only damage is just physical wear, not chemical deterioration.

The book press.

Leather, like paper, ended up on the alkaline side when processed. That was one of the reasons it lasted so long, because it was alkaline and acid is absorbed from the sulfur dioxide in the atmosphere. In the nineteenth century, the gas lighting produced some kind of acid that really affected libraries.

Natural ingredients

As I see it—and this is my overall philosophy—go back as close to natural ingredients as possible. The scientific way is the natural way rather than the synthetic way. A tanner in Philadelphia tells me they can do anything with leather, they know all the technology to do anything they want—make it supple, color it, make it hard—but I don't know if they've come up with the answer to longevity. If you tan leather the old way, you're not going to rush it, you're going to use natural tannins and not acids. You're not going to be so fussy about the finish. The new leather, they can get all the fats out of it and whatever, so when they color it, it's perfectly even. Whereas the old leather has an irregularity, a mottled look that has its own beauty. They're the leathers that weren't overscrubbed, that took months and months to tan. And they've held up.

A 1516 volume is brought back to life with sutures by the skilled hands of Shihadeh's wife.

Leather will last longer if it is properly cared for, if the conditions of storage are not too damp, not too dry, not too hot. When leather gets wet and dries out, it gets brittle. I developed a salve, now on the market, which will keep it soft. And by filling the pores, it can act as a buffer against pollutants in the atmosphere. Leather bindings have to feed or they'll dry out or absorb impurities from the air.

A lot of the leather-bound books that are advertised as edition books just use a thin piece of leather. They're not going to hold up very well. How would you know if it's cheap leather? I guess price has something to do with it. You can't buy a good, full-leather dictionary for $50. Good leather alone would cost $50. I'd say the standards on leather bibles are fairly good, though, with the best hand craftsmanship.

As far as I'm concerned, the right way to bind a book is to have the proper tightness in the back. I want the back tight against the spine for the appearance, the feel, and because it'll last longer. When it begins to pull away, you're putting a strain on the hinge, and the book begins to break down. A thin book won't have this problem. To build that tightness into a book would add an extra $5, because somebody's paying attention to those details.

Handbound books are custom-made according to whether or not you want it to lie flat. Of course, the tighter it is, the longer it's going to last, whether it's machine sewn or hand sewn.

I think the trend now is really downhill, and we're about down to the bottom. The paper's cheap and glued in, and hardbacks aren't even covered with cloth but with paper that can look like anything—cloth, grained leather. They look nice, but they don't last. Now the covers on this seventeenth-century book are laced in. They're sewn around a cord, which is then laced into the covering. Some of the cords are made of hemp, like rope. The leather wears away, but that cover is hanging on there just as strong as can be. In the monasteries, they used wood boards and double sewing, and it was a substantial book. But then shortcuts were taken. They stopped using wood and started using cardboard and paper just pasted together. The cords got thinner and thinner, and by the nineteenth century they got so thin that, even though the cover was in one piece, the cords just broke off.

Now the edition books, which are machine done, were cheaper and faster to do. There was the popular edition, and the fancier limited edition, which had better paper and better binding. That goes on even today. Smaller presses still print with lead type and use nicer bindings and paper in a variety of hand methods for a more durable binding.

But you take those Franklin Mint editions. They're just a shabby imitation. The peak of fine bindings was in the nineteenth century, with all kinds of beautiful, elaborate work—bindings that the Franklin Mint is trying to imitate, but today would cost thousands of dollars a book, and they're selling them for $39. Even the processes they use, if they did it on a one-by-one basis with a craftsman, could be improved on. First of all, the leathers they use could be better than just cowhide stamped all in one shot with a machine. The bands are just pressed into the leather, not artistically tailored. I'm not trying to put them down, I'm just saying that if somebody thinks they're getting a nice, handcrafted book and they're saving some money, they're not. It's not the kind of book that's going to go up in value, whereas a nicely bound book at any age will increase in value tomorrow. I guess it's like a print and a painting. Rembrandt's "Night Watch," the original, goes for $1 million, and a cardboard reprint is $2.

If you have a prize book you want to restore or put into a nice binding, you have to find the right hand binder. Some people are fairly well trained and some are awful. People bring in books to me to rebind that are supposedly hand bound by a library binder, and they're terrible in every way.

Shihadeh collects old dies with which he can duplicate traditional gilt work.

***Flight from the City*, published in 1938 by Ralph Borsodi**

Christie C. Tito

"Durability has resided in the ideas in our heads—the goal of self-sufficiency and 'do it yourself' which we espoused in 1938 and have been working on ever since. Books represent these ideas and have been among our most-durable possessions, including first and foremost, Ralph Borsodi's *Flight from the City.*"

KATE OLSEN
Martinez, California

Friends of the book

Fortunately, some well-placed people care dearly about the fate of the book. Librarians, publishers, and paper people make up the Committee on Production Guidelines for Book Longevity, under the aegis of the Council on Library Resources. The members study ways of improving the physical quality of publications, books in particular, and give their recommendations in a 1981 "Interim Report on Book Paper."

The committee laments that "books containing the acidic seeds of their own destruction continue to be produced by the millions, storing up problems for the future, failing to provide a permanent record of our own times." Not that they recommend printing *everything* on long-life paper. Attention should be paid to works judged of lasting importance, rather than formula novels, novelizations of films, textbooks, workbooks, and the like.

Books meeting the committee's guidelines could be distinguished by a statement on the copyright page:

> The paper in this book meets the guidelines for permanence and durability of the Committee on Production Guidelines for Book Longevity of the Council on Library Resources.

The committee's report lists the larger mills now producing acid-free paper at competitive prices. Copies of the 13-page report are available, upon receipt of a self-addressed mailing label, from the Council on Library Resources, Inc., Suite 620, One Dupont Circle, NW, Washington, D.C. 20036.

RY

On the other hand . . .

"Perhaps it is a saving grace that many modern books—to say nothing of magazines and newspapers—will not exist beyond a few decades. Could this be nature's subtle way of eliminating from posterity the records of an uncouth and slipshod age?"

DARD HUNTER, *Papermaking* (Dover, 1978)

Care

Some books, no matter what you do, are just going to deteriorate. If you want your books to last, you have to know what you're buying.

The first thing I would do is take off the dust jacket and have a close look. Now this particular cover is made out of paper. It's not going to last. I can push through this hinge with my finger. The thicker the book, the more it's going to sag and the faster it'll break down. The best way to store a thick book is on its side. Otherwise, what happens is you set it on the shelf and the weight of the book is going to cause the papers to sag forward and down. The book loses its shape and caves in at the back. Don't leave it standing by itself. It's going to sway and in time develop a set because the changes in humidity and temperature will affect the adhesive in the back.

When you take a book off the shelf, you never want to pull it by the top of the spine. That's where most books tear. Put your fingers flat on the papers and tilt it out. Or, push in the book next to it, so you can get a grip on the back of the book.

Like everything else, books keep longer at freezing temperature, or in an air-conditioned library. A humidity of around 40 to 50 percent is ideal. In summer, particularly around August, books can mildew, so I use a dehumidifier in the basement. It'll take a gallon of water out of there every day. Then in the winter, when it's dry, we need a humidifier. Keeping books in a box or glass case will protect them from dust, dirt, and air pollution.”

AMERICA'S RAILROADS: ANTIQUES AT WORK

The railroad is remarkable as one of the most enduring institutions of the Industrial Age. Other technologies have waxed and waned, or have so evolved as to bear but little resemblance to their origins. But the basic principles of the railroad—the simple, brilliant concept of a guideway system formed by flanged wheels running on parallel rails, and the inherent energy efficiency of overland transport afforded by a string of cars pulled along a track—have endured unchanged, as valid today as they were a century and a half ago. No less enduring have been the standards adopted in the nineteenth century that permitted the interchange of equipment between connecting railroads, thus linking together hundreds of independent railroad companies into one universal, continent-wide system. The 4-feet-8½-inch standard gauge (the spacing between the inner faces of the rails) was adopted from the English wagon gauge, and became nearly a world-wide standard.

As its technology evolved, the American railroad has had to make certain that what is built today must work with what was built generations ago; and today's technology must be compatible with what may be built generations into the future. One can find both faults and virtues in this continuum of railroad technology. On the one hand, it has engendered a sometimes fearful conservatism, a resistance to change, that has often handicapped the railroads in adapting to a changing society and transportation marketplace. On the positive side, continuity has led the railroads to build to last, and then to extract the full measure of service from their material and equipment. The railroad has come down through time as perhaps the most durable of all American industries.

R. Yepsen

Collection of William D. Middleton

For a century and a half, the B & O's Thomas Viaduct has carried trains of ever-greater weight.

Fred W. Schneider III

The B & O's eastbound *Diplomat* crosses the Thomas Viaduct in this modern-day view.

Railroad durability begins with the very roadbed itself. By and large, today's trains follow alignments staked out a century or more before. Thus it is that Conrail diesels now snarl across the Berkshire hills of Massachusetts on grades laid out a century and a half ago by West Pointer and pioneer railroad engineer George Washington Whistler for the Western Railroad of Massachusetts; the yellow-clad locomotives of the Union Pacific race across the great spaces of Nebraska, Wyoming, and Utah on a line laid down by General Grenville M. Dodge in the years after the Civil War; Amtrak's *San Francisco Zephyr* winds through the rocky peaks of Donner Pass and the High Sierra on a roadbed carved and blasted out of solid rock by Collis P. Huntington's Chinese laborers in the 1860s. Said James J. Hill, builder of the Great Northern Railway, "I've made my mark on the surface of the earth, and they can't wipe it out."

No less enduring have been some of the great engineering works that projected the rails across America's broad rivers and deep valleys.

As early as 1829, the pioneer American railroad—the Baltimore & Ohio—turned to the classical Roman masonry arch for the construction of Carrollton Viaduct, the first significant American railroad bridge. It was built to carry the B & O's main line across Gwynn's Falls, near Baltimore, Maryland, and the single 100-foot arch still serves the railroad today.

Far more ambitious than the Carrollton bridge was the B & O's great Thomas Viaduct at Relay, Maryland, which also employed stone-arch construction. Completed in 1835, it still carries the B & O's Washington main line across the Patapsco River on a curving line of eight masonry arches spanning a total of more than 600 feet.

The greatest of all early masonry structures is the extraordinary stone-arch viaduct with which the New York & Erie spanned the broad valley of Starruca Creek near Susquehanna, Pennsylvania, in 1848. More than 1,000 feet long, the Starruca Viaduct comprises 17 arches of 50-foot span and stands 100 feet high. It too continues to carry railroad traffic to this day.

Don Van Vliet

Two freights pass under the Starruca Viaduct, built 1848 in northeastern Pennsylvania by the Erie Railroad.

William D. Middleton

A westbound Boston & Maine freight leaves the west portal of Hoosac Tunnel in Massachusetts. Completed in 1874 after more than twenty years of construction, this was the first great American tunnel.

Iron can't match stone for durability, but the Baltimore & Ohio's Savage branch crosses the Little Patuxent River in Maryland over a Bollman truss bridge, erected on the B & O main line about 1869 and moved to its present site in 1887. It continued to carry railroad traffic until 1947 and now serves as a pedestrian walkway.

In 1917, a landmark year for railroad-bridge construction, North American railroads completed four spans that still stand today as record structures of their type: at Metropolis, Illinois, the Paducah & Illinois Railroad crossed the Ohio River with a simple truss span of 723 feet, still the longest of its type ever built; Gustav Lindenthal's massive Hell Gate Bridge carried New York-New England railroad traffic across an arm of New York Harbor on a 977-foot steel arch that still ranks as the longest and heaviest railroad arch of all time; in Canada, railroad-bridge builders spanned the St. Lawrence in 1917 with the great Quebec Bridge, whose 1,800-foot central span still stands as the world's longest cantilever bridge; and finally, the great bridge engineer Gustav Lindenthal completed a second record span in 1917 with a crossing of the Ohio

River at Sciotoville, Ohio, that incorporated a continuous truss with two equal 775-foot clear spans that was—and still is—the longest railroad bridge of its kind.

In the railroad's track structure, too, railroad men have employed materials of exceptional durability. The commonplace wooden cross tie often lasts for as many as 40 years. (Occasionally ties are marked with their date of installation by a date nail.) Steel rails can go on almost indefinitely. In the late 1950s, for example, the author traveled over a North Dakota branch line of the Northern Pacific Railroad that was laid with the same rails with which the line had opened in the 1880s. (Rails are marked along the sides with their date of manufacture.)

Cascading

As they wear, steel rails progress downward through several levels of service in a frugal process called "cascading." Rail may begin its service life on a heavily traveled main line. Then, when wear standards for this service have been exceeded, the rail is pulled up and relaid on a less demanding secondary or branch line. From there, they may be relegated finally to yard or side-track service.

The Smithsonian Institution

The *John Bull*, undergoing a steam test at the age of 149.

The rolling stock of the railroad has always been built with solidity and long life in mind. The steam locomotive, which was the predominant form of motive power for American railroads for close to a century and a quarter, was a piece of machinery that could last almost indefinitely. The extraordinary durability of this machine has been highlighted in recent years by the growing interest in reviving old engines for special excursions. The American Freedom Train was operated over much of its nationwide journey for the 1976 American Bicentennial by a Southern Pacific Golden State-type steam locomotive that had spent the previous 20 years sitting in a Portland, Oregon, park. Little more than a normal overhaul and a coat of paint were required to ready the 35-year-old locomotive for 80-mile-per-hour running.

But clearly the record for durability must go to the historic locomotive *John Bull* of the Camden & Amboy Railroad. Built for the New Jersey line by Robert Stephenson & Company of England in 1831, the *John Bull* was donated to the Smithsonian Institution in 1885 as one of its earliest engineering relics. Nearing 100 years in age, the John Bull was withdrawn from the Smithsonian's Arts and Industries Building in 1927 to operate in the Fair of the Iron Horse, the Baltimore & Ohio's Centennial pageant at Baltimore. After another half century of quiet repose in the Smithsonian, the *John Bull* was again to operate under steam generated in her wrought-iron boiler. The locomotive celebrated its 150th birthday on September 15, 1981, with an outing over the B & O's Georgetown branch at Washington.

The most famous of all American electric locomotives, the Pennsylvania Railroad's celebrated GG1, has endured for almost a half century in some of the most rigorous high-speed passenger service in North America. Produced between 1934 and 1943, the GG1 continued to operate in Amtrak Northeast Corridor service until 1980, and until the very end, one could often find a GG1 substituting for one of Amtrak's modern *Metroliners* in over-100-mile-per-hour service. A few GG1's still pull New Jersey commuter trains in and out of New York City.

Other, less famous electrics have lasted even longer. One of the New York Central Railroad's original electric locomotives of 1906 survived in switching duties on successor Conrail into 1981. And, the Canadian National Railroad still operates a daily commuter service through Montreal's Mount Royal Tunnel with the same sturdy electric locomotives built by General Electric that initiated tunnel service in 1914 and 1916.

William D. Middleton

A Pennsylvania Railroad GG1 pulls a northbound Washington-New York train at Bowie, Maryland. Number 4877 was built in 1939.

William D. Middleton

A Reading Company commuter train south of Jenkintown, Pennsylvania. These electric cars were built in 1930 and are still in service today.

William D. Middleton

These Canadian National locomotives date to 1914 and 1916.

Edward A. Lewis

Like returning alumni, boxcars advertise their longevity. Marked on each piece of rolling stock is the car's month and year of birth. This wooden car served "The Sole Leather Line," the Wellsville, Addison and Galeton, near the Pennsylvania-New York border. According to the numbers stenciled on the sides, it was built in March, 1930.

Fred W. Schneider III

An Erie-Lackawanna commuter train pauses to pick up Manhattan-bound passengers at Convent Station, New Jersey. These cars are at least 50 years old.

William D. Middleton

The cars of this Chicago South Shore & South Bend Railroad electric interurban train were built in the late 1920s and are still at work.

Fred W. Schneider III

A contemporary of the Model T, this 1923 streetcar continues to haul capacity crowds in New Orleans. The city uses nearly three dozen such cars.

R. Yepsen

Railroad locomotives last an average of 22 years.

In the very antithesis of the planned-obsolescence approach of the auto industry, diesel locomotive builders standardize the design of such principal components as trucks, traction motors, generators, and diesel engines over long periods. Refinements and improvements are made, but the basic product remains essentially unchanged. Electro-Motive's famous 567-series diesel engine, for example, remained in production for some 25 years. After these so-called first-generation diesels served for a quarter century or so, many of them cheated the scrapyard and returned to their builders to be remanufactured. Thus, diesel locomotives built in the 1940s and 1950s live on today.

Freight and passenger cars also have enjoyed exceptional longevity. Ancient wooden boxcars served Pennsylvania's little Wellsville, Addison and Galeton into the 1970s. Passenger cars are often downgraded through descending levels of service as they age. A car that served one generation in deluxe limited train service might serve the next as a commuter car, and yet another as a bunk car for track workers. Thus, today's Canadian National commuters at Montreal ride in heavyweight steel cars dating to early in the century. New Jersey commuters still ride in at least one of the Pennsylvania Railroad's P-70 heavyweight steel coaches, designed in 1907 and built into the 1920s. Amtrak has remanufactured 25- and 30-year-old coaches, sleepers, and diners for such long-distance trains as the *Broadway Limited*, the *Crescent*, and the *Silver Star*.

William D. Middleton

A San Francisco cable car at Union Square in 1979. Built in 1887, Number 23 continues to take passengers up and down the city's steep grades.

The PCC trolley car deserves mention. Developed in the early 1930s as a standardized, modern vehicle that would help the street-railway industry to survive, the PCC car remained in production through 1951, and a remarkable number of them run today in the several North American cities that still operate street railways. Remanufacturing projects promise to add a decade or more to the life of PCC cars that are now at least 30 years old. New Orleans never did get around to updating its service with PCC cars and still operates streetcars that date from the mid-1920s. San Francisco runs cable cars made in 1887. Some of Philadelphia's Broad Street subway cars were on hand for the line's 1928 opening, and a Philadelphia suburban line operates between Upper Darby and Norristown with wind-tunnel-designed, aluminum-bodied cars built in 1930. In the Midwest, the suburban Chicago South Shore & South Bend carries passengers in the cars it installed in the late 1920s.

There is something about the railroad that engenders lifetime careers of extraordinary length in the people who work on it. An Illinois Central engineer, Robert T. "Polecat" McMillan, went to work for the railroad in 1890 and stepped down from the cab of the 100-mile-per-hour *City of New Orleans* streamliner to retire on February 8, 1956, at the age of 83.

WILLIAM D. MIDDLETON

Courtesy of Ernest M. Dolan

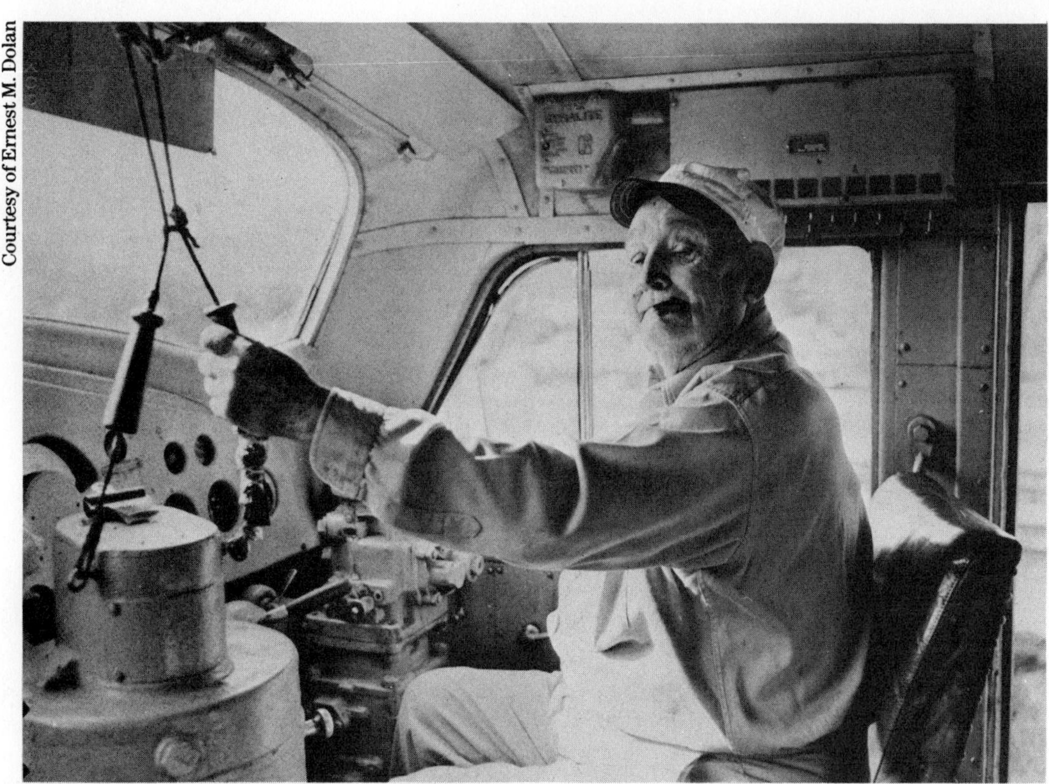

Bob "Polecat" McMillan in the cab of the famous streamliner, the *City of New Orleans*, southbound. Polecat preferred steam power to diesels. His fireman, Ernest Dolan, sent us the photo and remarks that it's "an excellent picture of him. He was just as much at home on an engine as he was sitting in an easy chair. I fired him a lot and never saw him excited or disturbed by anything that happened."

Dear Sir:

I am to inform you about my Zippo lighter, my little five year old brother came in the house one morning laughing, I asked him what had happened, and then I asked him where my Zippo lighter was. He took me out on the Railroad track and all I could find was a smashed case, afterward he told me the train run over it.

THE NO-DEPOSIT, NO-RETURN PLANET

11

Apocalypse no

The apocalypse is an old subject to my generation. I was seven when my parents' generation bombed Hiroshima. An earliest, vividest nightmare was of my Illinois hometown being bombed to rubble by the Russians because we had an unusual number of machine-tool factories. As I recall, all those science-fiction movies of the 1950s assumed a nuclear end of the world.

By and by we came to love it. Come our majority, in the 1960s, we were called the "Now Generation," accurately, because that's all we could talk about, figuring there wasn't any "then" we could count on. That was the overt, romantic side of it at least. The less noble side is that we were afraid there wasn't any future available that wasn't going to bore us to death, we children of affluence. So, simultaneously scared and bored and pretty well off, we embraced the situation and looked for exciting terminal times. Bob Dylan, 1963, the Cuban Missile Crisis: "It's a Hard Rain's a-Gonna Fall"—". . . I heard the sound of a wave that could drown the whole world." Have you noticed, that's the theme of nearly every unpleasant subject that's come up since. Overpopulation, pollution, cancer, cold war, hot war, nuclear power, nuclear weapons. It's always the end of the world, or of civilization—the terms are interestingly interchangeable.

Engelhardt in the *St. Louis Post-Dispatch*

Throwaway planet.

My own bunch was so avid, we made up crises. In the mid-1960s, thousands of California hippies whipped up a froth of dread about a prediction by the seer Edgar Cayce that California was going to fall off and sink in the Pacific Ocean. It didn't. (Not only didn't but couldn't, but we weren't into geology, man.) I myself, in response to the Energy Crisis of 1973,

went around saying to audiences and in print that America would be under martial law by Christmas. No such luck. That energy crisis was a lark, and so is the current one so far. Check your own response to the present war fever—pulse quicker, eye more glittering, ire a bit more focused? "Bloody Yanks, get us all in a war!"

My point is that these situations are serious, but we avoid taking them seriously by always taking them ultimately. "Do you realize the combined megatonnage of the major powers is enough to blah blah blah?" After this discussion, the deluge. There's no reason to do anything because it's all too hopeless.

What crap. Earth is not threatened. Life on Earth is not threatened. Civilization, such as it is, is not particularly threatened.

The major analyst of Earth's life these days is James Lovelock, deviser of the Gaia Hypothesis (which proposes that our planet's myriad biota use the atmosphere and oceans as a vast and subtle buffering device—making the Earth, in effect, one life). In his recent book, *Gaia*, Lovelock reports: "Towards the end of 1975 the United States National Academy of Sciences issued a report prepared by an eight-man committee of their own distinguished members, assisted by forty-eight other scientists chosen from those expert in the effects of nuclear explosions

A wood-frame house before and after a nuclear explosion of 5 psi peak overpressure.

A brick house before and after a blast of the same power.

and all things subsequent to them. The report suggested that if half of all of the nuclear weapons in the world's arsenals, about 10,000 megatons, were used in a nuclear war, the effects on most of the human and man-made ecosystems of the world would be small at first and would become negligible within thirty years. Both aggressor and victim nations would of course suffer catastrophic local devastation, but areas remote from the battle and, especially important in the biosphere, marine and coastal ecosystems would be minimally disturbed. . . . In the nineteen-seventies it still seems that a nuclear war of major proportions, although no less horrific for the participants and their allies, would not be the global devastation so often portrayed. Certainly it would not much disturb Gaia. The report itself was criticized then as now on political and moral grounds."

Some months ago, I was interviewing the eminent population biologist Paul Ehrlich for his views on genotoxins—the tidal wave of new chemicals that, like radiation, cause cancer, birth defects, and a possibly lasting pollution of the human gene pool. Though clearly against anything that would increase the human

A post-nuclear community

Ron Boutwell on a bluff above Terrene Ark 1.

In this nuclear age, bunkers are being built thousands of miles from the enemy's lines, not for soldiers but for civilian families. Some 240 underground condominium units are being built outside of La Verkin, Utah, by Ron Boutwell, a lawyer who has found that some Americans are worried enough to pay for their own civil-defense system. At his Terrene Ark 1, security will cost them about $40,000 for a shelter designed to keep its occupants out of roentgens' reach for 9 to 12 months.

The premise behind the project is that nuclear war is likely—"The odds are tremendous for nuclear war," according to Lane Blackmore, president of the firm that is constructing the complex. It's unpleasant to think through just what a nuclear attack would mean, he admits, but citizens have to accept the responsibility for their safety, because the government won't. In fact, the United States presents the vulnerability of its citizenry as assurance that we wouldn't use our nuclear arsenal. Meanwhile, says Blackmore, the Soviet Union is so far better prepared that a war would cost us "ten people to their one." The part-time residents of Terrene Ark 1 are paying dearly to improve their odds.

mutation rate, Ehrlich said, "It's very difficult for me to see exactly what the human-population consequences of the level of circulation of mutagens—or of radiation for that matter—is likely to be. It's a very difficult technical problem." He went on: "The argument for protecting nature by reducing mutagens is a crappy argument. In a fruit fly population or a lizard population, if you have a dose of radiation that causes a very high genetic load, selection will quickly reduce it. A fruit fly population doesn't go into shock if it loses half of its individuals or 90 percent of its individuals in a generation or for 20 generations."

During Rome's decline, the lament ran, "If Rome dies, the universe dies." What if that idea itself was one of the poisons that sickened the Empire? Megalomania is not exactly an adaptive mode.

Look at it another way (here's one for the quoters-out-of-context). Maybe an all-out nuclear war would be the best thing for our planet's ecology right now. It might set the misbehaviors of overpopulation back a couple of notches until more sanity could prevail. How severe a chastening will it take before we properly value the biological diversity we are ruining now for the sake of convenience? Our agricultural practices alone are more lethal than nuclear war. Not that they'll end the world either.

It is a most peculiar fallacy, full of contradictions, but perhaps for that very reason the premise, "the world is going to end before I do," throbs deep, hard to reach and harder to change. But out the other side is rather a comforting release, or so some of my crowd have found it. For us the mere idea of continuity is new and exciting. Imagine, working for a future beyond ourselves. We take up such interests as planting trees, working on our communities, or scheming up real space colonies. Not as exciting as an apocalypse perhaps, but there's more to do.

STEWART BRAND

Dear Sir:

I was working on the back of a dump truck and I layed it down while I was working on it. And I forgot about it. And I left it lay there and I let the back of the dump truck down on it.

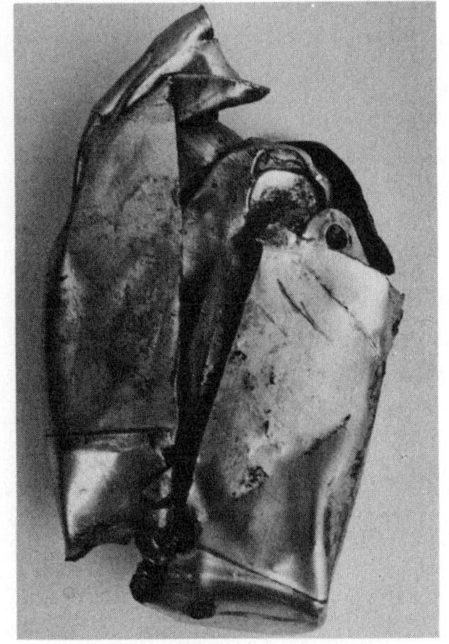

OUR CONTRIBUTORS

Max Alth has 14 books in print on home repair and a variety of other topics.

J. Baldwin is soft-tech editor for *CoEvolution Quarterly* and works with the New Alchemy Institute.

Tom Bender is an architect and writer on economics. He lives in a house he built, in Nehalem, Oregon.

John Blackford is a freelance writer and a book editor at Rodale Press.

Robert E. Cole is professor of sociology and director of the Center for Japanese Studies at the University of Michigan in Ann Arbor. His piece was based on extensive interviews with automotive officials in Japan and the United States.

Pamela W. Darling is a librarian, presently employed as Preservation Specialist for the Association of Research Libraries to develop manuals for libraries struggling to cope with the deterioration of books. She has worked for the Library of Congress, the New York Public Library, and the Columbia University Libraries, lectures widely, and has published many articles on book preservation.

Freelancer *Pat Donahue* lives in West Chester, Pennsylvania.

In his 20 years of testing and writing about consumer electronic equipment, *Herbert Friedman* has published some 3,000 articles.

Professional boatbuilder *John Gardner* is associate curator of small craft at Mystic Seaport, Mystic, Connecticut.

Harold Gessner is executive director of the Footwear Council.

Inventor *William Hauk* teaches at the Shelter Institute in Bath, Maine.

Ralph Keys once ran a sports car repair shop, and has made documentary films. He now is head of a corporate technical writing department in New Orleans and is working on a novel.

Rich Kline is a freelance writer who lives in the country outside of Auburn, Pennsylvania.

After earning his doctorate in sociology, *Dan Knapp* went on to become director of the Oregon Office of Appropriate Technology. He now runs Whole Earth Recycling in Berkeley, California.

Michael McClintock is the author of Scribners' *Homeowner's Handbook*.

Wayne Merry writes on camping from Atlin, British Columbia. He is working on a book about cold-weather expeditions.

William D. Middleton is assistant executive vice-president, Physical Plant, at the University of Virginia in Charlottesville. He has written several books and hundreds of articles on transportation and engineering, and is a contributing editor of the trade journal *Railway Age*.

After writing his piece for this book, *Joel Monture-Knecht* went back to college—Bennington—to study literature. He is working on a novel.

Peter Moore is senior editor at *Modern Photography*.

Alice Nass loves to shop for old clothes. She was an editor with *Bicycling* magazine and now studies graphic design.

Richard Sassaman is a freelance writer. His work has appeared in *CoEvolution Quarterly* and *Sports Illustrated*.

Greg Smith is managing editor of *Modern Tire Dealer*.

Freelance writer *Douglas C. Smyth* is working on a novel. He lives near Clinton Corners, New York.

Paul Suwijn has worked as a cabinetmaker and patternmaker, and now is a machine designer in Rochester, New York. He is a contributor to *Fine Woodworking* magazine.

Rosalind Williams is a research fellow in the Science, Technology, and Society Program at the Massachusetts Institute of Technology. The University of California Press recently published her observations on consumer society, *Dream Worlds*.

OUR ACKNOWLEDGMENTS

Chapter 2

Robert E. Cole, "The Japanese Lesson in Quality," *Technology Review*, July, 1981.

"Diesel Troubles," reprinted by permission from *Popular Science*. Copyright 1981, Times Mirror Magazine, Inc.

"Rust," reprinted from *The Family Handyman Magazine*, March, 1981. Copyright © 1981, The Webb Co., 1999 Shepard Road, St. Paul, MN 55116.

Chapter 3

Frank Berto, "A Dozen Bicycle Tires Compared," *Bicycling*, June, 1981.

Chapter 5

Survey data reprinted by permission of *Appliance Manufacturer*, a Cahners publication.

"Woodenware," *Entree* magazine. Reprinted by permission of Entree/The Fairchild Syndicate.

Chapter 7

"Component resale value," excerpted from "There's Gold (Well, a Little Silver, Actually) in old components," *High Fidelity*, December, 1980.

Marc Kirkeby, "Rock and Roll Is Here to Stay, but Not at 33⅓ RPM," *Rolling Stone* #346, June 25, 1981. Copyright © 1981, Straight Arrow Publishers, Inc. All rights reserved. Reprinted by permission.

"How to Get More Life from Your Records," *High Fidelity*, July, 1980. All rights reserved.

Peter Moore, "The Fading Image: How to Preserve Colored Pictures," *Modern Photography*, January, 1981. Reprinted by permission.

Chapter 9

"A Guide to Garden Hand Tools," from "Tooling Up," *Horticulture*, July, 1980. Text and illustrations by Aldren A. Watson. Reprinted by permission of the author.

APPENDIX: MEMBERS OF THE APPLIANCE PARTS DISTRIBUTORS ASSOCIATION

Alabama

Washer and Refrigeration Supply Co., Inc.
716 Second Avenue N
Birmingham, AL 35201

Napco, Inc.
709 North Memorial Parkway
Huntsville, AL 35801

Arizona

Appliance Dealer Supply Co., Inc.
P.O. Box 2017 (740 West Grant)
Phoenix, AZ 85007

Appliance Parts Co.
2333 North Thirty-fifth Avenue
Phoenix, AZ 85008

Akrit Appliance Supply Co.
1132 North Richey Boulevard
Tucson, AZ 85716

Arkansas

Mid-South Appliance Parts Co.
1020 West Fourteenth Street
P.O. Box 2722
Little Rock, AR 72201

California

Appliance Parts Co. Div. of Washing Machine Parts Co.
15040 Oxnard Street
P.O. Box 2787
Van Nuys, CA 91401

Cal Sales Corp.
641 Monterey Pass Road
Monterey Park, CA 91754

Coast Appliance Parts Co.
5915 North Kester Avenue
Van Nuys, CA 91401

Electrical Appliance Service Co.
290 Townsend Street
San Francisco, CA 94107

Colorado

Ray Jones Appliance Parts Co.
376 South Broadway
Denver, CO 80209

Akrit Appliance Supply Co.
402 Arrawanna Street
Colorado Springs, CO 80909

Connecticut

American Appliance Parts Co., Inc.
2516 Whitney Avenue
Hamden, CT 06518

Arcand Distributors, Inc.
845 Windsor Street
Hartford, CT 06120

Electric Appliance Parts Co.
175 Freight Street
Waterbury, CT 06702

Westchester Appliance Parts, Inc.
194 Richmond Hill Avenue
Stamford, CT 06902

Delaware

Jacoby Appliance Parts
226 West Market Street
Newport, DE 19804

District of Columbia

Trible's Inc.
2240 25th Place NE
Washington, DC 20018

Florida

Marcone Appliance Parts Center
777 Northwest Seventy-ninth Street
Miami, FL 33150

Georgia

D & L Appliance Parts Co.
5799 New Peachtree Road
Atlanta, GA 30340

Harris Appliance Parts Co.
5129 Montgomery Street
Savannah, GA 31405

Hawaii

Appliance Parts Co., Inc.
P.O. Box 17976
1550 Kalani Street
Honolulu, HI 96817

Idaho

W. L. May Co., Inc.
202 East 33rd Street
Boise, ID 83704

Illinois

Automatic Appliance Parts Corp.
7757 West Lawrence Avenue
Chicago, IL 60656

Midwest Appliance Parts Co.
2600 West Diversey
Chicago, IL 60647

C. E. Sundberg Co.
615 West Seventy-ninth Street
Chicago, IL 60620

Indiana

Appliance Parts, Inc.
P.O. Box 22350
1734 West Fifteenth Street
Indianapolis, IN 46222

Bell Parts Supply, Inc.
2819 Forty-fifth Street
Highland, IN 46322

Evansville Appliance Parts
920 West Pennsylvania Street
Evansville, IN 47708

Appliance Parts Supply Co.
1241 Wells Street
Fort Wayne, IN 46808

Iowa

The Ricketts Co., Inc.
801 Southeast Fourteenth Street
Des Moines, IA 50317

Dey Appliance Parts
323 Laparte Road
Waterloo, IA 50702

Kentucky

The Collins Co., Inc.
Appliance Parts Div.
819 South Floyd Street
Louisville, KY 40203

Marcone Appliance Parts Co.
4422 Kiln Court
Louisville, KY 40218

Louisiana

Bruce's Distributing Co.
509 East Seventieth Street
P.O. Box 6718
Shreveport, LA 71106

Sunseri's Inc.
2254 Sixtieth Street Claude Avenue
New Orleans, LA 70117

Appliance Parts Co. of Alexandria
2214 Lee Street
Alexandria, LA 71301

Maine

Appliance Parts Co.
255 Danforth Street
Portland, ME 04102

Supply Distributors
456 Riverside Industrial Parkway
Portland, ME 04103

Maryland

Coatline Parts Co.
818 Snow Hill Road
Salisbury, MD 21801

Trible's Inc.
771 Hungerford Drive
Rockville, MD 20850

Massachusetts

Appliance Parts Co., Inc.
112 Dartmouth Street
Boston, MA 02116

Hall Electric Supply Co., Inc. (HESCO)
33 Brighton Street
Belmont, MA 02178

M.G.M.S. Associates, Inc.
22 Water Street
Cambridge, MA 02141

Supply Distributors
50 Revere Beach Parkway
Medford, MA 02155

Michigan

Apco, Inc.
3305 South Pennsylvania
Lansing, MI 48910

Servall Co.
228 East Baltimore Street
Detroit, MI 48202

Minnesota

Appliance Parts, Inc.
250 Third Avenue North
Minneapolis, MN 55401

Dey Appliance Parts
P.O. Box 5086
525 North Snelling Avenue
St. Paul, MN 55104

Mississippi

Appliance Parts Co., Inc.
727 South Gallatin Street
Jackson, MS 39204

Missouri

Marcone Appliance Parts Co.
2300 Clark Avenue
St. Louis, MO 63103

St. Louis Appliance Parts, Inc.
2911-13 South Jefferson
St. Louis, MO 63118

Nebraska

Appliance Parts Supply, Inc.
14647 Industrial Road
Omaha, NE 68144

Nevada

Cal Sales Corp.
3453 Industrial Road
Las Vegas, NV 89109

Electrical Appliance Service Co.
611 Kuenzli Street
Reno, NV 89502

New Hampshire

Supply Distributors
148 Merrimack Street
Manchester, NH 03101

New Jersey

Jacoby Appliance Parts
269 Main Street
Hackensack, NJ 07601

Valley Appliance Parts Co.
2222 Hamburg Turnpike
Wayne, NJ 07470

Westchester Appliance Parts, Inc.
470 U.S. Highway #46
Teterboro, NJ 07608

New Mexico

Akrit Appliance Supply Co.
2820 Vassar NE
Albuquerque, NM 87107

New York

All Appliance Parts of New York, Inc.
1345 New York Avenue
Huntington Station, NY 11746

Westchester Appliance Parts
1034 Yonkers Avenue
Yonkers, NY 10714

Buffalo Appliance Parts Co., Inc.
1175 William Street
Buffalo, NY 14206

Nichols Appliance Parts, Inc.
3150 Erie Boulevard E
Syracuse, NY 13214

Rochester Appliance Parts Distributors
1130 Emerson Street
Rochester, NY 14606

Jacoby Appliance Parts
1023 Allerton Avenue
Bronx, NY 10469

North Carolina

D & L Appliance Parts Co., Inc.
2100 Freedom Drive
P.O. Box 31816
Charlotte, NC 28208

Moore and Stewart, Inc.
316 East Franklin Avenue
Gastonia, NC 28052

North Dakota

Appliance Parts, Inc.
20 North University Avenue
Fargo, ND 55108

Ohio

American Electric Washer Co.
1834 East Fifty-fifth Street
Cleveland, OH 44103

Appliance Parts Supply Co.
235 Broadway Street
Toledo, OH 43602

Dayton Appliance Parts Co.
122 Sears Street
Dayton, OH 45402

Dayco Appliance Parts
620 East Weber Road
Columbus, OH 43211

Mason Supply Co.
985 Joyce Avenue
Columbus, OH 43203

Pearsol Appliance Corp.
2319 Gilbert Avenue
Cincinnati, OH 45206

Pearsol Corp. of Ohio
1847 East Fortieth Street
Cleveland, OH 44103

V & V Appliance Parts, Inc.
27 West Myrtle Avenue
Youngstown, OH 44507

Oklahoma

Greer Electric Co.
1018 South Rockford
Tulsa, OK 74104

Pritchard Electric Co., Inc.
3100 North Santa Fe
Oklahoma City, OK 73101

Oregon

Hansberry's Appliance Parts Co.
1134 Southeast Stark Street
Portland, OR 97214

W.L. May Co., Inc.
1120 Southeast Madison Street
Portland, OR 97214

Pennsylvania

Collins Appliance Parts, Inc.
1533 Metropolitan Street
Pittsburgh, PA 15233

Parts Distributors Corp.
312 North Easton Road
Willow Grove, PA 19090

V & V Appliance Parts, Inc.
3738 West Twelfth Street
Erie, PA 16505

Wagner Appliance Parts, Inc.
1814 Tilghman Street
Allentown, PA 18104

Rhode Island

Appliance Parts Co., Inc.
316 Cranston Street
Providence, RI 02907

Twin City Supply Co.
885 Westminster Street
Providence, RI 02903

South Carolina

G & E Parts Center, Inc.
P.O. Box 2466
2403 South Pine Street
Spartanburg, SC 29304

Harris Appliance Parts Co.
P.O. Box 611
29 Bypass N
Anderson, SC 29621

Coastline Parts Co.
134 East Montague Avenue
Charleston, SC 29406

D & L Appliance Parts, Inc.
901 South Cashua Drive
Florence, SC 29501

South Dakota

Dey Appliance Parts
300 North Phillips
Sioux Falls, SD 57102

Tennessee

Brown Appliance Parts Co., Inc.
857 North Central Avenue
P.O. Box 3589
Knoxville, TN 37917

Curtis Co.
731 East Brooks Road
Memphis, TN 38116

Napco, Inc.
501 South Second Street
Nashville, TN 37213

Texas

Central Supply Div. of Central
Consolidated, Inc.
2612 McKinney
P.O. Box 3385
Houston, TX 77001

Pearsol Appliance Co.
3127 Main Street
Dallas, TX 75226

Standard Appliance Parts Corp.
4814 Ayers Street
P.O. Box 7488
Corpus Christi, TX 78415

Texas Parts & Supply Co.
P.O. Box 115
1209 South St. Marys
San Antonio, TX 78291

Washing Machine Parts Co.
704 North Main Street
Fort Worth, TX 76106

Akrit Appliance Supply Co.
1805 Montana
El Paso, TX 79902

Utah

Ray Jones Appliance Parts Co.
3336 South 300 East
Salt Lake City, UT 84115

Vermont

Supply Distributors
18 Chaplin Avenue
Rutland, VT 05701

Virginia

Refrigeration Supply Co., Inc.
1657 West Broad Street
Richmond, VA 23261

Booth Supply Co., Inc.
2621 Florida Avenue
Norfolk, VA 23513

Trible's Inc.
7273 East Arlington Boulevard
Falls Church, VA 22042

Wholesale Parts Distributors, Inc.
1141 Lance Road
Norfolk, VA 23502

Washington

Appliance Parts & Service Co.
400 9th Avenue, North
Seattle, WA 98109

W.L. May Co.
18840 Seventy-second Street
Kent, WA 98031

West Virginia

Mason Supply Co.
800 Virginia Street W
Charleston, WV 25303

Wisconsin

A & E Distributors, Inc.
1418 North Erwin Avenue
P.O. Box 8045
Green Bay, WI 54308

Power Equipment Co.
2373 South Kinnickinnic Avenue
Milwaukee, WI 53207

Canada

Mossman's Appliance Parts, Ltd.
1465 Gerrard Street E
Toronto, ON M4L 2A2

Reliable Parts Ltd.
860 Kingsway
Vancouver, BC V5V 3C3

Gentlemen:

The enclosed Zippo lighter was severely damaged by a Cocker Spaniel dog.

Would you please have it repaired to satisfactory condition. Also, would you personalize it the same way that it is now. That is, the Moore Business Forms, Inc. symbol on the front and the initials KO engraved on the back.

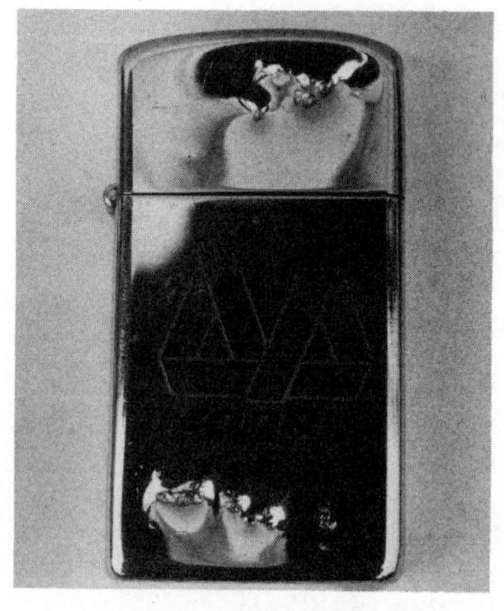

INDEX

Page numbers in italics indicate photos or illustrations. Car models are listed under the manufacturer.

D

T

U

V

W

Y

Z